CASE STUDIES IN MANAGEMENT

DR.SACHIN.S.VERNEKAR
Director
Bharati Vidyapeeth University
Institute of Management and Research, New Delhi (BVIMR)

DR. K.VENKATASUBRAMANIAN
Management Consultant and International Trainer, Visiting Faculty
Bharati Vidyapeeth University
Institute of Management and Research, New Delhi (BVIMR)

MRS. PREETY WADHWA
Associate Professor,
Marketing, Bharati Vidyapeeth University
Institute of Management and Research, New Delhi (BVIMR)

Student Editors

Kanika Sanduja, MBA
D/o Mr. Krishan Sanduja

Monika Chauhan, MBA
D/o Mr. B.S. Chauhan

Abhitosh Vatsal, B. Tech, MBA
S/o Mr. D.S. Chauhan

Himalaya Publishing House

MUMBAI • NEW DELHI • NAGPUR • BENGALURU • HYDERABAD • CHENNAI • PUNE
LUCKNOW • AHMEDABAD • ERNAKULAM • BHUBANESWAR • INDORE • KOLKATA

First Edition : 2012

Published by : Mrs. Meena Pandey
for **HIMALAYA PUBLISHING HOUSE PVT. LTD.,**
"Ramdoot", Dr. Bhalerao Marg, Girgaon, **Mumbai - 400 004.**
Phones: 2386 01 70/2386 38 63, Fax: 022-2387 71 78
Email: himpub@vsnl.com
Website: www.himpub.com

Branch Offices:

New Delhi : "Pooja Apartments", 4-B, Murari Lal Street, Ansari Road, Darya Ganj, **New Delhi - 110 002.** Phone: 23270392, 23278631 Fax: 011-23256286

Nagpur : Kundanlal Chandak Industrial Estate, Ghat Road, **Nagpur - 440 018.** Phone: 2738731, 3296733 Telefax : 0712-2721215

Bengaluru : No. 16/1 (Old 12/1), 1st Floor, Next to Hotel Highlands, Madhava Nagar, Race Course Road, **Bengaluru - 560 001.** Phone: 22281541, 22385461, Telefax: 080-22286611

Hyderabad : No. 3-4-184, Lingampally, Besides Raghavendra Swamy Matham, Kachiguda, **Hyderabad - 500 027.** Phone: 040-27560041, 27550139, Mobile:- 09848130433 Telefax: 040-27560041

Chennai : No. 85/50, Bazullah Road, T. Nagar, **Chennai - 600 017.** Phone: 044-28344020, 32463737, 42124860

Pune : No. 527, "Laksha" Apartment, First Floor, Mehunpura, Shaniwarpeth, (Near Prabhat Theatre), **Pune - 411 030.** Phone: 020-24496323/24496333/32326733

Lucknow : Jai Baba Bhawan, Near Manas Complex, Church Road, Aliganj, **Lucknow - 226 024.** Phone: 0522-2339329, 9305302158, 9415349385

Ahmedabad : No. 114, "SHAIL", 1st Floor, Opp. Madhu Sudan House, C.G.Road, Navrang Pura, **Ahmedabad – 380 009.** Phone: 079-26560126, Mobiles: 09327324149,09314679413

Ernakulam : No. 39/104 A, Lakshmi Apartment, Karikkamuri Cross Rd., Ernakulam, **Cochin – 682011**, Kerala. Phone: 0484-2378012, 2378016, Mob.: 09344199799

Bhubaneswar : 5 Station Square, **Bhubaneswar (Orissa) - 751 001.** Mobile: 9861046007, E-mail:- orissa@himpub.com

Indore : Kesardeep Avenue Extension, 73, Narayan Bagh.Flat No. 302, IIIrd Floor, Near Humpty Dumpty School, Narayan Bagh, **Indore (M.P.) 452 007,** Mobile: 09301386468

Kolkata : 108/4, Beliaghata, Main Road, Near ID Hospital, Opp. SBI Bank **Kolkata - 700 010.** Mobile: 09910440956, E-mail:- nkmitra@himpub.com

Guwahati : House No. 15, Behind Prajjyotish College, Near Sharma Printing Press, P.O. Bharalumukh, Guwahati - 781009 (Assam) Mobile: 07439040301; 07439040302

DTP by : Elite-Art, N.S. Marg, Daryaganj, New Delhi-110 002, Mobile: 9911297688

Printed by : Geetanjali Press Pvt. Ltd., Nagpur

Foreward

We have been using case studies in my classes to a large extent during our teaching tenure and also in executive development programs. We found them much better in getting the attention of students and giving them a learning experience. Adult learning is very different from the school learning. The students, who have attained an age where they can think of their own, will have to learn differently. Case studies help in learning differently, since they take the student to specific occasions

Management program have to contribute to the skill levels and not just to the knowledge base of the students. Today's students have access to various communication channels and they learn much from them. When the students of management come to the classroom, he expects the faculty to take him through some learning experiences. Thus, the case studies form an important tool for the faculty and the students in the learning process. Case studies can create an environment in the class, when everyone can freely put forth their views and also listen to other's views, analyze and come to a logical conclusion. Case studies also promote team work and encourage leadership. The communication skills of the students also improve in the process.

I am glad that BVIMR has brought out this book enlisting the cases presented during the case study completion Paristhithi. It shows their desire to share the knowledge gained to the academic community, instead of keeping them in their library. Educational institutions, should not only gather knowledge, but dispense knowledge as well. Then only they become the origin of knowledge

Life is a learning experience, and you can learn from anywhere. The teacher also learns from the students in a class room. The case studies invoke discussions, when both the students the teacher learns from each other.

The case study method, has a proven track record and I hope that everyone who reads this book utilizes the cases for learning and teaching management.

Dr. K.Venkatasubramanian
Management Consultant and International Trainer, Visiting Faculty
Bharati Vidyapeeth University
Institute of Management and Research, New Delhi (BVIMR)
Mrs. Preety Wadhwa
Associate Professor,
Marketing,Bharati Vidyapeeth University
Institute of Management and Research, New Delhi (BVIMR)

Preface

Case studies are a good learning experience for those who are in management functions and also the students who aspire to be tomorrow's managers. Case studies put us in the same environment when the case happened and also gives insight to the management problems and we can ourselves find out the solutions, as if everything happens now.

Even if the case study relates, to a period which has gone by, the problems to be addressed remain the same and the solutions will require a lot of analysis and decision making to come to the right conclusions.

At BVIMR, it has been a culture for the students to learn through case studies in the class room itself. So when the function Paristhithi is organized every year, especially for case study competition, there is an enormous amount of enthusiasm by the students of BVIMR as well as students from other institutions who participate in this competition. During this occasion case studies are received from all the participants and it is really heartening to note that they cover various functional areas, from attrition to Bankruptcy, from case study on Agro Processing industry to Special economic zones in India. The variety of the topics chosen by the participants is an indicator of the desire of learning by the participants.

This book is a compilation of the various cases presented by the participants on the occasion. BVIMR is of the strong opinion that these cases should not lie within the boundaries of the campus and would like to present the same to the student and academic community everywhere. It is good to have a management function and to facilitate those who have participated. But it feels much better to share the entire proceedings with the fraternity in education and the students who would like to benefit from the proceedings

A number of management competitions do happen everywhere, but they do not become available to those who are interested. BVIMR strongly believes in sharing the knowledge gained and hence this compilation of the case studies presented during Paristhithi.

These cases would benefit the teaching faculty in management institutions and they can take up these cases in the classroom, or the students, who can sit in a restaurant, read the case, discuss and benefit from the same.

We sincerely hope that this book will find a place in every library of the management institutes in India and abroad.

Dr.Sachin.S.Vernekar
Director
Bharati Vidyapeeth University
Institute of Management and Research, New Delhi (BVIMR)

Contents

PART - I : GENERAL MANAGEMENT

PART - II : HUMAN RESOURCES MANAGEMENT

PART - III : INTERNATIONAL BUSINESS

PART - IV : MARKETING CASES

PART - V : FINANCE CASES

1

Anna: Leader of Second Freedom Movement

Ms. Neelam Saraswat, (Assistant Professor), IPEM, Ghaziabad
saraswat.neelam@gmail.com
Mr. Gaurav Bhargava, (Assistant Manager), Syndicate Bank, Ghaziabad
gbhargava84@gmail.com

"There can be no doubt that corruption is a dreaded disease that needs to be weeded from the Indian Society. I am very happy that we have a very able and dedicated leader in Anna Hazare to lead us in this fight against corruption,"

Rajinikanth (Film star), Chennai chapter of India against Corruption, the NGO spearheading the anti-corruption campaign in various cities.

"We have accepted the will of a powerful movement, headed by a powerful leader"

Union Finance Minister Pranab Mukherjee,

Out of the blue, a person with angelic smile and composed face became center of attention in complete India. Anna Hazare, 74 year old man with his charismatic aura, is the most talked about person in India as of now. He with his divine intentions to eradicate corruption from India is ruling over the hearts of millions of Indian. It is very clear from the fact that thousands of Indians followed his words and accompanied him in his efforts against corruption and supported his non-violent movement 'fast unto death" by being in Ramlila Maidan in Delhi. Now he is known as "Second Mahatma Gandhi". This man has managed to awaken an entire nation and has motivated them to fight against corruption. But how has Anna Hazare managed all this when other people like Ram Dev ji Baba could not do it? Why are millions of people following him? How are thousands of youth ready to fast until death with him now? How as he managed to make an entire nation sit up and take notice ? What makes him so special? Answers to these questions lies in answers of few other questions like "Is Anna a great leader? Does he possess qualities of great leader? Does he have characteristics of transformational leader?

To answer these questions we need to look at the history and past life of Anna Hazare and we also need to consider the fight against corruption taken by him.

Anna Hazare: An Introduction

Anna a 74 year old man took birth as Kisan Baburao Hazare in a small village in Maharashtra to working class parents. He has played many powerful roles from a tenacious soldier to a social reformer, and a right to information crusader. Anna Hazare's journey of four decades has been unprecedented in terms of a non-violent yet effective campaign of resurrecting a barren village into an 'ideal village' model and empowering the faceless citizen through pioneering work on Right to Information. His efforts to empower grampanchayats, protect efficient government officers from frequent transfers and fight against the red tapism in government offices have also received accolades.

His tryst with the army came when many Indian soldiers became martyrs in the Indo-China War of 1962 and the Government of India had appealed to young Indians to join the Indian army. Being passionate about patriotism, he promptly responded to the appeal and joined the Indian Army in 1963. During his 15-year tenure as a soldier, he was posted to several states like Sikkim, Bhutan, Jammu-Kashmir, Assam, Mizoram, Leh and Ladakh and braved challenging weathers. At times, Hazare used to be frustrated with life and wondered about the very existence of human life. His mind yearned to look out for a solution to this simple and basic question. Fortunately for him, inspiration came from book of Swami Vivekananda. The book revealed to him that the ultimate motive of human life should be service to humanity. After reading the book, he realized that striving for the betterment of common people is equivalent to offering a prayer to the God. Anna was greatly influenced by Swami Vivekananda's teachings. At the age of 26, Anna took an oath to dedicate his life in the service of humanity. He decided to be bachelor to devote his life for the betterment of human life. After completing 15 years of service in army, he returned to his native place in Ralegan Siddhi, in the Parner tehsil of Ahmednagar district.

Development of Model Town

Anna Hazare saw miserable condition of farmers due to water scarcity in his village Ralegan Siddhi. Hazare visited the project of one Vilasrao Salunke, a resident of Saswad near Pune who had started a novel project of water management through watershed development in a joint venture with the Gram Panchyat and decided to implement it in Ralegan Siddhi. By keeping an eye on conserving every drop of water and preventing erosion of the fertile soil, he steered the villagers to begin working towards water conservation. The combined effort of Anna and villagers resulted in 48 Nala Bunding work, contour trenches, staggered trenches, gully plugs, meadows development and of forestation of 500 hectares of land, five RCC weirs and 16 Gabion Weirs thus increasing ground water level. After that, Hazare along with his team worked out the cropping pattern suitable to the quality of soil and the water volume available for farming. This led to increase in the water table by making water available for 1,500 acres of land instead of 300 acres. As a natural sequel, this effort led to yielding of food-grains and the villagers became self-sufficient in terms of food. The table turned turtle – earlier there was no work available for the villagers, now manpower was required to be imported from neighboring villages.

On the request of Anna, all the villagers came under one roof of unity and people voluntarily contributed in terms of labour and money to build a school, a hostel, a temple and other buildings. Mass marriages, grains bank, dairy, cooperative society, self-help groups for women and youth mandals helped develop the village in all aspects and gave a new face to it. Hazare's Ralegan Siddhi became the first role model of an ideal village and has become a tourist spot for many visitors across the nation, since it shows the metamorphoses from the worst village to an ideal village.

Right to Information Campaigning

Anna rightly thought that Development is marred by corruption and started a new venture in 1991 called Bhrashtachar Virodhi Jan Aandolan (BVJA) or public movement against corruption. It was found that some 42 forest officers had duped the state government for crores of rupees through corruption in confederacy. Hazare submitted the evidences to the government but the latter was reluctant to take action against all these officers as one of the ministers of the ruling party was involved in the scam. A distressed Hazare returned the Padmashree Award to the President of India and also returned the Vriksha Mitra Award given by then prime minister of India Rajiv Gandhi. He further went on an indefinite hunger strike in Alandi on the same issue. Finally, the government took action against the culprits. Hazare realized need to change the entire system that was studded with loopholes. Hence, he campaigned for the Right to Information Act and first agitated in the historical Azad Maidan in Mumbai in the year 1997 and he agitated at least ten times for the same cause. To create mass public awareness about RTI amongst the youth, Hazare traveled extensively throughout the state. Finally, again he went on an indefinite hunger strike at Azad Maidan in the last week of July 2003. At last, the President of India signed the draft of the Right to Information Act after his 12-day-long hunger strike and ordered the state government to implement it with effect from 2002. The same draft was considered as the base document for the making of the National Right to Information Act-2005. After the implementation of the RTI Act-2005, Hazare travelled for more than 12,000 Kms across the state creating awareness about the Act, interacted with more than one lakh college students and conducted mass public meetings across 24 districts of the state. Hazare deservedly won the coveted Padmashree and then Padmabhushan. Care International of the USA, Transparency International, Seoul (South Korea) also felicitated him. Apart from this, he received awards worth Rs 25 lakh and donated the entire amount for the Swami Vivekananda Kritadnyata Nidhi (social gratitude fund). Out of the two lakh rupees received from the above amount, mass marriages are carried of at least 25-30 poor couples every year.

Fight against Corruption

Anna Hazare's fight against corruption started during implementation of "Adarsh Gaon Yojana". While working in the scheme, he realized that development is getting hampered due to planned corruption in Government machinery and he decided to fight against this corruption. He gave evidence against two ministers who had amassed wealth disproportionate to their income and also started agitation and undertook fast for 10 days. Chief Minister intervened and he deleted these two ministers from ministry and appointed an Inquiry Commission.

He also forwarded evidence of corruption about 4 ministers in the regime of coalition Government of Congress and National Congress Party, and had asked the Government to conduct inquiry and also undertook fast for 9 days in August 2003 at Azad Maidan. One of the ministers had made allegations about corruption in the institutions in which Anna was associated. Government appointed retired Supreme Court Judge Shri P.B. Sawant to conduct the inquiry. In the report the commission had observed ministers guilty and had held Mr.Hazare also guilty for irregularities but not a single charge of corruption was proved against him. Mr. Hazare has offered the Government that it should take action against him as well as the ministers based on the findings of the enquiry commissions.

Afterwards, He realized that to stop big evil of corruption a change is required in the system and for this a strong movement should be initiated. He believes that decentralization of power is must if we need to change the system. Anna started his operation on big scale when the complete nation was burning because of spate of scams and scandals across the country. He formed his team of strong people from diversified backgrounds who are expert in their areas and who also considered as honest people. Anna appeared on the national canvas in April 2011, when he went on an indefinite fast at Delhi's Jantar Mantar to implement a strong anti-corruption bill. That fast lasted for only four days, but it tapped into the collective conscience of a nation. Middle India rose as one, and leading them was an unlikely leader, Kisan Baburao Hazare. When he felt reluctance from the side of Government in fulfilling their cimmitement, he again started he campaign and that is too on bigger level. This time he involved millions of Indians in his fight. He made people to believe in his vision of corruption free India which brought people in Ramlila Maidan to support anti-corruption movement. Anna was arrested before he went on his second fast. But this could shatter his confidence in himself and in his people. His 13days long fast came to the end with the victory of thousands of Indians who selflessly supported this big movement.

In all these fights for social betterment, Anna was eager to sacrifice his life for noble cause. That Hazare has given his life for social betterment is reflected thus: "I do have my home in the village but I have not entered it for the past 35 years. I have implemented schemes costing more than several crores of rupees but I do not have bank balance. Last 12 years I have been working in the field of eradication of corruption. This movement is run entirely by public support without and grants or sponsorships. I appeal for money wherever I go for a public meeting and urge them to contribute generously. The same money I use to carry out my campaigns. The money collected at such public meetings is counted in front of the villagers and my volunteers issue a receipt of the same on the spot". Baba Ram Dev also started similar movement but could not succeed because he could not instill required interest in the people. Even his response to the actions taken by state police made others to feel that he was not confident about his movement. Apart from this there were many other differences which made efforts futile.

Today Anna is considered as great leader and being compared with Leaders like Mahatama Gandhi, Jr. King martin Luther, etc because of his qualities and selfless motives. As Anna says his fight against corruption and other social evils is not finished yet. He is eating healthy and gaining weight to restart his fight with more energy, more zeal and new vision.

Teaching Objectives

This case study is having below given teaching objectives:

1. To make students understand leadership process.
2. To make students well versed with traits and qualities of effective leaders.
3. To make students aware about reasons for leadership derailment.
4. To give students understanding of behavior of transformational leader and process of transformational leadership.

Student Assignment

Students are required to give answers of below given question:

1. Identify leadership qualities posses by Anna.
2. Why Anna has been widely accepted as leader? Explain
3. Is Anna a Transformational leader? Prove it.

Potential Use of Case

This case can be used to make students understand continuous process of leadership. Even this case can be used to make students to inculcate qualities of great leaders if they want to be leader in future.

Sources

1. www.annahazare.org visited in between 1st September to 10th September, 2011
2. www.ndtv.com
3. *indiatoday.intoday.in/video/rajinikanth-supports-anna.../148906.html*
4. http://indiatoday.intoday.in/story/anna-hazare-a-powerful-leader-pranab-mukherjee/1/149751.html
5. http://timesofindia.indiatimes.com/topic/Anna-Hazare
6. Book "Anna Hazare: Reformer, Socialist and Anti-Corruption Leader" by J C Dua
7. http://ibnlive.in.com/news/the-rise-of-the-leader-anna-hazare/179169-3.html

2

E-Assessment : A Emerging Area for the Indian Education Sector

Mr. Daljeet Singh Bawa
Assistant Professor, Bharati Vidyapeeth Institute of Management & Research
daljeetsbawa@yahoo.com

Dr. S.L. Gupta
Professor, Birla Institute of Technology

Dr. Narayan is the Head of Department of Management of Nandan University. He calls for a meeting of the concerned faculty members. He is in a pensive mood. He says "Despite of providing you with adequate infrastructural and instructional facilities, no considerable improvement has been shown in the performance of the students in the term papers. Where we are heading to? The faculty members replied "It is very difficult for us to keep a track of all the students. We are trying to find possible alternatives to keep student motivated, engaged but it is practically impossible for us to keep a track of individual student." Dr. Narayan said "We need to find a probable solution to track individual student progress, the discrepancies and reasons for the deviations in the student's performance." The faculty members said "We need a system which can serve the purposes of assessment of a learner's knowledge and skills at the outset of course, that provides developmental feedback to a learner on his or her current understanding and skills and learner's achievement leading to formal qualification". "I think we need to contact an educational consultancy so that we can focus and track individual learning and performance."

The educational consultancy suggested them to make use of an automated solution of assessment (E-Assessment) which can enable them to track individual progress. E-assessment involves the use of information technology in the design, delivery and administration of assessment activities which can effectively contribute to the Qualifications Framework. The need is to identify the key stakeholders. Stakeholders are defined as Individuals and organizations with a vested interest in the assessment process. "Each stakeholder has its own perspective(s)". The key areas where e-assessment can have a possible impact in case of an educational institution can be teaching, learning, assessing and administration.

The consultant from educational consultancy explains to him that e-assessment involves the use of one or more technologies to support the overall assessment process. For example, an assessor may use an e-portfolio to gather information on candidate performance in the workplace or an online quiz to assess their knowledge of key concepts and processes. The assessor may use this information in combination with other assessment evidence, such as direct observation or a third party report, to evaluate candidate performance. In turn, the outcomes of the assessment may be captured in a management information system and used to produce rapid, reliable information on candidate progress. E-assessment may be used for diagnostic, formative or summative assessment purposes. In diagnostic assessment, e-assessment resources and materials are used to identify candidate's strengths and areas for improvement. This form of assessment often occurs at the commencement of a training program. In formative assessment or assessment for learning, evidence is used to provide developmental feedback to learners on their current skills and knowledge relative to a defined standard. This information may also be used by trainers so that instruction may be modified to suit learner needs. In summative assessment or assessment of learning, e-assessment resources and materials are used in gathering evidence and making decisions about the competence of the candidate.

Thus e-assessment can serve as a potential tool to comprehend the intricacies of the teaching-learning process keeping in view the importance of the evaluation system at different stages and possible feedback. This will enable data coaching and will prove to be an effective diagnostic tool for students' achievements

3

Darkness to dawn and dawn to darkness. What next?

Dr. Dattatry Ramchandra Mane
Associate Professor, Department of Management Sciences
University of Pune

An engineer and a post graduate in management from a premium institute. Nandu born in lower middle class family having two sisters and a brother. Father was a first member in family who came to city in search of job and joined an industry as a machine operator. Hence has to support his family in the village and manage his own family.

Since school days, Nandu has developed an interest in machines and their operations. Fortunately, he could get a chance to visit a Small Scale unit often as it was owned and managed by father of his friend Raju. After 10th standard, Nandu could hardly get any time to visit the unit, but his interest in machines made him complete mechanical engineering successfully.

As Nandu was interested in machines and industry, during vacations instead of enjoying vacations like other students. Nandu used to go to Small Scale units and request them to permit him to work in their industry for which they should not pay him any remuneration. He during his vacation went to different industries and had worked with pattern shop, forging unit, machine shop etc and got an overall idea of the mechanical industry. After his engineering he availed of B-School education from a premier institute.

He got a good job in a reputed company through campus placement programme. He was quite satisfied with his job, yet a feeling of discomfort was there as he was not using his talents and potential completely.

Once when Nandu was on a business tour and accidently met his old friend Raju from school whose father was having a small scale unit. They were meeting after a long gap of 10 years. They decided to have a dinner together that night. While discussion at the dinner all the past memories were cherished. During discussion Nandu realized that Raju had left education after 12th and was helping his father in his business and was thinking of starting his own unit. Through the discussion, Nandu realized that Raju was experiencing shortage of funds.

While offering the proposal, Nandu was highly convinced about his business partnership with Raju. Firstly, Raju had experience of working with his father for about five years. Secondly, his father's contacts would fetch order's for Raju and Nandu and eventually, they will develop their vendors. Thirdly, Raju was capable of handling the routine work of the unit like production, quality, machine setting, scheduling activities, delivery and follow up with customers. Nandu will continue with his job, but during free time he will pursue business development. Fourthly, partnership will enable them share the risk involved in their business.

The proposal of being partners started taking shape. Nandu taking initiative started to enquire for machines and check the best possible option. During this process he decided to install a machine of higher capacity so that there would not be a capacity issues and would be able to satisfy varied requirements of jobs where capacity of the machine would not be a problem. Nandu did not wanted be compromise on quality as well as on capacity issues from day one.

Meanwhile, Raju had identified a shop which was very close to their (Rajlaxmi) shop for which Nandu also agreed. As it was close to Rajlaxmi shop Nandu found advantages as initially they were going to get the workload from Rajlaxmi for which transportation would not be an issue secondly, it would also help in maintaining the quality as Rajlaxmi was in the business for a longer period of time and expertise advice would be useful, it would also help in achieving the schedule and also communication between units would be effective.

They finalized the machine and the shop. Nandu meet raju for his contribution as Nandu has paid the advance for the machine and also deposit for the shop on his own. Raju promised to give his share at the time of installation of the machine as some payment of him was pending with some parties.

The day of inauguration started knocking at the door, Nandu was desperate to get Raju's contribution. And a blow! Raju steeped down from the partnership.

Nandu got disheartened initially. He had reached a stage from where it was not possible to go back. As Nandu had by this time invested a lot of money, time and energy.

Nandu came home and for the whole night he was not able to sleep. He was thinking for an alternative, as time had already ran out of his hand. At last, Nandu decided to inaugurate the shop next morning as he had belief in himself and a fighting spirit. Decided to continue the biggest question before him was how he is going to start the machine as there was no job for operation which jobs should be installed on the machines at least for inauguration as Raju had back out there was no question of getting any workload from Rajlaxmi Enterprises.

Next day Nandu, went to a scrap yard and purchased some round bars so that at least he can install on the machine and carry out the operation for inauguration.

After inauguration Nandu came home and again started thinking seriously about his decision whether he should delete the idea of starting a unit by selling the machines or should start searching for the workload on his own which he know was very difficult.

As Nandu had a fighting spirit, he decided to work hard and search for a load for his shop. Nandu used to go for job and after the office hours he used to meet the companies officers for job (work load) but was unable to get them. This continued for about a month and a half. At last one company was ready to give the roughing work but asked for installing two more machines of smaller capacity as the job required three operations in a sequence.

Nandu was in a great trouble as there was no output of single rupee from the installed machine and also he had invested all his savings in the machine already and was not having any surplus for further investment in the machines and also there was no guarantee of the company that it will give regular supply of the jobs for machining.

As Nandu had no alternative he decided to purchased two new machines by taking loan and installed in the shop. The first lot of jobs Nandu himself loaded a vehicle and brought it in the shop. As there were only two operators and three machines Nandu used to work on the third machine by him after returning from his job till 12 in the night. This went for a longer period.

Many a times, there was shortage of jobs for operations as Nandu had only single party from whom they got the load. This was affecting the profits as the overhead and the operator's wages expenses had to be paid even though the machines were idle. Many times there was no profit left and Nandu had to manage the expenses from his own salary. One more problem was of not getting the payment in stipulated time for which Nandu had to incur the expenses from his own pocket.

Nandu was aware of the risk of dependency on a single customer and hence was always searching for some additional customers so that risk of dependency can be reduced and also utilization of facility can be increased further as current utilization was only 40% of the facility.

Eventually as days passed it was a regular schedule for Nandu to work on the machines after coming from the office till late night and on the next day before going to his office visit the units and give the direction to the workers. Nandu was determined and ready to work hard for getting his dreams true of becoming an entrepreneur.

His determination and hard work started giving results. He started getting more and more orders on account of quality of his product.

As the demand went on increasing, day by day, Nandu went on increasing the operational time from 8 to 12, 12 to 16 and finally 16 to 24 hours a day!

This trend of increase in demand continued and the demand was increasing and thus to satisfy the demand two more machines were installed in the same premises. It was not further possible to install any more machine in the same premises as there was no space available.

Known for quality and delivery schedules Nandu got an offer by Mumbai based company for machining the components who was ready to give sufficient load for the machines but the only requirement was the unit should be located outside octroi limits.

Nandu had two alternative to shift existing machines outside octroi limits or to install all together new machines in the new premises i.e. setting up an additional unit.

After giving a thought Nandu decided to install new machines in a new facility and let the old shop and the facility run in the old location. As there was no point in altogether closing down the existing business which is set for a longer period and also all the machines and operators were trained and set for performing the jobs. And over the period of time good relations with the suppliers are built. There was also a thought that if he shifts his existing plant outside octroi limits he will lose out the suppliers and the company for whom he had developed relations. Also there is a risk of dependency on a single supplier for whom he is new. He also felt that if he installs a new facility at the new location his business will also grow and risk is minimized. Hence he decided to install a new facility was taken.

As growth was fast and the requirements form the customers were increasing continuously nandu invested all the profits he generated from the business and some part of his earnings from job in expanding the facility. He had never thought of keeping some profits aside. The reason for doing so would be growth and also as he was not married there was no responsibility on him and he wanted to take advantage of these favorable conditions and grow the business.

As the business expended and there were two different units located approximately 18 kilometers away from each other it was getting more and more difficult in controlling these two units. Nandu had appointed supervisors at both the shops so that he will get some relief.

Due to quality and timely delivery the orders were continuously increasing and the Mumbai based company was putting pressure on Nandu to increase his capacity by adding more machines. It was very difficult for Nandu to invest more in new machines as he had already take the loan for the existing machines and the loan was not fully paid back.

Hence Nandu took the decision of closing down the first plant and shifting all the machines at one location as the load was sufficiently large which can satisfy the capacity requirements. He also felt that if sufficient load is assured by the company it would be better if he shift his machine from the first plant and install them at new location which will also help him to concentrate and planning and controlling would be easier it would also help to improve the quality. Taking all the factors into consideration he shifted the machines at new location which was outside octroi limits.

Mean while the customer who had asked Nandu to install the facility outside the octroi limit had identified a party for CNC operations which was done earlier by the company themselves. They also asked Nandu to affiliate with the new party and get load from the CNC party and supply the jobs after pre-turning to the new vendor. He was also directed to race the bill for pre turning on the CNC vendor and settlement of bill will be done by the new vendor and get the payment for the same party.

The CNC machining vendor was a partnership firm in which one partner was looking after the orders and the other one was looking after the day to day operations in house. But it seemed that both the partners was not serious and they had no control over the quality of the products which increased the rejection and rework and also delivery schedules were not meet and delays in supply was a regular complaints. As there was delays and rejections by CNC vendor the amount was deducted from their bills and due to delays in the supply of material the down time cost was recovered from the party which also lead to delay in payments.

This affected Nandu at large as to incorporate the rejection by the CNC party they insisted on price cutting and asked to reduce the machining cost for which they were not at fault. The delays in payments were also frequent phenomena.

Large amount of payment was blocked with the CNC party and it was getting very difficult to run the unit for Nandu as he had to pay the wages, rent, electricity charges and other expenses incurred.

Mean while Nandu had left the job and got married to a girl who was also career oriented and was working in government at a higher position.

During his pursuit of his goals, Nandu had observed ethics and good values.

As the payment (bills) were blocked it was very difficult for nandu to manage the day to day expenses for which Nandu had to take additional loan from the bank. The days started changing the downfall began! It happens!

The outstanding of the CNC machine shop increased. The CNC vendor was also not in a position to repay the bank loan in spite of the banks reminders for repaying the loan installments. There were disputes between the partners and the partnership was broken.

The partner who had taken over the shop with the loan was not from technical back ground and was unable to run the shop and the rejection increased further.

Finally the bank put seal on the shop and the operations were stop. But in the whole process Nandu suffered a lot as a huge amount of money was blocked and there were no chances of recovering the amount in near future and also there were not work load for his plant.

Mean while Nandu sensing the future had applied for a job and got selected and joined a job which was having an attractive package and an opportunity for growth. The job profile also matched with the area of interest i.e. manufacturing sectors where he can experiment on the machines and produce the products.

Now Nandu had to decide between the two options whether he should close the shop by selling the unit and enjoy the life with his daughter and wife or put some extra efforts again and try to rebuild the unit.

Questions

1. Which entrepreneurial qualities could be identified in Nandu's personality?
2. Do you feel he should learn out of his failure?
3. What would you advise Nandu- to continue with the business or to concentrate only on salaried job?

4

Climate Change and Water Poverty: Increasing Vulnerability of Women

Dr. Savita Aggarwal, Dr. Geeta Punhani**, Ms. Jagriti Kher***
Institute of Home Economics, University of Delhi
jagriti28@gmail.com
*Assistant Professor, Department of Communication and Extension, Institute of Home Economics, University of Delhi, ** Associate Professors, Department of Communication and Extension, Institute of Home Economics, University of Delhi

Water: An integrated resource

Water is one of the most important natural resource required for multiple uses across societies and cultures. Water is used for domestic, agricultural, industrial and environmental uses. Inadequate access to safe water profoundly affects most people in their lives and livelihoods. Access to water in an equitable manner and the improved management of water are therefore, imperative to the quality of life in a society, and for sustainable development and poverty alleviation. The role of water is so important that poverty itself is now recognized to be due to lack of access to different livelihood resources such as water (Sen, 1999). This is apparent by the fact that almost two third of the population without access to safe water lives on less than two dollars a day (Human Development Report, 2006).

According to the World Water Development Report, 2003, almost 1.1 billion people in the developing countries have inadequate access to water and 2.4 billion lack access to adequate sanitation facilities. According to the latest WHO/UNICEF Joint Monitoring Programme for

Water Supply and Sanitation (JMP 2010). 884 million people in the world still do not get their drinking water from improved sources and almost all of them are in developing regions. In India as well as many other developing countries, large numbers of households still do not have provision of adequate water for domestic use. This has resulted in a significant loss of time and effort, especially on the part of women, who most often have to bear the burden of water collection.

Women and Water

The role of women as water managers for the family is undisputed in most of the developing world. Women are very closely associated with water since it is at the core of their traditional responsibilities such as cooking, cleaning and sanitation as well as bathing and caring for the children. Further, women are instrumental in educating children about water and sanitation.

Since women and children spend greater amounts of time at home as compared to men, therefore they are more likely to be affected by the availability of water or the lack of it. Rural and semi-urban women spend considerable time procuring, transporting and storing water from different water bodies such as rivers, lakes wells or community taps. They carry water in different containers on their head or in their arms. They often have to travel long distances and pay heavy physical (time, energy), temporal (time), affective (negative feelings and attitudes) and cognitive (opportunities for formal education, training and intellectual development) costs. In times of sickness of family members, disasters and environmental stress, such as droughts or floods the burdens of women magnify several times, since they are the primary caregivers for the family.

Studies conducted in different parts of the world show a clear linkage between gender and water. According to an estimate by UNFPA, 2002, women in many developing countries walk for an average of six kilometers every day to collect water. One of the prime causative factors of the very large gender gaps in school attendance in many countries is the time burden of collecting and carrying water by the female children (Human development report 2006). There may be almost 50 million primary school age girls who are not in school in developing countries because of fetching water and firewood (UNICEF, 1998). A study conducted in Tanzania has depicted a very strong relationship between school attendance and distance of water source from home. It was found that when the source of water was 15 minutes or less from the home, the school attendance of girls was 12% higher as compared to homes where water source was an hour or more away (Hanchate and Dyson, 2004). This was not the case with boys since their attendance rates in school was far less sensitive to distance of water source from home, highlighting the role that girls play in fetching water.

A study conducted by WHO/UNICEF Joint Monitoring Programme for Water Supply and Sanitation in 35 developing countries in 2005-06, confirm the anecdotal evidence that women (64%) shoulder the bulk of the water collection. Women are more than twice as likely as men to go and fetch drinking water.

A study on time use pattern across 18,000 households spread across six states in India indicated that water collection is a deeply gendered task. Women are primarily responsible for water collection and bear 87% of the work burden of water collection, the rest being borne by men and children. Men have 76 percentage points less probability to fetch water as compared to women (MOSPI, 1998-99).

Translating the losses borne by girls and women in terms of man (woman) hours and economics shows a loss of human capital and reduces the ability of the household to capitalize fully on its other resources. As per a study conducted in India by Foundation for Science, Technology and Ecology it is estimated that women fetching water spend 150 million work days per year, equivalent to a national loss of income of 10 billion rupees.

The Millennium Development goals were put forward by the United Nations in 2000 to improve the quality of life of people of the world. It is significant to note that all the eight goals are directly or indirectly water dependant (WHO-UNICEF JMP, 2004). It is also important that though gender is mentioned only in two of the above goals, yet many of the goals are women dependant in addition to being water dependant.

The Government of India put forward The National Policy for Women Empowerment in 2001 which states that, "Special attention will be given to the needs of women in provision of safe drinking water, sewage disposal, toilet facilities and sanitation within accessible reach of households especially in the rural areas and urban slums." Despite all these concerns, access to safe water eludes a large proportion of women in the developing world.

Climate Change and Water

During the past century, mean world temperature has increased by 0.74° C and it is projected that in the next 100 years, global mean temperature may rise by 1.1 to 6.4° C (IPCC 2007). This, in turn, will lead to changes in all aspects of the hydrological cycle. It is projected that rainfall will become more variable and uncertain, leading to increased frequency of droughts and floods. All these would have an impact on the spatial and temporal availability of water in many parts of the world. It is estimated that climate change account for 20% of the increase in global water scarcity (World water Report, 2003). According to Human Development Report, 2006, almost 700 million people in 43 countries live below water stress threshold of 1700 meter cube per person by 2025 this figure will reach three billion.

The requirements of water are continuously increasing due to strong physical and industrial growth of the cities as well as rapid rural to urban migration. According to UN projections, by 2030, almost 60% of the global population will come to reside in the cities and put an additional pressure on the resources including water. Also a large proportion of the growth in urbanization will occur in the developing world with over two billion people moving to the cities between 2000 and 2030 (United Nations, 2005). This will further push the demand for water and other resources in the urban areas, thereby aggravating the already complex situation.

Climate Change and Water availability: Indian Scenario

In India also, the water availability in future is likely to be different as compared to the present due to changes in rainfall patterns. During the last fifty years, mean annual surface air temperature has risen by an average of 0.4^{0}C (Rupa Kumar et.al. 2002). There is an increased frequency of droughts and floods. It is projected that during the years 2041 to 2060, there will be increase in surface air temperatures across all seasons varying between 2-4^{0}C or even greater in the northern region. Not only the precipitation will become more variable, but also there will be an increase in the intensity of rainfall by 1-4 mm per day. There is also likely to be an increase in the highest one day rainfall (World Bank, 2009). By mid-century, annual average river runoff and water availability are projected to decrease by 10-30% over many parts of semi-arid and arid India some of which are already water stressed areas (IPCC, 2007). Such climatic changes, associated with increasing population, urbanization and industrialization, will significantly reduce the per capita water availability of water in the country. In India, the per capita availability of water was 5177 m^3/capita/ year in 1951. This value has drastically reduced to 1654 m^3/ capita/ year in 2007 and is likely to further go down to below 1140 m^3/ year by 2050 (MOWR, 2008). While the per capita availability of water is decreasing, the demand for water in the country is likely to rise significantly due to growing population and affluence. The total water consumption in India is expected to rise by 20-40% in the next 20 years (India vision, 2020). It is thus expected that in the coming years, problems of climate change coupled with urbanization will put increased pressure on water as well as other resources. Thus decreased availability of overall water supply in future is further likely to affect quality of life of people and is bound to impact the lives of women who are hitherto responsible for procurement and management of water.

Water Poverty Index: A tool to characterize water availability at household level

Several assessments of water resources through physical sciences and hydrological modeling are available. However, these do not link with our knowledge of human resources and their geographical distributions. The Human Poverty/Development Index although are very useful for assessing overall development of society, but are not able to capture entirely water related poverty problems. A more holistic approach is needed to address the questions of water availability, and its relationship to human and ecological needs with special focus on the gender issues related to water. The World Water Development reports 2003 and 2006 have reinforced the need for country specific indices on water related knowledge and capacities which can be instrumental in solving region specific problems and help set targets and monitor progress.

A water management tool, known as the Water Poverty Index (WPI) has recently become available which is able to bridge this gap. It is constructed with a methodology similar to HDI. WPI is a holistic water management tool developed by physical and social scientists, water practitioners, researchers and stakeholders. It involves quantitative and qualitative assessments of physical and socio-economic indicators to monitor the availability of water in communities (Sullivan, 2002). It is a simple and easy to use indicator and can be used by water managers, planners as well as people at the community level. This requires an interdisciplinary approach and is able to link physical estimates of water availability with the socio-economic drivers of household welfare at all levels from a community, village, district, region and nation and indicates the degree to which water scarcity impacts human populations. The index was developed as a tool to measure water stress at the household and community levels, designed to aid national decision makers, at community and central government level, as well as donor agencies, to determine priority needs for interventions in the water sector. The index combines into a single number, a cluster of data directly and indirectly relevant to water stress. It has already been used extensively for characterizing water poverty of nations (Lawrence et al., 2003), regions (Cullis and O'Regan, 2004) and communities (Sullivan et al., 2003).

The components of the index are resources, access, capacity, use and environment all of which impact the availability of safe water in the household as described in Figure 1. Further, each of the components has several subcomponents.

The '*Resource*' component aims to capture the overall availability of water. '*Access* to water' includes the access of population to safe drinking water and sanitation as well as access to water for other purposes. The '*use*' component focuses on the consumption of water at the domestic level, in industry and agriculture. '*Capacity*' is the ability of people to manage water and is interpreted in terms of education, investment in the health sector and income which indicate the capacity of people to lobby for water. The '*environment*' component is very complex, combining variables such as quality of water, water stress and environmental degradation. Each of these components put together are used to generate the WPI score.

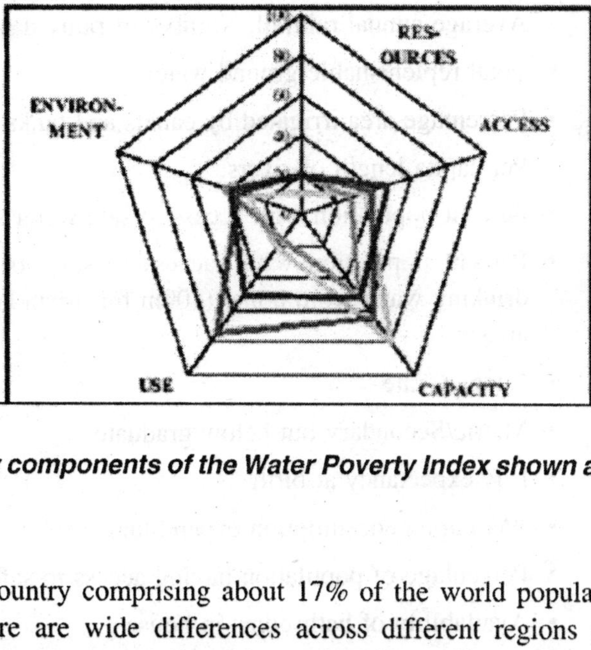

Figure 1. Key components of the Water Poverty Index shown as a pentagram.

The Present study

India is a large country comprising about 17% of the world population and just 4% of its water resources. There are wide differences across different regions and states in terms of availability of water resources, the level of human development, the access of people to resources such as water, the vulnerability of people and the state of environment. Assigning one value of WPI to such a large and diverse country does not reflect the regional variation in the household water availability. Thus the present study was undertaken to quantify the availability and management of water at the household level for different states of India. Despite much research on gender and natural resources management, there have been only a handful of studies on gender and water which, based on empirical data bring out the impact of household water poverty on gender. Since climate change coupled with demographic and socio economic factors are bound to impact the availability of water, also the close association of accession and management practices related to water and women empowerment, the linkages between water, climate change and women has also been studied. Thus the present study is on the impacts of Climate change on water and also its consequent impact on women.

Methodology

The WPI was calculated using the five components namely Resources, Access, capacity, Environment and Use. Their state level parameters were evaluated to quantify the value of WPI and an average was determined to arrive at a definite value. The following sub-components were used to quantify the WPI keeping the mind their suitability for the region and feasibility of obtaining data.

TABLE 1.

Components used to compute WPI in the present study (based on Sullivan et.al. 2002).

Components	*State level*
Resources	• Average annual rainfall, Number of rainy days
	• Total replenishable ground water
	• Percentage area irrigated by canals and tanks
	• Per capita length of rivers.
Access	• Percent population with access to safe water supply
	• Percent population with access to safe location of safe source of drinking water from home (100m for urban areas and 500 m for rural areas)
Capacity	• Literacy rate
	• Matric/Secondary but below graduate
	• Life expectancy at birth
	• Per capita consumption expenditure
Environment	• Percentage of population having access to safe toilet facilities
	• Availability of bathrooms in house
	• Percentage of wastes treated
	• Percent population living in slums.
Use	• Ground water used for
	• Domestic and Industrial sector
	• Irrigation purposes
	• Percent of net irrigated area to net sown area

In order to quantify WPI values for states of India, the index values for all the components were calculated. The sub components were classified in two categories- negative indicators, and positive indicators. Variables such as percentage of households, having access to safe drinking water facilities, percentage of households having bathrooms in the house lead to better development and hence were classified as positive indicators. On the other hand, the indicators such as percent population living in slums were negative indicators. These figures were converted into index numbers by normalization method, as used for calculating Human Development Index (For detailed methodology, refer to Sullivan, et. al., 2002).

The Index values of Water Poverty

An average of all the five values indicated the water poverty of people in various states of India. The results given in table 1 show that the WPI values ranged from as low as 0.24 in case of Jharkhand to as high as 0.64 in case of Punjab indicating that there are large differences in the management and utilization of water resources.

Jharkhand had the worst record in this because of generally poor scores in all the components of water poverty Index (Figure2; Table 2). As many as thirteen states had WPI values below or equal to 0.40 indicating highest level of water poverty. These included Bihar, Uttar Pradesh, Rajasthan, Jharkhand, Madhya Pradesh, Maharashtra and Orissa. This group included the populous state of Uttar Pradesh and even Maharashtra. The low values of WPI in all the above states were due to relatively small resource base, limited capacity to lobby for water and subsequently low use of water for different purposes.

Fifteen states and Union Territories (UT's) had WPI values ranging from 0.41 to 0.50 indicating moderate level of water poverty. This group includes Gujarat, Himachal Pradesh, Tamil Nadu, North eastern states such as Arunachal Pradesh, Sikkim and Mizoram and even the agriculturally well to do state of Haryana. These states attained these scores through different routes of sub components (figure 2), indicating scope for improvement in the overall management of water resources. Only four states and UT's had WPI values ranging from 0.51 to 0.60. These include Chandigarh, Delhi and Goa, these were relatively better off in terms of the accession and management of water. The only state of Punjab had an index value above 0.60 representing the least water poverty scenario.

The household water poverty Index value for India was 0.40 indicating high water poverty and considerable deficit in the accession and management of water at the household level.

While some of the states had high values of Environment others were high on Access or use and some others in Capacity. Over all there is a lot that needs to be done in these states

TABLE 2
State Level variation in the values of WPI

Name of the state	*Resources*	*Access*	*Capacity*	*Environment*	*Use*	*WPI*
Andaman & Nicobar Islands	0.44	0.73	0.65	0.36	0.27	0.49
Andhra Pradesh	0.22	0.74	0.32	0.19	0.30	0.35
Arunachal Pradesh	0.65	0.74	0.29	0.38	0.09	0.43
Assam	0.58	0.52	0.22	0.41	0.28	0.40
Bihar	0.20	0.83	0.08	0.24	0.40	0.35
Chandigarh	0.08	1.00	0.87	0.67	0.18	0.56
Chattisgarh	0.38	0.64	0.20	0.14	0.33	0.34
Dadra & Nagar Haveli	0.30	0.75	0.35	0.40	0.41	0.44
Daman & Diu	0.02	0.97	0.67	0.55	0.13	0.47
Delhi	0.05	0.96	0.78	0.69	0.52	0.60
Goa	0.38	0.68	0.92	0.56	0.28	0.56
Gujarat	0.13	0.81	0.41	0.51	0.35	0.44
Haryana	0.17	0.80	0.47	0.40	0.57	0.48
Himachal Pradesh	0.17	0.86	0.56	0.64	0.12	0.47
Jammu & kashmir	0.54	0.62	0.30	0.33	0.38	0.43
Jharkhand	0.22	0.37	0.19	0.23	0.18	0.24
Karnataka	0.23	0.76	0.41	0.43	0.31	0.43
Kerala	0.46	0.19	0.77	0.65	0.41	0.50
lakshadweep	0.13	0.00	0.67	0.75	0.44	0.40
Madhya Pradesh	0.21	0.61	0.16	0.23	0.35	0.31
Maharashtra	0.23	0.77	0.56	0.26	0.18	0.40
Manipur	0.47	0.30	0.54	0.48	0.07	0.37
Meghalaya	0.76	0.34	0.24	0.27	0.10	0.34
Mizoram	0.79	0.32	0.57	0.64	0.06	0.48
Nagaland	0.36	0.42	0.46	0.50	0.11	0.37
Orissa	0.37	0.54	0.19	0.18	0.32	0.32
Pondicherry	0.13	0.95	0.76	0.43	0.61	0.58
Punjab	0.20	0.98	0.59	0.44	1.00	0.64
Rajasthan	0.09	0.62	0.20	0.28	0.40	0.32
Sikkim	0.54	0.66	0.39	0.51	0.21	0.46
Tamil Nadu	0.21	0.82	0.47	0.37	0.37	0.45
Tripura	0.39	0.46	0.39	0.42	0.33	0.40
Uttar Pradesh	0.18	0.85	0.15	0.29	0.53	0.40
Uttarakhand	0.27	0.83	0.41	0.39	0.25	0.43
West Bengal	0.28	0.81	0.33	0.28	0.32	0.41
India Values	0.24	0.73	0.33	0.32	0.36	0.40

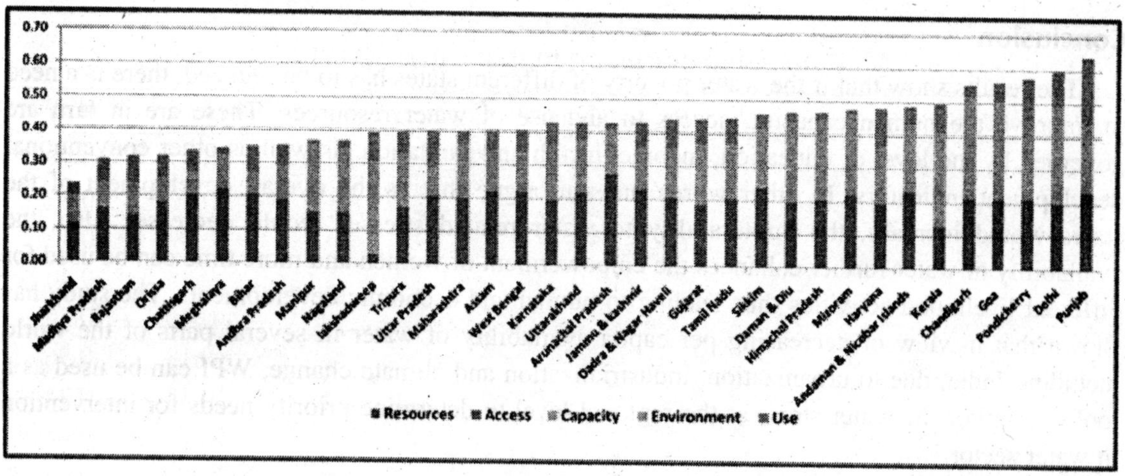

Fig 2: State level variation in Water poverty Index at the household level

Since water and women are very closely associated WPI was plotted against the Gender related index (GDI) values for the states of India.

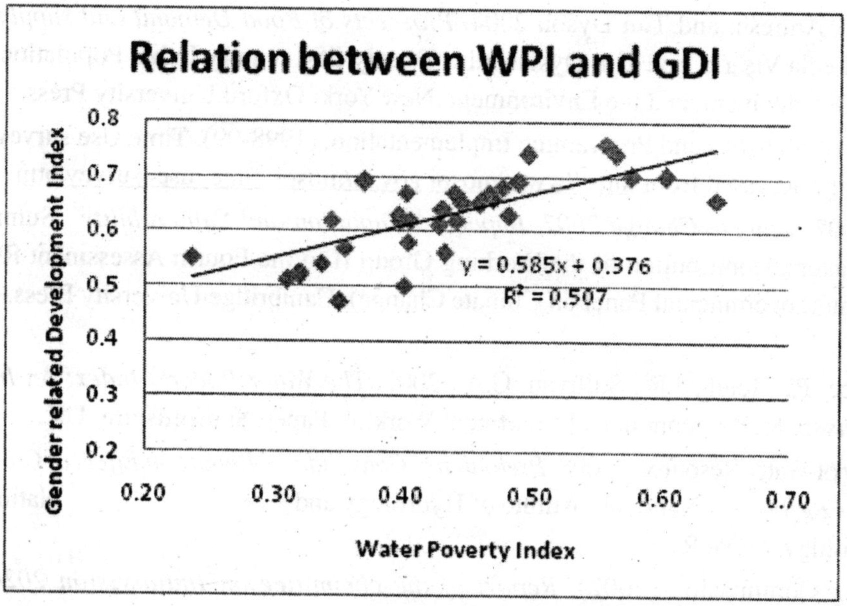

There was a direct and a highly significant relationship between water poverty index in the different states of India and Gender related development Index. The states with better availability, accession and management of water also had better status of women as was indicated by higher values of Gender related development Index. This is because women benefit by better accession and management of water through improved health, sanitation, nutritional status, better chances of education as well as economic empowerment.

Conclusion

The results show that if the water poverty of different states has to be reduced, there is a need to improve the human capacity, access to and use of water resources. These are in turn are governed by the level of education, income, health and sanitation, as well as other conventional development indicators. In other words one can argue that as the overall development of the states would increase, the vulnerability to water related stresses would decrease. Also, the availability of water further enhances the empowerment of women and more time can be used for different livelihood activities thus leading to human and economic development. The study has shown that in view of decreasing per capita availability of water in several parts of the world including India, due to urbanization, industrialization and climate change, WPI can be used as a tool to monitor the water stress at the regional level to determine priority needs for intervention in water sector.

References

- Department of Women and Child Development: *National Policy for the Empowerment of Women-* 2001 – India. Retrieved from http://wcd.nic.in/empwomen.htm
- Hanchate, Amresh, and Tim Dyson 2004. *Prospects of Food Demand and supply*. In Robert Cassen, Leela Visaria, and Tim Dyson, eds., Twenty first century India: Population, Economy, Human Development, and the Environment. New York: Oxford University Press.
- Ministry of Statistics and Programme Implementation, (1998-99). Time Use survey: Summary of Findings accessed from http://www.mospi.gov.in/mospi_time_use_survey.htm
- IPCC 2007. *Climate Change 2007. Impacts, Adaptation and Vulnerability*. Summary of the Policymakers. Contribution of the Working Group II to the Fourth Assessment Report of the IPCC (Intergovernmental Panel on Climate Change). Cambridge University Press, Cambridge, U.K.
- Lawrence, P., Meigh, J.R., Sullivan, C.A., 2002. *The Water Poverty Index: An International Comparison*. Keele Economics Department Working Paper, Staffordshire, UK.
- Ministry of Water Resources, 2008. *Preliminary Consolidated Report on Effect of Climate Change on Water Resources*. National Institute of Hydrology and National institute of Hydrology, MOWR
- Planning Commission (2002). *Report of the committee on India vision 2020*. Planning Commission, Government of India.
- Rupa Kumar K., Krishna Kumar, R.G Ashrit. S.K. Patwardhan and G.B. Pant.2002. "Climate change in India: Observations and Projections." *In Climate Change in India: Issues, Concerns and Opportunities*, eds. P.R. Shukla, K. Subodh, S. Sharma and P.V.Ramana. New Delhi: Tata McGraw Publishing Company Ltd.
- Sen, A.K., 1999. Development as Freedom. Clarendon Press, Oxford.
- Sullivan, C.A., (2002). *Calculating a Water Poverty Index*. World Dev. 30, 1195-1210
- Sullivan, C.A., Meigh, J.R., Giacomello, A.M., Fediw, T., Lawrence, 2003.

The Water Poverty Index: Development and application at the community scale. Natural Resource Forum. Retrieved from http://gisweb.ciat.org/wcp/download/water_poverty_index_Sullivan.pdf.

- Sullivan C. and Meigh J., 2005. Targetting attention on local vulnerabilities using an integrated index approach: the example of climate vulnerability index, Water Science and Technology, Volume 51, No. 5, pp 69-78, IWA Publishing 2005
- UNICEF, (1998) accessed from Morna Lowe. C, 2000. *Mainstreaming Gender in Water and sanitation: Literature Review for the SA Department of Water and sanitation*, Johannesburg.
- UN. 2002. United Nation's Report of the World Summit on Sustainable Development, A/CONF.199/20, 2002: 15-21.
- United Nations, (2005). *World Urbanization Prospects: The 2005 Revision.* Department of Economic and Social Affairs Population Division. New York, Retrieved from http://www.un.org/esa/population/publications/WUP2005/2005wup.htm
- UNDP, 2006. Human Development Report, 2006. *Beyond Scarcity: Power, poverty and the global water crisis*, New York: Oxford University Press.
- UNDP, 2007/2008. Human Development Report 2007/2008 *Fighting Climate Change: Human Solidarity in a divided world.* New York: Macmillan
- UN/WWAP (United Nations/World Water Assessment Programme), 2003. Executive Summary of the 1st UN World Water Development Report: *Water for People, Water for Life.* New York, Oxford. UNESCO (United Nations Educational, Scientific and Cultural Organization).
- WHO/UNICEF, 2004 *Joint* Monitoring Programme for Water Supply and Sanitation; *Meeting drinking water and sanitation target: a mid-term assessment of progress, Water.* World Health Organization and UNICEF, 2004
- WHO/UNICEF Joint Monitoring Programme for Water supply and Sanitation. *Progress on Drinking Water and Sanitation: Special Focus on Sanitation.* UNICEF, New York and WHO, Geneva, 2008.
- WHO/UNICEF, 2010. Joint Monitoring Programme for Water supply and Sanitation. *Progress on Sanitation and Drinking Water.* World Health Organization and UNICEF, 2010.
- World Bank. 2009. *Climate Change Impacts in Drought and Flood Affected Areas: Case Studies in India,* World Bank, Washington, DC.

5

"Challenges and Oppurtinety in Agroprocessing Industry in India w.r.t Maharashtra"

Prof J S Kadam
js_kadam@rediffmail.com
Prof Jayashri J Kadam
jayshree_nirmal@rediffmail.com
Pad Dr Vikhe Patil Foundation's
I B M R D Vilad ghat Ahmednagar

Introduction

The Agro processing sector is highly fragmented industry, it widely comprises of the following sub-segments: fruits and vegetables, milk and milk products, beer and alcoholic beverages, meat and poultry, marine products, grain processing, packaged or convenience food and packaged drinks. A huge number of entrepreneurs in this industry are small in terms of their production and operations, and are largely concentrated in the unorganized segment. This segment accounts for more than 70% of the output in terms of volume and 50% in terms of value. Though the organized sector seems comparatively small, it is growing at a much faster pace in this case we are studied some segments.

Industry Sub-Segments

Fruits and Vegetables

The installed capacity of fruits and vegetables processing industry has doubled from 1.1 mn tonnes in January 1993 to 2.1 mn tonnes in 2006. Presently, the processing of fruits and vegetables is estimated to be around 2.2% of the total production in the country. The major processed items in this segment are fruit pulps and juices, fruit based ready-to-serve beverages, canned fruits and vegetables, jams, squashes, pickles, chutneys and dehydrated vegetables. The new arrivals in this segment are vegetable curries in retortable pouches, canned mushroom and mushroom products, dried fruits and vegetables and fruit juice concentrates.

The fruits and vegetable processing industry is rather fragmented. A large number of units are in household and small-scale sector, having low capacities of up to 250 tonnes per annum. From the year 2000 onwards the industry has seen a significant growth in ready-to-serve beverages, pulps and fruit juices, dehydrated and frozen fruits and vegetable products, pickles, processed mushrooms and curried vegetables, and units engaged in these segments are export oriented.

	2001-02		*2004-05*		*CAGR*	
	Quantity	*Value*	*Quantity*	*Value*	*Quantity*	*Value*
Dried & Preserved Vegetables	209157.8	5371.5	351034.3	7657.5	18.8	12.5
Mango Pulp	76735.18	2413.4	90988.6	3008.5	5.8	7.6
Pickles & Chutney	38758.97	1203.4	67193.29	1205.8	20.1	0.1
Others Processed Fruits & Vegetables	61332.39	2017.4	80760.5	2755.3	9.6	10.9
Total	385984.3	11005.7	589976.7	14627.2	15.2	9.9

Milk and Milk Products

India is with highest livestock populations in the world, it accounts 50% of the buffaloes and 20% of the world's cattle population, most of which are milch cows and milch buffaloes. India's dairy industry is considered as one of the most successful development industry in the post-Independence era.

In 2005-06 total milk productions in the country was over 90 million tonnes with a per capita availability of 229 gms per day. During 1993-2005, the dairy industry recorded an annual growth of 4%, which is almost 3 times the average growth rate of the dairy industry in the world. The total milk processing in India is around 35%, of which the organized dairy industry accounts for 13% while remaining is either consumed at farm level, or sold as fresh, non-pasteurized milk through unorganized channels.

In an organized dairy industry, dairy cooperatives account for the major share of processed liquid milk marketed in India. Milk is processed and marketed by 170 Milk Producers" Cooperative Unions, which federate into 15 State Cooperative Milk Marketing Federations. Over the years, several brands have been created by cooperatives like Amul (GCMMF), Vijaya (AP), Verka (Punjab), Saras (Rajasthan). Nandini (Karnataka),Aanand (Gujarath) and Gokul (Kolhapur). Mahananda in Mumbai

The milk surplus states in India are, Punjab, , Maharashtra, Andhra Pradesh, Karnataka and Tamil Nadu. The manufacturing of milk products is very much concentrated in these states due to the availability of milk in huge quantity.

According to the Ministry of Food Processing Industries, exports of dairy products have been growing at the rate of 35% per annum in terms of quantity and 28% in terms of value since 2001. Significant investment opportunities exist for the manufacturing of value-added milk products like milk powder, packaged milk, butter, ghee, cheese and ready-to-drink milk products.

Marine Products

India is the largest fish producing country in the world it is the third largest fish producer in the world while ranks second in inland fish production. Categorically India's potential for fishes, from both inland and marine resources, is supplemented by the 8,000 km coastline, 3 mn hectares of reservoirs, 50,600 sq km of continental shelf area, 1.4 mn hectares of brackish water and 2.2 mn sq km of exclusive economic zone.

Processing of marine produce into canned and frozen forms is carried out fully for the export market. With regards to infrastructure facilities for processing of marine products there are 372 freezing units with a daily processing capacity of 10,320 tonnes and 504 frozen storage facilities for safe storage with a capacity of 138,229.10 tonnes, besides there are 11 surimi units, 473 pre-processing centres and 236 other storages.

Processed fish products for export include conventional block frozen products, individual quick frozen products (IQF), minced fish products like fish sausage, cakes, cutlets, pastes, surimi, texturised products and dry fish etc. total share of market 27./.

Exports of marine products have been inconsistent and on a declining trend which can be owed to the adverse market conditions prevailing in the European and American markets. The anti-dumping procedure initiated by the US Government has affected India's shrimp exports to the US.

Fish Production & Exports

Year	Production (in mn tonnes)			Exports	
	Marine	Inland	Total	Quantity (MT)	Value (Rs bn)
2000-01	2.81	2.84	5.65	440473	64.44
2001-02	2.83	3.12	5.95	424470	59.57
2002-03	2.99	3.21	6.2	467297	68.81
2003-04	2.94	3.45	6.39	412017	60.92
2004-05 (Prov.)	2.78	3.52	6.3	461329	66.47

Grain Processing

Processing of grain includes milling of wheat, rice and pulses. In 1999-00, there were more than 91,000 rice hullers and 2,60,000 small flourmills which were engaged in primary milling. There are 43,000 modernized rice mills and huller-cum-shellers. Around 820 large flourmills in the country convert about 10.5 mn tonnes of wheat into wheat products. Also there are 10,000 pulse mills milling about 75% of pulse production of 14 mn tonnes in the country.

Primary milling of grains is the considered to be the important activity in the grain-processing segment of the industry. However, primary milling adds little to shelf life, wastage control and value addition. Around 65% of rice production is milled in modern rice mills. However, the sheller-cum-huller mills operating give low recovery. Wheat is processed for flour, refined wheat flour, semolina and grits. Apart from the 820 large flourmills, there are over 3 lakh small units operating in this segment in the unorganised sector. Dal milling is the third largest in the grain processing industry, and have about 11,000 mechanised mills in the organised segment. Oilseed processing is another major segment, an activity largely concentrated in the cottage industry. According to estimates, there are approximately 2.5 lakh ghanis and kolus which are animal operated oil expellers, 50,000 mechanical oil expellers, 15,500 oil mills, 725 solvent extraction plants, 300 oil refineries and over 175 hydrogenated vegetable oil plants. Indian Basmati rice has gained international recognition, and is a premium export product. Branded grains as well as grain processing is now gaining popularity due to hygienic packaging.

Some of the key constraints identified by the food processing industry include

- Poor infrastructure in terms of cold storage, warehousing, etc
- Inadequate quality control and testing infrastructure
- Inefficient supply chain and involvement of middlemen
- High transportation and inventory carrying cost
- High taxation

SWOT Analysis of Agro–Processing Industry Strengths

- Abundant availability of raw material
- Priority sector status for agro-processing given by the central /state Government
- Vast network of manufacturing facilities all over the state
- Vast domestic market

Weaknesses

- Low availability of adequate infrastructural facilitie
- Lack of adequate quality control and testing methods as per international standards Inefficient supply chain due to a large number of intermediaries

Opportunities

- Large crop and material base offering a vast potential for agro processing activities
- Setting of SEZ/AEZ and food parks for providing added incentive to develop greenfield projects
- Rising income levels and changing consumption patterns

Threats

- Affordability and cultural preferences of fresh food
- High inventory carrying cost
- High taxation

Conclusion

At the end it is concluded that the key success factors of the Agro processing industry Are

Diversified product mix for as well as international market

Strong research and development domestic capabilities., marketing Support

Efficient Infrastructure

Efficient supply chain management

References

Ministry of Food Processing Industries, Annual Report 2005.

6

'Kaizen' Thinking Fires Productivity

Anisha Sahapathi,
DAV Institute of Management, Faridabad
sahapathi_anisha@yahoo.co.in

Mike Brookes, founder and co-owner of Ambi-Rad, when asked why he failed for many years to introduce new ideas aimed at increasing competitiveness, gives as simple answer: he was too busy expanding.

His Midlands engineering company is a European leader in gas-fires 'radiant tube' heating systems. But Mr. Brookes found little time to think about how to increase quality and productivity on the shop-floor.

'We were a top-down company with all the new ideas coming from the directors,; explains Mr. Brookes. Such stories of companies lacking the interest or resources to tackle deep-seated manufacturing problems concern **Stephen Byers, the trade and industry secretary**.

He is particularly keen that smaller manufacturers should take on board **'kaizen', or continuous improvement programmes** of the kind initially introduced by Japanese groups in past 20 years.

The competitiveness problem were highlighted in a report last year by the European Commission, which put Britain in 11th position out of 15 in the EU productivity league table.

At Ambi-Rad, Mr. Brookes decided two years ago that it was time to take action. He set about implementing 'Kaizen' thinking under which workers low down in the company hierarchy are given more control over decisions and encouraged to come up with suggestions for quality and efficiency improvements.

Most of the 150 workers at Ambi-Rad's main plant in Brierly Hill, near Wolverhampton, have been divided into eight groups which are each responsible for specific aspects of making the company's heaters.

Team leaders encourage new ideas and act as a link between the shop floor and senior managers. One recent idea came from **Jean Cox, an assembly worker** at Ambi-Rad for 13 years. She suggested punching holes in a piece of metal in a different place so as to shorten the overall production process. The proposal was implemented, leading to a small but worthwhile improvement.

'I feel I am much more involved,' says Ms. Cox. 'As a problem occurs, rather than carry on regardless, we are now encouraged to think of a way round it.'

Some of the ideas are very simple, but according to Mr. Brookes, suggestions from people like Ms. Cox have taken £300,000 a year off the company's costs. The Kaizen scheme has enabled Ambi-Rad to maintain profits at a time of severe difficulties in the engineering business. In the past two years, many comparable UK companies have seen orders and earnings hit by the strong pound and week demand in important markets.

'It's been hard going but partly because of the new manufacturing ideas we have kept pre-tax profits at 10 percent of sales, which is really excellent by the standards of other engineering companies,' Mr. Brookes says.

This year Ambi-Rad expects to have sales of £18 m, more than twice the figure five years ago and exports roughly a quarter of its turnover.

Mr Brookes wants savings from "Kaizen" based ideas to reach £500,000 annually over the next few years. From a combination of improved competitiveness resulting from this thinking, new products and a stronger export effort, he reckons Ambi-Rad can increase sale 25 per cent in the next three years, while keeping the profit ratio roughly similar.

Source : Peter Marsh, Financial Times, 23 November1999.

Problems highlighted:

1. Explain how Kaizen groups can help reduce costs for business such as Ambi-Rad.
2. Identify and evaluate the benefits for three stakeholder groups in Ambi-Rad from the firm adopting Kaizen.
3. Assuming sales increase by 25% of £18m over the next three years and the ratio of pre-tax profits remains at 10%, calculate the firm's expected level of pre-tax profits in year 3.
4. Examine the conditions that were necessary for the Kaizen philosophy to be successful at Ambi-Rad.
5. Using the case study as a starting point, assess the possible relationship between the use of Kaizen groups and the leadership style of an organization.

7

Fall of Satyam and Corporate Governance in India

Mr. Parikshit Anand anand364@gmail.com
Ms. Aarushi Malhotra aarushi1986@yahoo.com
Ms. Himani Grover g_himani86@yahoo.com
Bharati Vidyapeeth University, Institute of Management and Research, New Delhi

Corporate Governance

The corporate sector in India is governed by the Companies Act of 1956 which aims to ensure adequate protection of the interests of creditors and shareholders and regulates the issue, transfer and allotment of securities; the Securities Contracts (Regulation) Act of 1956 which covers all aspects of securities trading and regulates the operations of the stock market; the Securities and Exchange Board of India (SEBI) Act of 1992 which protects the interests of shareholders and promotes and regulates the securities markets; and the Sick Industrial Companies (Special Provisions) Act (SICA) of 1985 which deals with the financial reorganization (including bankruptcy procedures) of distressed companies. India's corporate sector consists of private limited and public limited comapneis. The Indian corporate sector has seen substantial and significant changes since 1993 when the phrase corporate governance came to prominence. Since then, a series of legal and regulatory reforms have transformed the corporate governance framework and improved the level of accountability and responsibility of insiders, fairness in the treatment of minority shareholders and stakeholders, board practices and transparency. Over the last few years, a series of corporate governance committees were appointed by the Confederation of Indian Industry (CII), the Department of Company Affairs (DCA) and the SEBI.

Most recently in the year 2005, the Ministry of Corporate Affairs, in partnership with the CII, the Institute of Company Secretaries of India (ICSI) and the Institute of Chartered Accountants of India (ICAI), has set up the National Foundation for Corporate Governance (NFCG) with the goal of promoting better corporate governance practices. In its assessment report comparing the observance of corporate governance in India with the OECD Principles of Corporate Governance, the World Bank (2004) finds that in India 10 of the 23 OECD Principles are observed, six are largely observed, six are partially observed, and only one is materially not observed. The 10 principles that were found to be observed were; protection of basic shareholders' rights; right to participate in fundamental corporate decisions; shareholders' AGM rights; functioning of markets for corporate control; respect of stakeholders' rights; a performance enhancement mechanism for stakeholder participation; stakeholders' participating in the corporate governance process to have access to relevant information; fair and timely dissemination of information; compliance with applicable law; and board members' access to accurate, relevant and timely information. The six principles which were found to be largely observed were; disapprotionate control disclosure; disclosure standards; high quality standard of accounting, financial and non-financial disclosure, and audit; boards to act with due diligence and care in the best interests of the company and the shareholders; boards to treat all shareholders fairly; and boards to fulfill certain key functions. The partially observed principles relate to the equal treatment of all shareholders; prohibition of insider trading and abusive self-dealing; disclosure interests of members of the board and managers; effective rederessal for violation of stakeholder interests; annual audit by an independent auditor; and the boards' ability to exercise objective judgment on corporate affairs independent from management. The only principle which was found to be materially not observed relates to shareholders' including institutional investors' consideration of the costs and benefits of exercising their voting rights, as pension funds seldom exercise voting rights, instead they exert influence through nominee directors on the board of their portfolio companies.

I. Fall of Satyam

A company named "Satyam" (truth, in Sanskrit) inspired trust. The IT boom in India, was fuelled by young, middle-class, educated, building Indian entrepreneurs and Western firms anxious to outsource to take advantage of high-skill, low-wage worker. This trend created a new breed of businessman for the 21st century and generated many fortunes literally overnight. Byrraju Ramalinga – Raju – founder and former chairman of Indian IT giant Satyam Computer Services – was one of these new millionaires. The son of a farmer from a middle class family with an American MBA degree and a 1999 Ernest & Young Entrepreneur, Raju started Satyam and worked his way to make the company a top 5 Indian IT firm with clients in 60 countries. Satyam is listed on the New York Stock Exchange (NYSE) and the Bombay Stock Exchange. Satyam was the 2008 winter of the covered Golden Peacock Award for Corporate Governance under Risk Management and Compliance Issues, which was stripped from them in the aftermath of the scandal.

About the fraud: Nature & Dimension: The Satyam Computer Services scandal was publicly announced on 7 January, 2009, when Chairman Ramalinga Raju confessed that Satyam's accounts had been falsified. Company Chairman Ramalinga Raju resigned after notifying board members and the Securities and Exchange Board of India (SEBI) that Satyam's accounts had been falsified. Raju confessed that Satyam's balance sheet of 30 September 2008 contained:

- Inflated figures for cash and bank balances of Rs. 5,040 crore (US $ 1.04 billion) (as against Rs. 5,371 crore (US $ 1.1 billion) crore reflected in the books).

- An accrued interest of Rs. 376 crore (US $ 77.46 million) which was non-existent.
- An understated liability of Rs. 1,230 crore (US $ 253.38 million) on account of funds was arranged by himself.
- An overstated debtors' position of Rs. 490 crore (US $ 100.94 million) (as against Rs. 2,651 crore (US $ 546.11 million) in the books).

Raju claimed in the same letter that neither he nor the managing director had benefited financially from the inflated revenues. He claimed that none of the board members had any knowledge of the situation in which the company was placed. He stated that: "What started as a marginal gap between actual operating profit and the one reflected in the books of accounts continued to grow over the years. It has attained unmanageable promotions as the size of the company operations grew significantly (annualized revenue run rate of Rs. 11,276 crore (US $ 2.32 billion) in the September quarter of 2008 and official reserves of Rs. 8,392 crore (US $ 1.73 billion). As the promoters held a small percentage of equity, the concern was that poor performance would result in a takeover, thereby exposing the gap. The aborted Maytas acquisition deal was the last attempt to fill the fictitious assets with real ones. It was like ridding a tiger, not knowing how to get off without being eaten."

Although B. Ramalinga Raju has sought to take full responsibility for cooking Satyam accounts, it is now clear that 'operation fudging at the company was a complex exercise and was meticulously planned and executed with precision. There were scores of meetings with dozens of people to falsify the accounts of the company that was listed on the New York Stock Exchange. Talluri Srinivas and S. Gopalakrishnan, the two Price Water House auditors arrested in the scam, have told cops that the agenda used to be clear in the meetings though the word fudging was not used. Everyone present was aware of the motive of the meetings which was to falsify the accounts, they said during their interrogation. The meetings were usually chaired by Ramalinga Raju himself but in his absence Rama Raju, his brother, or Srinivasa Vadlamani, the chief financial officer, would officiate. It is not known whether the PW auditors told police the identity of other company managers who were regular at these meets. But the auditors said that the internal audit department of Satyam with qualified chartered accounts was sully aware of the goings on. The fudging of accounts had been on for the last six years, the auditors reveled.

The two external auditors are also believed to have confessed that it was because of this environment that instead of independently verifying Satyam's balance with the banks they accepted written Statements by the company management. The statement, in the form of a letter was usually signed by Rama Raju or Vadlamani. They also told the Crime Investigation Department (CID) sleuths that they approved the accounts of Satyam because of Ramalinga Raju's 'towering presence' and did so without ever questioning him. "We did not dare raise questions when the client was a reputed company. Moreover, Ramlinga Raju himself took personal interest in the accounts," one of the auditors told CID sleuths. The investigating agency arrested Srinivas and Gopalakrishnan on January 23 on the charges of cheating and criminal conspiracy after the falsification of accounts of Satyam Computer Services Ltd. came to light.

The CID posed over 100 questions including whether they were aware of the falsification of accounts, how long the fudging of accounts happening, the role of former chairman, managing director, chief financial officer, and whether the company offered them bribes to certify accounts and if Ramalinga Raju forced them to sign on audit report and why the remuneration of PWC had shot up in the last few years.

After commitment in falsification of accounts: After the scandal broke, then-board members elected Ram Mynampati to be Satyam's interim CEO. Mynampati's statement on Satyam's website said: "We are obviously shocked by the contents of the letter. The senior leaders of Satyam stand united in their commitment to customers, associates, suppliers and all shareholders. We have gathered together at Hyderabad to strategize the way forward in light of this starting revelation." On 10th January, 2009, the Company Law Board decided to bar the current board of Satyam from functioning and appoint 10 nominal directors. "The current board has failed to do what they are supposed to do. The credibility of the IT industry should not be allowed to suffer" said the then Corporate Affairs Minister. Chartered accountants regulator ICAI issued show-cause notice to Satyam's auditor Pricewaterhouse Coopers (PwC) on the accounts fudging. On the same day, the Crime Investigation Department (CID) team picked up Vadlamani Srinivas, Satyam's then CFO, for questioning. He was arrested later and kept in judicial custody. On 11th January, 2009, the government nominated noted banker Deepak Parekh, former NASSCOM chief Kiran Karnik and former SEBI member C. Achuthan to Satyam's board. Analysts in India have termed the Satyam scandal as India's own Enron scandal.

Immediately following the news, Merrill Lynch (Now with Bank of America) terminated its engagement with the company. Also Credit Suisse suspended its coverage of Satyam. It was also reported that Satyam's auditing firm Price water house Coopers will be scrutinized for complicity in this scandal. The New York Stock Exchange has halted trading n Satyam stock as of 7th January, 2009. India's National Stock Exchange has announced that it will remove Satyam from its S&P CNX Nifty 50-share index on January 12. The founder of Satyam was arrested two days after he admitted to falsifying the firm's accounts. Ramalinga Raju is charged with several offences, including criminal conspiracy, breach of trust, and forgery.

The Indian Government has stated that it may provide temporary direct or indirect liquidity support to the company. However, whether employment will continue at pre-crisis level, particularly for new recruits, is questionable. On 14th January, 2009, Price water house, the Indian division of Price water house Coopers, announced that its reliance on potentially false information provided by the management of Satyam may have rendered its audit reports "inaccurate and unreliable. On 5th February, 2009, the six-member board appointed by the Government of India named A.S. Murthy as the new CEO of the firm with immediate effect. Murthy, an electrical engineer, has been with Satyam since January, 1994 and was heading the Global Delivery Section before being appointed as CEO of the company. The two –day-long board meeting also appointed Homi Khusrokhan (formerly with Tata Chemicals) and Partho Datta, a Chartered Accountant as special advisors.

Role of Auditors: There is intense debate about the role of Price water house Coopers, the external auditors of the company in clearing the accounts of Satyam. Auditors are supposed to have checked, verified cash balances, bank statements, assets with relevant confirmations. Satyam was a large company, not a street store; Price water house Cooper is a globally reputed firm.

Professional accounting bodies and police are currently examining the role of auditors in this incident minutely.

Role of Directors: The Companies Act in India has stringent corporate governance requirements of board members. Yet Raju was able to steer the fabricated accounts through this board members for 6 –years! This has bewildered the corporate sector and regulators. At times, the company was holding excessive cash, as per the books. This should have invited questions by board members. The Indian Government specifically delineates the role of independent directors in safeguarding the interests of the organization and the shareholders.

It is fair to expect independent directors, like Harvard Professor Krishna Palepu, the former, non-executive director of Satyam, to be more guardians of corporate governance. It is unfair to expect independent directors, meeting monthly or quarterly to be undercover detectives or crops! An independent director would normally assume that audited accounts have been rigorously examined. This is more so when an internationally credible firm like Price water house Coopers- has audited the numbers. But, they need to still ask the right questions and probe. Corporate governance goes hand-in-hand with the mitigation of risk, and effective risk management.

The questions, which have been raised are what role were independent directors playing in the process of the functioning of Satyam and how far was the audit committee effective in the transparent disclosures of financial of the company? An important gap in the whole process of corporate governance has been the weakness in accountability of the board through disclosures, which have become very crucial today in the current environment when a multiple of creative accounting practices involving inevitably ambiguities and many alternative methods of report the financial effects of transactions used largely and routinely by the promoters to mislead rather than inform the shareholders and the public. In this regard the composition of the board and the monitoring role of independent directors should be the corner stone of SEBI's regulatory check.

Any community that encourages, directly or indirectly, a feudal structure or dictatorship is bound to result in disaster. On the other hand, any community (company, city, town, nation etc.) that spouses the cause of democracy committed with fair, balanced, transparency and accountability will never see a disaster. What happened in Satyam is that it was a huge scandal. Nobody could stand up and say what is happening is wrong. Even those who thought what was happening was wrong did not have the courage and were not in an environment to say that it was wrong.

II: Satyam Fraud still in opaque: slow going system.

Can the judicial trial for Ramalinga Raju and his associates be also placed on the fast track? That is pity. Economic offences of such magnitude certainly deserve the creation of a special court, which could expedite the trial process and deliver its judgment on Raju. The CA institute's probe on the role of external and internal auditors in the scam-hit Satyam Computer Services' case has moved a step forward. An internal committee of the Institute to issue separate notices to the six found 'prima facie guilty' or professional misconduct. For persons of the statutory audit team of Price water house, Bangalore, including Mr. S. Gopalakrishnan and Mr. Srinivasu Talluri, both partners and the two signatories to the Satyam's accounts for different financial years, have been found prima facie guilty of professional misconduct. Both have been found 'prime facie guilty' for failing in the duty of carrying out statutory audit and for not qualifying their report (s) for all these years (2000-1 to 2007-8) that the financial statement does not give a true and fair view of the affairs of the company. The Enforcement Directorate (ED) has attached over a third of the 786 properties owned by Raju and 131 others, including his brothers and their wives, after it established that these were obtained through the ill-gotten gains from India's largest corporate fraud. The 280-odd properties attached by the ED through a provisional order are wroth Rs. 200 crore on paper, but their current market value is estimated to be about Rs. 1,200 crore. The ED found that the companies that were used to buy these properties had virtually no independent source of funding. The funds laundered by Raju and his associates were routed to these firms for purchasing real estate. The 786 properties identified by the ED were acquired between 2005 and 2008, and are spread across Andhra Pradesh, Tamil Nadu, Maharashtra, Karnataka and Uttar Pradesh.

Ten months after the Satyam scam, the investigating agencies are yet to get their act together. The process of getting B. Ramalinga Raju to court to face final charges will take quite some time. This is because a lot of work is still pending with all the four agencies tasked to track the Satyam accounting fraud. These agencies are the Serious Fraud Investigation Office (SFIO), stock market regulator Securities and Exchange Board of India (SEBI), ICAI and the Central Bureau of Investigation (CBI). So far, the only step taken by the government for Raju's trial is the plan to set up a special court for Satyam in Hyderabad. On April 7, a CBI team filed a 6,500 page charge-sheet including allegedly incriminating documents and statements against Raju and eight others who were involved in the execution of the Rs. 7,800 crore fraud. But CBI acknowledges that those are not enough to book the former promoters of the company for issues like diversion of funds, their misappropriation as well as the role played by the independent directors over the years. Those will come in the second phase, according to the agency. The nine were charged with various breaches of the IPC, including conspiracy, forgery of valuable security, cheating, falsification of accounts, using forged documents as genuine, causing disappearance of evidence etc. The present findings of CBI are enough (only) as far as the allegations in the charge sheet are concerned like conspiracy, cheating. It should be over by end of September or October. Incidentally the multi-disciplinary investigations team of CBI suspects the promoters might have diverted the funds of the company to foreign accounts in the US, Mauritius, England and even some countries in Asia. Just compare this with the $50 billion Bernie Madoff investments scandal in the US that came to limelight around almost the same time, in December 2008. Six months later, on June 29, 2009, Madoff was handed a 150 years in prison with restitution of $170 billion, which he begun serving [The Financial Express, September 09, 2009 and Mint, October 21, 2009]. The CBI would question several people in the US, UK, Mauritius, Singapore, Belgium and the British Virgin Islands. It is examining a possible diversion of funds from Satyam to these countries.

When India's fourth-largest IT company spiraled into spectacular riding the tiger anarchy, that was a big call for shifting corporate governance into higher gear in the country. Raju's confession still seems the strongest evidence against him. One emphasizes both how important it is to make an exemplary case of Satyam and how imposing severe penalties is the most effective deterrent to accounting manipulation. In addition, we should focused on ways to improve the quality of firms' financial reporting, whether by way of switching to IFRS or liberalizing the rules governing stockholder litigation. If an auditor fails in his duty in India, he faced a maximum imprisonment of two years as against the US Sarbanes – Oxley Act that handed out imprisonment for 20 years. Combine the fact that India has one of the poorest corporate fraud conviction rates in the world with that we have entered new waters with the Satyam case, and you have a lab case why Satyam must be dealt with most efficiently. All imperatives notwithstanding, nine months on, we still seem stuck with the bare bones of the Satyam soga. We don't for example, yet know how Satyam ADRs worth $100 million were deployed or how funds were siphoned off between Satyam and its sister concerns.

III: Action policy: what should be followed?

Unfortunately, even the audit committee does not look at information with the angle of corporate governance. The quality and structure of capital expenditure warrant a close examination by the board as well as audit committee. This situation warrants a merit- based constitution of the board of the companies, in particular the selection of independent directors.

The Satyam accounting fraud promoted market regulator SEBI to announce peer review certified auditing processes for Sensex and Nifty companies to bring in greater transparency and accountability. This peer review process has now been further strengthened by the decision of Institute of Chartered Accountants of India (ICAI) to make compulsory for all listed companies to be audited by Peer review-certified companies from April 1, 2009. This will instill public confidence in financial reporting, enhance effectiveness of the audit process and ensure better quality and consistency in accounting and auditing services across a cross – section of auditing firms. The institute has selected around 1,200 firms which would do the peer review. It would also cover financial statements of companies looking for IPOs once they file the Red Herring prospectus. For companies, the peer review process would enhance the quality of attestation services and provide guidance to improve their performance and adhere to various statutory and other regulatory requirements. The peer review would include scrutiny of an auditor's working notes by a chartered accountant and firm's which are denied peer review certificates would be barred from auditing. Currently, ICAI has a peer review board with a panal of chartered accountants, which conducts scrutiny of the notes of the auditors.

Corporate governance has got another shot in the arm by the positive outcome of SEBI's disclosure requirement on pledging of shares – another measure introduced after the Satyam scandal. About 500 listed companies have come forward with details concerning the shares pledged by their promoters since SEBI made it mandatory. It has helped investors, as many of their decisions are based on the disclosures which reveal how much control the promoter really has over his or her company. Earlier, promoters were not too keen to discloses share they pledged because they fared their stock price may take a hit. With economic slowdown and credit crunch, promoters pledged their shares to mostly raise working capital but also long term loans to increase their holding. The market regulator has indeed played a commendable role post the Satyam fraud and these two measures will indeed ensure higher standards of transparency in corporate India.

The SEBI report on corporate governance had expected that board members would be homogenous in terms of expertise, functions and affirmations. It is common knowledge that boards are homogenous only in one respect and that is that they work as a gang and not as a caretaker or trustee of the companies and shareholders. There is need for creating and promoting the culture of good corporate citizenship. As far as the quality of the expertise of independent directors is concerned, there are a few of them who can be considered as expects on the profit and loss account, balance sheet, other financial disclosures and regulatory compliances. They do not understand the significance and impact of various heads of income and expenditure given in the profit and loss account and implications of variation in components of the balance sheet.

Regulators need to turn proactive on the financial health of a company or issues of corporate governance. With regard to accountability there needs to be a zero tolerance policy towards violators. Only strengthen laws and regulations can help us curb frauds and white collar crimes. It is time that the role of the regulators changes, from a mere policymaker to playing a more proactive role such that they take charge of a company's books whenever they find discrepancy in the financial health of a company or on issue of corporate governance. Taking a cue from the RBI, which has complete control over the banking industry, it is time that the government/ regulator put in place a similar model for corporate India. Corporate governance consultants should be a part of the board of directors. They should be senior executives and have the power to stand up to the board members and point out wrong doings. The Registrar of Companies (ROC) has a wealth of information which can be used to spot distressed companies.

There are three priorities which corporate houses in developing countries should focus on, while experimenting with reforms in corporate and public governance mechanisms. The first is to focus on improving the quality of information' to the public in the context of disclosure practices. The second is to address the conflict of interest which has played havoc with the integrity of control system. And the third is to protect the interests of minority shareholders. These three priorities need to be considered by any corporate that wants to create value through a credible brand image. Such value creation through strong corporate governance ultimately leads to a strengthened socio-economic fabric. To improve the information quality, we need to go well beyond the legal fiats and proactively address the aspirations of information customers. Corporate governance is a trusteeship obligation that should be systematically integrated in a company's business processes; assets and resources entrusted to the managers must be judiciously and honestly utilizes for managers must be judiciously and honestly utilized for addressing interests of all stakeholders. The three-pronged reform in mindset of corporate managers may help strengthened stakeholder confidence which in turn will fetch good returns for the business corporate.

Conclusion

Corporate governance is a multi-faceted subject that covers the structural framework covering stakeholder relations, within which corporate decisions are taken. While most of the scholarly debates on corporate governance are fuelled by shareholder activism in developing economics like India, much of it has highlighted the symptoms rather than the causes. The entire corporate governance premises is very crucial as it is the foundation of the institution of Joint Stock Companies which has led to global economic development since last century.

The lesson of the scandals is that there are multiple things that can go wrong in modern economies built on complex financial systems. Negligence needs to be distinguished from structural failure. And it needs to be recognized that these problems can arise in the private and the public sectors. Solutions have to be matched to the nature of the cause and its institutional location. Bleeding the patient cannot be the treatment for every disease (Nirvikar Singh, 2009].

The current framework of corporate governance emphasizes on compliance, leading thus a checklist mentality. Performance oversight can be added to the compliance dimension of corporate governance. The Raghuram Rajan Committee on financial sector reforms has stressed the need for a regulatory review of accounting statements. In view of the Raghuram Rajan Committee's recommendations and experience in Western countries, especially in the US, it behoves the Governments and SEBI to start the process of setting up an appropriate accounting review board. The questions that need to be asked are: Can we prevent another one? And what are the lessons we would learn after the floor has been swept clean?

It scams and accounting scandals are breaking out often, why are regulators unable to spot it? Well, the regulators cannot do much. Regulators and their agencies have to peer into the rear-view mirror while laying out the law. Whenever a scam occurs, both investors and regulators are put on guard against that particular kind of scam. But the next one turns out to be quite different, exploiting a different loophole in the law. Regulators, by virtue of the urgency with which they are required to act, cannot place a fielder on every inch of the boundary. When they move one fielder, they are opening potential gaps for an expert batsman (the scamster) to score. The investor's cause is not helped when the boundary is thin and subject to interpretation.

References

Books and Journals

- Balasubramaniam, N. (1997) "Towards Excellence in Board Performance", The IIMB Management Review, January- March, 67-84.
- Butani, Mukesh (2009) Corporate governance: We don't need an Overdose, The Business Standard, February 2.
- Cadbury, A., Chairman, (1992) Report on the Financial Aspects of Corporate Governance.
- Dahiya, Sri Bhagwan (2008) Corporate governance developments in India, Chapter 13, available in Christine A. Mallin's Handbook on International Corporate Governance, Edward Elgar, Cheltenham, UK.
- Debroy, Bibek (2009) Phony Capitalism, The Financial Express, January 12.
- Dignam, A. and Lawry, J. (2006) Company Law, Oxford University Press.
- Gopalakrishnan, Adarsh (2009) "Scam Secret: Suspended Disbelief, The Hindu Business Line, October 25.
- Kar, Pratip (2009) Patterns in governance failures, The Business Standard, April 13.
- Khan, M.Y. (2009) Is an independent director an eyewash? The Financial Express, March 8.

Websites:

- www.outsourcing-pharma.com/.../**Satyam-fraud**-may-cost-it-GSK-Novartis-deals
- www.basissap.com/.../impact-of-**satyam-fraud**-on-outsourcing
- *www.financialexpress.com/.../**satyam-fraud***
- www.accountancyage.com/aa/.../**satyam-fraud**-methodology-revealed
- *www.amitbhawani.com/blog/**satyam-computers-fraud/***
- hubpages.com/.../Corporate-Governance-and-**Satyam**-Scam-Or-**Satyam-Fraud**

8

The Ratnakar Bank Limited: Keeping Pace with Time

Mr. Pavnesh Kumar
IILM Academy of Higher Learning
dr.pavnesh@gmail.com

Background Note

Modern banking in India could be traced back to the establishment of Bank of Bengal (Jan 2, 1809), the first joint-stock bank sponsored by Government of Bengal and governed by the royal charter of the British India Government. It was followed by establishment of Bank of Bombay (Apr 15, 1840) and Bank of Madras (Jul 1, 1843). These three banks, known as the presidency banks, marked the beginning of the limited liability and joint stock banking in India and were also vested with the right of note issue.

In 1921, the three presidency banks were merged to form the Imperial Bank of India, which had multiple roles and responsibilities and that functioned as a commercial bank, a banker to the government and a banker's bank. Following the establishment of the Reserve Bank of India (RBI) in 1935, the central banking responsibilities that the Imperial Bank of India was carrying out came to an end, leading it to become more of a commercial bank. At the time of independence of India, the capital and reserves of the Imperial Bank stood at Rs 118 mn, deposits at Rs 2751 mn and advances at Rs 723 mn and a network of 172 branches and 200 sub offices spread all over the country.

In 1951, in the backdrop of central planning and the need to extend bank credit to the rural areas, the Government constituted All India Rural Credit Survey Committee, which recommended the creation of a state sponsored institution that will extend banking services to the rural areas.

Following this, by an act of parliament passed in May 1955, State Bank of India was established in Jul, 1955. In 1959, State Bank of India took over the eight former state-associated banks as its subsidiaries. To further accelerate the credit to fl ow to the rural areas and the vital sections of the economy such as agriculture, small scale industry etc., that are of national importance, Social Control over banks was announced in 1967 and a National Credit Council was set up in 1968 to assess the demand for credit by these sectors and determine resource allocations. The decade of 1960s also witnessed significant consolidation in the Indian banking industry with more than 500 banks functioning in the 1950s reduced to 89 by 1969.

For the Indian banking industry, Jul 19, 1969, was a landmark day, on which nationalization of 14 major banks was announced that each had a minimum of Rs 500 mn and above of aggregate deposits. In 1980, eight more banks were nationalised. In 1976, the Regional Rural Banks Act came into being, that allowed the opening of specialized regional rural banks to exclusively cater to the credit requirements in the rural areas. These banks were set up jointly by the central government, commercial banks and the respective local governments of the states in which these are located.

The period following nationalization was characterized by rapid rise in banks business and helped in increasing national savings. Savings rate in the country leapfrogged from 10-12% in the two decades of 1950-70 to about 25 % post nationalization period. Aggregate deposits which registered annual growth in the range of 10% to 12% in the 1960s rose to over 20% in the 1980s. Growth of bank credit increased from an average annual growth of 13% in the 1960s to about 19% in the 1970s and 1980s. Branch network expanded significantly leading to increase in the banking coverage.

Indian banking, which experienced rapid growth following the nationalization, began to face pressures on asset quality by the 1980s. Simultaneously, the banking world everywhere was gearing up towards new prudential norms and operational standards pertaining to capital adequacy, accounting and risk management, transparency and disclosure etc. In the early 1990s, India embarked on an ambitious economic reform programme in which the banking sector reforms formed a major part. The Committee on Financial System (1991) more popularly known as the Narasimham Committee prepared the blue print of the reforms. A few of the major aspects of reform included (a) moving towards international norms in income recognition and provisioning and other related aspects of accounting (b) liberalization of entry and exit norms leading to the establishment of several New Private Sector Banks and entry of a number of new Foreign Banks (c) freeing of deposit and lending rates (except the saving deposit rate), (d) allowing Public Sector Banks access to public equity markets for raising capital and diluting the government stake,(e) greater transparency and disclosure standards in financial reporting (f) suitable adoption of Basel Accord on capital adequacy (g) introduction of technology in banking operations etc. The reforms led to major changes in the approach of the banks towards aspects such as competition, profitability and productivity and the need and scope for harmonization of global operational standards and adoption of best practices. Greater focus was given to deriving efficiencies by improvement in performance and rationalization of resources and greater reliance on technology including promoting in a big way computerization of banking operations and introduction of electronic banking.

The reforms led to significant changes in the strength and sustainability of Indian banking. In addition to significant growth in business, Indian banks experienced sharp growth in profitability, greater emphasis on prudential norms with higher provisioning levels, reduction in the non performing assets and surge in capital adequacy. All bank groups witnessed sharp growth in performance and profitability. Indian banking industry is preparing for smooth transition towards more intense competition arising from further liberalization of banking sector that was envisaged in the year 2009 as a part of the adherence to liberalization of the financial services industry.

Structure of the Banking Industry

According to the RBI definition, commercial banks which conduct the business of banking in India and which (a) have paid up capital and reserves of an aggregate real and exchangeable value of not less than Rs 0.5 mn and (b) satisfy the RBI that their affairs are not being conducted in a manner detrimental to the interest of their depositors, are eligible for inclusion in the Second Schedule to the Reserve Bank of India Act, 1934, and when included are known as 'Scheduled Commercial Banks'. Scheduled Commercial Banks in India are categorized in five different groups according to their ownership and/or nature of operation. These bank groups are (i) State Bank of India and its associates, (ii) Nationalised Banks, (iii) Regional Rural Banks, (iv) Foreign Banks and (v) Other Indian Scheduled Commercial Banks (in the private sector). All Scheduled Banks comprise Schedule Commercial and Scheduled Co-operative Banks. Scheduled Cooperative banks consist of Scheduled State Co-operative Banks and Scheduled Urban Cooperative Banks.

Trends and Outlook of Indian Banking Industry

A few other major developments in the performance of the Indian banking industry are briefly mentioned below.

Rise of Transactional Banking: Growth of retail lending including mortgage and personal loans is leading to numerous transactions, which banks are able to manage efficiently with the support of growing technology prowess and competencies. In view of the greater possibility of personal banking services in India, transactional banking will assume significance, thus giving scope for a new business model as also a wide range of technology solutions.

Outsourcing Gaining Significance: The rapid rise of personal banking, the need to service and track it in a consistent manner, has led to the outsourcing of several of the follow-up and customer service functions, with banks setting up separate processes and mechanisms to manage them. This trend will increasingly be evident in the marketing of products, maintaining client profiles, attending to customer requests and also in exploring new business opportunities.

Focus on Fee Income: Indian banks, including the Public Sector Banks, have become focused on the fee income, taking advantage of the enormous scope and potential for personal banking and related services. Several banks have shown sizeable growth in the fee/non-interest income in the recent period.

Thrust on SMEs and SSIs: The promotion and growth of small and medium enterprises (SMEs) has become an issue of policy thrust in recent years, in view of their significance in the domestic economy and contribution to the national output. The performance of the stock markets in the last three years was also largely on the back of surge in the share prices of stocks pertaining to SMEs. The environment governing SME financing has vastly improved with the setting up of rating agencies for SME financing. Banks look at this segment as a potential source of business and growth.

Product and Business Collaborations: Initiatives at deriving economies of scale are gaining importance in Indian banking. There is growing collaboration and partnerships amongst banks in promoting new business, distributing products and services as also in cross selling. In the recent period, instances of even some Public Sector Banks coming together to jointly develop business initiatives is increasingly evident In Sep 2006, Indian Bank, Corporation Bank and Oriental Bank of Commerce announced a business alliance that is envisaged to generate greater benefits to each of them, including expansion of international business. Similarly, several banks are distributing insurance products in collaboration with insurance companies.

Shared Services (ATM Networks): There is growing trend of pooling of resources for providing some shared services, such as ATMs and credit cards. In the 1990s, the first of such initiatives began under the aegis of the Indian Banks' Association, with the setting up of SWADHAN, a shared ATM Network. Following its dissolution, a new set up came into being, under the aegis of the IDBRT, known as National Financial Switch (NFS) which has 24 banks sharing the network of 8371 ATMS, the largest of such network of ATMs in India. Cash Tree is another ATM network with major public and private sector participating in it. MITR is a network of ATMs between six Public Sector Banks.

NRI Banking/International Services:. International liabilities consist of various items, including foreign currency deposits, non resident deposits, and equities of banks held by non-residents etc. International borrowings are growing at a pace higher than that of deposits. The strong surge in international liabilities has led to banks stepping up their focus on external activities, in the form of opening new branches outside India and forging business relationships and collaborations. The focus is more on the Middle East, European and North American markets, where significant presence of population of Indian origin is prevalent. A few banks have begun to explore China and Vietnam as new markets.

Technology and Core Banking Solution: Core banking solution (CBS) is critical to offer country-wide banking facilities, and has emerged as a key competitive and success factor for banks. CBS is more of a challenge for the public and the Old Private Sector Banks, since the New Private Sector Banks are already networked since their inception. Several public sector and Old Private Sector Banks have made significant advances in extending core banking solution to most of the branches, which will radically redefine the scope and quality of delivery and distribution of bank products as also the customer service..

Cross Selling: Globally, cross selling is a major component of the business of banks. In India too, it is catching up fast with several of the banks of the State Bank Group already making headway in selling products of other group banks and subsidiaries in the insurance and capital market services. Other banks are also building this business in an aggressive manner. Cross selling would help in banks boosting the fee income.

Internet/Mobile Banking: Taking advantage of the vastly improved and innovative telecom solutions, many banks are able to offer services on internet and mobile telephones. Internet banking and phone banking are becoming quite common place amongst all groups of banks that provide customers with ready information on certain banking services. Internet / and mobile based banking is expected to grow further in view of the expansion of capacity in the bandwidth and value added services introduced in the telecom sector.

Financial Inclusion: Following the government's policy initiative of pursuing inclusive growth, banking institutions have been advised to offer products that will cater to a wide spectrum of the population living in the rural areas. Following this, many banks have introduced exclusive no-frills accounts, which will provide banking access to a large segment of unbanked population. Banks, particularly in the public sector see a huge opportunity in this segment, as more people will now seek banking services. The advances in technology and computing could enable banks to manage growth of huge numbers in the accounts and transactions.

Risk Management/Asset Liability Management: One of the positive features of the Indian banking is its low cost of the turnaround. Following financial liberalization leading to the banking crisis, many emerging and mature economies spent huge amounts, sometime costing upto 50% of the GDP, in making successful banking turnaround. In India, however the cost of the turnaround is relatively low, somewhere in the region of 3% of the GDP. A greater challenge following the turnaround is keeping the loan book healthy. It is where banks are taking proactive measures in setting up efficient risk management systems and robust asset liability management processes. All banks have put in place several tiers of risk management processes and procedures that are helping them to contain the growth of bad debts.

Capital Adequacy Norms: Indian banking system has been proactive in adopting global standards in capital adequacy and are gearing up to adopt Basel II norms. Basel II norms provide banks and the regulatory agencies a range of options for determining capital requirements for credit and operational risk that are most suitable for the operations in financial markets. This framework consists of a three-pillared approach viz., minimum capital requirements, supervisory review of capital adequacy, and market discipline. The Reserve Bank of India stipulated that Foreign Banks operating in India and Indian banks with operational presence outside India should adopt the new standards in computing capital adequacy with effect from Mar 31, 2008 and all other scheduled commercial banks to move towards this system not later than Mar 31, 2009

Corporate Governance and Disclosures: There is a distinct improvement in the corporate governance norms and the disclosure standards in the banking industry. All listed banks are now required to follow Clause 49 of the listing agreement of stock exchanges that stipulates the structure of the corporate governance as also disclosure standards. All listed banks now disclose details of the governance and their functioning through various committees and forums and follow norms on reporting the financial details, consisting of quarterly announcements, segmental reporting etc. Enhanced quality of governance and disclosure standards have made the banking sector an attractive option for investors in India and abroad.

Standards in Customer Service: In Feb 2006, the Reserve Bank of India, with 11 other banks, set up the Banking Codes and Standards Board of India to monitor and ensure that banking codes and standards are voluntarily adopted by the banks and strictly adhered to, while providing customer services. The Code is a major development that would have significant impact on the quality of customer services and in fulfilling the obligations of the bank. The Code sets out minimum standards of banking practices that banks should follow in dealing with the customers. The Code envisages providing full information to the customers before a product is sold. Similarly, guidelines on credit card operations were also issued by the Reserve Bank of India in Nov 2005. These are envisaged to significantly enhance the customer service standards in Indian banking

Growing Investor Interest in Indian Bank Stocks: In view of the great potential and prospects, bank stocks have seen significant growth in the recent period with the support of investor interest from India and abroad. Non resident holdings in the New Private Sector Banks where foreign holding is allowed up to 74%, rose to 70.9% in ICICI Bank, 70.3% in Centurion Bank of Punjab, 53.6% in HDFC Bank, 50% in YES Bank for FY06. Among the Old Private Sector Banks, ING Vysya Bank (70.8%), Federal Bank (45.8%) has sizeable non-resident holdings. Among the Public Sector Banks, non-resident holdings vary across banks. The latest position in this regard indicates quite a few big banks reaching the threshold levels (20%) of foreign institutional investment.

Growth of Off Balance Sheet Operations: There is a sharp increase in the offbalance sheet operations of banks, particularly in the Foreign and New Private Sector Banks. Off-balance sheet exposures of banks in India, of which derivatives form a major component. This trend, which refl ects growing deregulation and new business opportunities for banks, also emphasizes the scope for robust risk management to overcome the challenges of market dynamics.

Challenges before Banking Industry

The enhanced role of the banking sector in the Indian economy, the increasing levels of deregulation along with the increasing levels of competition have facilitated globalisation of the India banking system and placed numerous demands on banks. Operating in this demanding environment has exposed banks to various challenges. The last decade has witnessed major changes in the financial sector - new banks, new financial institutions, new instruments, new windows, and new opportunities - and, along with all this, new challenges. While deregulation has opened up new vistas for banks to augment revenues, it has entailed greater competition and consequently greater risks. Demand for new products, particularly derivatives, has required banks to diversify their product mix and also effect rapid changes in their processes and operations in order to remain competitive in the globalised environment.

About Ratnakar Bank

Ratnakar Bank has made its mark in the commercial banking sector of India. The bank was established in 1943. The founders of Ratnakar Bank are Shri. Babgonda Bhujgonda Patil, a renowned advocate and Shri. Gangaram Siddhappa Chougule, a businessman from Kolhapur.

Inspired by the clarion call for self reliance given by National leaders in the pre-independence era, a group of patriotic, eminent personalities from various walks of life came together to launch a crusade for economic independence. On the then scenario of industrialist owned banks catering to the needs of the rich and realising the limitations of co-operative societies and co-operative banks, it was decided to establish a commercial bank with the avowed objective of meeting the needs of the low and middle income segment of the society engaged in trade and commerce. 'THE RATNAKAR BANK LTD.,' was born on 6th, August 1943. "Ratnakar" means an ocean, a treasure house of jewels.In a short span of just 16 years, The Reserve Bank of India conferred the status of SCHEDULED BANK on THE RATNAKAR BANK LTD., in 1959. The Bank, by its conscious decision of serving, basically, Kolhapur and Sangli districts, has in the past preferred to grow into an institution of immense internal strength in preference to size. Now, in keeping with the present day challenges the Bank has embarked on a modernisation and expansion programme with the objective of consolidating its strengths by achieving recognition for its development in size, as well.. Currently, the bank is run under the expert guidance of Shri Subhash G. Kutte, Managing Director & CEO of the bank. Ratnakar Bank Ltd. has tie ups with Kotak Life Insurance and Bajaj Allianz General Insurance Company Ltd. and offers life and general insurance products. The bank has a huge client base of more than 550,000 people. The bank carries out its operations through a network of 84 branches in Karnataka, Maharashtra, Gujarat, Goa, the Union Territory of Dadra & Nagar Haveli and New Delhi. Till date, 53 branches offer core banking solutions and 10 other branches are fully computerized branches.

Ratnakar Bank products and services

Ratnakar Bank has every product to meet the needs of every customer. The products and services offered by Ratnakar Bank are enumerated below:

- Loans
- Housing Loans
- Car Loans
- Two Wheeler Loans
- Agricultural Loans
- Educational Loans
- Consumer Loans
- Commercial Credit Loans
- Loans for Professionals/ Purchasing Medical Equipments
- Super Secured Loan
- Scheme Sanjeevani Mortgage Loan
- Scheme Ratna - Trade (Working Capital)
- Recurring Deposit Non-Resident External (Rupee) Account
- Deposits

- Fixed Deposit
- Ratnakar Tax Saving Term Deposit Scheme 2006
- Amrutkumbha Lakshadish Deposit
- Kalpavruksha Nirantar Deposit
- Monthly Interest Payable Deposit Scheme
- Cash Certificate
- Utility Deposit Schemes
- Reinvestment Deposit
- Unit Deposit Schemes
- Current Account
- Ratna Vyapar Plus Current Account
- Ratna Max Income Savings Account
- No - Frills Deposit Accounts
- Services Merchant Banking
- Western Union Money Transfer
- Depository Services and Dematerialization
- Leasing Finance
- Insurance and Investment Opportunities
- ATM Services
- Venture Capital Fund
- Credit Counseling Services
- Drafts
- Free Services

Ratnakar Bank Ltd. has an array of free services for its customers which includes the following:

- Issuing of 1st pass book, term deposit receipts, statement of accounts and cheques for saving deposit account
- Opening and maintenance of No Frill accounts
- Offering electronic clearing services apart from return cheques
- Balance enquiry (including enquiry for up to 2 years old transactions)
- Local cheques collection
- National Electronic Fund Transfer (NEFT) – only for inbound transactions.
- Cash payment through every type of account
- Cash Deposits for Term Deposit, Saving, cash credit and Current A/c up to Rs.5.00 lacs

- ATM services
- Deposit receipts collection of other banks
- Guidance for different types of deposits and loan accounts and additional banking services
- Standing instructions for debit/credit of internal transactions
- Inter branch transfer of Rs.10,000/- under CBS

With the inevitable focus on customer satisfaction through prompt service and decision conveyance, Bank has adopted a flat administrative structure. Except 19 branches all other 64 branches report directly to Head Office. A group of 19 branches which mostly include branches at metropolitan cities like Mumbai, Pune & Ahmedabad report through General Manager, Mumbai. With customer interests in mind, the chain of command is kept to the minimum.

Top Level Changes in the bank

Vishwavir Ahuja, who headed Bank of America's Indian unit till 2009, joined Ratnakar as its managing director and chief executive last year. It also appointed former Morgan Stanley India CEO Narayan Ramachandran to its board.

It has also built up a senior management by appointing executives from various private sector financial services firms. These include Rajeev Ahuja (ex-Head, Fixed Income Capital Markets and Sales, Citibank), Shashank Mukherji (existing leadership in the Bank), Nitin Chopra (ex-CEO of Bharti Axa Life Insurance), Sunil Gulati (ex-Group President, Corporate & Institutional Banking, YES Bank), Suhas Sahakari (ex-Head, SME Business, Axis Bank), Shanta Vallury (ex-Head, Liabilities Distribution, ICICI Bank) and Naresh Karia (ex-Country Controller, Citibank).

"The Indian Banking sector has one of the brightest opportunities today thanks to the growth being experienced by the country. We have taken a significant leap forward to participate meaningfully in this growth. We are keen to address this by providing modern financial services to Emerging Large Companies, Small & Medium Enterprises, Retail Banking segments and the largely untapped Financial Inclusion segment, and be the 'bank of choice' in the segments we operate," said Ahuja in a statement.

Failed attempt to acquire stake in Kolhapur-based bank seen as trigger

The Reserve Bank of India (RBI) is examining surrogate holdings of Indian companies in private sector banks. The move follows a hostile takeover attempt by a leading Mumbai-based real estate company to acquire around 42 per cent in Kolhapur-based Ratnakar Bank.

A top Ratnakar Bank executive said the company, which also has interests in financial services, had approached the bank in January-February this year to explore the possibility of acquiring a substantial stake in the bank. The bank's board, however, did not entertain the move and cited regulations that do not permit any single entity to hold more than 10 per cent in a bank.

RBI also stepped in and immediately appointed two observers on the bank's board. At the bank's board meeting towards the end of February, the move by the realtor was quashed in the presence of the RBI observers, but with a dissent note from some members.

RBI guidelines do not allow companies to hold shares in a bank directly and companies that have indirect holdings in banks do not get control or voting rights. On the single-entity holding limit, the guidelines stipulate that those that manage to acquire more than 10 per cent over a period of time will have their voting rights capped at 10 per cent, irrespective of the level of shareholding.

Sources close to the development said RBI is taking the issue of surrogate shareholding seriously, although scanning for such holdings is part of the routine audit of banks. They added that the issue has become significant, since RBI's attention has been drawn to the fact that surrogate shareholders have, in some cases, succeeded in wielding control over such critical decisions as lending, treasury, investment and key appointments.

Despite the single-entity holding norm, a source said it is difficult to trace the origins of all the surrogate companies till a full-fledged audit is complete. The source said many companies own shares in banks by floating firms in other names or through subsidiaries of shell companies or via special purpose vehicles.

Many companies float financial companies or insurance ventures that buy stakes in private sector banks through bilateral off-market deals or through stock market transactions. Banks resorted to a similar practice by floating non-banking finance companies to skirt exposure norms while lending.

The sources said the current audit season will focus on such investigations. If the investigations yield something concrete, prudential measures to close possible loopholes could be put in place.

The issue of surrogate shareholdings by companies is critical for old-generation and weak private sector banks, since they need capital for expansion and are, therefore, vulnerable to acquisition.

The SS Tarapore committee on fuller capital account convertibility had proposed allowing companies to own banks but RBI did not favour this suggestion, fearing potential conflict of interest.

Plans to Infuse Funds through Rights Issue

Kolhapur-based Ratnakar Bank has raised equity funding from India's largest mortgage lender HDFC Ltd and consortium of private equity investors including Norwest Venture Partners, Beacon India Private Equity Fund, Cartica Capital, Faering Capital, Gaja Capital Partners and Samara Capital, among others. The bank has raised Rs 720 crore through the issue. The firm has also opened its Mumbai Main Office at Lower Parel.

Ratnakar Bank may plan a rights issue of shares within a year to fund its expansion and seek to list its shares within four years, its new managing director and chief executive Vishwavir Ahuja has said. Ahuja, who headed Bank of America's Indian unit until September last year, recently took over the Kolhapur-based bank.

The bank plans to increase its focus on financial inclusion and has appointed a four-member committee that includes Vijay Mahajan, the chairman of microfinance firm Basix, to recommend a new strategic plan for the bank within a month, Ahuja said.

Ratnakar Bank, which has 87 branches mainly in Maharashtra, Karnataka, Gujarat and Goa, will increase its lending to small borrowers such as – small and marginal farmers, artisans and workers to up to half of all its loans, with the remaining amount going to existing borrowers like agriculture, traders and small businesses. It also aims to double the number of its customers to 1 million, he said. The bank, which had a capital of Rs 343 crore, aimed to spend money on acquiring new technology and upgrading branches, Ahuja said.

Futuristic Outlook

The Indian banking industry showed great resilience in springing back to shape as also adjusting to the impact of the reforms. From a high overhang of bad debts and large loan delinquency in the early 1990s, Indian banks turned the corner in a decade's time with a stronger balance sheet and surging profitability. Not deterred by the burden of bad debts that emerged in the aftermath of banking sector reforms and introduction of prudential norms, the banking industry showed sound growth and expansion in the post reform period. Capital levels have increased, profitability has risen, productivity improved and so has several developments in enhancing the quality of customer service. Integration of banking industry with other major segments of finance, notably the securities markets is also growing. Integration with international markets is also on the rise, where Indian banks are increasing their presence and operations. All these augur well for the prospects of the Indian banking in the future.

An important aspect of the Indian economy at present is having a vibrant domestic financial system and a strong external sector. Given the growing pace of globalization of finance, Indian domestic financial system in general and banking industry in particular stand to gain from opportunities arising within the country and outside. The Union Budget and the Monetary Policy statements in the recent period have greatly enhanced the scope and significance of the Indian financial sector by encouraging greater integration among the domestic and international financial markets. In this context the constitution of a Committee on Financial Sector Assessment by the Government and the The Reserve Bank to undertake comprehensive self assessment of the Indian financial sector as per global standards and laying down a road map for further reforms is an important initiative. RBI announced constitution of an internal working group to examine the report of the High Powered Expert Committee on Making Mumbai as an International Financial Center and implement the recommendations as appropriate. Making Mumbai as an international financial center would be of great significance for Indian finance and banking in view of the enormous opportunities such a development could bring in.

The stance of the monetary policy to get a hold on rapidly rising asset prices and growing inflationary tendencies in the back of high economic growth, though might appear to impact the business of banks, but could prove helpful in the long run since the prudential measures could ensure appropriate pace of business and better risk management.

At the same time there are challenges that may appear daunting. Banks in Asia, particularly in China have phenomenal size as compared to Indian banks. Liberalisation is leading to creation of global banks through growth and consolidation. In this background, an important and most urgent challenge for Indian banks is to create a size that would be effective in dealing with the global competition. Indian banking also needs larger amounts of capital to sustain their growth in the future for which they need to step up performance and efficiency that would attract investors. Another equally important challenge would be harnessing the benefits of technology. Though progress is made, technology solutions integrating the banking operations to derive synergies and efficiencies in Public Sector Banks need to move at a much faster pace. Similarly, Public Sector Banks need to step up the use of infrastructure related to Real Time Gross Settlement and Electronic Fund Transfer Systems that could benefit their customers. There is much scope to further increase the share of non-interest income, which will raise profitability and productivity.

In the next two years (2009) there would be significant changes in the banking landscape as per the road map announced for the presence of Foreign Banks in India. From Arpil 2009 onwards, the limitations on the Wholly Owned Subsidiaries of the Foreign Banks would be removed. Wholly Owned Subsidiaries of the Foreign Banks will also be allowed to list and dilute their stake and will be allowed to enter into mergers and acquisitions with the Private Sector Banks in India. These measures will greatly enhance the opportunities for Foreign Banks that will further intensify the competition for the domestic banks.

Notwithstanding these challenges, the Indian banking industry can look forward to a promising period ahead. High economic growth offers banks a host of opportunities in new businesses and also in expanding the existing ones. Growing international operations of Indian business will provide Indian banks with global opportunities in banking. Rising income levels of people will give scope to design and develop a wide range of personal financial products and fee based services. Focus on infrastructure development and certain key sectors like rural economy, health and education offer exciting business opportunities for the extensive branch network of Public Sector Banks located in the rural and semi-urban areas.

While opportunities could be numerous, responding to them positively and realizing them to a desired extent would be a great challenge. With right strategies in harnessing technology and human resources developing market segments, design of new generation products and services, focus on efficient customer service and pursuing global aspirations can take Indian banks to the next generation banking.

References

- Dr. Y.V. Reddy on Banking Sector Reforms in India An Overview at the Institute of Bankers of Pakistan, Karachi, Pakistan, May 18, 2005
- Dr. Alan Bollard, Corporate governance in the financial sector, Christchurch, New Zealand, 7 April 2003.
- Mark W. Olson, **Business Trends and Management Challenges for the Banking Industry,** Annual Economic Outlook Conference, Middle Tennessee State University, Murfreesboro, Tennessee, 16 September 2005
- Enhancing corporate governance for banking organisations, Consultative document issued by BCBS, July 2005.

- Malcolm D Knight, Banking and insurance regulation and supervision: Greater convergence, common challenges, Madrid, 22-23 September 2004
- UBS AG, The Bank for Banks Industry Challenges. August 2004
- Ms. K.J.Udeshi, Financial System Stability and Basel II - Way Forward, Sri Lanka, rbidocs.rbi.org.in/rdocs/Speeches/DOCs/68615.doc
- www.the**ratnakarbank**.com/index.html
- investing.businessweek.com/research/stocks/private/snapshot.asp
- awww.info2india.com/.../**banks**/...**banks**/the-**ratnakar-bank-ltd**.html
- www.rupeetimes.com

9

A Success Story of Indore City Bus

Ms. Payal Sharma
Lecturer, Mahakal Institue of Management-Ujjain (M.P.)
payalsharma.ind@gmail.com

Indore is a major city and commercial center of the state of Madhya Pradesh in central India. Indore is located 190 km west of the state capital Bhopal. According to the 2011 Indian census, Indore city has a population of 25, 24,912. It is the largest city of Madhya Pradesh, the 15th largest city in India and the 147th largest city in the world. It is also the commercial capital of the state and serves as the headquarters of both Indore District and Indore Division. Indore is the only city of India that has both an Indian Institute of Management (IIM) and an Indian Institute of Technology (IIT). These two premier education institutions are located in the city and many engineering and management institutes are also here. Indore not only known Indore Agro Industrial Region but also known as a software city , these are the few reasons which makes it metropolitan city of Madhya Pradesh also the reason of growing population. With the beginning of the 21st century, the ever-increasing intensity of traffic, congestion, delays, accidents and other transportation problems in the city compelled the municipal authorities to plan a way out of these traffic problems. Indore news constantly highlighted the plight of the common man, which forced the administration to take action. After months of discussions and planning, Indore City Transport Services Limited (ICTSL) was incorporated on December 1, 2005.

Organization Profile

The aforesaid company has identified and took permission for 18 high travel demand routes from RTA and has already started operation of its 37 ultra-modern low floor buses. These city buses with 2 broad doors are allowing passengers to board and alight quickly and easily, save time and fuel, and give better run-times and improved economy to the bus operators. Real time vehicle tracking and fully computerized ticket vending system are some other highlights. O&M and other regulatory measures are being exercised by the company. According to official data, Indore Municipal Corporation and Indore Development Authority invested an authorised capital of Rs 2,500,000 jointly. ICTSL runs through 277 kilometres of road network in the city and nearby areas. The city transport system currently functions as a public-private partnership. Six private partners along with the city administration manage the transport system.

The cost of living in the city should be such that the common man does not feel life is a burden for him. ICTSL adheres to the ideology as it offers pass system for regular travellers. The monthly pass that could be earlier made for Rs 300 is now available for Rs 350.

The model had to be designed keeping in mind the motto of 'Minimum Investment With Maximum Returns' for all parties involved in the business. Mr. Vivek Aggarwal (Collector, Indore) designed it with flawless technique and scientific approach. The financial model provides maximum profitability for the company as well as the operators. The operational aspect provides impeccable control for both the parties and fully computerized monitoring.

The Need

Effective Public Transport is the need of every metropolitan city. For cities that are growing at a rapid pace, it becomes the most essential vehicle for pace of growth. Indore could easily be identified as the fastest growing metropolitan city in central India and the most important feature missing here was a good public transport service. The senior officials of the city identified the need and a meeting was called in the month of November 2005. All the decision makers of the city were present. The decision taken was to create a solution that was Reliable, Affordable and Safe. The task sounded very difficult, especially looking at the availability of funds and relevant Infrastructure but it was the need of the city.

Various systems were discussed and several examples were talked on. The result of all the brainstorming was to create a SPV that would take the task of providing the service required to support the rapid growth of the city.

Concept

Cities with population of more than one million should have urban bus Transport Corporation that owns 30 percent of its own buses and contracts 70 percent of buses from private contractors and operators. Motivated by this World Bank recommendation note on 'India's Transport Sector, The Challenges Ahead (2002)' Mr. Vivek Aggarwal, Collector and District Magistrate, Indore conceptualized a financial model of public transport system through private partnership where in every player whether Government, the spv, local administration, operators and people are mutually benefited.

Looking to the high potential for development of competitive bus transport market through contracting or franchising arrangements, a Special Purpose Vehicle as a public limited company was formed which specifies the role of the market and government. It was felt that cities like

Indore should develop their own regulatory and enforcement capabilities to promote city service competition and put in place a mechanism that will ensure financial viability of such operations.

The main source of revenue for the company is the monthly premium amount received from the bus operators, advertising revenue and the share of revenue generated through passes. The sources of revenue for the bus operators are the daily fare box collection, share of revenue generated through advertising on buses and monthly passes. Cost effective and substantial finances to the operators has been made available by the bank. Operators were financed 100% by the bank and an agreement has been executed between the company, the bank and the operators to have an escrow account.

Other transport facilities are also available or the competitors of ICTSL figure 1 is showing the numbers

Figure: 1 Number of Registered Vehicle 1991-2010

Type of Vehicle	Nos.
Busses	3420
Mini Bus	28994
Motor Cab/ Metro Taxi	3534
Tempo	211
Auto Rickshaw	11876
Maruti City Van/ Tata Magic	792

Source: Regional Transport office

An estimated 22.7 lakh trips are performed everyday in the city by City busses of which central area contributes 19.4 percent, while the rest of Municipal Corporation area contributes 76.4 percent and extension area's share being 4.3 percent only. The shares of personalized vehicles (cycles, two wheelers & cars) and public/IPT transport in the total trips are 51.1 percent & 16.4 percent respectively. Work /Business trips accounts for maximum share (38.1 %) followed by education trips (37.6 %). Shopping trips share was 28.4 percent. The average trip lengths observed were 3.8 km and 4.4 km including and excluding walk trips respectively.

Company **"Atal Indore City Transport Services Ltd"** has been incorporated to operate and manage the public transport system. The new SPV is ideally constituted as a Public Limited Company incorporated under the Companies Act, 1956. The Registered Office of the company is situated at 30 Residency area, Indore. The authorized capital of the company is Rs 25 lacs divided into 2.50 lacs equity shares of Rs. 10/- each. The initial paid up capital of Rs. 25 lacs is being held by the Indore Municipal Corporation and Indore Development Authority in equal proportion. The main objects of the company are

- Create specialized and effective regulatory agency to monitor cost effective and good public transport services within the city of Indore with private partnership.
- To establish and maintain line of passenger coaches to transport passengers.
- To develop support system for improving transport infrastructure.

Implementation

The implementation of the whole process was to be carried out at war front as the target launch date was decided as January 26, 2006. That meant only 56 days to implement a public transport service in a town that was craving for it for more than 15 years. This is how it was done:

First Step

Finalization of routes:

A survey was carried out across the city to identify the major routes that would provide the maximum passenger traffic. Eighteen such routes were identified and finalized taking suggestions from the traffic department.

Selection of Bus Model:

Technical and Financial proposals were invited from various manufacturers of buses and Ultra-modern low-floor TATA Star bus was chosen to run on the streets of Indore. The beauty of the bus was a spectacle and the practicality provided is unmatchable.

Invitation of Bids from Operators:

A pre-bid meeting was hosted on December 20, 2006 to explain the various aspects of business to the prospective bidders. The idea was presented and questions were answered. After clearing all the doubts of the operators, bids were invited on December 23, 2006. The operators actively participated in the bid process and we had the routes booked.

This was it! The stage was set. Routès were in place, the operators were ready and the buses were booked.

Second Step

After the operators, some more people had to come on board to run the show. They were the marketers.

Advertisement:

Applications were invited January 17, 2006 from companies interested in taking the rights for advertising on the buses. Various advertisers participated and we had the highest bidder at Rs 25000 per bus per month. This should go as a record.

Passes:

The monthly pass system had to become the backbone of the financial modal. There were various options like Route Pass, Daily Pass, Student Pass etc. but the company decided to keep it simple and start with a single pass for all priced at Rs. 250. This would enable the passenger to travel unlimited for a month on any bus on any route. The bids for issuing passes were called and on January 20, 2006 we had a company ready to setup 15 Instant Pass Centers across the city to issue these passes.

The Grand Finale

Now we had all the people in place. The operators, the advertisers, the pass issuers, the drivers, conductors & administrative officers. The stage was set and 5 days were left. The buses were to be delivered, the advertiser's branding was left, the ticket issuing machines had to be programmed and the manpower had to be trained. The pass-issuing machine came from UK and it was all set to issue the first pass on 26th of January 06.

Republic Day added more jubilation to the city. Yes it was here! The buses were flagged off, the ticketing machine issued the first ticket and it moved.

This was a sight to watch. After 15 years Indore city had got a good public transport system. A system which was reliable and contemporary, affordable yet profitable, fashionable yet sustainable.

New Gifts From ICTSL To Indore

AICTSL Introduction:-With the objective of implementing reliable and efficient public transport service a Special Purpose Vehicle (SPV) in the form of limited company Atal Indore City Transport Services Ltd (AICTSL) was set up to operate and manage the public transport system in Indore. AICTSL currently is running 104 buses in the city through promoting private sector participation in terms of investment on and operation of high quality buses under the overall planning and control of AICTSL. Furthermore 125 SLF buses are being procured under JNNURM to improve the capacity .To meet the large demand and improve the capacity and productivity of buses, AICTSL has proposed to plan, to develop and operate Bus Rapid Transit System (BRTS) in Indore.

Bus Rapid Transit (BRT) system in the city will provide a safe and efficient transportation system that is environmentally friendly. The BRT system will provide an attractive alternative for motorists by reducing the delays traditionally found in regular bus systems by improving the infrastructure, utilizing bus runways, convenient bus stops/stations, modern vehicles, and adopting state-of-the-art technologies in the form of Intelligent Transportation Systems (ITS). the integration of ITS components into the proposed BRT system with the objective of improving the travel times, accessibility, ease of use, environmental impacts and attractiveness of BRT.

Indore ITS is a broad range of wireless and wired communications-based information and electronics technologies, which, when applied to the current transportation system, can help improve safety, reduce congestion, enhance mobility, minimize environmental impacts, save energy, and promote economic productivity. ITS are a cost-effective strategy that further enhances the BRT experience. ITS is the application of advanced communications and technologies to transportation systems providing advanced monitoring, control, and traveler information capabilities that allow better real-time management of roads and transit systems.

The first service got an overwhelming response from day one. A dream project was successfully implemented within 56 days. This was the one of the achievement for the Indore municipal corporation to implement the new transportation services merely in 56 days. This short span of time become the milestone for other cities which are going to be enter into the enhancement of there city transportation services.

Teaching Notes

Learning Objectives

1. This case study focuses on the future need of the proper transportation service in India, as population is increasing every second these will be needed.
2. Cities those are planning to start city bus services they can learn many think from Indore city bus for getting success.
3. Population create pollution; one of the major reason of pollution is rapid growth in vehicle, ICTSL is also planning to start CNG buses in future which is the eco friendly services beneficial to reduce pollution.

Assignment Questions

1. Did you think only need for better transportation service is the reason for ICTSL has come in existence? If no give the reason.
2. Identify the reasons behind the success of ICTSL in city like Indore.
3. Give the proper strategies to implement city bus policy in different cites like Indore.
4. Did you think that other transportation facilities like; Auto Rikshaw, Minibuses, Tata magic, etc. can beat the city bus in future when city bus will come with "Bus Rapid Transit System".

Bibliography

1. http://www.embarq.org/sites/default/files/Full%20Report%20-%20A%20Study%20on%20the%20Para-Transit%20System%20in%20Indore%20City.pdf
2. Indore City Bus Services, from http://www.citybusindore.com/management.asp
3. Sustainable Urban Transport Project, from http://www.sutpindia.com

10

Corporate Social Responsibility at Fab India

Ms. Ruchika Jeswal
Assistant Professor (Marketing), Institute of Management Studies, Ghaziabad
ruchikajeswal@yahoo.com

ABSTRACT

Corporate Social Responsibility (CSR) can be defined as the "economic, legal, ethical, and discretionary expectations that society has of organizations at a given point in time". The concept of corporate social responsibility means that organizations have moral, ethical, and philanthropic responsibilities in addition to their responsibilities to earn a fair return for investors and comply with the law. This case study aims to explore the concept of CSR at Fab India Pvt. Ltd. FabIndia works closely with artisans by providing various inputs including design, quality control, access to raw materials and production coordination. Fab India is Trying to work with its artisans closely and is trying to maintain a supplier base . Today Fab India has a number of retail outlets selling several products and trying to pass the benefits to its artisans .

Introduction

Social responsibility is an organization 's obligation to engage in activities that protect and contribute to the welfare of society . Social responsibility is a matter of intense debate. At one extreme, there are those who strongly believe that organizations are in business solely to produce goods and services that societies want –be they atomic weapons , legal advice ,or life saving drugs – and that they are entitled to make profits in return. For these people , social responsibility is, simply not an issue .At the other extreme ,there are those who believe that organizations should be allowed to do business only if they do not harm ,help solve social problems, and put some of the profits they earn back to work for society.

Concept of Corporate Social Responsibility

Corporate Social Responsibility (CSR) can be defined as the "economic, legal, ethical, and discretionary expectations that society has of organizations at a given point in time". The concept of corporate social responsibility means that organizations have moral, ethical, and philanthropic responsibilities in addition to their responsibilities to earn a fair return for investors and comply with the law. A traditional view of the corporation suggests that its primary, if not sole, responsibility is to its owners, or stockholders. However, CSR requires organizations to adopt a broader view of its responsibilities that includes not only stockholders, but many other constituencies as well, including employees, suppliers, customers, the local community, state, and federal governments, environmental groups, and other special interest groups'

Company Profile

Fab India was established by John Bissel in 1960 in order to fuse the best aspects of East/ West collaboration. He was determined to showcase Indian handloom textiles while providing equitable employment to traditional artisans and also to develop India's export potential in it's emerging textile industry. Over the years the focus of Fabindia's marketing shifted from exports to the local Indian retail market. What started as an export house has today become a successful retail business presenting Indian textiles in a variety of natural fibers, and home products.

Case Body

FabIndia was founded with the strong belief that there was a need for a vehicle for marketing the vast and diverse craft traditions of India and thereby help fulfill the need to provide and sustain rural employment. They blended indigenous craft techniques with contemporary designs to bring aesthetic and affordable products to today's consumers.

Their endeavor is to provide customers with hand crafted products which help support and encourage good craftsmanship.

Their products are sourced from villages all over India. FabIndia works closely with artisans by providing various inputs including design, quality control, access to raw materials and production coordination. The vision continues to be to maximize the hand made element in their products, whether it is handwoven textiles, hand block printing, hand embroidery or handcrafting home products.

FabIndia's managing director William Bissel ,who conceived and steered the model, says that unlike many Indian companies he doesn't believe in setting up a department to promote corporate social responsibility(CSR) .He created an air of hope ,anticipation and excitement in the sleepy village of Chanderi in the Ashok Nagar district of Madhya Pradesh .The local people include about 1000 –odd weavers who were disappointed not just by no rain or no water but by disappearance of the demand of their cherished fabric –Chanderi.

They were then introduced to the concept of becoming owners of shares in a community owned company .They were unsure but bought shares because they thought that it could change their lives in some ways.

That way has been paved by FabIndia ,A retail outfit that has grown from one store in mid 1990's to 85 .Dabbling in fabric , apparel, handicrafts and other products, it began an experiment with community –owned companies nine years ago in an attempt to include artisan in the wealth creation process. Fab India has created a fully owned subsidiary Artisans Micro Finance, a venture fund .It is owned 49 percent by the fund, 26 percent by the artisans ,15 percent by private investors and 10 percent by the employees of the community –owned company .The investment by these four categories of investors provides the paid up capital .The company promotes the sales of its artisan community to FabIndia ,Which is the principal buyer.

Walk into any of Fab India's high end retail outlets in major cities across India, and around the world - you would be tempted by their unique clothing and furnishing collection, surprised by the store's relentless focus on the customer and would probably walk out with a big bag in your hands. However, you would never guess that the profits made from that store and many others across the country are partly distributed among the weavers, about 20,000 of who are 'shareholders' of subsidiary companies floated by Fab India.

The artisans gain in many ways .The value of their shares goes up .They earn dividends when the company is in a position to declare them Eventually the company will try and offer loans to the artisans ,arranged through banks. The loans can be used to buy new looms or expand production of other products. Although the villagers see it as a gamble they are convinced that it would work.

William Bissel is convinced that involving artisans and sharing benefits of growth with them is the most sustainable of all models. The shares offer the artisans a divisible asset class and community owned companies help convert FabIndia's artisan base into an asset .

But the model is not desirable from a social point of view alone. Fab India has moved from being a primarily export house in the 1960's to a turnover of Rs 300 crore ,of which 90 percent is domestic sales.Its aim is to be a " lifestyle lternative to mass produced "

Artisans Microfinance Director Smita Mankad Quit ABNAmro to do something she believed was worthwile.

'If you want grow at the pace we have grown , you have to carry your supplier base with you," she says, emphasizing that FabIndia's growth will be hampered unless the artisans grew with it.

If FabIndia is changing the way the artisans work, the new model is changing the way FabIndia works .The typical central warehouses owned by community –owned companies from which goods travel directly to stores across India , This reduces logistics costs and minimizes the role of Middlemen.

While the system seems to be working for all concerned , challenges remain .One of them is developing secondary markets so that the companies can stand on their own feet .Critical to that will be introducing a consciousness of the design element in the artisans so that their products have a wider appeal. Bissel says the model will depend on the artisans beginning to understand the benefits of joining together in something that's not cooperative". A cooperative imposes many restrictions upon them and doesn't give them much in return ,If you get together ,you must create something that's bigger than the sum of it's parts. FabIndia's entry made the biggest difference as it began to source fabric worth Rs 1 crore a year from Chanderi .

Fabindia sources its products from over 15000 craft persons and artisans across India. They support the craft traditions of India by providing a market and thereby encourage and sustain rural employment. Today they have retail outlets in all major cities of India - 85 at last count - in addition to international stores in Rome, Italy; Dubai, UAE and Guangzhou, China.

Today FabIndia has expanded beyond textiles into furniture, stationery, pottery, organic foods and bodycare products. All merchandise is sold under the single FabIndia brand and the company owns all its stores as Bissell feels this helps the brand to maintain its identity.

FabIndia works closely with artisans and villagers to develop designs and colour palettes and to optimise production techniques and raw material inputs. For the textiles, mostly natural fabrics and vegetable dyes are used.

"We attract a specific type of customer and decided we want to give that customer the spectrum of products," Bissell says of the product diversification strategy, adding that FabIndia's customers do not fit an age or demographic profile, but are a loyal base of people who want to support craft.

But Bissell is also candid in admitting that some of the diversifications have had unexpected problems. For example, FabIndia's range of organic foods, which it launched in 2004, has a limited audience and as it is perishable has a shorter shelf life than other FabIndia products.

FabIndia recently forayed overseas and has had some early success. For example, its store in the Gulf has been quick to take off. But this has only reinforced Bissell's conviction that it is the Indian diaspora that makes FabIndia a profitable business. Penetrating overseas markets is a "focus but not a large focus", says Bissell, who sees customers in India as the mainstay. The business derives 90% of its revenues domestically. "Our global expansion will be targeted at places where there are a large number of Indians," clarifies Bissell.

Bissell is clear that it is the firm's decision to stay focused over the decades of its existence that is responsible for its success. "We have consistently operated in the niche we identified initially," sums up Bissell, explaining the firm's philosophy. "We are like a restaurant which serves only one kind of cuisine." And with takers abounding for that one type of cuisine, it is clear Bissell is on to a good thing.

Questions

1. What is the relationship between Fab India, the parent company and the subsidiaries - If the subsidiaries have a claim on Fab India's profits or just act as a supplier unit?
2. What do you think of the model that Bissel has proposed?
3. Would FabIndia really be able to transfer the benefits to its artisans as they have proposed?
4. FabIndia's community-owned companies are converting artisans into assets while sharing the benefits of growth with them .Explain?
5. Would Diversification in some other areas help Fab India to provide better to its shareholders- the artisan community?

Teaching Notes

Overview

Corporate Social Responsibility (CSR) can be defined as the "economic, legal, ethical, and discretionary expectations that society has of organizations at a given point in time". The concept of corporate social responsibility means that organizations have moral, ethical, and philanthropic responsibilities in addition to their responsibilities to earn a fair return for investors and comply with the law. A traditional view of the corporation suggests that its primary, if not sole, responsibility is to its owners, or stockholders. However, CSR requires organizations to adopt a broader view of its responsibilities that includes not only stockholders, but many other constituencies as well, including employees, suppliers, customers, the local community, state, and federal governments, environmental groups, and other special interest groups.

John Bissel , who had worked in India as a consultant for the Ford Foundation, founded FabIndia in 1960 to showcase Indian handloom textiles to the world. He opened the flagship Greater Kailash, New Delhi, store in 1975 to retail home furnishings, and subsequently expanded into garments. At the time, the business largely catered to overseas buyers.

William Bissell his son took over as managing director of FabIndia in 1999 and today heads a network of 87 stores in 39 cities in India as well as branches in Rome, Dubai and Guangzhou with a turnover in excess of Rs3 billion ($68 million). Bissell went one step further in trying to ensure he is sharing the wealth FabIndia creates with those who are helping him to create it. FabIndia floated a wholly-owned subsidiary, Artisans Micro Finance, which will create community-owned companies. For each company, a calculation is done of how much working capital it needs, then this is financed two-thirds through debt and one-third through equity.

Applications

This case study would be best for a management student trying to explore about Corporate social Responsibility and its effects on our Indian community.

Objectives of the Case

This a type of decision case. It will introduce to the reader the following concepts:

1 Corporate Social Responsibility

2. Social responsibility and Organizational Stakeholders

References :

1. www.fabindia.com
2. Business World
3. Vipin Gupta ,Kamala Gollakota ,R. Srinivasan,(2008) Business Policy and Strategic Management, Prentice Hall of India Private Limited .

11

Streamlining Discharge: A Systems Approach

Dr. Sunanda D. Amonkar
Professor, Department of Medicine.
sunandaamonkar@yahoo.co.in
Meena Parulekar, Faculty
meena.sahib@marianinstitute.in,
sahib.meena@gmail.com
Ajit Parulekar
Associate Professor (Marketing)
ajitp@gim.ac.in
Marian Institute of Health Care Management (MIHM)

ABSTRACT

In a large hospital in a public setting, discharging patients from the hospital can prove to be a difficult task. There are a host of activities that function interdependently to make this happen. The entire discharge process can thus be viewed as a complex system working within constraints to enable smooth operations. The sheer volumes of patients attended to on any particular day along with limited availability of resources can create a unique blend of complicated situations for the hospital administration.

Dr. Shikha Gupta has been preoccupied with questions about the discharge process at her hospital. She has planned to bring this forth to the management during the meeting scheduled later in the week. Considering the additional burden of post –operative conditions which contributes to the total patient load in the department, managing the discharge process becomes even more

critical. Primarily, she is concerned about tracking of her patients once they are relocated from the medicine department to other areas of the hospital. This in fact could be one of the contributing areas that alters/ affects the discharge process in the department. Her search for probable factors affecting patient transfers helps her to discover some crucial system errors that need prompt attention.

The discharge process in the above situation has been viewed as a system composed of distinct processes and tasks that need to be fulfilled in order to ensure safe discharge of the patient. The vast majority, i.e. unpaid category of patients was the focus area for the study. Key problem areas have been identified while also attempting to understand the dynamics of discharge in a public hospital setting.

Streamlining Discharge: A Systems Approach

It was January 3rd 2011, a bright start to the New Year and life as usual in the medicine OPD of the Government Hospital in Goa. Yet another grueling OPD session had just come to an end, but for Dr. Shikha Gupta, a junior resident in Unit 2 of this department, the day had just begun. Already there were a couple of phone calls from the staff nurses that the ward beds were full and the newly admitted patients were waiting for beds in the wards; not only were they sitting on the stools but some were on the trolleys and even on the floor. Of late this was becoming a regular feature on almost all units' admission day. As she proceeded to the wards in a very pensive mood, she stopped to grab a bite at the food counter while trying to recollect her duties for the day. Briefly running through her list of patients she could identify only two patients who could be discharged today; hardly sufficient to make place for the waiting patients. May be she could ask the residents from other units to try and discharge some of their patients if possible. Also she was not sure about the bed availability in the other wards to transfer stable patients out. If admissions kept pouring in at this rate and with another 18 hours to go before closure of admissions in her unit, accommodating all the patients would indeed be a herculean task. With a prayer in her heart, as she stepped into the ward these were the words in her mind and on her lips "Good lord here I come......"

The government hospital in Goa is a public hospital providing secondary and tertiary level care to patients within and from neighboring areas of the state. A 1400 bedded facility, the hospital boasts of a 24x7 pharmacy facility and a hi-tech laboratory for testing of blood samples. The specialty services provided at this hospital includes oncology care, fertility treatment and trauma surgery. The major achievements for this hospital in the past year were its least infant mortality rate when compared to other public hospitals in the country, a 5% decrease in the ICU associated infections and the installation of the latest MRI (magnetic resonance imaging) machine for diagnostic purposes.

Since there are not many providers of secondary and tertiary healthcare in the nearby areas, this hospital is always overloaded with patients from remote areas of the state as well as adjoining areas of Karnataka and Maharashtra. Patients arriving at the hospital are asked to make a case paper initially followed by them being checked by the respective doctor/consultant. Depending on the nature of condition and treatment required they get admitted to the medicine department as inpatients. It is interesting to note that the average length of stay for an inpatient was between 3 to 4 days but in the last year this trend had seen a change with the ALOS (average length of stay) in some cases going up to 7 days for some patients. Known for its capability to handle up to 300 OPD and close to 150 inpatients on any given day, the IPD satisfaction levels in the medicine department had gone low in the past year. Increasingly, managing the patient load had become problematic with an additional burden of post-operative conditions on the rise. Dr. Shikha was also particularly concerned about tracking of her patients once they were shifted outside the medicine ward to other departments of the hospital. With a staff strength of 40 doctors and around 70 nurses working in three shifts per day this delay in discharge had in turn begun to affect the normal functioning of the department.

Organization of the Medicine Department

The medicine department was organized into six units; the reporting structure of each unit is as given below:

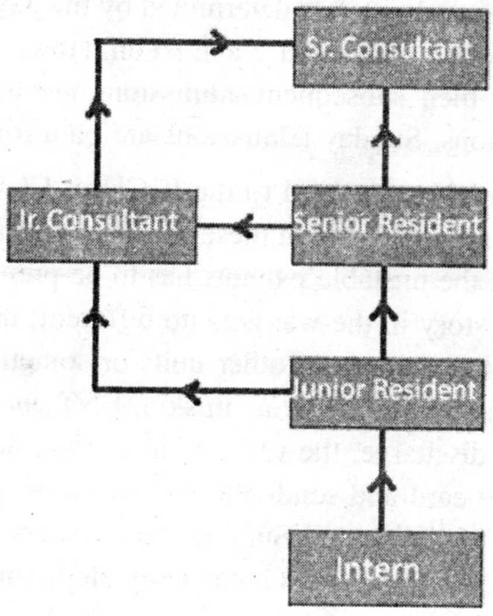

The junior resident doctor reports to the senior resident while the senior resident doctor reports to the junior /senior consultant. The interns are included as and when based on their availability during rounds.

The department of medicine has a total of seven wards; the bed strength of each is as given below:

Type of ward	Number of wards	Bed strengthPer ward
Males	3	30
Females	2	30
ICCU*	1	15
CCU**	1	15

*- Intensive Coronary Care Unit

**-Coronary Care Unit

Patient Procedure in the Medicine Department

New patients are admitted to this department on Fridays and Saturdays starting from 9.00 am on Friday to 9.00 am on Saturday every week. After patients are admitted on friday, they are first seen by the junior residents and then by the senior residents. Depending on the nature of the case, the patient may get referred to the consultant also. The next day on Saturday grand rounds are conducted in which senior and junior consultants along with other doctors including interns evaluate all patients in their individual units.

The IPD(in patient department) patients in medicine wards are comprised of patients admitted at the OPD, through the casualty and those transferred to the medicine ward from other specialty wards if and when they develop medical complications. All routine patients are evaluated at the OPD level of which only those that are unstable and require monitoring and/or supervised treatment or those that pose diagnostic dilemma are admitted as in patients, the rest are sent home after prescribing them the necessary investigations and treatment. On the other hand, the emergencies are attended to at the casualty and patients are admitted to the wards on priority basis. The unit under which they are admitted is determined by the day of the admission; Monday admissions are under unit 1, Tuesdays under unit 2 and so on. However if the patient was earlier admitted under a particular unit then subsequent admissions are always under the same unit irrespective of the day of admissions. Sunday admissions are on a rotation basis.

The critical patents are invariably admitted to the ICCU or CCU where they are stabilized and then shifted to the general wards. The stay in these wards is determined by the admission rate and very often the most stable of the unstable patients has to be prematurely shifted out to make way for the new admission. The story in the wards is no different; in case of these patients they are transferred either to the medicine wards of other units or sometimes even to wards of other specialties where the bed occupancy rate is low as in skin, ENT and ophthalmology wards. The moment the patients are fit for discharge, the resident in charge, despite his/her busy schedule immediately writes the discharge card and sends the patient home there by generating a bed to accommodate fresh admissions. Medicine and Surgery departments usually compete for beds in the hospital followed by the Obstetrics and Gynecology department as well as orthopedics department.

Hierarchy of consultation for inpatient admissions

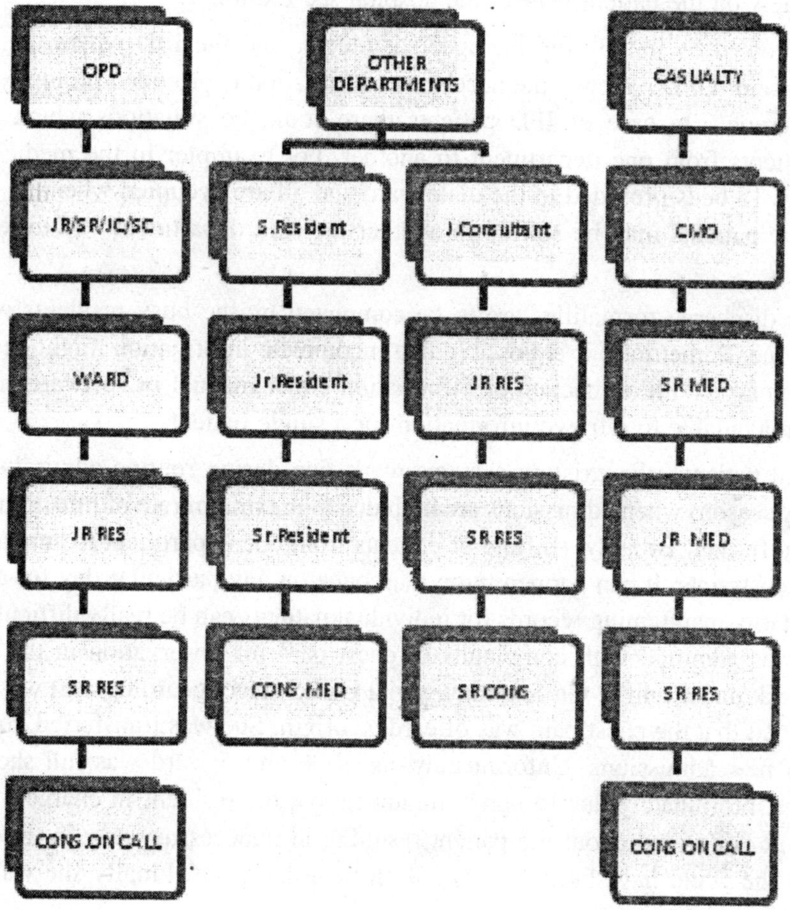

JR-Junior Resident
SR-Senior Resident
JC-Junior Consultant
SC-Senior Consultant
CMO-Casualty Medical Officer

In order to understand the dynamics of discharge, Dr.Shikha tried to first identify the factors that affect discharge. Her interactions with the senior residents and nurses gave her a better perspective on these factors and helped her to understand the nuances of discharge in her unit.

Factors Affecting Discharge

To begin with, completion of diagnosis in the case of a single patient would require a waiting period of 24-48 hours on an average. This is the time required for collection of clinical data and conduct of investigations depending on the disease condition of the patient. In certain patients when the diagnosis is not clear, based on differential diagnosis number of tests are carried out to ascertain the nature of the exact clinical condition and treatment started accordingly. For a detailed overview on the patient flow at the hospital see Exhibit 1.

This is followed by identifying the specialist/doctor and the IPD where the patient can be admitted. In case of OPD patients, the necessary consultation is provided promptly and discharge proceeds thereon. In case of IPD patients there could be situations which might demand transfer of patients from one department to another. For example: In the medicine department where there are 15 beds provided in the male ward and all are occupied when the need arises for more beds, few patients may be shifted to another the skin department to make room for the new patients.

Again the discharge formalities are to be completed by the busy residents who are always hurrying for time. Sometimes, it is possible that incomplete information might get entered in the discharge summary. With no backup of information either manual or software enabled, there is no mechanism available to retrieve information for a single patient.

For unpaid patients, the existing systems work fine during routine admissions however, in July (the rainy season) when admissions are high due to maximum rate of infections, the problems get aggravated further. Broadly, shifting of patients from one department to another occurs based on resource constraints. It can happen more than once on any particular day for a single patient. In such a scenario, maintaining records for individual patients can be really difficult. For example: Mrs. Radha was admitted with complaints of chest pain for observation in the ICCU ward on Friday last week under unit 5. On Saturday, serial ECGS (electrocardiogram) was performed and it was confirmed that the chest pain was of cardiac origin. She was transferred out to the ward to make bed for new admissions. Unfortunately since the unit 5 ward was full she was shifted to unit 2 wards. Unfortunately due to non communication, the resident in charge of Unit 5 female patients was not informed about the patient resulting in unnecessary stay in the hospital for the patient when she could have been discharged on Saturday itself. Finally she was discharged on Monday after rounds.

In her detailed discussion with fellow residents of medicine Dr. Shikha discovered that generally the stakeholders in the discharge process are few comprising of doctors, NGO's (non-government organizations), social workers and the patient. In most cases, if the diagnosis is rightly made treatment begins in time and the discharge can be planned accordingly. In some cases however, the diagnosis might take time due to many reasons like waiting for second opinion, test results not yet obtained or evaluated, non-co-operative patient and so on. Rarely, the diagnosis may terminate in non-identification of the clinical condition in which case again, the discharge process for the patient remains a big question.

IPD Issues

As Dr.Shikha sat down to understand the interdependencies among the factors listed above she recollected the case of Mr. Hans who was admitted in an intoxicated state at 8 am on Monday last week .Towards evening his consciousness levels had improved considerably despite which he was not willing to divulge any information as to what he had consumed. Since it was a MLC (Medico-legal case), the police who had come to record his statement had to be called the next day. At the rate at which he was improving Shikha was certain she would be able to discharge him the following day once his statement was recorded. However at the end of her rounds she realized that Mr. Hans was no longer there in the ward. When questioned the staff nurses too were not able to provide any information of his whereabouts nor was anything mentioned in the admission register. Where had the patient gone? Was he transferred to another ward due to bed shortage; had he quietly slipped out of the hospital? Had he jumped out through the windows in his inebriated state? And so a search was launched for him. It was only after much hue and cry was raised, one of the interns who was on call when Mr. Hans was admitted informed Shikha that he had spotted the patient at the bus stop and the only reason he had not bothered to inform the staff was because he thought that the patient had been discharged. Once this was known all the legal formalities like informing the Medical superintendent were completed in a jiffy. What a sheer waste of precious time this was ....

One of the most common situations encountered during rounds of the medicine ward is discovering a patient to be in "no man's land". This is probably the most difficult to handle and implies the period when the patient is both untraceable and has probably not been attended to. Dr. Shikha vividly recollected the case of Mr. Pednekar who was admitted on Saturday, last week at 10 am under unit 6. However when it came to light that he was admitted under unit 5 six months ago, he was again transferred to unit 5 on Sunday. Unfortunately, the resident in Unit 5 was informed about the said patient only at 4pm on Monday. Thus the patient was missed on rounds and status quo was maintained. It was only on Tuesday after the consultant rounds that further investigations etc was under taken for the patient thereby delaying the discharge of the patient.

Dr. Suman Arya, senior consultant and one who shared a good rapport with Dr.Shikha added to her findings on the discharge process by raising issues concerning other departments. For example, she cited the case of Mr. Priolkar who was posted for suprapubic cystostomy by the urology surgeon last month at the hospital. In view of his uncontrolled diabetes he was admitted under medicine for control of the same. After about a week of close monitoring when the sugar levels were finally brought within the normal limit he was referred back to urology for transfer and further management. However, the treating surgeon had proceeded on leave and the patient continued to be in the medicine wards occupying a bed, till the surgeon resumed and transferred him to urology ward.

As Dr. Shikha pondered over various such issues and their complexity, she was also forced to think from the patient's perspective in situations of DAMA (Discharge against medical advice). She still could not forget the case of Mrs. D'costa last year. Mrs. D'costa was admitted in the ICU as a case of snake bite with poor respiratory efforts, low blood pressure and failure of the blood to clot with resultant acute renal failure. Every time she needed to be dialyzed she had to be shifted to the nephrology ward and back. . Once her vitals had stabilized she was transferred out to the general wards for further stay, however her back and forth journey to the nephrology wards continued due to bed shortage there .To add to their misery on a couple of occasions when she was brought back following dialysis she was relocated to different wards. With this regular relocation subject to bed availability she and her relatives were already frustrated and wanting to go. Thus far we had managed to pacify them. However on one such occasion she along with a few other female patients was transferred to the male ward since beds were available only in this ward. That was the final straw and they finally left the hospital against medical advice to get her admitted in a private hospital thereby denying us the satisfaction of discharging her after having literally got her back from the jaws of death.....

How does the discharge status get affected for such a patient? What are the mechanisms that can be put in place to make sure discharge proceeds smoothly?

Owing to the inherent nature of complexity of the discharge process and the associated issues with it, the average length of stay for patients in the IPD had increased by 3 days (Exhibit 2). This in turn implied a drain on the minimum resources available with the department. The stress level of the residents was also at a high because of the sheer increase in the number of patients treated in the department.

As Dr. Shikha continued to think about ways and means to approach the discharge process, she was suddenly interrupted by Dr. Anuj Sharma who wanted some advice on his patient in the ICCU. It was then that she realized that she had accidentally stepped into the ICCU instead of the female medicine ward where she was supposed to check on two of her patients......

EXHIBIT 1

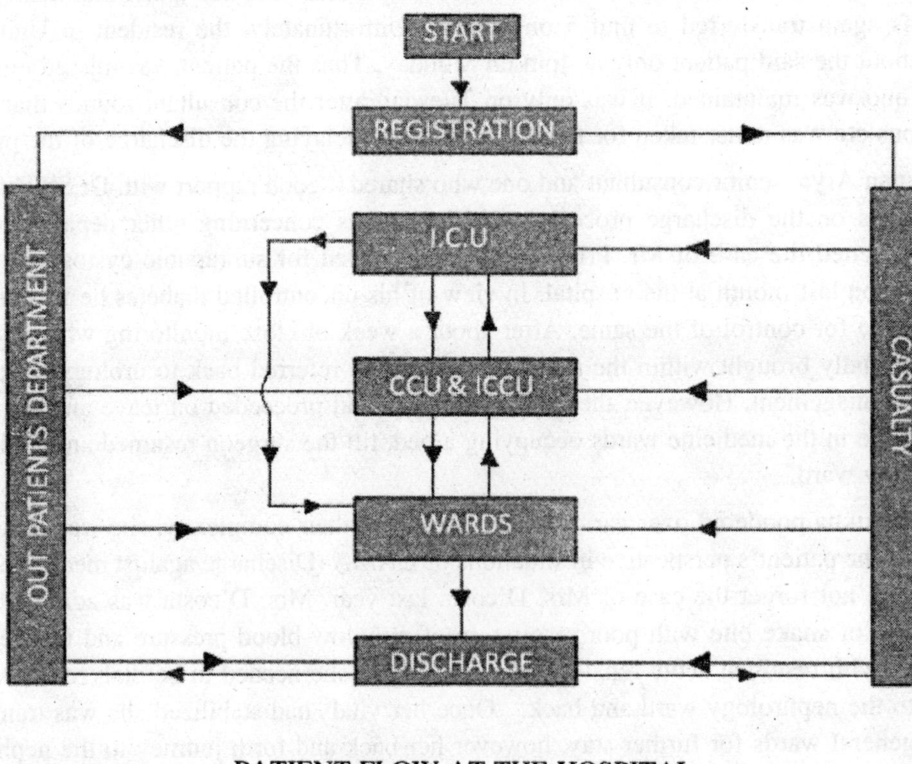

PATIENT FLOW AT THE HOSPITAL

EXHIBIT 2

Month	Admission	Discharge	Length of stay	Avg. Length of stay
9-Jan	1039	836	5847	7
9-Feb	907	721	6651	9.2
9-Mar	845	701	7153	10.2
9-Apr	941	733	7356	10
9-May	988	700	7412	10.6
9-Jun	1102	945	7365	7.8
9-Jul	1252	1144	7451	6.5
9-Aug	1174	980	7329	7.5
9-Sep	1148	1029	6968	6.8
9-Oct	1206	1098	7136	6.5
11-Nov	1232	1150	6424	5.6
9-Dec	1219	1050	6547	6.2
10-Jan	1141	987	6413	6.5
10-Feb	1110	983	6220	6.3
10-Mar	1095	968	6467	6.7
10-Apr	999	999	6459	7.1
10-May	1159	964	6834	7.1
10-Jun	1137	93	5343	5.6
10-Jul	1196	1023	5912	5.8
10-Aug	1223	1001	6284	6.3
10-Sept	1129	896	4455	5
10-Oct	1056	909	4994	5.5
			SUM	155.8
			AVERAGE	**7.08**

Statistics for alos* in the medicine department (jan 2009-oct 2010)

(* ALOS-Average length of stay)

EXHIBIT 3

Month	*No of patients admitted*	*No of patients discharged*	*Occupancy*	*Old*	*New*	*Total*
Jan-09	1039	836	92	3583	2377	5960
Feb-09	907	907	94	3129	2349	5478
Mar-09	845	701	92	3313	2514	5827
Apr-09	941	733	97	2937	2186	5123
May-09	988	700	95	2645	2270	4915
Jun-09	1102	945	97	3177	2888	6065
Jul-09	1252	1144	95	1913	1738	3651
Aug-09	1174	980	94	3004	3548	6552
Sep-09	1148	1029	92	3423	3929	7352
Oct-09	1206	1098	91	3480	3681	7161
Nov-09	1232	1150	85	3243	3557	6800
Dec-09	1219	1050	84	3002	3388	6390
Jan-10	1141	987	82	3134	3134	6268
Feb-10	1110	983	88	2973	3438	6411
Mar-10	1095	968	83	3002	3950	6952
Apr-10	999	913	85	2607	3227	5834
May-10	1159	964	87	2401	3423	5824
Jun-10	1137	953	71	2605	3530	6135
Jul-10	1196	1023	76	2774	4221	6995
Aug-10	1223	1001	80	2676	4195	6871
Sep-10	1129	896	59	2475	4213	6688
Oct-10	1056	909	73	2597	4117	6714
Nov-10	-	-	-	2441	4022	6463

Number of indoor patients admitted to the medicine department (jan 2009-oct 2010)

Teaching Note

Synopsis

Set in 2011, the case describes the difficulties faced by Dr Shikha Gupta with respect to the patient discharge process in a large hospital in a public setting. The case presents the host of activities that function interdependently to make patient discharge happen. The entire discharge process is a complex system working within a variety of constraints ranging from skewed seasonal demand for beds, to inter-ward and inter-departmental patient transfer and the related issue of monitoring & tracking patient health, medico-legal cases and the attached protocols, and managing patient & their medical records movement. The sheer volumes of patients attended to on any particular day, especially in a public hospital, along with limited availability of resources creates a unique blend of complicated situations for the hospital administration.

Dr. Shikha has been preoccupied with questions about the discharge process at her hospital and she has planned to bring this forth to the hospital management during the meeting scheduled later in the week. Primarily, she is concerned about tracking of her patients once they are relocated from the medicine department to other areas of the hospital. This in fact could be one of the contributing areas that alters/ affects the discharge process in the department. Her search for probable factors affecting patient transfers helps her to discover some crucial system errors that need prompt attention.

The discharge process in the above situation has been viewed as a system composed of distinct processes and tasks that need to be fulfilled in order to ensure safe discharge of the patient.

Case Objectives

This case is intended to be taught at the MBA level or in executive education programs as part of the courses for managing public health or hospital administration and could also be used in an operations strategy course. The teaching note focuses on the use of the case for students enrolled in a managing public health or hospital administration course.

This is possibly the only case that focuses on the discharge process in hospital. Thus, the case gives the reader an overview of the patient flow in the hospital with an emphasis on the normal discharge process, highlights issues faced in hospitals (both public and private) like planning of facilities such as hospital beds (when demand for beds is seasonal) and managing patient records especially when they are moved from ward to ward and department to department in a large multi-specialty hospital (the entire records for a patient from registration to getting admitted, examined and discharged in most Indian public hospitals is paper-based). Also presented are the handling of medico-legal cases and the importance of tracking patient movements of such patients as well as facing the issue of discharge against medical advice.

Discussion Areas

The three main areas that the classroom case discussion will revolve around are:

A. How should public hospitals manage with varying demands of beds during the year? For example, in the monsoon months they might run short of beds while it may not be the same during lean months. The case presents information on month-wise data on the number of patients admitted, discharged and the average length of stay. Can some conclusions be drawn regarding the number of beds that the hospital needs? How do they go about determining the optimum number of beds? A related issue is that the seasonality in terms of demand for beds could be different in different departments (such as surgery, medicine, obstetrics and gynecology).

B. How to monitor the health (and records) of patients especially when they are transferred from one ward to another due to unavailability of beds (for example, generally beds in the medicine department are unavailable and hence patients are shifted temporarily to the ophthalmology ward)? This has 3 aspects to it: 1. Doctors and staff are responsible for taking rounds and monitoring patients in a particular ward – hence it is highly probable that patients moved outside the department may not get time from the doctor; 2. Due to the inconvenience faced by the patient (a non-ambulatory patient being shifted from place to place) and their relatives, there is a higher chance of them asking for a discharge against medical advice; and 3. Since the medical records of the patient are paper-based, remotely and regularly monitoring patient progress becomes difficult.

C. The patient flow process.

Assignment Questions

1. Outline the most important issues that Dr Shikha needs to highlight to the management of the hospital with respect to the problems in the discharge process?
2. What should the hospital authorities do to alleviate the dissatisfaction of patients like Mrs D'Costa (page 8 of the case)?
3. How can patients like Mr Hans (pages 7 and 8 of the case) be monitored? What kind of systemic interventions would you suggest?
4. How should the problems faced by Mr Pednekar (page 8 of the case) and Mrs Radha (page 7 of the case) be dealt with? Will computerizing medical and patient records solve these problems? What could be the measures adopted to track patient information with respect to discharge formalities?
5. How to fix the situation encountered in the case of Mr Priolkar (pages 8 and 9 of the case)?
6. Suggest possible ways and means to reduce the dependencies associated with patient transfers.

Analysis

Ans 1. Dr Shikha's brief to the management

From the case it is evident that the discharge process works as a complex set of activities which contribute in many ways to the overall delay in many cases. Considering the volume of patients seen on any particular day the problem can get aggravated because of resource constraints. In such a scenario, adjustments become the norm which though temporarily takes care of the problem, does not help to identify the cause or the underlying reason for the inefficiency. What is required is a systems approach to discharge process that helps to identify and relate to the individual interdependencies and helps minimize the same.

Time for diagnosis:

The total time involved in getting a diagnosis of the clinical condition of the patient is in question. Sometimes, this can get extended because of reasons like detailed testing, second opinion, non-co-operative patient etc. Till then the patient remains admitted.

Consultant and Bed Availability:

Despite the other processes facilitating discharge being in place the fact that the consultant on call may not be available for consultation can add to the delay in discharge for specific patients. This also becomes important both because the consultant understands the patient condition best and also there is a certain level of comfort that the patient has developed with the specialist.

Bed availability is a dynamic requirement that cannot be predicted accurately at any time because of demand fluctuations. It can be viewed as literally a hand-to-mouth situation at times with arrangements being made at the last minute .

Completion of Discharge summary: A routine procedure that takes time nevertheless and requires co-ordination with respect to patient information and flow in the medicine department

Peak admissions and transfer of patients: During peak season (especially the rains in June-July), the medicine ward falls short of beds due to patient load. This is the time when many patients are transferred to other wards and thereby it becomes difficult to monitor these patients.

Ans 2. The Case of Mrs D'Costa

The ICU should have dialysis facilities. If patient is shifted from the wards for dialysis he/she should be shifted back preferably to the same ward if not the same bed. Multiple transfers for a single patient should be avoided at all costs. The number of visits outside the ward should be restricted to a maximum of 2-3 during their stay.

Ans 3. The Case of Mr Hans

The wards should preferably have a single entry and exit point. The door should be manned by security. The windows have to have grills in order to avoid casualties. Standard dictum should be that MLC cases are not to be shunted from one ward to the other. They should be necessarily discharged from the same wards in which they are admitted.

Ans 4. Cases of Mr Pednekar and Mrs Radha

The resident transferring the patient out should inform the resident in charge of the case about the shifting out of the patient. The residents should have a list of patients admitted under his unit at all times and unless his records show that the patient has been discharged he should make every effort to trace the patient. There needs to be a systems intervention and computerization of this system will improve the results by allowing doctors and staff to access patient movement, records and progress from any computer terminal in the hospital.

Ans 5 The Case of Mr Priolkar

This is a case of poor communication across departments. This is common in any large organization, with hospitals being no exception. Improved communication between the doctors in the same department and interdependent departments will reduce the incidence of such problems. In case the treating doctor has to go on emergency, an adequate provision should be made to see that patients under his care are adequately taken care of in his absence – either discharged if they are ready for discharged; or moved under the care of another doctor..

Ans 6 Common measures to deal with problems due to patient transfers

- Computerization of medical records - easy to maintain records and also to access the records from any ward.
- Over the years the patient turnover rate has increased but the staff and the bed strength has remained the same. These need to be revisited. Also, since seasonality of different departments occur at different times – the resources must be flexible enough to be used/ shared by departments.
- Patient admission, transfer and discharge records should be displayed in the respective wards in such a manner as to be easily visible. e.g. Board with magnets color coded for specifics units.

Teaching Approach

You can begin the case by asking students to list down the issues that Dr Shikha should bring to the attention of the management. You would expect the following issues to be highlighted by students:

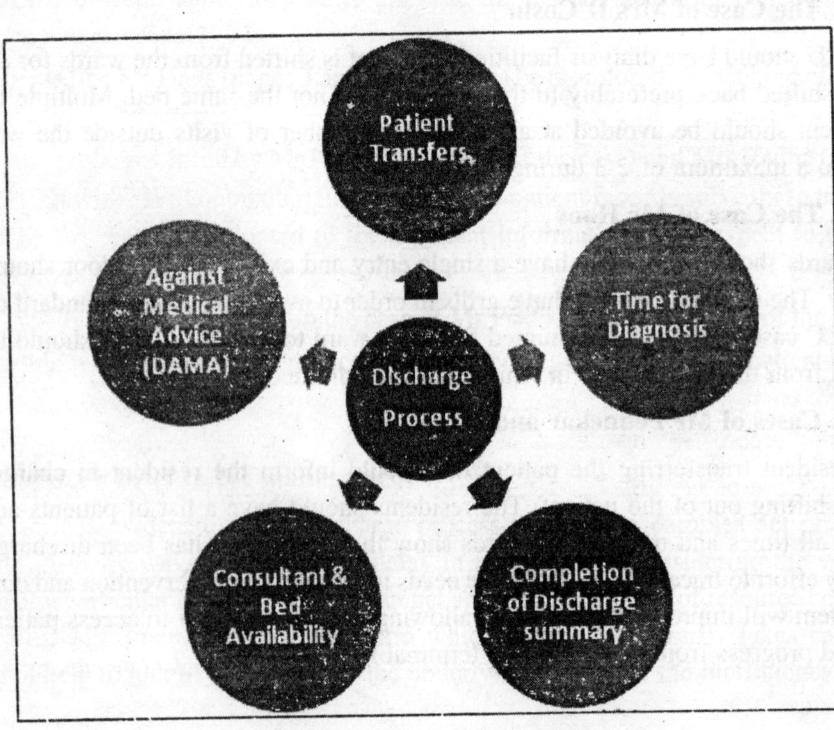

The related issues of patient inconvenience, movement of records, loss of information, difficulty of follow-up for doctors will also be listed in addition to the above factors.

It will seem that there are only problems with the system. The class is primed for the next step: critically evaluating the process flow from registration to discharge. Present the system (on a slide):

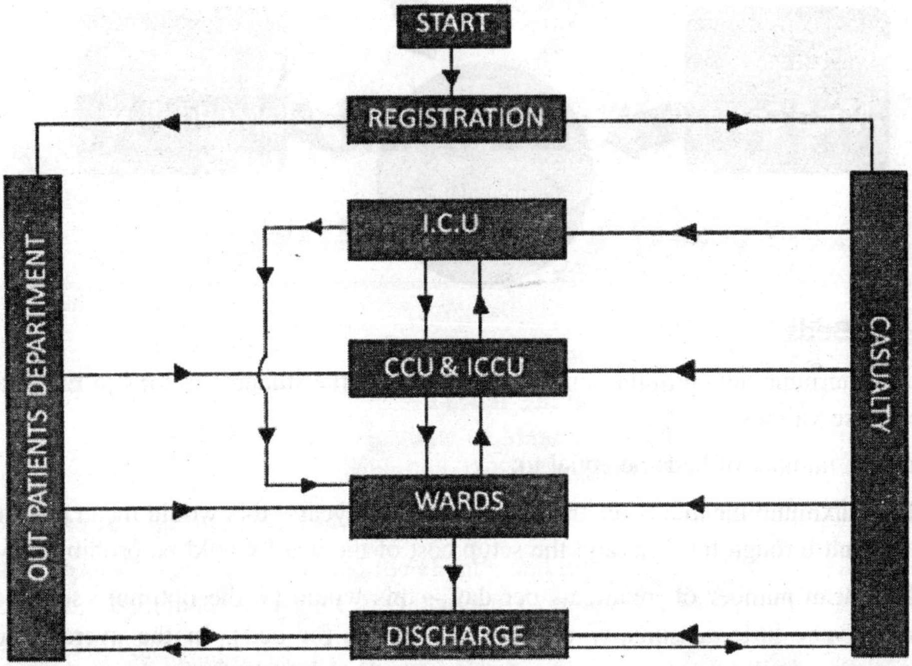

Now pose the question: Are these problems because of a problem in the process flow and if yes, then what are the specific gaps in the system.

Whilst there are many issues identified about the discharge, then process flow is well thought of and there are very few gaps in the process per se.

Now you can address each of the cases:

Case 1: Mrs D'Costa – and the dialysis facility

Case 2 – Medico Legal Cases like Mr Hans and the need for high security and concrete paper-work in such wards

Case 3 – Mr Pednekar and Mrs Radha – Monitoring transferred patients and the importance of maintaining records (computerization of records).

Case 4 – Case of Mr Priolkar. Highlight the issues of managing patient information, doctor/ consultant availability and communication intra- and inter-department.

The above cases will throw up the 2 most important problems:

1. Planning for beds

2. Managing Information – patient records, doctor availability, discharge history etc & computerization of all this information to enable ease of storage and access.

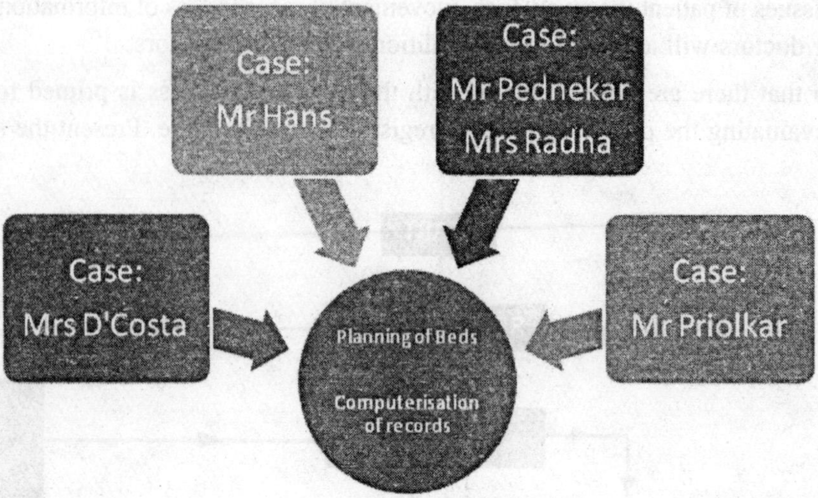

Planning of Beds

How to determine the optimum number of beds? Ask the students to look at Exhibits 2 and 3 make their observations.

Should the number of beds be equal to:

1. The maximum inpatients on any single day in the year – this would mean that many beds would lie vacant through the year and the setup cost of the ward would be prohibitively high.

2. The mean number of inpatients per day – this would be the optimum solution only in case there is very little seasonality or skewed demand for beds. In the average number of inpatients is very similar day to day and month to month, only then the mean is the good way to plan for bed capacity.

3. The mode of the number of patients of the day or any other number – This would be closer to an optimal solution. But the count for the mode must be reasonably high. If out of 365 days, the modal solution is shared only by 10 days, then it is a poor solution. However, on the days of abnormally high inpatient load, the number of beds would be inadequate.

Multi-department hospitals can also explore models of sharing facilities between departments based on complementary seasonality's.

Computerization of Records

Whilst computerization is undoubtedly beneficial, computerization alone is not the solution. The solution is more systemic and computerization will only make the records easier to maintain and access. The issue is whether the patient records must be with the doctor, with the patient, or must reside with the ward (i.e must move from ward to ward or department to department along with the patient).

12

SATYAM - The Story of Governance Failure

Tushar Jindal
Assistant Profesor, Institute of Management Studies(Ghaziabad)
tusharjindal1984@yahoo.co.in

"Better to see the face than to hear the name"

The Corporate world of India and the client's and investors all over the world were taken by surprise when B.Ramalinga Raju,C.E.O Satyam Computers had written a letter to board of directors regarding what he has cooked over a period of time and what exactly is the situation of the company. The financial statements were not genuine and the figures were bogus. This had a direct impact on the share prices of the company and it showed a single day fall from a high of 188.7 to 30.8.The money of the investors was eroded and it raises the question on the corporate ethics, the work of Auditors (Price Water House Coopers), functioning of Companies. Hence this case is presented regarding the various aspects of this corporate disaster, functioning of auditor and corporate governance and certain suggestions are given to avoid such situations in future.

ONE COOK "RAJU", SPOIL THE PARTY

Introduction (About company):

Brief about Satyam Computers

Satyam Computers Services Ltd. Is a consulting and information technology services Company based in Hyderabad India. It was founded in 1987 by B.Ramalinga Raju. The main functioning of the company was that it offers Information Technology Services to many top big companies of the world and was also listed on Newyork Stock Exchange and Euronext. It was a major player in this sector and had whopping revenue of over a billion dollar at certain time. In terms of employability and vast presence, this company had a network in somewhere about 67 countries across 6 continents and it employs over 40,000 professionals all over the world with it's presence in countries like United States, United Kingdom, U.A.E, Canada etc. It's clientage covers over 654 globally recognized companies ,among which 185 companies were Fortune 500 companies. This represents the name, fame and ideology of the company. Apart from this Satyam was also keen on its research and development part and hence had a strategic corporate tie ups with over 50 companies. They also had there development centers in various other parts of India like in Bangalore, Chennai, Pune, Mumbai, Delhi, Nagpur, Bhubaneswar And Vishakhapatnam. *All was going well for the company till the Balloon of Fault, incorrect information, misleading facts busted and its true position was revealed.*

"There are two levers to set a man in motion, fear and self interest" —*Napolean Bonaparta*

The Breaking News

On morning of January 7, 2009, Satyam Computer Services Ltd's Chairman Mr.Ramalinga Raju resigned after notifying its board members and SEBI that he falsified accounts and assets. The shares of the IT Company were down by more than 82% touching low of Rs 30.70. He mentioned in his letter which he sent to Board Of Directors the following important facts:-

1. The Balance Sheet carries as of September 30, 2008
   - Inflated (non-existent) cash and bank balances of ₹5,040 crore (as against ₹ 5361 crore reflected in the books)
   - An accrued interest of ₹ 376 crore which is non-existent
   - An understated liability of ₹ 1,230 crore on account of funds arranged by me
   - An over stated debtors position of ₹ 490 crore (as against ₹ 2651 [cr.] reflected in the books)
2. For the September quarter (02) we reported a revenue of ₹2,700 crore and an operating margin of ₹ 649 crore (24% Of revenues) as against the actual revenues of ₹ 2,112 crore and an actual operating margin of ₹ 61 Crore (3% of revenues). This has resulted in artificial, cash and bank balances going up by ₹ 588 crore in Q2 alone.

Reason of this Gap

- The gap in the Balance Sheet has arisen purely on account of inflated profits over a period of last several years (limited only to Satyam standalone, books of subsidiaries reflecting true performance).
- What started as a marginal gap between actual operating profit and the one reflected in the books of accounts continued to grow over the years.
- It has attained unmanageable proportions as the size of company operations grew significantly (annualized revenue run rate of ₹ 11,276 crore in the September quarter, 2008 and official reserves of ₹ 8,392 crore).
- The differential in the real profits and the one reflected in the books was further accentuated

by the fact that the company had to carry additional resources and assets to justify higher level of operations thereby significantly increasing the costs.

Efforts of Raju to Cure the Problem

"It was like riding a tiger, not knowing how to get off without being eaten"

This was quoted by Mr. Raju in his letter as he was not able to eat the curry which he has been cooking over couple of years without letting it to fall down and spoil his clothes. He tried to take couple of efforts to fill the gap in the financial statements but the gap was too wide to be cured.

All Eyes on MAYTAS Acquisition Deal.....

- Satyam Computers on Dec 16, 2008 announced that it will acquire two group firms – Maytas Properties and Maytas Infra.
- The BOD of Satyam had approved the founder's proposal to buy 51% stake in Maytas Infra for US $ .3 bn and 100% stake in Maytas Properties for US $ 1.3bn.
- This was the move that sparked the row over alleged violation of Corporate Governance Laws.
- This Deal was not supposed to be profitable for investors; hence after its announcement they started to raise their voice.

Satyam Justification for the Deal.....

- To De-risk or spread the risk of core Business.
- The new organization would be stronger and more diversified to deal with uncertainty of the Market.
- They felt that it was difficult in recent times to make strategic deals with other IT Companies hence they thought of diversifying into Infrastructure Sector.

The aborted Maytas acquisition deal was the last attempt to fill the fictitious assets with real ones. Maytas' investors were convinced that this is a good divestment opportunity and a strategic fit. Once Satyam's problem was solved, it was hoped that Maytas' payments can be delayed. But that was not to be.

Reaction of Investors after the Announcement Of Accusation Of Maytas...

- Investment giant Templeton and Brokerage house CLSA opposed to this decision
- It result that part of the investors succeeded to thwart an attempt by the minority shareholding promoters, to use the firms cash reserves to buyout two companies owned by them—Maytas Properties & Maytas Infra.
- That attempt of Expansion lead to the fall in price of the Company's stock and shocking confession of Ramalinga Raju about his manipulations.

Were the Auditors Supposed To Be Blamed?

Who is an Auditor: Auditor is a person /firm which check the financial statements of the company and try to form an opinion wether the financial statements are representing true and fair position of the company or not. Basic work of the auditor is to check and report if there are any irregularities in the books of accounts.

Need of Auditor: It is a part of compulsion in respect of companies to get there accounts audited. This is called Statutory Audit. As the investors are not in a position to take care of their money and day to day affairs of the company , auditor is appointed to check whether what is shown or represented by company's financial statements is true and fair or not.

Auditor in case of Satyam : After the confession of Ramalinga Raju about his cooking and manipulation of books for such a long period of time, the very first question was asked regarding the credibility of Auditing Firm..Price water House Coopers, Were they sleeping when such a blunder was taking place or were they also involved in that conspiracy. This case has itself raised so many questions on the functioning of Auditors.

Investors raise questions over PwC Satyam audit

Satyam's bogus accounts had been audited by Price Waterhouse, the Indian-based auditor, which is a member firm of PricewarterhouseCoooper International, since the financial year 2000-2001.

"It's hard to miss $1 billion of cash," Dennis Beresford, a former chairman of the Financial Accounting Standards Board, the US accounting watchdog, said.

PwC's role in "India's Enron" comes under the spotlight amid allegations that large Indian companies regularly use misleading accounting techniques and bully analysts, accountants and auditors into staying quiet.

The information which Mr Raju disclosed in a letter to the board regarding the false pile up of cash– a straightforward falsehood which the company's auditors might have detected they had run a rudimentary check of the group's bank accounts, according to experts.

It was really hard to believe that how could auditors miss this big discrepancy…they usually do bank reconciliation, check various bank certificates and statements and perform various other procedures than how they were not able to detect such a fraud…this again raises a question that there was lack of supervision or were the bank statements forged.

The company's balance sheet as of March 31, 2008 was signed off by Srinivas Talluri, a partner of Price Waterhouse in Hyderabad, the southern Indian city where Satyam is based.

PwC Reply over Allegations……

In response to the allegations PwC said: "The audits were conducted by Price Waterhouse in accordance with applicable auditing standards and were supported by appropriate audit evidence".

"Given our obligations for client confidentiality, it is not possible for us to comment upon the alleged irregularities. Price Waterhouse will fully meet its obligations to cooperate with the regulators and others."

PWC had written a letter to the BOD of Satyam that it's audit may be rendered "inaccurate and unreliable" due to the disclosure made by Satyam's Ex-Chairman.

Note:

- It is to be noted that the Auditors are supposed to follow auditing and assurance standards; they have also to follow the basic principles governing the Audit.
- Maintaining Confidentiality about Client's Information and conducting audit with the help of Evidences are necessary on the part of auditors.
- In case of any allegation all these workings act as an evidence in support of the auditor.
- It should also be taken into consideration that the auditor depends upon the company for various informations which under normal circumstances he can assume to be correct.

Why shareholders cannot take any action against the Auditor?

"The contract that the auditor has with the company is not a contract the shareholders or other stakeholders are privy to. Hence, under Indian law, it would be difficult for the shareholders to take any action against the auditors under the Law of Contract."

Investor's money eroded and lesson need to be learned by investors...

Imagine somebody putting all his money in Satyam stock or Satyam ADR. The price went down from 170 to 6 in just two days. In fact even before that the price was 300 and then went down to 170. It would have wiped away your entire earnings had you put everything in the Satyam stock.

The lesson for people who are trying to understand how to build your stock portfolio that never put all your eggs in one basket. Diversification is the name of the game. Try to diversify with the stock composition and invest sensibly in various company's stocks.

Analysis and Expert opinion

- Analysts said that the Satyam scandal had underscored the need for urgent reform to India's creaking corporate governance standards. That means strict corporate governance standards should be introduced.
- There should be restriction on Auditors providing with consultancy work in our country, for instance, there is no restriction on auditors from carrying out consulting work for the companies they audit. This gives chances to some unfair practices.
- Saurabh Mukherjea, of Noble, the London-based investment bank, said: *"We have run into listed companies where the advisory arms of the audit firm earn consultancy fees for help with M&A, new entity structuring and tax minimisation."* In most Western countries rules limit such activities, which could trigger conflicts of interest for auditors. Mr Mukherjea suggested that the Satyam fraud should not come as a shock. *"Our experiences ... suggest that manipulative accounting and aggressive promoter [owner] practices are more common in India than is generally believed to be the case,"* he said. *"Many [Indian] firms have become so convinced of their own invincibility that they do not even bother denying irregularities when confronted with the evidence. They simply threaten you."*

- Foreign institutional investors are also weary of the influence exerted by India's politicians over the country's regulatory system.
- PwC's role in the Satyam scandal will now be probed by the Securities and Exchange Board of India, the markets watchdog, and the Indian government's anti-corruption office.
- The Institute of Chartered Accountants of India is also investigating and has the power to bar Price Waterhouse from working in the country indefinitely, a spokesman for the body said. Satyam was also listed on the New York Stock Exchange and faces a class action lawsuit in the US.

Inferences of the case...

There has been a lot of controversy regarding the misuse of the post by the CEO of the company

The fake number of jobs which was shown by the CEO was an abuse of power and it was a clear violation of the prevailing laws in India. This gives the impression that in India the power and position is what matters and the people in the top position make a clear violation of the rights provided to them.

This scam has seriously affected the corporate bodies in India. The role of an incorporated company is to satisfy desires of investors, and to channelize their investment. But most of the time entrepreneur's play with money of the investors

There are laws to safeguards investors' interest but the Satyam scam has raised the question on the fundamental role of the government and corporate governance

The main objective of the paper is to analyze relevance of corporate law in contemporary world and whether it is a time to revisit corporate governance.

The resulting action by the government has been that they have put three independent directors on the board and that these are people of repute which are Mr. Deepak Parekh, Kiran Karnik and C. Achuttam.

People are talking about good corporate governance models from the companies but I am sure we have not seen the end of it as there are scamsters and fraudesters in every society who think of loopholes and then eventually will be caught making the common man lose money.

Solutions

- There should be restrictions on Auditors in providing consultation services to the company in which they Audit.
- Strict Corporate Governance Standards should be there.
- The ICAI should come up with strict Auditing standards and principles.
- Penalty for default on the part of the auditor should be severe.
- Some independent auditors, beside those who are doing audit of the company on the regular basis should be sent for surprise checking in the company.
- SEBI should become stricter about the rules, the violation of which may lead to de-listing

of the company and imposition of penalties.

- It was find out that Satyam used international accounting mechanism which are yet to be introduced in India , which were supposed to bring more clarity about the financial position to the investors. but it didn't work..hence the way company is maintaining it's accounts should be well scrutinized.
- Importance should be given to the physical checking of various items of the balance sheet as there crucial scrutiny is necessary.
- The code of professional misconduct should be strict and clear.
- More and more independent verification should be done and in some cases direct confirmation from the client's parties should be obtained.

EXHIBITS

Exhibit 1: LETTER TO BOD OF SATYAM

To

The Board of Directors
Satyam Computer Services Ltd.

Dear Board Members,

It is with deep regret, at tremendous burden that I am carrying on my conscience, that I would like to bring the following facts to your notice:

1. The Balance Sheet carries as of September 30, 2008

   o Inflated (non-existent) cash and bank balances of ₹5,040 crore (as against ₹ 5361 crore reflected in the books)

   o An accrued interest of ₹ 376 crore which is non-existent

   o An understated liability of ₹ 1,230 crore on account of funds arranged by me

   o An over stated debtors position of ₹ 490 crore (as against ₹ 2651 [cr.] reflected in the books)

2. For the September quarter (02) we reported a revenue of ₹2,700 crore and an operating margin of ₹ 649 crore (24% Of revenues) as against the actual revenues of ₹ 2,112 crore and an actual operating margin of ₹ 61 Crore (3% of revenues). This has resulted in artificial, cash and bank balances going up by ₹ 588 crore in Q2 alone.

The gap in the Balance Sheet has arisen purely on account of inflated profits over a period of last several years (limited only to Satyam standalone, books of subsidiaries reflecting true performance). What started as a marginal gap between actual operating profit and the one reflected in the books of accounts continued to grow over the years. It has attained unmanageable proportions as the size of company operations grew significantly (annualized revenue run rate of ₹ 11,276 crore in the September quarter, 2008 and official reserves of ₹ 8,392 crore). The differential in the real profits and the one reflected in the books was further accentuated by the fact that the company had to carry additional resources and assets to justify higher level of operations — thereby significantly increasing the costs.

Every attempt made to eliminate the gap failed. As the promoters held a small percentage of equity, the concern was that poor performance would result in a take-over; thereby exposing the gap. It was like riding a tiger, not knowing how to get off without being eaten.

The aborted Maytas acquisition deal was the last attempt to fill the fictitious assets with real ones. Maytas' investors were convinced that this is a good divestment opportunity and a strategic fit. Once Satyam's problem was solved, it was hoped that Maytas' payments can be delayed. But that was not to be. What followed in the last several days is common knowledge.

I would like the Board to know:

1. That neither myself, nor the Managing Director (including our spouses) sold any shares in the last eight years — excepting for a small proportion declared and sold for philanthropic purposes.
2. That in the last two years a net amount of ₹ 1,230 crore was arranged to Satyam (not reflected in the books of Satyam) to keep the operations going by resorting to pledging all the promoter shares and raising funds from known sources by giving all kinds of assurances (Statement enclosed, only to the members of the board). Significant dividend payments, acquisitions, capital expenditure to provide for growth did not help matters. Every attempt was made to keep the wheel moving and to ensure prompt payment of salaries to the associates. The last straw was the selling of most of the pledged share[s] by the lenders on account of margin triggers.
3. That neither me, nor the Managing Director took even one rupee/dollar from the company and have not benefitted in financial terms on account of the inflated results.
4. None of the board members, past or present, had any knowledge of the situation in which the company is placed. Even business leaders and senior executives in the company, such as, Ram Mynampati, Subu D, T.R. Anand, Keshab Panda, Virender Agarwal, A.S. Murthy, Han T, SV Krishnan, Vijay Prasad, Manish Mehta, Murali V. Sriram Papani, Kavale, Joe Lagioia, Ravindra Penumetsa, Jayaraman and Prabhakar Gupta are unaware of the real situation as against the books of accounts. None of my or Managing Director's immediate or extended family members has any idea about these issues.

Having put these facts before you, I leave it to the wisdom of the board to take the matters forward. However, I am also taking the liberty to recommend the following steps:

1. A Task Force has been formed in the last few days to address the situation arising but of the failed Maytas acquisition attempt. This consists of some of the most accomplished

leaders of Satyam; Subu D, T.R. Anand, Keshab Panda and Virender Agarwal , representing business functions; and A.S. Murthy, Han T and Murali V representing support functions. I suggest that Ram MynampÃ ti be made the Chairman of this Task Force to immediately address some of the operational matters on hand. Ram can also act as an interim CEO reporting to the board.

2. Merrill Lynch can be entrusted with the task of quickly exploring some Merger opportunities.
3. You may have a testatement of accounts' prepared by the auditors in light of the facts that I have placed before you.

I have promoted and have been associated with Satyam for well over twenty years now I have seen it grow from few people to 53,000 people, with 185 Fortune 500 companies as customers and operations in 66 countries. Satyam has established an excellent leadership and competency base at all levels. I sincerely apologize to all Satyamites and stakeholders, who have made Satyam a special organization, for the current situation. I am confident they will stand by the company in this hour of crisis.

In light of the above, I fervently appeal to the board to hold together to take some important steps Mr T R Prasad is well placed to mobilize support from the government at this crucial time. With the hope that members of the Task Force arid the financial advisor, Merrill Lynch (now Bank of America) will stand by the company at this crucial hour, I am marking copies of this statement to them as well.

Under the circumstances, I am tendering my resignation as the chairman of Satyam and shall continue in this position only till such time the current board is expanded. My continuance is just to ensure enhancement of the board over the next several days or as early as possible.

I am now prepared to subject myself to the laws of the land and lace consequences thereof.

(B. Ramalinga Raju)

Copies marked to:

1. Chairman SEBI
2. Stock Exchanges

Exibit 2

Date	*Open*	*High*	*Low*	*Close*	*Volume*	*Adj Close*
1/1/2009	175	183.25	173.25	182.4	23936000	182.4
1/2/2009	184	185.9	173.55	177	32711300	177
1/5/2009	178	181	161.6	166.1	24865400	166.1
1/6/2009	167.5	180.5	161.1	178.2	20378700	178.2
1/7/2009	179	188.7	30.8	41.05	3.3E+08	41.05
1/9/2009	36	36	6.3	22.75	2.16E+08	22.75
1/12/2009	28.5	39.9	28.5	34.7	1.17E+08	34.7
1/13/2009	32	39	30.1	31.4	68222600	31.4
1/14/2009	32	34.85	28.35	29.9	56418400	29.9
1/15/2009	27	27	19	20.45	1.01E+08	20.45
1/16/2009	21	28.4	21	24.6	1.15E+08	24.6
1/19/2009	25.2	26.7	23	25.6	45974300	25.6
1/20/2009	24	27.5	23	26.6	80508800	26.6
1/21/2009	24	29.35	24	27.9	70298100	27.9
1/22/2009	28.5	30	28.1	29.6	54015200	29.6
1/23/2009	29.25	39.35	27.5	38.85	2.03E+08	38.85
1/27/2009	41	54.4	41	46.65	1.04E+08	46.65
1/28/2009	47.85	56.1	47.1	55.6	1.64E+08	55.6
1/29/2009	57	60	39	49.4	2.12E+08	49.4
1/30/2009	52.15	54.4	45.5	53.5	72627200	53.5

Source: *www.yahoo.com*

This is the representation of the share prices of Satyam stock during the month of *January '2009*

Exhibit 3. Profit & Loss Account

	Mar ' 11	Mar ' 10	Mar ' 09	Mar ' 08	Mar ' 07
Income					
Operating income	4,776.10	5,107.60	8,432.50	8,137.28	6,228.47
Expenses					
Material consumed	-	1	154.9	-	-
Manufacturing expenses	44.8	224.3	589.8	83.79	69.35
Personnel expenses	3,292.00	3,731.00	5,592.70	4,964.84	3,692.92
Selling expenses	-	61	117.3	87.51	62.87
Adminstrative expenses	963.6	899.2	2,142.50	1,170.83	873.42
Expenses capitalised	-	-	-	-	-
Cost of sales	4,300.40	4,916.50	8,597.20	6,306.97	4,698.56
Operating profit	475.7	191.1	-164.7	1,830.31	1,529.91
Other recurring income	289.9	69.2	10.6	277.87	168.07
Adjusted PBDIT	765.6	260.3	-154.1	2,108.18	1,697.98
Financial expenses	9.2	25.4	39	5.94	7.61
Depreciation	149.9	190.8	297.2	137.94	129.89
Other write offs	-	-	-	-	-
Adjusted PBT	606.5	44.1	-490.3	1,964.30	1,560.48
Tax charges	53.7	16.2	150.7	226.12	150
Adjusted PAT	552.8	27.9	-641	1,738.18	1,410.48
Non recurring items	-680.4	-99.1	-1,073.80	-22.44	12.75
Other non cash adjustments	-	-	-6,221.20	-	-
Reported net profit	-127.6	-71.2	-7,936.00	1,715.74	1,423.23
Earnigs before appropriation	-2,462.20	-2,334.60	-2,818.30	5,564.06	4,260.04
Eonity dividend	-	-	67.4	234.89	231.85
Preference dividend	-	-	-	-	-
Dividend tax	-	-	11.4	39.86	37.55
Retained earnings	-2,462.20	-2,334.60	-2,897.10	5,289.31	3,990.64

Source: *www.money.rediff.com*

Balance Sheet

	Mar ' 11	Mar ' 10	Mar ' 09	Mar ' 08	Mar ' 07
Sources of funds Owner's fund					
Equity share capital	235.3	235.2	134.8	134.1	133.44
Share application money	1230.4	1230.5	1230.4	1.83	7.85
Preference share capital	-	-	-	-	-
Reserves & surplus	1925.9	2061.7	-657.1	7221.71	5648.07
Loan funds					
Secured loans	31.5	42	641	23.67	13.79
Unsecured loans	-	-	-	-	-
Total	3423.1	3569.4	1349.1	7381.31	5803.15
Uses of funds					
Fixed assets					
Gross block	2020.4	1818.9	2155.3	1486.53	1280.4
Less : revaluation reserve	-	-	-	-	-
Less : accumulated depreciation	1406.7	1285.9	1404.4	1062.04	930.45
Net block	613.7	533	750.9	424.49	349.95
Capital work-in-progress	268.3	373	389.5	458.63	290.05
Investments	532.1	726.6	93	493.8	201.15
Net current assets					
Current assets, loans & advances	4519.1	3793.3	2614.7	7451.13	6003.75
Less : current liabilities & provisions	2510.1	1856.5	2499	1446.74	1041.75
Total net current assets	2009	1936.8	115.7	6004.39	4962
Miscellaneous expenses not written	-	-	-	-	-
Total	**3423.1**	**3569.4**	**1349.1**	**7381.31**	**5803.15**
Notes:					
Book value of unquoted investments	532.1	726.6	93	493.8	201.15
Market value of quoted investments	-	-	-	-	-
Contingent liabilities	1365.8	1581	2350.73	623.28	267.2
Number of equity sharesoutstanding (Lacs)	**11765.66**	**11761.86**	**6738.95**	**6704.79**	**6671.96**

Source: *www.money.rediff.com*

References :

1. En.Wikipedia.org/wiki/satyam-scandal
2. www.money.rediff.com/companies/satyam
3. www.moneycontrol.com/stocks/company
4. www.indiastudychannel.com
5. www.financialexpress.com/news/satyam
6. www.indianepress.com/fullcoverage/satyamscam
7. articles.economictimes.indiatimes.com
8. www.business-standards.com
9. www.pressreleasepoint.com/satyam-fraud-case-scandal
10. Satyamscam.in

13

Use of Quality Management System for Operational Effectiveness in the Garment Sector

Nazimuz Zaman
Institute of Productivity and Management
Ghaziabad

Ellile Export (pvt) ltd. mainly deals with garment manufacturing specialized in gents wearing. They are based at Noida ,UP and has a show room and material collection and dispatch centre in Karol Bagh , New Delhi. It started its business in 1996 with just 15 employees and they now have 159 employees working in full time basis. Their business model is b-2-b and also engaged in trading activity. They takes order of garments like t-shirts, shirts, trousers etc. They mainly targets those organizations who has minimum of 200 employees. It is basically done having seen the requirements in terms of uniforms, special occasion wearing , gifts to the employees or delegates. They also has license of manufacturing specific brand's products for them.

Amresh Kumar after trying his hands in several areas finally found his place in terms of Ellile Export. With his employees and their performance he was quite happy. His client coordinator Mr. Saroj Kumar is an efficient person and has never disappointed him in terms of performance and trust. He has been with him since the inception . At any point of time , whenever Mr Amresh finds any problem solved to be difficult he call on Saroj and finds out a rout.

Ellile Export has a production capacity of 100000 shirts in a month. 98% perfection is normal average performance rate per employee. What ever machines they have is at par with the industry standard. They has proper co ordination with their vendors and they have never failed in supplying the right quality of raw materials at the right price at right time . What Mr. Amresh thinks is that all this has been possible only because of the sincere efforts of his client coordinator.

What is happening in his business for the last 4-5 years is quite satisfactory and he is happy with the performance. He has been witnessing a growth of 20% over the last 4 years which is above the industry level. But what he discovers in his factory wastage house made him bit tensed. Every day he takes a round of his factory and he discovers that as his production level is increasing day by day the bins of waste material is gradually increasing. From his experience he finds the period of October to march is a pick season The production level goes up significantly in this season. To meet the industry demand they outsource a major part of its production . Outsourcing has always been a major strategy of their production schedule. But in house production gives them significant cost effectiveness. Amresh comes to his cabin and thinks over the waste . He calculates out that a near about Rs-400000/month has been drain out in terms of waste material. He calls on his supervisor to discuss the problem and what to do with this .This factory supervisor Mr Sudhir is an aged person, working for him for the last 6 years. He is efficient and very popular among employees. His politeness and the art of presentation adds an edge to his personality. Mr. Sudhir answering the question of his boss says that it is normal part of their business. It is all of human error from which perhaps we can not expect 100%. Sudhir pointed out that the workers are expert in their business and also well motivated. Most of them are working since long and also improving in their performance. But he assured his boss that he will study the fact and try to find out a solution.

Amresh , perhaps did not get what he expected from his factory supervisor. He really took the matter very seriously which fueled his head-ache. As usual he called on Mr. Saroj. He is now with his full statistics. The average cost per shirt is Rs-200/. Complying with his production capacity he can produce near about 100000 shirts in a month. Thus with a 98% of perfection level he could have produce 102040 no shirts. Thus he is loosing a revenue of 2040no shirts/month. If it is calculated in the yearly basis it is near about 24480no shirt. Thus they are wasting out a handsome amount of Rs-4896000/year. This amount is just on the total cost basis . Adding a minimum 40% profit margin the amount rose up toRs-6854400/. Mr. Saroj gone through the data. The drainage of such an amount really embarrassed him. He even never thought that such a thing also may happen. As an old employee and his attachment with the firm it is his turn to do something to kill this evil of wastage. He took some time from Amresh and assured his boss that he will come up with solution. Amresh is now a bit relaxed . he has faith on his best employee.

The solution:

The problem what Ellile Export is facing is mainly of quality driven and also increasing the employee performance level up to a significant level. They are as not being a big player in this field had faced the problem of competitiveness in terms of proper utilization of resources. it is observed that most of the firm which are not working at very big size and operation level but still we can not ignore their existence in the society , often tend to ignore the fact of optimum utilization of resources . as in the case of Ellile Export if we analyze the fact we find that they are working at below the 3-sigma level. Though it seems to be a matter of simple quality control, yet it is not so simple controlling quality and improving performance above a normal standard level and is indeed a matter of constant review and observation.

Analyzing the system

Thus to study the work performance and to develop a systematic production procedure we have o study the work process. This work process will help in determining the bottleneck in production process. Following steps can be identified in the whole production process i.e. from the supply of raw material to the final production and distribution.

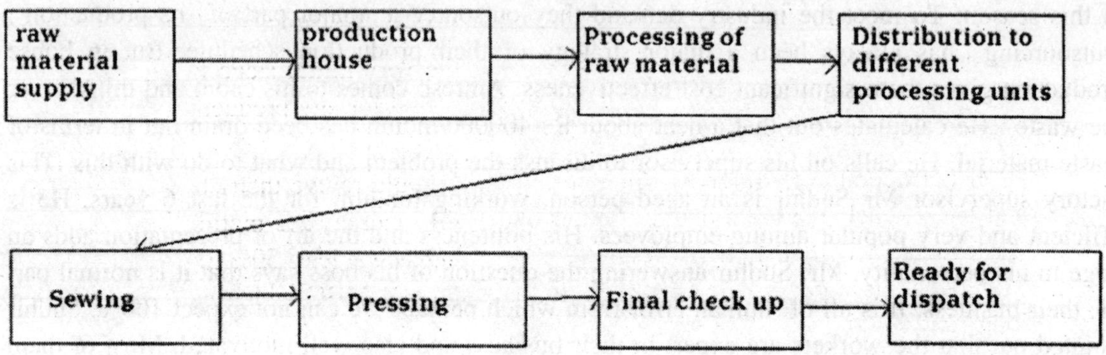

Diagram-1

The raw material comes from their vendors and collected at their production house. The raw material is in the form of roll of cloth for shirts and in t-shirts we can have separate component in different roll. In the processing house the raw material is checked out and the different component are separated and send to the respected processing unit. After processing they are assembled them into the required size and format. After sewing pressing and final check out is done and send to respective packaging unit. Packaging is the final step at production unit and they are ready to dispatched to the dispatched centre at Karol Bagh.

I visited the production house at Noida to understand the real situation. It is worth understanding that quality is not only based on the material and equipment. A lot of human and environmental factors are associated with it. For proper understanding the problem we have to study all these factors.

What I found there is mentioned bellow

1. The production house is a huge one where the entire employee works together. There is no separation of any form between the workers and they have easy access to each other.
2. The material given to the tailors lies on the floor and they are given at bulk what is to be consumed in the whole day.
3. The raw material collection unit is nothing but a separate corner of the hall also same for raw material processing.
4. There is only one technical person to see all the problems of more than 150 machines. In general most of the problems are handled by the workers themselves.

5. There is rough and disturbing sound of the machine within the hall which disturbs the general communication.

The points discussed above, indeed reveals significant facts about the company. What we see is that the solution is also lies beneath these facts. It is significant to see that the company is under going a significant operational and quality drawback in terms of work environment and the infrastructure. It also further can be sub divided into improper assembling and shorting process.

Whatever we analyze we the process is integrated indeed. Before moving towards the solution we have to intensively study the processing system. It is seen from the above discussion that the production system has a loophole in the process. To provide the solution we can move towards the following direction. In overall quality control process they should adopt the following measures.

1. They should adopt a better shorting process at the very initial stage of production. The identification and the traceability function is very vital for any production unit which can always result in a efficient production flow.
2 After considerable (3/4months) time period they should revive their short term activities and try to achieve them one by one in which they can always motion the reduction of wastage and accomplish these. In this way they can reach at least 50% t0 60% of reduction. Moreover this process will give them the advantage of MBO which will leverage in the long run.
3. The whole process should be documented in a proper follow up and proper implementation of updated process
4. This will bring transparency and accountability as well.
5. The site visit reveals tat the production house is not systematic one. They should arrange all the assembly line in systematic order witch can provide them a proper flow of material and information between the units. For this they should go for proper departmentation under the roof. This may not involve too many money indeed. As they can use the basic design with cheapest material. Moreover this is a long term and one time investment, they can see for permanent installation also.

The present production house can be diagrammatically represented as follows.

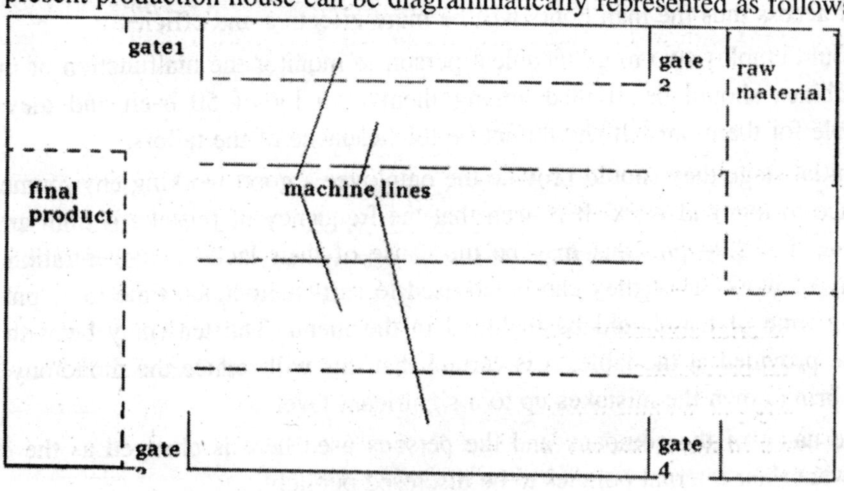

Diagram-2

The above production house can be re structured as bellow. This will give the advantage of a structured production house. It will also provide a psychological advantage to the employee and hence will improve the quality.

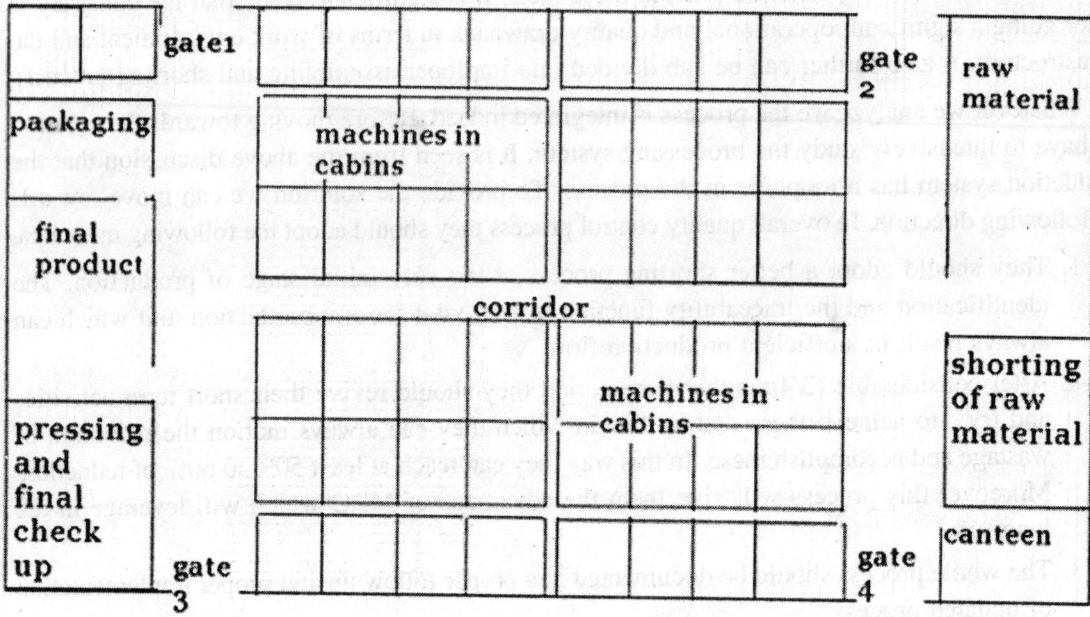

Diagram-3

Through the corridor the material will be supplied systematically. There will be no over flow and the supervisor should monitor the process. Ultimately this will lead to the adoption of just in time for the company which will definitely be an added advantage for them. The departments are arranged in a systematic order so that there be a flow Information and the material. The pack aging house and the final product are separated so that there be no bottleneck among them. Due to the separate cabins among the employees there will be no direct access thus the man hours will be more effective and efficiently.

6. They should employ two more technical person to monitor the malfunction of machines. The machines should be divided among them as a lot of 50 each and they will be responsible for them only. It should not be the headache of the tailors.
7. At the initial stage they should provide the employee a good working environment and a good place to live and work. It is seen that the frequency of mistake is high around the lunch time .i.e. 2:00 pm .this may be the cause of their lack of concentration and the monotony of work. Thus they can be advised to shift their lunch time to 1: pm and the refreshing time of tea should be included in the menu. The tea (may be with snacks) should be provided at the table. It is certain that this will reduce the monotony of work and will bring down the mistakes up to a significant level.

N.B: The name of the company and the persons used here is changed as the company doesn't want their internal policies to be disclosed publicly.

Exhibit

The Indian textile industry consists of both the organized and unorganized sector. In unorganized sector we can identify processing, knitting and garmenting and in unorganized sector we have manufacturing, trading. The growth and capacity utilization of this sector is significantly high. It is the sector which provides the highest employment opportunity among all the industry. Following table exhibit the growth and capacity utilization of the sector.

Industry	Growth rate		Capacity utilization	
	04-05	05-06	04-05	05-06
Cotton textile	7.4	8.5	91.4	97.4
Wool, silk and man made fiber textile	3.6	00	89.2	98.0
Jute and other vegetable fiber textile	3.7	0.5	83.6	83.5
Textile products	19.2	16.3	81.5	92.7
All industries	8.4	8.1	82.2	82.7

It can be seen from the above table that the growth rate of product from textile industries is more than that of all industries average growth rate in the two years and the capacity utilization of cotton textile was estimated at 97.4% (highest) and the textile product industry 92.7% (second highest) in 2005-06 an was well above all industries figure of 82.7%.

Human Resource Management

1

Migration of Higher Education Faculty

Dr. A. M. Gurav
D. R. K. College of Commerce, Kolhapur
annasahebg@yahoo.co.in

Indian higher education is on sea-saw position in the globalized world due to Indian doors having opened for Foreign educational entrepreneurs. India has vast base in education from 'Takshashila' university to the present modern universities. The Indian universities have been increasing in number but quality of higher education is in the reverse gear which will push away the talented faculty from Indian universities to foreign universities. The basic Indian higher education was and is rich but it may be floating in coming future in the areas of quality and faculty. The world higher education is marching from Glob to India, Student Brain to Faculty Brain, Talented Brain to Talented Universities, Local Teaching to Virtual Teaching, Indian Culture to Foreign Culture, Macro to Nano, Quantity Education to Quality Education, Indian Culture to Western Culture, Lesser Prospects to Better Prospects, Large Size Family to Small Size Family is today's trend. Human Hardware Education to Human Software Education. In higher education factory one has to write vision statement, mission statement, define core values and strategic planning for the education in order to develop the human resource and this is possible only with the visionary faculty. India has one of the largest higher education systems in the world, with more than 17000 colleges, 544 Universities, 13 Institutes of national importance and various other vocational institutes. We, the teachers in higher education, should build various remedial models for stopping the migration of Indian faculty to the foreign campuses. Intellectual, spiritual and ethical combination is required for stopping migration in higher education. The matrix model can be used for stopping migration of teachers in higher education.

Questions:

1. Analyze the case carefully and give appropriate title for it.

2. Analyze the Higher Education, Indian and Foreign Universities, Indian Students aspects of this case.
3. Is Indian University Faculty doing well?
4. What is your alternative plan(s) for Indian University Faculties?

Teaching Note:

- **Clear teaching objectives:**
  - a. To know the Indian Management Education scenario.
  - b. To understand the foreign education trend.
  - c. To compare and know the required the talented brain.
- **Suggested student assignment:**
  - a. Go through the Government of India resolution regarding foreign university draft bill.
  - b. Visit to the private university for knowing the present position.
  - c. Discuss with the Professors in this regard.
- **Suggested readings/references:**
  - a. Government Publication regarding higher education.
  - b. Government draft bill about foreign university permission.
  - c. University News.
- **Possible discussion questions:**
  - a. Analyze the case carefully and give appropriate title for it.
  - b. Analyze the Higher Education, Indian and Foreign Universities, Indian Students aspects of this case.
  - c. Is Indian University Faculty doing well?
  - d. What is your alternative plan(s) for Indian University Faculties?
- **Potential uses of the case:**

  This case is useful to students, Professors and Policy makers.
- **Analysis and Suggested teaching approach:**

1. Analyze the case carefully and give appropriate title for it.

India has vast base in education from 'Takshashila' university to the present modern universities. Our higher education is on sea-saw position in the higher education level. In the globalized world, Indian doors have opened for Foreign educational institutions, especially very recently bill has about to pass. Due to WTO social, cultural and economical changes have taken place in the Indian educational environment. The number of Indian universities has been increasing but the quality of higher education is in the reverse gear, which will push away the talented faculty from Indian universities to foreign universities. The world is full of opportunities in the area of higher education. It indicates that there are various issues and challenges in higher education. The basic Indian higher education was and is rich but it may be floating in coming future in the areas of quality and faculty. Although it is true, at present drastic changes have taken place in the globalized higher education and the Indian faculty has started draining to the foreign universities at abroad and very soon foreign universities in India. The Indian government is seriously thinking to allow the foreign investors in education sector under dimmed, autonomous and private universities with 100 acre, 50 acre and 10 acre of land and 100 crores of rupees capital for starting universities in India. All stakeholders in higher education like students, society, parents, government, employer etc are the 'Arjunas and we teachers are the 'Sarathis' in higher education scenario. We, the Sarathis, are the great warriors in the Indian higher education who fight and win without lifting any weapon but these 'Sarathis' will migrate from Indian universities to the foreign universities in coming future. Today's Economics Times and Indian Express (5-9-2011, Teacher's Day) has mentioned that the good salary, which is more than MBA qualified employee is getting in corporate sector, has to offer to the MBA class teaching professor, then only the good teachers will available to the Management educational Institutions. This view indicates that the management educational institutions are not offering attractive salary and perks (except exceptional), which may affect adversely on maintenance of Indian faculty in Indian higher educational institutions.

Title:

a. "Migration of Faculty from Indian Universities to Foreign University Campuses"
b. "Indian Faculty to Foreign Universities in India"
c. "Quality Education for future"

2. Analyze the Higher Education, Indian and Foreign Universities, Indian Students aspects of this case:

Indian higher education is marching towards 2020. ... Hon'ble the then President of India, A. P. J. Abdul Kalam believes, Our vision is predicted on the belief that HUMAN RESOURCES are the most important determinants of overall development.... It means that the Indian higher education is the factory where human resource develops. In this higher education factory one has to write vision statement, mission statement, define core values and strategic planning for the education in order to develop the human resource and this is all possible only with the visionary faculty, but, if the faculty is draining from Indian universities to the foreign university campuses, what will be the fate of pure Indian education. India has one of the largest higher education systems in the world with more than 17,000 colleges, 544 Universities, 13 Institutes of national importance and various other vocational institutes. Indian higher education is rich at present. India has significant advantages in the 21st century knowledge race. India is the third largest in the world in student number, after China and the United States. Considering this positive situation, the foreign universities are going to come to India for selling or imparting knowledge in the vast Indian market and therefore, there are different issues, challenges and causes in the faculty migration. At present the world higher education is marching from glob to India. It means that, education and knowledge have expanded considerably. World eminent players are interested to start their colleges in India. It is observed by a case writer that hereafter more faculty brain will be migrated in comparison with student brain to the foreign university campuses. It was desirable until a few years back that the student brain would migrate away for their betterment and for the betterment of India at large. But now if the faculty brain migrates, it will be like losing the weapon along with the bullet. It is predicted that the good and reputed foreign universities will start their educational activities in coming future in India. In this situation the Indian talented brain will take VRS and join in the foreign universities. It is a serious thing since what happened in the experiment of the nationalized bank employees VRS that the good brain took VRS from nationalized banks and joined in private banks, though a few exceptions. It can be interpreted that the same thing will happen in the Indian talented brain bank. It is observed that due the LPG the concept of communication has changed in the educational world. Earlier majority of the students and teachers were using local teaching i.e. classroom teaching only for learning and teaching, but at present with the advent of internet and virtual learning from the foreign university, the faculty will be involved more in virtual teaching. **I**ndian **C**ampus of **U**niversity to **F**oreign **C**ampus of **U**niversity, benefits analysis reveals that this migration is today's mantra in the higher education business. The parents least bother about ICU for higher education but they bother more about FCU. The great challenge before the Indian universities is how to maintain ICU itself alive in the face of migration of faculty from Indian university to foreign university campuses. The migration from Indian universities to foreign campuses is because of higher education is marching from Macro to Nano specialization. ***Quantity Based Education to Quality Based Education*** means, there had been quantity based education so far, but at present there is a quality based education, which is a challenge in higher education. The foreign universities will focus on quality based education, so they are in search of quality faculty, which they expect to migrate from Indian universities to foreign university campuses. The Indians blindly imitate the western educational culture without studying our educational culture and without accepting western work culture. The case writer does not claim that the western education is completely bad or vice-a-versa, but those bad things we are copy, they become the external threat in higher education due to globalization. Another important point is to be noted here that majority of the Foreign Universities (except exceptions) are very much fond of Indian culture and environment, due to this attraction of foreign universities will start their campuses in India and then our faculty will migrate to foreign university campuses.

3. Is Indian University Faculty doing well?

Yes. But how much is the question. It is observed by the case writer that there is shortage of talented teachers (at large scale) who can teach and impart the quality education for betterment of the students in the higher education. Talented fresh brain is going to professional sectors like IT, Medical and Corporate and slow brain is coming to traditional mode of education. The talented brain left with Indian higher education and migrating to foreign university campuses. It is a journey of Lesser Prospects to Better Prospects in getting education and imparting education. The culture and perception of the educated family have been changing and it motivates to admit our child in foreign universities for any course with any damn amount of fees. Due to parent's perception about the child, Indian parents will opt for foreign universities and this will lead our faculty to migrate to the foreign university campuses. Human Software Education is nothing but Physical approach to education and not Brain development approach to education. It is observed by the case writer that the foreign universities will focus on student's skills development and this will attract our faculty brain migration to their campuses. It is observed by the case writer that in

Indian universities (except exceptions), it is found that there is lack of sufficient opportunity for students, quality of education, resources allocation, research, good salary to teachers, interdisciplinary approach, feasible workload to teachers, motivational factors to teachers, sufficient infrastructure, ICT, flexible working hours. Due to these issues, challenges and reasons, the Indian brain will definitely migrate to foreign university campuses.

4. What is your alternative plan(s) for Indian University Faculties?

Considering the above mentioned reasons behind migration of Indian teachers to foreign university campuses, it is true that, one who is competitive, will migrate and not all teachers. We, the teachers in higher education, should build various remedial models for stopping the migration of Indian faculty to the foreign campuses. The model should be need based and suitable to all brilliant faculties who are thinking to migrate to foreign campuses. Intellectual, spiritual and ethical combination is required for stopping migration in higher education. One can use the following Matrix Model for minimization of migration from Indian campuses to foreign university campus.

Stakeholders ⇨ ***Values*** ⇩ Needs	*Students*	*Employers*	*Employees*	*Society*	*University*	*Government*
Quality in Education						
Change in Curriculum						
Methods of Teaching						
International Requirements						
Soft Skills						
Financial and Non financial Benefits						
Employability etc.						

The matrix model for stopping migration of teachers in higher education demands an integrated approach. Vertical and horizontal integration is essential. In short, the world should move from capitalistic education to sustainable development of students. At present it is the challenge before the higher education to develop the students. Here, we have to consider that the students are the input and afterward; some students become an output; after completion of their education. Here measurement of input – output relationship is nothing but the measurement of value addition in the students and this is one of the reasons for migration and at the same time it is a solution for stopping the migration of faculty from Indian universities to the foreign university campuses.

References:

1. S. Sadri, S. Jayashree and M. Ajgaonkar, (2002), *Geometry of HR, Himalaya Publishing House – Mumbai.*
2. S. N. Pathan, (2005), *Quality Improvement Programme Through NAAC – A success Stories of Maharashtra, Intellectual Book Bureau - Bhopal.*
3. S. V. More, (2007) *Bharatrtna Dr. Sarvapalli Radhakrishnan, Sukhada-Sourabha Prakashana – Patan – Satara.*
4. Shankar Acharya, (2007), *Can India Grow Without Bharat, Academic Foundation - New Delhi.*

2

Human Resource Planning in ABC Corporation

Ms. Aman Aggarwal
Assistant Professor, IILM Graduate School of Management
aman.agrawal@iilmgsm.ac.in

ABC Corporation, a mid sized high-end IT consulting company has sales offices in the US and Europe and offshore development centres in Delhi and Bangalore with over 5000 employees.

To ensure a healthy bottom line and to stay competitive, the company needs to ensure that it has high utilization, low administrative costs and cost-effective delivery of projects.

AS the global markets recover from the recent recession, business is fast picking up and sales are improving. The company is however, running into problems with delivering the sold projects. Due to the recession, sales cycles are long. When a project is sold, it needs to be staffed with software engineers, managers, and architects with the right set of skills to deliver that kind of project. As new projects are sold, the HR department is finding it harder and harder to staff the required people on those projects. The people available on the bench do not have the relevant skill set for the projects and no immediate in-house training can be provided to address this. The project has aggressive time lines, so, the HR department decides to hire people from outside the company at high rates for the project and somehow get the project started with the existing people in the time being.

The people who have been in the company for some time are disillusioned by these things because they are forced to work on projects for which they do not have the correct skill sets and people hired from outside the company are paid a lot more than them.

The project may be one of its kind sold so far in the company and there is no long term career plan for the people hired suddenly for this project. The hiring has happened at such short notice and under so much client pressure that the hiring department has had to cut corners and not stick to their usual high standard of hiring and close scrutiny of whether the person will fit well with the organization's values. This has led to a steady decline in the quality of work done on projects and a definite dilution of the company's strong culture.

On the one hand there is a rush of hiring new people and on the other hand there are a large number of people on the bench who have rolled off some projects that have recently been completed but cannot be staffed to new work because all new work is on completely different technologies. So, the company is faced with a paradoxical dual problem of low utilization and low people availability at the same time.

The HR department is not able to make much improvement in the situation because they do not have any relevant data about the current skill-sets of the existing pool of people. The HR department is also not informed by the sales people about the specific technologies on which new work is being sold until the time when the project is ready to be staffed. The HR department is also not able to leverage the right level and combination of people for a project and most projects have become top-heavy with too many architects and managers being needed to get the work done on time.

Points for Discussion:

1. What are the reasons for employee dissatisfaction and high turnover?
2. Are there any problems with their hiring strategy?
3. Why employees not performing?
4. Is there any problem with the job analysis?
5. How can they improve their human resource planning

This case study describes problems of acquiring human resource in a IT consulting company. It also discusses the reasons for low employee morale, dissatisfaction among employees in spite of being given good salaries. .

There is US based IT consulting company ABC having around 5000 employee in India. It's a project based company having its offices across world. Acquiring resources is biggest problem faced by this company. Because of number of reasons:

1. There are resources available in the company. On the basis of which they keep selling their projects.
2. There is no match with the skill set available with the requirements of new projects
3. Employees get staffed and can not perform effectively because of wrong skill set
4. Employee dissatisfaction increases because of poor performance, low motivation, no recognition, lack of training etc.
5. in spite of being a good pay master employee engagement become low
6. Employee turnover increases

Approach

Sales department should be providing capacity forecast along with the skill set required. This will help in making optimum utilization of internal resource, at the same time HR department will get an insight what types of employees are to be hired.

2

Managing Attrition Rate in Kenelex BPO

Mr. Anubhav Tiwari
Assistant Professor, Bharati Vidyapeeth University
Institute of Management and Research, New Delhi
anubhavtiwari2001@rediffmail.com

The BPO or **Business Process Outsourcing** Industry as is well known is one of the biggest money spinners in the modern business scenario. It has led to making India the Back office of the World. The revenue contribution of BPO Exports to the Indian GDP has risen from 6.2 Billion US$ in 2006-07 to 8.1 Billion US$ presently and even not stopping here. The double digit growth rate has provided tremendous opportunities but this Industry is also beset with a number of problems and Challenges. This was quite evident in case of KENELEX BPO, The Third party service provider Indian Company providing valuable services to foreign Clients in Industry verticals such as Customer Interaction Services, Banking and Finance & Insurance. The motto being **"Innovating Thoughtfully"** was conceived to serve them most Innovatively and in a prompt manner .The firm's set up at Gurgaon with a working capacity of 450 people was a true state-of – the –art facility with most modern equipments available but still the company is grappling with most burning Human Resource problem ie **Rising Rate of Attrition**. The Bleeding Human Capital had assumed alarming proportions in the tune of more than 45% particularly at the Middle Management and the Lower levels.

The firms turnover was quite fine and healthy still it could not stop the mass exodus. The CEO of the firm Mr. Benjamin was quite concerned and depressed by this. He was simply clueless what to do as it was really a deadly challenge to keep the figure down particularly as the demand level out strips the supply of the good workforce by a big margin. He was constantly holding meetings with his Senior Managers to resolve this Issue but with no success.

In one of the meetings he discussed this matter at length. The senior manager Mr. Naik reported to him that this is really bad time for them. They train the newly recruited Workforce with the requisite skills such as Soft-skills and in Technicalities spending good amount but suddenly one fine day they find that they stop coming to the office altogether without assigning any specific reason. It is really a huge loss to the company. The chief HR Manager Mr. Prabhu also added that if this trend persists than they can also lose their market share heavily as in this Inflationary Economy the training costs are tremendous. Something must be done immediately to counter this Monster.

The CEO told them that Company policies would be reviewed and they would also take the help of an outside Consultant for this. They took the help of a well known Consultant (DGA Consultants) who with his team studied the system in depth and came out with certain startling facts. He was of the view that the younger workforce in the teens as employed by the firm is having its own aspirations and ambitions regarding job. Furthermore their working style is different from the older generations.

They feel that the BPO industry is still a low brow Industry and do not consider it as a serious career option but only as a stop gap arrangement. They work for some time here and after making fast buck just disappear. The other reasons as cited by him were such as the prevalent Odd working Hours in the Company.

The level of stress Build-up due to continuous Call frequency thereby resulting in Employee Burn-out, Non-Availability of any standard Training Program for the Employees, No proper Benchmarks for the Compensation/Benefits Performance and HR policies, The Health related issues such as Sleeping Disorder, Digestive system getting Upset, Depression, Eyesight Problem, Ear Problem, Indiscipline in Behavioral Issues, Friendship and Interpersonal Relationships. This along with the shortage of the people with right kind of skills in the Industry has made rival companies hop for them thereby leading to this kind of problem, further more the issues like Imported Inflation ,The Economic Slowdown in US and the Appreciating Rupee has made this Industry Unattractive.

Mr. Benjamin was amazed to find these problems and asked for the rectifying measures along with the likely future course of Action. The chief Consultant Mr. Gupta smiled and provided him a comprehensive list of Do's and Don'ts to combat this menace. He told him to follow the Innovative approach of Increasingly employing the Part-timers and Middle aged people and even the House wives for the job. The firm must also start searching at the B-Class cities and Towns the quality workforce thereby leading to lower costs along with the employee availability & stability, A system of pre-employment Check must be initiated which must include rigorous reference checks, relieve letter from previous Organizations etc. The system must be organized through the National Skills Registry to check defection, The proper training programs to be conducted on continuous basis along with the use of ancient practices of Yoga and Dhyan or Meditation to increase the quality of Life as a part of firms Culture, Creation of Spiritual Workplace by the firm is a must.

A proper Industry Academia Interaction must be initiated, A policy of **'Learn while you earn'** must be followed so that the Undergraduates/ graduates working in the organization also get a chance to enhance their credentials, A No-poaching agreement with other Companies will also be a help to curb this problem, Adequate focus on the motivational aspects of Individuals is a must as it is most difficult to implement it in the routine and repetitive jobs. Innovative techniques like providing Horizontal Career options and Handling of entire processs rather than Individual Task performance can lead to substantial success in containing this problem. Moreover the company must also try to climb to the next higher rung of the Value pyramid ie More Analytical jobs of KPO rather than mere Transactions.

The CEO nodded his head and thanked the Consultant to provide such a timely and valuable information. He immediately gave the approval to implement these suggestions. The Company prudently applied those corrective measures and it was found that with in a span of around six months the scenario was totally changed in favor of KENELEX. It was now a totally transformed organization with sound intellectual character as well as Wealth.

Discussions Questions:

1. "BPO is a people driven Business" Do you agree with statement Why or Why Not?
2. " The Rising rate of Attrition is good for health of BPO Companies as they get ready-made talents available easily" Do you agree with the statement?
3. Please suggest some more Innovative Ideas besides the one mentioned here to combat the monster of Attrition

4

Emotional Engagement at Work

Ms. Aparna Marwah
Assistant Professor, Bharati Vidyapeeth Institute of Management & Research
aparnamarwah@gmail.com
Dr. S.L. Gupta
Professor, Birla Institute of Technology

Do you encounter situations on a rare or routine basis that personally affect you?". This was the question that was asked by a team comprising of an HR Counselor Srinivasan and HR Psychologist Dr. Negi. Aastha replied in a pensive mood "The company expects me to only show positive emotions to customers";

"the requirement to hide negative emotions and never to show negative emotions (e.g., irritation) to customers" sometimes becomes emotionally cumbersome.

The requirement to empathize and place oneself in the situation of the customer (e.g., "The company expects me to imagine myself in the situation of customers"), and the requirement to be authentic in client contacts (e.g., "The company expects me to be sincere and authentic in the contact with customers") tends to drain out my zeal to work and excel in my area.

"How often do you have to show feelings to customers that do not correspond with the way you feel at that moment?," Aastha told "Quite often and "How often do you have to show positive feelings to customers, while in fact you feel indifferent?". "Seeing my profession, I feel always".

Dr. Negi and Srinivisan asked unanimously "Did you always feel the same when you joined this profession?"."No, Aastha replied but today I feel like leaving the job. My colleagues work from 9 to 5. They leave at 5pm sharp, enjoy their life, do not take customers, their calls; sometimes grievances seriously but I from day one tend to handle everything as my own is the sufferer.I think I have developed psychological problems"

Dr. Negi and Mr. Srinivasan asked how can you say this? "I feel emotionally drained from my work", and "I feel tired when I get up in the morning and have to face another day on the job."

Dr. Negi and Mr. Srinivasan replied "You are suffering from emotional dissonance and emotional exhaustion. In people – oriented careers this happens quite often. All you need is to develop Emotion Work-related Self-Efficacy (e.g., "I am capable of successfully handling situations with demanding or difficult customers (e.g., drunk or aggressive)") and to emotional dissonance. (e.g., "I am capable of being cheerful and friendly with customers, even if I actually donot feel well because of, for example, problems at home").

They continued "Resolution of customer problems is your work – a part of your duty. You need to maintain an appropriate work-life balance."

"During my work I feel full of energy" (vigor), "I am enthusiastic about my job" (dedication), and "When I am working very intensively, I feel happy" (absorption). Feelings rules make interpersonal interactions more manageable and predictable, and over employees a (sometimes much-needed) shield to protect their personal feelings.

Dr. Negi and Mr. Srinivasan suggested "The relationship between emotionally charged interactions with recipients with both emotional exhaustion and work engagement is fully mediated by emotional dissonance. That is, as a result of emotionally charged interactions with customers, you experience a discrepancy between felt and displayed emotions which, in turn, leads to emotional exhaustion and reduced engagement.

Self-efficacy may help individuals in not experiencing a discrepancy between felt and expressed emotions in reaction to drunk, demanding, and aggressive customers. Also, highly efficacious employees do not become emotionally dissonant from strict and severe display rules, while low-efficacious individuals clearly experience a discrepancy between displayed and authentic feeling when confronted with strict versus non-strict rules for display of emotions. This understanding will form a fruitful start for a further exploration of the role of personal resources in buffering the detrimental consequences of emotion work.

Self-efficacy not only buffers the detrimental effects of performing emotion work, but also plays a crucial role in maintaining and enhancing its positive effects. High levels of emotional dissonance do not affect the levels of work engagement of high (vs. low) efficacious cabin attendants. In contrast, low-efficacious individuals clearly loose their vigor, absorption, and dedication when they cannot express their true feelings. This shows that highly efficacious persons are better able to deal with emotional dissonance, which is often considered to be an intrinsic part of human service work, than individuals with low levels of efficacy since it does not affect their feelings of vigor, absorption, and dedication.

Self-efficacy can be considered as a personal resource that enables employees to deal with job demands (resources mainly predict motivational effects, while job demands rather evoke negative health effects (such as emotional exhaustion).

Self-efficacy proves to be promising in decreasing the negative consequences of performing emotion work, and in enhancing its positive effects on employee's work engagement.

Highly efficacious persons are not only better equipped to cope with threats or demands in their working environment, but are also better able to generate available resources, such as social support, which, in turn, may lead to positive effects on health and well-being.

Just try to maintain an appropriate work-life balance, don't mix the two. Social interactions provide tremendous opportunities for us to deepen learning but not at the cost of personal growth. You will find kindred spirits who fuel joint explorations and productions, reinforce understandings, and provide divergent opinions and clarification of understandings as discussions ensue. In many cases, social interactions enable levels of learning that simply wouldn't be possible for us to accomplish on their own. Successful leveraging of such opportunities requires some degree of social and emotional maturity on the part of the employee - especially when interactions occur outside the company environment.

5

IT Governance and CRM Beyond CBS in the Indian Banking Industry – A Case Study of Leadership in Robust, Resilient Punjab National Bank

Dr. Deepak Tandon
LBS, Dwarka, New Delhi
deepaktandon0@gmail.com

Dr. Neelam Tandon
JIMS , Kalkaji New Delhi

Dr. Samiksha Ojha,
IMI, New Delhi

Mr. Pulkit Ahuja,
LBS, Dwarka, New Delhi

Having successfully implemented the CBS , the Indian Banking Sector is ready for an optimisation level surmounting the problems and Risks in It Revolution. A new forward Journey of analysing the need of IT Governance. Methodological and Operational Risk Management in the Indian b Banks has already begun. The functional and implementation of best practices in IT Governance is the need of the hour post Basle II & Basle III norms amidst domain of IT transformation.Not only the speed but the delivery of the Banking services has changed the total face of the Banking sector,Post stabilisation of the CBS and E- Comerce products adoption the authors have suggested Models for a Robust and reliable Banking services to the customers at a lower cost and generate measures for an effective information management . Punjab National Bank , a pioneer Bank has taken a lead in IT as an enabler and has used a two-pronged strategy to IT-enable itself and support present and future business needs. The authors through a Litmus Case Methodology through Sections have categorically emphasised the journey of IT Transformation, SWOT analysis, Culture and technology issues in Punjab National Bank . The steps being taken beyond CBS implementation by Punjab National Bank have been elaborated.Modelling of the S-curve framework w.r.t Bank products like RTGS/NEFT , Cards has been also depicted vis a vis the total Indian Banking sector. Econometric tests like Pearson Correlation, Test of equality , Granger Casuality tests performed by the authors suggesting to substantiate the need for Enterprise architecture for Punjab National emerging it as an IT Giant in the recent forthcoming years .

Key Words

1. EA – Enterprise Architecture
2. RTGS = Real Time Gross settlement enabled services
3. CLC – Cutomer Life Cycle
4. NEFT = National Electronic Fund transfer
5. CBS – Core Banking Solution
6. IT – Information Technology

JEL classification G21,G28,L13

INTRODUCTION

The Indian banking system, in the last decade, has come a long way with the total assets increasing more than five times from $250 billion to more than $1.3 trillion (between March 2000 and March 2010), registering a cumulative annnual growth rate of 18 percent compared to average GDP growth of 7.2 percent during the same period. Banks have added more than 14000 branches and 41000 ATMs to their network in the last decade, besides broadening the scope of delivery channels to internet banking, mobile banking, phone banking and call centers, thus rolling out technology to the advantage of the customers. The deregulation, disintermediation, emergence of advanced technologies, along with the consolidation wave in the banking sector have been instrumental in making banks to diversify their operations. As a result the banks are transcending their normal business operation and are venturing into investment banking, leasing, merchant banking, factoring, hire purchase and mutual funds etc., through separate subsidiaries. One aspect of overall financial change is a shift in the pattern of business undertaken by banks. This is thought to be manifested in a relative increase in fee and other non-interest income vis -à-vis the net interest income. As a result, there has been a manifold interest amongst the foreign banks also to expand their operations to India.

(a) Transformation of Indian Baking Industry:

New private sector and foreign banks emerged - equipped with the latest technology. These banks opted for a different model of having a single centralized database through a network infrastructure, instead of having multiple databases for all their branches. These changes were market driven, having the influence especially of globalization. The crux is Indian banks have no control over developments abroad but are subjected to their effects. Hence these changes were not the outcome of internal changes but of external changes.

In other words, deregulation has opened up new opportunities for banks to increase revenues by diversifying into investment banking, insurance, credit cards, mortgage financing, depository services, securitization, etc.Now all the banks have started with the concept of multi- channels, like ATMs, credit cards, debit cards, telephone/mobile banking, internet banking, call centers, etc.

(b) Forces for change in Indian Banking

Underlying forces for change

- Developments in communication systems, coupled with blurring of differences between banks and non - banks and globalization have aggravated the competitive environment.
- Technology became a key differentiator for the new private sector banks. The technological superiority helped these private sector banks to have upper edge over public sector banks. The traditional source of income (Net Interest margin = Interest Earned – Interest Expended) was compressed due to the pressure of competition. As a result commercial banks had to face the challenge of finding out new sources of income and curtailing overhead expenses.
- The operating conditions are different for private sector and public sector banks in India (wage bill, legacy of non-performing assets and extensive network of Public sector banks) which results in imperfect competition in the market.
- With increasing competition among banks products through diverse distribution channels including upgraded branches, ATMs, telephone and Internet. The mantra to attract and retain customers lies in efficient customer service including customized and value added products to meet various needs of individual customers as also to meet the need of diverse types of customers.

(c) Manifestation of Underlying Forces:

Concern Issues are:

- Use of technology to be increased substantially in banks to cope with rising volumes and reduce transaction costs and processing time. In Public Sector Banks, legacy systems and interoperability is a major hurdle in the integration of all delivery channels. A major problem of banks in India is the availability of excessive data, the relevance and quality of which are both suspect. The inculcation of a proper attitude towards technology adaptation and proper security systems is an urgent need of the hour.
- Very low level of computer literacy and the existing mind set of some senior bankers are road blocks in the IT implementation in banks to 100% level.
- Information Technology related security issues in Indian banks are also a matter of concern.

(d) Innovations in Technology at Indian Banking Sector

Under the guidance and directions of the Board for Payment and Settlement Systems (BPSS), policies of the Reserve Bank continued to be transparent and oriented towards promoting orderly development of the payment systems ensuring that the systems functioned in an efficient and secure manner. The policies encouraged participants to shift from paperbased/cash-driven payment systems to safer and faster electronic modes of payments in a nondisruptive manner.

The process of issue of authorisation to entities for operating payment systems under the Payment and Settlement Systems Act, 2007, was made rigorous and in alignment with these objectives, ensuring that only entities with sound financial position, adequate expertise, and technology support and good corporate governance are authorised to operate such systems. Thirty seven entities have so far been issued certificate of authorisation to operate various payment and settlement systems in areas of credit-debit card management, ATM networks, cross border money transfer services, and issue of pre-paid payment instruments.

Technological innovations give:

Safety – Keeping the risks in various payment system products minimum and manageable if they are necessary and unavoidable.

Security – Giving confidence to stakeholders that the payment systems can be trusted and are reasonably protected from threats and vulnerabilities.

Soundness – Demonstrating the capability and ensuring the payment systems function in a non-disruptive manner.

Efficiency – Providing measures to assure that the payment systems are costeffective, reliable and promote financial and economic stability.

(i) Paper Based Payment Systems

Paper based transactions account for 60 per cent of total transactions processed through both (Magnetic Ink Character Recognition) MICR and Non-MICR clearing houses. To enhance the safety, security and efficiency of paper based system, the Reserve Bank took steps like (i) discontinued high value clearing in a non-disruptive manner over a period of one year; (ii) extended speed clearing which facilitates local clearing of outstation cheques, to 66 MICR centres; (iii) Initiated steps to roll out Cheque Truncation System (CTS) in Chennai covering all the southern centres after successfully implementing the same in the National Capital Region; (iv) issued a new cheque standard styled CTS-2010 to enhance the integrity of images procured under CTS by mandating minimum security features covering quality of paper, watermark, banks logo in invisible ink, and void pantograph on cheque forms.

(ii) Electronic Payment Systems

The large value electronic payment systems, viz., Real Time Gross Settlement System (RTGS) and the Retail Electronic Payment Systems, viz., National Electronic Clearing Services (NECS and ECS), National Electronic Fund Transfer (NEFT) and Card Payment Systems are the electronic payment systems available in India. The trend of shift of transactions from paper to electronic mode continued during 2009-10. The share of electronic transactions to total transactions increased from 32.8 per cent to 40 per cent volume-wise and from 83.9 percent to 89 percent value wise during the year. To encourage the electronic transactions, the waiver of processing charges for ECS/NECS/NEFT/RTGS was further extended up to March 31, 2011.

(iii) Real Time Gross Settlement Systems

The implementation of RTGS systems by Central Banks throughout the world is driven by the goal to minimize risk in high-value electronic payment settlement systems. In an RTGS system, transactions are settled across accounts held at a Central Bank on a continuous gross basis. Settlement is immediate, final and irrevocable and thus the credit risks due to time lags in settlement are eliminated. India introduced RTGS system in 2004 and since then, each yearthe volume and value of transactions transacted is increasing in multiples. Reserve Bank in consultation with participants has been continuously striving to bring about improvements. Keeping this in vie Punjab National Bank , a pioneer Public Sector Bank Bank in India went for Technologocal upgradation for the four reasons . "Firstly, technology has the capacity to reduce the transaction cost to a great extent, plus it saves time. Secondly, it limits data entry time as replication, report generation etc, can be done automatically. Thirdly, it offers immense scope for improvement on the customer relationship front, as computers help deliver quick and enhanced value-added services to customers like smart cards, ATMs, Internet banking, etc. And lastly it also helps keep track of the business.

II. OBJECTIVES OF THE STUDY

1. To study the need for technological transformation in the Banking Industry with special reference to E-products in the Banking sector in India

2. To study the technological developments in Banking Sector of India and the journey beyond CBS

3. To study the impact of Technological Products in post e-transformation saga reforms of the Indian Banking Industry with special emphasis on RTGS and NEFT and prepare the S Curve

4. To study the performnance of Banks under the study is significantly improvised by implementation of E- Banking Products namely MICR /Non MICR, RTGS, NEFT, ECS/NECS and CTS.

5. To identify new horizons of technological products in Indian Banks keeping and suggest Vision 2020 action plan in view of the progressive Entrepneurial areas of concern in E- Products.

III. METHODOLOGY

(a) Research Methodology

The present paper is concerned with the technological advancement and its role in performance in the Indian Banking Industry. The Banks have been divided in Five (5) Categories namely State Bank Of India (SBI) , Nationalised Banks, Foreign Banks , Private Banks and Others.

Secondary Data of RTGS and NEFT in terms of number of transactions in millions for the annual years 2008-09 and 2009-10 has been collected from Reserve Bank of India, New Delhi.

Paired sample T- Test is used as a statistical tool to analyse the significant product contribution in termsof technological advancements for two succeeding years.

Paired sample t-test is a statistical technique that is used to compare two population means in the case of two samples that are correlated. Paired sample t-test is used in 'before after' studies, or when the samples are the matched pairs, or the case is a control study.

Paired sample t-test

Assumptions in Paired sample t-test:

1. The first assumption in the paired sample t–test is that only the matched pair can be used to perform the paired sample t-test.
2. In the paired sample t-test, normal distributions are assumed.
3. In a paired sample t-test, it is assumed that the variance of two samples is same.
4. In a paired sample t-test, observations must be independent of each other but can be matched for (technological set of characteristics) set of charateristics.

b) Software used – SPSS (18 versions)

c) Hypothesis

Ho: There is no significant difference between the means of the two variables namely RTGS and NEFT

Ha: There is a significant difference between the means of the two variables namely RTGS and NEFT

d) S-Curve has been made in the Indian Banking Industry analyzing technological cycles. Major chunk of the National Banks' RTGS and NEFT is by 8 players as substantiated with PNB as the leader

IV.ANALYSIS

The Reserve Bank has taken a series of initiatives to facilitate use of electronic mode for various retail and large value transactions. RTGS is a large value payment system which processes both customer and inter-bank transactions of '1, 00,000 and above, while the NEFT is essentially a retail system. Further, while RTGS is a realtime gross settlement arrangement, NEFT is a near-real time system with settlements taking place at hourly intervals. Both systems are operated by the Reserve Bank. The facility of RTGS and NEFT is available in over 70,000 branches with 119 members and 99 banks participating in the respective systems.

The volume and value of transactions processed through the two systems has shown an impressive growth over the years. Considering the fact that RTGS is a large value payment system as against NEFT, the value of transactions processed in the former are much larger. However, the growth trend in the value of transactions in the two systems reveals that the amount of transactions processed in NEFT has increased exponentially since 2007-08, while RTGS has exhibited a relatively steady growth.The signifcant contributory product can further be analysed with the help of Pairesd t-test.

Table 1 - Bank Group-wise Number of Transactions in RTGS and NEFT

(Number of transactions in million)

Bank Group	RTGS		NEFT	
	2008-09	2009-10	2008-09	2009-10
SBI group	3.3	7.4	2.7	6.7
Nationalised Banks	3.5	9.0	2.2	7.7
Foreign Banks	2.2	5.3	12.4	21.6
Private Sector Banks	4.2	11.3	14.4	29.3
Others	0.1	0.3	0.03	0.2

Note: Others include State Cooperative Banks, RBI and Urban Cooperative Banks Under NEFT, and under RTGS, apart from these three entities, SEBI-regulated entities Bank group-wise data for 2008-09 and 2009-10 of RTGS and NEFT systems from table one depicts that private sector banks were major participants in the systems and accounted for over one-third of total transactions. The SBI Group accounted for 22 per cent of the total transactions in the RTGS system but their presence in NEFT was only 10 per cent. Further, the volume and value of transactions in the RTGS system was concentrated among a few participants. It is worth to know trhat the top eight players namely SBI, Punjab National Bank, AXIS Bank, HDFC Bank, ICICI Bank, Bank of India, IDBI Bank and CitiBank accounted for more than 50 per cent of total volume and value of transactions as at end-March 2010.

The paired sample statistics depicts that the NEFT mean score is 6.3460 for 2009 and 13.1000 for the year 2010 but RTGS mean transaction in milion is 2.6600 in the year 2009 and 6.6600 in the year 2010. It is evident that there is higher growth rate of NEFT and RTGS transaction in the year 2010 as compared to the year 2009. It is also true that NEFT mean transaction is higher than the RTGS transaction for both the years; namely 2009 as well as 2010. There is a moderate correlation between RTGS and NEFT transaction at 0.476 degree during 2009 but in the year 2010 the degree of correlation between two products has increased to a higher level at 0.642 degree. The t-value of paired sample during the year 2009 is -1.382 and significance value at 95% of confidence is 0.234. The t-value of paired sample during the year 2010 is -1.469 and significance value at 95% of confidence is 0.216. This is higher than 0.05. Hence there is no signficant difference between NEFT and RTGS products of Banking as technological contributory factors in performance of the bank groups into consideration for the years 2009 as well as 2010. Hence we reject the alternative hypothesis and accept the null hypothesis. It can be concluded that though RTGS is a large value payment system as against NEFT but the mean value of transactions processed in the later are much larger. However, the growth trend in the value of transactions in the two systems reveals that the amount of transactions processed in NEFT as well as RTGS has increased exponentially from 2009 to 2010. This is a positive trend in the growth path of banking sector and benefits of this will definitely trickle down to the corporates and bank's customers in coming years.

Table 2 - Paired Sample Statistics

		Paired Differences					t	df	Sig. (2-tailed)
		Mean	Standard Deviation	Standard Error Mean	95% Confidence Interval of the Difference				
					Lower	Upper			
Pair 1 (2008-09)	RTGS & NEFT	−3.6860	5.96242	2.6664	−11.0893	3.7173	−1.382	4	.239
Pair 2 (2009-10)	RTGS & NEFT	−6.4400	9.80449	4.3847	−18.6138	5.7338	−1.469	4	.216

V. SUGGESTIONS:

1. Integration of core banking systems with common inter-bank payment systems such as NEFT and RTGS, in a straight through processing (STP) mode be made available

2. Approach towards centralisation in banks to facilitate customer relationship management (CRM) in a large scale and better MIS based decision making for the enterprise as a whole be looked into

3. Large scale electronification of payment processes should be catered to the Customers by the Banks. This can be done by :

a. providing for adequate business continuity plans, including disaster recovery systems

b. giving greater importance on IS Audit;

c. give emphasis on risk management relating to outsourcing;

d. IT related requirements for ensuring time bound compliance to the needs for Basel II be stringent

4. This will help in large scale usage of standardized message based financial transaction processing;

PART II New S CURVE in Technology in Banking

S Curve in the Banking Industry:

In this study we discuss the S-curve framework in the Indian Banking in view of advent of new technologies which are changing the way customers make transactions through their banks, which include technologies like ECS, Card Payments, NEFT, RTGS, among others. We examine whether the adoption of shared electronic banking network technologies in the financial services industry exhibit S-curve growth patterns as in case of other technologies.S curve is a radical model leveraging technologies discontinuities ,which will be ableto create a significant advantage over their peers .

Various dynamic models such as the 'Tushman/Rosenkopf Technology Adoption Life Cycle Model (1992)' and 'The Revised Technology Adoption Life Cycle Model' state that the evolution of an innovation ends with the arrival of a technological discontinuity. However, it is difficult to predict when this discontinuity will arrive. It can be argued that the rate of advance of a technology is a function of the amount of effort put into the technology and follows the S curve (Foster, 1986), as shown in ***Figure 1***. For a given technology, the evolution is as follows: Initial efforts result in little advancement until the technology becomes successful. This success point, at the lower knee of the curve, is where the technology has finally demonstrated its utility and superiority over the previous technology. After this point significant progress and improvements are made as several embodiments are produced and the technology becomes widely established. Eventually, however, the physical limits of the technology are reached, and continued effort results in little additional advancement. To go beyond the limits of the top of a predecessor's S-Curve, a new alternative must be created.

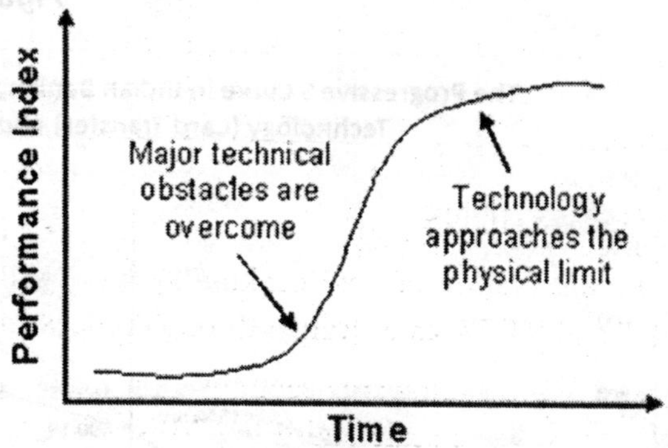

Figure 1

The S-curve is particularly useful for analyzing technological cycles and predicting the introduction, adoption and maturation of innovations. It emerged as a mathematical model and was afterwards applied to a variety of fields including physics, biology and economics. It has been helpful in describing the utility gained by people as the number of their consumption choices increase.

In the innovation management field the S-Curve illustrates the introduction, growth and maturation of innovations as well as the technological cycles that most industries experience. In the early stages large amounts of money, effort and other resources are expended on the new technology but small performance improvements are observed. Then, as the knowledge about the technology accumulates, progress becomes more rapid. As soon as major technical obstacles are overcome and the innovation reaches a certain adoption level an exponential growth will take place. During this phase relatively small increments of effort and resources will result in large performance gains. Finally, as the technology starts to approach its physical limit, further pushing the performance becomes increasingly difficult. This can be seen in ***Figure 2*** in which case the total value of RTGS transfers shows a small increase in the initial year followed by a jump in the adjacent years and finally normalization phase following the high growth phase.

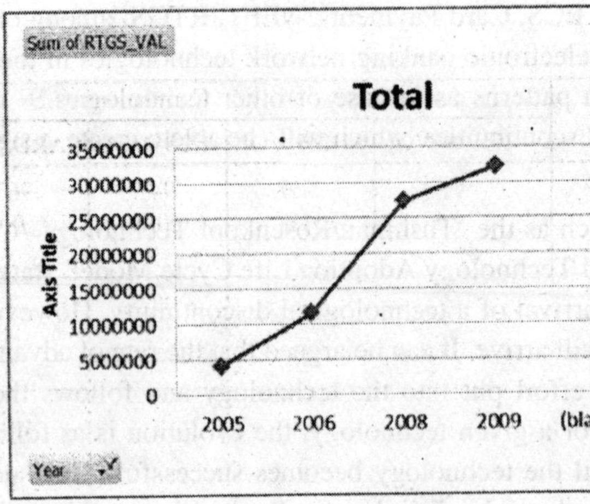

Figure 2

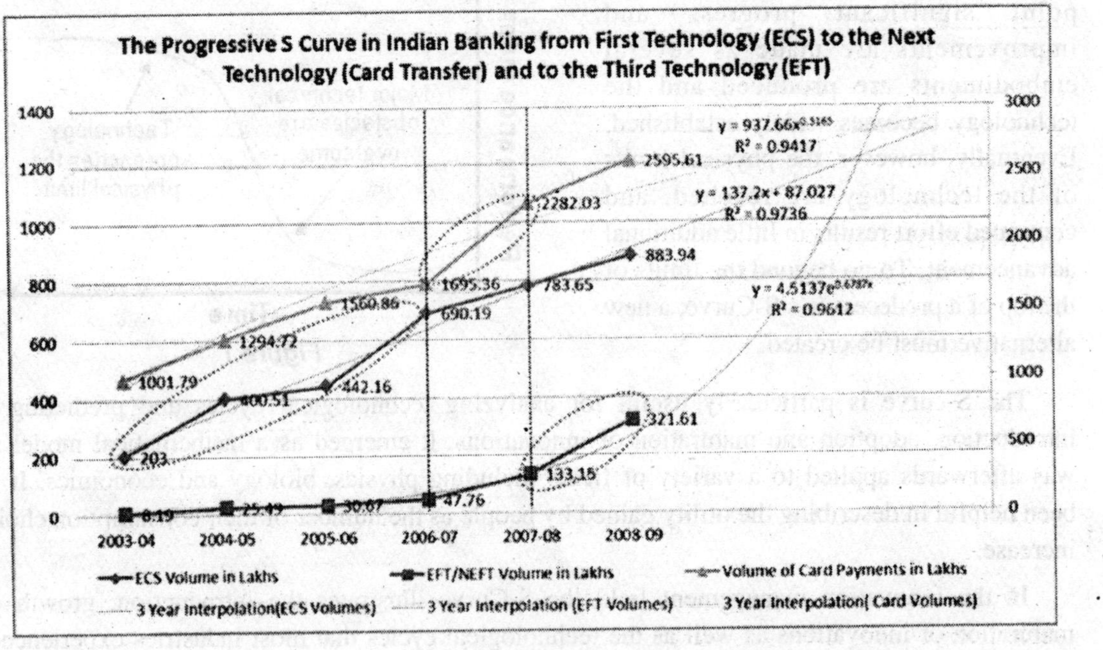

Figure 3

Correlation Analysis

		Correlations				
		RTGS_VOL	MICR_VOL	ECS_VOL	CARDS_VOL	NEFT_VOL
RTGS_VOL	Pearson Correlation	1	.657	.947*	.963**	.984**
	Sig. (2-tailed)		.229	.015	.008	.002
	N	5	5	5	5	5
MICR_VOL	Pearson Correlation	.657	1	.850	.784	.562
	Sig. (2-tailed)	.229		.068	.116	.324
	N	5	5	5	5	5
ECS_VOL	Pearson Correlation	.947*	.850	1	.988**	.911*
	Sig. (2-tailed)	.015	.068		.002	.031
	N	5	5	5	5	5
CARDS_VOL	Pearson Correlation	.963**	.784	.988**	1	.950*
	Sig. (2-tailed)	.008	.116	.002		.013
	N	5	5	5	5	5
NEFT_VOL	Pearson Correlation	.984**	.562	.911*	.950*	1
	Sig. (2-tailed)	.002	.324	.031	.013	
	N	5	5	5	5	5

* Correlation is significant at the 0.05 level (2-tailed).

** Correlation is significant at the 0.01 level (2-tailed).

Paired Samples Test

		Paired Differences		t	df	Sig. (2-tailed)			
		Mean	Std. Deviation	Std. Error Mean	95% Confidence Interval of the Difference				
				Lower	Upper				
Pair 1	RTGS_VOL - CARDS_VOL	-2.562E5	84001.335	37566.539	-360482.234	-151879.366	-6.819	4	.002

Annual Growth Rate

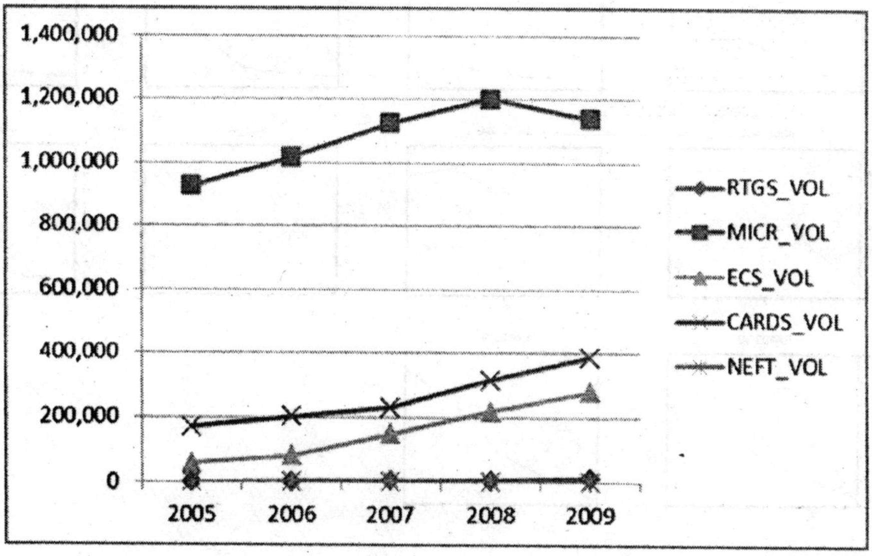

Figure 4

Test of Equality of RTGS and NEFT

Test for Equality of Means Between Series

Date: 07/17/11 Time: 21:41

Sample: 2005 2009

Included observations: 5

Method	*df*	*Value*	*Probability*
t-test	8	2.180557	0.0608
Anova F-statistic	(1, 8)	4.754828	0.0608

Analysis of Variance

Source of Variation	*df*	*Sum of Sq.*	*Mean Sq.*
Between	1	61257834	61257834
Within	8	1.03E+08	12883292
Total	9	1.64E+08	18258241

Category Statistics

Variable	Count	Mean	Std. Dev.	Std. Err. of Mean
RTGS_VOL	5	5061.800	5074.538	2269.402
NEFT_VOL	5	111.7360	125.1086	55.95027
All	10	2586.768	4272.966	1351.231

Payment Systems Performance

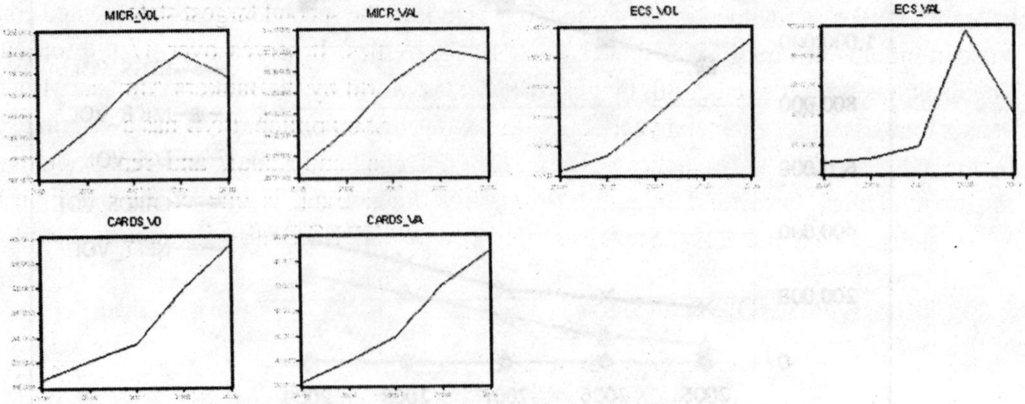

Granger Causality

Pairwise Granger Causality Tests

Date: 07/17/11 Time: 22:16

Sample: 2005 2009

Lags: 1

Null Hypothesis:	Obs	F-Statistic	Probability
NEFT_VOL does not Granger Cause RTGS_VOL	4	16.7204	0.15269
RTGS_VOL does not Granger Cause NEFT_VOL	6.40049	0.23964	

Thus it can be inferred that neither the usage of RTGS nor NEFT has caused each other and the users for both the technologies are independent of each other.

PART III

CASE STUDY: PUNJAB NATIONAL BANK AS LEADING IT ENABLER BANK

About Punjab National Bank

Punjab National Bank (herein referred to as PNB) is one of the leading banks in India and offers a wide variety of banking services, which include corporate and personal banking, industrial finance, agricultural finance, financing of trade and international banking. Among the clients of the Bank are Indian conglomerates, medium and small industrial units, exporters, non-resident Indians and multinational companies. PNB is the second largest PSU bank in India with a dominant presence in north India. Keeping in tune with changing times and to provide its customers more efficient and speedy service, the Bank has taken major initiative in the field of computerization. All the Branches of the Bank have been computerized. The Bank has also launched aggressively the concept of "Any Time, Any Where Banking" through the introduction of Centralized Banking Solution (CBS) and over 2000 offices have already been brought under its ambit. **PNB** was founded in 1894 and today is indeed the second largest state-owned commercial bank in India with about 5000 branches across 764 cities. It serves over 37 million customers. The bank has been ranked 248th biggest bank in the world by theBankers Almanac, London. The bank's total assets for financial year 2007 were about US$60 billion. PNB has a banking subsidiary in the UK, as well as branches inHong Kong, Dubai and Kabul, and representative offices in Almaty, Dubai, Oslo, and Shanghai. Punjab National Bank is one of the Big Four banks of India, along with ICICI Bank, State Bank of India and HDFC Bank—its main competitors.

CORPORATE MISSION & VISION

Vision

"To be a Leading Global Bank with Pan India footprints and become a household brand in the Indo-Gangetic Plains providing entire range of financial products and services under one roof"

Mission

"Banking for the unbanked"

With over 60 million satisfied customers and more than 5100 offices including 5 overseas branches, PNB has continued to retain its leadership position amongst the nationalized banks. The bank enjoys strong fundamentals, large franchise value and good brand image. Besides being ranked as one of India's top service brands, PNB has remained fully committed to its guiding principles of sound and prudent banking. Apart from offering banking products, the bank has also entered the credit card, debit card; bullion business; life and non-life insurance; Gold coins & asset management business, etc. PNB has earned many awards and accolades during the year in appreciation of excellence in services, Corporate Social Responsibility (CSR) practices, transparent governance structure, best use of technology and good human resource management.

Bank always looked at technology as a key facilitator to provide better customer service and ensured that its 'IT strategy' follows the 'Business strategy' so as to arrive at "Best Fit". The Bank has made rapid strides in this direction. All branches of the Bank are under Core Banking Solution (CBS) since Dec'08, thus covering 100% of its business and providing 'Anytime Anywhere' banking facility to all customers including customers of more than 3200 rural & semi urban branches. The Bank has also been offering Internet banking services to its customers which also enables on line booking of rail tickets, payment of utilities bills, purchase of airline tickets, etc. Towards developing a cost effective alternative channels of delivery, the Bank with 5050 ATMs has the largest ATM network amongst Nationalized Banks. With the help of advanced technology, the Bank has been a frontrunner in the industry so far as the initiatives for Financial Inclusion is concerned. With its policy of inclusive growth, the Bank's mission is "Banking for Unbanked". The Bank has launched a drive for biometric smart card based technology enabled Financial Inclusion with the help of Business Correspondents/Business Facilitators (BC/BF) so as to reach out to the last mile customer. The Bank has started several innovative initiatives for marginal groups like rickshaw pullers, vegetable vendors, dairy farmers, construction workers, etc. Bank has launched a welfare scheme of adoption of village viz., "PNB VIKAS". Under the scheme, Bank has selected 117 villages (60 in lead districts and 57 in non lead district) in different circles for all-round improvement in the living standards of the villagers. Besides, Bank has formed "PNB PRERNA", an association of the wives of the Bank's senior management. The association through its voluntary initiatives has undertaken activities like distribution of food to the poor and needy, provision of computers, books, stationary items to poor girl students at various orphanages and schools etc. Backed by strong domestic performance, the Bank is planning to realize its global aspirations. Bank has opened one branch each at Kabul and Dubai, two branches at Hong Kong and an Off Shore Banking Unit at Mumbai. In addition to the above, Bank has Representative offices at Almaty, Dubai, Shanghai and Oslo, a wholly owned subsidiary in UK with 7 branches and a subsidiary each in Kazakhstan & Bhutan, and joint venture with Everest Bank Ltd. Nepal. During the year, Bank acquired majority equity stake of 63.64% in Dana Bank of Kazakhstan.

BANK'S BUSINESS

(Amt in Rs. Cr.)

Business Parameters[1]	31.03.10	31.03.11	26.08.11
Total Global Business	4,35,931	5,55,005	**5,48,979**
Global Deposits	2,49,330	3,12,899	**3,16,163**
Core Domestic Deposits (ex. IBDs)	1,93,898	2,23,801	**2,23,052**
CASA Share %	40.85%	38.45%	**35.43%**
Net Advances	1,86,601	2,42,106	**2,32,816**

Other Information[2]

Core Deposit:	Circles shown positive variation :	**41**
Credit:	Circles shown positive variation :	**27**

as on 12.08.2011[2]:

Deposits growth:	Banking system 18.4% ;	PNB **22.1%**
Net Bank Credit growth:	Banking system 20.2% ;	PNB **22.4%**

Technology initiatives of Punjab National Bank are:

- Alternate Delivery Channel Products including various types of Cards
- New Age payment and settlement mechanisms e.g. RTGS, NEFT,ECS, CTS etc.
- Other initiatives e.g. ASBA. Xpress money transfer, CMS, CRM.
- BCP Guidelines

PNB's IT set-up

As any other financial institution PNB also has a number of applications running on its network. The bank has plans to standardise all its platforms on UNIX operating system and RDBMS on Oracle. As far as the hardware platform is concerned, PNB has Sun Microsystems' Web servers at the data centre. For the Base 24 switch, they have gone in for Compaq Servers. Apart from this, they are also using RISC Servers, IBM and Xeon servers. PNB has around 500 servers across the country and around 13,000-15,000 PCs placed in different offices across the country. At some locations, the bank is still using DOS machines to run some of their ATMs.

Networking hardware: The bank is using Cisco products (routers, switches) at the data centre for networking hardware. It has around 100 routers and 8-10 switches across the country, mainly from Cisco. Initially TechNet was the network integrator for the bank. But, as the bank's requirements increased, it shifted to HCL Comnet to design and implement its network as HCL Comnet was better equipped to handle the load, says Bajwa.

Storage: Considering the size of its operations, PNB needs to have an effective storage system, but it doesn't have a centralised storage system yet. The data for all its 2,700 branches is still stored on PCs. But the bank is in the process of storing all its data on CD-ROMS by March 2003. It is also in the process of implementing a data warehousing solution called Ladders.

Through this solution, all the data from the branches will be sent to the corporate office through regional and zonal offices respectively. For this solution, PNB has opted for a Xeon server and UNIX operating system. National Institute of Bank Management (NIBM) has developed this solution for PNB.

Security: The bank already appointed IDRBT as its security consultant. IDRBT is in the process of creating documentation on the security set-up of the bank. PNB has hired Network Systems to implement the selected solution and is considering solutions like Firewall, Biometrics, PKI and is tendering for the same.

WAN: Today, the bank has a network of around 400 ATMs installed and this number is expected to grow very soon. All these ATMs are connected through a Base-24 switch from FSS. Recently, the bank has also decided to share its ATM network with other banks. So PNB's customers will be able to use other banks' ATMs and vice versa.

This will help the bank to increase the reach of its customers. For wide area connectivity of all its ATM machines, PNB has taken 160 VSATs from Comsat Max. Though hired, the VSATs are used exclusively by PNB.

PNB also has another network on INFINET, a financial network set up by RBI under which more than 800 VSATs are installed all over the country. PNB is using 60 VSATs as part of INFINET.

Benefits

One of the biggest benefits that the bank has derived out of IT has been the tremendous saving on recruitment front—the bank has not recruited more staff even while the business and work pressures have gone up five times. Consequently, PNB's profitability has also increased. To train users the bank has set up 14 computer training labs across the country.

Future

As part of its future roadmap the bank has lined up some interesting projects. This includes the launching of its debit cards. For its CRM initiatives the bank plans to set up a customer relationship centre, in addition to a virtual Internet branch. It is also thinking of setting up a videoconferencing system at 30 locations. It has already placed an order with Siemens Information Systems for the same.

To further strengthen its position in the industry, PNB has plans to set up PNB IIT (PNB Institute of Information Technology) in Lucknow. Apart from providing technical training to bankers, this autonomous body will also research and develop technical products for the banking industry.

SUGGESTIONS AND CONCLUSIONS

(a) Suggestions

1. Integration of core banking systems with common inter-bank payment systems such as NEFT and RTGS, in a straight through processing (STP) mode be made available

2. Approach towards centralisation in banks to facilitate customer relationship management (CRM) in a large scale and better MIS based decision making for the enterprise as a whole be looked into

3. (c) large scale electronification of payment processes should be catered to the Customers by the Banks This will be :

a. providing for adequate business continuity plans, including disaster recovery systems

b. giving greater importance on IS Audit;

c. give emphasis on risk management relating to outsourcing;

d. IT related requirements for ensuring time bound compliance to the needs for Basel II be stringent

4. This will help in large scale usage of standardized message based financial transaction processing;

(b) Conclusions

The Authors implicit from the Case analysis:

1. That it is a time that we launched ourselves in the next orbit and touch new heights of excellence in the performance and efficiency of the Banks.

2. Research & Development , Trainings , Consultancy and IT specific up gradation tools be implemented in Banking Industry

3. Precautions in terms of firewalls, data encryption , digital certification are some of the precautionary security measure which should be well embedded in the software used by the bank

4. ERP (enterprise resource planning) auto reconciliation for one to one fund transfer , bulk fund transfers , statements be generated at a nominal cost . The concept of E- CRM (Customer relationship Management) is the way forward to CBS .

5. Continuous quest for up gradation of skills, vision, mission and commitment to perform efficiently for profitability and productivity are some areas needing urgent attention.

6. The innovative technological products RTGS and NEFT have shwon tremendous progress over 2009 and 2010 and it is expected that this growth rate is further going to accelerate in coming years.

7. Major projects intended to be pursued would include implementing a new and feature rich RTGS system – The need to migrate to a new version of RTGS that could leverage on advancements in technology, Provide for scalability in volumes, parameterise more features in line with similar facilities available in other countries, result in more flexibility and reliabilty in operations, better liquidity saving features, etc., would be pursued.

8. E CRM – Effective,Analytical & Collabotaive CRM is to be implemented in light of Risk Management , advent of BasleIII. Data storage, Data Mining & warehousing about customers will model new customer characteristics implementing assess affinity to a product, service or message.

Thus against the backdrop of their success, RTGS, NEFT, Cheque Truncation, would make payment systems exceedingly quick. Bank customers will have a *Universal Account number and thus make the system flawless and scamless in the Vision 2020.

References & bibliography

1. Anarade, C "Banking products and services" in Indian institute of banking and Finance Mumbai
2. Gupta V, "Risks of E-banking in India" in E-Banking, the ICFAI university press, 2004.
3. Priyanka "Technology-Future in Banking" in banking in the new millennium by R.K.Uppal, Rimpi Kaur
4. Santhanakrishnan, M.S and Chetan, D "Information systems for banks" in Indian institute for banking and finance, Taxman publications
5. Toor, N.S "computer and banking" handbook of banking information, Skylark publications
6. Indian Banker, June 2007 Vol II No6 Indian Banks' Association Mumbai
7. Indian Banking 2010 Special issue 2004, vol 26 No I, IBA bulletin, IBA Mumbai
8. Elements of Mercantile Law by N D Kapoor – Sultan Chand & Sons, New Delhi, 2006, P – 353
9. Frauds in Banks by N Pitchandi and A Sivamurthy – The Indian Society of Criminology, Deptt of Pychology, University of Madras, Madras, 1984 – P-5
10. Banking Law and Practice by P N Varshney, Sultan Chand & Sons, New Delhi
11. Banking Frontiers, July, 2005
12. Avasthi G P M (2000 - 01), "Information Technology in Banking: Challenges for Regulators", Prajnan, Vol. XXIX, No. 4, pp. 3 – 17
13. Eapen P G (2000), "Automated Teller Machines – Security Issues", IBA Bulletin, Vol. XXII, No. 9 (September), pp. 23 – 26
14. Murali S., "Ombudsman Scheme - 2006", The Indian Banker, Volume 1, No. 10
15. Jain Sudhir, "Fraudulent Encashment – Impact and Safeguards", The Indian Banker, Vol. 3 No. 3
16. Uppal R.K., "Customer Perception of E – Banking Services of Indian Banks: Some Survey Evidence", The ICFAI Journal of Bank Management, Vol. VII No.10
17. Shanti S (1984), Customer Services in Banks, Himalaya Publishing House, Bombay
18. Pathrose P P (2001), "Hi Tech. Banking Prospects and Problem", IBA Bulletin, Vol. XXIII, No. 7 (July)
19. Kulkarni R V (2000), "Changing Face of Banking from Brick and Mortar Banking to E - Banking", IBA Bulletin (January)
20. Metzer S R (2000), Strategic Planning for Future Bank growth", The Banker's Magazone (July - August), pp. 57 – 65

6

The Journey of Leadership From Anna Hazare to 'Hazar Anna'— A Case – Study on Leadership

Ms. Hema Mirji
Bharati Vidyapeeth University
Institute of Management & Entrepreneurship Development, Pune
bab_hema@yahoo.com

Keywords:

Anna : a term used for describing the person or ideology who is against corruption.

Hazar Anna : a term used for describing the growth of ideology of anti – corruption.

In 1962, despite not meeting the physical requirements, 25-year-old Hazare was selected, as emergency recruited Indian Army. During the Indo-Pakistani War of 1965, Hazare was posted at the Indo-Pak border. On 12 November 1965, he was the only survivor of a convoy when Pakistan launched air attacks on Indian bases. This led him to dwell on the purpose and meaning of life and death. In 1978 Hazare went to his native village Ralegan Siddhi which was one of the many villages of India plagued by acute poverty, deprivation, a fragile ecosystem, negligence, and hopelessness. He reinforced the normative principles of human development – equity, efficiency, sustainability and made remarkable economic, social and community regeneration in the village without any inputs of industrialization and technology-oriented agriculture.

Haraze identified the key problem among villagers is alcoholism. He understood that without solving the problem of the menace of alcoholism, no effective and sustainable reform would be successful in the village. He justified the punishment like mother administers bitter medicines to a sick child as she cares for the child. He successfully used the system of Gram Panchayat, Gram

Sabha (Village meeting) as a platform for collective decision making process to discuss the issues relating to the welfare of the village. All these decisions were taken in a simple majority consensus. The decision of the Gram Sabha was accepted as final decision. Using the collective decision platform, Hazare made many decisions like bans on alcohol, bans on cutting tree, bans on drugs, etc. He also started some unique concepts like, Grain Bank, with the objective of providing food security to needful farmers during times of drought or crop failure. Rich farmers, or those with surplus grain production, could donate a quintal to the bank. Farmers could borrow the grain when they need but have to return the same amount of grain they borrowed, plus an additional quintal as an interest.Starting with small project, he solved many bigger problems in the village like water scarcity and made irritation possible. He persuaded the villagers to construct a watershed embankment to stop water and allow it to use for agriculture and increase the ground water level.

In 1991 Hazare launched the People's Movement against Corruption, a popular movement to fight against corruption in the village, Ralegaon Siddhi against 40 forest officials and timber merchants. This protest resulted in the transfer and suspension of these officials. In May 1997 Hazare protested against alleged malpractices in the purchase of powerlooms by the Governor of Maharashtra. He was arrested in this movement and was released on later. In 2003 Hazare raised corruption charges against four ministers of the government. He started his fast until death on 9 August 2003 and ended his fast on 17 August 2003 after then chief minister formed a one-man commission to probe his charges. The commission report forced the ministered to resign from the cabinet in March 2005.

In the early 2000s Hazare led a movement in Maharashtra state which forced the state government to pass a stronger Maharashtra Right to Information Act as he believe all corruption can end only if there is freedom of information. He also opposed the government's policy to promote making liquor from food grains in Maharashtra, argued the government that Maharashtra is a food-deficit State and there was shortage of food grains and it is not logical to promote producing liquor from food grains.

In 2011, Hazare initiated a Satyagraha (Fasting for a nobel cause) movement for passing a stronger anti-corruption Lokpal (ombudsman) bill in the Indian Parliament as conceived in the Jan Lokpal Bill (People's Ombudsman Bill). The bill is for a stronger anti-corruption bill with stronger penal actions and more independence to the ombudsmen in the states. He started hunger strike when the demand was rejected by Indian government. The movement attracted attention in the media, millions of supporters inside and outside of India, and also identified one of popular movements in India after independence. People also supported through Internet social media such as Twitter and Facebook. Online Signature Campaigns like avaaz got more than 10 lakh signatures in just 36 hours. The middle class people and the youth power were participating voluntarily in this movement. The demand was propagated as a nation-wide general demand against corruption. In this movement he was arrested and didn't compromise with his ideology of nonviolence by protesting against violent movement of his supporters. He became from a well-acclaimed social activist to the most powerful influencer and visionary leader of modern India.

Questions

1. Describe the Leadership style of Anna Hazare.
2. Explain the characteristics of his leadership movements.
3. Explain why is Anna Hazare successful.

References:

1. "Moving the masses Anna's way". *The Hindu Business Line*., 19 July 2011
2. Wikipedia.org, "Anna Hazare"
3. Dynamics of rural development: lessons from Ralegan Siddhi Publisher- Foundation for Research in Community Health, 2002. Original from The University of Michigan. Digitized 21 Jul 2009

7

The Plight of Setup and Transition Function of Managed Services in Nokia Siemens Networks, India - Challenges and Opportunities

Ms. Hilsa Mishra
Faculty-IT, New Delhi Institute of Management
hilsathestar@gmail.com

Ms. Abha Grover
Assistant Professor, New Delhi Institute of Management,
groverabha@yahoo.co.in

Abstract

Nokia Siemens Network (NSN), the world's leading managed services provider is facing tough time in India due to disagreements and conflicts in one of its most important functions of Setup and Transition. The case in point deals with the various challenges faced and strategies undertaken by the protagonist Tarun who has taken up the role of MS Setup and Transition manager. The case portrays his dilemma of loosing his line manager time and again because of their conflicts and disconnect with the top management. The case sees leadership, foresight and vision at the top as the vital elements of a function and also that of the organization on the whole. The point put forth is that its high time a few bold steps are taken that can revamp the company's future.

Keywords: Setup and Transition , leadership, vision, conflict.

Case study

Nokia the leader in mobile device market and Siemens a German engineering conglomerate largest of its kind in Europe merged together in 2007 aiming at making both companies bigger players in fixed-mobile convergence (FMC) market, where consumers use a single device to make calls over both mobile and landline networks. The combined company will also allow the pair to offer play services of TV, broadband access, fixed and mobile telecoms. This joint venture primarily aimed at fighting the key competitions in the market like the telecom leader Ericsson, Alcatel-Lucent and Chinese vendors like Huawei and ZTE and also to enable them to fight global price pressures.

One of the results of this union was their becoming one of the key players in providing Managed Services which became very popular in the last decade. Facing increasing competition and commoditization from traditional telecom products, service providers like Nokia Siemens Networks along with Ericsson which first introduced the concept in 2003 and Huawei etc. moved to next generation, converged, network infrastructures in order to offer new, revenue-generating services. Making this transformation can be complex and difficult. However, if done correctly, working with a managed services provider and outsourcing all or part of the next generation network planning, implementation and management, the transition to the new infrastructure can occur quickly and efficiently and with reduced risk. Managed Services on the whole includes functions like Network planning and optimization, Network operations, Network implementation, technical support and Setup and Transition.

The key reason for managed services market growth in India is not just cost savings, but the use of managed services as a business optimization and growth driver. Another key reason for adoption of managed services over strategic outsourcing is access to best of breed services without the fear of losing control of IT. Managed services provide opportunities for enterprises to focus on their core business competencies while leaving day-to-day IT operations to a third-party service provider. Also, enterprises gain access to high-quality, expert support and best-of-breed management tools with a minimum investment.

Changing market trends, increasing customer expectations and ever-fiercer competition are challenging businesses as we know it. Communications Service Providers (CSPs) are looking at newer ways to improve operational performance and the customer experience. Doing this while exploiting new growth opportunities can, however, be complicated. And this is exactly where the third-party experts enter to take the ownership of all your troubles make life seem easier. Their focus is to make operations simpler for the companies. When we see at the new age businesses in Telecom it can be believed that those communications service providers who focus on their core activities to provide a superior service experience, increase the customer base and service usage will build the most valuable customer relationships in the market. Managed Services helps them to do just that. The service providers can take responsibility for the quality and efficiency of their networks and processes so that they can better concentrate on your customers.

The Nokia Siemens Networks in the core believes that the key to delivering results is our ability to combine customer focus, delivery excellence and the most competitive operations. Their consultants work on finding a solution for Communications Service Provider's (CSP) challenges. Our deployment backbone – the Global Service Delivery framework – will then be utilized to provide the best in people, processes and technology – in that order. They take responsibility for the results. Networks and services enable your business. They can help the company in need in optimizing both. They can enhance your operational efficiency by managing the network or enhancing the customers' experience by ensuring the quality of your services.

This Hi-tech era was in its full bloom when Tarun Basu one of the brightest and dynamic Telecom Professionals was appointed as MS-Setup and Transition Manager in Nokia Siemens Networks Ltd., Gurgaon, India. He joined under the very talented and one of the senior most professionals in the Telecom Industry Mr. Rajeev Sharma who was heading the Managed Services. Rajeev was also new to the system as he joined just 11 months back and was still getting accustomed to the new organization. In his study he learned that there were some flaws in the system and ways of working could be improved. In his long career he had seen it all and was certainly well versed with the best practices in the industry.

Rajeev noticed that the framework was very much there. But due to lack of commitment by the Top management, the systems and processes did not reach to the implementation level in the true sense. Also he could see that there was a person dependency in the system. So when the personnel in question left the organization, the programs, ways of working and the vision changed with the change in the leader.

Rajeev being an action oriented leader, wanted to align to global processes, apply best practices to the MS Domain, and bring synergy and overall efficiency in the productivity of people and system of managed services. Even after having repeated meetings with them, the Top management did not appreciate his approach and seeing no encouragement and buy-in from the Top management on his plans which could shape the better future of MS, he decided to quit.

Immediately after his resignation the grapevine started flowing in the organization, about his conflict and difference of opinion with the organization which was not known to any body till that time. And this had shaken the confidence of many employees in the management very badly as Rajeev was very popular because of his stature and experience, he was a person whom everybody looked up to.

Tarun was shaken by the sudden exit of his manager and dream leader in a jiffy. And gave him a call to seek guidance and understand the impending situation, in the evening."Hello Sir, How are you?" he said. Rajeev replied"I am fine Tarun. You tell me. How have you been?" Tarun replied "Sir, I am shocked by your leaving the organization. And I have no clue what lies ahead. You have left me completely perplexed"."My dear boy", Rajeev said," I could see this coming since long, but was hoping against hopes and this was the reason I could not give you any hint about what my decision eventually would be." "But Sir, this is the most extreme step. What made you plan this?" Rajeev took a pause and went into deep thinking mode. After a while he said "Tarun, in due course of time I have realized that there has been a big disconnect between my thinking process and vision and that of the company management. I tried to fill the gap with more and more communication, but all seems to be in vain. My efforts, plans and recommendations were not being acknowledged. And I was not getting the *go ahead* for some key programs. I waited for things to improve but eventually I realized that the gap can not be filled since the top management was adamant on their look out. It was clear that we were not made for each other. As you know my dear friend an alliance has no point if it is not mutually beneficial, it has to break sooner or later."

Tarun was quiet and reviewed the whole situation again and again. He could not sleep that night because of the stress of being on his own without his guiding star, his mentor and philosopher.

Rajeev had joined with so much of energy and was heading the function with such a great level of enthusiasm that people were looking for changes in organization tools and systems which were not proficient enough when today's dynamic market was taken into consideration. They had to stick to the older system which lacked efficiency, vision, and had duplicacy and overlapping of roles and non-uniform ways of working across regions and circles and customer teams. The employees are disturbed demotivated, waiting for things to get cleared and see a new ray of hope. The same applied to Tarun as well just that he could feel the loss more as he was directly affected as Rajeev was his line manager and source of immense motivation and learning.

The thought of leaving the organization occurred to Tarun as well but he could not as he had completed only 8 months time in the coveted company and he was reluctant to ruin his CV because it obviously sends a wrong message to an employer and is definitely a question on one's credibility. Therefore he kept waiting for some one to take Rajeev's place. Weeks passed as it was not easy to get a substitute of such calibre. Finally the day came when Karan Grover, another senior professional heading operation from NSN itself took the position of Head Managed Services, through internal transfer.

Tarun pepped himself up as he waited outside Karan's cabin to see him. "Come in Tarun" said Karan. "Good morning Sir" said Tarun. Karan took the updates of projects and programmes undertaken by the Managed Services function from Tarun. After patiently listening to him, Karan said "Tarun I am indeed lucky to have dynamic, sharp and experienced professionals like you in the key role in my team". Tarun said "Thank you very much Sir. I look forward to achieve excellence in what we, as a function set out to do. I hope our association will prove to be fruitful to everybody associated. Sir please share your vision regarding the same". He said "We will establish this function like never before and a highly experienced person should lead this. You should be the person coming and telling me the need future business. Your role will be highly distinct I promise". A wave of motivation filled Tarun's heart and he again became hopeful about his work life.

He immediately got the assignment for the setup of managed services delivery organization in four telecom circles for the tier-1 operator Idea Cellular's 3G network. In next two months time he had to understand the scope of work from the signed MS contract, which was unique in nature as NSN had to operate in supervisory mode only and NSN was supposed to provide On-the-Job Training (OJT) to Idea Cellular's technical staff in next one year's time to enable them to manage the newly launched 3G technology.

Meanwhile Karan appointed George Mathew from the Vodafone account from NSN itself as Head of MS-Setup and Transition who further gave visibility of this function to the whole organization.

Things were looking perfect for Tarun when one fine morning he got a call from George .He was sounding grim. He said "Tarun, There's a bad news for us. Karan has left the company. After a pause he continued, "It is said that he was made to leave as a result of some heated argument with the top management." "Sir did you talk to him" asked Tarun. George said "Not yet. He is too upset to talk right now". Tarun drove to office, still thinking about the conversation he had with George and once again found himself being insecure and sceptical about the future.

Tarun had no choice but to wait for the situations to improve. Meanwhile he was assigned few Non technical projects purely related to resources on-boarding and allocation. These were General management projects not at all appropriate for the expertise and technical prowess of a candidate like him. This added to his dissatisfaction. And he was not at all happy about how the function was shaping up.

He got a call from George to see him. George said "Karan has left and now we have to wait and watch till the time a new MS Head takes command." Tarun said "Sir, Why is this gap and conflicts between the various MS Heads and the Top management persistent since so long?" George gave it a thought and said "As I can see it's a leadership issue. People at the top are not aggressive, they don't have the right business mindsets, have lack of competitor analysis, and they are not following the best practices in the industry. And this might lead to very serious consequences. I am afraid. Apart from this, the costing of the managed services is also an issue because it is not appropriate and well-planned and therefore achieving the target gross margins is becoming highly challenging."

Tarun wonders on the insight given by George. And weighs options of leaving the reputed organization and the coveted role he joined with so much of excitement and the alternative of staying back and wait for the things to work out and streamline on their own. He is on the cross-roads again and has no clue, which way to choose.

The Plight of Setup and Transition Function of Managed Services in Nokia Siemens Networks, India - Challenges and Opportunities

Teaching Note

This teaching note was written by Prof. Hilsa Mishra, New Delhi Institute of Management, and Prof. Abha Grover, New Delhi Institute of Management. It was prepared to accompany the case 'The Onset of 3G Technology for the Idea Network implemented by the Nokia Siemens Networks Ltd. in Uttar Pradesh - Challenges and Opportunities'. The case was made possible by the Managed services department of the coveted company Nokia Siemens Networks Ltd.

1. Abstract

Nokia Siemens Network (NSN), the world's leading managed services provider is facing tough time in India due to disagreements and conflicts in one of its most important functions of

Setup and Transition. The case in point deals with the various challenges faced and strategies undertaken by the protagonist Tarun who has taken up the role of MS Setup and Transition manager. The case portrays his dilemma of loosing his line manager time and again because of their conflicts and disconnect with the top management. The case sees leadership, foresight and vision at the top as the vital elements of a function and also that of the organization on the whole. The point put forth is that its high time a few bold steps are taken that can revamp the company's future. The case highlights the foresight and deep analytical skills and patience of the Setup and transition manager which help him withstand turbulent times. The case also emphasizes on the fact that talented professionals must be valued and retained leaving no stone unturned as they are the ones who write the company's future. The case uses third person storytelling narration in the introductory part and the main problem is highlighted through dialogue form narration.

2. Teaching Objective and Target Audience

The case deals with the requirement of understanding and analyzing the situation and getting to the root of what an employee goes through when the person he reports to leaves his job, leaving him at cross roads absolutely clueless about future prospects. The objective is to make the users of the case aware of the problems encountered when different people with varied mindsets come together to setup a new business with apparently meager resources amidst cut-throat competition. The case highlights the strategies undertaken by the Setup and Transition manager to deal with the serious survival issues. Thus providing opportunity to the case users to use their wits to the fullest. The case can also be used for teaching the above concepts to executives and postgraduate management students for individual analysis and small group discussion.

3. Teaching Approach and Strategy

The case and the references should be provided to the executives and the students one day prior to the discussion for individual analysis and write up. Next day the case should be discussed among a small group. The outcome of the small group discussion should be presented in front of the whole batch by representative of each group and in order to evaluate each option in detail.

4. Analysis

The case does not have any quantitative data and should be analyzed using SWOT analysis method. Some part of the case has been written in dialogue form and is therefore suitable for role play. The case is suitable for written assessment or examination and oral presentations.

5. Bibliography

http://www.nokiasiemensnetworks.com/portfolio/services/managed services

6. Feedback

The case has been tested in the MBA class. Most of the students identified the problems correctly and were able to develop alternatives that the organization could follow in a scenario

depicted in the case. The case was also able to generate lot of arguments in favor and against the alternatives suggested by individual participants. In all, the case was found to be suitable for individual write up and small group discussion. The intra-group and inter-group analyses were also lively and added a number of new ideas. Therefore, individual analysis and discussions should be followed by intra-group and inter-group discussions to get maximum learning benefits for the participants.

Questions:

1. **What will be your strategy and modus operandy if you happen to be at Tarun's place?**
2. **"Failing to Plan is planning to fail." Justify the statement keeping the case in perspective.**
3. **Human resource is the most important resource of an organization. And when talented personnel leave the motivation levels of the other employees is badly hit.Comment.**

8

HR Implications in Lenovo's Take Over of IBM PCs: A Case Study

Mr. Indranil Mutsuddi
Acharya Institute of Management & Sciences, Bangalore
indranilmutsuddi@yahoo.com

Abstract

Uncertainty in the fast changing business scenario tends to lead to buy-outs and mergers and acquisitions. Companies are thereby trying to improve their competitive positions by paying more attention to opportunities in the market that could be leveraged through mergers and acquisitions. These have facilitated organizations to streamline complex operations, challenge competitors, foster innovation and higher technological capabilities, deal with other complexities and contingencies in the business environment by turning two organizations into one. The given case illustrates the Lenovo's acquisition of IBM PCs and makes an attempt to involve readers and students in order to understand the strategic dynamics of the acquisition process and the HR issues underlying the same. The case also invites its readers to analyze Lenovo in the present scenario where reports on the organization's performance had not been overwhelming according to the expectations of business experts.

Key Words: Lenovo, IBM PCs, Acquisition, Cultural Integration, Integration

HR IMPLICATIONS IN LENOVO'S TAKEOVER OF IBM PCS: A CASE STUDY

Introduction

There has been an unprecedented growth in the numbers of mergers and acquisitions that took place (or were announced) in last calendar year. The total number of M&A deals announced during the year 2007 rose up to 661 with a total announced value of $51.17 billion as compared to 2006 in which only 480 such deals took place. Sectors like steel, telecom and aviation witnessed amalgamation of big brands and thus, was clear leaders in sectoral values. With such a whooping number of M&As taking place every year, some concerns of employees also rise apparently. One such case attracting tremendous attention in terms of both strategic management and HR perspectives has been Lenovo's takeover of IBM PCs.

Lenovo's takeover of IBM PCs

Lenovo, the reputed Chinese computer company now in charge of IBM's legendary PC business said it will waste no time in proving itself in the global marketplace. In a statement released recently, Lenovo Group said it has completed its $1.25 billion acquisition of IBM's (Quote) "Think" brand, including its ThinkPad laptops, ThinkCentre desktop PCs, ThinkVantage software tools and ThinkVision monitors.

On December 7, 2004, IBM signed an agreement to sell its Personal Computing Division (a division of the Personal Systems Group segment) to Lenovo Group Limited. Lenovo according to the deal will acquire substantially all the assets and assume certain liabilities of the Personal Computing Division. Under the terms of the agreement, IBM will receive consideration at closing in the form of cash and equity in Lenovo Group. IBM, as part of the agreement, retained the right and will be given a preference to provide maintenance, warranty and financing services to Lenovo Group. In addition, IBM had agreed to provide certain agreed to transition services to Lenovo Group. This transaction is expected to close in the second quarter of 2005 (IBM, Annual Report, 2004).

"This acquisition will allow Chinese industry to make significant inroads on its path to globalization," Lenovo chairman Liu Chuanzhi said at a media conference. The acquisition, according to industry experts, has been described remarkable as it has been predicted to change the structure of the global PC manufacturing business. Lenovo as a part of the deal would take over IBM's desktop PC business, including research, development and manufacturing for $1.25 billion in cash and shares, while IBM will retain a 18.9 percent stake. Lenovo had also agreed to take on liabilities that raise the total value of the deal for IBM to $1.75 billion (Anonymous, 2004).

While Lenovo commands one-third of the Chinese marketplace, it is now considered third in the worldwide PC business behind market leader Dell (Quote) and HP (Quote). According to a recent report by US consulting firm IDC, Lenovo had a 17.8 percent PC market share in Asia, excluding Japan, in the first quarter of 2007, compared with 16.8 percent a year earlier. HP had a 15.4 percent share, followed by Dell, with 8.1 percent. Analysts said the result beat their expectations (Liu, L., 2007).

Lenovo's strengths from the Acquisition

According to the Lenovo top management the company is well-positioned, with competitive strengths in branding, world-class scale and industry-leading efficiency. The company firmly believed that, Lenovo's leading R&D and product differentiation capabilities, experienced management team and global distribution network — through this unique alliance with IBM – would give the organization a powerful competitive position in global markets. (Exhibit 1)

The new Lenovo: Post Acquisition picture

The new Lenovo would be expecting a worldwide workforce of more than 19,000 people who seem to be elated with the deal. As a leading global business, the new Lenovo will have facilities, operations and people located around the world, with sales offices in every corners of the globe. According to an announcement by the management of IBM, post acquisition the worldwide headquarters will be in New York, with principal operations in Beijing and Raleigh, North Carolina. Worldwide research and development will be led out of the Raleigh location, with additional research centers in China and Japan. Other centers of business activity are located throughout Europe and Latin America (IBM, 2004).

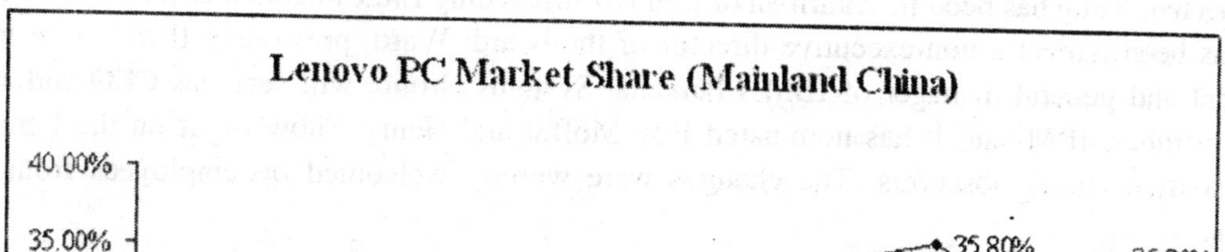

Fig 1: Lenovo PC Market Share (Mainland China)

Note: Calendar year 2004-2006, results before acquisition reflect combined shares of Lenovo and IBM PCD,

Source: Market share is based on industry and company estimates (www.pc.ibm.com/ww/lenovo/2006annualpopup.html)

"The closing of this transaction is an historic event for Lenovo and marks a new era for the global PC industry," Yuanqing Yang, Lenovo chairman of the board, said in a statement. "The new Lenovo's strategy would be based on what our customers want: high-quality products and world-class service." Although the market share of Lenovo came down in early 2005 it slowly picked up post acquisition with the organization gradually consolidating its business (Fig 1).

Lenovo executives further believed that due to this M&A, the quickest path to transitioning IBM's "Think brand" lines to Lenovo would come through their procurement and marketing expenses as well as expanding to new markets. The new Lenovo would have combined annual PC revenue of approximately $13 billion and volume of approximately 14 million units.

"We expect to capture synergies starting today through leveraging the complementary nature of Lenovo and PCD's customer bases, product offerings and geographic coverage while utilizing Lenovo's highly sophisticated operating platforms," the top management of Lenovo said in a statement to the media.

The Changes in Top management

As part of the acquisition announcement, Lenovo firmed up its executive management team. As expected, Yang has become chairman of Lenovo succeeding Liu Chuanzhi, Lenovo's founder, who has been named a non-executive director of the board. Ward, previously IBM senior vice president and general manager of IBM's Personal Systems Group, will serve as CEO and as a board member. IBM said it has nominated Bob Moffat and Henry Chow to sit on the Lenovo board as non-voting observers. The changes were warmly welcomed by employees from all corners.

Which employees of IBM would be affected?

- There are approximately 10,000 IBM regular and supplemental employees globally whose employment would transfer to the new Lenovo. Excluded from this transfer would be those who are approved for and receiving benefits under the Medical Disability Income Plan (MDIP) and the Long Term Disability (LTD) Plan at closing. Those employees currently on pre-retirement bridge leaves of absence would also also excluded.
- All employees who are part of IBM.s Personal Computing Division (PCD) and whose primary work responsibility is in support of the PCD mission/business.
- Employees in other IBM business units whose primary work responsibility is in support of the PCD mission/business.
- Additional employees deemed necessary to meet the new Lenovo requirements may be selected based upon business need and an assessment of their current job responsibilities.
- Employees defined above who are receiving benefits under the IBM Sickness and Accident Income Plan as well as those on leave of absence will also become employees of the new Lenovo.

New employment terms & conditions

Accordingly, Lenovo will maintain compensation and benefits that are comparable in value in the aggregate to those currently offered by IBM. This guarantee will be extended at least through the end of 2007 and perhaps beyond. This commitment to maintain comparable compensation and benefit value is intended to reassure employees making the transition to the new Lenovo about the level of the company's investment in its human resources and in the future strength of the business.

In the U.S, this means that at the time employees join the new Lenovo, their base salaries will remain the same, and performance bonus opportunity and sales commission plans will provide a substantially similar opportunity. The new Lenovo will also offer comprehensive retirement and health benefits that are comparable to current IBM programs. Generally, IBM employees who join the new Lenovo will receive service credit for benefit purposes. The new Lenovo employees can expect continued professional growth and challenge, along with the opportunity to participate in a new and expanding business venture. Lenovo and IBM are committed to making this a smooth transition that minimizes personal disruptions and loss of work productivity.

Issues related to organizational changes

As the two company structures are highly complementary, industry experts have commented that there could be the need for rebalancing the new organization and its structure would be minimal. If resource reductions are foreseen, Lenovo had agreed to provide affected employees with severance benefits equal to those provided by IBM, with service credit for employment with both IBM and the new Lenovo. But in the case of the new Lenovo, things are different from the usual merger situation, since in this case this is an acquisition of an already lean division which will take over much of the management duties for the new parent. So the typical overlap that would generate layoffs, for the most part, would not exist in the Lenovo's acquisition of IBM. And given that Lenovo is using the acquisition to move into additional markets, a staffing uplift is part of its strategic goal of business expansion and the end result could well be more akin to a mass hiring than it is a typical merger (Barry Zellen, 2005)

Compensation and Benefits

Lenovo has agreed that at the time an employee joins the new Lenovo, base salary would remain the same, and current performance bonus targets would be initially maintained for the first year, with new targets established for the new Lenovo thereafter. Incentive and sales commission plans would provide a substantially similar opportunity, with targets based on the objectives of the new Lenovo. Lenovo has also agreed to maintain the same compensation concepts that IBM has used, with key measurements tied to the new Lenovo's business performance and success.

Lenovo had also agreed to offer an overall package of benefits that is comparable in value in the aggregate to the current IBM program. Special provisions and a five-year guarantee apply to pension and savings benefits, as follows:

Prior retirement formula under the IBM Personal Pension Plan (Prior Plan): The new

Lenovo would deliver comparable pension benefits to Prior Plan participants through a new pension plan (the new Lenovo Pension Plan) that would be established by the new Lenovo.

Personal Pension Account (cash balance) formula under IBM Personal Pension Plan: The new Lenovo would deliver comparable benefits to Personal Pension Account participants through a defined contribution plan (the new Lenovo Defined Contribution Plan).

Match with IBM Savings Plan: Lenovo had indicated an intent to continue the current IBM Savings Plan.

Health benefits: Regarding this aspect, the new Lenovo employees would have immediate access to a comprehensive program of health benefits coverage, with no exclusions or pre-existing condition limitations other than those currently found in IBM.s plans. Participants will receive credit for amounts applied to 2005 deductibles, if any.

Share option schemes for employees and executives

The Old Share Option Scheme at Lenovo was adopted on 18th January 1994 and was terminated on 26th April 2002. The Old Share Option Scheme was designed to provide qualified employees with appropriate incentives linked to share ownership. Only employees, including directors, of the Group could participate in the Old Option Scheme. This scheme was replaced by a new scheme in March 2004. As at 31st March 2004, the maximum number of shares available for issue under the New Option Scheme was 563,081,810, representing approximately 7.5% of the issued share capital of the Company. The maximum number of shares issued and to be issued upon exercise of share options granted to each qualified participant (including both exercised and outstanding options) in any 12-month period up to the date of grant shall not exceed 1% of the shares of the Company in issue (IBM Annual Report, 2004). The new share option schemes were definitely meant to engage employees and executives during the post acquisition scenario.

HR lessons learnt

The success of M&A always depends on the how well the HR issues are managed after the merger takes place. HR issues that formed the cornerstone of the success of Lenovo's acquisition of IBM PCs can be as follows:

Engaging employees: The uncertainties created in Lenovo's acquisition had been efficiently been dealt by the management of both the companies. Particularly the management of IBM had been successful to clarify all the doubts and contingencies and preventing the shift of focus of its employees from productive work to issues related to interpersonal conflicts, layoffs, career growth with the acquirer Company (Lenovo), compensation, etc. Moreover, employees at IBM were reported to be concerned with how well they will go with new colleagues.

Cultural Integration: This perhaps had been the greatest challenge ably managed by both IBM and Lenovo. The management of the new Lenovo were been able to clearly define the factors influencing the cultural integration prior and post acquisition. The organization conducted several orientation sessions to orient the new members in the organization's culture, norms and values. Although Lenovo followed a well disciplined and highly routinized work environment

(Company song, strict time and attendance monitoring etc) as compared to the free environment at IBM (Exhibit 6 and 7) where diversity is valued and managed effectively, yet the senior executives of both the organizations were instrumental in creating conducive environment in the new organization to address diversity and use it to the best for the organization's success.

Employee communication: Both IBM and Lenovo were good enough to emphasize on maintaining a constant and clear communication between the employees at all levels and the top management before, during and post amalgamation of the new organization. The top management made it sure every time that messages and information were openly shared at all levels and this really enhanced the effectiveness of the acquisition that could have been a challenging perspective for any other organization.

Solidification and Post integration: Clearly after the evolution of the new Lenovo, a new entity of an organization was defined and most importantly what went in favor of the acquisition was the ability of the top management to define, clarify the boundaries and integration related dimensions. These initiatives involved:

- Meddling two cultures need assessment, fine-tuning and implementing the change
- Role of the top management as a change facilitator
- Revising the new model with constant feedback and communication
- Deciding the leaders who are going to chalk out the culture of the new entity

The present scenario

The new Lenovo had indicated that International Assignees would continue in their current assignments until they are completed, and that the terms and conditions currently in place would continue for the assigned duration of the international assignment. The company moved its headquarters to Raleigh, North Carolina, after taking over IBM's PC unit in 2005. PC sales in China, the world's second-biggest market, account for 36 percent of Lenovo's total revenue and are expected to rise 21 percent to $19 billion this year (Liu, L, 2007).

Yet inspite of these remarkable achievements, things seem to be really challenging for Lenovo. The company had been reported to be struggling in order to improve its balance sheet since taking over IBM's PC arm, returned to profit in the fourth fiscal quarter. The world's third-biggest PC maker posted a net profit of $161 million for 2006-2007 fiscal year, a strong year-on-year increase of 625 percent. Full-year revenue was $14.6 billion, up by 10 percent. The company's net income was $60 million in the three months ended on March 31, compared with a $116 million loss a year earlier, which included $70 million expenditure in internal restructuring. Although Its worldwide PC shipments grew more than 17 percent, well ahead of the industry average of approximately 11 percent, helping it eat into the market share of Hewlett-Packard and Dell in Asia.

Conclusion

Market reports (Jane Spencer, 2008) have indicated that post acquisition Lenovo's computer shipments rose 8 percent in the third quarter, but its growth was eclipsed by the overall market, which grew nearly twice as fast. That left Lenovo's global market share at 7.3 percent, down from 7.8 percent a year ago, according to research firm Gartner. Analysts have scaled back their expectations for Lenovo, which reports its quarterly earnings Thursday. Morgan Stanley, for example, expects a weak quarter and projects Lenovo's net income will fall 20 percent in the current fiscal year, the first year of decline since the IBM PC acquisition, which was completed in May 2005.

The new Lenovo and its HR policies are expected to reap rich dividends for the organization in its future performance. But to what extent it would be effective in the present economic downturn would well be worth watching for most academicians and management experts.

Questions for analysis

1. Discuss the strategic and HR challenges associated with this take over?
2. What factors do you think had ensured effective amalgamation of these two organizations?

References

Anonymous, (2004): "IBM sells PC business to China's Lenovo", Economic Times, December 8th, 2004, http://www.msnbc.msn.com/id/6666170/

Barry Zellen (2005): "IBM/Lenovo Deal Presents Fewer Integration Risks Than Skeptics Fear", http://wirelessinnovator.com/index.php?articleID=4827&sectionID=45

IBM (2004): "IBM Human Resources Transition Questions & Answers", http://www.allianceibm.org/hr_us_qa.pdf

IBM Annual Report (2004), http://www.ibm.com/annualreport/2004/

Jane Spencer, (2008): "Lenovo's global ambitions take a hit", http://www.charlotteobserver.com/business/story/299477.html

Lenovo Financial Highlights (2003-2004), http://www.pc.ibm.com/ww/lenovo/2004annualpopup.html

Liu, L, (2007): "Lenovo back in the black in Q4", http://www2.chinadaily.com.cn/bizchina/2007-05/24/content_879737.htm

Mutsuddi, I, Mutsuddi, R., (2008): "Has the growth of Indian conglomerates been a threat to foreign multinationals", ICFAI Journal of marketing management, Vol: VII, No: 3, August 2008, pp: 52-53.

Exhibit 1: The Lenovo SWOT Analysis *(Mutsuddi et al, 2008)*

Strengths:

- National Image (China)
- Knowledge about the local market
- Strong R&D
- Mass manufacturing capability
- Quick responsiveness

- Government policies in favour of Industry includes infrastructure development, reduction in excise duty
- Capability of integrating the overseas operations

Weaknesses:

- Little knowledge about Indian market
- Poor brand perception (global)
- No pure electronics sales
- Low inventory turnover
- After sales services are not adequate
- Limited knowledge of global market

Opportunities:

- Import barrier
- Increasing global demand
- Internet boom
- Growing wireless PC/Notepad/Thinkpad/Laptop market
- Government association

Threats:

- Heavy competition from global counterparts
- Industry reaching maturity
- Software piracy and clone market in China
- Little firm's growth

Exhibit 2: Snapshots of IBM Annual Report (2003-2004)

Courtesy: http://www.ibm.com/annualreport/2004/

For the year ended December 31st	2004	2003	Yr to yr % margin change
Revenue	$ 96,293	$ 89,131	8%*
Gross Profit Margin	37.4%	37.0%	0.4 points
Total expense and other income	$ 24,004	$ 22,144	8.4%
Total expense and other income to Revenue Ratio	24.9%	24.8%	0.1 points
Provision for taxes	$ 3,580	$ 3,261	9.8%
Income from continuing operations	$ 8,448	$ 7,613	11.0%
EPS from continuing operations:			
Diluted	$ 4.94	$ 4.34	13.8%
Basic	$ 5.04	$ 4.42	14.0%
Weighted-average shares outstanding:			
Diluted	1708.9	1756.1	(2.5%)
Basic	1675	1721.6	(2.7%)
Assets	$ 1,09,183	$ 1,04,457	4.5%
Liabilities	$ 79,436	$ 76,593	3.7%
Equity	$ 29,747	$ 27,864	6.8%
* 3.4% adjusting for currency			

Exhibit 3: Financial Highlights from Lenovo Annual Report (2003-2004)

Courtesy: http://www.pc.ibm.com/ww/lenovo/2004annualpopup.html

Particulars	*2004 HK $ mn*	*2003 HK $ mn*	*Increase/ Decrease*
Operating Results			
· Turnover	23176	20233	14.5%
· EBITDA	1125	1175	(4.3%)
· Profit attributable to shareholders	1053	1017	3.5%
· EPS-fully diluted (HK cents)	13.19	13.55	3.3%
Financial Position			
· Total Assets	8342	6756	23.5%
· Cash & cash equivalents	2650	2808	(5.6%)
· Shareholders' fund	4489	4189	7.2%
Financial Ratio			
· ROA (Return on assets) (%)	14.42	14.5	(0.7%)
· ROE (Return on equity) (%)	4.7	25.6	(3.5%)
· Current ratio (times)	1.9	2.1	(9.5%)

Exhibit 4: Lenovo Financial Summary (1st Q 06-07, 05-06 & 4Q 05-06)

Courtesy: http://www.pc.ibm.com/ww/lenovo/2006annualpopup.html

Particulars	*1Q 2006-07*			*1Q 2005-06**		*4Q 2005-06*	
	US $ mn	*%*	*Y/Y*	*US $ mn*	*%*	*US $ mn*	*%*
Turnover	3,476		38%	2,514		3,125	
Gross profit	497	14.3%	- 1 pts	385	15.3%	437	14.0%
Operating Expenses	465	13.4%	+ 0.9 pts	315	12.5%	456	14.6%
Other expenses/(income)**	(2)	0%		4	0.2%	21	0.7%
Pre-tax income/(loss) before restructuring cost	34	1%	- 48%	66	2.6%	(40)	- 1.3%
Restructuring Cost	19					70	
Profit attributable to shareholders	5		- 89%	46		(116)	
EPS (US cents)·							
Basic·	0.06		- 89%	0.53		(1.3)	
Diluted	0.06		- 88%	0.52		(1.29)	

* Included only two months of contribution from acquired IBM's personal computer business

** Including finance income, finance cost and share of profits/(losses) of jointly controlled entities and associated companies

Exhibit 5: Lenovo Condensed balance sheet (March & June 2006)

Courtesy: http://www.pc.ibm.com/ww/lenovo/2006annualpopup.html

Particulars	*US $ mn As on June 30, 2006*	*US $ mn As on March 31, 2006*
Non Current Assets	2308	2305
Current Assets	2865	2736
Total Assets	5173	5041
Shareholders' fund	1007	1044
Minority Interests'	1	1
Total Equity	1008	1045
Non-current Liabilities	826	814
Current Liabilities	3339	3182
Total Liabilities	4165	3996
Total Equity + Liabilities	5173	5041
Net Current Liabilities	(474)	(446)
Total Assets less Current Liabilities	1834	1859

Exhibit 6: Cultural Dimension @ IBM

Courtesy: http://www-01.ibm.com/software/globalization/topics/diversity/diversity.jsp

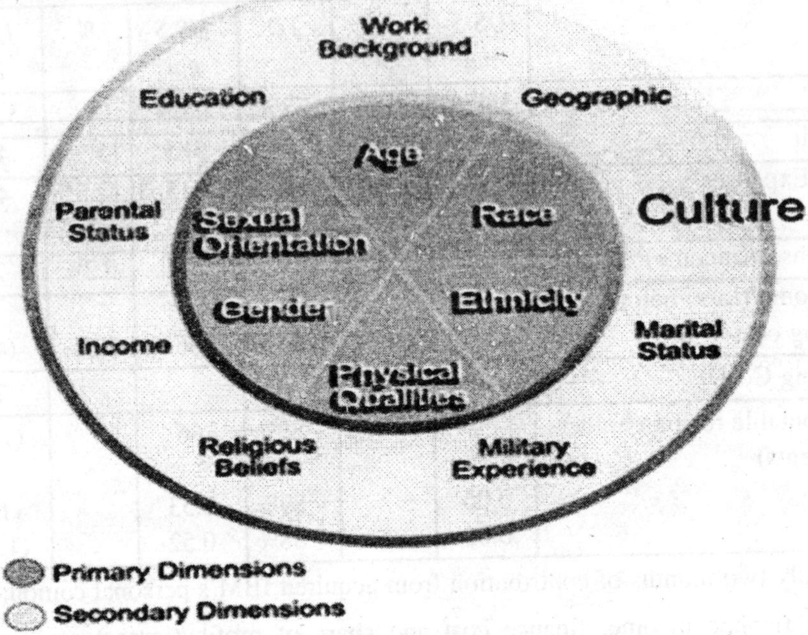

Exhibit 7: Cultural Orientations Model at IBM

IBM uses the COM (Cultural Orientation Model) developed by TMC of Princeton, NJ. This model is based on common tendencies of the people on a number of dimensions or values and has identified the dimensions as:

Courtesy: http://www-01.ibm.com/software/globalization/topics/diversity/com.jsp

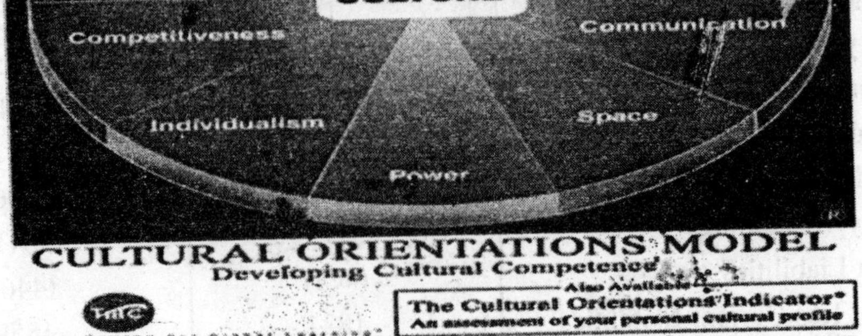

9

Bharat Forge LTD: The Success Story

Khushbu Singhania **Anjali Modak** **Neha Chawla**
Bharati Vidyapeeth University
Institute of Management and Research, New Delhi

BHARAT FORGE LTD.(BFL)

Bharat Forge Ltd. is a global company, which is now the second largest forging company in the world and aspiring global leadership position in the next few years.

Bharat Forge is engaged in the manufacture of automotive components. They started their operations in 1966 and by 1990; they had grown to become the country's largest and most technologically advanced forging company.

Bharat Forge Ltd. is the supplier to virtually every Indian auto manufacturers, and their revenues were generated from the domestic market. If they had continued in the same way they would have steady incremental growth. However, their vision was different, and this prompted them to take what were perhaps the most defined decisions that permanently changed the course of the company and propelled them to completely different platform.

BHARAT FORGES AHEAD

In 1989, company invested in creating first state of the art forging facility at a cost of almost a 100 crores of rupees at a time when the total company turnover was about a 120 crores. Many of their friends, well-wishers, customers and financial analysts advised them against taking this decision. It got to a stage when the project was even termed as a *white elephant in the pink media.* It was this vision of Mr. Kalyani that enabled the company to respond to the emerging challenges.

However, the vision of Mr.Kalyani to make Bharat Forge a global company persisted. He banked on the ability of his people to perform and deliver. Even they did not disappoint him. They performed way beyond his expectations, and fully justified his faith and confidence in them. With the benefit of hindsight, Mr.Kalyani felt that if he had decided not to make that investment in 1989, Bharat Forge would have been a completely different company today.

While preparing a vision for the company, it was also necessary for the company, to factor in developments in the environment that would have an impact on their future. The role of management leadership is to anticipate change and to put in place strategies that will enable the company to respond to emerging challenges.

Bharat Forge's exposure to the international markets had given them a reason to believe that it would become imperative for Government of India to liberalize the economy sooner rather than later. As it turned out, their assessment was fairly accurate. In 1991, when the first steps of liberalization was initiated by Narsimha Rao government in which our present Prime Minister, Dr. Manmohan Singh, was the finance minister, Bharat Forge was already on course to establish domestic market leadership, and continued to increase the gap between themselves and rest of the industry. The downturn in the domestic automotive industry in 1997 prompted them to launch a strong export thrust that radically changed their approach and gave the company a strong outward orientation.

THE WORLD IS NOT ENOUGH

The success in the international market encouraged them to dream big. Bharat Forge wanted to establish themselves as global leaders. They decided to take on the challenge and were convinced that if they did things correctly, they could achieve their goal. Since then there was no looking back. The first forging line of the company that went into commercial production in 1993 was the backbone towards aggressive initiative into international market.

In the strategic plan of1997; company set following objectives for themselves.

- To aggressively grow their business by accessing global markets.
- To be among the top three players in the world in heavy complex forges, which was the business that they were in.
- To set global benchmarks in cost, quality, technology, speed to market and customer service, and to create sustainable competitive advantage through focus on product development, on operations and most importantly – on people.

HUMAN RESOURCE STRATEGY

In the early 1990's company made one of the important decisions that is creating a human resource strategy. This strategy was centered on creating a lean and qualified organization. Their challenge was to change embedded mindsets, to create conditions for bottom-up change.

The company made a 3 level organization through significant reduction in the tiers of the middle management, by multi-tasking various functions and inter-disciplinary jobs. They had a qualified cadre of over 500 engineers who could absorb and implement modern manufacturing methods and operate high technology equipments. The most significant change was that the company substituted blue-collar workers with white-collar work force that is hiring of skilled workers. They hadn't hired a single non-skilled worker in their company over so many years.

Continuous training included exposure in Germany. The company considered overseas customers integral to their people development initiatives. The employees had gradually understood the traditional methods of developing, making, selling and servicing. The company rated engineers by radically re-designing their business processes to achieve a dramatic improvement via factor of 2:10. They moved from a task-based approach to a process oriented organization in which complete end to end activities were undertaken that helped them to create unmatched value with their customers.

If we were to summarize their strategy, they were pursuing the hairlines of their vision. They started by building the organization, by placing emphasis and focus on improving cost, efficiencies, enhancing product quality and rationalizing their internal processes.

This helped in having a leadership position in the domestic market. They leveraged the domestic market, built an export orientation in the company by creating world-class international sale capabilities, and followed this up with an organization structure that enabled them to respond to the requirements of the global customers efficiently. Then they decided to conduct the operations across the globe. An important element of their global vision was "to become one of the largest forging companies in the world." One more objective was to de-risk their business by developing a diverse range of customers across markets, products and geographies. The first step they took was therefore to increase market size by exporting to customers in the global automotive industries.

By 2003, Bharat Forge ltd. had built a fairly significant presence in the global markets. They had 24 international customers (refer annexure) and significantly they became the first automotive component company to start exports to OEMs for automotive companies in China. Their breakthrough into China gave them immense satisfaction and popularity, because it came at a time when China was increasingly being regarded as the manufacturing workshop of the world. They were able to establish when it came to skill-intensive manufactured products; the company had a clear comparative advantage as compared to Chinese competitors. In fact, the company's designing and machining capabilities were at power with Germany.

In 2003-04, the United States accounted for about 68% of their export business. China accounted for about 24% followed by Europe which only accounted for about 8% of the business (refer Annexure 1).

As part of their 'nearest kin' strategy, they started developing customers in segments of the automotive industry other than heavy commercial vehicles, which was their commercial forte. They started developing customers in passenger and other non-automotive segments like oil and gas exploration and construction equipment industries. As far as Europe is concerned, it was necessary to follow slightly different strategy that took into account the special circumstances that prevail in the European automotive industry.

The Peddinghaus wedding

They had experienced that the companies in Europe prefer that the component manufacturers should be located near their factories. They therefore thought of establishing a manufacturing footprint in Europe so that they get the advantage of attracting large number of European customers. In January 2004 the company acquired Carl Dan Peddinghaus, the second largest forging company in Germany, which was recognized for its strong design and engineering capabilities, in a view to capture European markets as they prefer component manufacturers to be located close to their factories. They floated a 100% subsidiary in Germany and acquired two CDP plants along with about 800 employees, order books and the intellectual property.

The company is now known as CDP Bharat Forge Gmbh. The acquisition resulted in much larger and wider market presence, larger product offer and deeper penetration in the passenger car segment and a manufacturing presence in one of the most developed countries in the world. They had realized that the acquisition success would greatly depend upon a comprehensive, well structured and clearly defined integration programs. Thus they took an initiative and constituted for an inter-company cross-functional integration team and gave them a 100-day directive to focus on following areas:

- Integration at people level
- Marketing and customer integration strategies
- Manufacturing and Technology and quality benchmarking
- Purchasing strategies to leverage volumes
- Communication
- An organization plan and Human Resource strategy

They had successfully completed the integration process. There were several hard issues concerning synergies, integrating project planning and financial due diligence. Having identified the differences between both the organizations, i.e. the 'people' and the 'cultural' aspects Bharat Forge Ltd. took the challenge, and was in a position to take initiative to bridge the gap and harmonize the best aspects of both the organizations without losing time.

The company conducted a cultural due diligence, which effectively was a practical step-by-step approach for making a rapid, cost effective, cultural assessment of both the companies.

Simple things like when you say 'yes', a German woul mean' yes' and India would probably mean 'maybe', preferences for open or closed offices, recruitment practices, platform for employee interactions etc. the company had a challenge since it was a cross-border deal, so there were issues regarding language barriers, cultural differences, different work practices etc. So the company followed Human Resource Integration strategy.

The company's human resource integration strategy was based on three major platforms:

- Strong and effective communication.
- Selection of management team from the existing organization in Germany to run CDI.
- A process to resolve cultural issues.

Mr. Kalyani before acquisition of the company sensed that the employees were demoralized. They had concerns over the job security. They also were worried about the company's future. Thus he conducted a meeting of all the employees in Germany. During his address, he assured the employees that the company would remain the same in the future as it was in the past but he emphasized on cost reduction, improved productivity and product innovation. He also motivated them by saying that their co-workers in Bharat Forge India are keen to learn and get exposure in precision engineering skills that are integral to German manufacturing industry.

BRIDGING THE CULTURAL DIVIDE

Mr. Kalyani had a Global vision. He considered the relationship as the bridge to unite people from diverse religions, cultures and backgrounds so as to achieve faster progress and prosperity for countries, companies and people all over the world.

The CDP acquisition hastened Bharat Forge's transformation into a global company. It contributed to a radical change in the attitudes and embedded mindsets. Employees of Bharat Forge are ready to take the world.

To be termed as 'global' a company should meet the following criteria:

- It should have a presence and investment in multiple countries. One should not only be an exporter.
- There should be a constant movement of people from the parent to other operation and vice-versa.
- There should be learning and sharing of experiences.
- One should have a meaningful market share in the products and markets that one operates in.
- One should be plugged into global capital markets and should have global investors.
- One should have key alliance partners in one's business, should work and hire a local talent, especially I the market where it operates in.

Bharat Forge also acquired another company in Germany called as CDP Aluminum Technical that manufactured forged aluminum components for high end customers such as Volkswagen, BMW, Audi, Ford and others. This acquisition helped Bharat Forge Ltd. to offer their customers with a larger bouquet of product encompassing steel and Aluminum.

DOMESTIC CUSTOMERS OF BHARAT FORGE

GLOBAL CUSTOMERS OF BHARAT FORGE

FORGING A GLOBAL BRAND

Bharat Forge Ltd. has been the largest exporter in automotive components from India for the past consecutive 3 years. The company is among the very few Indian companies in the Indian industry to have a global footprint and it in the second largest company in its field in the world. The vision of the company to be the no.1 company in this business will contribute in making "Made in India", a global brand in the automotive industry in the world.

According to Mr.Kalyani, India has an advantage in terms of high-quality manpower and availability of good quality raw materials such as steel and aluminum at prices that are comparable with the international prices. These types of success stories are making man other companies to believe in their own abilities. These initiatives need to be complemented by government initiatives through facilitation in the area of indirect taxation, improving the quality of infrastructure, accelerating the labour reforms and facilities for development of skills. If this can be done, then Indian automotive component manufacturing industry can surely have 5-6 global leaders in their businesses.

To conclude, Bharat Forge therefore, meets virtually all the criteria of a global company. They have transformed from a small, low-technology domestically oriented company, to the one that is now at the threshold of global leadership. This has been possible due to effective implementation of strategies which were planned through intense people participation and by fully involving the employees at various stages of the organization's value chain.

The Director's interest in long term development of employees, to give them opportunities to reveal their talents for the benefit of the organization and to achieve their personal goals, an unflinching adherence to the value system, empowering the employees and constantly motivating them to perform at high levels of efficiency and making them partners in organization's progress and prosperity distinguishes the company from most of their national competitors.

QUESTIONS

1. Critically analyse Bharat Forge Ltd ?
2. What are the strategies responsible for Bharat Forge's success into a top global company ?
3. What impact did the acquisition of CDP have on Bharat Forge Ltd. ?
4. What is the road ahead for Bharat Forge Ltd. ?

10

Training and Development : The E-learning Way

Mr. Lokinder Kumar Tyagi
Associate Professor
Bharati Vidyapeeth University
Institute of Management and Research, New Delhi
lokinder.tyagi@gmail.com

Ms. Nuzhat Khan
Assistant Professor
Sharada University
itsnuzhat@yahoo.com

INTRODUCTION

E-learning is an instruction that is delivered electronically. Almost anything that teaches a skill or conveys information in an organized fashion online can be considered elearning. E-learning programs are administered through what are called learning management systems (LMSs).E-learning includes asynchronous-meaning it is not delivered to every user at the same time-text-based courses, job aids, educational games and video and audio segments, As well as synchronous media like videoconferencing and chat rooms.

Just as IBM's Basic Blue has achieved its success the question; whether e-learning is restricted to only big organization or is it economically viable for the small medium size enterprises." Small businesses are often overlooked. Most of the services are designed for big companies," says Brandon Hall,Ph.D., lead researcher and CEO of brandon-hall.com.

Another potential problem with a small firm is that you want to ensure that employees will have the hardware and software they need to take full advantage of the courses.

In the meantime the industry is refusing to admit that e-learning is simply a warmed-over version of the computer-based training systems that made a brief appearance in the early 80's and were dead just a few years later. The fact that the internet makes the same ineffective programs cheaper to deliver does not justify the continued flogging of this dead horse. The industry's own studies show a lack of quality, retention, and above all the failure to even complete the programs by a majority of students.

IBM'S BASIC BLUE

In 1999, IBM launched the pilot Basic Blue management training program, which was fully deployed in 2000. Basic Blue was an in house management training program for new managers. It imparted 75 percent online and the remaining 25 percent through the traditional classroom mode. The e-learning part included articles, simulations, jobs aids and short courses.

The founding principle of Basic Blue was that 'learning is an extended process, not a one-time event.' Basic Blue was based on a '4-Tier blended learning model' (Refer Annexure). The first three tiers were delivered online and the fourth tier included one-week long traditional class.

But was e-learning restricted to only big companies or are small firms also looking for an e-training of their employees. In 2001, Walker and Associates—a Welcome, N.C., telecommunications equipment distributor with just under 300 employees—got a new president who encouraged training and development. He spearheaded a move toward online training by forming a partnership with GeoLearning Inc., a web-based training solutions and learning management system provider in West Des Moines, Iowa.

Together, they created the Walker Institute of Training and Development, an online corporate university that offered dozens of courses from GeoLearning's library. "We wanted to make sure we were addressing the learning needs of our salespeople our in the field," says Randy Turner, director of corporate learning and development at Walker and Associates. "We wanted to give them learning opportunities that didn't tie them down to a classroom."

Small businesses are often overlooked. Most of the services are designed for big companies," says Hall. However, some providers had started to pay attention to smaller firms, which was good news because elearning can be especially beneficial to smaller organizations.

Proponents also point out that elearning saved significant money in travel costs-which can be especially important for small companies with far-flung offices. For example, instead of flying a dozen salespeople to a product seminar in Chicago, you can have them plug in their laptops from hotel rooms around the country and download the information at their convenience.

E-learning also cuts down on opportunity cost-a boon for companies with smaller staffs and limited staff redundancy. "Traditional training was very expensive, especially in a small company where it is difficult to take everyone away from day-to-day responsibilities," points out Ellen willen, director of marketing for Quelsys, an e-learning firm in Norwalk, Conn.

Smaller companies with limited budgets also appreciate the fact that e-learning can avoid wasting precious training dollars on lost tuition and fees due to last-minute cancellations. As one HR professional quoted: "With classroom training, you're paying for 20 people whether 20 or 10 show up. With e-learning, when you're using it, you pay for it; when you're not, you don't."

Companies that didn't had the staff to serve as software experts also used e-learning as a continuous, on-demand resource. For example, many employees at Walker and Associates used online courses as a reference tool. "If they need to learn Microsoft Word, they can access it on an as-needed basis," says Turner, who adds that "people are using it as an online resource.

Willen says, "In most e-learning systems you can go back and access pieces of information" or job aids for a year after completion of the course.Perhaps most importantly, with e-learning, "a small organization that couldn't afford to have its own training department could still offer a variety of training courses", said Frank Russell, president and CEO of GeoLearning. "E-learning helps small organizations act like bigger ones".

SIMULATIONS FURTHER STRENGTHENING E-LEARNING

Recent research demonstrated that even when employees were provided access to eLearning, few participated (only 69% for mandatory courses and 32% for voluntary), and of those who did, few actually completed the course. The reason for failing grades were obvious: most people simply didn't enjoy the process of studying, writing tests, and being evaluated. Not to mention the requirement to take time away from work and personal commitments, all of which piled up during the training.

The only answer for successful training was E- Simulations. Simulations made learning exciting by combining education, entertainment, and technology to provide highly visual, interactive, and engaging learning experiences. For the individual, this meant a greater likelihood of participating and completing the training. For the organization, it meant employees who have gained experience, and made mistakes inside the simulation, not the real world.

GROUND REALITIES OF E-LEARNING

One thing that e-learning boosters never wanted to talk about is the simple fact that very few people ever actually finish an e-learning course when it involves a technically complex or lengthy subject such as software training or programming. Shockingly, the majority of the multi-billion dollar e-learning market had been for IT training, a sector for which e-learning is uniquely unsuited!

Upon close inspection, the ugly truth was self-evident, borne out by both industry studies and individual experiences - the longer was the e-learning track, the lesser were the number of participants who successfully completed the program. Why was this? In large part, it could be chalked up to human nature. We're simply not designed to learn well in a vacuum; people perform the complex process of assimilating information best in socially interactive environments.

Learning Tree, an IT training firm, uncovered the problem when its e-learning development team designed a pilot course to test an elearning program's efficacy. The results surprised them - despite enlisting the skills of their very best instructors who consistently used email and phone messages to encourage participants, only 30 percent of students managed to complete the pilot course. That's a 70% drop out rate, even after Learning Tree's best efforts at facilitation!

According to a poll which was conducted by Forrester Research, over half the people enrolled in e-learning programs in general failed to complete them because of "lack of interactivity." The numbers got worse as the duration of the e-learning track lengthened.

A follow-up study by Learning Tree revealed that the drop out rate steadily increased with the course time: in a multi-part, 25-hour e-track, 72% completed the first three-hour course, but only 52% completed two courses, and just 19% - not even a quarter! - Of the participants completed the full 25-hour e-track. Why such poor results?

Technical training was and will always be difficult. And the increasing complexity of software had created an exploding demand for timely, cost-efficient, effective training. The siren call had been to accomplish that through e-learning. But the fact of the matter is that e-learning didn't work for complex technical topics, it's being proved daily that it doesn't work, and a lot of time and money is being burned.

The industry's own studies show a lack of quality, retention, and above all the failure to even complete the programs by a majority of students. Organizations and individuals who require more than an "appearance" of training ignore these warnings at their peril.

QUESTIONS

1. What do you think are the potential benefits of e-learning in Training and Development?
2. Can smaller firms also target for e-learning in their training and development?
3. Will Simulation be helpful to make e-learning successful?
4. What was the reason for students not to complete the e-learning program?
5. In spite of the drawbacks of e-learning why do we have such a rosy picture about the future of e-learning.?

TEACHING NOTES:

Overview

The case primarily gives an overview of the benefits of E-learning technique of Training given by Human Resource Department. There are various methods and techniques of training people, amongst which e-learning is gaining popularity. It is very important for any HR manager to decide on the methodology of training given..Also, weigh the pros and cons of e-learning before adopting it.

Moreover , e-learning alone does not suffice, the HR department should also provide the trainee with the Simulation of the actual situation..Simulation is believed to build on e-learning but skyrockets all the elements of ROI. The case also gives a brief insight on the on that not all the industries are benefitted by e-learning.

Application

The reader is a Mangement student who has knowledge abcut the HR practices.

Objective

This is a Complex case.The objective of the case is to make the students understand the benefits of e-learning and the potential drawbacks.Also to pay attention to the cost involved in such type of training.Nonetheless, to take into account of situation where e-learning has failed and why.

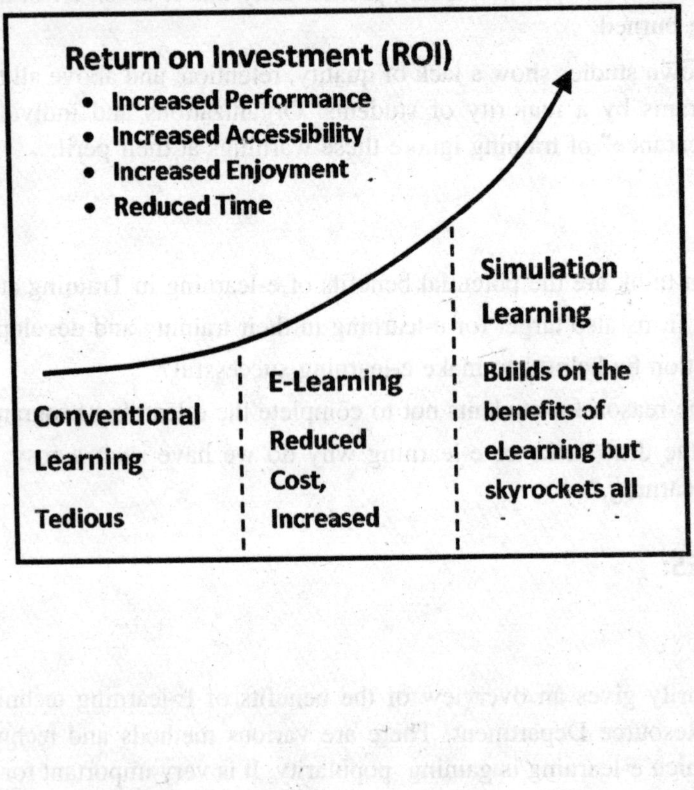

ANNEXURE

IBM's BASIC BLUE FOUR TIER MODEL

TABLE I

Tier 1	Performance support andreference material	Read it, watch it, listen to it, Be directed to it	Websites, Audio, Seminars, Video, Books, e-books	Internet
Tier 2	Interactive learning, gamessimulations	Examine it, try it, play at it, interact with it	Inetractive games, Multimedia, or Actaul solutions	Multimedia
Tier 3	Collaborative learning	Discuss it, practice with others, Create virtual communities of practice or purpose	e-labs, e-teams, Live virtual classrooms, Web conferences	Collaborative
Tier 4	Experience-based Learning	Get togther, meet as a community, Develop relationship, live it, do it	Mentoring, role Playing, case studies, coaching	Face to Face

IBM's COST SAVINGS THROUGH E- LEARNING PROGRAMS

TABLE II

Program	*Saving in 2000(in US $ million)*
Basic Blue	16.0
Going global	0.6
Coaching simulator	0.8
Manager Quick Views	6.6
CustomerRoom	0.5
Sales Compass	21.0

11

The Challenge of Managing Organizational Culture

Prof. Madhu Shridhar
Professor
Bharati Vidyapeeth University
Institute of Management and Research, New Delhi
madhushridhar@yahoo.com

This is a about the cultures of a very successful and well known company. As invariably happens, the culture of a company, over time, reflects the beliefs and values of the founders and impacts its performance on multiple dimensions.

This is a case of a traditional first generation unit which over a period has become a force to recon. ABC the Flagship company of the Rathore Group is an Indian manufacturing company that commenced production in 1966, it is one of the largest domestic player with a share of 80% in axle components and engine components, it also has to its credit World's largest single-location forging capacity and boasts of an elaborate product profile besides having a deep Global OEM Customer base.

The company was inherited by the foreign returned scion. Capital was never an issues for the company, it has a strong value system, determination to grow and have a name in the market. Hard work and attention to detail is considered an asset. The foreign returned scion hired a professional management team that enabled him to diversify into newer businesses.

ABC operates in two business segments: Forgings and General Engineering Trading. The Company has developed products, such as rotor forgings for thermal power, headers for nuclear power and crankshafts and portal axles for locomotives, and parts like blow out preventers and fluid ends for the oil and gas sector. The Company's automotive forgings business has manufacturing facilities in three continents: Europe, North America and Asia. And its main markets are India, USA, Europe, China, Japan, Australia.

ABC's Vision is

- To be among the top three global players worldwide in chosen activity
- To aggressively grow business by accessing global markets
- To set global benchmarks in
  - * Cost
  - * Technology
  - * Speed-to-market parameters
  - * Customer Service
- To create sustainable shareholder value through successful implementation of growth plans

Product Profile

- Axle Components
- Engine Components
- Machined Components
- Oil & Gas Sector Forgings
- Construction Equipment Components
- Speciality Forgings

User Industries

- Auto
- Oil and Gas
- Construction Equipment
- General applications

The company has a strong awareness of its social milieu and wants to make a difference inspite of it being focused on building a profitable company. The company was very significantly owned by a single individual and was less sensitive to employees in general. The company was operationally very tightly run with a strong focus on cost management and cash-flows. The company valued integrity, ethics, and quality and created a professional and apolitical working environment. It favored low-key management styles and valued simplicity.

Over time as the environment changed, the company still continued to operate with the mind set of profit as its aim and spent on employee amenities as per their standards. The company felt that such investments were wasteful. It felt that costs of operation would go up thereby hurting its financial performance. Investing in marketing was seen as an unnecessary expense by the company since business was pouring in thanks to market dynamics.

The company kept a low profile and **stuck to its goals of delivering shareholder returns.** Its leaders were socially and politically aware and were involved in trying to fuel social change but over time, bowed to media, peer and market pressures and set up campuses and provided amenities to its employees. It also tried to become far more visible in social upliftment causes. The company thanks to smart marketing and PR and due to its unique employee strength always understood the market pulse and kept ahead of its competitors.

The company listed itself also in the US thereby raising its profile and enhancing its access to customers and capital. It understood the value of market capitalization even while being more focused on operating cash-flows. Its board of directors consisted of internationally leading corporate and academic leaders.

The company set up relationships with national and international manufacturing academic institutions to interact with the employees thus building brand imaging and brand positioning. It invested in R&D, supported entrepreneurial employees when they spin out ventures, and invested in building relationships with various international entities. The company was always inclined to support new initiatives and was focused on low investments, cost management, cash flows, and did a world class job in driving operational efficiencies. The company has made several acquisitions.

The leader of the company read books like "How to cut costs and double your profits". Almost all those who have quit the company appear to be less socially conscious.

Though the company is at the top in the market, and enjoys a higher market capitalization, revenues, margins, reputation and brand image. The company is very significantly owned by the head who's several times richer than when he started. The company has employed the foreign return son of the largest shareholder who is the heir apparent.

ABC the flagship company took a decision to float a new company " Mathur Ventures Ltd." which will be predominantly the market arm of the group with a strategic viewpoint of giving stiff competition to its domestic competitors. In the year1997, DBA Ltd. was launched with Mr. Mathur Jr. becoming the Director and a major share holder of the company. Mathur Ventures Ltd. virtue of its close association with the ABC and having a common Group Name had no problem in creating ruffles in the market. The appointment letter of the CEO was given by the ABC but the Vice president was appointed by the Mathur Ventures Ltd. The Sr. HR person was on deputation from ABC to Mathur Ventures Ltd.

Business plans and budget funding was approved by a committee of Sr. Vice Presidents Mktg., Prod., Finance , Exports and HR of ABC's. Regular meetings were held with the committee members but day to day functioning was the responsibility of the newly appointed CEO. The company hired officers of various ranks and within a short span of 6 months had a strong 250 team of officers of different levels working in the various dept. with salaries more than what the market was offering. The HR and the Accounts dept. reported to the CEO where as the rest reported to the VP Mktg. The company in a short span of 6 months had opened 16 branches in various parts of the country and on an average each branch had 3-4 marketing team with the team leader reporting to the Head office. Each branch was equipped with a clerical staff who was looking after accounts, admin and reporting to both the CEO and the VP were as the mktg. team was directly reporting to the VP Mktg.

The Officers for induction visited the HQ and would be taken to the ABC Comp. and shown around the Campus and allowed to interact with the concerned dept. of ABC. This created a mixed feeling in the officers, a sense a belongingness and also a sort of complex from the ABC's staff just by virtue of them being on rolls of the ABC. "Good performers will be absorbed by ABC" was a standard line given by the CEO to the new appointees.

First year's performance was very miserable as expected but the growth projection for the second year was a challenge. At the end of the second year things did not change much. The Mktg. and Sales Dept. of ABC was not very cooperative for the simple reason that they realized it is a erosion in their domain as their sales figure for that year had shown a slight dip. They were all concerned about their performance. The local market feed back was also not very encouraging their association with the ABC staff was coming in the way of capturing the market. In one of the committee meeting this issue was taken up and it was decided that Mathur Ventures will have to develop their own base and will not be given piggy ride as was the understanding earlier. This decision was a big dampener on the Mathur Ventures morale. The situation became more grim because of the recession the market was facing during that time. Rumors started floating that the company's future does not look bright and in the midst of all this the CEO put in his papers and requested to be relieved at the earliest, this further affected the functioning of the branches and the officers started coming to the Head office to get a clearer picture. The recession was not allowing the market to grow added to that the ABC staff was also trying their best not to part with their customers all this resulted in the poor performance of the company. The committee took a decision that looking at the situation it will be a wiser step to withdraw from this venture.

The HR was informed to start working on this decision. VP Marketing reacted very strongly to this and made it very clear that he will not put in his papers in fact if need arises he will go to the courts to fight it out.

HR manager participated actively in the overall exercise. The team developed a employee plan, which included the identification of skills needed by employees to take new responsibilities and the development of training and reskilling programs for employees. Since it may be necessary to acquire other skills in the future, the plan also addressed the issue of recruitment planning.

HR's role at this point while dealing with a subject as traumatic (to employees) as downsizing was to maintain proper balance between formal and informal forms of communication. A few common methods of communication included small meetings, face to face interaction, one-on-one discussion, breakfast gatherings, all staff meetings, video conferencing and informal employee dialogue sessions, use of newsletters, videos, telephone hotlines, fax, memoranda, e-mail and bulletin boards; and brochures and guides to educate employees about the downsizing process, employee rights and tips for surviving the situation.

Employees were encouraged to voice their ideas, concerns or suggestions concerning the issue at hand. There was a common problem faced by all and this acted as a binder. Many officers gave valuable ideas regarding the restructuring, increase in production, and assistance required by employees in such situations.

Reports and information became critical it had to be acquired from internal as well as external sources (the HR department was responsible for providing it) to provide various opportunities available for employees outside the organization. And from internal sources, such companies need to gather demographic data (such as rank, pay grade, years of service, age, gender and retirement eligibility) on the entire workforce. In addition it gave information regarding number of employees that were normally expected to resign or be terminated.

HR developed an inventory of employee skills to help management take informed decisions. Major steps in the downsizing process included offering career transition assistance to the employees, and providing support to help them cope with their situation.

Periodic review of the implementation process and immediate identification and rectification of any deviations from the plan minimized the adverse effects of the downsizing process. the progress was reviewed quarterly and was published in order to help every manager monitor reductions by different categories. These categories could be department, occupational group (clerical, administrative, secretarial, general labor. HR tracked the progress and achievement of every division separately and emphasized the application of a different strategy for every department as reaction of employees to downsizing varied considerably from department to department.

Though the above measures helped minimize the negative effects of downsizing, but the emotional trauma of the concerned people could never be eliminated. The least HR could do was to downsize in a manner that did not injure the dignity of the discharged employees or lower the morale of the survivors. The whole process took six months from the date the decision was taken by the committee.

20% of the staff were absorbed by the group companies and roughly 30% were placed in outside units because of the HR dept. hard work. The VP was finally convinced about the decision and the poor working style which led to this situation. He was paid more than he expected to protect the Mathur brand does not suffer. The HR guy went back to the ABC wiser now.

One thing was clear that the company was unafraid to lead and take steps that were unusual at the time they were. It is not a matter of good versus bad, right versus wrong kinds of judgmental decisions. It is a matter of company and leadership culture and if it works, it works.

QUESTIONS FOR DISCUSSION

1. As part of an organization's HR team responsible for carrying it through such an exercise, discuss the measures you would adopt to ensure the exercise's success. Given the uncertainty in the job market, what do you think employees should do to survive the trauma caused by downsizing and prepare themselves for it?
2. What should the new entrants take into consideration while taking up jobs? And why

12

Strategic Planning : Time and Opportunity — It is Easy to Come First but Difficult to Remain at that Position

Nakul Chaturvedi
Bharati Vidyapeeth University
Institute of Management and Research, New Delhi

This is a very true statement which I have tried to substantiate through this case wherein conduciveness of strategic planning in terms of time element involved and knack of analysis of upcoming opportunities required is being emphasized on.

Movieplex cinemas limited, company that ushered multiplex revolution in India in 1997, by starting the first multiplex with five screens and a seating capacity of 1150 in Delhi. Movieplex redefined cine viewing experience by providing its audience with comfortable, well-cushioned, reclining chairs with ample leg space. It was the first cine exhibitor in India to offer state-of-the-art screens using superior & advance projection & audio visual sound system & it was the first one to provide computer generated movie tickets and online booking of tickets. By the year 1999, it expanded its chain of multiplexes in New Delhi & other parts of National Capital Region (NCR) like Gurgaon, Faridabad & Noida. It coined the punch line "think movies" to promote its multiplex chain, & to make Movieplex cinemas synonymous with movies and movie viewing.

The multiplexes developed by Movieplex cinemas were all stand alone properties that attracted several well-known food and non-food retailers to their premises. Retailers like Pizza Hut,

Barista, Archies etc. featured prominently in most of the multiplexes, which, in turn increased the footfalls to the multiplex, especially during weekends.

These moves slowly elbowed out a number of major single screen cine exhibitors in and around New Delhi. At this point of time industry experts felt that time was ripe for Movieplex to expand to other parts of the country but insiders within the company stuck to their business policy of expanding in a region till the point of saturation and then moving into other locations. They believed that, apart from the metros, country was not yet ready to experience the multiplex revolution and the markets would be very narrow. Moreover, the company felt that they were way ahead and created almost invincible entry barriers for any new entrant to enter the value added cine exhibition industry.

However there was a substantial increase in the number of malls across the country. The mall developers wooed the multiplex owners as they found that multiplexes were good 'irrigators' at the mall because they brought in the footfalls. As Movieplex was the most established and recognized multiplex chain in and around New Delhi, it received several proposals by mall owners to establish multiplexes at various malls but it stuck to its business policy of stand-alone properties for its multiplexes.

A few new entities quickly entered the industry via the mall route. Popular pictures posed the most significant challenge to shivam cinemas. Apart from employing all the best practices in terms of comfortable movie viewing & state-of-the-art technology, the company adopted differential pricing strategy for its tickets by classifying its auditoriums into two classes – the General class & the Executive class. The prices of the tickets were also based on the quality of the movies. It also initiated a system of booking tickets through SMS. Movieplex charged a flat rate irrespective of movie quality.

Moreover, Popular picture was quick to realise that it needed to have a pan Indian presence & so it established its multiplex chain in Delhi, Mumbai, Gurgaon, Chennai, Hydrabad, Kolkata, Indore & Bangalore. These moves have enabled popular to surpass Movieplex, not only in terms of revenue but quality of services it offered.

Screen Entertainment was another company, it focused on establishing its multiplex chain in smaller cities like Pune, Kochi, Coimbatore, Kanpur, Nasik and Jaipur. The company promoted its chain as "Multiplex Experience at the Cheapest Price". Apart from adopting differential pricing based on classes it added another dimension by basing it on the days of the week.

The term strategy means "The determination of basic long term long-term goals and objectives of an enterprise and the adoption courses of action and the allocation if resources necessary for carrying out these goals."

- Determination of goals
- Selection of alternatives
- Resource allocation

Thus a strategic planning is not the process of implementing business policy and keep working on time tested activities to achieve the soul aim of the enterprise but to ascertain the aptness of alternatives time to time, regardless of them being very profitable in the past and analyzing the opportunities and changes being imposed by internal and external factors influencing the functioning of the enterprise.

There is an indispensable role of analysis of opportunity or change in the environment and a decision taken after been thought upon several times from different standpoint. As in this case discussed above Movieplex was erroneous at times in scrutinizing the opportunities.

In the corporate world, the pioneer or the first movers in any industry often fails to maintain its competitive advantage when its followers or later entrants start making their presence felt in that industry. This happens because pioneer fails to constantly innovate, or take time an effective competitive decisions. The first movers tend to cling to their time-tested strategies, which yielded positive result when they were the sole entity in the market. This phenomenon is called 'active inertia'. The second movers in the industry on the other hand, the followers in the industry learns from the experience of the pioneer and take full advantage of the pioneer's weakness & strategic mistakes.

Same has been the case with Movieplex cinemas.

1. At this point of time industry experts felt that time was ripe for Movieplex to expand to other parts of the country but insiders within the company stuck to their business policy of expanding in a region till the point of saturation and then moving into other locations. They believed that, apart from the metros, country was not yet ready to experience the multiplex revolution and the markets would be very narrow.

2. As Movieplex was the most established and recognized multiplex chain in and around New Delhi, it received several proposals by mall owners to establish multiplexes at various malls but it stuck to its business policy of stand-alone properties for its multiplexes.

In both of the situations being mentioned above the company underestimated opportunity for growth against the risk involved and somewhere conflicting the business policy and strategies designed. At the same time they condone the point that strategies are for goals not goals for strategies. The decision to stick to time tested course of action a taking less risk backfired perhaps the opportunity was not properly analysed.

Now this was the trouncing faced by Movieplex due to lack of knack or, not to be sarcastic, erroneous & inaccurate scrutiny of the opportunity. The opportunity, when exploited by others gave them entry and chance of establishment in the industry with had strict entry barriers and capability, again due to apt strategies, to compete the pioneers of an industry in a race for success in their track and defeat them.

To make a come back in the industry Movieplex needed to develop a fight back strategy to be developed, which could be done gradually over a considerable period of time. The plans that Movieplex formulated to make a comeback included the followings;

1. For Movieplex to gain lost ground, it needs to have a pan Indian presence at the earliest.
2. The establishment of pan Indian presence should happen ideally via the mall route.
3. Movieplex should not only consider the metros for its expansion, but also the cities that are literally untouched, and the multiplex revolution has yet to take place in a big way.

4. Pricing policies is another area of immediate attention. Price is something which makes demands elastic the most it can either adopt differential pricing based on different parameters or can go for establishment of economy multiplexes along with the normal ones. The area of establishment should be critically decided.
5. It can go for well-planned backward integration. It can either focus of movie production, post-production or distribution apart from cinema exhibition, which would enable them to exercise more control on the overall within the industries.
6. They can take up promotional activities synchronized with their punch line, "Think Movies". They can take up activities on large scale, which could be conducive to make Movieplex synonymous with movies, as they initially vision.

Now this is again due to strategic planning that the pioneers of the industry could make themselves sustain their existence in the market. This time there were no opportunity or economies of scale but gradual strategic planning over the period of time and its effective and efficient implementation.

This justifies the inevitability of the analysis of opportunities and process of gradual thinking and observing for strategy formulation and decision making towards achievement of long-term goals.

13

Changing Face of Compensation in PSUs : An Attempt to Compete with Private Sector

Ms. Neelam Saraswat, IPEM, Ghaziabad
saraswat.neelam@gmail.com
Mr. Gaurav Bhargava, Syndicate Bank, Ghaziabad
gbhargava84@gmail.com

"If public sector banks are required to compete with private banks on a level playing field, there is a good case for compensating them too on a competitive base".

- Reserve Bank of India Governor D Subbarao (www.in.news.yahoo.com)

This case is not only relevant in the banking sector but also matter of focus in other industries. To compete with private sectors, Public sector units are doing changes in their work procedures. They are changing their organization structure in order to become more prompt in response to the changing environment which includes competitors also. Employees become the very important source of competitive advantage for an organization. To attract and to retain employees, one organization needs to have sound compensation strategy supported by other HR functions. Compensation in PSU has many reasons for revision. "The executive compensation in the public sector, as is well known, is lower than that in the private sector. Notwithstanding the historical reasons for this, there is perhaps a good reason to revisit this. There is also the risk that if the public sector bank compensation is not improved, the public sector may lose talent to the private sector", Subbarao said (www.in.news.yahoo.com). Talent acquisition and talent retention is the basic problem faced by most of the PSUs. PSBs seem to be facing a crisis with almost half the top management cadre retiring in the next couple of years, with no identifiable talent to replace them (www.moneylife.in). Situation becomes more appalling for PSUs when people are handsomely paid in private sector organizations. So this issue has started to gain attention of policy makers in India. Payment according to the industry norms is becoming part of compensation determinates for PSUs. Apart from pay hike, PSUs are adopting other effective components of compensation in private sector units. Variable pay or pay for performance which is more popular in private sector is now gaining its popularity and acceptance in public sector units also.

Committee which is Chaired by A.K. Khandelwal, former CMD, Bank of Baroda, and constituted of five other members – Dr. T.V. Rao, Professor, IIM-Ahmedabad, Dr. Deepak Pathak, Professor, IIT Mumbai and M.V. Nair, ex-chairman Indian Banks' Association and H.N. Sinor, former executive IBA (www.expressindia.com) has proposed that PSB should be allowed to adopt the CTC (cost to the company) concept, something that is more attuned with the corporate sector than the public sector. The committee has also suggested that variable pay should be a major component of wages (www.news.in.msn.com). One of the major recommendations given by the committee includes introduction of employee stock options plans (ESOPs) for top performers of the banks to retain talent in public sector banks. The committee has proposed that banks must acknowledge 25 per cent of the top performers through ESOPs and performance linked incentives. ESOPs may help PSUs to pull up the productivity level of employees and to curb attrition rate. Few other recommendations given by the committee include (www.expressindia.com) (www.moneylife.in):

- Introduction of separate positions for chairman and the managing director
- Outsourcing of non-core operations and incentivize mobility of clerical staff to the rural areas in PSBs.
- Wage settlement at the individual bank level, with each bank deciding its own wage structure depending on its profitability and capacity to pay instead of industry-wide wage settlement.
- Changes to the archaic recruitment criteria of PSBs. For clerical staff minimum qualification should be graduation, instead of the current SSC requirement. Also, for the officer cadre, candidate should hold a banking diploma, apart from graduation.
- Formation of a board committee on HR in each bank. Banks having business worth Rs 3 lakh crore and a staff of 30,000 will be required to appoint an executive director-HR on their board.
- Succession planning by bank's board for each key leadership position by identifying three potential successors. The Committee has also suggested for the setting up of a national level Banker's Leadership Development Institute which will develop leaders for banking industry.
- Introduction of performance management systems.

Incentive structures have started to gain ground in PSUs other than banks also. "An incentive system is being worked upon as. recommended by the sixth pay commission. It could be implemented by next year". Prajapati Trivedi, secretary, performance management, said at the annual economic editors' conference (www.economictimes.indiatimes.com). This incentive scheme would be based upon performance of the employee and would also depend upon cost savings on account of reduction in the use of office stationary and savings in the electricity consumption. Government has started to prepare the system for performance monitoring and evaluation for the same.

Government officials are very optimistic about the changes in compensation structure. This might help PSUs to attract best talent and to retain the same. This change in PSUs can help organizations to outperform private organizations. It can even solve the problem of low motivation of government employees which has always been the major issue in PSUs. This is the accepted outcomes but reality may even be opposite it. Bureaucratic structure of Government organization may proved to become blockage in this path. Introduction of variable pay will increase the financial burden on already loss making PSUs. Employees at PSUs may oppose the incentive system.

Questions

1. Will new pay structure help PSUs to compete with their counterparts in talent acquisition? Critically evaluate.
2. What kind of problem may be faced by PSUs in introduction of incentive schemes and pay for performance? How should these issues be addressed? Explain.

References

1. http://in.news.yahoo.com/48/20100908/1238/tbs-rbi-pushes-psu-bankers-case-for-fatt.html, Access on 20/11/2010
2. http://www.moneylife.in/article/8/6797.html, Access on 23/11/2010
3. http://www.expressindia.com/latest-news/PSU-banks-may-link-pay-with-performance/643167/, Access on 23/11/2010
4. http://news.in.msn.com/business/article.aspx?cp-documentid=4123753, Access on 25/11/2010
5. http://economictimes.indiatimes.com/news/news-by-industry/jobs/Incentive-system-for-govt-staffers-next-year-Secy/articleshow/6818946.cms, Access on 28/11/2010

14

Performance Incentive: What Changes will it bring in Indian PSUs?

Ms. Neelam Saraswat, IPEM, Ghaziabad
saraswat.neelam@gmail.com
Mr. Gaurav Bhargava,
Syndicate Bank, Ghaziabad
gbhargava84@gmail.com

"There is no difference between a horse and a donkey in the government. And till you create the difference, nothing will improve"[1]

This statement clearly indicates the problem related to lack of efficient pay structure in Indian government sector. It is widely believed that performance of government organizations is lesser than satisfactory because there is less distinction between high performance and low performance In India; traditionally government employees are paid on the basis of length of service. The salary is mostly covered by basic pay, DA and other allowances that are admissible depending upon the nature of the job. This pay structure leads to the situation where employees do not exert themselves for higher performance. They do not strive hard to improve the efficiency and quality of the system, services and product. Government employees also do not have other motivating factors available. Employees can also be motivated by attraction of promotion. But promotional avenues are also limited in government sector.

Statement made by Reserve Bank of India Governor D Subbarao[2] "If public sector banks are required to compete with private banks on a level playing field, there is a good case for compensating them too on a competitive base" is also directed towards problem in pay structure which is broadening the gap between the private sector and government sector players. This case is not only relevant in the banking sector but also matter of focus in other industries. To compete with private sectors, Public sector units are doing changes in their work procedures. They are changing their organization structure in order to become more prompt in response to the changing environment which includes competitors also. Employees become the very important source of competitive advantage for an organization. To attract and to retain employees, one organization needs to have sound compensation strategy supported by other HR functions.

Compensation in PSU has many reasons for revision. "The executive compensation in the public sector, as is well known, is lower than that in the private sector. Notwithstanding the historical reasons for this, there is perhaps a good reason to revisit this. There is also the risk that if the public sector bank compensation is not improved, the public sector may lose talent to the private sector", D Subbarao said.[3] Talent acquisition and talent retention is the basic problem faced by most of the PSUs. PSBs seem to be facing a crisis with almost half the top management cadre retiring in the next couple of years, with no identifiable talent to replace them (www.moneylife.in). Situation becomes more appalling for PSUs when people are handsomely paid in private sector organizations. So this issue has started to gain attention of policy makers in India.

Private sector corporations extensively use Performance Related Incentive (PRI) to compensate higher performers and also to differentiate them from non-performers. PRI is the concept which is built on the premises that better performance can be achieved when pay is linked with performance. Essence of PRI is that differential performance must be differentially rewarded. PRI in private sector is mostly concentrated on higher level managers as means of awarding them higher performance by giving them stock options or cash for organizational performance. Lower level employees are given bonus for individual and group performance. Private corporations such as Maruti Udyog Ltd., Indian Pharmaceuticals Corporation Ltd., Larson & Turbo Ltd., Apollo Tyres Ltd., have successfully implemented PRI. This is the factor where public sector organizations should pay attention in order to compete with private sector organizations. Differentially rewarding employees according to performance becomes powerful tool to improve government performance. Performance related incentive have been debated since the fourth pay commission in the mid 80s, but yet has not been implemented. The government of India faced lot of criticism that increased burden on public exchequer without bringing in the desired ethos.[4] In July 2006; Government of India approved setting of Sixth Central Pay Commissions (SCPC). SCPC examined the issues of PRI more seriously.

The rational for using performance linked system in government organizations is based upon several potential benefits that can accrue to public organization. First, it can motivate individual; to improve individual or team performance, similar to the prevailing philosophy of private sector where such schemes are popular. Another benefit is to enable government to attract and retain talent, particularly in times where private sector compensation is much higher than government.[5] Accountability and efficiency of government employees have become very crucial for competent public administration. One of the key ways for achieving this is performance linked incentives. Expectations from PRI are to provide motivation to employees and to compete with private sector for managerial and to reduce undue burden on central exchequer.

Even the experience of government around the world also shows positive side of PRI. Experience of several OECD countries indicates, PRI schemes can also be seen as way of facilitating broader organizational change in the functioning government departments.[6] PRI concept is not new in the government. PRI system is more prevailed at senior managerial level in developed countries like USA, UK, France, etc[7, 8]. OECD 2005 report also indicates that increasingly non-managerial employees have also covered in the last few years. Started in Private Corporation, PRI has also started gaining more and more ground in government organizations, for improving the overall performance of government organizations.

"Mercer Human Resource Consulting 2006 CEO Compensation Survey"[9] performance related pay is the norm and more than 50% of the CEOs receive performance based shares. In the US Government, agencies such as The General Accounting Office, The Internal Revenue Service, and the Federal Aviation Administration have also implemented performance related incentive. Some Africa and other developing countries have also introduced performance linked incentive to ensure employee performance improvements, especially in service delivery to citizens.[10] More counties like Ethiopia, Ghana, Indonesia, Mali, and Myanmar are also implementing PRI. Experience of Asian countries has also been good with PRI. Singapore government provides a highly successful example of implementing PRI for civil servants (Government Employees). They have replaced traditionally seniority based pay with PRI. The most important rational behind implementation of PRI is to minimize the corruption in government as well paid employees do not succumb to the temptation of corruption.[11] Pakiastan has also taken initiatives in area of performance related incentives government and public sector organizations. Even certain public sector organizations have also implemented the PRI. NTPC have been successfully implementing performance related incentive schemes and result has been positive so far.

Indian Government can also accept the same kind of results by implementing the PRI on large scale. According to study done by G Raghuram and Prof. Narayan Rangraj[12] the Indian Railway was required to introduce the PRI to compete with private players on the salary related aspects and also to retain their employees. PRI will also help IR to attract talented entry level managers.

PSUs in India are adopting effective components of compensation which are widely used in private sector units. Variable pay or pay for performance which is more popular in private sector is now gaining its popularity and acceptance in Indian public sector units also. Even payment according to the industry norms is becoming part of compensation determinates for PSUs.

Committee which is Chaired by A.K. Khandelwal, former CMD, Bank of Baroda, and constituted of five other members – Dr. T.V. Rao, Professor, IIM-Ahmedabad, Dr. Deepak Pathak, Professor, IIT Mumbai and M.V. Nair, ex-chairman Indian Banks' Association and H.N. Sinor, former executive IBA[13] has proposed that PSB should be allowed to adopt the CTC (cost to the company) concept, something that is more attuned with the corporate sector than the public sector. The committee has also suggested that variable pay should be a major component of wages.[14] One of the major recommendations given by the committee includes introduction of employee stock options plans (ESOPs) for top performers of the banks to retain talent in public sector banks. The committee has proposed that banks must acknowledge 25 per cent of the top performers through ESOPs and performance linked incentives. ESOPs may help PSUs to pull up the productivity level of employees and to curb attrition rate. Few other recommendations given by the committee include[14, 15]:

- Introduction of separate positions for chairman and the managing director
- Outsourcing of non-core operations and incentivize mobility of clerical staff to the rural areas in PSBs.
- Wage settlement at the individual bank level, with each bank deciding its own wage structure depending on its profitability and capacity to pay instead of industry-wide wage settlement.
- Changes to the archaic recruitment criteria of PSBs. For clerical staff minimum qualification should be graduation, instead of the current SSC requirement. Also, for the officer cadre, candidate should hold a banking diploma, apart from graduation.
- Formation of a board committee on HR in each bank. Banks having business worth Rs 3 lakh crore and a staff of 30,000 will be required to appoint an executive director-HR on their board.
- Succession planning by bank's board for each key leadership position by identifying three potential successors. The Committee has also suggested for the setting up of a national level Banker's Leadership Development Institute which will develop leaders for banking industry.
- Introduction of performance management systems.

Incentive structures have started to gain ground in PSUs other than banks also. "An incentive system is being worked upon as recommended by the sixth pay commission. It could be implemented by next year". Prajapati Trivedi, secretary, performance management, said at the annual economic editors' conference[16]. This incentive scheme would be based upon performance of the employee and would also depend upon cost savings on account of reduction in the use of office stationary and savings in the electricity consumption. Government has started to prepare the system for performance monitoring and evaluation for the same.

Government officials are very optimistic about the changes in compensation structure. This might help PSUs to attract best talent and to retain the same. This change in PSUs can help organizations to outperform private organizations. It can even solve the problem of low motivation of government employees which has always been the major issue in PSUs. Even it can help government to fight with biggest evil that is corruption which is deeply rooted in public sector units. This is the accepted outcomes but reality may even be opposite it. Bureaucratic stricture of Government organization may prove to become blockage in this path. Introduction of variable pay will increase the financial burden on already loss making PSUs. Employees at PSUs may oppose the incentive system. Implementing PRI is strategic change for the organizations and will require greater decentralization and autonomy which may be opposed by officials who are holding and enjoying the powerful positions as the new pay system may result in change of power structure.

Questions

1. Will new pay structure help PSUs to compete with their counterparts in talent acquisition? Critically evaluate.
2. What kind of problem may be faced by PSUs in introduction of incentive schemes and pay for performance? How should these issues be addressed? Explain.

References

1. Excerpt taken from Synthesis Report of Studies on Formulating the Concept, Principles and Parameters for Performance related incentives (PRI) in Government for Sixth Central Pay Commission, Prepared by Prof. Biju Varkkey, Prof Prem Pangotra, Prof Rekha Jain, Prof Manjari Singh, Prof Abhishek Mishra, Prof. G Raghuram, Prof Narayan Rangraj, and Dr Swati Mishra, IIM Ahemdabad, 2008.
2. http://in.news.yahoo.com/48/20100908/1238/tbs-rbi-pushes-psu-bankers-case-for-fatt.html, Access on 20/11/2010
3. http://in.news.yahoo.com/48/20100908/1238/tbs-rbi-pushes-psu-bankers-case-for-fatt.html, Access on 20/11/2010
4. Excerpt taken from Study on Formulating the Concept, Principles and Parameters for Performance related incentives (PRI) in Government for Sixth Central Pay Commission, Prepared by G Raghuram and Prof. Narayan Rangraj
5. World Bank 2001, Salary Supplements and Bonuses in Revenue Department, WP 33328, Vol 1 , Accessed at www.wds.worldbank.org
6. OECD 2005, "Performance Related pay Policies for Government Employees" OECD Publishing.
7. World Bank 2001, Salary Supplements and Bonuses in Revenue Department, WP 33328, Vol 1 , Accessed at www.wds.worldbank.org
8. OECD 2005, "Performance Related pay Policies for Government Employees" OECD Publishing.
9. www.mercer.com/pressrelease/details.html/dynamic/idcontent/1263210
10. OECD 2005, "Performance Related pay Policies for Government Employees" OECD Publishing.
11. Part of excerpt taken from presentation made by Shri Suresh C Gupta IAS at IIM A during a workshop on "Pay for Performance" May 1, 2007 as mentioned in Synthesis Report of Studies on Formulating the Concept, Principles and Parameters for Performance related incentives (PRI) in Government for Sixth Central Pay Commission, Prepared by Prof. Biju Varkkey, Prof Prem Pangotra, Prof Rekha Jain, Prof Manjari Singh, Prof Abhishek Mishra, Prof. G Raghuram, Prof Narayan Rangraj, and Dr Swati Mishra, IIM Ahemdabad, 2008.
12. Excerpt taken from Study on Formulating the Concept, Principles and Parameters for Performance related incentives (PRI) in Government for Sixth Central Pay Commission, Prepared by G Raghuram and Prof. Narayan Rangraj

13. http://www.expressindia.com/latest-news/PSU-banks-may-link-pay-with-performance/643167/, Access on 23/11/2010
14. http://news.in.msn.com/business/article.aspx?cp-documentid=4123753, Access on 25/11/2010
15. http://www.expressindia.com/latest-news/PSU-banks-may-link-pay-with-performance/643167/, Access on 23/11/2010
16. http://www.moneylife.in/article/8/6797.html, Access on 23/11/2010
17. http://economictimes.indiatimes.com/news/news-by-industry/jobs/Incentive-system-for-govt-staffers-next-year-Secy/articleshow/6818946.cms, Access on 28/11/2010

15

What Went Wrong at Techo-soft?

Ms. Neelam Saraswat, IPEM, Ghaziabad
saraswat.neelam@gmail.com
Mr. Gaurav Bhargava,
Syndicate Bank, Ghaziabad
gbhargava84@gmail.com

"The day is much colder than any other day" Rita said to Sumit, Assistant Manager in HR Department, at tea. Rita is currently working as Senior Manager HR in Techno-soft Corporation Pvt. Ltd. She is working with Techno-soft from last 25 years. Since that, time has never been as tough as it was in last one and half year. Economic slow down had badly hit all the businesses all over the world and Techno-soft was not an exception.

Techno-soft is an IT company. It was enjoying good reputation, huge client base and high market share till year 2007. The MNC had profit of $1.3 billion in financial year 2007-08. It was having 15,000 employees globally out of which 4,000 were working in India only. Employees were paid handsomely and well taken care by the organization. Employees were provided excellent career opportunities. Company won many awards for its employee friendly practices. Most of the employees of Techno-soft were working in the company from minimum 3 to maximum 30 years. Employees were very much committed to Techno-soft.

Every thing was smoothly happening when economic slow down hit major economies all over the world. As Techno-soft was having its operation in many counties, it lost on huge number of client base. Company started to loose profits from first quarter of financial year 2008-09. Also company notified loss of around $500 million in first quarter of FY 2008-09. And the loss kept on increasing till the first quarter of FY 2009-10. Management of Techno-soft became concerned about increasing loss and they made strategies to reduce the cost. The top management notified

HR department to cut the work force as soon as possible and cut the cost on employee related issues. HR department also did not think on long term basis and started giving pink slip to the employees without filtering talented employees and without knowing their worth to the company. At the end of the FY 2008-09 Techno-soft was having only 1300 employees in India. The HR department which was known for its employee friendly practices was now loosing its credibility and trust. Remaining employees also started feeling insecurity regarding the job. Their productivity level came down as work load was high and they were working under pressure. Employees who were shown pink slip were now negative about the company.

Good days came back when the global market started to show improvement from the mid of year 2009. Techno-soft again got new assignments and projects. Those projects were demanding highly capable people. HR department of Techno-soft contacted the old employees for re-recruitment. But now those employees were also working somewhere else and they were not willing to come back to the company which did not value their contribution in the success of the organization. So Techno-soft had to look at other resources for recruitment. Techno-soft had to invest huge amount of money and time in the process of recruitment. But this huge investment was not giving proper return on investment to the company as huge lay off had created bad image of Techno-soft. Now only one day left for recruitment process to be over and Rita was not vary optimistic about getting highly talented employees as they were having earlier. After finishing her talk with Sumit she again resume back to interview desk for taking interviews.

Questions

1. What went wrong at Techno-soft? What is the main issue of concern in the case?
2. What should have been done by Techno-soft to avoid the problem which they were facing currently?
3. Put yourself at the place of Rita and suggest the ways to fix the problem.

16

Training Need Assessment through Skill-Will Mapping of Shop Floor Employees with Special Reference to Perfetti Van Melle

Dr. Manjula Jain
Director
School of Business Management
IFTM University
manjulajain@iftmuniversity.ac.in

Ms. Ritika Khanna
Assistant Professor
School of Business Management
IFTM University
ritikakhanna@iftmuniversity.ac.in

Ms. Nishtha Sharma
Assistant Professor
School of Business Management, IFTM University
nishthasharma@iftmuniversity.ac.in

Introduction

Perfetti Van Melle is a privately owned company, producing and distributing candies and chewing gums in more than 130 countries worldwide. The company was established in March 2001 through the merger of Perfetti and Van Melle.

In July 2006, the group acquired the Spanish company Chupa chups, thus strengthening its position as the third largest confectionery (sugar confectionery + gums) group in the world, and becoming the first player in the global sugar confectionery market.

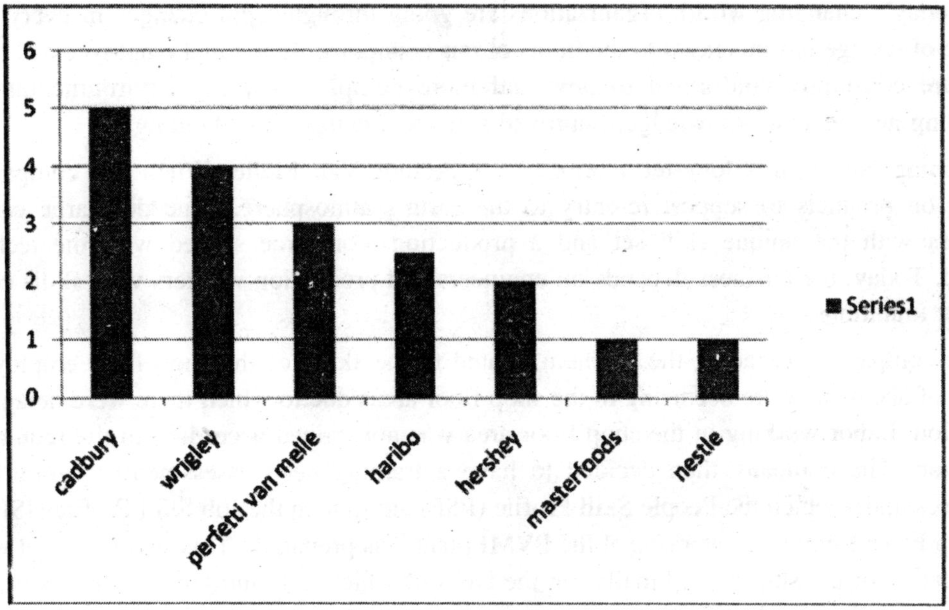

It is now the third largest confectionery group in the world, and the first to be present in the main Asian market. Employing over 14000 people and operating 32 companies throughout the world. Perfetti Van Melle has a true global reach. It is present in the Asia pacific region, Europe, Middle East, Africa, and the America. Its corporate headquarters are located in Lainate (Italy) and in Breda (the Netherlands).

Some of the main brands offered by Perfetti includes: **Mentos, Frisk, Fruittella, Alpenliebe, Golia, Happydent, Vivident, Big Babol, Airheads, Chupa chups, and Smint.**

In addition to these global brands, Perfetti Van Melle offers a wide range of products, the popularity of which is rooted in individual, local, and regional markets. The ability to develop products, versions, and flavors that suit the different demands and opportunities of the local market is indeed one of the group's key to success.

The significance and value of training has long been recognized. Consider the popular and often repeated quotation, *"Give a person a fish and you feed him for a day. Teach a person to fish and you feed him for a lifetime."* This simple but profound saying is attributed to the wisdom of Confucius who lived in the 5th century BC. Given today's business climate and the exponential growth in technology with its effect on the economy and society at large, the need for training is more pronounced than ever. (McClelland S.D., 2002)

With the new emerging organizational reality where change, competition, workforce demographic changes and business upheavals are eminent, training and development is becoming ever more an important method that equips organizations with the flexibility, adaptability and durability required for survival (Al Khayyat, R. Elgamal, M. 1997).

The Key Challenge

It's all to do with training : "You can do a lot if you're properly trained".-ELIZABETH II

In today's changing world, organizations are going through rapid changes in every sphere. The rate of change has increased to the limits of our endurance. Individual employees all over the world are constantly conformed to new and more complex working environmental forces, demanding new level of knowledge, improved skills and better understanding.

Training has been a long-term priority for Perfetti Van Melle. When the company was focused on products to support re-entry to the earth's atmosphere, it needed large cadres of engineers with the unique skill set and a production workforce skilled with the techniques required. Today, the business depends on engineers and production workers with skills centered on smart munitions.

The company was facing the problem related to the skills of the shop floor employees. A number of accidents were occurring in the shop floor areas due to which there were delays in the production. Labor working in the shop floor area was not trained according to the requirements of the job. The company then decided to have a training need assessment program for the employees under which the People Skill Profile (PSP) along with the Job Skill Profile (JSP) of all the Shop Floor Employees working at the PVMI plant was prepared. This was followed with the identification of the skill gaps. Finally, on the basis of which, a training calendar was drafted to address the skill gaps identified.

Identification of Workstation

A workstation was recognized as an area that was manned or required monitoring by a shop floor employee (SFE). At the PVMI plant there were three Center Fresh lines, one Chlormint line and a Cream fill line. As such twenty three workstations were identified. Few amongst them are as follows:

1. Center Fresh Molding Area
2. Center Fresh Mixing Area
3. Chlormint Mould Area
4. Sugar Conveying Section
5. Glucose Unloading and Syrup Preparation
6. Primary Packing-Chlormint
7. Secondary Packing
8. Forklift Operator
9. Quality Assurance – Flavor Mixing
10. Quality Assurance – Laboratory

Identification of General Skills

General Skills are those which are common across workstations and are necessary to perform jobs across the plant. Hence no matter what task the SFE is involved in the general skills set will be applicable to each of them.

The primary focus of the general skill was to create awareness amongst the SFE on areas critical to maintaining an environment which was accident free and conducive to the production of a quality product keeping in mind the standards set by the FDA and other regulating bodies.

However since the plant was in the start-up stage a lot of the skills that would normally be expected from an SFE were not applicable. Hence a number of SFE's (in particular the general helpers) were found wanting in certain areas. Although this skill deficiency was acceptable at the present moment, three to four months down the line when all lines were up and running and the necessary systems were in place it would have been expected that the SFE's meet the desired efficiency level for every skill set.

A specimen of the General Skills set is given in Annexure 1.

Identification of Specific Skills

Every workstation was having a different set of skill requirements. This was followed from the fact that the task requirements demanded from the SFE differ depending on the machines/ process involved in the particular workstation – to meet the demands of that job. Hence there were twenty three different sets of skill sets for the twenty three workstations that have been identified.

The specimen of the different sets of specific skill sets is detailed in Annexure 2.

Soft Skill Profile

Unlike a job skill profile the soft skill profile did not focus on the technical skills of an individual, rather it was essentially a guide to determining crucial factors such as the commitment, dedication and ability of the SFE to adapt to different conditions and to work in a team.

The soft skill profile was designed to capture those skills which are a necessity over and above those technical skills that form an eliminating factor and not the deciding factor.

A specimen of the Soft Skill Profile is given in Annexure 3.

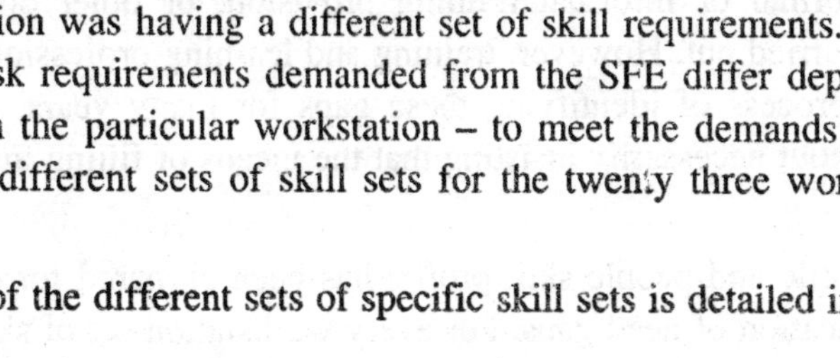

People Skill Profile

The People Skill Profile often known as the Skill–Will Profile identified how the individual SFE will measure up on the Job Skill Profile drawn up for that particular workstation. The Job Skill Profile which was made up of the Generals Skills, Specific Skills and the Will Parameters would have benchmarks given by the respective department managers. For every SFE the ratings given for a skill set will constitute the Individual Skill Profile (ISP). All the individual skill profiles will then together make up the People skill Profile.

In each of the team interviews, the employees expressed a deep commitment to acquiring new skills and abilities. They indicated that new skills and training make it possible to periodically move from one team to another and that being on the right team is critical when the business shifts direction. As one team member noted, "People must upgrade their skills to stay state of the art." Another pointed out, "Change does exist – needing new skills doesn't mean that you aren't a good employee." They also indicated, however, that it was hard to get timely and definitive information about just what the future directions of the business were.

A specimen of the People Skill Profile is given in Annexure 4.

Analysis:

The analysis of gaps in knowledge and skills identifies what employees will need to learn in order to be fully competent in the jobs they will be doing now and in the future. How these gaps are filled may involve formal or informal training provision, or other opportunities for the necessary learning to be carried out. However, training and learning professionals were using the acronym 'TNA' for the process of identifying these gaps for many years, and this fact sheet follows that tradition, without necessarily insisting that the means of filling the gaps was through formal training.

Once the job skill profile and people skill profile has been prepared for each SFE, the next stage involved the identification of need gaps. For every workstation set of skills were identified which focused upon the skills that the SFE's were found wanting in and a training program was designed for the same. These programs were targeted on the specific skill sets of every workstation.

For the general skill sets that the SFE's were found deficient in, the training program was conducted for the SFE's shift wise. All SFE's attended the programs that were conducted on the skills identified as falling in the general skills category.

The skill gaps were identified by comparing the rating given to the SFE for a particular skill by the shift executive/associate manager and the benchmark set by the manager of the respective department.

Once the skill gaps had been identified for every individual a skill will matrix was prepared by taking the average score of each SFE for the general skill set, specific skill set and the will parameters. It was desired that the SFE's will score more in the general and specific skill set as well as in the will parameters. Hence there are four quadrants on the graph and the aim of the training programs that were conducted was to equip the SFE's with the necessary skills that result in their ratings moving to the top right quadrant i.e. to the quadrant which is high both in skill and will parameters. The skill will matrix of the shop floor employees of the plant has been shown below:

SKILL WILL MATRIX

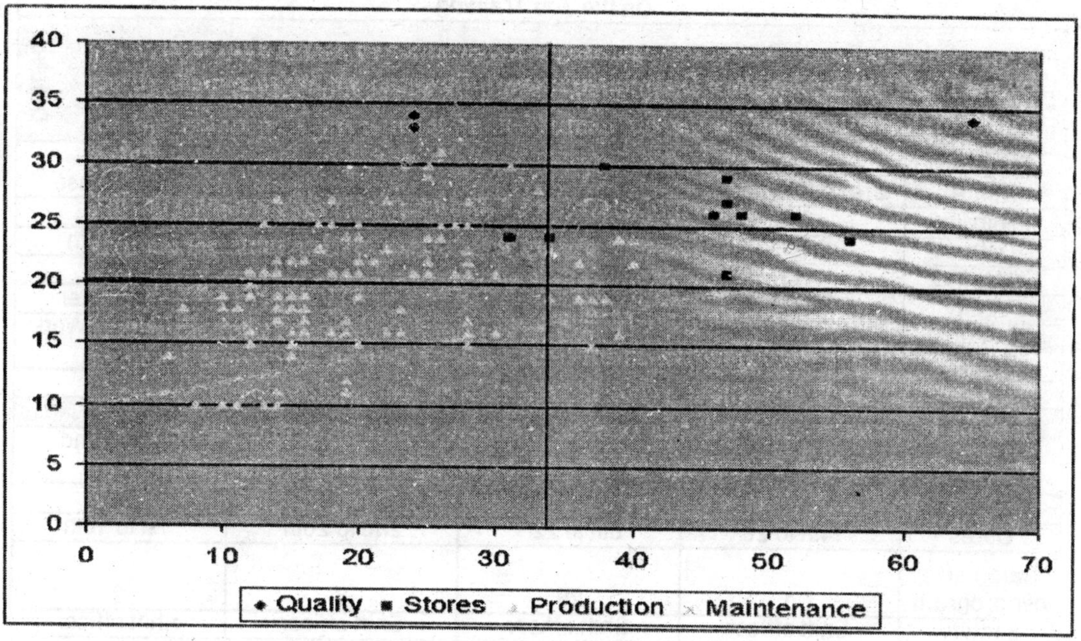

The matrix above shows that majority of people lie in the quadrant of high will and low skill .i.e.; they need to improve upon their skill parameters so that they can be moved to the high skill high will quadrant.

Training Calendar

Having identified the specific area in which training needs to be imparted, a training calendar was designed to equip the SFE's with the skills essential to the efficient operation of the workstation.

Training Calendar-2009				
On the Job Training				
	July	August	September	October
Program Name	Creamfill Process	Sugar Conveying Section	Forklift Operator	Boiler House
Eligibility	SFE	SFE	SFE	SFE
Dates	8th to 22nd	6th to 22nd	2nd to 9th	6th to 11th
Batch Size	13	7	3	4
Faculty	Shift officer	Shift officer	Shift officer	Shift officer
Venue	Respective Work Station	Respective Work Station	Respective Work Station	Respective Work Station
Target	13	7	3	4
Program Name	Sugar Conveying Section	Primary and Secondary packing	General Fitter	Turner and Welder
Eligibility	SFE	SFE	SFE	SFE
Dates	14th to 28th	6th to 22nd	2nd to 20th	1st to 10th
Batch Size per program	1	29	8	2
Faculty	Shift officer	Shift officer	Shift officer	Shift officer
Venue	Respective Work Station	Respective Work Station	Respective Work Station	Respective Work Station
Target	1	29	8	2

Conclusion

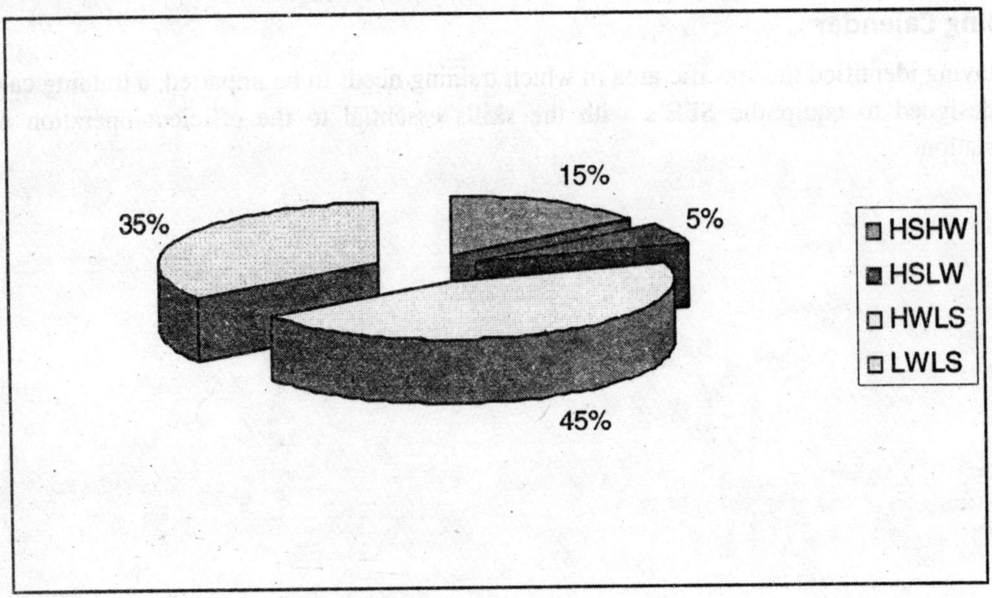

From the above chart it can be interpreted that 15% people were lying in the high skill high will quadrant, 5% employees were in the high skill low will quadrant so they need to develop more will.

45% employees were in the quadrant which is high in will but low in skill which means that they have the will to do but they lack in the skills required to perform the tasks.

35%employees were in the low skill low will quadrant which means that they were low in both the parameters and need to improve so that they can become more perfect and move to the high skill high will quadrant.

Training is the base for personnel mgmt. If we expect the performance of high level from our employees we must train them. Changes take place in technology and mgmt every day. Therefore, it becomes necessary that the workers and employees of the enterprise must be trained so that they discharge their duties easily and effectively and may adjust with the changed circumstances.

Training could be compared to this metaphor - if I miss one meal in a day, then I will starve to death. The survival of the organization requires development throughout the ranks in order to survive, while training makes the organization more effective and efficient in its day-to-day operations.

Exhibits

Exhibit 1

	1	2	3	4	5
General Skills:					
Knowledge of Safety Parameters/PPE (goggles, safety					
shoes, face mask)					
Knowledge of Emergency Response Plan					
Knowledge of First Aid					
Awareness of Basic Manufacturing Process					
Awareness of organizational Objectives					
Understanding of diagnostic procedures in the manual					
Maintenance and use of log books and history books					
Maintenance of tool kit					
Awareness of 5S					
Awareness of HACCP					
Awareness of SQF					
Awareness of Standard operating procedure					
Knowledge of work Permit System					

Exhibit-2. MOLDING LINE - CENTER FRESH

	1	2	3	4	5
Specific Skills:					
Awareness of temperature of the electrical heater in the pre-extruder and forming extruder					
Knowledge of the percentage of filling syrup required for the centre filling					
Knowledge of the weight and shape of the candy					
Knowledge of the allowable temperature and RH for conduction of the process (for cooling tunnel as well as environment)					
Knowledge of operation of the machines in the process					
Awareness of the impact of change in speed of forming machine on the process					
Knowledge of the type of dies to be used					
Knowledge of the type of lubrication oil to be used					
Knowledge of the function of the inner and outer cam					
Awareness of reason for fluctuations in weight, leakage in pieces and deformation in pieces of candy					

CHLORMINT MOLDING

	1	2	3	4	5
Specific Skills:					
Awareness of the impact of rework on the process					
Knowledge of operation of the machines in the process					
Knowledge of the weight and shape of the candy Knowledge of the rope sizer calibration/adjustment process					
Knowledge of the function of the pressure chain Awareness of operating temperature and pressure of the solvomat and cooker					
Awareness of reason for fluctuations in weight					
Knowledge of the allowable temperature and RH for conduction of the process (for cooling tunnel as well as environment)					
Knowledge of Die set fixing , dismantling and working of die set					

MIXING SECTION - CENTER FRESH

	1	2	3	4	5
Specific Skills:					
Knowledge of time for the mixing process					
Knowledge of the sequence in which to add the materials					
Knowledge of quantity of material to be added together					
Knowledge of the cleaning procedure					
Knowledge of operation of machines in the process					

GLUCOSE UNLOADING AND SYRUP PREPARATION

	1	2	3	4	5
Specific Skills:					
Knowledge of time for the mixing process					
Knowledge of the sequence in which to add the materials					
Knowledge of quantity of material to be added together					
Knowledge of the cleaning procedure					
Awareness of technical settings					
Awareness of importance of valve and fuse check (glucose section)					
Basic parameters for operating the machine					
Check for quantity of liquid that can be further filled in the tank					

PRIMARY PACKING

	1	2	3	4	5
Specific Skills:					
Skill level in Packing					
Awareness of the different types of Defects					
Knowledge of machine speeds					
Awareness of different temperature settings - cutting and sealing temperature					
Awareness of technical settings of the machine					
Basic parameters for operating the machine					

SUGAR CONVEYING SECTION

	1	2	3	4	5
Specific Skills:					
Skill at Operation of blower					
Capability to troubleshoot basic problems					
Knowledge of function of the purging valves					
Knowledge of the cleaning procedure					
Knowledge of diversion valves for separate sections					

SECONDARY PACKING

	1	2	3	4	5
Specific Skills:					
Skill level in Packing					
Awareness of the different types of Defects					
Knowledge of machine speeds					
Awareness of technical settings					
Calibration of the Machine (Yamato - weight check)					
Basic parameters for operating the machine					

QUALITY ASSURANCE - FLAVOR MIXING

	1	2	3	4	5
Specific Skills:					
Knowledge of the procedure used to prepare the flavors and colors					
Knowledge of the cleaning procedure					
Awareness of safety procedures while handling flavors					
Knowledge of clearance and rejection procedures					
Awareness of importance of cleanliness and maintenance of basic hygiene					

QUALITY ASSURANCE – LABORATORY

	1	2	3	4	5
Specific Skills:					
Knowledge of water testing					
Skill at troubleshooting					
Knowledge of storage conditions					
Awareness of process parameters (temperature, humidity, weight)					
Awareness of quality control systems					
Knowledge of instruments, their calibration and their use					
Knowledge of the sampling plan					
Knowledge of testing for raw materials/finished goods					
Knowledge of cleaning procedures					
Skill at identification and classification of defects					
Knowledge of the manufacturing process					
Awareness of safety procedures while handling chemicals					
Awareness of packing parameters (weight, counts, wrapping quality, sealing quality, mfg/exp date)					
Knowledge of clearance and rejection procedures					

FORKLIFT OPERATOR

	1	2	3	4	5
Specific Skills:					
Knowledge of nature of goods					
Knowledge of cutting angle					
Knowledge of cleaning procedure					
Battery Charging procedure					
Driving Skills					
Basic troubleshooting skills					
Basic maintenance (Checking of air and oil pressure, lubricant and distilled water level, brakes and horn, nuts and bolts)					

Exhibit3

Soft Skills Profile	
Qualification:	
No Schooling	1
High School Pass	2
Inter Pass	3
ITI Trained, Diploma	4
Graduate, post graduate	5
Work Experience:	
Fresher	1
1-2 Years	2
2-3 Years	3
3-4 years	4
More than 4 Years	5
Will Parameters	
Punctuality/Attendance:	
Below 80%	1
80-85%	2
86-90%	3
90-95%	4
>95%	5

Exhibit4

CHLORMINT MOLDING

	1	2	3	4	5
General Skills:					
Knowledge of Safety Parameters		❒			❒
Knowledge of Emergency Response Plan			❒	❒	
Knowledge of First Aid		❒		❒	
Awareness of Basic Manufacturing Process			❒	❒	
Awareness of Organizational Objectives		❒			❒
Maintenance of log books			❒	❒	
Tool kit			μ		
Capability to troubleshoot basic problems		❒	❒		
Awareness of 5S			μ		

Awareness of HACCP			μ		
Awareness of SQF		❐	❐		
Awareness of importance of cleanliness of the machine and maintenance of basic hygiene				μ	
Awareness of Standard Operating Procedure			❐	❐	
Specific Skills:					
Awareness of the impact of rework on the process			❐	❐	
Knowledge of operation of the machines in the process			❐	❐	
Knowledge of the weight and shape of the candy			❐		❐
Knowledge of the rope sizer calibration/adjustment process			❐	❐	
Knowledge of the function of the pressure chain			❐	❐	
Awareness of operating temperature and pressure of the solvomat and cooker			❐	❐	
Awareness of reason for fluctuations in weight				❐	❐
Knowledge of the allowable temperature and RH for conduction of the process (for cooling tunnel as well as environment)				μ	
Knowledge of Die set fixing , dismantling and working of die set			❐	❐	

Work Experience:		
Fresher	**1**	
1-2 Years	**2**	
2-3 Years	**3**	
3-4 years	**4**	❐
More than 4 Years	**5**	#

Will Parameters					
Punctuality/Attendance:					
Below 80%	**1**				
80-85%	**2**				
86-90%	**3**	❐			
90-95%	**4**				
>95%	**5**	❐			

	1	2	3	4	5
Team Work			❐		❐
Adaptability			❐	❐	
Physical fitness/ hygiene			❐		❐
Dedication and commitment		❐			❐
Reaction to criticism/errors		❐		❐	
Degree of involvement in task			❐		❐
Awareness and practice of safety and quality standards			❐		❐

❐ - Benchmark

❐ - Below the Benchmark

µ - At Par with Benchmark

 # - Better Rating than Benchmark

17

Benchmarking of Personnel Practices & Mapping of Organizational Culture: A Manufacturing Industry Perspective

Mr. Puneet Bansal
Department of Management Studies, IIT, Delhi
puneet@iitdmba.com

Introduction

In a manufacturing belt such as Gurgaon and Manesar, the shop floor workers' opinions and behaviour depend a lot on the neighboring and surrounding manufacturing organizations. The policies of the neighboring manufacturing organizations and the benefits being offered by them play a major role in employee dissatisfaction and unrest, which leads to conflicts and finally gives rise to attrition. Therefore, it is always better in such organizations to carry out regular benchmarking surveys and keep up with the pace of the belt and also be able to exceed it in a few areas to retain the talented manpower in the organization. Thus, this benchmarking study had to be done for Perfetti Van Melle India Ltd. to help the human resource managers to update their policies and increase or keep up the existing benefits as per any lacunae highlighted in the study.

Moreover, as a fundamental shift is occurring in across the business world, we are moving progressively further away from a world in which national business were relatively isolated from each other by barriers by distance, time zones and language; and by national culture differences, and business systems. To map the various aspects of culture in the organization and their inter-linkages formed the second part of our project. Both the projects have been summarized in the form of research design, methodology and conclusion.

The Manufacturing Plant at Manesar, Haryana The Manufacturing Plant at Manesar, Haryana

The manufacturing plant at Manesar, Haryana is located amidst the scenic beauty of the Nakhraula village situated around 15 kms. from Gurgaon. The plant was established in 1994. Product brands like Alpenliebe, Big Baboi, Center fresh, Chlormint, Happydent, Center Shock and Cofitos etc. are produced at this manufacturing facility.

The various departments at this fully air conditioned plant are Production, Maintenance, Packaging, Accounts & Finance, Supply Chain, Personnel, Quality control, Research & development and Information technology. The plant boasts of the latest manufacturing techniques and sophisticated equipment. The plant has 280 permanent workers and about 450 contractual workers under temporary contracts and also permanent contracts.

The shop floor workers are classified into 8 grades:

E1 (1); E1 (2); E2 (1); E2 (2); E3; E4; E5 and E6.

The working hours at the plant are as follows:

Shift Working Hours with break durations

	Shift 1	Shift 2	Shift 3	General Shift
Working hrs.	7:00a.m-3:00p.m	3:00p.m-11:00p.m	110:00p.m-7:00a.m	9:00a.m-5:30p.m
Break duration	**20 + 15 mins.**	**20 + 15 mins.**	**15 + 15 mins.**	**20 + 15 mins.**

The plant has a friendly and informal work culture which is very conducive to healthy information sharing. Everyone in the plant believes in respect for the individuals and equality irrespective of hierarchy. The plant undertakes many welfare activities for the workers such as free meals, free transport, free uniforms, loans, medical facility etc.

Project 1: Benchmarking Personnel Policies & Practices

Research Problem

Human resource policies and programs are that set of organisational policies which seek to establish and maintain the employment relationship. Most treatments of human resource management tend to be normative and generally have sought to identify ways in which human resource management can be conducted in order that the results would lead to a more effective organisation and / or greater employee satisfaction, while also taking into consideration that human resource management policies vary widely from one organisation to the next.

First, however, it is important to have a clear understanding of what benchmarking is and how it can be applied to improve the overall performance of an organisation.

Benchmarking Process

Benchmarking is the search for industry best practice which leads to superior performance. The pioneer of competitive benchmarking was the American company, Xerox Corporation. The company demonstrated the usefulness of observing and learning from superior performers by benchmarking their competitors. Through the knowledge they gained they managed to dramatically improve their productivity and significantly reduce their cost of production.

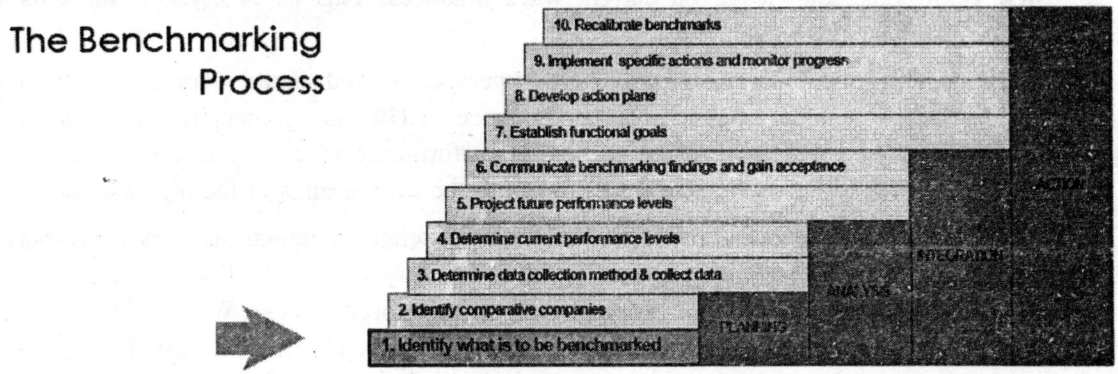

Figure 1: The benchmarking Process

The process of benchmarking can be broken into 10 steps which progress through 4 phases:

1. Planning
2. Analysis
3. Integration
4. Action

Step 1: Identify what policies, benefits and functions are essential practices and should be benchmarked.

Step 2: Identify external organisations or functions within own organisation with superior work practices for comparison.

Step 3: Determine what data sources are to be used. If an organisation has up to date personnel systems it should be able to measure a range of HR practices and outputs relatively easily. Valuable information may be available through personnel records, surveys or even interviews.

Step 4: Determine the current level of policy performance. This will enable the gap in policies to be identified. Emphasis lies on the importance of a "full understanding of internal business processes before attempting a comparison with external organisations."

Step 5: Develop a vision for future operation based on the benchmarking findings. Focus is directed on the quality of best practice procedures and how these can be not just emulated, but improved upon by the organisation.

Step 6: Report progress to all those concerned on an ongoing basis. Communication and feedback are crucial components of benchmarking.

Step 7: Establish functional goals linked to the overall vision for the organisation.

Step 8 & 9: Develop action plans and implement the best practice findings. This should be the responsibility of the people who actually perform the work. Periodic measurement and assessment of achievements should be put into place.

Step 10: Update knowledge on current work practices. This is, in essence, the crux of continuous quality improvement.

Assessment must be undertaken from a holistic perspective and should involve looking out or through the narrow window of functional performance. If HR management is ever to be taken seriously as a major contributor to the successful performance of an organisation, it needs to adopt a strategic focus and look at measures linked to the overall aims of the organisation.

Unlike the manufacturing and production sector, areas related to human services and resources have less experience with identifying and defining industry standards. Take for example the common HR measure of the rate of absenteeism within an organisation. What is included as a measure of absenteeism - certified sick leave, uncertified sick leave, sick leave full pay, sick leave half pay, short leave, leave-without-pay, maternity leave, etc? All, some or none of the components of absence may be relevant in different situations.

This, therefore, means that comparing HR information from one organisation to another or even within the same organisation may be misleading due to the use of different:

1. Definitions;
2. Methods of data collection, storage and/or retrieval;
3. Methods of calculation; and
4. Organisational structures.

Industry Standards

Far too often HR is viewed as a collection of loosely associated functions rather than an integrated system. Any HR department is a system containing a range of interrelated subsystems. It is useful to view HR in this way when discussing measurement because some factors (both internal and external to the HR department) can often influence a number of HR subsystems.

Figure 2: HR subsystems

In most cases it is relatively easy to identify who wants or needs HR information - usually the Chief Executive Officer (CEO), corporate executive, line managers or HR professionals. In our case it is the Factory Personnel manager. The next step is to identify what information would prove the most useful.

The performance indices selected should take into account:

* The different HR subsystems,
* The priorities of the organisation and
* The frequency with which the information will be reported. Some indices are more meaningful when reported on a frequent basis, while other information has a long term focus (e.g. Turnover).

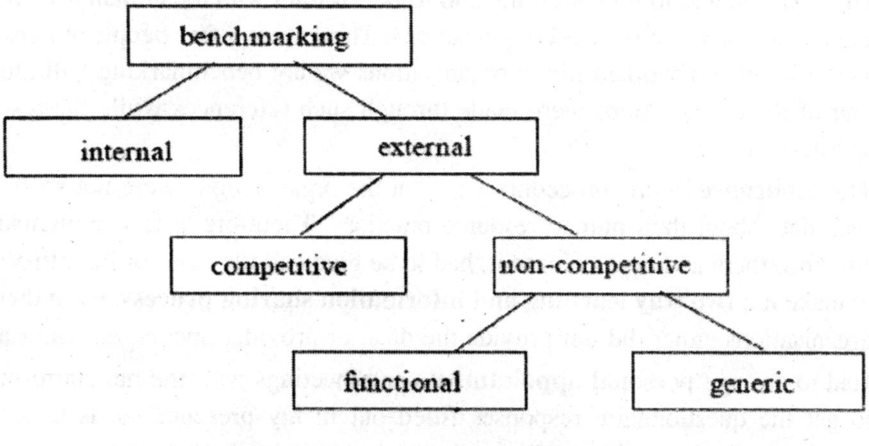

Figure 3: Facets of benchmarking

Research Design

Methodology &Procedure:

The stepwise data collection procedure and research methodology is as follows:

- Developing and formulating a questionnaire as per the requiem of the organisation i.e. **chalking out and planning what is to be benchmarked:**
    - The questionnaire encompasses all the policies and benefits being currently extended by Perfetti Van Melle India Pvt. Ltd. to the shop floor members.
    - It takes into account all the policies and benefits that matter to the shop floor members to maintain the employment relationship at its utmost level.
    - The importance of the policies and benefits has been decided upon through discussions with 6 of the most senior shop floor members and the personnel department executives.
    - Accordingly, a comprehensive questionnaire had been prepared to collect data from the management of the organisations decided upon.
- The next step was to **decide upon the organisations** with which to compare and analyse: The Gurgaon – Manesar manufacturing belt, which is under consideration in this project, is **not a very employer friendly labour market** and has frequent lock outs and strikes in a few of the neighbouring organisations and a considerably high attrition rate overall. In such a volatile market the **workers are directly influenced and that too, very quickly by the policies, benefits and governance of the neighbouring organisations**. It is not uncommon to see the workers demanding new benefits or schemes recently extended in any of the other organisations in the belt. Therefore, it was decided to benchmark the policies and benefits here with those of the organisations in the Gurgaon - Manesar manufacturing belt rather than food processing and manufacturing organisations even though the organisations being considered are of totally different manufacturing fields (mostly auto ancillaries) than Perfetti Van Melle India which can be considered a food processing FMCG organisation.
- The next step was to find out **links and make contact** with the human resource departments and managers of the selected organisations. There were a few people at Perfetti Van Melle who have earlier worked in the organisations we are benchmarking with, the contacts for four of the organisations were made through such references while the rest were directly approached.
- **The hindrance** in this procedure was that the organisations were not willing to part with such data about their human resource practices. Therefore, a few mails had to be sent to convince them and urge them to it, had to be given all the data for Perfetti Van Melle so as to make it a **two way learning and information sharing process**. Even then, a few of the organisations either did not provide the data, or provided incomplete, unusable data.
- Had to arrange **personal appointments** and meetings with the human resource managers to get the questionnaire responses filled out in my presence so as to ask questions to clarify any doubts and to understand their working methods better.

Observations & Findings

Table 1: Comparison of facilities with other companies

	Personal Loan (Rs.)	Meal Charges	Transport	Training Days/ employee	Leaves/ year	Communi-cation	Meetings Health centre
Perfetti Van Melle	1,50,000	40	Yes	4	32	Yes	No
HMSI	2.50.000	25	Yes	8	25	Yes	Yes
Denso	2,00,000	20	Yes	5	30	No	Yes
Career Aircon	3,00,000	23	Yes	4	35	Yes	Yes
Rico Auto	3,00,000	20	Yes	6	25	Yes	Yes
Gillete	4,00,000	25	Yes	10	35	No	Yes
Purolator Filters	2,50,000	23	Yes	8	35	Yes	No

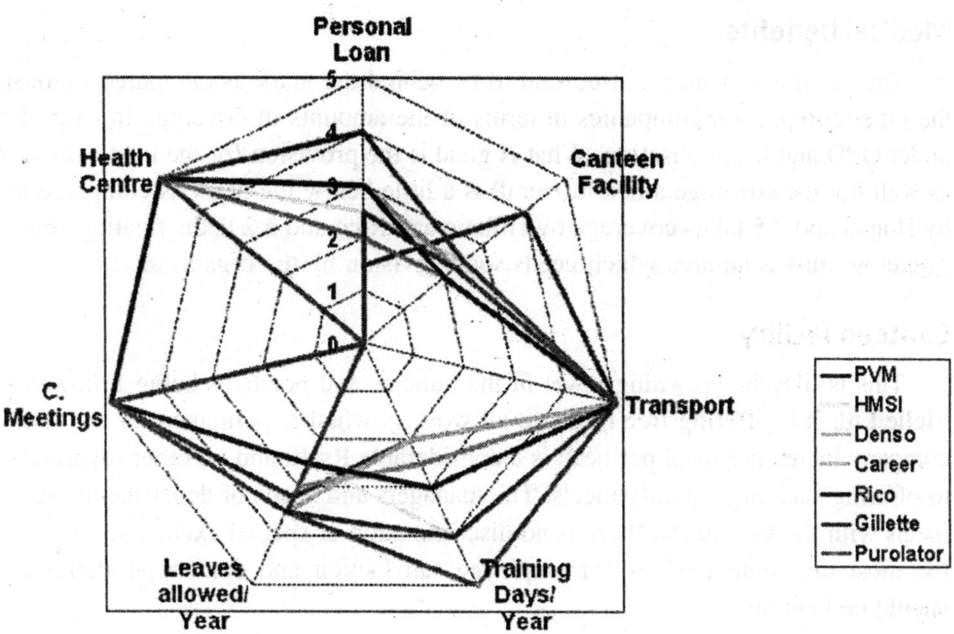

Figure 4: Radar Chart showing benchmarking practices with other companies

Results & Conclusions

The major conclusion that can be drawn through the information available is that the current policies being followed at Perfetti Van Melle India are at par and mostly above the market i.e. the neighbouring manufacturing units.

The individual comparisons are as follows:

Leaves and holidays

The system of leaves and holidays followed by Perfetti Van Melle is at par with most in case of the number of holidays but lagging behind a few in terms of maximum leaves which can be encashed or carried forward, with Gillette leading the way in terms of encashment scheme which is based on twice the amount of basic pay. The current leaves structure of Perfetti is a balanced and feasible structure which does have a little margin for increase but above that it would not be feasible in terms of cost-benefits.

Employee Loans

The good thing here is the salary advance benefit that PVM India (Perfetti Van Melle) is extending to its workers which works as a personal loan or advance but is cost free to the worker as it is adjusted in the next month's salary. What can be included in the loan scheme is a provision for housing loans to the employees through bank tie-ups so as to not cause a cost increase but just to facilitate the employees in easier procurements and lesser formalities.

Medical benefits

This is an area which can be said to be behind the mark as compared to most, but not all of the other comparison companies in terms of the amounts of coverage in case of the entitlement under OPD and hospitalisation. What is good is the provision for the medical coverage of parents as well but the coverage amount overall is a little below the mark as compared to the 1.75 lakhs by Honda and 2.5 lakhs coverage by Gillette and Rico and a 2 lakhs floating coverage by Carrier. Therefore, this is an area which needs some revision by the organisation.

Canteen facility

This is like the crowning jewel in the policies and practices being followed by Perfetti Van Melle Ltd. It is offering free meals to all workers whether permanent or not. The cost which the company incurs per meal per head is a considerable Rs.40 and no other organisation comes close to offering such high quality meals. The managers and heads of departments enjoy the very same meals with the workers so there is no discrimination or special extensions as well. This is one of the most important reasons for employee satisfaction and content at Perfetti Van Melle and should be kept up.

Employee transport

Another golden area in the policies here is the free transport facility provided by the company for all shop floor members. Even for those using there own transport for commuting to and fro from the factory are paid Rs.15/each way i.e. Rs.30 per day which is a considerable convenience for the workers. Though most of the other companies are providing transport, with some its just subsidized but none have as convenient a system as Perfetti Van Melle. Therefore, this system should be maintained at its current standards.

Employee Communication

The company organizes a communication meeting every month to communicate about the performance results of the company. They share about the problems being faced by the company, about the competitors and other information. They also reward the award winning employees in that meeting for various activities like productivity reward, safety programmes, sports meet etc. Such practices are followed in Rico and Purolator only.

Employee training

This is an area which needs some serious reprisal. The training of employees is the lowest compared to other companies. Other companies have developed mechanisms of training such as Gillette has "Train the trainer" programme in which they encourage the people who are already trained to share their learnings with other. Although they are having a team initiative called "HUM" but other group activities such as Quality circles, SGA are almost non-existent in the company.

Project 2: Analysis of organization culture through OCTAPACE

Research Problem

A lot of focus is being brought in by the organizations towards organizational culture. Organizations need to address the 'culture' perspective in their approach towards people management. A hospital's success is largely dependent on the quality of work efforts of its employees. Therefore, the HRD function focuses on the crucial role of human resources in the "organization culture", which may be understood from the following:

1. Employees constitute the principal component in accomplishing organizational objectives.
2. An employee's value is measured not only in terms of the cost of employing him, but also in terms of the investment in training and development, and on-the-job experience.
3. Employees have reciprocal obligations to and interest in each other; they both gain from these relationships.
4. Employer and employee share goals that make for greater employee identification and involvement with the organisation.

Human resources are also treated as indispensable because of their potential to activate the other factors of production of goods/services in modern organisations. In the manufacturing sector it has been increasingly recognised as inevitable and crucial to the effective functioning of hospitals as they are more people intensive than equipment is. Despite its developing stage in manufacturing organisations, HRD as a function is appreciated and initiated in hospitals only recently and there still seems to be a lack of proper orientation with regard to the design of HRD function.

About OCTAPACE

Organisation culture thus starts up with a common life style adopted by its members in form of shared learning, behaviours, values & interests & provides the employees with a clear understanding of the way things are done around them in their organisation thus guides their further actions. It is considered to be a common perception held by the employees regarding their organisation.

Culture in an organisation plays at different levels, dominant culture which is shared & accepted by the majority of the organisations members, the next level to come are the subcultures that exist at the micro level that reflect the common problems & situations faced by every member in the organisation within his own group or department. A culture adopted in the organisation may be quite possibly based on the national culture or even the local societal & religious norms.

Thus in a nutshell view it may said that the organisational culture is a social glue that helps to hold the organisation together.

OCTAPACE stands for Openness, Commitment, Trust, Authenticity, Proactivness, Collaboration and Experimentation. It is not a one-time thing. It is an ongoing process of diagnosis, fact-finding endeavours, team building, and activities such as survey feedback, training – education, socio-technical systems, process consultation and organisational goals and inter-group activities. It is daring to dream and bringing to life vision and working towards mission whilst remembering our values and principles in Pefetti Van Melle.

OCTAPACE results through statistics will help us in knowing the culture and belief in Perfetti Van Melle

Objectives:

- Collection of the responses from all middle management employee from Executive level to Factory Manager level
- Tabulation of the data
- Graphical and numerical description of the data
- Calculation and interpretation

Checklist

OCTAPACE PROFILE

1. Free interaction among the employees, each respecting others, feelings, competence and sense of judgment.
2. Facing and not shying away from problems.
3. offering moral support and help to employees and colleagues in a crisis.
4. Congruity between feelings and expressed behavior (minimum gap between what people say and do).
5. Preventive action on most matters.
6. Taking independent action relating to their jobs.

7. Team work and Team sprit.
8. Trying out innovative and ways of solving problems.
9. Genuine sharing of information, feelings and thoughts in meetings.
10. Going deeper rather than doing surface-level analysis of inter personal problems.
11. Interpersonal contacts and support among people.
12. Tactfulness, smartness and even a little manipulation to get things done.
13. Senior encouraging their subordinate to think about their development and take action in that direction.
14. Close supervision of, and directing employees on, action.
15. Accepting and appreciating help offered by others.
16. Encouraging employees to take a fresh look at how things are done
17. Free discussion and communication between seniors and subordinates
18. Facing challenges inherent in the work situation.
19. Confiding in senior without fear that they will misuse the trust.
20. Owning up to mistakes.
21. Considering both positive and negative aspects before taking action.
22. Obeying and checking with seniors rather than acting on your own.
23. Performing immediate tasks rather than being concerned about large organization goals.
24. Making genuine attempts to change behavior on the basis of feedback.
25. Effective managers put a lead on their feelings.
26. Pass the buck tactfully when there is a problem.
27. Trust begets trust.
28. Telling a polite lie is preferable to telling the unpleasant truth.
29. Prevention is better than cure.
30. Freedom to employees breeds indiscipline.
31. Usually, Emphasis on team work dilutes individual accountability.
32. Thinking out and doing new things tones up the organization vitality.
33. Free and frank communication between various levels helps in solving problems.
34. Surfacing problem is not enough; we should find the solutions.
35. When the chips are done you have to fend for your self (people can not relay in others in times of crisis).
36. People generally are what they appear to be.
37. A stitch in time saves nine.
38. A good way to motivate employees in to give them autonomy to plan their work.
39. Employees' involvement in developing a organizations' mission and goal contributes to productivity.
40. In today's competitive situation, consolidation and stability are more important than experimentation.

Observations & Findings

Item No.	*Maximum score*	*Awarded score*	*Average score*
1	156	116	3
2	156	118	3
3	156	125	3.2
4	156	84	2
5	156	92	2
6	156	88	2
7	156	129	3.3
8	156	94	2.4
9	156	116	3
10	156	118	3
11	156	125	3.2
12	156	87	2
13	156	92	2
14	156	89	2
15	156	129	3.3
16	156	89	2.3
17	156	116	3
18	156	108	2.8
19	156	127	3.3
20	156	92	2
21	156	99	2.5
22	156	100	2.6
23	156	131	3.4
24	156	93	2.4
25	156	107	2.7
26	156	109	2.8
27	156	126	3.2
28	156	95	2
29	156	100	2.7
30	156	104	2.8

31	156	131	3.4
32	156	91	2
33	156	115	2.9
34	156	117	3
35	156	122	3.1
36	156	84	2
37	156	92	2.4
38	156	88	2.3
39	156	129	3.3
40	156	94	2

Results & Conclusions

S.No.	*Characteristics*	*Maximum average score*	*Average Score Achieved*
1	Openness	4	2.9
2	Confrontation	4	2.9
3	Trust	4	3.2
4	Authenticity	4	2.0
5	Proactivity	4	2.4
6	Autonomy	4	2.3
7	Collaboration	4	3.3
8	Experimentation	4	2.1

Graphical presentation

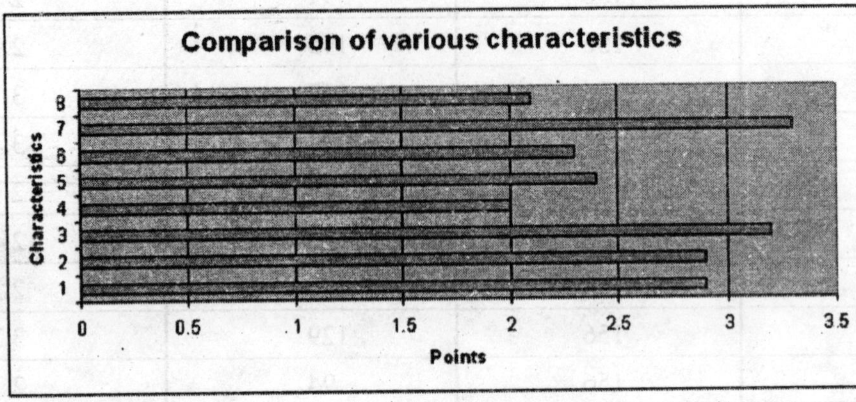

Figure 5: Graphical representation of OCTAPACE profile in the company

Conclusion

Authenticity and experimentation have been awarded least points around 2 which shows that only some persons share these beliefs in the organization.

These things are affecting Perfetti Van Melle as if out of eight pillars, two pillars are week. And it requires immediate action on the part of every one to improve on these particular areas.

References

1. Schutz H.; Speckeser S. and Gunther S. (1998), Benchmarking labour market performance and labour market policies, Berlin.
2. Todaro, Julie B. (1993), A practical guide for personnel management: The essential elements, Texas State Library, Austin.
3. Saad S.; Carter, Gary W. and Rothenberg M. (1999), Testing and assessment: An employer's guide to good practices, Employment and training administration, Washington.
4. http://wikipedia.com
5. Research Paper "A study on the relationship of Ethical work climate and Organization culture in public organization" by Rod Erakovich, Visiting Assistant professor at Texas Wesleyan University, Arlington. A paper presented at American Society for Public Administration National Conference, Phoenix Arizona, March 23-26, 2002.
6. www.citehr.com
7. Research Paper "Competitive Benchmarking in the Air cargo Industry", Ingrid Lobo, Mohammad Zairi, European centre for TQM, University of Bradford,UK
8. Research Paper. "Image & effectiveness of Hospitals: An HR Analysis", D.M. Pastonjee, Kajal S. Sharma, Sonal Patel, Journal of Health Management, 2005.

18

"HCL Learning as a Strong Brand in the Education Industry"

Dr. Rachita Rana
Professor and PGDM Director
Institute of Information Technology and Management, New Delhi.
Mr. Om Sharat
Institute of Information Technology and Management, New Delhi.
Mr. Ashish Kathpal
Institute of Information Technology and Management. New Delhi.

INTRODUCTION

As companies across Industries are increasingly turning to e-Learning to deliver custom-built solutions, e-Learning is fast becoming the preferred mode of content delivery. The disruptive trends in the e-Learning industry like enterprise wide deployment of content, qualitative and dynamic content, new content and new media for content delivery, multichannel delivery, have poised several challenges for enterprises like technology enterprises, content interoperability, dynamic course designs, and content management solutions. With enterprises expanding at break-neck speed and ramping up their capacities and employee skill levels, they are also faced with multiple challenges of:

1. Improving efficiency and reducing-cost
2. Increasing workers' performance
3. Meeting regulatory requirements

4. Fulfilling compliance goals scalable to thousands of employees spread across geographies, achieving an optimized completion rate
5. Speeding up the process of doing business
6. Being ready for growth opportunities

Managing Knowledge with learning objects

The first wave of e-learning was focused on cost displacement solutions associated with administering classroom training, i.e. the LMS (Learning Management System). However, the market has matured and expanded to a second wave of adopters who want a more sophisticated e-learning solution. This second wave requires an e-Learning Content Management System to fulfill the needs of personalized and adaptive e-learning along with the economic benefits of reusable Learning Objects.

HCL and e-Learning practice

HCL's e-Learning practice with its deep strengths in enabling a spectrum of e- Learning solutions help both e-Learning providers and enterprises to develop, deploy, and manage e-Learning content across their own enterprise and their customers' enterprise. HCL is one of the leading offshore e-Learning service providers and offers services that range right from Consulting to Courseware Authoring & Management, providing professional servicing around Learning Management Systems (LMS) and collaborative learning for market segments spanning Publishers, Universities and Corporate Groups. HCL has implemented successfully the maintenance, re-engineering and testing of various systems for a leading human capital management solution provider.

Introduction to the company HCL Infosystems

HCL is a $5.9 billion leading global technology and IT enterprise comprising two companies listed in India – HCL Technologies and HCL Infosystems. HCL Infosystems Ltd is one of the pioneers in the Indian IT market, with its origins in 1976. It is India's premier hardware, services and ICT systems Integration Company offering a wide spectrum of ICT products that includes Computing, Storage, Networking, Security, Telecom, Imaging and Retail. HCL is a one-stop-shop for all the ICT requirements of an organization. India's leading System Integration and Infrastructure Management Services Organization, HCL has specialized expertise across verticals including Telecom, BFSI, e-Governance & Power. HCL has India's largest distribution and retail network, taking to market a range of Digital Lifestyle products in partnership with leading global ICT brands, including Apple, Cisco, Ericsson, Kingston, Kodak, Konica Minolta, Microsoft, Nokia, Toshiba, and many more.

Vision:

A global corporation enriching lives and enabling business transformation for customers, with leadership in chosen technologies and markets. Be the first choice for employees and partners, with commitment to sustainability.

Mission:

To deliver defect free products, services and solutions to meet the requirements of external and internal customers the first time, every time.

Values:

- To be a responsible corporate citizen
- Committed to Quality, Innovation and growth in every Endeavor
- Honoring all commitments
- To uphold the dignity of the individual

Quality:

"To develop and impart Industry relevant ICT Education to meet the requirement of customers, Industry and society by continually updating technology content and improving our processes"

"In its pursuit of excellence", the company has developed a quality management system in line with **ISO 9001:2000** standards.

Organizational Structure

HCL TECHNOLOGIES

↓

HCL INFOSYSTEMS

↓

HCL LEARNING

Figure 1

About HCL Learning (empowering Learning)

HCL Learning is a division of HCL Infosystems, a $ 2.6 billion ICT enterprise which covers the entire length and breadth of education, learning and training needs across schools, colleges, individuals and enterprises. The company's initiatives are driven through passion, innovation and imagination to create learning interventions that are engaging, effective, and rewarding. They have created high quality educational content for a wide range of target audiences. The highly engaging content solutions have been creating value for clients and users in schools, higher education institutions, universities, and professional educational settings.

The pedagogy encourages the use of rich visuals and animations in the course material, and provides scope for a consistent interaction between the teacher and the student. The intent is to make the teaching and learning process purposeful and relevant.

The HCL Advantage

- Partnership with leading LMS providers and Content Vendors
- End to end service offerings in e-Learning from Consulting and Implementation, to BPO support and Infrastructure management
- Value Based delivery models designed for maximum customer satisfaction
- Proven Global Delivery model using 3i methodology
- Quality and Processes : CMM level 5 delivery processes
- Rich pool of design specialist including Instructional designers, Copywriters
- In-Depth domain expertise - Extensive experience in K - 12, university, higher education, lifelong learning and corporate training
- Reusable IPs and frameworks like QuickLearn to reduce time to market and improve operational efficiencies
- Compliance to Industry standards - SCORM, AICC, IEEE , W3C, and QTI

Functional Analysis (HCL Learning)

HCL Learning develops markets and delivers training and educational programs along with instructional products related to sophisticated information technologies. The company provides its products and services through instructor-led courses, and corporate training. HCL Learning markets its services to K12, K2 segments with information management systems professionals, system integrators, value-added resellers and others with systems management responsibilities.

HCL Learning has a focus to become the best independent IT training company in India. It offers more courses, with affiliations and in more locations. There are many reasons, but most important are the Technological, Financial and Quality imperatives.

- World-class technical expertise based on our quality instructors & delivery methods ensure excellent training at centers and corporate venues.
- Industry-leading custom content development for hands on training in the classroom including onsite labs for real skill transfer to corporate.
- Regular upgrades in course contents and course materials in line with the breakthroughs in IT industry.
- Strong reputations among Employers, who hire graduates from HCL as a training organization that prepares students to evaluate situations, analyze solutions and apply practical knowledge to produce effective results.

HCL Learning announced the launch of the special IT training programs for Green Computing, in partnership with **Global Science and Technology Forum (GSTF)**. As part of this partnership, HCL with Global Science and Technology Forum (GSTF) will offer introductory training programs across 130 cities expected to reach out to over 12,000 students by the end of this year.

Green Computing holds great significance in the current business environment and has become an integral part of every organization's development across the globe. With more and more green practices being adopted, there is a need to develop a pool of highly trained Green IT professionals.

GSTF and HCL Learning apart from introducing the new are also in the process of upgrading its existing programmes. The partnership is also expected to launch some special programmes based on computing concepts and is also working on integrating next generation platforms like cloud computing, which is expected to drive the next IT revolution.

Quality Instruction

At HCL Learning, instructors provide a high quality, interactive and productive learning experience for students. A rigorous training program ensures the instructors to follow strict guidelines for consistently delivering a high level of instruction.

Accelerated Training and Certification from HCL Learning has developed an innovative method of training that involves hands on experience in a given technology. The end result is accelerated training that leads to greater retention of subject matter.

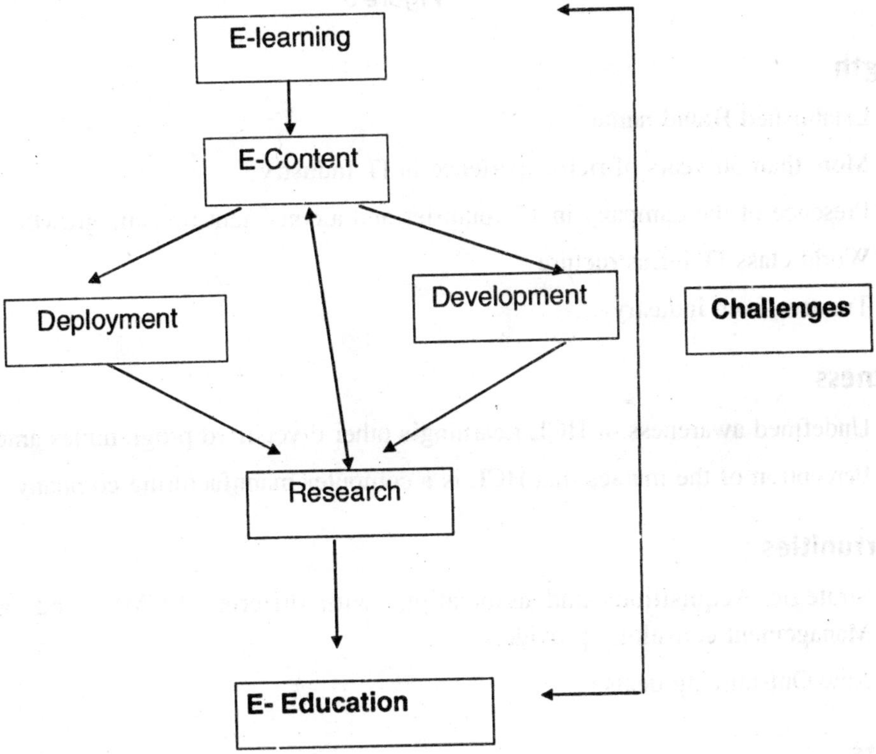

Figure 2. Algorithm Showing the E-Content Model

SWOT Matrix

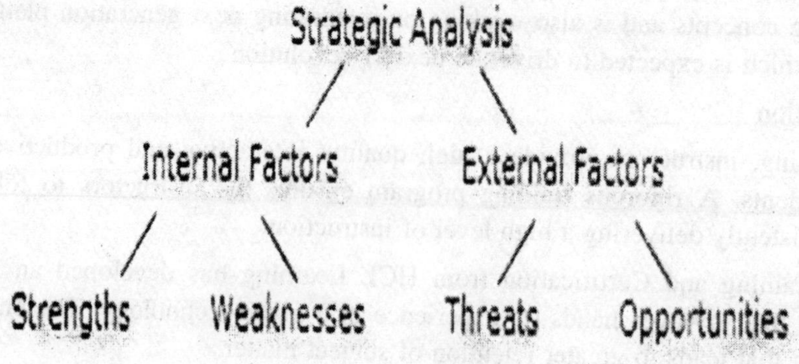

Figure 3

Strength

- Established Brand name
- More than 30 years of rich experience in IT Industry
- Presence of the company in 17 countries and a consistent revenue growth
- World class IT infrastructure
- Trainers from industry

Weakness

- Undefined awareness of HCL Learning's other diversified programmes among the people
- Perception of the masses that HCL is a computer manufacturing company

Opportunities

- Strategic Acquisitions and associations with different LCMS and other Strategic Management consulting providers
- New Outsourcing deals

Threats

- Competitors

BCG Matrix Model: HCL Learning

The **BCG matrix** or also called **BCG model** relates to marketing. The BCG model is a well-known portfolio management tool used in product life cycle theory. BCG matrix is often used to prioritize which products within company product mix get more funding and attention and thus with the descriptive research carried out, it helped in formulating an analytical model of the same.

The BCG model is based on classification of HCL Learning programmes (and implicitly also company business units) into four categories based on combinations of ***market growth*** and ***market share*** relative to the largest competitor.

Matrix Table 1

Matrix	*K12*	*K2*	*Colleges*	*HCL CDC*
BCG **Stars**	• DigiSchool • LearnIT • SMS	• DigiCampus		
BCG **Cash Cows**	• Xcelerate • Teachers Training		• Corporate Training	• ICT Training • Corporate Training • Government Skill Development • e-Learning Solutions
BCG **Question Marks**	• Language Lab		• Career Ace • Language Lab	• SAP Training • Language Lab

HCL Learning as a BRAND in the Education Industry

In order to analyze and to determine the scope of HCL learning as a BRAND in the Education Industry an empirical study was conducted. Market Analysis provided in bringing a thought delivery and actionable market insights, marketplace data, and expert opinions in order to have an informed executive decision-making, both within and across business units and functions given below.

- Identified critical intelligence topics, investigated relevant market research and information, in order to identify and communicate, through written and oral presentations and reports, significant market insights and concepts, and their implications, in order to extract some relevant findings and recommendations.

Other Responsibilities:

Lead Generation - the ability to clearly define the potential market that leads to the appropriate project scope, its objective and its planning.

Role:

- Understanding the Client wants and needs.
- Analyzing the competitive landscape.

- **Assessing the marketplace online and gathering qualified and prospective clients for the next business development cycle.**
- **Identifying emerging growth trends and opportunities across various dimensions in the specific market.**

Social Media Optimization Marketing for two of the product offerings of HCL Learning in the 'Private Sector Initiative' criteria nominated for the **"WORLD EDUCATION SUMMIT – 2011"**

Role:

- Promotional activities carried out through SMO marketing for **'DIGISCHOOL'** and **'DIGICAMPUS'**

RESEARCH METHODOLOGY

Research Design

The research design used in the study is Descriptive and empirical case study analysis: To apply this methodology the primary data was collected through Questionnaires and personal interviews with several respondents in order to see the scope of HCL Learning in providing effective learning during the time of need.

The population of the study has 50 respondents in Delhi/NCR which includes professional candidates, students, and teachers.

Sample Size

- 20 Professional candidates
- 20 Students
- 10 Teachers

The analysis of data required operations such as establishment of categories, the application of these categories, and the application of these categories to raw data through coding, tabulation and then drawing statistical inference. The unwieldy data was condensed into a few manageable groups and tables for further analysis and then the classification of data into purposeful and usable category. Coding, editing and tabulation were done simultaneously and then analysis was based on computation of various percentages.

The reason was to gather and analyze the response of the Professional candidates, Teachers and Students as to how far they are interested in taking up HCL's e-Learning medium as the most preferred mode of Content Delivery.

Findings

Tabulated Analysis of the Research

Table 1: Awareness about HCL Infosystems as a Brand

		Frequency	*Percent*	*Valid Percent*	*Cumulative Percent*
Valid	Yes	42	84.0	84.0	84.0
	No	8	16.0	16.0	100.0
	Total	50	100.0	100.0	

Interpretation:

HCL Infosystems, being one of the leading pioneers has very well established its name in the market. Therefore, it reflects that 84% of the respondents are well aware about the Organization as a whole. The research carried had no hassles as all the respondents were keen observers and listeners due to the pre-existing brand image.

Table 2: Awareness about HCL Learning as a Brand

		Frequency	*Percent*	*Valid Percent*	*Cumulative Percent*
Valid	Yes	40	80.0	80.0	80.0
	No	10	20.0	20.0	100.0
	Total	50	100.0	100.0	

Interpretation:

As far as HCL Learning is considered, we all can assume from the above tabulated interpretations that 80% of the people already knew about the e-Learning initiative taken by HCL Infosystems and that is why the HCL learning is furthermore gaining a competitive advantage in terms of its methodologies and programmes adopted, which will keep on boosting up to maintain a consistency which is one of the core values of the Organization.

Table 3: Interest in knowing more about other Programmes of HCL Learning

		Frequency	*Percent*	*Valid Percent*	*Cumulative Percent*
Valid	Yes	36	72.0	72.0	72.0
	No	14	28.0	28.0	100.0
	Total	50	100.0	100.0	

Interpretation:

HCL Learning's e-Learning initiatives has put across a relevant impact on the respondents and thus it can be observed that 72% of the respondents are interested in knowing more about other programmes of HCL Learning.

Table 4: Reason for their association with HCL Learning

		Frequency	*Percent*	*Valid Percent*	*Cumulative Percent*
Valid	Brand Name	14	28.0	28.0	28.0
	Job assistance	15	30.0	30.0	58.0
	Edge over others	21	42.0	42.0	100.0
	Total	50	100.0	100.0	

Interpretation:

When being considered in terms of what will make them join HCL Learning or being a part of any of its offerings, 42% of the people came out with a conclusion that they might want to get an edge over others and 30% for getting Job assistance, but although the brand name shows a comparatively 14%, we should not assume that the Brand name of HCL has given the lesser frequency as it already has shown a powerful impact in the previous interpretation.

Table 5: Overall rating of the HCL Learning Programmes

Occupation	*DigiSchool*	*Xcelerate*	*DigiCampus*	*Language Lab*	*ICT Training*	*Corp. Tr.*
Professionals	14.76	16.43	18.33	18.81	14.52	17.14
Students	25.24	16.19	17.62	18.33	10.48	12.14
Teachers	21.90	20.00	18.57	15.71	11.90	11.90
Overall	**20.38**	**17.05**	**18.10**	**18.00**	**12.38**	**14.10**

Interpretation:

Amongst the categories, it seems that the programme DigiSchool gets the highest percentage and is preferred most by the students followed by Teachers and then Professionals.

However, DigiCampus and Xcelerate and Language Lab Solutions can be a leader in preparing the youths in this highly competitive world.

Competitive Analysis

The main objective of framing a competitive analysis is related to getting the information about competitors existing in the Market and how HCL Learning is ready to accelerate its pace and finally emerge as the market leader in the world of e-Learning programmes.

Table 6

Occupation	*HCL Learning*	*CMC*	*Smartlink Networks*	*D-Link India*	*PCS Technology*	*MRO-TEK*
Professionals	5.71	25.71	19.52	19.05	10.95	19.05
Students	6.67	25.71	20.95	20.00	11.43	15.24
Teachers	7.62	23.81	20.48	18.57	12.86	16.67
Overall	**6.48**	**25.33**	**20.29**	**19.33**	**11.52**	**17.05**

Interpretation

Taking few competitors in terms of e-Learning practices being followed by other peer companies, it seems that it is only lack of adequate knowledge about various other programmes, but this being one of its challenges can actually help in accelerating the pace of increasing the perception of HCL Learning amongst masses and the days are not far when HCL e-Learning initiative can emerge as the leading Brand as compared to other competitors.

The findings also pointed out that most people are in the favor of DigiSchool programme along with Xcelerate and ICT training Programmes. A further deprived interpretation based on the analysis suggests that those days are not far when HCL Learning will emerge as the best in the e-Learning initiatives taken so far yet by any of its close competitors in aspects of its varied programmes offerings.

We are just beginning to harness the power of the internet for the delivery and management of education. Even without a clear demonstration that e-learning is superior to traditional lectures; the use of online learning provides solutions can overcome some problems with traditional education. With increasing constraints being placed on educators, one needs to explore other avenues for effective knowledge transfer to trainees especially with the help of an upto date Content Delivery Model.

E-learning provides flexibility in both time and location, while accessing curriculum presented online. The harnessing of computer technology, more specifically web-based tools open the door for collaboration amongst both students and teachers. E-learning adds many dimensions to the educational process and if utilized well, has the potential to enhance both the students and instructors educational experience. It will not replace the traditional teaching but can certainly augment the magnitude of knowledge dispensation to the ever increasing knowledge hunger of a student that essentially remains the driving force to excel in this world's-learning has come to stay for long.

It seems that undoubtedly, e-learning could provide an enormous boost to opportunities for training, learning and development. The e-learning market is still in its infancy. It is an unstable and non-transparent market, which complicates the forecasting of its future.

Furthermore, the demand of customers is evolving constantly, due to insights gained during implementation of products, but also due to shifting concepts at national and international levels. In addition to the initial requirements, focused on 'provision of technology' and 'user friendliness', there are also rapidly changing demands of the users.

The database Collection with HCL Learning, from the position about verifying leads and how to execute the actual generation process, conversely now depends upon the sales team who are working off on the leads. HCL Learning has the right people, who can now convert those into the qualified leads.

There are many things that make up a quality lead and a quality lead generation person. By understanding how the process works and what makes it work can best choose the right lead generation an organization demands and using a perfect match proving a long way to support the business. A successful and aggressive lead generation program can make all the difference in the world. Not only does it provide you with quality leads that you may not have ever been able to capture before, it also frees up your sales force to do what they do best – sell.

Social Media Optimization is a form of online marketing using a set of methods, generating publicity through social media, online communities and community websites.

Social media measurement thoughts are different and emphasize to remove all jargons and helps that executives understand and ultimately help tie results to the bottom line.

With all those relevant information and an enthusiastic response from the visitors by attracting them, and creating an image for HCL e-Learning's practice, made programme **'DIGISCHOOL'** receive an award in the **"WORLD EDUCATION SUMMIT, 2011"**, for the category in the **'Most Innovative Learning and Teaching process in the Private Sector Initiatives'** which totally relates to the mission of HCL that **'Only a Leader can transform to a Leader'**

Competitor's Analysis

To plan effective marketing strategies, the company needs to find out all it can about its competitors. It must constantly compare its marketing strategies, products, prices, channels, and promotions with those of close competitors. In this way company can find areas of potential competitive advantage and disadvantage. Competitor's analysis involves first identifying and assessing competitors and then selecting which competitors to attack or avoid.

Competitor analysis in marketing and strategic management is an assessment of the strengths and weaknesses of current and potential competitors. This analysis provides both an offensive and defensive strategic context through which to identify opportunities and threats.

Summary

- **Traditional courses are bulky**. A course contains what everyone might need to know about a topic. A learner wants only part of what that course has to offer, specifically, what he or she wants to learn. To accomplish this, old-style courses must be atomized — broken down into reasonably sized chunks (learning objects) and reassembled in right-sized packages. LCMS were designed to deal at the atomic level.

- **Old-style Learning Management Systems** ("LMS") were created for tracking registration, attendance, class lists, grades, test results, class scheduling, and other administrative requirements of schools and instructor-led classes. They aren't so hot at delivering chunks of learning, be they personalized learning paths made up of objects or the introduction of a new product next week.

LMS are reporting systems and generally do not include ways to create new content or to deliver small packets of learning.

• **Learning Content Management Systems** were created to overcome these difficulties. Learning objects, those small chunks or "granules" of learning, are at the heart of an LCMS. They are maintained in a database or "repository."

• LCMS provide authoring tools to create new learning objects for the repository. In the crudest form, this may consist of converting PowerPoint presentations and Word memos into learning objects. Most authoring packages use templates, storyboards, and/or forms to enable non-technical subject matter experts to create learning objects directly, by-passing an intermediary who knows how to code. Some authoring tools provide batch modes to convert libraries of legacy content into learning objects. The most sophisticated incorporate version control, multiple authors, and project management as well.

• LCMS have the ability to assemble and consolidate learning objects into lengthier "learning paths" or learning experiences that are personalized to a learner's profile, job description, assessment results, or requests. A learning path can obtain up-to-the-minute information because it is assembled "on the fly" rather than taken off the shelf.

• LCMS track who takes what. Many lack the depth of reporting available in a traditional LMS but this is because LCMS are relatively immature products; the LMS have been around for a while. A year from now, I expect the LCMS to incorporate LMS functions. An LCMS can roll up information to create rich reports. An LMS, which does not operate at the level of learning objects, cannot roll down to get that level of detail.

References

- http://hcllearning.com/AboutHCLLearning.aspx
- http://www.siliconindia.com/shownews/HCL_Infosystems_gearing_up_for_future_growth_opportunities-nid-82859.html
- http://iimjobs.com/content/view/22100/28/
- http://en.wikipedia.org/wiki/Below_the_line_(advertising)
- http://edelweiss.in/company/HCL-Infosystems-Ltd.html
- http://openeducationresearch.org/
- http://www.yousigma.com/comparativeanalysis/hcltechnologies.html
- http://www.maxi-pedia.com/BCG+matrix+model
- http://www.netmba.com/strategy/matrix/bcg/
- www.teleark.com/ lead-generation
- http://www.hclinfosystems.in/news217.htm
- http://en.wikipedia.org/wiki/HCL_Enterprise
- http://mashable.com/2010/10/22/social-media-optimization/

19

Infosys in Ferment over New HR Policy - iRace

Ms. Reena Shyam,
MS Ramiah College, Bangalore,
reena_shyam01@rediffmail.com
reenashyam1@gmail.com
Ms. Ritu Bali
Assistant Professor, BVIMR, New Delhi
koc_ritu@yahoo.co.uk

For over a decade, Infosys Technologies has been seen as one of the best places to work and an epitome of employee friendliness. However, that reputation has now taken a big knock. Several measures initiated by the company under growing pressures of shrinking profits during recession and client demands insisting on better quality of service. Nandita Gurjar , the global head for HR in Infosys, initiated its new changed management system christened " iRace-Infosys Role and Career Enhancement program" that was rolled out last year. It is a career architecture that aligns talent management activities with client priorities, business focus and employee aspirations. It is said to be a platform that clearly defines roles, competencies and proficiency requirements while linking career movement to performance and business focus. It offers 26 career streams. It is about how people move in the organization levels. The objective is to focus on people with deep domain knowledge who can add high value in quality of service.

iRace was designed by consulting firm Mercer with the idea of mapping positions with experience and skill levels. Previously, positions and promotions were often given arbitrarily, based on an employee's bargain strength, which often was substantial considering jobs were aplenty. Many were given managerial responsibilities within three to four years, often leading to clients complaining about their lack of technology skills. While iRace objective appeared laudable, it suffered in its implementation, the worst of which was to reassess all employees based on the new standards .Many employees were demoted on the ground that they did not meet iRace's experience norms. So, senior project mangers went down to project managers, project managers to technical leads, some even went down two levels. iRace has affected over 4,000 employees who felt it was blocking their career growth. Some employees believe certain aspects of iRace are irrational. It looks at not just an employee's overall industry experience, but also the employee's tenure in the particular vertical he or she is currently in. It discounts the earlier experiences of the employee in multiple other verticals. Over the last few months Infosys has witnessed a rise in attrition levels, a clear indication of employees not receiving the new changes too happily.

The HR initiatives seem to have the full backing of the Infy management. Many in the industry regard this partly as a cost cutting move by Infosys. During brighter years companies resorted to mad hiring, giving employees huge monies and fancy designations. Today, when the situation has changed, companies are looking for innovative ways to bring down cost. Some of these exercises defy logic and are traumatic to employees.

Key Words: Change, Resistance to Change, Change management

References:

1. "Infosys in ferment over HR policy – Employees demoted following new norms"- Sujit John & Mini Joseph Tejaswi,18th March, Times of India , 2010
2. "Infosys sees higher employee activism – **Infoscions** vent anger on HR issues in blogs,want to be part of future decisions –Bibhu Ranjan Mishra, 14th April ,The Hindu 2010

Teaching Note

Case Objectives and Use

The case revolves around Infosys Technologies, a company that has been seen by many as the epitome of employee friendliness. However that reputation has now taken a big knock. Several changes initiated in the HR policies of the company recently led to discontent among employees. The biggest grouse of employees relate to an HR initiative called iRace- Infosys Role and Career Enhancement a change management system to map the technology skills of the employees. This initiative, which aimed at "improving the technology depth "of the software professionals, reportedly affected over 4,000 employees who felt it was blocking their career growth .Employees showed their angst towards these changes in various social networking sites and official internal blog. The case further reiterates the fact that any change process within an organization requires the involvement of employees to facilitate smooth implementation

The case analysis should enable students to

1. Understand the forces that trigger change in organizations
2. Appreciate the problematic and processual nature of organizational change, and the centrality of *human agents* in the change process;
3. Understand individual and organizational strategies for *coping with change* and overcoming *resistance to change*

Case Synopsis

Infosys Technologies has initiated several changes in its HR policies under growing pressures facing the IT industry in the form of shrinking profits during recession and client demands insisting on better quality of service. The biggest grouse of employees relate to an HR initiative called iRace- Infosys Role and Career Enhancement a change management system to map the technology skills of the employees. While iRace objective appeared laudable, it suffered in its implementation, the worst of which was to reassess all employees based on the new standards. Many employees were demoted on the ground that they did not meet iRace's experience norms.

Employees started showing angst in various social networking platforms and websites when Infosys won the Business Today award for being the "Best Employer". Many of them questioned this and wanted to know under what criteria the company was adjusted best employer when employees were asked to work for 9.15 hours a day. There was also a rise in attrition level of the company indicating employee discontent to the new changes affecting them.

Suggested Student assignments

1. Analyze the changes which have affected an organization recently. Emphasize on the reasons for change and the likely consequences of change. And suggest strategies for effective change management

   (Eg: Hero Honda – end of a successful partnership)
2. Identify changes affecting employees in case of mergers or acquisitions and necessary change management strategies to be adopted by firms

   (Eg:Indian Airlines and Air India)
3. "An effective manager is one who can bring about a smooth change whenever require". Comment on the manager's role as a change agent in the light of the above statement, citing examples from your organization or in an organization you are familiar with. Briefly describe the organization you are referring to.

Suggested approach and Case Assignment

Prior to giving the case we can discuss, the importance of change in an organization and how important it is to overcome employee resistance to change. We can also discuss how important it is for organizations to ensure employee involvement and contribution in assimilating change in its practices.

We then assign the following questions which lead the student towards a rigorous analysis of the change process within an organization

1. Do you think iRace was a necessary change in the HR initiatives for Infosys?
2. iRace has resulted in employee dissatisfaction and increase in attrition rate of the company. Discuss the reasons why employees have shown such extreme resistance to the new promotion policy of the company.
3. What role should the HR play in ensuring that iRace can be effectively implemented within the organization?

4. What are the necessary steps that can be taken by the company to ensure easy implementation of changes in future?

Possible Discussion Questions

Change is unavoidable in today's business environment, and individuals, managers and companies have a choice: **Be controlled by, and reactive to changes in their environments, or, Be proactive and manage the change process to maximize benefits, and reduce negative impacts.**

1. What is change?

Organizational change is as "the movement of people from a current state to a defined state, different, improved and desired new state through a set of planned and integrated interventions"

2. What are the forces of change?

The external forces effecting change could be summarized with the following headings.

1. Demographic characteristics
2. Technological developments:
3. Market changes:
4. Social and political pressure

Internal forces: Internal forces for change are operative from inside the organisation.

1. Human resource factors
2. Managerial behavior/decisions

3. What are the types of change?

The two main types of change – step and incremental

Step change

- Dramatic or radical change in one fell swoop
- Radical alteration in the business
- Gets it over with quickly
- May require some coercion

Incremental change

- Ongoing piecemeal change which takes place as part of an organisation's evolution and development
- Tends to more inclusive

Why is change resisted?

There is a human tendency to resist change, because it forces people to adopt new ways of doing things.

Resistance to change	Some common reasons why change is resisted
Parochial self interest	Individuals are concerned with the implications for themselves; their view is often biased by their perception of a particular situation
Habit	Habit provides both comfort and securityHabits are often well-established and difficult to change
Misunderstanding	Communications problemsInadequate information
Low tolerance of change	Sense of insecurity
Different assessment of the situation	Disagreement over the need for change Disagreement over the advantages and disadvantages
Economic implications	Employees are likely to resist change which is perceived as affecting their pay or other rewardsEstablished patterns of working and reward create a vested interest in maintaining the status quo
Fear of the unknown	Proposed changes which confront people tend to generate fear and anxietyIntroducing new technology or working practices creates uncertainty

There are also several organizational barriers to change, including:

- Structural inertia
- Existing power structures
- Resistance from work groups
- Failure of previous change initiatives

Change is also resisted because of the poor way in which change is managed! For example, a failure by management responsible for the change to:

- Explain the need for change
- Provide information
- Consult, negotiate and offer support and training
- Involve people in the process
- Build trust and sense of security
- Build employee relations

As a result of change resistance and poorly managed change projects, many of them ultimately fail to achieve their objectives. Amongst the reasons commonly associated with failed change programmes are:

- Employees do not understand the purpose or even the need for change
- Lack of planning and preparation
- Poor communication

- Employees lack the necessary skills and/ or there is insufficient training and development offered
- Lack of necessary resources
- Inadequate/inappropriate rewards

How can change be implemented effectively?

Implementing change effectively

Given the likelihood that change will be resisted, what can management do to plan and implement a change programme more effectively?

The key stages in a successful change project are likely to be to:

- Identify the changes required (a role here for SWOT and PEST analysis)
- Determine the major issues
- Identify and assess the key stakeholders
- Win the support of key individuals
- Identify the obstacles
- Determine the degree of risk and the cost of change
- Understand why change will be resisted and how it can be managed

People are the key factor in overcoming resistance to change. The successful implementation of new working methods and practices or integrating new businesses into a group is dependent upon the willing and effective co-operation of employees and management. Many change initiatives and programmes fail because they are derailed by the "people factor"!

A key part of successful change is, therefore, building and communicating the reasons & the vision for change.

Employees need to be clear about what a change involves and how they are involved in it:

- What is involved?
- What are the proposed changes?
- What is the timescale?
- Why should we do it?
- What will the major effects be?

Various techniques can be adopted which help ease a change process, including:

- Cross-functional teams
- Stronger internal communication
- Negotiation
- Action planning
- Appointing "change agents" or "champions of change"
- And a certain amount of compulsion manipulation and coercion

Analysis of the case

1. Do you think iRace was a necessary change in the HR initiatives for Infosys?

Yes, iRace was a necessary career architecture that aligns talent management activities with client priorities, business focus and employee aspirations.

- It is said to be a platform that clearly defines roles, competencies and proficiency requirements while linking career movements to performance and business focus. The objective of iRace is to focus on people with deep domain knowledge who can add high value to the business.
- With the IT industry grapples with problems like shrinking profit margins and clients insisting on quality in projects. In extremely competitive markets, to achieve sustainable growth , Infosys has to ensure that its human capital have competencies aligned to meet client expectations.
- A change in the promotion policy of the company christened as iRace would ensure that important projects of the company are in experienced and knowledgeable employees also assuring superior service delivery to clients

2. iRace has resulted in employee dissatisfaction and increase in attrition rate of the company. Discuss the reasons why employees have shown such extreme resistance to the new promotion policy of the company.

Although iRace was initiated by the company with the aim of "improving the technology depth "of software professionals, it suffered in its implementation as it reassessed employee competencies based on new standards.

- At the time of global slowdown, Infosys launched iRace program under which the company's staff are required to wait longer for their promotions so that only the professionals with proven managerial skills can lead project teams. Many employees were demoted on the ground that they did not meet iRace experience norms. Senior project mangers went down to project managers, project managers to technical leads, some even went two levels. The change initiated by the company has been perceived by employees as a step that will delay their progressive growth in the company.
- Some of the major concerns of employees are new roles introduced in the hierarchy, extended work timings and lower salaries than industry standards. The employees are also upset about the compulsory certification being introduced by the company for each level of the role and leadership, and the improper management of acknowledging the promotions.

Although the company may deem iRace as a necessary change, employees fear the change may threaten their existing job designations and compensation, which was not dealt with by the company before the new policy was implemented.

3. What role should the HR play in ensuring that iRace can be effectively implemented within the organization?

- The HR of the company has to acknowledge that for any change to be implemented, employees are the key.

- It is 'difficult of individuals to resist a change decision in which they participated' Employee participation could be emphasized on
- The company can encourage employees to voice their opinion on the new polices and what aspects causes dissatisfaction
- Employees have expressed their discontent on social networking sites about the new policy. This would be damaging the reputation of Infosys as an employee friendly company. Employees can communicate the same through the intranet of the company so that necessary solutions can be worked internally.
- Proper communication about the intricacies of the policy and the necessity to introduce the policy has to be conveyed to all employees.
- Training programs could be initiated for those who are deemed less competent to handle superior positions, removing fears and insecurities of employees.
- Open house sessions between management and employees with complete transparency in expressing views and probing on the issues unearthed is necessary.

The company has taken efforts to tame the disgruntled employees who were earlier venting their anger in public forms and social networking sites by giving them a blogging platform on the company's intranet "Sparsh". "My voice" the dedicated company website has developed to seek the opinion of employees on important policy matters. The website is getting about 4,000 hits every day. Owing to the overwhelming participation, Infosys has now developed software which brings the summary of them employee's comments to which the company's HR Head Nandita Gurjar replies religiously. This effort to open the window for employees to air their opinion on these platforms is likely to bring about tolerance and receptivity to the policy changes initiated by the company.

References

1. "Infosys in ferment over HR policy – Employees demoted following new norms"- Sujit John & Mini Joseph Tejaswi, 18th March, Times of India , 2010
2. "Infosys sees higher employee activism – Infoscions vent anger on HR issues in blogs,want to be part of future decisions –Bibhu Ranjan Mishra, 14th April ,The Hindu 2010
3. Promotion at Infosys strictly for performers-Peerzada Abrar, 4 Feb, 2010,The Economic Times
4. http://www.ciol.com/News/News-Reports/Is-Infy-a-good-place-only-for-freshers
5. http://tutor2u.net/business/strategy/change-management-resistance-barriers.html

Bibliography

1. Moorhead ,Griffin Organizational Behaviour-Managing people and Organsiations, Biztantra,2009
2. Stephen Robbins, Orgnaistional Behaviour - Concepts, Controversies, Application, PHI 2008
3. McShane,Von Gilnow,Sharma, Orgnaistional Behaviour,Tata McGRawHill,2008
4. Fred Luthans . Orgnaistional Behaviour, Tata McGRawHill,2006

20

Creche Systems: An Insight into The H.R.M of Biocon, India

Ms. Richa Joshi, Ms. Shipra Taneja, Ms. Shivangi Tewari
Bharati Vidyapeeth University
Institute of Management & Research, New Delhi

BIOCON INDIA: AN INTRODUCTION TO THE COMPANY

Biocon is india's leading biotechnology enterprise. Established in 1978, the company today is an integrated biotechnology enterprise focused on the development of biopharmaceuticals. The company serves partners and customers in over 50 countries. Within the biotechnology space, the company ranks first in Asia in terms of revenues and market capitalisation and sixteenth globally

THE HUMAN RESOURCE MANAGEMENT AT BIOCON

Intellectual Profile of 3000 PersonnelBiocon, together with Syngene and Clinigene, employs 3000+ highly qualified biologists, chemists, computer scientists, medical practitioners, pharmacologists, engineers, financial, legal, marketing analysts, HR generalists and general administrators.

Biocon, Syngene and Clinigene together employee approximately 3000 qualified personnel - from biologists, chemists, medical practitioners, pharmacologists, engineers, finance / legal / marketing analysts, HR generalists to general administrators. 5% of our employees hold PhD degrees, 40% have a masters degree in science and the remaining are graduates with a bachelors degree in science, commerce or arts. 15% of Biocon employees are women(across the group). The employee attrition last quarter was 4% and last year it was over 20%. The average age of the employee is 28.8.

HUMAN RESOURCE PRACTICES

1. Strong Human Base

An organisation is as dynamic and effective as its people. At Biocon, the vast experience of distinguished Board of Directors, the invaluable learning of the Scientific Advisory Board and the strategic focus of the Key Management Team steer us towards our goals. They are amply supported by a 3000-strong team of exemplary bioscientists, engineers and business managers who build intellectual capital and drive growth.

2. Induction, Training, Recruitment and Automated HR

Taking into account Biocon's processes for induction and recruitment; training and inhouse development; and automation of HR processes it won an award. Induction process can be quite tedious, not in the least because of the huge number of applications. Last year, the company received close to 40,000 job applications and recruited 300 Induction, like other HR processes, is automated and helps bring in accuracy and saves time and costs. Applications are screened automatically and ready made regret letters generated to those who do not make the mark.

For recruitment the HRM chalks out an annual manpower plan wherein all the department heads draw up their requirements. It reviews manpower needs every quarter and decides on how to fill the vacant slots. They recruit mainly through networking and apart from that also have a career section on website.

3. In House Heath Care Centers For Employees

Biocon also has an inhouse healthcare centre, where the annual health check-up is done by doctors of Clinigene, a Biocon subsidiary, helping the company bring down spending to 1/10th of the cost.

4. Corporate Social Responsibility

Today enlightened companies understand the need for having a comprehensive corporate social responsibility (CSR) agenda. This has brought into focus non-financial issues such as business ethics, community service, corporate governance and workplace issues The four pillars of CSR are at biocon, community investment, employee relations, environmental practices and ethical conduct. Biocon has always taken pride in being upright corporate citizens committed to contributing significantly to the quality of life in society. It supports innovative and effective programmes in the fields of healthcare, education and environment and understand that our future is closely intertwined with that of our community.

Since its inception, Biocon has been involved in various social initiatives like Swacha Bangalore (BATF) and Towards a Polio-Free World (Rotary International)., Biocon organises regular polio camps to reach children under the age of three with vital polio centre.

5. Crèche: Day Care Centers

6. Miscellaneous

Biocon stands out because of focus on its HR practices - offering employees freedom while fixing accountability - which is rare in other result oriented environments.

It offers a variety of provisions from offering red roses to new employees to women portals.

Creches For Employee's Children: A Deeper Insight Into Hrm At Biocon

For Kiran Mazumdar Shaw, chief of Biocon, it's a matter of care. "People are our most valuable asset," she says. "In a knowledge driven industry such as ours, scientists and technologists are busy throughout. A day care centre would certainly ease parental pressure and would enhance productivity," says Nirupa Bareja, head of Human Resource (HR) at Biocon. Biocon has built the futuristic creche in the St. Francis School compound. "Our design has been made in such a way that we can expand the premises easily. We have a plan ready for an identical building in the next plot, and if needed, we will build a storey above the existing one." Park amusements such as a sand pit, jungle jim and slides make it a child friendly zone. The creche can accommodate about 25 children between six months and three years, "but we only have seven children now." Landscaping around the building has just begun and will take time to make the surroundings look green and more inviting. Headed for international quality! It's interiors look as spacious as its surroundings, far from the overcrowded commercial day care centres in the City. Riding toys to push or peddle around, cuddle toys, and colours that please the child's eye, the interior design has room to teach language, Maths, Science and games. Employees of Biocon have shown good response, "especially men," Stereotypes would expect women to take advantage of it more than men! "Most of our male employees have their wives working in other companies. These companies don't have day care centres. This becomes useful." Children can be seen scampering in the sand pit, jungle jim, slides in glee. "The Biocon day care's role as a child care and early childhood education provider compliments the primary role of parents in providing for their children. From casual conversations and daily notes to parent-teacher conferences, our day care has it all," says Nirupa. Parents (Biocon employees) of these toddlers can drop in at any time of the day to share those loving moments they long for. "We encourage communication between parents and teachers." "The home offers a secure environment. We're looking forward to putting my little son Neel (18 months old) in the day care, as it will allow him to interact with others," says Senior Manager (Finance), Chinnappa who's son is in Biocon daycare.

Q1. Why does the creche system catch the fancy of employees?

Women tend to continue with their jobs because they are relaxed about the fact that their children will be taken care of. It is a general tendency amongst women to leave jobs after motherhood because career then takes a backseat. This concept is changing with the new concept of crèches.

Better time management Optimum utilization of resources and efficiency in work.

Q2. What are the benefits of day care creches at biocon to its employees?

- Most of our male employees have their wives working in other companies. These companies don't have day care centres. This becomes useful."
- The Biocon day care's role as a child care and early childhood education provider compliments the primary role of parents in providing for their children. From casual conversations and daily notes to parent-teacher conferences, the day care has it all.
- Better productivity and efficiency at work
- Relaxed mindsets
- The environment at the day care center has park amusements and other international quality standards concepts such as a sand pit, jungle jim and slides make it a child friendly zone.

Q3. How is the company influenced by the strategy of innovative hr practises especially the creche system?

- Lower attrition rates as low as 2%
- Enhanced productivity
- Employee satisfaction and retention
- As jobs become complex and roles get diverse, employee motivation is top of mind among corporates.
- For working couples, it's convenient to manage home and office given the crazy hours at work these days.
- Working mothers abound in Biocon at managerial levels, so it lowers the chances of them leaving the job after motherhood
- Lower work breakdown
- Lower revenue losses when employees take less leaves or the ones related with hr practices of employing new personnels.

Other areas to be highlighted are:

The success story of biocon's creche system so far

Lower attrition

Women empowerment

Better organizational commitment and job satisfaction

Major challenges in future.

- Challenges of the biotechnology industry are the challenges of Biocon and its HR as well Despite having established drug development firms and reknowned research expertise, the Indian biotechnology industry is facing a cash crunch. Inherent challenges facing the biotech outsourcing business are the lack of appropriate infrastructure, issues arising under the Intellectual Property Rights ("IPR") laws, product liabilities, ensuring exclusivity and the need for increased industry-academia partnerships. Other issues that require attention include but are not limited to: Exchange Control regulations; labour laws; contract terms and conditions; mechanisms for dispute resolution and the tax issues relating to withholding tax, transfer pricing, tax holidays/exemptions, etc

- Better and innovative HR practices being developed
- Competitors and other firms coming up with idea of office day care centers ICICI Bank, where a majority of women rule the roost at senior positions, too has a crèche which charges a monthly fee to look after employees' children. The crèche has trained teachers, a library, gym, computer room and its own kitchen.

  Xansa technologies also has a crèche while firms like TCS, Wipra etc. are planning to follow the suit which is a competitive signal for Biocon.

Summary and Conclusion

Pamela Anderson loves Kid Rock. So does India Inc — now that it's smitten by the crèche crush. Parents in corporate India are being encouraged to bring their kids to work and meet up with them over tea-break or lunch. Tagging along children to the workplace is becoming a necessity in verticals with long (wo)man-hours and stretched schedules. Tech companies may have pioneered the idea of crèche and other child-friendly policies to maintain that crucial work-life balance, others such as ICICI Bank and JW Marriott Hotels are fast realising that childcare is no child's play. As jobs become complex and roles get diverse, employee motivation is top of mind among corporates. And with more women coming into the workforce, child-friendly policies of organisations are gaining ground

BIOCON has been successful in its strategy of crèches and day cre center

Findings and Reccomendations

We questioned a few working married people in Delhi who gave a few recommendations and suggestions on this concept. It can be summarized as below

- Options of nutritious and wholesome meals at crèche
- Availability of food and options like vegetable kiosks for employees witjin the offices
- More Informal get togethers and family days
- Birthday celebrations of children in office day care centers
- Proper training and recruitment of employees for day care centers e.g through psychometric tests etc
- 'Happy minutes' so that employees get sometime from office hours to spend with their children.
- Quality and conducive environment in crèches
- Motherly touch

21

Organizational Politics

Mr. Shanker Chatterjee
Professor
shanker_1945@yahoo.com

Mrs. Preety Wadhwa
Associate Professor
pwadhwa77@gmail.com

Bharati Vidyapeeth University, Institute of Management and Research, New Delhi

Mr Vivek Sharma passed a post Graduate Diploma in Human Resources from XLRI, Jamshedpur in 1995 with second rank. He was one of the lucky 10 young management graduates to get a job of a management trainee in **Zenith Engineering Company Ltd,** a large engineering firm in Mumbai manufacturing Machine tools and forging equipments. The Company had an excellent track record of performance with a consistent growth record in term of production ,sales and profits

The company was headed by its Chairman and Managing Director Mr Shankar Raman, (Age 58 years) a professional with over 30 years of experience in various organizations. It was in one of the informal get together with company officers during a cultural programme that Mr Shankar Raman got to meet Mr Vivek Sharma. He was greatly impressed with his good manners, dress sense and his communication ability. Mr Vivek was, therefore, pleasantly surprised when the next morning he was called by the Chairman in his office. Mr Raman was even more impressed after meeting him. It was an extended meeting during which Mr Raman enquired about his academic and family background, his present assignments, hobbies and so on. Towards the end of the meeting, the following conversation took place:

Mr Shankar Raman: " I am greatly impressed with your background. I have received good reports about you. How will you like to be a part of my office? Your responsibilities will include going through the mails and dealing with routine matter and thus relieving me from unproductive paper work. You will also meet my visitors and deal with them unless some of them require to meet me. You will also attend all senior level meetings and ensure that the decisions taken in such meetings are implemented in time. You will also be required to travel to our other offices and plants. Please think about it. You do not have to take up this assignment unless you want to. Tell me about your decision by tomorrow so that we can get started. Good luck to you.

Mr Vivek Sharma: " Thank you very much Sir for your kind words. I will certainly inform you about it by tomorrow. Good day Sir"

Mr Shankar Raman: " Good Day."

Mr Vivek returned to his desk greatly elated after this meeting His friends and other staff members enquired about what transpired during his long meeting with C&MD. He gave them some evasive replies and continued with his work. It was only towards the day that seriously considered the proposal. When studying at XLRI, his professor and mentor gave him this advise" Vivek, no matter how complex the situation is, learn to take your decisions independently and accept responsibility for the same." Vivek , however, consulted his father in Jamshedpur who advised him to accept the offer without delay. The following day, he sought an appointment with Mr Shankar Raman. He was told to meet him after office hours in the evening. The meeting was very brief.

Mr Vivek Sharma " Sir, I shall be delighted to take up my new assignment and assure you that I will meet your expectations.

Mr Shankar Raman : " Very well. I will instruct the Administrative Department to make necessary arrangements for your desk, You may go now"

Mr Vivek was surprised by this curt behavior by the Chairman, but thought nothing about it. The next day, he shifted to the Chairman's Secretariat and was very happy with the posh environment and his air conditioned office. His name was added to the few selected high ranking officials who were served lunch and tea from the Chairman's private pantry. He enjoyed other facilities like telephone at his residence, staff car and air travel facility for which he was not eligible at his level. But, with all these facilities, Mr Vivek remained a friendly, modest and and approachable young man ever ready to help anyone who cared to ask for it.

As days passed by , he impressed the Chairman by his hard work, integrity and his ability to deal with important matters independently. He attended all senior level meetings during which he gave valuable suggestions. His work required him to meet important dignitaries and visitors who were impressed with his manners and his ability to solve their problems. Overtime, he was drawn close to the family of the Chairman and had dinner with them on a number of occasions.

Something else was happening unnoticed. The Directors particularly, Mr Raina Director (Operations) was angry that so much importance was given to Vivek and wanted the Chairman to replace him with a senior officer with whom the Directors would feel comfortable dealing with. Mr Raina got a chance when the Chairman instructed Mr Vivek to get the annual production budget prepared on priority so that the same can be put up for approval of the Board of Directors in the next Board meeting. Mr Vivek promptly requested Mr Raina to get the production budget prepared. The next day, Mr Shankar Raman called Mr Raina to his office and the following conversation took place.

Mr Shankar Raman 'Hello Mr Raina did you get the production report prepared. We have to take it to the Board next Tuesday. I asked Vivek to inform you in this regard.

Mr Raina" Why, No Sir In fact, I asked Vivek specifically in this regard and he told me that there is no hurry in this regard. However, I knew it will be considered in the next Board meeting. So, I got it prepared anyway. I have brought it with me. It is here.

Mr Shankar Raman: " Thank you very much. You have saved me from an embarrassing situation. Leave your report here. I will go through it and call you in case I require any clarification.

Mr Raina :" Thank you very much Sir"

Unknown to Mr Vivek, a number of other senior executives were ranged against him in the office who spared no opportunity to backbite against him, spread misinformation and rumors to downgrade him in the eyes of Mr Shankar Raman. Other officers at his level were either jealous of him or were indifferent. Mr Vivek felt cut off from the mainstream and found it very difficult to function in this high profile assignment. All through this difficult times, he had sympathetic support from Ms Jyoti Gupta, personal secretary to the Chairman for the last ten years. She felt sorry and helpless at the way a devoted and hardworking young man like Vivek was treated by the strong lobby of senior executives in the organization. Mr Vivek could meet Mr Shankar Raman only occasionally due to his busy schedule. The following conversation took place between Mr Vivek and Ms Jyoti on day during lunch hours.

Ms Jyoti: Vivek, I feel sad for your condition. You should not have accepted this assignment. Remember, Chairman gave you a chance to decline this assignment. I wish you had consulted me. In that case, I would have given you a clear picture of the situation.

Mr Vivek: " I am indeed very disappointed. What should I do now"

Ms Jyoti: " Please get another job and do it fast.

Mr Vivek: " Thank you very much. I will consider your suggestion seriously.

The crunch came soon there after. One day, Mr Shankar Raman called him to his office and told him: " Vivek you have proved to be a big disappointment. You cannot work as a team. I realize I made a mistake in taking an inexperienced person like you in my office. But, considering your loyalty and hard working nature, I will not ask you to leave. I am shifting you to Materials Department as a junior officer.You may go now.

Dejected, Mr Vivek returned to his room and considered his future. Over the next six months, Mr Vivek applied for various jobs. Most organizations rejected him on the ground that he did not have any worthwhile experience. Some offered him a starting level job for an executive. Finally, he got a job as a personnel officer in a public sector company after serving as a senior executive in large private organization.

He resigned from his present assignment and took up the new job.

Questions:

1. Did Mr Shankar Raman do a right thing by creating a new position for Mr Vivek Sharma.
2. Where did Mr Vivek go wrong in creating the difficult situation for him in the office. Is Organizational politics like this avoidable? If so, how?
3. What are the other options available to a CEO to relieve him from routine work in order to concentrate on organizational and policy matters

22

A Case on Industrial Indiscipline

Mr. Shanker Chatterjee
Professor
shanker_1945@yahoo.com

Mrs. Preety Wadhwa
Associate Professor
pwadhwa77@gmail.com

Bharati Vidyapeeth University, Institute of Management and Research, New Delhi

Triveni Spun pipes and Structural Ltd is a large engineering company located in Bhopal. The company is engaged in manufacture of spun pipes and transmission towers, gear boxes, electrical stampings and motors in its plant spread over 100 acre of land. The offices are located within the plant premises. The plant employs around 2000 employees for its various departments and offices. The Company had also set up a well equipped Training centre within its plant to provide technical skills to the workers on various operations like lathe operations, milling, drilling, welding, cutting, fitting etc. The Training Institute is headed by Mr Ashok Sengupta and is assisted by the following staff:

Mr Pramod Verma	:	Training Officer
Mr Kamal Dheer	:	Training Officer
Mr Khalid Ansari	:	Training Officer
Mr Awas Tiwari	:	Librarian
Mr Raja Munde	:	Clerk-cum-typist
Mr Ramesh Nair	:	P.S. to Manager (Training)
Mr Abdul Hamid	:	Peon

In addition to the above staff, there were six training instructors who were deputed from the plant to impart specialized training to the workers as per the need of the plant. Senior plant executives were also invited to deliver lectures on operational processes, discipline, standing orders, communication skills and so on.

Mr Ashok Sengupta is a graduate in mechanical engineering with over 20 years of experience in plant operations. He is well respected in the Training Institute and in the plant for his competence and leadership qualities. A strict disciplinarian and a workaholic, he was given two out of turn promotions for his achievements as a training manager.

One day' he returned to his office half an hour early after lunch break. Having nothing particular to do, he went to have a look at the Workshop which was located at the far end of the Institute building. A strange sight confronted him. Mr Raja Munde Clerk-cum-typist was standing at the far end of the workshop and was loading expensive scrap and costly spare parts in a big gunny bag with the help of Devi Lal, casual labour in a jute gunny bag. Mr Sengupta immediately sensed the motive for this unusual activity. On some previous occasions, Mr Raja was caught stealing old newspaper and magazines from the Library, for selling in the scrap market. Mr Raja sensing the presence of a third person in the Workshop,looked around to find Mr Sengupta glaring at him.Mr Raja quickly unloaded the stolen articles and left the room. Mr Sengupta kept his cool and said nothing.

Returning to his office,Mr Sengupta decided that such indiscipline from his staff cannot be tolerated or ignored. He decided to have a word with Mr Tarsem Lal, the head of Personnel Department before initiating any disciplinary action action against Mr Raja.The plant had a strong INTUC dominated Union of which Raja was an active member. The same afternoon, Mr Sengupta went to the office of Mr Tarsem Lal and narrated the whole incident in the Institute's workshop to him. The following conversation took place between Mr Senguta and Mr Tarsem Lal:

Tarsem Lal: I am very sorry to hear this. Please try to understand my position.The plant has a very powerful union.There are well laid down procedure for dealing with disciplinary cases as per the standing orders and the provisions of law.

There has to be legally tenable proof of his stealing like photograph or eye witnesses. You will appreciate that arbitrary actions will lead to industrial unrest and slow down of production. I suggest that you ensure proper locking arrangements for Institute property.

Sengupta : You mean to say that such gross indiscipline has to tolerated because there was no eye witness. How will my staff feel about me. At least transfer this man from my Institute.I don't care if I do not get any replacement for him.

Tarsem Lal: (laughs) Who will take this idiot? You may have a word with other HODs. If someone want to take him as an additional hand in his Department,I will have no problem in transferring him from your Institute. But please remember, I do not have any replacement to give in his place.

Dejected, Mr Sengupta returned to his office. He knew that counseling Mr Raja will not have any effect. After Mr Raja was caught stealing old newspapers and magazines, Mr Sengupta and his colleagues had a long session with him advising him to mend his ways but without any success. He repeated the same thing after a few months. This time, he was let off with a strong written warning.

The fact was that Raja was addicted to alcohol and used to steal Institute's material for selling to provide him with money to purchase liquor when he needed. He was also a heavy smoker.

After, Mr Sengupta returned to his office, Mr N.K. Murty, Private Secretary to Mr Tarsem Lal who overheard the conversation between Mr Sengupta and Mr Tarsem lal , rang up and informed Raja that his boss had come to complain and to suggested disciplinary action against him. Nothing happened for the next few weeks.

One day, Mr Sengupta returned to his office early after lunch. There were no other officer or staff present at that time in the Institute. He was going through the office mails, when Mr Raja entered his office and started abusing him in most filthy language and went then away.Mr Sengupta, stunned by this behavior, managed to keep his cool and remained silent. He did not discuss the incident with his colleagues or staff when they returned after lunch, but was determined to handle the situation on his own. He took Mr Abdul Hamid,peon, into confidence and asked him to report to him immediately whenever Mr Raja comes to office after consuming alcohol.The occasion came soon. One day, the peon reported to him that Raja has come after consuming lots of alcohol. Mr Sengupta rang up the Security Department at the factory main gate to send a jeep and two strong security guards to the training Institute immediately.

When they came,Mr Sengupta asked them to bodily lift Raja and take to the plant dispensary. Mr Raja could do nothing to escape the situation. In the dispensary, Raja was put through breath analyzer test in presence of the Medical officer and hospital staff. A detailed medical report was prepared and was duly signed by the medical officer and entered in the records.

In the office, Mr Sengupta summoned Raja and informed him in presence of all the officers and staff that his services will be terminated though after enquiry and due process and there is nothing that he can do to save himself. Mr Raja fell on the feet of Mr Sengupta and pleaded for mercy saying that he has wife and two small children totally dependant on him. He said he will commit suicide if his service is terminated. He also started crying bitterly. At this, the officers and staff of the Training Institute pleaded with Mr Sengupta to give one more chance to Raja as he is without any means to support his family in absence of his job.

Mr Sengupta relented, but made it clear to Raja that now he has a documented record of his gross indiscipline and he will not hesitate to use the same if there is a the slightest act of indiscipline on his part in future.

Questions

1. Do you agree with the decision taken by Mr Sengupta in respect of Mr Raja.? If not,how should he have handled the situation?
2. Do you support the approach of Mr Tarsem Lal Personnel Manager towards industrial indiscipline.
3. What preventive measures do you suggest in such cases.

23

Organizational Behaviour

Mr. Shanker Chatterjee
Professor
shanker_1945@yahoo.com

Ms. Shipra
Lecturer

Bharati Vidyapeeth University, Institute of Management and Research, New Delhi

Prism Cements Ltd is a large cement company, which is owned and managed by a big private sector industrial group. The company is engaged in operating ten cement factories located in the states of Madhya Pradesh, Andhra Pradesh, Gujrat and Rajasthan. The Head office of the company in located in New Delhi.

The Company is engaged in implementing major expansion and diversification projects. To meet this objective and to build a professional management cadre, the company had drawn up an ambitious plan to induct in a phased manner batches of management trainees, in different functional areas: marketing, HR, finance, material management and in various engineering streams to manage the new cement plants.

Komal was inducted in the first batch of management trainees. She had done her MBA degree in first division from a reputed management Institute in Himachal Pradesh. After attending a month long induction program in New Delhi and in one of the company's plant in Raipur in Madhya Pradesh, she was posted in the HRD department of the Personnel Department, for her on the job training.

Mr P.K.Singh who had joined the company after leaving his job in another cement company headed the HRD department. Director (Personnel) of the company was Mr.R.D.Gupta. He was 53 years of age with about 30 years of experience in handling various functions in the personnel departments in several companies in the private and public sectors.

Mr P.K.Singh was a competent executive and organized the activities of HRD department in an efficient manner. He was very happy to have Miss Komal to assist him in organizing training programs for the executives and non-executive. There was a good understanding between the two and they supported each other in meeting the deadlines and commitments. Komal was a tall and very good looking girl. In fact, she attracted lots of attention (mostly unwanted) among the executives working in the Head office. Often executive from other departments: Finance, Projects, MIS will come to HRD department just to chat with her. This irritated and disturbed Mr P.K. Singh. But, being new to the organization, he preferred to keep quiet. Some executives also started back biting against Mr Singh to spoil his relations with Komal.

One evening, the peon of Director (Personnel) came to HRD department with the message that Komal and Mr P.K. Singh should see the Director and apprise him about the activities of their department. Both of them were very excited because it was unusual for the Director to meet executives at their levels; and that too for a routine matter. Both of them organized their information and program details to show to the Director and waited for a call from the Director's office for the meeting. Around 6 PM, they were asked to meet him. They entered his office to find the Director very busy studying some files.

Finally, he looked at them and asked them to work hard and achieve the targets set for their department. They then left his office.

Some days later, the Director called only Komal to his office. He then discussed about her family, hobbies and so on. She was visibly uncomfortable with him alone particularly since her boss, Mr. Singh was not there. She was also surprised that the Director had all the time to discuss irrelevant things just to retain her in his office. Subsequent, the Director would call Mr. Singh and Komal frequently to his office. There, he would ignore

Mr. Singh and continue talking to Komal. One day the following discussion took place between Komal and her boss, Mr. Singh.

Mr.P.K.Singh: Komal, are you aware why the Director is calling you on some pretext or the other. Let us be very frank. Both of us are mature adults. The main issue is ,we are both career oriented adults. The Director's behaviour is clearly affecting our department's work. We were working as a tea and achieving good results. What can we do now?

Ms Komal: Sir, a woman understands these issues very well. It is nice that you raised this issue. Otherwise, I was planning to discuss this matter with you Anyway. Frankly, I am embarrassed and upset with Director's behavior.

You have probably observed how the office staff smiles when we go to his chamber. You probably know my answer, but I will tell you. I cannot continue in this organization any longer. In fact. I have already a good job offer and I am planning to accept it.

Soon thereafter, Komal resigned from the job and joined another organization.

Then,

Trouble started for Mr.P.K.Singh. Since the Director believed that he encouraged Komal to leave and he will not have more occasions to see her. Mr. Singh's facilities were withdrawn one by one. A room cooler replaced his room air conditioner. A typist replaced his stenographer. His files were not cleared for days together. Other senior officers of Personnel Department taking a hint at the annoyance of Director for him started ignoring him. In short, his continuance in the organization became almost impossible.

Not surprisingly, he resigned and took up another job in a small company on a lower salary. After Mr Singh left Prism Cements Ltd, The HRD department was entrusted to a junior officer in the personnel department with the task of attending day-to-day paper work. He was assisted by only a typist to do the typing and clerical work. Thus, the HRD department virtually collapsed due to undesirable attraction of the Director (Personnel) for a young and beautiful woman executive.

Questions

1. Analyse the situation to find out the cause of the collapse of a promising HRD Deptt.
2. What could have been done to prevent the situation?
3. Do you see any role of the top management that such situation does not arise and Competent executives are retained in the organization?

24

Employee Engagement: A Case Study of LPS-Bossard Pvt. Ltd.

Mr. Himanshu Dembla
Regional Manager (North)-LPS-Bossard Pvt. Ltd,
Ms. Swaty Wadhwa,
swatyswaty@rediffmail.com
Kasturi Ram Collegeof Higher Education, Sonepat

The age-old dictum goes that 'satisfied employees create satisfied customers" by constantly striving for the best, by their motivation and enhanced performance. It is believed that an engaged employee always acts positively in the interest of the organization and takes unconcealed pride in the success and prosperity of his employer.

In general it refers to employee "involvement, commitment, passion, enthusiasm, focused, effort, and energy" (Macey & Schneider, 2008)

Feeling "engaged" depends on the "strength" of the workplace not necessarily on the corporate leadership"

- Buckingham & Coffman, 'First Break all the Rules'

ABSTRACT

Employee engagement is the level of commitment and involvement employees have towards their organizations. In simple words, it is just figuring out how much of a person's heart is in the job. It is a positive attitude held by employees towards the organization and its values. An engaged employee is aware of context and works with colleagues to improve performance within the job for the benefit of the organization. The case discusses the level of employee engagement or employee commitment at LPS-Bossard Pvt. Ltd. Rohtak and shares the result of questionnaire that was administered on the employees. The organization believes that an engaged employee is more productive; create higher quality results; will stay longer and above all is passionate and self-motivated throughout his stay in the organization.

Key Words: LPS-Bossard, Employee engagement, Employee satisfaction index Trending

Learning Objectives:

- To develop an understanding of what Employee Engagement is?
- To explore the difference between Job Engagement and Job Satisfaction.
- To discuss why engagement is important.
- To highlight the "Top" Best Practices.
- To study how LPS-Bossard has developed a culture of engagement.

Introduction:

The concept of employee engagement is playing a vital role in the modern organizations. In simple words, it is just Figuring out how much of a person's heart is in the job.

An engaged employee is a person who is fully involved in, and is enthusiastic about, his or her work. Such employees are attracted to, and inspired, committed and fascinated by their work.

The term Employee engagement refers to 'a positive attitude held by employees towards the organization and its values. An engaged employee is aware of context and works with colleagues to improve performance within the job for the benefit of the organization.

Conceptualization:

Employee engagement has its roots in classic work done in employee motivation, in the form of intrinsic motivation (Herzberg, 1966). Bateman and Grant (2003) state that intrinsic motivation is said to exist when behavior is performed for its own sake rather than to obtain material or social reinforces. Although Deming (1993) placed great weight on the value system, he also acknowledged the vital role of intrinsic motivation and the need to engage workers in their work.

It would appear that employee engagement is strongly linked to the work of classic motivation theorists and researchers. Engagement at work was conceptualized by Kahn, (1990) as the 'harnessing of organizational members' selves to their work roles. In engagement, people employ and express themselves physically, cognitively, and emotionally during role performances.

The second related construct to engagement in organizational behavior is the notion of flow advanced by Csikszentmihalyi (1975, 1990). He defines flow as the 'holistic sensation' that, people feel when they act with total involvement. Flow is the state in which there is little distinction between the self and environment. When individuals are in Flow State little conscious control is necessary for their actions. Employee engagement is the thus the level of commitment and involvement an employee has towards their organization and its values

Difference between Job Engagement and Job Satisfaction:

Being *satisfied* with your job doesn't mean that you're *engaged* with it (you can be happy at work but do a poor job of it!)

If you're ***engaged*** with your work you will not only be more *satisfied* with it, but you will also be more productive, create higher quality results, and demonstrate better customer service

Aspects of Employee Engagement

Three basic aspects of employee engagement according to the global studies are:-

- The employees and their own unique psychological make up and experience.
- The employers and their ability to create the conditions that promote employee Engagement.
- Interaction between employees at all levels.

Thus it is largely the organization's responsibility to create an environment and culture conducive to this partnership, and a win-win equation.

Categories of Employee Engagement

According to the Gallup the Consulting organization there are there are different types of people:-

Engaged—"*Engaged*" employees are builders. They want to know the desired expectations for their role so they can meet and exceed them. They perform at consistently high levels. They want to use their talents and strengths at work every day. They work with passion and they drive innovation and move their organization forward.

Not Engaged—*Not-engaged* employees tend to concentrate on tasks rather than the goals and outcomes they are expected to accomplish. They want to be told what to do just so they can do it and say they have finished.

Actively Disengaged--The "*actively disengaged*" employees are the "cave dwellers." They're "Consistently against Virtually Everything." They're not just unhappy at work; they're busy acting out their unhappiness. They sow seeds of negativity at every opportunity.

Components of Employee Engagement:

- Career Development- Opportunities for personal development.
- Leadership- Clarity of company values.
- Leadership – Respectful treatment of employees.
- Empowerment
- Equal opportunities & fair treatment.
- Performance Appraisal.
- Pay & benefits.
- Health & Safety.
- Job satisfaction.

- Communication.
- Family friendliness.
- Co-operation.

Best Practices Facilitating Engagement

- Leadership concern
- Talent Management System
- Freedom to contribute to their own job and progress
- Clear and **accessible** HR Policies
- Periodic Performance reviews
- Active Participation in decision making
- High Levels of team work
- Least biased and discriminated Work environment
- Proper exchange of Information

Normally every organization is interested in measuring employee engagement. One level of measuring it includes:

- Overall opinion about their working experience in the organization;
- Loyalty intent;
- Recommendation likelihood; and
- Feeling inspired to give their best efforts

These are called the engagement measures. The second level would be the key drivers that impact employee engagement. The drivers provide specific inputs to enhance employee engagement to the organization's goals. In addition, there would be inputs to control attrition.

Broadly, the dimensions that would go under the microscope of an employee engagement study are as follows:

- **Quality of Experience:** Role, Infrastructure, Managerial support, Inter-departmental interfaces, Team-work, Compensation, Communication.
- **Student orientation and practices:** Opinions about organization's services vis-à-vis employee's needs, complaint resolution and other relevant aspects.
- **Work processes:** Quality, efficiency and productivity.
- **Vision / Mission:** Awareness and related practices.
- **Views about brand image:** Pride in working with the organization.

While the above dimensions are a starting point, the specific and relevant dimensions as well as the areas under each dimension to be studied in an organization are finalized based on a rigorous research process that encompasses the organization's needs as well as employees expectations and experiences.

LPS Bossard Pvt Ltd.- A Case Study

LPS Bossard Pvt Ltd. is a joint venture between M/s Lakshmi Precision Screws Ltd., Rohtak and Bossard AG, Switzerland. It was incorporated in November 1997 and became operational in 1998 with specialization in Industrial Assembly Technology and now a 45-member family serving to their customers all over India with a sales over Rs. 55 million with a steady growth.

They deal in fasteners and have a range of more than 50,000 of fasteners in Stainless steel, High tensile steel, MS, Brass, Copper, Aluminum, Titanium Alloy and Plastics. Their range includes standard items (as per DIN, ISO, JIS, NFE, and other National & International Std.) and Multifunctional fasteners like, Self drilling screw, Thread cutting, Thread Forming screws, EcoSyn, EcoFix and many more. Apart from these they also develop and supply items as per customer specifications.

They have joined hands with many world repute companies like ***Panduit Corp.*** for distribution of *Cable ties and Wiring Accessories, **Recoil Fasteners Australia** for Thread Damage Repair Kits, Inserts and Insertion Tools, Fairchild Fasteners for Tension Latches, ¼ Turn Fasteners, Push Button Fasteners, **Richco** for Injection Moulding Parts and other Plastic Parts, BarSplice for Construction fasteners to cater to the needs of customers for 'C' items.*

In their main operational activity Fastening Technology, they are headquartered in Rohtak, Haryana and have formed regional offices at New Delhi, Bangalore & Pune. In an effort to be closer to their customers, they also have offices in Ahmedabad, Chennai, Hyderabad, and Kolkatta & Mumbai.

A word about their Parent Companies

LPS Ltd.

Founded in March 1972, LPS is one of the leading manufacturers and suppliers of high tensile fasteners such as Bolts, Screws, Nuts and similar parts for Automobile and other Industrial Sectors and has acquired the state of art technology. LPS is Accredited in Mechanical and Chemical Testing since 1995 by A2LA (American Association for Laboratory Accreditation, USA) and NABL (National Accreditation Board for Calibration & Testing Laboratories) and is ISO certified since 1996. LPS also got QS 9000 in March 2000.

Bossard AG

Bossard a leading logistic-oriented group for fastening technology was founded in 1831 in Zug, Switzerland and today is managed by the seventh generation of the Bossard Family with roughly 1100 employees. Bossard is the first company in this sector to get an ISO 9001/9002 & 14001 certification (since 1986). Bossard has its global presence with regional business units in Europe, United States and Asia/Pacific and operations in over 15 countries having a turnover of over US$ 350 Million.

Overall we can say that they are the leading OEM supplier offering global solutions for local requirements.

Their Guiding Principles for their activities

Customer Focus

They focus on the real needs of their customers. They understand their problems and can solve them. That's why they develop custom-tailored products and services for every customer.

Value Added

Not all products and services add value – but they all lead to costs. Key for the customer is the perceived value. That's why they cannot be inexpensive but, instead, offer the best value.

Quality

All their stakeholders can rest assured that they invariably deliver what the promise. That's why they can offer their customers security, convenience and cost-effectiveness.

Independence

They have always put their trust in creativity, innovation and unconventional thinking.

People

They rely on highly motivated employees, empower them to contribute to the group's success and let them participate in it. That's why they are having teams to coordinate the activities. According to them:

"Their employees are their greatest assets."

Some Japanese systems used: Currently we can offer our Two-Bin, Kanban Card, Kanban Barcode, Edifact and SmartBin systems.

Globally the group has a specialization in handling the needs of many industries like:

Air Conditioner	Home Appliances	Aero Space	Wind Mill
Medical Equipment	Instrumentation	Energy Meter	Locomotive
Automobile and	Electrical & Electronics		

Accredited worldwide

Within the first year of their operations, they have been certified as an ISO 9002 certified by UL USA. Many of their customers have rated them as best suppliers and this is the biggest certificate they have, and will always achieve.

Their Major customers

Asea Brown Boveri	Adtranz	All BHEL
All Bharat Electronics Ltd.	Amtrex Hitachi	Enercon India
Crompton Greaves	MICO	Behr India

ISRO	VSSC	DRDL
DLW	TATA	Defence Customers
Tecumseh	Secure Meters	GE Medical Systems
Moser Baer	ITL	Wipro GE
SIEMENS	Alstom	JCB India
Havell's		

"They believe in long lasting business relationship"

And for the same they believe in developing their greatest assets i.e. their employees and thus have dedicated teams of talented professionals. It is an organization that doesn't rest on concrete pillars but on the shoulders of dedicated and committed teammates. In order to motivate employees awards are given to them for different categories.

- Best Customer support officer (inside).
- Best Customer support officer (outside).
- Best Regional Manager.
- Best A/R management (accounts receivables).
- Best BIR management (Bad inventory report).
- Best new conversion.

The management regularly does a survey to find out the status of employee engagement or commitment in order to find out what employees feel about their organization, whether they feel engaged or not. In order to do the same, they did an employee commitment survey in order to find out Employee Satisfaction Index. This survey is done on trimester basis.

Results 2010: As compared to year 2008 and 2009, employee engagement in 2010 was increased as concrete Improvements were done in the year 2010:

- **Team Building Activities-**
- They have organized Kite, Rangoli and Mehandi competition in the month of August & got very active participation from Team
- **Technical Trainings:** Now they have catalogue training session once in 15 days for CSO & ISP so that they can be very much confident while talking to their customers
- **Group Training & workshop** - They had done a successful CSO workshop in August for 4 days, all CSOs from all regions were involved & now their Sales workshop is in pipeline which will be in 3rd week of March 2011
- **Trainings –** All Training's Hardcopy are kept in Library with Indexing for New Joinees & Existing employees.

A Comparison of Employee Satisfaction Index Trending from Annual 2008 to 2010

BIN – Employee Satisfaction Index Trending

ECS Trending from Annual 2008 to Annual 2010 average points

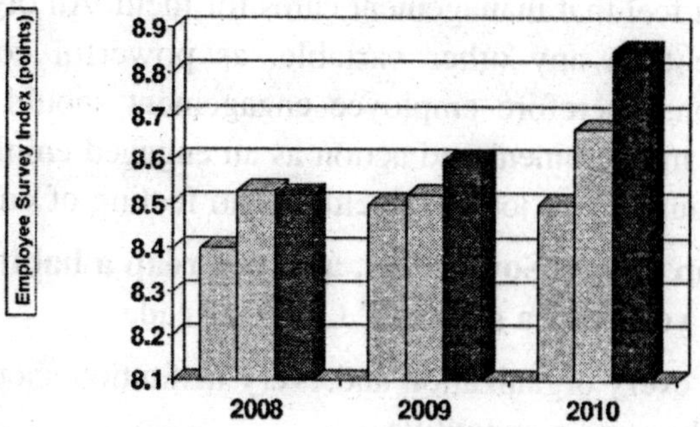

Employee Survey Index	2008			2009			2010		
Avr Score	8.58	8.6	8.7	8.72	8.57	8.9	8.65	8.67	8.85

Period (By Trimester)

BOSSARD

Findings & Interpretations:

- 99% participation in ECS Annual 2010
- They have got an average of 8.72 score in Annual 2010
- They got an average score of 8.80 on question no.1,2,7,8,13 which shows they are proud to be associated with the organization and enjoying the work environment.
- They got an average score of 8.85 on question no. 8,9,10,11,14 which shows they have a strong and dedicated leadership.
- They got an average score of 9.38 on question no.12 and13, which shows they their engagement in the organization.
- They got an average score of 8.34 on question no.5 and 6, which shows that they find the job very challenging and innovative.
- This time they got to know the higher satisfaction of employees regarding their feedback on trainings, work environment & towards their Leaders, they got more than 9 points from Q-11 to Q-14.

An additional and continuous 5 Step Programme at LPS-Bossard for making the culture full of engagement:

- Creation of Work Place…
- Like: Temple
- Like Garden
- Removal of Disparity &Bringing Uniformity at Work Place
- Open Communication
- Respect & Concern for Each other
- Employees Involvement

Conclusion

Thus we can say that Employee Engagement is the buzzword term for employee communication. Overall where there is a need for recognition, provide them in order to make employees feel special, make them feel that management cares for them. An organization should thus recognize employees, more than any other variable, as powerful contributors to an organization's competitive position. Therefore employee engagement should be a continuous process of learning, improvement, measurement and action as an engaged employee experiences job satisfaction, organizational commitment, job involvement and feeling of empowerment.

"Sow a thought, and you reap an act. Sow an act, and you reap a habit, and you reap a character. Sow a character, and you reap a destiny." Charles Reade

From this, it is very clear that every organization and every institution should strive towards this emerging concept in order to become competitive.

TEACHING NOTE

Synopsis

The Case describes how LPS-Bossard created a culture of engagement in their organization. Previously few attention was given to the employees working there but when the organization realized its importance, they added few activities in their normal routine in order to make the employees feel disengaged i.e they realized that Intentional disengagement (rest and recovery) is essential to sustain full engagement. The case also discusses the level of employee engagement or employee commitment at LPS-Bossard Pvt. Ltd. Rohtak and shares the result of questionnaire that was administered on the employees. The organization believes that an engaged employee is more productive; create higher quality results; will stay longer and above all is passionate and self-motivated throughout his stay in the organization. Overall with the help this case, students will be able to understand the concept of Employee engagement or commitment and they will also be able to link it with them also in the manner that the same concept if applied to them also, a better learning and understanding develops about the clarity of the subject they study. The more the student engagement more will be the learning.

Case Objectives

This case is made for the students at the MBA level or in executive education programs in order:

- To develop an understanding of what Job Engagement is?
- To explore the difference between Job Engagement and Job Satisfaction.
- To discuss why engagement is important.
- To highlight the "Top" Best Practices for employee engagement.
- To study how LPS-Bossard has developed a culture of engagement.

Assignment Questions

1. "Employee Engagement policies are becoming increasingly important in the current scenario". Do you agree with this statement? Discuss with respect to LPS-Bossard Pvt. Ltd.
2. If the organization would not have taken specific initiatives for developing the culture of engagement, what would have been the repercussions?
3. As a student of management, what additional steps you would have taken to improve employee engagement in the organization?
4. Can you suggest some more areas where this concept can be applied?

TEACHING PLAN

The teacher will use a story of mother and housewife that how they are able to deliver every thing right at the time, consistently all 365 Days in a year without any failure and that also with Good Quality, delivery Just in Time, In the Desired Quantity with Low Cost. It's only because of 'Her Emotions & Concerns' towards her family as she feels that.........

This is 'My Family'.

- He/She is 'My Son/Daughter'.
- He is 'My Husband' etc. etc.
- This is 'My House'

just to make the students understand how an ATTITUDE can be developed in the employees for engagement.

Then the teacher will give few theoretical concepts about the topic and with the help of case-study , the students would be able to know why engagement is important, what are the "Top" Best Practices for employee engagement and how to develop a culture of employee engagement in the organization.

The teacher can use a power point presentation or a video to show the culture of engagement in the organization.

Suggested / Possible Answers to Assignment Questions

After understanding the concept and watching a power point presentation or a movie, the students will definitely able to give all the answers. Answer to question number 4 would not be told but the students will apply logic to find its answer.

Suggested Teaching Approach

Interactive session with the students

Audio Visual Support

The teacher can use point presentation with a video to show the actual scenario of the organization.

Bibliography

Davenport Thomas; Prusak Laurence. (2000) "*Working Knowledge: How Organizations Manage What They Know*" Harvard Business School Press.

Heskett, Jame L (1994) "Putting the service profit chain to work" Harvard Business Review, Vol. 72 Issue 2.

Jones James R.; Harter James K (2005) "Race effects on the employee engagement-turnover intention relationship" Journal of Leadership & amp; Organizational Studies.

Kalburgi Mohammed Javed; Dinesh G. P.(2011) "A Study of Employee Engagement in NEKRTC Bellary" Eighth AIMS International Conference on Management.

Mukherjee Ashok (2005) "Engagement for the mind body, and soul" Human Capital

Vazirani Nitin "Employee Engagement" SIES College of Management Studies, Working Paper Series 05/07

Woodruffe Charles (2006) "Employee Engagement – The Real Secret of Winning a Crucial Edge over your rivals" Manager Motivation

Websites:

- http://www.opcuk.com/downloads/defining_employee_engagement.pdf
- www.bossard.com

Data was also collected from organization's brochure, discussion with the senior members of the organization.

25

People Issues in Family Owned Business

Vidya M.Iyer
IILM Graduate School of Management
vidya.mahesh@iilmgsm.ac.in

Introduction

The small and medium enterprises contribute about 40% of India's export and play a very vital part in the country's industrial growth. Most importantly, this is the sector that employs the population closest to the bottom of the pyramid.

Definition of MSMEs in India

Manufacturing Enterprises – Investment in Plant & Machinery

Description	*INR*	*USD($)*
Micro Enterprises	upto Rs. 25Lakhs	upto $ 62,500
Small Enterprises	above Rs. 25 Lakhs & upto Rs. 5 Crores	above $ 62,500 & upto $ 1.25 million
Medium Enterprises	above Rs. 5 Crores & upto Rs. 10 Crores	above $ 1.25 million & upto $ 2.5 million

Service Enterprises – Investment in Equipments

Description	*INR*	*USD($)*
Micro Enterprises	upto Rs. 10Lakhs	upto $ 25,000
Small Enterprises	above Rs. 10 Lakhs & upto Rs. 2 Crores	above $ 25,000 & upto $ 0.5 million
Medium Enterprises	above Rs. 2 Crores & upto Rs. 5 Crores	above $ 0.5 million & upto $ 1.5 million

(*Source:* SME Chamber of India)

Many manufacturing and service organizations grow from being micro to small then medium. A few of them manage to grow into large over a reasonably long span of time.

Most of the SMEs start as family or proprietorship businesses. Depending on the potential of the business and the strength of the owner the business flourishes over generations. It has been observed that only 1/3rd of the family owned businesses grow from small to medium and lare across 3 generations and the other 2/3 rd barely manage to reach the second generation. the growth rate of these businesses too is low.

In Indian context the reasons for the stunted growth are multi-dimensional. These reasons include, lack of professional approach form the owners, improper management of people, lack of financial incentives for the employees because of the slow growth and low affordability of the owners towards expansion.

Some of the common industrial sectors in the SME band are manufacturing, jewelry, food and agri-product processing, printing and other service organizations.

This case relates to the print industry and is set in a medium sized organization. The print industry in India is going through difficult times. Beginning with paper, ink, packaging material and including technology, India depends largely on imported products for its printing demands. Though printing in India has existed for a long time now, the market has become dynamic with the influence of technology and entry of cash rich international and domestic business houses. The world print market too is evolving rapidly with technological changes. The long-established small print houses in India have been facing testing times in the recent past. They are presently in a transition phase from small and medium level enterprises to the next higher level. Some of the companies that could not survive the sweeping changes have diversified out of the industry and some others have been bought over the rich and bigger.

Pedagogical Objective of the Case

— To provide an understanding of the working of small companies; it is aimed to create a sense of inquisitiveness in areas other than mainstream businesses.

— Many family-owned businesses in India lack professional managerial skills. Along with conventional wisdom, professional ideas are essential to grow the business from one level to the next higher. Thus there is a learning objective for the reader to identify, appreciate and understand the working of family-owned businesses.

— To specifically highlight and discuss the people issues in traditional and family run businesses. The case subtly conveys the importance of employee-engagement and training. In situations of financial crunch and the increased complexities due to market competition and various opportunities available for the employees the art of man-management is put to test.

Growth of Printart

The organization was founded by Mr. Amardas Ramraj and his brother Mr.Dharmaraj. The initial years were focused on printing brochures, religious content and other forms of off-set printing works. After the demise of Mr. Dharmaraj, the entire management came into the hands of Mr. Ramraj. He was a qualified chartered accountant and was astute at managing the numbers and client relationship. He laid emphasis on quality of work and timely delivery. His reputation in the industry grew over time as a person with unquestionable personal qualities. Therefore the business grew without many obstacles. With time, the technology too advanced and the company tied up with manufacturers of machinery from Japan and Germany. This gave the company an edge over its competitors. The company now hired more workers, gave then training and expanded business across India. The quality of the work brought them visibility in the international market too. This meant, they catered to large parts of Western and Northern parts of India and exports to selected countries in about 20 years of their existence. The growth was by all means commendable for a print company and that too a family owned organization. By 2005, the organization had completed 50 years of existence and had a turnover of INR 60 Cr.1975 was a landmark year in the company's map, as they launched products solely for export markets in the year 1975 and entered into a higher league of printers in India.

By the year 1980, PRINTART had established itself among the top companies in India and Mr. Ramraj began inducting his son and daughter into the organization. Both of them began taking part in the organization's activities. The son, Mr. Rajat took into Sales and Client Management and the daughter, Ms. Rajitha took into the technical aspects and operations of the company.

The second generation started off well because they learnt quickly and worked hard towards sustaining the momentum initiated by their father. They were conscious of the fact that the industry was growing rapidly and competition too was growing. Thrust was given to increasing the product portfolio and simultaneously forge new collaborations. With the guidance of Mr. Ramraj, by the turn of the century, the company grew to almost double its size in terms of its operation. He kept a close watch in the working of his children and was planning gradual withdrawal. All along he ensured that he maintained personal relations with his senior employees who were with him since inception of the business. The employees too had developed a comfortable relationship and the psychological contract worked more than the lettered word.

By now, product lines grew steadily and strategic acquisitions were made, both domestically and internationally. The company entered printing books in foreign languages, books of fine quality printing at international standards, printing on imported paper, using the most advanced inks and dyes. They also tied up with ink-manufacturers, small scale screen printers and a laser printer to integrate backwards.

Philosophy of Mr.Ramraj

Clients are the heart of the company and commitment to quality is the soul of the business. Beyond these profit is the motive of every business. These were the tenets on which Mr. Ramraj constructed his business. He went on to believe that while profits were necessary, the client should be kept satisfied at all costs. It was due to this ideology of his that the company was a preferred business partner for many of his clients. The principles and philosophy of the company stood the company in good stead for long, despite sometimes leading to reduced profits.

Towards his employees, he believed in treating each of them as per their individual abilities and needs. He believed less in structured compensation. This policy of Mr. Ramraj had worked well for him and employee loyalty had never been an issue for him. His employees too were ready to walk the extra mile for the company owing mostly to the relationship with Mr. Ramraj.

The People Challenge

The growth of the business led to expansion. It was inevitable for the management to recruit professionally trained technical and managerial personnel now. To keep up with the technological changes, demands of the customers and market competition, the company decided to recruit management trainees and engineers into the organization. The new comers were allowed to move freely in the organization and understand the working. The overall management of Human Resources and other related issues were usually taken care of by Mr. Ramraj himself and recently by Ms. Rajitha began getting involved in understanding her father's ways of man-management. They had so far avoided hiring a professional HR manager. The infrastructure and administrative needs were taken care of by Mr. Ramraj's right-hand man, Mr. Paul in the organization. There was not much clarity in terms of work allocation, performance measurement and compensation systems. The promotions and increments came in whenever the management thought it right. But, most of the old employees were silent, because the management generally met their expectations of work and compensation. The new comers and the freshly qualified ones had their questions. They were not convinced with the unscheduled way of declaring promotions, incentives and rewards. Also, they had questions like, why the older employees continued to get importance in spite of remaining backward in technology and low in aggression to compete.

The young employees could not appreciate the extent to which loyalty was being appreciated in the company. The management trainees also found a total lack of organization. This was in contrast to their educational knowledge. Since, the owners and the top management were open to meeting the new comers, ideas were given and thoughts were exchanged. But to their disappointment, there were no major changes in the organization.

In about 2 years, around 2007 while the company grew in financial worth, challenges started brewing from within. The senior most manager who had been handling purchases had decided to quit. There were changes in the sales teams handling domestic and exports respectively.

Upon having freewheeling talks, some of the exiting employees confided that it was humiliating to be coached by the new generation of management and employees. The increased involvement of Mr. Ramraj's children meant the older employees perceived a threat from the generation next. The rapid changes in technology meant loss of importance for some of the skills of the earlier times like manually setting the machine every time for printing. The computerized setting machines took their place.

The technical team too started facing problems, essentially because the most experienced technical hands were ageing. A couple of them had brought in their sons into the organization. Their sons had got trained in the organization while working. They learnt the work after they joined as apprentices. The new technical team was updated in terms of qualification. They had print technology engineers form leading colleges, trained and experienced technicians. Despite all this, Ms. Rajitha faced regular problems in building her team. The main contention was, the middle-aged employees did not get opportunities to upgrade themselves, because the freshers came in with the new technology.

Mr. Rajat too began seeing cracks in the sales team. The upcoming competitors were the most favorite places were the employees joined after they quit PRINTART. The new companies started with higher capital and to build their reputation offered high incentives to the sales personnel. The new sales force did not see reason to join and then continue with PRINTART in times of such fluidity. in some ways, Mr. Ramraj's philosophy of compromising on the margins to keep clients happy, meant the costs could not be increased at the rate proportional to the production and operational costs. This meant lower fraction of profit growth, thereby meaning lesser increase in incentives and commission.

The company could not go deeper into their pockets to keep the employees happy. Striking the balance between increasing the prices and increasing the compensation was becoming challenging with everyday.

The company was contemplating hiring consultants to enable them come out of this web if issues that they found themselves in. But, then it was felt that they will be the best judges to re-invent their processes and decide on the future steps.

After long thought within the family it was identified that the first need was a full time devoted HR manager, so that communication between the employees and the management can be stream lined. This was the first of the many changes that were intended to be the remedy for the many challenges facing PRINTART. They also contemplated training the people.

Mr. Ramraj's children were looking at the option of totally revamping the employee set up in the organization by introducing "Voluntary or early Retirement schemes." Mr. Ramraj personally was not convinced that employees should be retrenched, he was in a dilemma. The family was examining a variety of options to bring about quick and smooth change as long periods of uncertainty would cause damage to the reputation. Already the new companies were forging ahead to meet the changing market trends and savvy generation of employees. Additionally the international market too was getting tighter with the rapid entry of Chinese companies.

26

Catch-22 Situation at ABC Pvt. Ltd.

Mrs. Rupali Kumar
Associate Professor
rupali.bvimr@gmail.com
Bharati Vidyapeeth University, Institute of Management and Research, New Delhi

Synopsis

The case "Catch-22 situation for an HR Manager at ABC Pvt. Ltd." describes the problems occurring between two employees and its negative impact on their productivity in the work affecting on-the –job performance for them as well as leading to impairment of the organizations image or goodwill and the steps an HR manager has to take to tackle such situation in the company.

Case objectives

This case aims to make readers aware about various ways to tackle employees conduct and its possible effect on the working environment and productivity of the company. More importantly is to learn how to make employees behave in a desired or orderly manner to make their actions effective and productive.

Discussion Areas

- **The effect of bad personal relations effecting the working environment of the employees in the company.**
- **The method by which HR manager should handle such a problem.**

Teaching Approach and Strategy

The case should be provided to the readers one day prior to the discussion for individual analysis and write up. Next day the case should be discussed among a small group. The outcome of the small group discussion should be presented in front of the whole batch by representative of each group and in order to evaluate each option in detail.

Frame work for Analysis

The case does not have any quantitative data and hence should be analyzed using SAPLAP framework, SWOT and PEST analysis method. Some part of the case has been written in dialogue form and is therefore suitable for role play. The case is suitable for written assessment or examination and oral presentations.

The Case

ABC Pvt. Ltd. is a small company dealing in employment consultancy sector. The employee strength of the company is not much but has a very strong culture which binds the employees together. The team leader along with his team members would report to the operational head. But since past few days the branch has been witnessing severe difficulties. The reputation of the company was going down and considering this the director of the company hired new personnel Mr. Adam for this post. Mr. Adam is a humble person and tries to keep its employees happy. The new manager gave good results and within a short period of time the company revived back again. The director threw a party in the evening for all the employees along with their family members after the grand success for the company. Mr. Adam drank too much and misbehaved with Mr. Bob's wife. Mr. Bob who is the team leader saw this happening and went up to Adam and threatened him for his act. The superior-subordinate ego in Adam's mind led him to indulge in a heated argument between the two. This fight between the operational head and the team leader is now visible in their work also. They have become a hot topic in the office among the employees too. The whole environment of the office has changed because of one wrong act in a social gathering. This was becoming a big concern as it led to bad performance of Bob's Team. Whatever the team did, could not register in the eyes of company as Adam would never let Bob's efforts come forward, by exercising his authority for his own benefit. As a result the respect and trust between senior and the team was not there.

The HR Manager tried to resolve the complete situation with a request to both the employees to quit fighting and to keep their personal matter at home. But to the amazement of the HR Manager neither of them changed after the request made by him. Hence the HR manager issued an oral warning and as an organizations practice a temporary record of this warning was placed in the respective employees file and once the employee shows the changed behavior and a willingness to adhere to rules and regulations, the record of the oral reprimand is removed from his/her file. But this action was also not taken supportively by Mr. Adam and Mr. Bob. He felt helpless when he realized that both the employees are stubborn and are not ready to listen no matter what.

Now the HR manager is in a flux and needs a suggestion regarding what should be the future course of action.

QUESTIONS

1. According to you whether such issues of informal gathering should be considered by the HR manager?
2. Giving a warning letter to both operational manger and team leader was the right decision of HR manager?
3. What else HR manger could do to solve such a problem?
4. The punishment for both of the official should be same or different according to you?

International Business

1

Indian Economy Winning Inflation through Economic or Political Ways

Dr. Navneet Gera,
gerasir@yahoo.com

Ms. Neetu Jain
myaccount.jain@gmail.com

Bharati Vidyapeeth University, Institute of Management and Research, New Delhi

Objectives

- The objective of the case is to understand the causes of inflation in Indian economy.
- To study the problems that India is facing in calculating inflation.
- To analyse the political, economical and the socio-cultural measures to control the inflation.
- To identify and invite suggestions to curb the inflation and maintain the growth.

Abstract

Rising prices in India is a subject of concern for every household in India and has emerged as a major policy challenge for the government and the RBI. RBI has raised interest rates seven times since March 2010 to tame inflation and the cost of borrowing has increased. Both RBI and government now expect inflation, as measured by the WPI, to ease to 7% by the end of March 2011 but economists are of the opinion that we can not ignore the global environmental factors.

This paper explains that inflation is a sign of disequilibria in the economy. This paper points out that soaring prices often are generated by the excess demand over supply or may be because of continuous increase in cost of raw material. Inflation is increase in supply of money without increase in the supply of goods and services. High inflation has emerged as a major policy challenge for the government and Reserve bank of India.

Introduction

Inflation is the most controversial concept which has undergone modification since the days of neo-classical economists. Inflation was then regarded as a continuous rise in prices as a result of the excessive increase in the quality of money. This view was propounded on the assumption of full employment.

According to him, there being unemployment in the economy, an increase in the money supply leads to increase in Aggregate Demand, output and employment. According to Keynes the true inflation is when the money supply increases beyond the full employment level, output ceases to rise and prise rise in proportion with the money supply.

Till the middle of 1950's, Keynesian model of inflation, based upon excess demand, remained valid. However in the later 1950's there was a prolonged debate between Demand-Full inflation and cost push inflation.

Inflation is commonly understood as a situation of substantial and general increase in the level of prices and consequent deterioration in the value of money over a period of time. Inflation in India is explained by money factors. The identification of the fundamental source of inflation has always been a subject of controversy. If inflation is caused by an excess of aggregate demand over the existing supply of goods and services, it is demand pull inflation.

A group of economists hold the opposite view that the process of inflation is initiated not by an excess of general demand but by an increase in costs, as factors of production try to increase their share of the total product by raising their prices. Therefore such a price rise is termed as "Cost push Inflation" as prices are being pushed up by the rising factor costs. Cost-push inflation is induced by the wage-inflation process. This is especially true for a country like India, where intensive techniques are commonly used. It has been said that a rise in wages causing a rise in prices and this is turn generate an inflationary spiral because an increase would motivate the workers to demand higher wages.

How does India calculate Inflation

Inflation is statistically measured in terms of percentage increase in the price index, as a rate percent per unit of time-usually a year or a month.

Some economists assert that India's method of calculating inflation is wrong as there are serious flows in the methodologies used by the Government. India uses the wholesale price index (WPI) to calculate and then decide the inflation rate in the economy.

Whereas most developed countries use the consumer Price Index to calculate inflation.

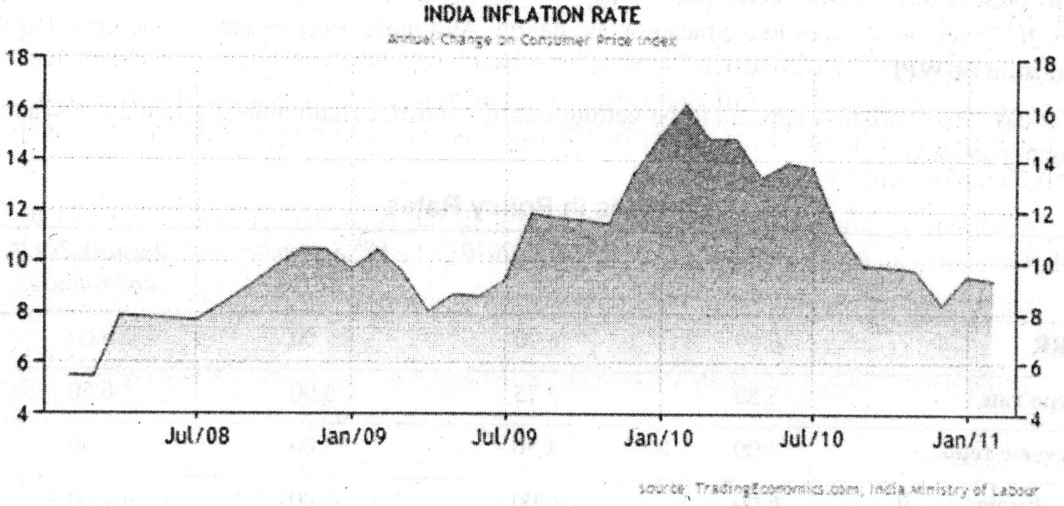

Year	Jan	Feb	Mar	Apr	May	Jun	Jul	Aug	Sep	Oct	Nov	Dec
2011	9.30											
2010	16.22	14.86	14.86	13.33	13.91	13.73	11.25	9.88	9.82	9.70	8.33	9.47
2009	10.45	9.63	8.03	8.70	8.63	9.29	11.89	11.72	11.64	11.49	13.51	14.97
2008	5.51	5.47	7.87	7.81	7.75	7.69	8.33	9.02	9.77	10.45	10.45	9.70

But why is India not switching over to the Consumer Price Index Method of calculating Inflation

There are many intricate problems from shifting from Wholesale Price Index to Consumer Price Index model.

First of all, in India there are four different types of Consumer Price indices and make switching over to the index from Wholesale Price Index fairly 'risky and unwieldy'. CPI Industrial workers, CPI urban non-manual employees, CPI agricultural labourers and CPI rural labour. Secondly as per official CPI cannot be used in India because there is too much of a lag in reporting CPI numbers. Thirdly WPI is published on a weekly basis and the CPI on a monthly basis. And in India inflation is calculated on a weekly basis.

Most of the major economics like US, UK, Japan, France, Singapore and even china have selected CPI as its official barometer to weight its inflation. India however uses WPI. Economists say that main problem with WPI is that more than 100 out of 435 commodities included in the index have abstained to be important from consumption point of view. WPI is supposed to measure impact of prices on business. But India uses it to measure the impact on consumers. Many commodities not consumed by consumers get calculated in the index. WPI measures general level of Price change either at the level of wholesaler or at the producer and does not take into account the retail margin.

In present day service sector plays a key role in Indian economy. consumers are spending loads of money on services like education and health. And these services are not incorporated in calculation of WPI.

Today when inflation appears to be getting out of control, certain anti-inflationary measures are being adopted.

Changes in Policy Rates

Key rate	*3rd July 2010*	*27th July 2010*	*16th September 2010*	*January 2011 and Current*
CRR	6.00	6.00	6.00	6.00
Repo rate	5.50	5.75	6.00	6.50
Reverse repo	4.00	4.50	5.00	5.50
Bank rate	6.00	6.00	6.00	6.00

Sources - RBI

Rising prices in India is a subject of concern for every household in India and has emerged as a major policy challenge for the government and the RBI. RBI has raised interest rates seven times since March 2010 to tame inflation and the cost of borrowing has increased. Both RBI and government now expect inflation, as measured by the WPI, to ease to 7% by the end of March 2011 but economists are of the opinion that we can not ignore the global environmental factors. One of the reasons for inflation is cited from the rise in crude oil prices. The major cause of inflation is food inflation due to high prices of milk, egg, meat and fruits. Prime Minister said inflation had become a problem in the last 18 months and there were reasons beyond the government's control which had contributed to the price spike.

The finance minister Pranab Mukherjee stated in economic survey -"It is observed that a rise in savings and investments and pick up in private consumption has resulted in 9.7 per cent growth of GDP at market prices (constant) in 2010-11.Savings rate has gone up to 33.7 percent while the investment rate is up to 36.5 percent of GDP in 2009-10. In order to check food inflation, the economic survey has suggested, the Government should improve the delivery mechanisms by strengthening the institutions and addressing corruption.

The budget of Feb 2011 has taken various steps to curb the inflation and have announced in the budget to check price rise, such as boosting farm productivity and cutting fuel use. The budget announced funding for production of pulses, oil palm, cereals and vegetables, increased credit flow to farmers and said cold chains would be augmented, but lacked immediate measures to douse high prices of food. Finance minister Pranab Mukherjee announced for lowering fuel consumption and also the customs duty exemption on hybrid vehicle parts and batteries for electric vehicles, and announced direct transfer of subsidies to needy people using kerosene and cooking gas, but did not directly lower oil prices flared by political tensions in West Asia and North Africa.

Conclusion

The challenges to curb the inflation will be a tough exercise and challenge both for the Indian Government as well as the Indian consumer. There is immediate need to address the inflationary pressures building in the mindsets of Indian household else it may pose severe problem in the economy. However, there have been political as well as economic measures taken up by the Government from time to time to curb the same. The socio-cultural role of Indian households plays a vital role by cutting their expenditure from fast-food retail chains and controls the emotions by consuming less of junk and fast foods in their diet. The collective efforts of Government and every household are equally important to win the inflation from the economy in the long run.

2

Journey of 51% FDI in Retail to 100% - Economical or Political

Dr. Navneet Gera,
gerasir@yahoo.com
Bharati Vidyapeeth University, Institute of Management and Research, New Delhi

Abstract

FDI in retail sector has been on half of its journey by getting approval of 51% investments in single brand outlets. There had been a debate among academics and other policy-makers about the far-reaching implications of arrival of global retailers in the economy. This is one area where the level playing field argument is not only meaningful but also significant. Indian retail players have forecasted that the retail boom currently sweeping the nation will usher in a golden era. India's vast middle class & its almost untapped retail sectors are the key attraction for the global retail giants waiting to explore new markets. Industry trends for retail sector indicate that organized retailing has major impact in controlling inflation because large organized retailers are able to buy directly from producers at most competitive prices.

Key Words

FDI in Retail, India's Retail Segment, Multibrand in India, FDI Policy on Retail

Introduction

FDI in retail had many discussions both politically & economically. Indian retail chains would get integrated with global supply chains since FDI will bring in technology, quality standards and marketing thereby, leading to new economic opportunities and creating more employment generation. The opposition to FDI in retail rests on several planks. The entry of large global retailers such as Wal-Mart would kill local shops and millions of jobs. The argument that the advent of FDI and supermarkets will displace a large number of kirana shops is similar to the argument used during the era of industrial licensing, which was meant to protect small-scale industries. The Government is seeking for these options keeping in view the existing social framework of India and they will ensure that the entry of global retail giants do not displace the existing employment in the retail business. The implementation of 6-pay commission on 15 August 2008 has already given additional income as well as arrears to the Government employees wherein the total salary has increased by about 21%.

Retail trade takes place through different types of outlets — kirana shops, more modern retail shops, departmental stores, supermarkets, and hypermarkets. Kirana shops and retail shops are a feature of our traditional businesses. Every village and town has them and are usually family-owned and managed. Most kirana shops store goods unpacked in bulk containers, from which they are measured or weighed out in paper packets by the owner. They take cash but give credit to known customers. As generations pass and villages become small towns, kirana shops graduate into modern retail outlets with shelves and cupboards and packaged goods. They then begin to store packaged goods and over-the-counter drugs. As the populations of towns are larger than those of villages, retail shop owners cannot know all customers and therefore credit becomes more selective. When towns become cities, departmental stores appear. Supermarkets are the next stage in the evolution of retailing. They are viable only in the bigger cities. It is worthwhile analyzing the pros and cons of the proposed policy of allowing FDI in retail trade.

51% FDI in Retail – More advantageous for Consumers or More harmful for Job losers

One key point is that we must differentiate between the interests of consumers, who constitute big chunk of population than the interests of retailers. It is obvious that the interests of the consumer should take precedence over those of the retailer. FDI in retail and the development of larger stores and supermarkets have both advantages as well as disadvantages in one way or the other. Consumptions is the driving force for production followed by economic growth of the country. Increase in consumption is also the factor for fast developing shopping malls. Mr. Kamal Nath stated – "India is a growth story not driven by exports but driven by the domestic market."

The supermarkets offer a wide range of products and services, so the consumer can enjoy single-point shopping. The fact that a well-known chain of supermarkets sources from a manufacturer speaks of better quality.

With the availability of finance, the supermarkets are investing in much better infrastructure facilities like parking lots, entertainment for children, Fast food chains, ATM machines, etc. All this makes shopping a pleasant experience for Indian consumers. The larger supermarkets, which tend to become regional and national chains, can negotiate prices more aggressively with manufacturers of consumer goods and pass on the benefit to consumers thus controlling Inflation. On the other hand, the ability of supermarkets to demand pricing and quality standards from manufacturers is likely to benefit even kirana shops, who can even buy from the supermarkets to sell the same products in smaller towns and villages.

To the extent the large retailers establish a direct linkage with the farmers by cutting out many layers of middlemen, develop the processing facilities and export the products to meet their global requirements, farmers would get better prices and bigger markets while the consumers would benefit in terms of lower prices, better quality and greater variety. The resultant rural prosperity may open up markets for other industrial goods and help a more balanced regional development as also job creation in other sectors. The benefit will flow from higher exports when the global chains are allowed in other sectors such as readymade garments. As for monopolistic pricing practices, the best safeguard would be in permitting all global chains to set up shops. The competition among retailers would ensure better prices for consumers and suppliers alike.

World Bank attributes the opening of the retail sector to FDI to be beneficial for India in terms of price and availability of products as it would give a boost to food products, textiles and garments, leather products, etc., to benefit from large-scale procurement by international chains; in turn, creating jobs opportunities at various levels.

Global trends have important implications for Indian retailers. The Indian consumer is very value conscious; willing to spend money in most cases, but constantly cost conscious, evaluating every rupee spent. It is therefore imperative for retailers to offer a price advantage through sourcing and operational efficiency, as well as a strong private label programme to attract customers. Existing and new entrants need to achieve scale quickly to drive efficiencies in procurement, supply chain and marketing.

Retail is also a driving force for the real estate Industry. In fact, in emerging country like India, the construction activities for malls and establishing new markets are directly generating huge employment. Real estate and human resources will be the critical drivers to build scale. There are a few hundred malls under various stages of development across the country. It may include acquiring and developing the real estate themselves, rather than wait for mall development. Given the rising demand for retail real estate, retailers will need to take a long-term view on rentals and look at alternative options like ownership or very long leases. Retailers that invest in training will be able to ensure the availability of quality manpower in a rapidly growing market. India is a fast growing and emerging economy. There will be additional disposable income in the coming years and that will provide a big boost to various sectors. The implementation of 6-pay commission on 15 August 2008 has already given additional income as well as arrears to the Government employees wherein the total salary has increased by about 21%.

It may be a challenge for local player to create strategic advantage through customer service via all the touch points in a retail store activities like selling, merchandising and using them to give the customer the best possible experience that leads to a sale. Utilizing loyalty programs as differentiators and structuring the loyalty programmes for maximum customer and retailer benefits could be some other strategies for retailers.

The retail sector in India is severely constrained by limited availability of bank finance. Other challenges the local players will realize from giant foreigners will be in establishing and improving a brand's identity, including giving the brand a set of values that the consumer wants, recognizes, identifies with, and trusts. Measuring the strength of the retail brand by examining the extent of consumer loyalty, and their willingness to pay a premium to shop there. Retail Brand Building in order to build a long-term commitment from customers, and driving conversion opportunities among non-customers.

Impact of FDI in Retail on Employment

Opening the retailing to FDI means dislocating millions from their occupation and pushing vast number of families under the poverty line. The fear expressed by some people is that allowing FDI in retail trade and the entry of international retailers could lead to a diminution of kirana shops and retail stores. Many consumer goods manufacturers could find that supermarkets account for an increasing share of their sales and will be afraid of losing this valuable and reliable customer to competition.

The benefits from higher exports are likely to offset any direct job loss in the local kiranas as result of competition from big global retailers. Even, if the domestic big players are allowed to operate, the job loss problem for the small shops would remain, while the benefits from larger exports would not be there. So, clearly, if big players are to be permitted in retail, this must extend to FDI.

India's vast middle class and its almost untapped retail sector are key attraction for the global retail giants waiting to explore newer markets. Moreover, they can easily attract the unemployed youths by giving opportunities in their outlets, paying fair salary. They can also be used for canvassing local people in buying things from the shops where they work. They may initially offer some incentives for higher sales. These unemployed youths can be attracted by the giant players and could develop better inter personal relations as well as can exercise innovative practices – Loyalty cards to attract customers.

Global retail giants Wal-Mart, Tescos and Carrefour and Metro have shown keen interest in tapping the growing Indian retail market. However, even as the entry of foreign retail players was being opposed several domestic giants like Reliance Industries, Aditya Birla group and Kishore Biyani, among others have been setting up network at a rapid pace.

Government Policy on FDI

100% FDI in retailing is not allowed, foreign retailers can operate in India through joint ventures, where the Indian partner is an export house, Franchising/Local manufacturing/Sourcing from small-scale sector, Cash and carry operations. The key research reports states FDI will help the retail businesses to grow from the present $300 billion to $700 billion by 2015.

The Indian Government wants to ensure that foreign direct investment (FDI) will not replace the unorganized sector in the retail market before allowing international players in the sector. Under the new FDI norms for retail announced by the government, multi-product, single brands are permitted to enter the country. The commerce and industry ministry has set a target of $25 billion for FDI inflows for 2007-08. Government data shows that in 2006-07 FDI inflows stood at $19 billion, a significant increase of 153.86 per cent a year ago. Between August 1991 and September 2007 India has received FDI worth $60 billion.

Budget 2008 is a populist budget rather than an economy booster. Experts predict that it will have a positive impact on the Consumption patterns. The growing trend of consumers to allocate larger share of income to consumption and gradual improvement of lifestyle provides bountiful opportunity to the retailers and will provide the necessary stimulus to organized retail. Union Budget 2008-09 provides for 16% excise duty concession on certain cold chain refrigeration equipment could encourage retailers to set up their own back-end logistics. It is effectively a 16% saving on the capital cost, which is substantial. The supply chain infrastructure is made of many other expensive components, besides refrigeration, but this is definitely a step in the right direction.

Retailing is the largest private sector industry in the world economy with the global industry size exceeding $7 trillion and a latest survey has projected India as the top destination for retail investors. And the further upsurge is anticipated in the retail sector as the Government of opened up 51% FDI in single brand retail outlets.

As the government is in a process to initiate a second phase of reforms, it is cautiously exploring the avenues for multi-brand segment. Industry experts are sensitive to the point that local markets have an edge over the retail investors in India as they have unique advantages such as an understanding of local needs and extended service like home delivery. As the FDI, influence on the Indian retail sector sets in, the total size of the retail trade is expected to grow extensively in the coming years and the consumer segments patronizing the big malls will create frenzy for organized retailing predicting a growth of 25-30 per cent per annum over the next decade.

Retail Formats

In India, it may be difficult to transplant a successful international format directly and expect similar performance. Local conditions and insights into the local buying behavior have to shape the format choice. A good point to note in the retailing industry today is the level of experimentation happening locally in terms of formats. Players like Subhiksha and Margin Free Markets are providing convenience with discounts on goods, while internationally convenience formats typically charge a premium over market prices.

The Indian retail format comes with opening n number of retail outlets in various parts of the country – **(Reliance Fresh)** than comes the political agenda and then the turnaround strategy. Should we have the **Retail Act – 2010** to decide upon the various parameters for opening of outlets. Similarly, ITC is experimenting with a model, which brings together a two-way flow of goods in the retail outlet — farmers sell their produce and purchase goods to fulfill their consumption needs. While the experience of these retailers as they scale up beyond their current geographies may provide new insights and lead to modification or fundamental re-engineering of their formats in future, such experimentation and identification of an appropriate format for the local conditions would differentiate winners from losers in the Indian retail market of the future. It is now the time for Government to decide about FDI in retail markets as well as a wait of green signal for the giant players.

Case Questions

1. What are the advantages and disadvantages of FDI in retail?
2. In your opinion what should be the decision of Indian Government on allowing FDI in retail? Discuss.
3. Analyze the competitive models of local and foreign retailers?

References

1. Kamal Nath defends retail FDI policy, Feb 2008, The Hindu
http://www.thehindubusinessline.com/2008/02/09/stories/2008020952401000.htm
2. Policy on FDI in Retail Soon – Kamal Nath, Jan 06 , Sify Business
http://sify.com/finance/fullstory.php?id=14119902
3. Kamal Sharma and Jeevan Prakash, "FDI in Retail – A question of Job, not ownership" Business Line 2005
4. http://www.cpim.org/upa/10272005_fdi_retail%20trade.pdf

3

Hutch Essar Ltd – On Sale

Mr. Neha Kalra
Ms. Ravi Ranjan Gupta
Bharati Vidyapeeth University, Institute of Management and Research ,New Delhi

About Hutchison Whampoa

Hutchison Whampoa Limited (HWL) is a leading international corporation committed to innovation and technology with businesses spanning the globe. Its diverse array of holdings range from some of the world's biggest port operators and retailers to property development and infrastructure to the most technologically advanced and marketing-savvy telecommunications operators. HWL reports turnover of approximately HKD242 billion (USD31 billion) and HKD 124 billion (USD16 billion) for the year ended 31 December 2005 and for the unaudited results for the six months ended 30 June 2006 respectively. With operations in 56 countries and over 220,000 employees worldwide, Hutchison has five core businesses - ports and related services; property and hotels; retail; energy, infrastructure, investments and others; and telecommunications.

A shadow over the war of acquisition of Hutch:

The tussle over the acquisition of Hutchison Essar Ltd has created quite a furore overseas. "Whatever be the outcome of the tussle to acquire Hutchison Essar, it signals to other global mobile telecom service providers who are absent in the world's fastest growing mobile telecommunication market that there is ample room to enter, atleast inorganically," said Rishi Sahai, board director, IndusView.

Hutchison Telecommunications, the telecom arm of Hong Kong-based Hutchison Whampoa, has announced its intention to sell off the majority stake it holds in Hutch-Essar. It has invited bids from potential buyers, which include global telecom giant Vodafone, US-based private equity funds, domestic major Reliance Communications and the Essar group, which currently owns 33 per cent of Hutch-Essar.

Some of the large mobile telecom service providers such as Telefonica SA of Spain, Deutsche Telecom AG of Germany and the French service provider France Telecom are among those missing out on the opportunities that exist in the Indian market, which is growing at more than six million subscribers a month and expected to reach a mobile subscriber base of 348 million by 2010 from the current 143 million. Hutchison has reportedly rejected indicative bid of around $13.5 billion from Malaysia's Maxis Communications and US-based private equity firm Texas Pacific. The acquisition of Hutchison Essar will be India's largest merger and acquisition (M&A) deal. With an expected bid of at least $14 billion for Hutchison Essar, the total value of M&A deals will touch $45 billion. The acquisition will also give the telecommunication sector top slot in the sectoral ranking of the M&A table with deal value of $16 billion and a share of 35 per cent in the total deal value ($45 billion), said Sahai.

If the acquisition of Hutchison Essar goes to **Britain's Vodafone Group Plc**, it will be the largest cross-border deal involving an overseas firm acquiring a company in India (inbound). Secondly, the acquisition will also swing the balance between inbound and outbound deals (involving Indian companies acquiring companies overseas) in favour of inbound deals at $18 billion vs. outbound at $16 billion. Infact, the deal value will be higher than the acquisition of UK's largest steel company Corus Group Plc, if it ends up with India's Tata Steel Ltd.

However, going by the regulatory provisions, Vodafone will have to go with an Indian partner and its stake in the acquired company cannot exceed 74 per cent. Looking at the current stake holding of Hutchison Essar - 67 per cent owned by Hutchison Telecom International Ltd (HTIL), a subsidiary of Hong Kong-based Hutchison Whampoa Ltd and 33 per cent by domestic diversified Essar Group, the swing vote is in the hands of the later.

India's telecom growth story is particularly interesting as many of the big operators who had earlier exited returned to its shores. These include AT&T Inc., BT Group PLC and Vodafone Group PLC.

The Cold War between Ruias and Ambanis:

In business, it's said, there are no permanent friends and no permanent enemies, only permanent interests. For those who might recall the much-discussed-but-never-confirmed rivalry between the Ambanis and the Ruias (of Essar) back in the 1990s, there's a certain irony to the unfolding drama over the acquisition of Hutch Essar. Hutch Essar's 67% owner, Hutchison of Hong Kong, has made it known that it is prepared to receive an offer.Anil Ambani's Reliance Communications is interested in buying Hutch Essar. But, here's the catch. It isn't enough for Hutchison to agree to Ambani's offer to buy its 67% even though it would give him majority control of Hutch Essar. Under law, it's all or almost nothing: he has to stay below 10% — which is neither here nor there — or he has to buy out the entire 100%.

This is where the Ruias come in (or get out, depending on one's point of view). Unless they agree to sell their 33% and exit Hutch Essar, Anil Ambani cannot enter. Ambani, therefore, must convince the Ruias to sell him their part of the business. Right now, everyone's talking to everyone or at least planning to — even as the list of would-be suitors grows by the day, from Maxis of Malaysia to Orascom of Egypt to Qatar Telecom to UK's Vodafone, besides Reliance

Comm and who knows, Sunil Mittal's Bharti Airtel. The Ruias are in the unique position where they're being sought after for their stake even as they seek to buy out Hutchison's holdings and acquire full control of Hutch Essar.

The Ruias have had their share of problems with Hutchison and the strong-willed Hutch Essar CEO Asim Ghosh, but they also recognise that Ghosh and his team have built enormous value for them: 33% of an enterprise value of $15bn (give or take a billion) tots up to almost Rs 15,000 crore. The best part is that they haven't had to seriously sweat for it, since the day-to-day management of the company has been Ghosh & Co's headache.

But Hutchison is said to have indicated to investment bankers that it would not be averse to an offer it cannot refuse. People in the know say the company's multi-multi-billionaire owner Li Kashing is unsentimental about everything except his family and his dog (in a manner of speaking, since we don't know if he has one). If someone's willing to pay him a silly price, he'll sell like any hardheaded businessman would, said a person close to the situation.

If Hutchison were to exit, Ruias would have a headstart on the rest of the field. Unlike all the other potential suitors, who would need to convince both Hutch and Essar to sell, the Ruias need to buy out only the Hutchison stake, either on their own or in conjunction with partner/partners. And money isn't likely to be a problem. Their core businesses — steel, shipping, oil — have been doing well and indications are that bankers would be more than happy to lend.

The question that the Ruias might ponder is: Would it be wiser to trade possible future uncertainty for a here-and now mega windfall? Or, given the fact that the telecom markets are growing at such a scorching pace, should they hold out for an even better valuation in the future?

The key contenders:

List of would-be suitors is growing by the day - from Reliance Communications to Essar Group to Maxis of Malaysia, besides Orascom, Qatar Telecom, Vodafone and perhaps Bharti Airtel.

Reliance Communications is believed to have tied up with four American equity funders — Blackstone, Texas Pacific Group, KKR and Carlyle. For Reliance it makes sense to acquire Hutch Essar. Reliance Communications has a subscriber base of about 24 million, second only to Bharti Airtel's 30 million and a shade larger than Hutch Essar's 22 million. Reliance's acquisition of Hutch Essar would propel him to a dominant numero uno position.

But it isn't enough for Hutchison to agree to Reliance's offer to buy its 67% even though it would give him majority control of Hutch Essar. Under law, it's all or almost nothing: he has to stay below 10% or he has to buy out the entire 100%. Therefore, unless Essar's Ruias agree to sell their 33% and exit Hutch Essar, Reliance cannot enter. But regulatory guidelines do not pose hurdles in the way of Reliance acquiring Hutch.As per the guidelines, the combined entity can't hold more than 15 MHz of spectrum in Metro and A category circles and 12.4 MHz spectrum in B & C circles. RCL faces the spectrum regulatory issues only in two circles.RCL's GSM arm, Reliance Telecom, offers services in eight circles, of which it overlaps with HEL in West Bengal and Kolkata. HEL is not present in RCL's other GSM circles — MP, North-East, HP, Bihar, Orissa and Assam.Also, the market share of the combined entity should not exceed 67% in any circle. However, this will not be the case in any of the 23 circles for RCL.

Bharti Airtel: There are speculates on the plans of Sunil Mittal. Is he talking to Vodafone and Singtel? Reliance's acquisition of Hutch Essar would have serious implications, leaving him a distant no. 2 in the game.

But when asked if Bharti Airtel would team up with its strategic investors, Singtel and Vodafone, to bid for HEL, Mr Mittal said the speculation was baseless and Bharti had never considered the move. Bharti has refrained from making a bid for HEL as the company is focused on its own expansion, and don't want to be dragged into legal and regulatory issues associated with the buy-out.As per the Indian telecom mergers and acquisitions guidelines, no company can have more than 15 MHz of spectrum in a licence area. A merged entity of Hutch and Bharti would therefore have to vacate spectrum in all circles where they jointly have more than 15 MHz.

Vodafone: The UK-based giant is quietly drawing up plans to throw its hat in the ring for Hutch-Essar. Talks are on with bankers and advisors on the strategy to be adopted.The Company is also believed to be exploring options of selling its stake in the Bharti group. It is believed that UBS, Vodafone's house banker, has been asked to explore options of selling its combined 10% stake in Bharti Airtel. But the shareholding agreement with Sunil Mittal's Bharti group has a non-compete clause that bars Vodafone from competing with Bharti for one year after the sale of shares in the Indian company.

Maxis: The Malaysian operator headed by Anand Krishnan, which operates Aircel in India, is understood to have engaged Standard Chartered as their adviser. But Hutchison is believed to have rejected a $13.5 billion bid from Maxis with private equity firm Texas Pacific Group. This implies that Hutchison is looking at a higher valuation.

Orascom: The Egyptian telco, which has over 19% stake in Hong Kong-based HTIL, is understood to have appointed Deutsche Bank as their adviser. Orascom, a key player in Pakistan, has raised security concerns among intelligence agencies.

Essar Group: The Ruias of Essar groups are in talks with various European and US banks to raise funds. They have recently appointed J M Morgan Stanley to advise them on the transaction. The group is also seen to have invited Qatar Telecom and Isthitmar - the private equity arm of Dubai government.There are reports that Essar would not be averse to exit from the venture if the valuation was right.The Ruias have had their share of problems with Hutchison and the strongwilled Hutch Essar CEO Asim Ghosh. From various accounts, Shashi Ruia and Ghosh share a certain bond based on mutual respect and fondness; but it's Ravi Ruia who's been the pointman for Essar on Hutch and it's not known whether there's happy co-existence on that front. There have been unconfirmed stories in the past that Ravi believes that their 33% stake in Hutch Essar entitles them to a greater say in management. But they also recognise that Ghosh and his team have built enormous value for them.

Though names like Singtel, Deutsche Telecom, France Telecom, Telstra, NTT DoCoMo and Telenor are also doing the rounds, the frontrunners are Reliance Communications, Vodafone and

Essar. Maxis may consider a higher bid but may not be willing to take it very high. Egyptian company Orascom had ran into a security controversy in India over its indirect minority holdings in Hutch-Essar as Orascom also has a presence in Pakistan.

Market Capitalisation:

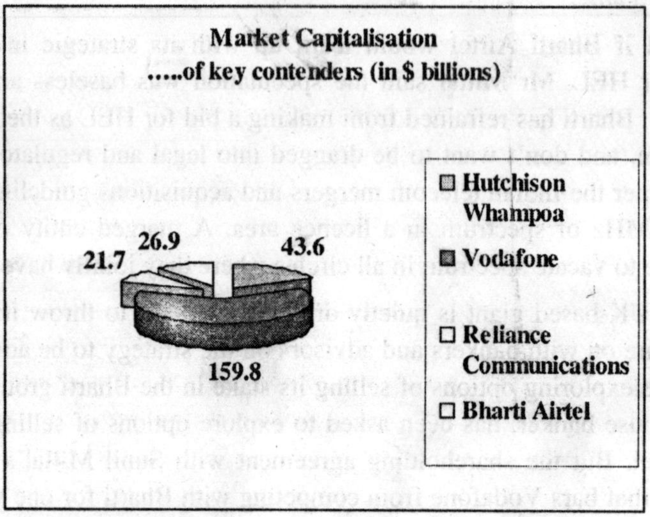

What the regulators have to say ?

Even as Reliance Communications, Essar and UK's Vodafone bid for the 67% stake of Hong Kong-based Hutchison Telecommunications International Ltd (HTIL) and its associates in Hutch Essar, domestic mobile operators have begun lobbying with various regulatory agencies to review telecom merger and acquisition guidelines. Industry sources say the aim is to nudge various regulators like the department of telecommunications (DoT), Telecom Regulatory Authority of India (Trai), Sebi, MRTPC and the Competition Commission to raise questions about a possible monopolistic situation should Reliance Communications succeed in taking over Hutch Essar.

According to the current merger and acquisition (M&A) guidelines:

- An operator cannot acquire more than a 10% stake in a competing company in the same circle.
- The total market share of the combined entity cannot exceed 67% in any circle.
- The combined entity cannot hold spectrum of more than 15 MHz in metro A category circles and 12.4 Mhz in B and C circles.
- Any M&A needs government approval, since it involves the transfer of the licence granted under the Indian Telegraph Act.

If Reliance wants total control of the company, they would have to acquire the entire 100% equity in Hutch Essar and merge it with Reliance Communications. In such a scenario, Reliance would emerge the largest mobile operator with around 52 million of the total subscriber base of around 130 million. The scenario has rattled rivals who are now using the bogey of a possible monopolistic situation in the future and are, therefore, urging the government to re-examine the M&A guidelines to prevent such a scenario. If Reliance acquires Hutch Essar, the merged entity's highest marketshare would be in Kolkata (53%), Gujarat (52.2%) and West Bengal (51.7%). Industry players say these marketshares would be close to 67%.

They have questioned what the government's move would be if the marketshare hit 67% in a circle?

How will the acquisition benefit Vodafone ?

If Vodafone acquires Hutch, the country's fourth largest mobile operator with 22 million subscribers, then India will account for its third largest customer base. The UK-based company operates in 27 markets globally. Germany is the largest market for Vodafone with 29 million subscribers, while the US (where it has a 44.4% stake in Verizon) is the second largest.If the deal goes through, India would become the country with most potential for expansion for Vodafone with only 11% teledensity. Most countries where Vodafone operates currently are reaching saturation. Switzerland has 96% teledensity followed by Germany (80%), US (76%), France (78%), Turkey (67%) Romania (70%).

Vodafone will acquire about 22.10% market share of the 100 million Indian mobile subscribers through Hutch. This will also corroborate with Vodafone's strategy of being in the top three mobile operators wherever it operates.Currently, Vodafone operates by way of subsidiaries, joint ventures or affiliates across globe. It enjoys controlling stake in only small or saturated markets. It has about five joint ventures and five affiliates in big markets where it enjoys stakes like 3.3% (China), 10% (India), 44.4% (US), 44% (France). The company's strategy clearly is to concentrate its resources on emerging markets. This month, Vodafone sold 25% in Swisscom (oe1.8 billion) in Switzerland, a market with 96% saturation. In August, this year, Vodafone sold 25% stake in Belgium's Proximus for euro 2 billion.

This comes after the world's largest operator in terms of subscriber base, Vodafone, (with 577.4 million subscribers) reported losses of oe14.9bn for 2005-06, coupled with plans to cut 400 jobs at its headquarters at Newbury, UK.In a statement issued earlier this month, the company states that its focus will now be markets of EMAPA (Eastern Europe, Middle East, Africa, Asia Pacific and affiliates) rather than developed markets of the UK, US or Germany.

The company is struggling to increase its stake in US' Verizon but can't find anyone selling its stake to Vodafone. Verizon's shareholders though don't seem to excited about the Hutch buyout as Vodafone has been reporting losses for five years in a row with this year's loss being the highest. The company's stock on the NYSE has fallen this week from $28.5 level on Monday to $27.7 on its last closing on Friday, with reports of a Hutch bid becoming stronger. Nevertheless, a majority stake in a major operator in Indian mobile market (which is adding about five million subscribers per month) may bail out the $14.65 billion telecom giant - as it cannot hope to increase its stake in highly regulated Chinese telecom market.

Vodafone has lost its battle once in 2004 when it was outbid by Cingular for a controlling stake in AT&T. A second battle lost may prove too costly for Vodafone in the long run. On the other hand its Indian partner, Bharti may also like its partner Vodafone win the bid, as RCL winning over Hutch could prove too costly both for Bharti and Vodafone.

Vodafone is looking froward to enter the Indian market and has a minority stake (about 10 percent) in Bharti Airtel. Vodafone is looking to increase its profile and footprint in the hot Indian market.As in India the growing sectors as of now is telecom as well besides Retail and Insurance. By acquiring Hutch Essar it will mean that Vodafone will be able to make its entry into the Indian market in a big way and not be a marginal player in the Indian market place. However there is a bit of a challenge for Vodofone and that is it has a non-compete with India's largest mobile operator Bharti Airtel. Sunil Mittal of Bharti Airtel has refused to join the bid for Hutch Essar reports the Financial Times. One option for Vodafone is to sell its minority stake in Bharti Airtel if its bid for Hutch Essar goes through.

This is a game with of high stakes and it is going to be interesting to see how this plays out. It is also not clear who is selling what. Is Essar selling its 33 percent share or is Hutchison Whampoa selling its share? Or are they both looking to sell their shares? Equipped with imperfect information it is difficult to asses the situation and we can only make an educated guess of how this game is going to be played out.

There are various numbers being quoted for the deal, but it will be a multi-billion dollar deal. An intense bidding war has begun. There are reports that Anil Ambani and Blackstone are offering $14 billion for the deal and that Hutchison Whampoa might exit out of the Indian telecom market. Maxis is reportedly offering $13.5 billion and might team up with Reliance and Blackstone. Vodofone is reportedly offering $13.5 billion for Hutch Essar.

The hurdles faced by the players:

Each of the suitors that have lined up to buy into or buy out GSM operator Hutchison-Essar has its own distinctive hurdle to overcome. For a suitor who is an existing telecom player, such as Reliance Communications or Bharti Airtel, it would involve 100 per cent buyout as these companies already have operations in the telecom circles in which Hutch-Essar operates. Indian regulations do not allow the same promoter to have more than 10 per cent stake in two operations in the same circle. They would have to do a complete buyout and merge the acquired company's operations with their existing ones in every circle.

Tough negotiations

A 100 per cent buyout necessarily means the persuading the Essar Group to sell. This might call for some rigorous negotiating skills for some of the Indian corporate suitors, according to analysts.The Essar group holds 33 per cent stake in Hutch-Essar through Essar Teleholdings.Bharti Airtel may additionally have other problems because it is already a GSM player and may exceed its spectrum limits if it acquires Hutch-Essar. Also, with the Hutch-Essar enterprise valuations currently circulating in the market - varying between $12 billion and $15 billion - Bharti will probably not be interested and may find it cheaper to expand its existing operations, said analysts. Essar Teleholdings could itself increase its stake in Hutch-Essar, but may find it difficult to raise the resources at current valuations.

Problems faced by other bidders:

The other possible suitors, according to sources close to the talks (that are happening in various permutations and combinations), are Maxis Communications - already a stakeholder in Aircel that operates only in two circles but has licences for several circles; Egypt-based operator Orascom, which may have regulatory problems because it owns stakes in telecom companies in Pakistan and Bangladesh; and several private equity players who may have to join hands with others to buy into Hutch-Essar. But these suitors can largely do without the co-operation of Essar, according to analysts. Ever since it became evident that the Hong Kong-based Hutchison group, which controls 67 per cent stake directly and indirectly in Hutch-Essar, wanted to exit, there has been hectic speculation on who will net the company, the most high-profile of the suitors being Reliance, which has already announced its intention to move into GSM play. Such an acquisition would allow it a speedy GSM entry, said analysts.

Composition of subscribers:

Subscribers are generally classified as active and inactive. It is prudent to verify the figure of active subscribers and evaluate their demographic profile. The quality of the subscriber base acquired and the value placed on it affects the profitability of the venture from a long-term perspective. Similarly, a clear understanding of the ARPU trend shows the usage behavior of the active subscribers.

Why global companies are keen on Hutch Essar? The bunch of benefits…

No other acquisition in the Indian telecom space has managed to get so much interest as Hutchison Essar has. And one does not have to go too far to know the reason for at least three large telecom majors lining up to pick up Hutchison's Indian mobile operations.

As per the number available with the Cellular Operators Association of India (COAI), Hutchison Essar's ARPU (average revenue per user) is among the highest in the Indian industry at Rs 373, compared to Rs 348 for Bharti. It also has the highest revenues per minute, beating rivals Bharti and Reliance Communications. The minutes of usage per subscriber per month for Hutch are also higher compared to other operators.

No wonder that Vodafone the world's second largest mobile company in terms of subscribers, is willing to bet nearly 10 per cent of its market capitalization in acquiring Hutch Essar.At $15 billion, which is what industry sources believe that Vodafone is willing to fork out to acquire 74 per cent stake in Hutch Essar, the British telecom company would pay about $682 for each of 22 million Hutch Essar subscribers. In contrast, Cingular bought AT&T Wireless for $41 billion, acquiring 21.98 million subscribers at $1,891 a subscriber. If Vodafone gets the deal, it will get a direct foothold into the largest growing market in the world at a lower price.

The company has had to face severe losses in the recent past and this may be its last chance to get into a rapidly growing market. On the other hand, for Reliance Communications, acquiring Hutch Essar would fast-forward its plans to foray into the GSM cellular space.

The company is already the largest CDMA operator in the country with 25 million users and adding 20 million more subscribers would catapult it to the largest telecom operator in the country. For Malaysia-based Maxis, Hutch Essar would give it a pan-Indian presence, which it has been looking to do ever since it acquired Chennai-based Aircel. While Aircel has cellular services in the Northeast and Tamil Nadu, Hutch Essar covers the other circles in the country. Though Maxis has applied for fresh licences, it will have to wait for spectrum before it can roll out a network. Acquiring Hutch Essar would save the company a lot of time in investing in a new network.

Why Indian Telecom market?

Hutchison Essar has suddenly become the hottest telecom asset on the block, anywhere in the world, and for very good reasons, too. India is the hottest telecom market in the world, having overtaken China in monthly subscriber additions, and Hutch is one of the larger players in the country. Hutch also enjoys a premium brand image and has the highest average revenues per user (ARPU) among all domestic telecom companies.

The board of Vodafone continues to believe the mobile market in India has great potential and is therefore considering the acquisition of a controlling interest in Hutchison Essar, the company said Friday. Such a transaction would be consistent with Vodafone's stated strategy of seeking selective acquisition opportunities in developing markets, the company said, while cautioning that the process is at an early stage, and may not lead to a transaction. At a time when the Indian telecom market is the fastest growing in the world — faster than even China — and pre-tax profits for the top three or four telcos are said to be in the region of 40%, why would they want to rock this cruiseliner when its on high sea?

Hutchison Essar's majority stakeholder Hutchison Telecommunications International, a subsidiary of Hutchison Whampoa, is said to be interested in selling its stake in the company. Hutchison Essar is a joint venture between Hutchison and India's Essar Group. Indian government rules limit foreign holdings in mobile services companies to 74 percent. If Vodafone's bid is successful, it will have to retain Essar Group as a partner or find another Indian partner that will buy out the Essar Group's stake in Hutchison Essar. Essar was not immediately available for comment.

Retaining the brand HUTCH after acquisition…….

Analysts also added that retention of the Hutch brand during the "window period" after a deal is signed was vital for two reasons. First, the brand plays a key role in consumers' choice. Second, the association with the telecom operator in India. This implies, an overnight change is unlikely to be welcomed by the subscribers.

Besides, brand migration, as witnessed during Hutch's successful image makeover from 'orange' to 'pink', is a lengthy exercise that can take months. Hutch-Essar had to undertake an extensive campaign to replace the brand catch line that was its very identity - 'The future is bright, the future is Orange', with the new slogan, 'Wherever you go, our network follows' along with the color 'pink'

Hutch Essar :Who will finaly win the race ?…..

The plot thickens every hour about the future of Hutch Essar India's third largest mobile operator. First there were reports of the various players that were interested in acquiring Hutch Essar. There were a couple of global private equity companies like Blackstone and Pacific Texas that were partnering with Anil Ambani's Reliance Group to bid for Hutch Essar. Then there was some interest from Bharti Airtel. Then came along Maxis of Malaysia. But in the background there were reports that the Ruia brothers were not interested in selling their assets of Hutch and that things were in great shape between them and Hong Kong-based Hutchison Whampoa led by Li Ka Shing. Hutchison Whampoa is reportedly looking to exit the Indian market.

A couple of days ago there were reports that Anil Ambani's Reliance and the global PE companies were all set to acquire Hutch Essar and the deal was almost done. Suddenly there are new reports that UK-based Vodofone that is headed by Arun Sarin, a telecom veteran, is also in the run and they might bag the deal. We will have to wait and see how this is going to play out.

What is clear is that the race to serve the next 100 or 200 million <plug in whatever number you want mobile customers in India will be an intense one. It has taken close to 10 years to get the first 100 million mobile customers in India. The last 10 years has been a period of trial and error for various mobile operators and service providers in India. India is perhaps the only country where both the CDMA (Reliance is a major player) and GSM phone subscribers are growing at a fast clip. Early on in the play Qualcomm courted the Indian market aggressively to market its CDMA technology. However the company has run into sum rough weather with its largest partner Reliance over the price of handsets etc. At the same time Reliance is also looking to get into the GSM market and that is where Hutch Essar fits in. By acquiring Huch Essar it will mean that Reliance gets instant access to a large customer base and can vault into the first place.

India is an interesting market along with many other markets in Asia and we are constantly on the look out for opportunities and will be evaluating many interesting prospects...Spokesperson, Telenor, Norway's largest telecom company, to Business Today

Even if you aren't one of India's 143 million cellular phone users, it wouldn't take you too long to single out Hutchison Essar Ltd (HEL) as one of those "interesting prospects". India's fourth-largest wireless operator with a subscriber base of a little over 22 million has become the most sought after asset in the recent history of global mergers & acquisitions, what with Li Ka-shing, the promoter of the Hong Kong-headquartered $3.13-billion Hutchison Telecom International (HTIL), putting its 67 per cent holding in HEL on the block (19.55 per cent of it is held indirectly via a company called Telecom Investments India, which has HEL Managing Director Asim Ghosh and Max India Chairman Analjit Singh as shareholders). With HEL in play as the backdrop, and going by the reams of speculation generated in recent days, one would be tempted to assume that the company that made the statement about evaluating prospects in India could be Vodafone. Or Verizon. Or Maxis. Or Orascom. Or even the UK-headquartered Hinduja Group. After all, each of these global majors has either evinced, or is said to have evinced interest, in the assets of HEL, which stood at Rs 4,052 crore for the first half of 2006. Also in the running are domestic corporations Reliance Communications (R-Comm) and the Essar Group, which holds 33 per cent in HEL via its holding company Essar Teleholdings Ltd (ETHL).

Top GSM Players in India:

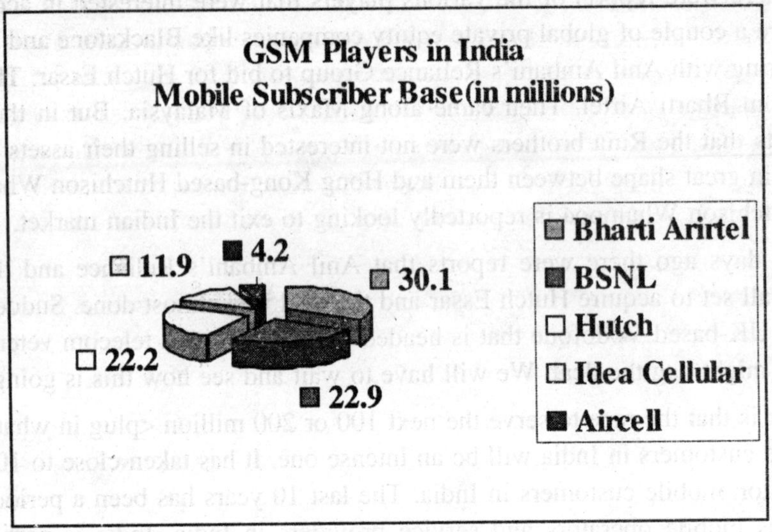

Why Hutch wants to leave Indian Telecom Market?

Hutchison Whampoa seems to have struck gold in India with the valuation of its 67% stake in Hutch Essar touching $14bn. But why does the group want to move out of the promising Indian Telecom Market is a question that industry watchers are looking to answer.

The biggest question that arises at present is that inspite of Indian Telecom Market being one of the booming sectors at present why does Hutch plan to exit at this moment. The telecom industry continues to grow at ascorching pace and the GSM industry has set a new world record by adding over 5 million subscribers in the month of November 2006. Besides this approximately 2 million subscribers added by the CDMA industry in November to an all time high of 7 million.

Even the board of Vodafone continues to believe the mobile market in India has great potential and is considering the acquisition of a controling interest in Hutch Essar.

The ultimate reason:

According to sources, Hutchison's 3G mobile business in Europe is in disarray as it has failed to register an impressive performance since its very inception. Due to sluggish subscriber growth, the European telecom giants like orange are eyeing o acquire controlling stake in 3G. Hutchison's Italian venture 3 italia is also in trouble due to poor performance and scrappingof an Initial Public Offer. Due to all these reasonsCRA's like standard & Poor's are maintaining a constant negative rating on Hutchison Whampoa. As a result of these flailing ventures the group is in urgent need of cash to repay its debts and fuel money into its ailing businesses. Earlier it had sold Star TV to Rupert Murdoch in 1995 for $950 mn and hived off its 20%stake in port business in 2006 for $4.3 bn Now again hutchison Whampoa headed by billionaire Li Ka Shing , is not even ,is not even blinking before selling its stake in the profitable Hutchison Whampoa Joint Venture. Anyways money is much needed, but it seems a high price to pay for exciting the very lucrative Indian telecom mart.

Conclusion:

No matter who wins the race, it will remain a pot boiller that showcases ambition, greed enterpreneurship, risk taking and global fantasies that are becoming the stuff of corporate legend.The emerging scenario in the telecom sector requires both policy as well as regulatory actions. The government on its part should revisit some of the pending issues and TRAI should be geared to keep a constant vigil on the behaviour of the big players.Large number of negotiations have occurred as *yet regarding the final player(s)* who would join hands for hutch be it Vodafone and Essar or Vodafone and Reliance or may be only Essar who is preety kee*n on acquiring the entire stake*. It is the last sizeable acquisition target that would be available in the Indian telecom market in the short to medium term. Any global player looking at entering the Indian market or a domestic player looking to would be willing to give his right hand for such an asset. The ball is in their court now ,lets see who finally wins the game.

Marketing Cases

1

Is Packaging The Real 5th P?

Ms. Amanpreet Kaur
Mr. Gaurav Sharma
Mr. Pushkar Pandey
Bharati Vidyapeeth University, Institute of Management and Research, New Delhi

What could have driven consumers to buy Temptations, Cadbury latest launch apart from the tempting television commercials? Or for that matter animal shaped soaps, see through toothpaste tubes, detergents packed in boxes which looks like washing machine tubs, exquisite perfumes bottles, easy- to- pour ready- to-drink juice packs or even zip locks in shampoo sachets? What is it in a product that instantly appeals to a consumer?

Though the brand and its popularity in the market do play an important role in attracting consumer, its Package act as the silent seller. Packaging is more than wrapping a product or cushioning it from breakage. It is referred to as a media for branding and stimulating recall in a crowded retail outlet. Little wonder that marketers are looking at innovative packaging solutions to make their brands look unique and exclusive.

Packaging, as defined by Kotler and Keller, refers to all the activities of designing and producing the container for a product. It is customary in Japan to appreciate the gift packaging when one receives a gift. The shopper in this day and age is influenced by the packing quality and attractiveness. It is little wonder that the marketer, like the Japanese, takes special care and attention to use packaging as an attractive element of marketing mix, which the customer would hopefully cherish.

Earlier it has been witnessed how the quantity in packaging, especially lower quantity has lead to increased usage and penetration in categories like shampoo, oils. There are some other benefits one can derive from effective packaging, apart from the basic functions like protection, making them easy to identify and enhance their presence at the point of sales. Packaging can be used as a way to assure the consumer about the products quality. When one uses a see through packing, it induces customers to try the product and in cases the nature of the product is such that physical experience is required then the see-through packaging helps provide a substitute.

When a shampoo manufacturer comes up with a new bottle, which can be kept inverted so that every time you don't have to struggle trying to force the shampoo down the bottle it will attract customers. The packaging used by parachute coconut oil increases the convenience for its customers. It has the option of a wide necked bottie from which consumers can remove the oil in winter when the oil would freeze .it also changed its pack from tin to plastic on simple consumer insight that they might get hurt from tin packs.

In Indian context one also finds that companies try to use packaging as a means of protecting their products from counterfeiters. The special crimp packing used in the case of Bisleri to assure customers that the bottle has not been tampered with. And even the fact that we as Indians like to find use of old products and if the packaging helps us in that we would be more happy dealing with that company. This can be seen by how we reuse used containers of paints and oil as substitutes for buckets and PET bottles of coke and Pepsi finding its way to the fridges of most homes. Some homemakers are observed buying many products like Mazaa 500 ML bottle and Priya pickles just for the after use of the bottles and also the packaging for easy storage like garlic mix and other food items that cam be squeezed into any corner of the fridge.

Packaging is also an effective tool to distinguish from spurious products .Using holograms and distinctive packaging helps to keep cheap imitators at bay. Attractive and innovative packaging definitely helps in enhancing sales, provided the packaging gives a tangible benefit to the customer. We can take the example of Fevi-quick; famous adhesive which came out with a pack worth Rs 5 and its innovative tube helped the consumers to avoid the mess while fixing something. Similarly the aluminum foil companies like Home foils have come up with innovative corrugated box for the packing with a cutter to easily cut the foil.

Amul butter is a classic example of innovative packaging. Though the packages have not changed frequently but the cartoon strip relating to the current issues has become a part of the day-to-day life of the Amul consumers.

Packaging also adds to the proposition of the product in the sense we can take the example of Colagate's product that emphasized on the whiteness and shininess after the use spent 1% extra of the cost just to use metallic film on their carton to signify shine.

An important aspect of packaging is convenience. A product should be packed in such away that it is easy to use. There are easy to pour in the juices and oil refill pack segments with which one can conveniently pour the liquid in the container. Colgate came out with plastic cover that guards the braces from the insects .some products like shampoo sachets also have zip locks by virtue of which the product can be used repeatedly. Cavinkare spokesperson, remarks that their innovative packaging methods have helped them to grow by 48% in the last 10 years. It markets its perfume Spinz, in sachets which are meant for one time use.

Packaging in addition to this is a very important source of information, like batch number, expiry date, date of manufacture etc. Maggi was great success due to the availability of method to prepare printed on its pack and not to forget its yummy taste!

BUT

Products that are premium in looks! But then when you want to make a good impression, you know its all in the looks. Beauty may be skin deep but if it helps to sell, it makes sense to capitalize on it. But the flipside to packaging do exist and emphasize on the question as "is packaging the real 5th P?"

Packaging, and not the product, is the first touch point that customers comes into contact with. A substandard product within a unique packaging might be earlier to sell as against superior product packaged in a substandard pack. Superior packaging would not ensure repeat sales.

The packaging cost can contribute to anywhere between 4-20% of the total cost of the product depending on the type of packaging. The added cost of innovate packaging also act as a major cost-disadvantage to the company.

Packaging- an effective differentiator or an ineffective differentiator

Boroline, the antiseptic cream comes in dark green cover, easy for the consumer to recognize the product. Boroline, though considered a good antiseptic cream, is a sticky cream. Borosoft, a competing brand used the sticky nature of Boroline as a possible consumer pain area and targeted Boroline directly in its advertisement campaign using a dark green tube. Boroline was recognizable.

Brand matters! Does packaging???

Nirma, the largest selling detergent in the world, found success in the rural market by using unelaborated packaging to position their product as one that cleaned well, yet was affordable. While this technique is not the most eye catching, it allows rural Indian consumer to experience the benefits of a branded product without requiring elaborate or expensive packaging.

But…Packaging is considered to be a part of the product strategy in the marketing mix. To emphasize the importance that packaging carries in the marketing mix, some marketers have gone to the extent of calling it the 5th P, the four others being Product, Price, Place and Promotion.

Questions

1. Justify the statement "It is ultimately the product quality that decides the success or repeat purchase of the product in the market, Packaging just acts as a stimuli"?
2. State few examples in context of innovative packaging that has forced the marketer to call it the 5th P in the marketing mix?

2

An Efficient Marketing for Sustainable Agricultural Development - A Case Study in Solapur District of Maharashtra

Mr. B.B. Shitole
Associate Professor, Dept. of Commerce
Arts and Commerce College, Solapur
bbshitole@gmail.com

Inroduction

Agriculture is one of the major contributor of economic growth for indian economy and still Agriculture is livelyhood of about 70% Indians living in the villages. At this juncture for the growth and development of rural area and to improve the "Human Development Index" (HDI); Production, Productivity and Marketing are the important aspects in the development of Agriculture sector in India. Today India is on first rank in the production of fruits and second largest country in the production of vegetables in the world; the country also achieved highest growth in the rice, wheat, pulses and oil seeds. However it is the need of the hour to improve the efficiency of Agricultural Marketing both at local and global level.

At present due to inefficient Marketing inadequate marketing infrastructure and poor post harvest management the loss of foodgrains is estimated 5-10% of the total production of the foodgrains and for perishable Agriculture produce it is estimated 25-30% of the total production;, Many times these perishable products are thrown on the roads. The NHB (National Horticulture

Board) Report 2009 shows the great success of fruits and vegetable growers in India. Since the last two decade the area and production of fruits and vegetables are continuously increases mostly the state Maharashtra, Karnataka, Andhra Pradesh and Punjab are the Leading states in Production of fruits and vegetables, Mainly grapes, mango, banana, orange and pomegranate are the important fruits and in class of vegetables onion, brinjal,cabbageand potato shows the great achievement. However Agricultural producers are facing many problems in maketing process at domestic and global level.All India data of production of fruits and vegetables in recent five years is given below.

Table. All India Area and Production of Fruits and Vegetables

Sr. No.	*Year*	*Fruits*		*Vegetables*	
		Area '000' ha	*Production '000' MT*	*Area '000' ha*	*Production '000' MT*
1.	2004-05	5049	50867	6744	101246
2.	2005-06	5324	55356	7213	111399
3.	2006-07	5554	59563	7581	114993
4.	2007-08	5857	65587	7848	128449
5.	2008-09	6101	68466	7981	129077

Source: Indian Horticulture Database 2009 page no. 22 & 23

The above table reveals that the area and production of fruits and vegetables for recent five years from 2004-05 To 2008-09. It is absolutely showing the area and production is continuousely increasing. It indicates potential for marketing of fresh and processed fruits and vegetables at domestic market and export marketing.

An Efficient Agricultural Marketing

Agricultural Marketing is a process in which Marketing functions are performed to show the results that reduction in production cost, distribution cost and improving in the quality of products which helps to keep remunerative price to the Agril producer and reasonable price to the final consumer. Each agril producer should try to save the cost of production right from the plantation to harvesting of the produce. In addition to this distribution cost during packaging , transportation, cleaning , grading, warehousing and cold storage should kept adequate. Direct Marketing and Marketing through co-operative organization helps mostly in saving the distribution cost. This results final consumer can buy the commodity in reasonable price.

Essentials of An Efficient Marketing

Agricultural Marketing involves all the activities of moving of Agril produce from farm to final consumer. To keep entire process on proper track in producer and consumer point of view important point should kept in mind -

1. Sound product planning
2. Effective quality improvement programme

3. Good packaging
4. Effective Marketing channels
5. Sound Marketing infrastructure
6. Ideal Marketing information system
7. Continuous Marketing research

Success Story of KrishibhushanMr. Ganesh Kulkarni

"Need of an efficient Market process for sustinable development of Agricultural sector "

KrishibhushanShri. Ganesh Kulkarni(Kaka) born in medium farmers family in a small village named Upalai (Khurd) of MadhaTaluka in Solapur District. Today at the age of 43 years he shares his experience of 20 years; in this occupation since 1991. His father lateBhalchandra was medium farmer, however the family income was good due to additional source of income from dairy farming. He completed his primary education in local Z.P. primary school and he was sent to nearby town to complete his highschool and college education. Even his father sent him to urban place for higher education. He was against the employment through seeking the job. He believes on self employment;after completion of degree Ganesh Kaka directly entered in the farming. Historically the area of Solapur District is known as drought -prone area hence majority of farming was on rainfall. Due to this adversities father of Ganesh Kaka was taking the traditional crops that are Jowar, Bajara, Grams, Moong, Horsegram and Groundnut . This results less marketable surplus therefore scope for marketing was limited to local market. To change entire situation of farming Ganesh kaka decided to use new technology in farming as an educated farmer and change in cropping pattern;on the basis of availability of water average rainfall and fertility of soil. He started horticulture farming with plantation of grapes on only one and half acre of land. With continuous efforts, guidance through reading of books and periodicals, visit to the farms of successful farmers in nearby villages, farms of Pune, Solapur and Sangli District and use of modern technology for water management, soil conservation;he achieved saving in the cost of fertilizers and chemicals. An experiment to improve in the quality of produce gives him great success in exporting grapes and banana.

At present he created job opportunities to the local people on his 85 acres of land; with production of banana, grapes, pomegranate and papaya. Today he exports both fresh and processed grapes and good quality of banana. Recently government of Maharashtra awarded him by prestigious award " KRISHIBHUSHAN -2009 " for his achievement in his occupation.

Cropping Pattern :

Cropping pattern he adopted after considering availability of water, local climatic changes, soil health and Marketing. He utilizing his land for growing grapes , banana, papaya and fodder.

Table. Cropping pattern adopted by Ganesh Kaka

Sr.No.	*Crop*	*Area in acers*	*Percentage*
1.	Grapes	50	59
2.	Banana	20	23.50
3.	Papaya	10	11.75
4.	Fodder and Misc.	5	5.75
	Total	85	100

Primary Source : Direct Interview by researcher

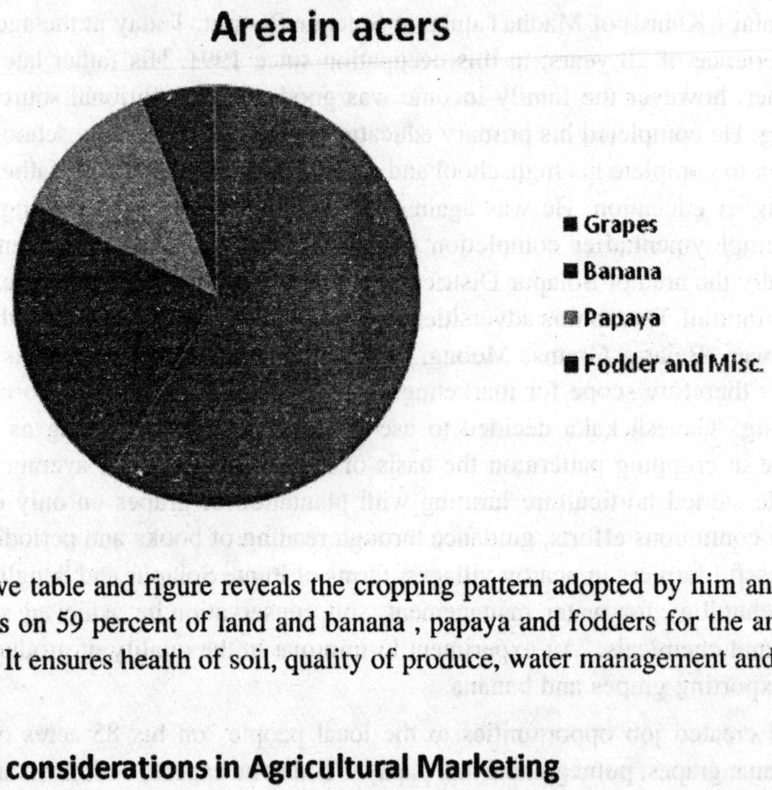

The above table and figure reveals the cropping pattern adopted by him and crop grown, he grown grapes on 59 percent of land and banana , papaya and fodders for the animals on the rest area of land. It ensures health of soil, quality of produce, water management and saving in cost of production.

Marketing considerations in Agricultural Marketing

Mr. Ganesh Kaka express his view and opinion on Marketing consideration that he practices

1. Production planning for maintain good quality of produce - He told that it is very complicated to prepare the quantitative plan for produce to be produced. However some precautions should be taken for good quality of produce such as preparation of soil for plantation, use of certified seeds, scientific plantation, prevention of diseases and water management.These measures helps in maintaining good quality of produce.

2. Cleaning, Grading and Packaging - Mostly for the fruits and vegetables cleaning, sorting, grading and packaging are the important processes for value additions, This results good remunerative price to the Agril producer and consumer can satisfied their needs due to freshness and good quality. He also viewed that for the export marketing these processes are more important than the Marketing at local level.

3. Own transportation vehicle -Transportation plays significant role for timely and adequate reaching of the commodities in the Market. It also avoid the inconvenience and save the cost of distribution.

4. Warehousing and Cold Storage Facilities - Changing trend towards high value crops including fruits and vegetables required scientific warehousing and cold storages for efficient marketing. Present efforts of the government are not sufficient for adequate growth and development, therefore government should directly participate in strengthening the cold storage chain in villages.

5. Group Farming - He suggested that group farming is the suitable remedy for small and marginal farmers with spirit of "One for All and All for One", and also focused on skill based division of work which helps in improvement of production and productivity of Agri. produce in their farms and efficient marketing process.

6. Enrichment in Agricultural Marketing Information System (AMIS) - At present AMIS provides information for arrivals and prices of the Agril. produce, However it is a need of the hour that aims should include production, variety and seasons of rivals countries for the purpose of export marketing and modern marketing techniques.

7. Marketing Training to the Agril. producers - Majority of the farmers are unknown about basic marketing skills and primary processing such as cleaning, sorting and grading.Agril. Department of the state government should prepare and organize basic training programmers with practical. The farmers can easily obtain the marketing skills and knowledge through this programmers which helps in promoting them towards efficient marketing.

8. To promote Agril. research towards efficient marketing - Finally Mr. Ganesh Kaka expected that to promote Agril. research towards efficient marketing system. He expressed that present research trend of all the Agril. Universities, Govt. organization like ICAR, NHB, DIM and NIAM are covers production, productivity, HYV seeds and modern technologies of Post Harvest Management. However it is a need of the hour to promote research towards strengthening the Agril. Marketing Process at local and global level.

In addition to this he suggested to promote village level Agro-processing industry which helps in value addition and creates employment opportunity to village youth.

"EVERY THING ELSE CAN WAIT BUT NOT AGRICULTURE"

- Pt. Javaharlal Nehru.

References

1. Angadi V.B., Cheema H.S. and Das M.R.(Edi.) - 2009, Himalaya Publishing House, Mumbai -4
2. Chaudhary C.M.,2009,Economics of co-operation,Sublime Publications, Jaipur-6
3. Memoria C.B. &Tripathi B.B.,2003, Agriculture Problems of India, KitabMahal, New Delhi - 2

4. National Horticulture Board,2010,Indian Horticulture Database, Aristo Printing Press, New Delhi
5. Planning commision of India, 2007, Maharashtra Development Report, academic foundation, New Delhi.
6. Times of India, Daily, 22nd March 2011
7. http://indiangov.in.commerce
8. http://agricoop.nic.in
9. http://mahaagri.nic.in

3

Looking beyond the Frontier for Market Growth

Mr. Sumod Khanna
Mr. A.V. Narula
Assistant Professor, Sharda University
Mr. Gagan Grover
gagangrover2001@yahoo.com
Bharati Vidyapeeth University, Institute of Management and Research, New Delhi

Abstract

The Case deals with International Market Development efforts by computer Peripherals Company which is trying to increase its market base through export. The case highlights macro factors for country screening through Market Share Index and Competitive Advantage Index leading to calculating Market Potential and Export Potential index for a logical decision to conclude choice of Foreign Market. This case hypothetically simulated from the adopted learning of Global Marketing Management (PHI) by Warren J. Keegan (Pace University), will help Management students understand basic Country Selection Process.

The summer had just begun and NCR region climate was warming up. The sudden downpour of showers was a welcome relief. It was raining heavily on Wednesday evening. Thunderstorm and stealth lightning tearing into the thoughts of Mr. Shailendra Jha (SJ) National Product Manager of Intex Technologies (India) Limited (ITL); who was standing next to the wide glazed window of his 13th Floor glass cabin and looking across the Taj express highway. Far into the horizon beyond Yamuna River, the rainbow was looking awesome and the refreshing aroma from the steaming hot coffee tumbler firmly held in his hands was racing into his mind, and so were his thoughts today.

SJ was indeed happy and proud of his achievement, when Managing Director Mr. N Bansal announced his promotion as International Business Manager just an hour ago. Nevertheless, his thoughts racing around the plans he was working upon to launch ITL's products in foreign markets.

Having established a significant presence in India, ITL had certainly taken a lion's share in IT hardware components in the domestic market since 1994. The competition from MNCs and Gray market products from Korean, Taiwanese and Chinese products in domestic market was stiff and price sensitive.

ITL started its business with networking hardware solutions such as network cards, bridges, adopters etc and slowly expanded its product width into Desktop speakers, headphones, joysticks, game pads, digital probes, cameras, alarms, specialized cables, connectors etc. Lately they had grouped their product lines into

(a) Computing like Personal Computers and Laptops

(b) IT Peripherals

(c) Entertainment Electronics

(d) Mobiles and Telecommunications

(e) Power Electronics

(f) Automobile electronics

The underlined were the new Product initiative by the company. A Product manager who was the virtual CEO of that product line solely managed each product category. The responsibilities spanned across product feature management, forecasting, budgeting, sourcing, packaging, pricing, promotional schemes, market development, market penetration as well as positioning etc.

Each Product Manager was supported by a team of Regional Managers and Area sales managers who were located in North, South, East and West of the Country. They managed the entire Channel Network of the company as well company sponsored direct outlets for product demos. The company sold its products through a distribution channel network of Wholesale Dealers, Retailers, and Direct Selling Agents. The company had adopted selective distribution strategy.

In the entire Product mix range there were many cash cows, stars and question marks, however stars and question marks accounted for a major percentage in the product mix. They had overall 20 % market share in computing and IT peripherals and ITL's overall CAGR was an impressive 30%.

ITL's strategic alliances with the sourcing company in Taiwan supplemented with technological association with few other Asian companies gave them an edge over competition in rapidly conceiving new products and launching them into the markets customized to local consumer needs. ITL had an in-house training and development cell, which provided the overall technical and training support to the marketing and sales department.

Flexible organization structure, strong knowledge centric professional team, and best management practices had contributed enormously in creating a competitive advantage for ITL through cost effective manufacturing practices, product quality (6 sigma), and excellent customer service. Moreover the company's business share was further consolidated due to professional salesmanship and effective relationship marketing adopted by them in India.

The company had integrated vertically for various components and established a Research and product development centre for keeping abreast with technological innovations. ITL through its partner company in Taiwan networked with small business enterprises across the globe for product innovation, patents, intellectual property rights, and product design organizations. ITL also had two assembly manufacturing lines at Jammu and Baddi in Himanchal Pradesh. ITL was patron to leading IT hardware-engineering institutions from where it successfully harnessed knowledge management activities. ITL also actively involved Management Educational Institutions for Business Problem Research through Summer Trainees.

All these activities helped ITL in extending quickly alternate product uses of its peripherals and components customized to various industries like defense, aeronautics, space, automobiles, security, chemicals, and Heavy engineering. These industries found use of ITL products mainly for alarms, security alerts, and networking.

Not only did the Board of Directors recommended action plan to sustain this competitive advantage in the domestic market with the launch of new innovative IT hardware products customized to Indian needs; but also had concluded to enter into the international markets.

The board of directors had just concluded a meeting with Managers of all departments and Set the Goal of a ROI of 20% in 2007-2008, which was 10% above the 2006-2007 figures. The Company's strategy from marketing perspective to achieve this ROI was clear – "Increase the Market share by 10%".

ITL had been profitable so far and was looking beyond the borders. This was clearly reflecting over the transformation of an ethnocentric ITL to polycentric stage. Although ITL had limited exporting business in Singapore, Dubai and Hong kong but it had not established a sustained International marketing initiative in the neighboring countries around Indian Ocean and Arabian Peninsula. SJ knew that the challenges facing him were tough and that he would have to reinvent his approach for successful international initiative once again.

First thing first, and SJ started working with the pool of country data spread over his table that consisted of Macro environment indicators, micro environmental issues etc. Against these factors, SJ started giving rating to each region on a scale of 1 to 10 with '1' lowest and '10' highest, so that he could hypothetically arrive at ITL's competitive advantage index for each region.

Country Screening and Market selection criteria.

Available DATA (hypothetical)

	Market Population	*Market Gnp*	*Business Terms of Access Index*
China	1.2 Billion	1000	0.2
Gulf	150 Million	500	0.6
East Africa	100 Million	300	0.9

Key macro and micro environmental factors assumed by weight age

	Technological	*Economical*	*Political*
China	40	30	30
Gulf	35	50	15
East Africa	25	20	55

According to SJ the possibilities of doing business in Gulf and Africa were promising, but he was not sure which region to select, so a structured analysis was necessary to arrive at the Market Size Index, Competitive advantage of each region and indicative Market Potential Index

Questions

1. What would be the MARKET SIZE INDEX of each Region?
2. How do you think would have SJ calculated the COMPETITIVE ADVANTAGE INDEX?
3. What would have been the MARKET POTENTIAL for each Region?
4. Which region do you think would SJ shortlist having high EXPORT POTENTIAL?
5. Prepare a neat flow chart of Country Screening criteria for this case and submit your recommendations in bulleted points

4

Luxury Branding in India: A Study

Mr. Aditya Vij
Mr. Gagan Grover
gagangrover2001@yahoo.com
Bharati Vidyapeeth University, Institute of Management and Research, New Delhi

This case studies the concept of Luxury branding coming onto the Indian shores in a big way in the last half of decade ; the reasons behind the same and an analysis if they have come in too late and in plenty and are they going in for the over kill ...will the market here in India support it or would it be a case of an overkill .

Most expensive suit

Early December, the world's most expensive men's suit, priced at a neat $113,000 - that's a whopping Rs 51 lakh - was launched in India. In London, its designer, 'luxury architect' Alexander Amosu, was already armed with a list of high-net worth Indians to reach out to personally after the event.

Two prospective customers, got in touch with Amosu's office ; immediately.

The suit, made from gold and platinum threads and embellished with nine 18-carat gold and pave-set diamond buttons, is the latest acknowledgement that luxury marketing has finally arrived in India.

A princely obsession Indian princes had patronized the top luxury brands in the world before Independence, especially during the Great Depression: Louis Vuitton bags, Rolls-Royce cars, Cartier watches, Van Cleef and Arpels jewellery et al.

The recent rise in wealth has seen the return of several luxury brands to our shores.

The Asia-Pacific Wealth Report of Merrill Lynch and Capgemini said there were 123,000 dollar millionaires in India in 2007, up almost a quarter from 2006.

The 2008 edition of the report said that the worth of the average Indian millionaire was $3.6 million, higher than the Asia-Pacific average of $3.4 million, but lower than the world average of $4 million.

At the recent Luxury Goods Forum, Minister of State for Commerce and Industry Jyotiraditya Scindia estimated that the $5 billion market will grow five times in size in the next five years.

There are clear indications of this.

The personal touch

So how does luxury sell in India?

Normal rules of sales and marketing do not work.

The customers are well-informed and do not hunt for value-for-money. The luxury experience, therefore, has to be superior and personalized.

Take the example of the Rs 51-lakh suit which uses 'Vanquish II', the most expensive fabric from Dormeuil made from blends of extremely soft and rare fibers like Himalayan Pashmina, Qiviuk and Vicuna. The suit is only made to order.

Once the order is placed, 'Amosu and his team will visit the clients wherever they want, anywhere in the world, for fitting,' says Dormeuil Mode SAS Commercial Director Frederic Dormeuil. 'Our target customers include businessmen, grooms, socialites and industrialists.'

Ermenegildo Zegna sends the customer's request straight to its experts in Italy for Made-To-Measure suits, jackets and coats. All for a price, of course, that begins at Rs 1.20 lakh and can go well beyond Rs 10 lakh.

Here's how it works: the customer has to choose from over 450 exclusive fabrics, patterns and colours, and zero in on a style. Trained staff at the store then takes the measurements which are codified and transmitted to a central computer in Italy.

The computer simulates and reproduces the pattern and design, which is then sent to the sewing department. At this stage, the artisans enter. The finished suit bears more than just the brand's label - it also carries the customer's name inside. The process takes about six weeks, after which the suit is delivered at one of the four Zegna stores in Mumbai, Delhi, Bangalore and Hyderabad.

Convenience is an integral part of the luxury experience.

Last year, when premium automobile brand Porsche introduced a 24x7, 365-day helpline service, this was an aspect it addressed. But it went beyond offering the conventional roadside assistance and towing facility: It also decided to arrange and pay for 'hotel stays or flight tickets back home if a Porsche owner happens to get stranded,' says Porsche India Director .

For the record, it sells models ranging from the Rs 59.22 lakh Cayenne Diesel to the Rs 2.9 crore 911 GT2 RS.

Some have gone a step further and started to customize luxury for India, like Cavalli and its Nehru jacket.

The right address

The challenge is to find the right address to retail luxury. Only, there aren't too many such locations in the country. And whatever there is, is prohibitively expensive.

The Porsche Design store in Delhi at 44 sq m is, therefore, its smallest store anywhere in the world.

The Emporio mall in New Delhi (it has 74 international luxury brands) and the Palladium (65) in Mumbai are visited by about 80 per cent of the potential consumers in the country!

The other option is to go to luxury hotels, which is what Mont Blanc and Louis Vuitton have done.

HermÃ¨s of France, for instance, has come to India in a 51-49 venture with Neelam Khanna, the wife of Ashok Khanna of Ananda in the Himalayas and Ista hotels and the granddaughter-in-law of MS Oberoi.

The first HermÃ¨s store opened at The Oberoi in Delhi, and the second is slated to come up at the Ista in Pune. But this is not an option exercised by all.

Current rules do not allow single-brand overseas retailers more than 51 per cent equity in the country. So, most luxury brands operate through dealers, though with tight control over display and promotion.

To get over the problem, many luxury brands have started to market directly.

It's a simple concept traditionally followed by jewelers who would carry ornament samples to customers' homes during special occasions like weddings and festivals.

Only now the samples include high-end clothing and lifestyle products, even premium watches. And the customer is often a rich industrialist or a business tycoon.

Epoca, a new multi-designer store that retails Dolce & Gabbana, Ferre and Trussardi at its Delhi outlet, claims it has seen success through the personal viewing of merchandise - which is considered far more convenient by its rich clients - than shopping at the store itself.

Here, the choice of partner becomes important.

Porsche Design, for instance, has partnered with Bird Group which is also a dealer for luxury cars. It thus has a ready database of rich people and also contacts in big companies that could buy Porsche Design gifts for their employees.

Porsche Design, the German maker of accessories, tracks 10 brands such as Louis Vuitton, Mont Blanc, Prada, Ferragamo and Dunhill; if eight of these set up shop in a city, it follows suit.

It has opened one store in Delhi, and could look at a second one, as well as one more in Bangalore

A pricey issue

In spite of the high real-estate prices, luxury brands know that they need to write their price tags carefully.

They know that the Indian buyer travels all over the world and is conversant with prices in Dubai, Singapore, London and New York. They cannot charge higher in India, the import tax of 112-127 per cent notwithstanding.

'We understand that buyers who come to Alfred Dunhill stores are well-travelled. You can't fool a customer about the fact that what he pays in India is more than he would in a European store,' says the head of Alfred Dunhill in India.

By and large, most of them know the price points that sell. Jay Makhijani of Mumbai-based Dia Precious Jewellery, which retails brands like Chopard, says that while watches priced between Rs 50,000 and Rs 3 lakh are bought regularly, it's the price tag of Rs 1 crore and upward that scares people away.

Dinesh Dayal, COO of L'Oreal India, believes that price is not a barrier. 'Our skincare serum, Secret De Vie from LancÃ´me, has fiercely loyal customers willing to pay Rs 14,500 for a 50 ml bottle,' he says.

Image: The Aqua Terra XXL Small Seconds Limited Edition is on display in a vitrine of the Omega booth at the world watch and jewelry show 'Baselworld' in Basel, Switzerland

Making contact

The promotion strategy, too, is different.

Conventional media which are consumed by the masses are a strict no-no, there is too much wastage. (Some Swiss watches are so exclusive that they do not advertise at all!) What works, apart from niche lifestyle media, is direct customer contact and word of mouth.

Abhay Gupta, executive director, Blues Clothing Company which retails brands like Corneliani, Versace and Cadini in India, says, 'Brand associations, social networking clubs, promotional events and media created events will encourage audiences to venture into luxury malls.'

The Porsche World Road Show at Aamby Valley near Pune was an example of this. Certified instructors took prospective customers through test drives and courses specially designed to highlight 'the Porsche experience'.

Iconic motorcycle manufacturer Harley-Davidson goes a step ahead with a multi-media 360-degree approach that has a clear focus on experimental marketing.

The one-point aim is to spread the Harley culture and further expand the global HOG (Harley Owners Group) family that currently has about 1.4 million members.

For a bike whose owners share a bond not only with their motorcycles but also with each other, this hasn't been too difficult to achieve.

Marketing strategies include 'regular riding events and boot camps across dealership cities, where a prospective customer can come, test ride the bike and experience the brand,' says Harley-Davidson India Director (marketing) Sanjay Tripathi.

This year, Harley Rock Riders, an annual rock music property, was also kickstarted in India with a three-month tour across the five cities that Harley-Davidson has ridden into with its dealerships: New Delhi, Chandigarh, Hyderabad, Mumbai and Bangalore.

That leaves one gap: trained customer-facing staff.

Since India had blanked out luxury for several decades, there isn't enough talent available. Every member of the Porsche staff - technicians, sales staff and customer care - has to undergo three to four training sessions every year.

Some of them are sent to Germany and West Asia for training. Recently, a session was also held in India. Porsche also has an online training module which every employee has to study and is then quizzed on.

Clearly, the rules of the game have started to evolve The brands coming in now seem to have missed the boat against the ones who docked in the ports earlier ; but the analysis of the markets say it is still a virgin market and lots can be still captured . India and Indians are hungry for more and to an extent desperate to be equaled / equated to the developed world ....The brands will survive and succeed like anything in the next 30 years to come , riding on the India growth and needs for up gradation. It is the Market to be in .

5

Smart AD Company: Challenges Ahead

Mr. Gaurav Kumar Tripathi
NLSIU, Bangalore

Young and dynamic entrepreneur Rahul Bahal started an Ad company at Bangalore in 1987. By 1994 the company emerged as a top company with100 percent growth rate and was the first one to tap financial markets and public issues in the city. The company in a short span became a leading name in this business and was ranked No 1 by Business India in the year 2007.With growing competition and changing business environment the company under went a joint venture with Smart Ad Company which was the subsidiary of ZIMBO (largest network in the world of advertising company, Japan).With the objective of meeting requirements of the clients and to meet the targets of channel groups the company started offering wider operations in the areas of advertising, celebrity management, event management, market research, media services, public relations and strategic brand corollary.

Smart Ad Company had thirty five employees and the organization had five departments namely Creative, Media, Finance and Account, Account Planning and Research Department (Annexure-1).The senior management of the Smart Ad Company identified a list of prospective clients through process of networking and by the data bank generated by their executives during their cold calls. Most of their account were either bulk or were generated by word of month. If the client was a corporate client then the director along with the copywriter, art director, director of client services met the client at his premises. Moreover, the company also accepted all kind of accounts depending upon the priority of the company as well as the clients. The eligibility of the clients was tested on account of planning department and depending upon the vision, background, balance sheet, size of the company and quantum of business of last three years. There after the client met the creative designer and discussed their requirements. The project was then handed over to the copy and design stream for further execution. They then worked upon the product positioning of the product brand name, packaging and distribution. They prepared a rough graph and discussed it with the client along with the alternative ideas. Each draft was charged separately. Any modifications if asked for by the clients were entertained then and there. There after the final draft of ad was pre-tested by the company using techniques and tools like memory test, observation test, waiting test and reaction test. The post testing was done through review of retail sales generated and by the kind of inquiry by customers after the ad had been launched. The company also collected commission from the media.

Smart Ad Company was ranked amongst the first three ad company in the city of Bangalore and their major clients included LG, Philips, Sony, Samsung and leading regional corporate. Smart Ad Company offered its services to exporters like Lalita Syntex Ltd., Jai Corp. Ltd,etc. The company owned all the prime hoardings in the city with more than 900 hoardings all over the state. Smart Ad Company arranged various hoarding sites to display their advertising messages and during this process they also provided additional services like identifying right hoarding locations, preparing estimates, fabrications of glow/neon/back-lit signs, paintings, making and fixing of viny1/ flex submitting photographs as copy of proof of display, subsequent supervision and upkeep of the sites, etc. In essence, it managed all problems associated with highly unorganized industry. The company also insured a consistent innovation and successful execution of new ideas and had leveraged their strength like quality, commitment, responsiveness, deliverance to their benefit. It had exclusive concessionaire of ground advertising in not one, but three one day international cricket matches played at Bangalore. It also marketed the first ever Celebrity Live show in the country and also organized road shows and other events. The company had organized a number of national level exhibitions on IT industry consecutively for two years.

Besides this the ad agency also facilitated big brands like Airtel and HPG in the introductory stage and helped them in generating sales in a very short span by providing them with market research from time to time. The company enjoyed good corporate relationships in the region and had lately diversified into painting which had helped them in reduction of overhead costs. Being the only company in the city, with a joint venture with ZIMBO it could to retain 85 percent of its loyal clients. Depending upon the target market needs it provided customized services. It held review meetings with the clients from time to time focusing on their future agenda as well as suggested strategies to build their brands with the changing market scenario. The company also assured to the deadlines with better coordination and interaction. Soon they started tapping the accounts from neighboring regions of western, northern and central India.

Although, being a joint venture with multi-national and possessing a techno-savvy studio, the company started facing a stiff competition from regional players for chasing regional clients. The company was more into print media and failed to explore their creative skills in audio-visual media and internet advertising. They also suffered a client shift on media's recommendation in spite of sharing healthy media alliances (both personal and monetary terms). The company was trying to enhance its creative skills of its employees but failed to retain the creative minds for not more than two years time as the nature of the Industry was dynamic and budding professionals looked for greener pastures. Moreover, the company failed to attract Bangalore based national accounts, who were giving a business of Rs.5-6crore to Mumbai based Ad company.

According to Saurabh Bahal Smart Head Smart Ad Company the educating the clients of the city and creating ads which were more brilliant in nature was the real challenge for them as jazzy looking ads could create gimmicks in business world, he felt. The business opportunities in the city were immense, and it was important to update their staff to cope up with the vibrant business environment. Off late the company had started sending experienced employees for field training to enhance their pitching, prospecting and creative skills. It also planned to focus on the visibility of their company through press release and more special campaigns. Yet Saurabh was not sure that these steps were enough to address the challenges ahead.

Questions

1. Do a SWOT analysis of the case.
2. Suggest the strategies to attract the major account in the region?

Annexure

Organizational Structure

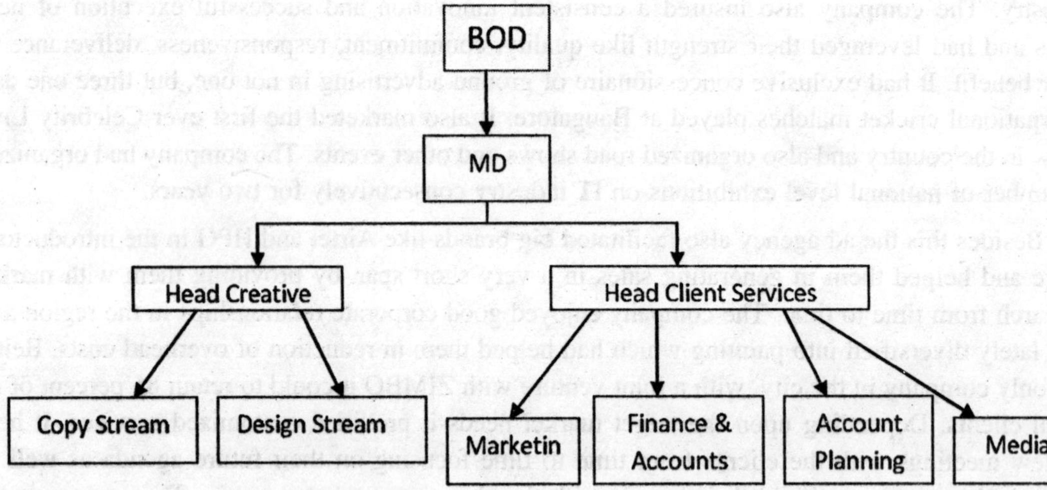

6

"Rising Prices - Causes, Impact and Remedies"

Mr. Lokinder Kumar Tyagi
Associate Professor
Bharati Vidyapeeth University, Institute of Management and Research, New Delhi
lokinder.tyagi@gmail.com
Dr. A.S.Rao
drsajeevan@gmail.com
Bharati Vidyapeeth University, Institute of Management and Research, New Delhi

An increase in the general level of prices implies a decrease in the purchasing power of the currency. That is, when the general level of prices rises, each monetary unit buys fewer goods and services. The effect of inflation is not distributed evenly in the economy, and as a consequence there are hidden costs to some and benefits to others from this decrease in the purchasing power of money.

In a developing economy, prices usually display an upward trend. But if prices keep rising persistently, they cause great hard-ship to the people. They spare neither the rich nor the poor, neither the producers nor the consumer. They make a economic activities uncertain and unstable, causing great unrest in the minds of the people.

The term "inflation" originally referred to increases in the amount of money in circulation, and some economists still use the word in this way. However, most economists today use the term "inflation" to refer to a rise in the price level. An increase in the money supply may be called monetary inflation, to distinguish it from rising prices, which may also for clarity be called 'price inflation'. Economists generally agree that in the long run, inflation is caused by increases in the money supply. However, in the short and medium term, inflation is largely dependent on supply and demand pressures in the economy.

In a developing economy a certain rise in prices in inevitable for at least three major reasons. First, the programmes of econo-mic development generate larger employment and money incomes and this increase the demand for basic consumer goods and services. The new incomes are not proportionately reflected in saving because a majority of the beneficiaries have to spend most of the additional money they get on satisfying unfulfilled needs. Secondly, the same programmes of economic development as generate the new money incomes push-up the demand for certain goods wanted also by the consumer, such as agricultural products, fuel, housing materials and the like. A third reason, of which the first two may be looked upon as special cases, is the large increase in currency in emulation and the operation of the law of supply and demand. Unless the production of basic consumer goods keeps pace with the increase in currency that is rendered inevitable by large scale, long term planning, prices are bound to rise even of the production of consumer goods is maintained at the old level.

India is faced today with one of the most critical economic situations. At no other time did Indians witness the horrible pheno-menon of spiralling prices as they do today, prices are soaring like rackets and each day one finds a rise in prices of more or less all essential commodities. Inflationary pressures are doing plenty of mischief and the people of middle class families are finding it a Himalayan task to make both ends meet.

Prices are expressed in terms of money. When the rupee or any other currency buys much less than what it used to, and more is to be paid for practically every item, then the problem of rising prices comes into being. In economic terminology it is known as 'Inflation'. Where the balance between money supply on the one hand and goods and services on the other is disturbed, a critical problem arises. If money supply increases more than goods and services available prices will rise.

Numerous factors can be cited to explain price rise in India First, our economic planning has suffered from serious drawback, right from the beginning. During the various Five-Year Plans, while the public expenditure persistently increased, the production targets were never realized. Secondly, this forced the Government to resort to deficit financing. The resulting imbalance inevitably led to infla-tion. The Third, major factor responsible for price rise is that due to great emphasis laid on heavy industries in our Five-Year-Plans, agriculture and consumer goods industries, which produce the items required by the people, have received insufficient attention. Con-sequently, agricultural production has not kept pace with consump-tion. Fourthly, in an underdeveloped economy like ours, the first increases in income always tend to be expended on food articles. In other words, the level of consumption tends to increase with increases in income.

By the nineteenth century, economists categorized three separate factors that cause a rise or fall in the price of goods: a change in the *value* or production costs of the good, a change in the *price of money* which then was usually a fluctuation in the commodity price of the metallic content in the currency, and *currency depreciation* resulting from an increased supply of currency relative to the quantity of redeemable metal backing the currency. Following the proliferation of private banknote currency printed during the American Civil War, the term "inflation" started to appear as a direct reference to the *currency depreciation* that occurred as the quantity of redeemable banknotes outstripped the quantity of metal available for their redemption. The term inflation then referred to the devaluation of the currency, and not to a rise in the price of goods.[21]

This relationship between the over-supply of banknotes and a resulting depreciation in their value was noted by earlier classical economists such as David Hume and David Ricardo, who would go on to examine and debate to what effect a currency devaluation (later termed *monetary inflation*) has on the price of goods (later termed *price inflation*, and eventually just *inflation*).[22]

Measuring the Rising Prices:

Inflation is usually estimated by calculating the inflation rate of a price index, usually the Consumer Price Index.[26] The Consumer Price Index measures prices of a selection of goods and services purchased by a "typical consumer".[4] The inflation rate is the percentage rate of change of a price index over time.

For instance, in January 2007, the U.S. Consumer Price Index was 202.416, and in January 2008 it was 211.080. The formula for calculating the annual percentage rate inflation in the CPI over the course of 2007 is

$$\left(\frac{211.080-202.416}{202.416}\right)\times 100\%=4.28\%$$

The resulting inflation rate for the CPI in this one year period is 4.28%, meaning the general level of prices for typical U.S. consumers rose by approximately four percent in 2007.[27]

Other widely used price indices for calculating price inflation include the following:

- **Producer price indices** (PPIs) which measures average changes in prices received by domestic producers for their output. This differs from the CPI in that price subsidization, profits, and taxes may cause the amount received by the producer to differ from what the consumer paid. There is also typically a delay between an increase in the PPI and any eventual increase in the CPI. Producer price index measures the pressure being put on producers by the costs of their raw materials. This could be "passed on" to consumers, or it could be absorbed by profits, or offset by increasing productivity. In India and the United States, an earlier version of the PPI was called the Wholesale Price Index.
- **Commodity price indices**, which measure the price of a selection of commodities. In the present commodity price indices are weighted by the relative importance of the components to the "all in" cost of an employee.
- **Core price indices**: because food and oil prices can change quickly due to changes in supply and demand conditions in the food and oil markets, it can be difficult to detect the long run trend in price levels when those prices are included. Therefore most statistical agencies also report a measure of 'core inflation', which removes the most volatile components (such as food and oil) from a broad price index like the CPI. Because core inflation is less affected by short run supply and demand conditions in specific markets,

central banks rely on it to better measure the inflationary impact of current monetary policy.

- **GDP deflator** is a measure of the price of all the goods and services included in gross domestic product (GDP). The US Commerce Department publishes a deflator series for US GDP, defined as its nominal GDP measure divided by its real GDP measure.
- **Regional inflation** The Bureau of Labor Statistics breaks down CPI-U calculations down to different regions of the US.
- **Historical inflation** Before collecting consistent econometric data became standard for governments, and for the purpose of comparing absolute, rather than relative standards of living, various economists have calculated imputed inflation figures. Most inflation data before the early 20th century is imputed based on the known costs of goods, rather than compiled at the time. It is also used to adjust for the differences in real standard of living for the presence of technology.
- **Asset price inflation** is an undue increase in the prices of real or financial assets, such as stock (equity) and real estate. While there is no widely accepted index of this type, some central bankers have suggested that it would be better to aim at stabilizing a wider general price level inflation measure that includes some asset prices, instead of stabilizing CPI or core inflation only. The reason is that by raising interest rates when stock prices or real estate prices rise, and lowering them when these asset prices fall, central banks might be more successful in avoiding bubbles and crashes in asset prices.[*dubious – discuss*]

Impact:

Increases in the price level (inflation) erode the real value of money (the functional currency) and other items with an underlying monetary nature (e.g. loans and bonds).

Debtors who have debts with a fixed nominal rate of interest will see a reduction in the "real" interest rate as the inflation rate rises. The real interest on a loan is the nominal rate minus the inflation rate (approximately [30]). For example if you take a loan where the stated interest rate is 6% and the inflation rate is at 3%, the real interest rate that you are paying for the loan is 3%. It would also hold true that if you had a loan at a fixed interest rate of 6% and the inflation rate jumped to 20% you would have a real interest rate of -14%. Banks and other lenders adjust for this inflation risk either by including an inflation premium in the costs of lending the money by creating a higher initial stated interest rate or by setting the interest at a variable rate. As the rate of inflation decreases, this has the opposite (negative) effect on borrowers.

Negative

- High or unpredictable inflation rates are regarded as harmful to an overall economy. They add inefficiencies in the market, and make it difficult for companies to budget or plan long-term. Inflation can act as a drag on productivity as companies are forced to shift resources away from products and services in order to focus on profit and losses from currency inflation.[11] Uncertainty about the future purchasing power of money discourages investment and saving.[31] And inflation can impose hidden tax increases, as inflated earnings push taxpayers into higher income tax rates unless the tax brackets are indexed to inflation.

- With high inflation, purchasing power is redistributed from those on fixed nominal incomes, such as some pensioners whose pensions are not indexed to the price level, towards those with variable incomes whose earnings may better keep pace with the inflation.[11] This redistribution of purchasing power will also occur between international trading partners. Where fixed exchange rates are imposed, higher inflation in one economy than another will cause the first economy's exports to become more expensive and affect the balance of trade. There can also be negative impacts to trade from an increased instability in currency exchange prices caused by unpredictable inflation.
- High inflation can prompt employees to demand rapid wage increases, to keep up with consumer prices. In the cost-push theory of inflation, rising wages in turn can help fuel inflation. In the case of collective bargaining, wage growth will be set as a function of inflationary expectations, which will be higher when inflation is high. This can cause a wage spiral. In a sense, inflation begets further inflationary expectations, which beget further inflation.
- People buy durable and/or non-perishable commodities and other goods as stores of wealth, to avoid the losses expected from the declining purchasing power of money, creating shortages of the hoarded goods.
- Inflation can lead to massive demonstrations and revolutions. For example, inflation and in particular food inflation is considered as one of the main reasons that caused the 2010–2011 Tunisian revolution[33] and the 2011 Egyptian revolution,[34] according to many observators including Robert Zoellick,[35] president of the World Bank. Tunisian president Zine El Abidine Ben Ali was ousted, Egyptian President Hosni Mubarak was also ousted after only 18 days of demonstrations, and protests soon spread in many countries of North Africa and Middle East.
- If inflation gets totally out of control (in the upward direction), it can grossly interfere with the normal workings of the economy, hurting its ability to supply goods. Hyperinflation can lead to the abandonment of the use of the country's currency, leading to the inefficiencies of barter.
- A change in the supply or demand for a good will normally cause its relative price to change, signaling to buyers and sellers that they should re-allocate resources in response to the new market conditions. But when prices are constantly changing due to inflation, price changes due to genuine relative price signals are difficult to distinguish from price changes due to general inflation, so agents are slow to respond to them. The result is a loss of allocative efficiency.
- High inflation increases the opportunity cost of holding cash balances and can induce people to hold a greater portion of their assets in interest paying accounts. However, since cash is still needed in order to carry out transactions this means that more "trips to the

bank" are necessary in order to make withdrawals, proverbially wearing out the "shoe leather" with each trip.

- With high inflation, firms must change their prices often in order to keep up with economy-wide changes. But often changing prices is itself a costly activity whether explicitly, as with the need to print new menus, or implicitly.
- According to the Austrian Business Cycle Theory, inflation sets off the business cycle. Austrian economists hold this to be the most damaging effect of inflation. According to Austrian theory, artificially low interest rates and the associated increase in the money supply lead to reckless, speculative borrowing, resulting in clusters of malinvestments, which eventually have to be liquidated as they become unsustainable.

Positive

- Keynesians believe that nominal wages are slow to adjust downwards. This can lead to prolonged disequilibrium and high unemployment in the labor market. Since inflation would lower the real wage if nominal wages are kept constant, Keynesians argue that some inflation is good for the economy, as it would allow labor markets to reach equilibrium faster.
- The primary tools for controlling the money supply are the ability to set the discount rate, the rate at which banks can borrow from the central bank, and open market operations which are the central bank's interventions into the bonds market with the aim of affecting the nominal interest rate. If an economy finds itself in a recession with already low, or even zero, nominal interest rates, then the bank cannot cut these rates further (since negative nominal interest rates are impossible) in order to stimulate the economy - this situation is known as a liquidity trap. A moderate level of inflation tends to ensure that nominal interest rates stay sufficiently above zero so that if the need arises the bank can cut the nominal interest rate.
- The Nobel laureate Robert Mundell noted that moderate inflation would induce savers to substitute lending for some money holding as a means to finance future spending. That substitution would cause market clearing real interest rates to fall.[37] The lower real rate of interest would induce more borrowing to finance investment. In a similar vein, Nobel laureate James Tobin noted that such inflation would cause businesses to substitute investment in physical capital (plant, equipment, and inventories) for money balances in their asset portfolios. That substitution would mean choosing the making of investments with lower rates of real return. (The rates of return are lower because the investments with higher rates of return were already being made before.)[38] The two related effects are known as the Mundell-Tobin effect. Unless the economy is already overinvesting according to models of economic growth theory, that extra investment resulting from the effect would be seen as positive.
- Economist S.C. Tsaing noted that once substantial deflation is expected, two important effects will appear; both a result of money holding substituting for lending as a vehicle for

saving.[39] The first was that continually falling prices and the resulting incentive to hoard money will cause instability resulting from the likely increasing fear, while money hoards grow in value, that the value of those hoards are at risk, as people realize that a movement to trade those money hoards for real goods and assets will quickly drive those prices up. Any movement to spend those hoards "once started would become a tremendous avalanche, which could rampage for a long time before it would spend itself."[40] Thus, a regime of long-term deflation is likely to be interrupted by periodic spikes of rapid inflation and consequent real economic disruptions. Moderate and stable inflation would avoid such a seesawing of price movements.

- The second effect noted by Tsaing is that when savers have substituted money holding for lending on financial markets, the role of those markets in channeling savings into investment is undermined. With nominal interest rates driven to zero, or near zero, from the competition with a high return money asset, there would be no price mechanism in whatever is left of those markets. With financial markets effectively euthanized, the remaining goods and physical asset prices would move in perverse directions. For example, an increased desire to save could not push interest rates further down (and thereby stimulate investment) but would instead cause additional money hoarding, driving consumer prices further down and making investment in consumer goods production thereby less attractive. Moderate inflation, once its expectation is incorporated into nominal interest rates, would give those interest rates room to go both up and down in response to shifting investment opportunities, or savers' preferences, and thus allow financial markets to function in a more normal fashion.

Suggested Teachings:

A variety of policies have been used to control inflation.

Monetary policy

Today the primary tool for controlling inflation is monetary policy. Most central banks are tasked with keeping the federal funds lending rate at a low level, normally to a target rate around 2% to 3% per annum, and within a targeted low inflation range, somewhere from about 2% to 6% per annum. A low positive inflation is usually targeted, as deflationary conditions are seen as dangerous for the health of the economy.

There are a number of methods that have been suggested to control inflation. Central banks such as the U.S. Federal Reserve can affect inflation to a significant extent through setting interest rates and through other operations. High interest rates and slow growth of the money supply are the traditional ways through which central banks fight or prevent inflation, though they have different approaches. For instance, some follow a symmetrical inflation target while others only control inflation when it rises above a target, whether express or implied.

Fixed exchange rates

Under a fixed exchange rate currency regime, a country's currency is tied in value to another single currency or to a basket of other currencies (or sometimes to another measure of value, such as gold). A fixed exchange rate is usually used to stabilize the value of a currency, vis-a-vis the currency it is pegged to. It can also be used as a means to control inflation. However, as the value of the reference currency rises and falls, so does the currency pegged to it. This essentially means that the inflation rate in the fixed exchange rate country is determined by the inflation rate of the country the currency is pegged to. In addition, a fixed exchange rate prevents a government from using domestic monetary policy in order to achieve macroeconomic stability.

Under the Bretton Woods agreement, most countries around the world had currencies that were fixed to the US dollar. This limited inflation in those countries, but also exposed them to the danger of speculative attacks. After the Bretton Woods agreement broke down in the early 1970s, countries gradually turned to floating exchange rates. However, in the later part of the 20th century, some countries reverted to a fixed exchange rate as part of an attempt to control inflation. This policy of using a fixed exchange rate to control inflation was used in many countries in South America in the later part of the 20th century (e.g. Argentina (1991-2002), Bolivia, Brazil, and Chile).

Gold standard

Under a gold standard, paper notes are convertible into pre-set, fixed quantities of gold.

The gold standard is a monetary system in which a region's common media of exchange are paper notes that are normally freely convertible into pre-set, fixed quantities of gold. The standard specifies how the gold backing would be implemented, including the amount of specie per currency unit. The currency itself has no *innate value*, but is accepted by traders because it can be redeemed for the equivalent specie. A U.S. silver certificate, for example, could be redeemed for an actual piece of silver.

The gold standard was partially abandoned via the international adoption of the Bretton Woods System. Under this system all other major currencies were tied at fixed rates to the dollar, which itself was tied to gold at the rate of $35 per ounce. The Bretton Woods system broke down in 1971, causing most countries to switch to fiat money – money backed only by the laws of the country.

Economies based on the gold standard rarely experience inflation above 2 percent annually.[51] Under a gold standard, the long term rate of inflation (or deflation) would be determined by the growth rate of the supply of gold relative to total output. Critics argue that this will cause arbitrary fluctuations in the inflation rate, and that monetary policy would essentially be determined by gold mining, which some believe contributed to the Great Depression.[54][55][56]

Wage and price controls

Another method attempted in the past have been wage and price controls ("incomes policies"). Wage and price controls have been successful in wartime environments in combination with rationing. However, their use in other contexts is far more mixed. Notable failures of their use include the 1972 imposition of wage and price controls by Richard Nixon. More successful examples include the Prices and Incomes Accord in Australia and the Wassenaar Agreement in the Netherlands.

In general wage and price controls are regarded as a temporary and exceptional measure, only effective when coupled with policies designed to reduce the underlying causes of inflation during the wage and price control regime, for example, winning the war being fought. They often have perverse effects, due to the distorted signals they send to the market. Artificially low prices often cause rationing and shortages and discourage future investment, resulting in yet further shortages. The usual economic analysis is that any product or service that is under-priced is over consumed. For example, if the official price of bread is too low, there will be too little bread at official prices, and too little investment in bread making by the market to satisfy future needs, thereby exacerbating the problem in the long term.

Cost-of-living allowance

The real purchasing-power of fixed payments is eroded by inflation unless they are inflation-adjusted to keep their real values constant. In many countries, employment contracts, pension benefits, and government entitlements (such as social security) are tied to a cost-of-living index, typically to the consumer price index.[57] A *cost-of-living allowance* (COLA) adjusts salaries based on changes in a cost-of-living index. Salaries are typically adjusted annually in low inflation economies. During hyperinflation they are adjusted more often.[57] They may also be tied to a cost-of-living index that varies by geographic location if the employee moves.

Annual escalation clauses in employment contracts can specify retroactive or future percentage increases in worker pay which are not tied to any index. These negotiated increases in pay are colloquially referred to as cost-of-living adjustments or cost-of-living increases because of their similarity to increases tied to externally determined indexes. Many economists and compensation analysts consider the idea of predetermined future "cost of living increases" to be misleading for two reasons: (1) For most recent periods in the industrialized world, average wages have increased faster than most calculated cost-of-living indexes, reflecting the influence of rising productivity and worker bargaining power rather than simply living costs, and (2) most cost-of-living indexes are not forward-looking, but instead compare current or historical data.

Sources

Rising Prices – The Scourge of the Present Time", Completition Success Review September 2011 Issue, New Delhi, p-

Abel, Andrew; Bernanke, Ben (2005). *Macroeconomics* (5th ed.). Pearson

Barro, Robert J. (1997). *Macroeconomics*. Cambridge, Mass: MIT Press. p. 895. ISBN 0-262-02436-5

Blanchard, Olivier (2000). *Macroeconomics* (2nd ed.). Englewood Cliffs, N.J: Prentice Hall. ISBN 013013306x

Mankiw, N. Gregory (2002). *Macroeconomics* (5th ed.). Worth

Hall, Robert E.; Taylor, John B. (1993). *Macroeconomics*. New York: W.W. Norton. p. 637. ISBN 0-393-96307-1

Burda, Michael C.; Wyplosz, Charles (1997). *Macroeconomics: a European text*. Oxford [Oxfordshire]: Oxford University Press. ISBN 0-19-877468-0

Websites:

http://en.wikipedia.org/wiki/Inflation

http://www.preservearticles.com/rising-prices-in-india.html

http://www.preservearticles.com/457-words-essay-on-unprecedented-price-rise-in-india.html

7

Rise and Fall of the Organized Retail Sector in India

Mr. Lokinder Kumar Tyagi
Associate Professor
Bharati Vidyapeeth University, Institute of Management and Research, New Delhi
lokinder.tyagi@gmail.com
Mr. Amitabh Singh
Regional Sales Manager, Dabur
amitabh.singh@daburindia.com

Introduction

Organized retail penetration in India is growing slower than estimates due to the slowdown. The earlier estimates was a 16% growth by 2012 which fell to 10.4 % . Almost every corporate house forayed into the retail sector , believing it would bring them easy , definite returns but they are soon beginning to realize that the business is not all that rosy & glamorous as it seems to be . The Subiksha debacle is just the tip of the fast melting iceberg & it has led to the discovery of many more skeletons in the organized retail closet .. Subiksha is grappling with a Rs 750 Cr debt burden & has downed shutters for all its1600 outlets.

Vishal retail - one of the fastest growing retail chains with 181 outlets has defaulted on its loan payment & is struggling with a debt burden of Rs 750 Crs .The fact remains that in spite of its restructuring some of its non profitable stores & a renegotiation of its rental contracts. Vishal still could not cough up enough money to pay its interest.

Case Body

"We have the best cost structure & business model that has worked beautifully on the ground .With a Rs 300 Cr liquidity injection the business can get back to its peak levels," says R.

Subramanium . The only hitch is that the decision still hangs precipitously in the hands of the bankers , who have become extremely risk averse in these uncertain & recessionary times.

Until October last year the retail industry was riding high , expanding at a frenetic pace & making heady investment plans . The Indian council for Research on International Economic Relations (ICRIER) report 2008 estimated that organized retail will grow by 45-50 per cent annually & constitute a 16% slice of the Indian retail market by 2011-12 as against its current size of 4 percent (in 2006-07) . Of course these estimates were dependent on India's GDP growing at 8-10% annually for the next 5 years . But a sudden slowdown of in the Indian economy , catapulted by the crash in the global economy & the macabre terror attacks in Mumbai , has thrown everything out of gear .

Now ICRIER says that it had assumed a growth of 8-10% during 2007-12 in the report which it feels is impossible for at least 2008-09 & 2009-10, hence organized retail cannot grow at 45-50 % as per earlier estimates.

A recent KPMG study has revised the estimated growth of organized retail to 10.4 % versus the earlier estimated 16 % by 2012. The Indian retail story is a recent phenomenon.

About 40 years ago , the country saw its first retail chain Samvaika – the first of its kind in the 1960's which was a primeval version of the supermarket concept sans the air conditioning , well planned aisle displays , Plano grams & high tech RFID (Radio frequency identification) technology at POS (point of sale) which are commonly seen today .

The next retail outlet came decades later in the form of Shopper's Stop set up by K Raheja group in 1991 in the bustling suburb of Andheri in North Mumbai & for years it stood alone catering to millions of customers walking through its doors . It was only after 2000 that it expanded to other cities in the country to become a full – blown retail chain .

But the real retail story began in 1999 when Piramal holdings opened India's first world class shopping mall , Crossroads , in south Mumbai – a " must visit" destination on a visitors Mumbai darshan expedition . So large were the hordes thronging the place that the mall decided to screen visitors whether they owned a mobile phone or not . That was in its hey days . Alas , Crossroads soon succumbed to the phenomenon of high footfalls & low conversions & was eventually sold of to the future group in 2006 , which is still in the process of deciding its fate . Nevertheless , despite its death , Crossroads marked the beginning of India's exciting retail trip . It inspired several other budding retailers to try their hand at the sunrise industry , which has since taken India by storm .

There was a sudden mushrooming of malls in the country . The until then non descript town of Gurgaon became the mall capitol of India , with 18 malls lining its barren landscape . According to a KSA –Technopak report in 2005 , India was to grow to 300 malls by 2010.

Another Mc Kinsey study conducted in 2007 predicted that organized retail will constitute 9-10% of the total retail market by 2010. The study also went on to list the numerous opportunities that lay in the nascent sector such as employment benefits to the tune of 35 million people , profitability & overall economic progress of the country . The industry was growing at a double digit when suddenly at the end of last year it came to a screeching halt.

India's GDP growth fell to 5.3% in the October – December 2008 quarter & is expected to fall further to 5% in 2009 . December was surprisingly a dark month for the retail industry as footfalls at malls fell drastically in December & almost all retailers posted negative growths. Retail stocks have also taken a severe beating in the past few months – Vishal Retail fell from a peak of Rs 880 in April 2008 to a low of Rs 26.70 in this March 2009 & Pantaloon plummeted from a high of Rs 576 in May 2008 to a low of Rs 105 in March 2009 . These were hot favorites of Private Equity players who had invested large sums of money in their futures . ICICI ventures sold of 10% stake in Subikhsa last year to the Aziz Premji owned investment firm – Premji Invest , reducing its exposure to 23 %. Now most of these PE firms are reeling under crashed valuations of these retail stocks by 60 – 90 % but one of the PE player says " Future of organized retail is bright because the shift from unorganized retail to organized retail is inevitable ."

As per some industry experts, it was a pure case of growth planned disproportionately with supply . When consumption was growing rapidly owing to the burgeoning middle class , their rising incomes, hence, higher disposable spends , retailers borrowed heavily to make provisions for working capital & property in order to fund their growth . Then suddenly , consumption levels slowed & the retailers by this time had already locked their money in capital & property which eventually led to issues in inventory & human resources " Retailers did not have the money to purchase new inventory & consumers did not want to buy old merchandise."

Some say that retail requires a high operating leverage & a lot many had raised a large amount of debt to expand . It was fine till the sales grew but with a small dip in revenue these retailers were unable to meet their interest payments . A classic example is Subiksha – it raised a debt of Rs 750 Crs on a capital base of Rs 32 Crs with shareholder funds of Rs 180 Crs . When growth slowed down , it couldn't repay its debt, ditto with Vishal Retail.

A dearth in appropriate real estate for organized retail coupled with growing competition amongst retailers led to a surge in rentals to unprecedented levels.

Retailers started trampling on each other's toes & real estate players began charging hefty rentals . India pays for the highest retail rentals as a percentage of total cost . Both rent & human resources constitute the majority of a retailers cost & both had climbed to levels which were unsustainable.

Adding salt to injury , the equity markets also crashed in 2008 – 09 drying up potential funds for retailers who were banking on raising equity to grow & bankers became increasingly cautious in lending money . India's regulatory environment (FDI policy on retail) anyways prevents retailers from seeking assistance from foreign players .Currently only 51 per cent FDI is permitted in single brand retail , FDI in multi brand retail is not allowed & 100% FDI is allowed in wholesale cash & carry business.

Though, many international retailers like Metro , Wal-Mart , Tesco , Carrefour & Bookers have entered India through the FDI route for the wholesale Cash & Carry business set up , none except Metro – Cash & Carry have been able to commence business so far owing to the high real estate process & economic uncertainty on account of political & social reasons.

Questions

1. What are the possible reasons of fall of the Organized Retail Sector in India?
2. What kind of business environment is best suited for putting the Organized Retail Engine back on track ?
3. Will relaxing FDI norms benefit the Retail Sector ?
4. What impact can a steadily growing organized retail business in Inidia put on the local Kiranawalas ?

Teaching Notes

Overview :

The issues covered in this case were the problems which the retail industry is facing today viz. heavy debt burden , slowdown in consumerism , high operating costs , old inventory , stringent FDI norms , lower GDP growth & lower sales .

Other issues covered were – origin of organized retail , restructuring of formats by prominent retailers to prevent further losses , change in buying behaviour of consumers.

Application :

This study is best suited for management undergraduates (BBA & MBA) students as it puts them to analyze the causes of downfall of this sector & also compels them to find out solutions to bring it "back on track."

Objectives of the case :

The case type is "Complex" & it carries the following key objectives for the reader

1) Offers a crisp introduction of the organized retail sector to the reader .

2) Forces the reader to analyze the issues which caused the downfall of this sector.

3) Compels the reader to arrive at the possible solutions for the problems faced by the organized retail sector currently.

Teaching Suggestions :

The country has so far not allowed any FDI in multi-brand retail due to strident political opposition, particularly of the Left, to the entry of multinational retail giants in India, who in their opinion, could ruin livelihood security of small traders and a large number of persons employed with traditional form of retail business.However, as fears of foreign fund flows into India diminishing in the next few months are becoming real, the government has begun to seriously think in terms of revisiting its policy on FDI in the retail sector.This, if allowed, will open up floodgates of new capital as foreign retail majors are too keen to foray into India's retail sector.

While, infusion of 100 per cent FDI in 'cash and carry' (B2B) retail is currently permitted, only 51 per cent FDI is allowed in single brand retail. No FDI is, however, permitted in case of multi-rand retail.While, the likes of Metro AG (Germany) and Shoprite (South Africa) have already taken advantage of 100 per cent FDI in 'cash and carry' business and likes of Carrefour (France) and Tesco (UK) have announced their intention to do so, single brand retailers like Marks & Spencer (UK) and Vision Express (Netherlands) have been forced to accept partnerships with local business houses for entry into single brand retail. Given the choice, many of them would have liked to go on their own.

Multi brand retail giants like Wal-Mart, Carrefour, and Tesco, on the other hand, due to current FDI policy, have been compelled to either take franchise route or provide technical (back-end) services. Some have even chosen to wait until the policy is completely changed to meet their requirements.Although, no major policy decisions are expected as the general elections are due in the next six months, the government is believed to be considering relaxation in FDI norms for both single and multi-brand retail.

Kamal Nath, the union minister of commerce and industries, at a recent trade conference in Paris, had announced that the government is seriously considering permitting up to 100 per cent FDI (as against 51 per cent at present) in single brand retail, specifically in the area of luxury retail. The official line so far has been to consider allowing 100 per cent FDI in single brand retail in the segments that do not adversely affect local employment.

It is also believed that, despite pronouncements to the contrary, the commerce ministry has mooted a proposal that seeks to allow up to 49 per cent (as against Zero per cent at present) FDI in multi-brand retail. Although, this will require a lot of political courage on part of the government, if both proposals of the commerce ministry are accepted, the country can expect to receive a large inflow of FDI in the retail sector from MNC retailers, as modern retail is growing at 40 per cent or more every year

References

1. Biyani, Kishore & Baishya (2007). *"It happened in India."*
2. Sheth, Hiral & Saraf , The Bubble Bursts , May 2009. Business India

8

Changing Consumer Preferences for Buying Car

Dr. Monika Sethi
DIMAT ,Raipur.
monicasethi22@yahoo.co.in

Changing consumer behavior

It's a reflection in general there is rise in demand of the four wheeler especially by the Double Income nuclear families. As there is increasing spending power in the 22-35 category of Indians the four wheeler industry can look forward to strong growth in the years ahead provided that the concerns regarding the infrastructure are addressed .Data from the consumer data survey also indicates that the spending tendency of the people has increased .Consumers with incomes of 15-25k have also actively considered / purchased cars when the earlier tendency was to save the money so that it could be used later for some other purposes . Cars are now viewed as a necessity / means of comfort rather a luxury item earlier.India's automobile sales expanded by 15.9% in the year ended March 31, 2005 to 7,896,475 vehicles as against 6,810,537 vehicles sold in the fiscal year 2003-04.This includes sales of passenger cars, two-wheelers and commercial vehicles. Sales of passenger cars grew by 17.7% in the year ended March 31, 2005, data released by the Society of Indian Automobile Manufacturers (SIAM) showed.

India was the fastest-growing large market for passenger cars in the world in 2004. Automotive demand was especially robust as the beneficial effects of a strong agricultural crop in the preceding year filtered through into rising incomes. With bank credit still cheap, the middle class expanding in size and a steady stream of new models entering the market,demand was buoyant, with sales of passenger vehicles rising by an estimated 24% in calendar year 2004. Sales of commercial vehicles, which are being driven by rising investment,government infrastructure spending and strong industrial production, will grow by around 22% in 2004/05 after expanding by close to 30% in 2003/04.

Although the outlook for the automotive sector is buoyant, growth is occurring from a low base: India remains poor and largely undeveloped, with only a small proportion of the population able to aspire to car ownership. Yet, a low average income obscures wide urbanrural disparities and the influence of a growing middle class that is increasingly able to afford personal transport. Growth in car sales in India has moved roughly in line with trends in disposable personal income. With gains in disposable income during the forecast period, in the range of around 10-15% a year. More importantly, the percentage of the population that can afford a car is also rising. According to India's National Council of Applied Economic Research,in 2002 only 6.1m households out of a total of 176m were classified as "affluent or very rich",and therefore able to afford a personal car. However, another 56.8m households were considered to be "well off"—able to afford motorcycles and scooters, but not cars. Some of those aspiring consumer households will have already moved into the "affluent" group during the current economic boom.

If only 10% of these "well-off" households can move to the next level in the next five years, the number of car-owning households could rise by nearly 6m, nearly doubling current levels. Although this structural shift seems eminently achievable, economic shocks—such as a drought or a fiscal crisis that leads to much higher interest rates—could stem demand for a period of time.

The table below shows the past record and the future estimates for the registrations of Automobiles The growth of the passenger car segment in absolute terms is the maximum .

	2004	2005	2006	2007	2008	2009
New passenger car registrations ('000)	1,117	1,343	1,479	1,624	1,747	1,911
Stock of passenger cars (per 1,000 population)	6.7	7.5	8.4	9.4	10.3	11.4
New commercial vehicle registrations ('000)	327	382	413	449	483	520
Light commercial vehicle registrations ('000)	122	144	153	173	191	210
Heavy & medium truck registrations ('000)	204	238	259	276	291	310

Source: Economist Intelligence Unit.

A broad commitment to low interest rates, plus easier financing arrangements for car buyers, should also stimulate greater demand for cars. A car loan that once took two weeks to approve can now be cleared in two or three days. In 2003 more than 85% of car sales were financed with loans, compared with 65% in 1998. Interest rates on car loans have fallen from around 19% five years ago to about 10% today. As in much of Asia, India is also seeing the birth of a youth-driven credit culture that places greater stock on consumption than in savings.

These factors, combined with the gradual deregulation of the car market and the entry of foreign investors, have improved price competition in a highly pricesensitive market, and have expanded the range of models on offer. Around 25 new car models will be introduced in India in 2005, most in the medium and luxury. Car producers are already opening more dealerships in semi-urban and rural regions to tap rising incomes and demand, and these areas now account for a growing share of overall sales.Several factors will restrain growth. Scooters and motorcycles are the dominant form of personal transport in India, and will remain so until incomes rise enough to allow average consumers to afford cars. Sales of motorcycles and scooters exceeded car sales by a factor of nearly six—roughly 6m units to 1m. Car sales will also be held back by the poor condition of roads. In 2007, however, a major roadbuilding project, the Golden Quadrilateral, is due to be completed. This will link the country's four major cities through a massive new road network, and should make car travel easier and more appealing.

Companies and competitors in the passenger car segment.The Breakup of the Market share of the car manufacturers for the period Apr-Dec 04

Major passenger-car manufacturers, Apr-Dec 2004

Market share (%)	
Maruti Udyog	51.0
Tata Motors	17.3
Hyundai Motor India	17.0

a As a percentage of total sales.

Sources: Centre for Monitoring Indian Economy; Society of Indian Automobile Manufacturers.

The Recent Industry Trends

In May 2005, total passenger car sales (including export sales) showed a growth rate of 10 % to 81976 units. Out of 11 players 4 players saw a dip in sales during the month. Maruti Udyog, Tata Motors and Hyundai Motor are the major players in the passenger car segment. Of these players, Hyundai motor showed a spectacular increase of 82% at 23080 units while Tata motors showed a marginal increase 6% in sales at 12698 units. Maruti Udyog registered a negative growth rate of 5% at 36579 units as compared to the corresponding period of previous year.

During the month of May 2005 Passenger car segment showed a 4% decline in exports at 13460 units while domestic sales grew by 13% as compared to corresponding period of previous quarter. The rise in domestic sales export was mainly contributed by Hyundai motors, which contributed a 85% increase at 9205 units. The players, which led to a fall in the exports, were Maruti Udyog which posted a 64% fall in sales at 2197 units.

For the two months i.e. April 2005 – May 2005 passenger cars have registered a growth of 12% to 156410 units. Market leader Maruti Udyog recorded a fall in sales by 5% to 69267 units, while Hyundai Motor registered a rise of 97% to 42774 units. Tata Motor also posted an increase of 10% in sales to 24375 units during the period. Among other players Skoda Auto India posted a highest growth rate of 23% at 1102 units. This was due to lower base in the corresponding period of previous year. While Fiat India recorded highest fall of 72% to 334 units.

Due to arrival of newer, more aggressive models and segment fragmentation, market shares of major players' have remained static or changed marginally despite growth in sales. Among the passenger car manufacturers, share of market leader Maruti Udyog dropped to 44% (against 52% earlier), while that of Hyundai Motor increased to 27% (against 15%). Market share of Tata Motors remained static at 16%. Apart from above the other players like Ford India's market share decreased form 6% to 4% at 5743 units. Toyota Kirloskar Motor Pvt. Ltd., did not have a change in the market share of 1% at 1681 units.

Tractor and utility vehicle major, Mahindra & Mahindra (M&M) planning to launch Renault's popular mid sized and low-cost sedan car Logan in India by 2007. For this M&M has joined hands with French carmaker Renault SA to form an Rs 700 crore joint venture.

The Swift, Maruti's latest model, was launched on May 25, 2005, at an attractive introductory price. The response has been overwhelming; over 18,000 customers from across the country have already placed orders for the Swift.

Under pressure after the instant success of Maruti's Swift, Hyundai Motors launched an offensive by reducing prices of its Santro Xing by over Rs 19,000. A virtual price war has broken out in the domestic car market. To beat Hyundais price cuts on its Santro Xing models,Maruti is resorting to discounts and freebies such as free stereos and insurance. The Maruti Focus is now shifting towards B segment, since it is the biggest segment in terms of volume as A segment is losing its ground. The sudden popularity of Maruti's Swift has left carmakers wondering if they will all have to cut prices to stay in the race. More cars are slated to be launched this fiscal. General Motors plans to re-launch Daewoos Matiz in a re-tooled avatar as the small-car Spark.The launch is likely to challenge conventional pricing of entry-level cars like the Alto and Zen in a big way and could force a fresh bout of price wars in the auto market. Maruti could cut prices of the Alto and Zen by this month-end or in July as its position under threat from GM's plans. Moreover, Hyundai's aggressive pricing strategies, which saw the Korean car-maker launch a non-AC Santro variant at Rs 2.79 lakh, are a challenge too.

Ford wants to introduce a family coupe being developed in Australia which could be priced to beat competitors like the Honda City and the Chevrolet Optra. Base model could be priced in a way that makes it more attractive than its competitors by offering more value for money.Launches usher in fresh waves of competition and this will bring down prices, even though vehicle makers here have been affected by the rising cost of raw materials such as steel, plastics, aluminum and rubber.

Fords moves could see Honda and Chevrolet reacting in a manner similar to the Hyundai-Maruti price jousting. Volkswagen also plans to bring in a small car based on the Volkswagen Fox within the next year. This too will impact the price of entry level cars.

Hindustan Motors is planning to roll out a car in the luxury 'D' segment from the Mitsubishi stable in 2005. This model is likely to compete with Honda Accord, Toyota Camry, Skoda Octavia and Opel Vectra. It is also planning to introduce new models in Pajero a premium segment car. The company has decided to emphasize on the premium 'D' segment of the car market. Hyundai Motor India, the wholly-owned subsidiary of Hyundai Motor Company is gearing up to launch redesigned versions of the Sonata, Accent in mid-2006 and a hatchback in 2007.

Czech car maker Skoda Auto will nearly double capacity in India and begin exporting to Bangladesh this year as part of its plan to use India as a regional hub. Skoda Auto, which is fully owned by Germany's Volkswagen AG, will also step up investment in India. The company has already invested Euro 100 million ($132.7 million) in its Aurangabad plant in Maharashtra, its only manufacturing facility outside Europe.

Discussion:

1. Analysis the changing scenario of customers buying for small cars & big cars.
2. What should be the different promotion programme of different Companies to maintain strong markert competitiveness.

9

Supply Chain Management Practices and CSR of McDonalds in Indian Market

Dr. Navneet Gera
Assistant Professor
BVIMR
gerasir@yahoo.com
Mrs. Preety Wadhwa
Associate Professor
pwadhwa77@gmail.com
Bharati Vidyapeeth University, Institute of Management and Research, New Delhi

Objectives:

- To study the SCM practices of McDonalds for becoming the leader in fast-food restaurants.
- To study the promotional strategies of McDonalds in India.
- To envisage the Corporate Social Responsibilities by McDonalds.

Abstract

McDonald's has been able to establish itself in the Indian market with its customised and customer sensitive market and has been a leading international fast food restaurant chain with 30,000 restaurants spread across the globe. The caselet discusses the Supply Chain Management Practices, Corporate Social Responsibilty promotional Strategies of McDonald's in India. The caselet focuses on marketing strategies of McDonalds as well as also emphasises on training and development of its employees. The caselet also describes the physical environment at McDonald's outlets and the marketing strategies followed by the company.

Key Words – CSR of McDonalds, Promotion Strategies of McDonalds, Positioning of McDonalds in India, SCM of McDonalds

Introduction

The business began in 1940, with a restaurant opened by brothers Richard and Maurice McDonald in San Bernardino, California. The first McDonald's restaurants opened in the United States, Canada, Costa Rica, Panama, Japan, the Netherlands, Germany, Australia, France, El Salvador and Sweden, in order of openings. In October 1996, Mc. Donald's opened its first Indian outlet in Vasant Vihar, an affluent residential colony in New Delhi. Indians have welcomed the fast food chains by accepting their products and in turn making them deliver the Indians taste of Food. Indians have nurtured their business in profitable as well as establishing global trust in economy. The key resource for food chain belongs to young generation and children in tier 2 and tier 3 cities having major share of population in Indian economy. McDonalds came into existence in the year 1954 but has entered in Indian market in the year 1996 through franchise business model. However, in terms of market share McDonalds is the world's largest fast food chain. McDonald's India has a joint venture with Connaught Plaza Restaurants and Hard Castle Restaurants. Connaught Plaza Restaurants manages operations in North India whereas Hard Castle Restaurants operates restaurants in Western India.

Global Competitors of McDonalds

- Burger King – Second largest burger chain
- Wendy's - World's third largest hamburger fast food chain
- Jack in the Box - American fast food chain
- Subway – Largest single-brand restaurant chain
- Carl's Jr. - Fifth largest American fast food chain
- Five Guys - American fast food chain
- Whataburger - American fast food chain
- Krystal - American fast food chain
- White Castle - American fast food chain
- Yum! – Largest multi-brand restaurant chain

The Indian food service industry

India has a diverse population. Indian consumers maintain their distinct food habits even after migrating to different parts of the country.

Demography of Indian Economy

- Growing income – The economic has positive sentiments is growing at a higher rate of above 8% and the income of households is also increasing due to hike in salaries, 6th pay commission and the entry of MNCs in India.

- Population growth and urbanisation – The size of Indian population is large and the composition comprises of young generation giving rise to the consumption.
- India's economic liberalisation – The era of liberalisation in India initiated in the year 1991 and has given way for the entry of FDI as well as the entry of McDonalds in India in 1996 is post-liberalisation.

McDonald's in India

McDonalds is the result of globalisation that is integration of Indian economy with the American giant and integrating the culture. In this era of globalisation, ultimately the real beneficiary is richer or poorer is a subject of debate. In nut shell who is the customer of fast food chains the poor rickshaw man or the labour class or none of them. In fact it is Indian food which is widely accepted from centuries in India like 'Roti Sabzi' or 'Dal-Chawal' and that too by every citizen of India. McDonald has developed its own niche market with the generation who is actually the key driver of population as well.

McDonalds is selling which kind of product that has become so popular and the taste of global population. In fact it is the standardised process which is sold to different markets through franchise stores by giving training and their established brand support. Just order your favourite menu and get instant delivery in no time. Indians use to have homemade food with less fats and religious values include avoiding onion in majority of cases. However, Indians have adapted themselves to 'Masala Dosa' or 'Idli sambhar' from south Indian dishes. The entry of McDonald has increased the variety for young Indian customer but also has given them new choice.

McDonald has continually adapted to the customer's tastes, value systems, lifestyle, language and perception. Globally McDonald's was known for its hamburgers, beef and pork burgers. Most Indians are barred by religion not to consume beef or pork. To survive, the company had to be responsive to the Indian sensitivities. So McDonald's came up with chicken, lamb and fish burgers to suite the Indian palate. McDonalds has also considered the huge Indian population and the Vegetarian customer has been offered items like McAlooTikki and the McVeggie burger.

McDonalds has not only imbibed the Indian culture in their menu but has also understood the behaviour of families and children of India. As a result it also provides special facilities like 'Play Place' where children can play arcade games, air hockey, etc. This strategy is aimed at making McDonald's a fun place to eat. This also helps McDonald's to attract the young urban families waiting to spend some quality time while their children have fun at the outlet. Moreover, the outlet ambience and background music highlight the comfort that McDonald's offers to Indian customers. Though, it may increase obesity but the commitment of quality of food and service in a clean, hygienic and relaxing atmosphere has ensured that McDonald's maintains a positive relationship with the customers.

McDonald's success in India is vested with the limited menu, fresh food, fast service and affordable price and has marked its presence in the minds and taste on the tongues of Indian consumers. Intense competition and demands has also encouraged the fast food giant to customize product variety without hampering the efficacy of its supply chain. Around the world (including India), approximately 80% of McDonald's restaurants were owned and operated by independent franchisees. McDonald's was able to run the show seamlessly by outsourcing nine different ingredients used in making a burger from over 35 suppliers spread all over India through a massive value chain.

Suppliers of Mc Donald's in India

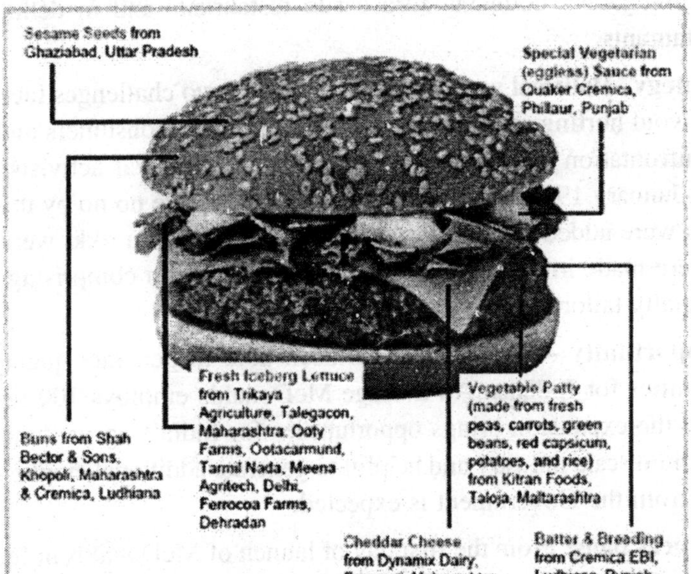

Fig-1 Supply Chain Management of McDonalds

Supply chain management: McDonalds has consistently followed the best supply chain management practices and had three objectives -

The first objective has been to operationalise its globally practiced QSCV-quality, service, cleanliness and value strategy. The second objective was to enjoy flexibility in pricing and the third was to launch new products whenever necessary. McDonalds uses Outsourcing in all its markets. In India due to higher import duty and currency fluctuations, McDonalds decided to source its raw materials from local suppliers to the maximum extent and import only process control equipment that allows it to dish out burgers and other orders in its super fast time frames. McDonalds 95 per cent of sourcing is done from 38 local suppliers as shown in Fig-1. The entire supply distribution is the responsibility of AFL logistics Ltd. A joint venture between airfreight and Coughlin in US and Radhakrishna Foodland (P) Ltd. In Thane, Maharashtra. Setting up supply chain in India was difficult due to poor transportation and storage infrastructure as well as lower quality agricultural products. They worked closely with local suppliers, farmers and also installed ERP software in Radhakrishnan Foodland to provide data of what is selling where and anticipate demand in each retail outlet and place orders accordingly. Company's delivery trucks had three degrees of refrigeration- a freezers section for meats, cold refrigerator for vegetables, non refrigerated for paer cups, napkins, plastic cutlery, etc. To maintain quality further company has obtained American Institute of Bakersa dn HACCP certification for quality standards. They have minimized costs, optimized quality control and ensured customer satisfaction with meticulous planning.

McDonalds –Do it differently in different countries

Emphasis on local management – McDonalds has focused on think global, act local and has opened two joint ventures on 50:50 joint venture with local entrepreneurship in Mumbai and Delhi. In Mumbai, amit jatia's company-hard castle restaurants and in delhi vikram bakshi's Connaught plaza restaurants.

McDonalds Strategy –Political and Social: There were two challenges faced by McDonalds the first one how to avoid hurting religious sensibilities of Indian consumers and the second how to avoid political confrontation with Indian government and political activists as was faced by KFC in Bangalore in January 1996. Beef and pork were a complete no no by this giant company. Instead new products were added like mutton maharaja mac and aalu tikki were introduced. The following changes were made in response to the cultural adaptation comprising of 75% of menu made Indianised specially tailored for Indian customers.

Employment opportunity – McDonalds has been able to generate quality and long term employment opportunities for Indians. An average McDonalds employs 100 people as cashiers, cooks, managers; and the expansion brings opportunities for India's agricultural workforce. It is seen as a small or medium scale industry and helpful to generate additional employment opportunity and thus the support from the Government is expected.

Packaging in Papers bags: From the first day of launch of McDonalds in India, the company has implemented paper bags use in packaging the food as the use of polythene in packaging is not safe and spreads pollution as polythene cannot be recycled but paper can be recycled. On the wrapper of McDonald's products it's clearly mentioned that the burger is Veg or Non- Veg and also the name of the burger is clearly mentioned on the wrapper and the color of the wrapper of burger is different for every burger like green, purple etc.

Re-engineering and designing the menu - McDonald's has continually adapted to the customer's tastes, value systems, lifestyle, language and perception. Globally McDonald's was known for its hamburgers, beef and pork burgers. Most Indians are barred by religion not to consume beef or pork. To survive, the company had to be responsive to the Indian sensitivities. So McDonald's came up with chicken, lamb and fish burgers to suite the Indian palate.

The vegetarian customer – India has a huge population of vegetarians. To cater to this customer segment, the company came up with a completely new line of vegetarian items like McVeggie burger and McAlooTikki. The separation of vegetarian and non-vegetarian sections is maintained throughout the various stages.

To counter these changes McDonalds has continuously introduced new products and has phased out the old ones which were at the decline stage of their PLC. The introduction is timed such that the new product does not cannibalize the product already in the maturity or growth stage. Thus the secret lies in getting profits with different products in the different stages of the PLC. The French Fries have been an important part of the McDonalds menu worldwide. But now it was in the stage of decline and was actually not generating proper return. In an attempt to revitalize it, a new variant was introduced namely Shake Shake Fries. This is being served with chatpata spice mix which has resulted in increase in the sales of French Fries and has elevated it from to the decline stage. This is used to delay the decline of a well established product which has the potential of generating further revenue.

McDonaldization

McDonald's has become emblematic of globalization, sometimes referred to as the "McDonaldization" of society. The Economist newspaper uses the "Big Mac Index": the comparison of a Big Mac's cost in various world currencies can be used to informally judge these currencies' purchasing power parity. Norway has the most expensive Big Mac in the world as of July 2011, while the country with the least expensive Big Mac is India (albeit for a Maharaja Mac—the next cheapest Big Mac is Hong Kong).

McDonalds Marketing Strategies in Indian Market

Segmentation -McDonald's uses demographic segmentation strategy with age as the parameter. The main target segments are children, youth and the young urban family.

Outsourcing

Table 1. Strategy of Outsourcing the Ingredients

Cheese	Dynamix Dairy Industries Ltd., Pune
Dehydrated onions	Jain Foods, Jalgaon
Iceberg lettuce	Trikaya Agriculture, Pune
Chicken patty	Vista Foods, Taloja
Veg. Patty, Veg. nuggets, Pineapple/Apple pie	Kitran Foods, Taloja
Chicken (dressed)	Riverdale, Talegaon
Buns	Cremica Industries, Phillaur
Eggless mayonnaise	Quaker Cremica Pvt. Ltd., Phillaur
Sesame seeds	Ghaziabad
Iceberg lettuce	Meena Agritech, Delhi
Fish fillet patties	Amalgam Foods Ltd., Kochi.
Iceberg lettuce	Ooty Farms & Orchards, Ooty
Vegetables for the patties	Finns Frozen Foods & Jain Foods (Nasik, Jalgaon)
Mutton and mutton patties	Al Kabeer, Hyderabad

Source: Business India, October 4, 1999.

McDonald's Indian Menu

Vegetarian	Non Vegetarian
McVeggie	Chicken Maharaja Mac
McAlooTikki	McChicken Burger
Paneer Salsa Wrap	Shahi Chicken McCurry
Crispy Chinese	Wrap Chicken Mexican
McCurry Pan	Fillet-O-Fish
Pizza McPuff	

"Mc Donald's mein hai kuch baat" projects McDonald's as a place for the whole family to enjoy. When McDonald's entered in India it was mainly perceived as targeting the urban upper class people. Today it positions itself as an affordable place to eat without compromising on the quality of food, service and hygiene.

McDonalds Promoting its Breakfast through psychological pricing

Source: http://www.mcdonaldsindia.com/promotions.html

McDonald's Brand Positioning and Messaging

One of the greatest attributes of McDonald's is its "everyday affordability" message that drives customers to McDonald's restaurants. McDonald's wanted to position itself as 'Indian' and a promoter of 'family values and culture', as well as being 'comfortable and easy'. One of the aims of McDonald's is to create a standardized set of items that taste the same in different countries. McDonald's learned that, although there are substantial cost savings through standardization, being able to adapt to an environment ensures success. Therefore the concept of "think global, act local" has been clearly adopted by McDonald's.

The Happy Price campaign has also been promoted via virals. Outdoor has also promoted a home delivery option in a country where home delivery is common in urban areas.

McDonald's has also been exploring strategic tie-ups with Indian sports properties such as the IPL cricket tournament, where it was one of the event's food providers.

McDonalds Tie up with Symbiosis

McDonald's, India's leading food service retailer has tied up with Symbiosis International University – SCCE as part of their continuous effort to promote education among its employees and provide them with 'skills for life'. 'People' are thus one of McDonald's most important assets and knowledge and education hence plays an integral role in the development & growth of the employees. McDonald's believes in giving its employees 'skills for life' so that they can achieve success in every aspect of their lives. The post graduate programme has been exclusively designed for McDonald's employees with an extensive syllabus on efficient business management.

Location: The entry of McDonalds has been well planned and an extensive research was carried on before actually making the decision with an initial opening in delhi and Mumbai which was driven by affordability and brand recognition factors. Logistics play a critical role in location strategy. As a part of its QSR-quich service restraurant business, McDonalds decided to open outlets only within 500 km radius of its main distribution centres so it did not initially enter Kolkatta despite of huge urban and metropolitan character. It opened up outlets in satellite cities near Delhi like Gurgaon, Noida, Faridabad and near Mumbai like Pune. It also entered into tourist cities like Jaipur, shimla, Mathura and cities with eating out culture like Bangalore, Chandigarh and Ahmedabad. It tied up with state owned Bharat Petroleum Corporation and opened up outlets at petrol stations ion and around delhi. Keeping large Indian lower middle class in view, outlets were opened in railway stations, bus stations, delhi metro rail corporation and crowded ISBT of Delhi, highways specially Delhi - Agra, Delhi -Jaipur, Delhi - Ludhiana, Mumbai – Pune. Moreover McDonalds has also targeted towards the shopping malls and new multiplexes in metros like Delhi and Mumbai.

Green sensitivity – From the political point of view Maneka Gandhi group opposes McDonalds and KFC. According to them junk food destroy ecological balance and cause behavioural disorders since they have excessive levels of monosodium glutamate (msg). They cater to only rich segment of society so they are anti social. So McDonalds instituted a special fund to support green movement in Delhi. In Mumbai, in addition to financial contribution, it sponsored community related activities as "keep your city clean", to promote environmental consciousness. In noida and vasant vihar it put up pro environmental advertisements like we love green. McDonalds also sponsored "Olympic Day run" in Vadodara, Gujarat. McDonalds also introduced baked dishes instead of fried like Mc Curry pan.

Customer Perception and Customer Expectation

Customer perception is a key factor affecting a product's success. Many potentially revolutionary products have failed simply because of their inability to build a healthy perception about themselves in the customers' minds. McDonalds being an internationally renowned brand brings with it certain expectations for the customers.

Target Segment	What is McDonald's for me?
A Family with children	A treat to children, a fun place to be for the children.
Urban customer on the move	Great taste, quick service without affecting the work schedule
Teenager	Hangout with friends, but keep it affordable.

Customers expect it to be an ambient, hygienic and a little sophisticated brand that respects their values. The customer's expect the brand to enhance their self-image. Customer responses obtained at the different franchisees in Delhi outlet confirmed the fact that they connect strongly with the brand. However, fulfilling some of the customer expectations like a broader product variety provide McDonald's a great scope for improvement.

Conclusion

McDonald's faces some difficult challenges. Key to its future success will be maintaining its core strengths—an unwavering focus on quality and consistency—while carefully experimenting with new options. These innovative initiatives could include launching higher-end restaurants under new brands that wouldn't be saddled with McDonald's fast-food image. The company could also look into expanding more aggressively abroad where the prospects for significant growth are greater.

The company's environment efforts, while important, should not overshadow its marketing initiatives, which are what the company is all about.

References:

http://www.economia.unimore.it/marchi_gianluca/Marketing%20internazionale%20M2/Materiali/McDonalds_India.pdf

http://d.scribd.com/docs/1f7bb4nqz9vuw6i1tn3h.pdf

http://www.mcdonaldsindia.com/aboutus.html

http://216.139.227.101/interactive/mcd2007- McDonalds Corporation

http://www.slideshare.net/guest47c65d/mcdonalds- McDonalds India

http://www.slideshare.net/guest47c65d/mcdonalds

http://www.scribd.com/doc/4980239/mcdonalds1193592835386271?autodown=pdf

http://www.scribd.com/doc/13142703/Marketing-MixMcdonalds-India

www.123oye.com/companies/**mcdonalds**-jobs-**india**.html

www.scribd.com/doc/2303069/Case-McDonalds-India-Launch

Adapted from –http://www.indiainfoline.com/Markets/News/McDonalds-ties-up-with-Symbiosis-Institute/5239209360

10

Wal-mart In India - Boom or Doom

Ms. Priyanka Virmani
Ms. Pradnaya Deshpande
Bharati Vidyapeeth University, Institute of Management and Research ,New Delhi

Wal-Mart - ?

Wal-Mart Stores Inc operates Wal-Mart discount stores, Super centers, Neighborhood Markets and Sam's Club locations in the US. The first Wal-Mart store was opened in 1962 in Rogers, AR. The Bentonville –based $316billion Wal-Mart has more than 6,600 stores worldwide. As of January 04, 2007, revenue was $33.3 billion higher than it was one year ago. It is the largest private employer in the United States and Mexico. Wal-Mart is the largest grocery retailer in the United States, with an estimated 20 percent of the retail grocery and consumables business, and is also the largest toy seller in the United States, with an estimated 45 percent of the retail toy business, having surpassed Toys "R" Us in the late 1990s. The company operates in 15 countries worldwide which include Argentina, Brazil, Canada, China, Costa Rica, El Salvador, Guatemala, Honduras, Japan, Mexico, Nicaragua, Puerto Rico and the UK. The company's securities are listed on the New York Stock Exchange and NYSE Arca, formerly the Pacific Stock Exchange, under the symbol WMT.

Motivation to expand to Global Markets

Organic growth: Wal-Mart has been growing organically by the introduction of new products and services on a regular basis. It is also constantly improving its service management to reduce the cost of logistics and thereby generate more profits. Same store sales is a key metric used to measure organic growth.

Acquisitions: Over the years, Wal-Mart has acquired many companies in the US as well in other countries to expand their business.

Market expansion: The retail industry was growing at a rapid pace when Wal-Mart realised the scope for expansion in the global market. Same store sales for Wal-Mart have not increased at a decent pace in recent years and therefore the need for market expansion has evolved. It has been a huge success across the world like North America (Canada), Central America (Mexico and Costa Rica), Asia (China and Japan), South America (Brazil and Argentina) and Europe (UK).

Wal-Mart's ability to transport the company's unique culture and effective retailing concepts to each new country has been the bottom line for Wal-Mart's successful international operations. The management and staff reconcile themselves to local cultures to ensure best service. They also participate in local community events. Wal-Mart International has realised a huge growth with potential for much greater development worldwide because of its understanding of local needs and satisfying them.

Wal-Mart International acquired Asda (UK's retailer) on July 26, 1999. Since then Asda claims it has gained one million more customers.

Although efforts to expand in some parts of Europe (Germany) and North-Eastern Asia (Korea) have failed, Wal-Mart learns and adapts to newer environments much faster than any other retailer in this world.

A Failure in Germany and Korea

Wal-Mart failed in Germany because of several reasons. Wal-Mart's biggest strength is competing on price, but because local German stores Aldi and Lidl were able to deliver good quality grocery at very affordable prices, Wal-Mart could never compete. Aldi and Lidl promoted weekly sales and heavily discounted merchandise, which drew the customers back to it. Wal-Mart opened all the stores in the suburbs and customers were very reluctant to drive that far for grocery. With the local shops providing better rates, customers had no need to drive to the suburbs. People were not even comfortable with the idea of the hypermarket.

Even in South Korea, local retailers provided huge discounts and therefore Wal-Mart could not compete on pricing. Many Koreans have never heard of Wal-Mart. There is only a single store in Seoul that has a population of 10 million.

Wal-Mart's typical business model

It has a highly efficient service channel management, which make it possible to buy directly from producers. Also, the company's innovative information technology (like use of satellite communication to link corporate headquarters with stores nationwide) has given Wal-Mart an edge over its competitors. It tries to compete on price with local merchants and is always located in a neighbourhood that is convenient to the customers.

Keenness to enter India

India is witnessing an unprecedented consumption boom. The economy is growing at the rapid rate of 7-8 per cent and has resulted in greater income dynamics, driven by factors such as favorable demographics and growth in aspirational consumption.

Retailing in India is currently estimated to be $300 billion; of which organized retailing (i.e. modern trade) makes up 5 per cent. Organized retail is expected to grow at a rate of approximately 35 per cent per annum till 2010.

The factors driving Indian retail growth are:

- **Sixty per cent** of the total population below 30 years of age is expected to have high purchasing power.
- **Increasing** double income families in cities have resulted in a higher disposable income for consumers.
- **Salary hike** is another reason for extra spending power, which may result in more consumption.
- Shopping has replaced outing as a most favoured option among the increasing tribe of **DINK couples.**
- Changing consumption patterns specially in the urban areas are helping the cause. With more families going nuclear, buying additional household products become necessity products.
- Indian consumers' **self-esteem needs** are satisfied by purchasing things from big multinationals like Wal-Mart. The new concept of shopping under one roof (super centre) is also what the Indian consumers have always wanted to experiment with.

Joint venture with Bharti Enterprises

Bharti Group and Wal-Mart have joined hands to tap the retailing opportunities in India. Bharti, with its deep knowledge of India's fast growing consumer market, and Wal-Mart, with its extensive global retail experience, share the same commitment to building relationships with producers to provide great quality at reasonable prices to consumers everyday.

Wal-Mart's alliance with Bharti Enterprises appears to be prompted by a need to get around restrictions on foreign companies, which are currently barred from operating multi-product retail chains in India. Under the deal, Wal-Mart and Bharti Enterprises will set up a joint venture to manage procurement, inventories and logistics, while stores will be set up under a franchise agreement.

Bharti will manage the front-end of the business, while Wal-Mart will take care of the supply chain, logistics and other back-end operations. The joint venture helps Wal-Mart easily understand the Indian market. This is possible because Bharti has a strong grip over the needs and wants of customers while Wal-Mart provides cost-effective logistics, helping Bharti sustain the price competition. Bharti Enterprises already has a retail network and is a household name in telecom, and this deal will prove its capabilities as a company with strong execution capability.

The competitors

Reliance Industries has entered the retailing industry and will operate hypermarkets, convenience and specialty stores as well as business-to-business operations, sell food, clothing, electrical consumer durables, luxury goods and financial and travel services. It is setting up distribution infrastructure to enjoy the benefits of competitive pricing.

Infiniti Retail Ltd (a Tata Group company) has also entered the market to make most of the growing retail sector in India. The Tata Group has partnered with Woolworths Ltd, Australia's biggest retailer, for sourcing and technical support. It opened the first store in Mumbai in October 2006.

Pantaloon Retail India, which has stores like Big Bazaar spread all over India, is also ready to expand the business and is planning to open 100 stores by December 2007.

Retailer	Brands
Early Birds	
K Raheja Group	Shopper's Stop, Crossword, Inorbit, Mall Hyper City, Café Brio/ Desi café
Future Group	Pantaloon, Big Bazaar, Food Bazaar, Fashion Station, Blue Sky
TATA Group	Trent
Landmark	Landmark
RPG	Spencer's, Music World
Debutantes	
Reliance	Reliance Fresh
Bharti-Wal-Mart	Field Fresh
In The Pipeline	
Aditya Birla	Madura Garments, Birla Sun life Insurance, Idea cellular, Planet Fashion and Trouser Town
Hero Group	Easy Bill
Carrefour/Tesco	Multi–Format Retailers

Will Wal-Mart succeed?

Wal-Mart has been a global company for many years. Apart from a couple of failures, it has been a huge success because of its understanding of the local markets. In India, it will be able to succeed because it has the best know-how to provide the right set of products to the right set of customers.

Customers are also hungry for new ways of shopping. The joint venture with Bharti Enterprises will prove a smart move as Bharti is one of the biggest consumer players in the market and has adequate knowledge about the Indian market. This will make the cultural transition easy for Wal-Mart.

Questions to be answered

1. Wal-Mart in India - what lies ahead?
2. Entry of Wal-Mart & hence the turnaround in the Indian Retail Industry?

11

Launch and Marketing Strategy of the "Business and Economy" Magazine – "Pinnacle"

Mr. Puneet Bansal
puneet@iitdmba.com

Mr. Shivendu Pratap
shivendu@iitdmba.com

IIT, Delhi

Executive summary

The launch of a new product is always a challenge for any organization where the organization has to initially address the issues of its survival and then the issue of sustainable growth. To attain both the objectives, the product launch and marketing strategy become one of the core issues. In case of a consumer non durable product launched in an already flooded market of competitors, this concern becomes even more important. Through our work, we have touched upon the aspects of the strategy of marketing & launching of Business & Economy magazine by Planman media house. The paper covers the full spectrum of marketing: brand positioning, segmentation, pricing, distribution, sales promotion and advertising. The financials of the company have also been worked out in terms of fixed and variable costs so as to judge the company's ability in recovering the costs and its present status. The Parent Company Planman Group has adopted a long term strategy for the initiative and has pumped money in the past when it was not able to recover its operating cost. The case leads us to know the impact of the decisions taken in the corporate world regarding branding decisions. Based on our findings, we have also made certain recommendations which will help the company to improve upon the future revenues.

Introduction

Planman group is India's leading multi interest consulting and business Services Corporation engaging a variety of organizations, institutions and enterprises in diverse industry and government verticals. Planman group has been involved in the education business for a long time. With that background, launching of a business magazine seemed to be natural extension of business service of the group. The magazine Business & Economy was launched on June 16, 2005 in Delhi and June 17, 2005 in Mumbai. The product has been launched on a rough ground which is already flooded with the likes of Business world, Business Today. Not to mention the already increasing business sections of news dailies & news channels, already posing to be an overdose of news. That way, to make a brand successful and more importantly, to achieve an early break-even, the strategies have to be dot-on-target. That's why an attempt has been made to make an analysis on various branding constructs.

Brand Positioning

Beyond deciding which segments of the market B&E will target, the company has decided what positions it wants to occupy in those segments .Positioning involves implanting the B&E 's unique benefits and differentiation in customers minds. B&E's competitor Business today is positioned as a product which gives an insight in latest business dealings and each issue contains a survey related to either business functioning or business education. Similarly business week is positioned as the cheapest digest of business environment every issue of which contains an in-depth analysis of a business situation. Consumers are overloaded with information about the products and services. To simplify the buying process, consumers organize products, services, and companies into categories and position them in their minds .A products position is the complex set of perceptions, impressions and feelings that consumers have for the product compared with competing products.

Planman media believes that B&E should aggressively promote only one benefit to the target market. It has developed a unique selling proposition which hinges on providing international quality information without sacrificing the quality of magazine. Not all brand differences are meaningful or worthwhile, not every difference makes a good differentiator .Each difference has the potential to create company costs and company benefits. Planman has adopted "More for more" brand positioning strategy which involves providing the most upscale product and charging a higher price to cover the higher costs. Not only is the marketing offered high in quality, it also gives prestige to the buyer. It symbolizes status and loftier lifestyle. From this view point Planman has priced B&E at Rs 20, which is the expensive by Rs5 as compared to Business today and by Rs10 as compared to business world. Planman media wants to create an image of B&E as the most influential business magazine by providing information which deals with business as well as economy. This differentiation is done by including foreign articles on business dealings, snippets of foreign economy, national business analysis and economy update. Brand positioning can be achieved through either aggressive marketing or providing a different touch and appeal in the product as compared to the competitors or using a brand ambassador for promoting the image of the product. Planman media uses Prof.Arindham choudhary as its brand ambassador for promoting B&E as a product which is tried and tested by eminent economist's .Every issue contains Prof .Arindham's editorial article which discusses a pressing issue at hand.

Pricing

Price is the amount of money charged for a product or service or the value exchanged for the benefits of the product or service. For a new product like B&E, it is necessary to understand its positioning before a price is set. It is necessary to make sure that it is not too low, or the product will not be taken seriously. If it is too high, the potential customer will not take the risk. Planman has identified the following general pricing strategies: ***Product Line:*** Setting price steps between product line items ***Optional Product:*** Pricing optional or accessory products ***Captive Product:*** Pricing products that must be used with the main product ***By-Product:*** Pricing low value by product to get rid of them ***Product Bundle:*** Pricing bundles of products sold together B&E being a new product, Planman has adopted new Product Pricing strategy viz.: ***Market Penetration:*** Set a low initial price in order to penetrate the market quickly and deeply to win a large market share. Works when:

- Market is highly price sensitive.
- Production and distribution costs fall as sales volume increases
- Low price must help keep out the competition

Market-Skimming: Set high prices to "skim" revenue layer by layer from the market. Works when:

- Quality and image support the higher price
- Enough buyers want the product at that price
- Cost of producing a small volume cannot be high
- Competitors should not be able to enter the market easily

Price Adjustment

The following are price adjustments strategies used by Planman media based on changing situations: ***Discount & Allowance:*** reduced prices to reward customer responses such as paying early or promoting the product ***Discriminatory:*** adjusting prices to allow for differences in customers, products, and locations ***Psychological:*** adjusting prices for psychological effects. ***Value:*** adjusting prices to offer the right combination of quality and service at a fair price ***Promotional:*** temporarily reducing prices to increase short-run sales ***Geographical:*** adjusting prices to account for geographic location of customer. ***International:*** adjusting prices in international markets In many markets, a high price contributes to the perception of the product as being of premium value. The perception of product or service is important. Will this be the image that will get customers to buy? Are customers more price-conscious? These are some of the questions which B&E has tried to figure out and decide about the pricing of the magazine. Planman continuously keeps a tap about what competitors are doing. It is probably unwise to set prices too much higher or lower without a good reason. If price is too low, B&E will just be throwing away profit. If price is too high, B&E will lose customers, unless it can offer them something they can't get elsewhere. B&E has found out that it can be useful to charge different prices to different customers, e.g. to customers who purchase repeatedly, or buy add-on or related products, as a thank you for their loyalty. To increase the reach of its product, Planman media has a free internet edition of every B&E issue. This way it has been able to attract the net savvy customers who are more prone to internet reading than going through the hard copy edition.

Brand Loyalty

Brand Loyalty is the consumer's conscious or unconscious decision, expressed through intention or behavior, to repurchase a brand continually. In order to create brand loyalty, Planman's advertisers has been trying to break consumer habits, help them acquire new habits, and reinforce those habits by reminding consumers of the value of their purchase and encourage them to continue purchasing those products in the future. The image surrounding a B&E's brand is the principal source of its competitive advantage and is therefore a valuable strategic asset. The challenge for B&E is to avoid the pitfalls of portraying a muddled or negative image, and instead, create a broad brand vision or identity that recognizes a brand as something greater than a set of attributes that can be imitated or surpassed. In fact, a Planman views its brand to be not just a product or service, but as an overall brand image that defines a company's philosophies. A brand needs more than identity; it needs a personality. Just like a person without attention-grabbing characteristics, a brand with no personality can easily be passed right over. A strong symbol or company logo can also help to generate brand loyalty by making it quickly identifiable. From the design of a new product to the extension of a mature brand, effective marketing strategies depend on a thorough understanding of the motivation, learning, memory, and decision processes that influence what consumers buy. Theories of consumer behavior have been repeatedly linked to managerial decisions involving development and launching of new products, segmentation, timing of market entry, and brand management. Subsequently, the issue of brand loyalty has been examined at great length. Branding is by far one of the most important factors influencing B&E's success or failure in the marketplace, and has a dramatic impact on how the "company behind the brand" is perceived by the buying public. In other words, the brand is not just a representation of a company's product; it is a symbol of the company itself, and that is where the core of brand loyalty lies.

Brand positioning

Planman media has been trying to make it certain that the development of a brand and market positioning strategy encompasses much more than a logo or slogan. An effective brand position must capture the distinctive mission, aspirations, and strengths of Planman Group and appeal to the motivations and interests of the marketplace. These are the overriding objectives of Planman media's approach to branding. Planman media's work on branding and market positioning typically includes the following:

- Evaluation and determination of an it's differentiating strengths vis-à-vis its competitors and the translation of those into preliminary brand ideas and concepts that can be further tested among prospective subscribers and other markets.

- Rigorous, empirically sound testing of brand and market positioning ideas to evaluate the effectiveness of presenting new ideas and its characteristics, programs, and initiatives to targeted customers or other key audiences.

Identifying where a specific brand is placed within the marketplace and its relationship to competitive brands, brand positioning is determined by defining the brand's benefits to the consumer, opportunities for which the brand is best suited, the brand's target audience, and who its main competitors are.

To achieve the benefits of brand positioning, it is necessary to research in-depth the market position (or lack thereof) of the brand. Brand maps and forms are created to profile the brand positioning, comparing the results with competitive brands. In realizing the benefits of brand positioning, it is important to understand that not all brands are competitors. A consumer may be presented with six brands of one product and only consider three out of the six as a purchasing choice. The consumer may have encountered a negative experience with a specific brand and may never consider purchasing it again, or there may be a brand that simply does not stand out to the consumer and it is passed up. Keeping these key points in mind the Planman media has initiated an annual B&E awards for corporate excellence .This has helped in creating a brand association and recall for the magazine. Special issues like collectors issue are published every year; this issue focuses on ranking industry sectors and brands, creating great awareness for the magazine.

Readership Profile

Indian Council for Market Research (ICMR) Circulation Survey for Planman Media (2005) has come out with the results which have been portrayed in the form of pie chart (fig 1) and bar chart (fig2) .The pie chart shows the profile of the average urban graduate readers across the country. Through this pie chart it can be seen that the major portion of the readership is taken up by age group 25 -34 years while the least contributing age group is 55 plus years.

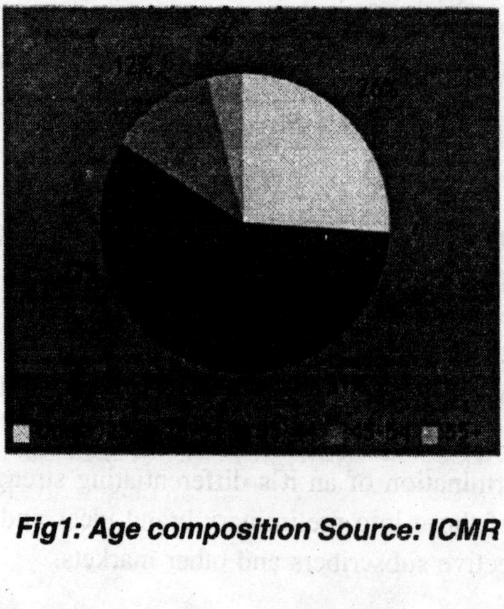

Fig1: Age composition Source: ICMR

This survey has helped Planman media to know on which age group it should focus more to increase the market penetration. The bar chart shows the industry wise breakup of B&E magazine. From the bar chart it can be seen that the professionals and business services contribute the maximum of the B&E's readership.

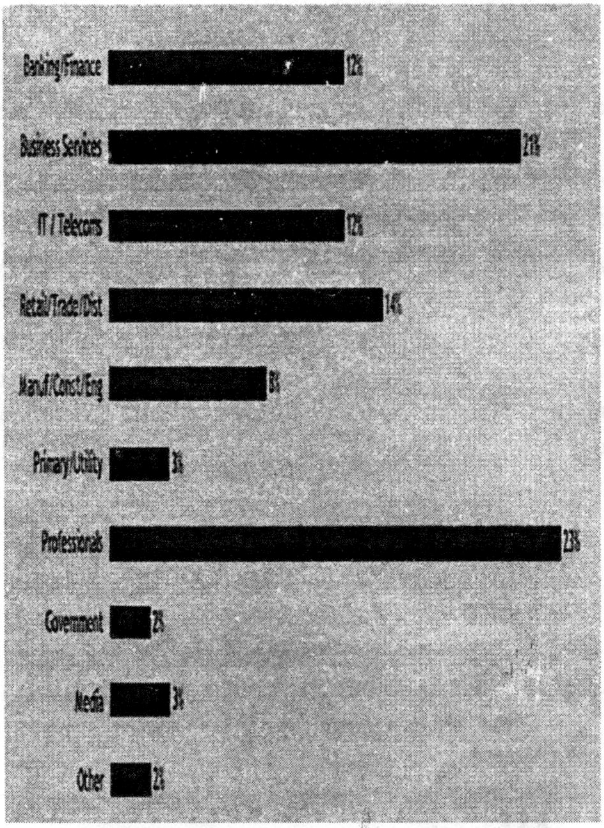

Fig 2: B&E's penetration across industries

Source: ICMR Circulation Survey for Planman Media (2005)

Product life cycle

Various stages in product life cycle of the product are:

• **Introduction stage:** In the introduction stage, the firm seeks to build product awareness and develop a market for the product. The impact on the marketing mix is as follows: **o** Product branding and quality level is established and intellectual property **o** protection such as patents and trademarks are obtained. **o** Pricing may be low penetration pricing to build market share rapidly, or high **o** skim pricing to recover development costs. **o** Distribution is selective until consumers show acceptance of the product. **o** Promotion is aimed at innovators and early adopters. Marketing communications seeks to build product awareness and to educate potential consumers about the product.

• **Growth stage** In the growth stage, the firm seeks to build brand preference and increase market share. **o** Product quality is maintained and additional features and support services may be added. **o** Pricing is maintained as the firm enjoys increasing demand with little competition.

o Distribution channels are added as demand increases and customers accept the product. o Promotion is aimed at a broader audience.

• **Maturity stage** At maturity, the strong growth in sales diminishes. Competition may appear with similar products. The primary objective at this point is to defend market share while maximizing profit. **o** Product features may be enhanced to differentiate the product from that of competitors. **o** Pricing may be lower because of the new competition. **o** Distribution becomes more intensive and incentives may be offered to encourage preference over competing products. **o** Promotion emphasizes product differentiation.

• **Decline stage** As sales decline, the firm has several options: **o** Maintain the product, possibly rejuvenating it by adding new features and finding new uses. **o** Harvest the product - reduce costs and continue to offer it, possibly to loyal niche segment. **o** Discontinue the product, liquidating remaining inventory or selling it to another firm that is willing to continue the product. **o** The marketing mix decisions in the decline phase will depend on the selected strategy. For example, the product may be changed if it is being rejuvenated, or left unchanged if it is being harvested or liquidated.

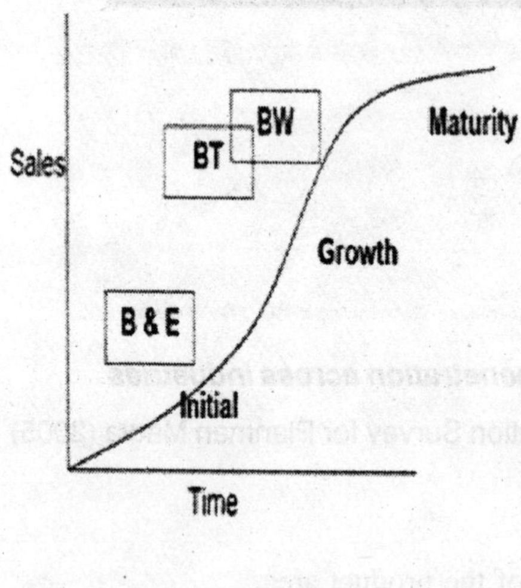

BW - Business world

BT - Business today

B & E - Business & Economy

The price may be maintained if the product is harvested, or reduced drastically if liquidated. Under the above conditions and after discussing with the B&E's official we came to conclusion that B&E is in initial stage of product life cycle while its competitors Business Today and Business World are both in the growth stage as shown fig3.

Distribution Network

The magazine is exclusively distributed by IBH (Indian Book House) at metros and other major cities like Hyderabad, Pune, Bangalore, Chandigarh, Trivandrum and Ahmedabad.

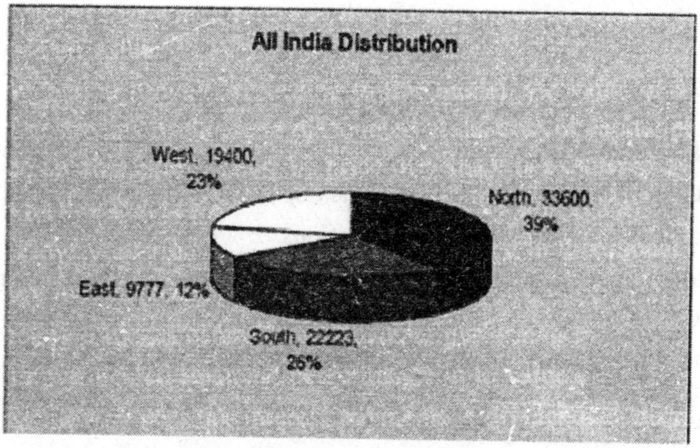

Fig 4: Region wise breakup of distribution of B&E in India. Source: Indian Council for Market Research (ICMR) Circulation Survey (2005)

According to the research conducted by the Indian Council for Market Research (ICMR) Circulation Survey (2005) for Planman media ,it was found out that northern part of India contributes maximum towards the distribution of B&E magazine(as shown in fig 4). It can be seen for the pie chart that the eastern region comprises only of 12,% of the total distribution of the B&E magazine.

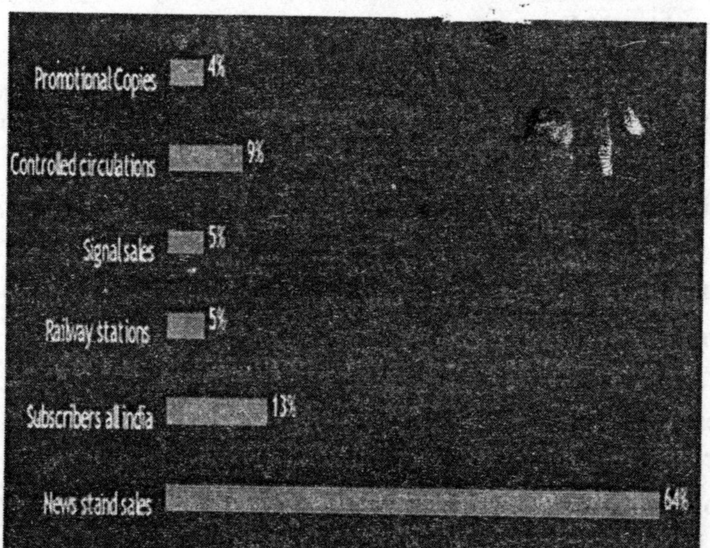

Fig 5: Ways of distribution of B&E Source: Indian Council for Market Research (ICMR) Circulation Survey (2005)

The bar chart (fig 5) shows the ways of distribution channels adopted by Planman media for selling the B&E magazine. The way of distributing and selling the magazine includes subscription, signal sales, sales at railway stations, newsstand etc. From the fig 5 it can be noted that news stand sales is the major contributor towards the sales of the magazine.

Advertising

To advertise its product, Planman consulting is

1. Using its in house ad-agency
   - For its ad-campaigns in dailies like Times of India, Hindustan Times etc.,
   - For cross advertising in its other publications.
2. Using an outdoor agency called MOMS (Madison outdoor media servicing) for hoardings, advertising at POP's etc.
2. Recently it has also started advertising on Television.

Sales Promotion

Sales promotion is any initiative undertaken by an organization to promote an increase in sales, usage or trial of a product or service (i.e. initiatives that are not covered by the other elements of the marketing communications or promotions mix). Sales promotions are varied. Often they are original and creative, and hence a comprehensive list of all available techniques is virtually impossible (since original sales promotions are launched daily!). Sales promotions can be directed at the customer, sales staff, or distribution channel members (such as retailers). Sales promotions targeted at the consumer are called consumer sales promotions. Sales promotions targeted at retailers and wholesale are called trade sales promotions. Some sale promotions, particularly ones with unusual methods, are considered gimmick by many. The various sales promotion technique sued by B&E are:

- **Price deal:** A temporary reduction in the price
- **Price-pack deal**: The packaging offers a consumer a certain percentage more of the product for the same price (for example, 25 percent extra).
- **Free-standing insert (FSI)**: A coupon booklet is inserted into the local newspaper for delivery.
- **On-shelf couponing**: Coupons are present at the shelf where the product is available.
- **On-line couponing**: Coupons are available on line. Consumers print them out and take them to the store.
- **Contests/sweepstakes/games**: The consumer is automatically entered into the event by purchasing the product.
- **Promotional copies** : During the launch around 5% of the total copies are distributed to educational institutes, corporate, institutions etc in various
- **Subscription Discounts**: Frequent discounts are floated to give fillip to sales.

Point-of-sale displays

- Aisle interrupter: A sign the juts into the aisle from the shelf.
- Dangler: A sign that sways when a consumer walks by it.
- Dump bin: A bin full of products dumped inside.
- Glorifier: A small stage that elevates a product above other products.
- Wobblers: A sign that jiggles.
- Lipstick Board: A board on which messages are written in crayon.

Findings

The analysis shows that the magazine has still not achieved break even with existing level of price and volume sales unless the subscription increases further to boost the advertising revenues, it may take several years for the magazine to recover its fixed cost. An estimate of the revenues generated per annum: — Rs. 9 crores Detailed financial analysis of B&E can be seen in the following attached file Puneet_Shivendu_IIT Delhi_FINANCIAL WORKING FOR B&E

What is also noticeable is that the magazine doesn't generate that high a revenue from advertising, since it is not as established as some of its competitors like BT, BW, and BI etc.

The Parent Company Planman Group has adopted a long term strategy for the initiative and has pumped money in the past when it was not able to recover its operating cost. The main profitability of a magazine is based on its advertising revenues which essentially depends on authentic subscription/readership surveys and also the image that magazine creates for itself.

Recommendations Pricing

A price of Rs 20 for an 'Initial Stage' magazine is an overprice as compared to its competitors Business Today and Business Week which are priced at Rs 15 and Rs 10 respectively

Product image

- Highly Diverse Content and with less focus on information when compared to that of competitors
- Foreign articles can be business oriented in nature
- Avoiding content on glamour and fashion to correctly position the brand **Distribution**
- Increase the number of Distributorship towns **Widening the target segment**
- Introduce a section 'Careers and Education' to attract student population
- Increase subscription figures by tie-ups with hotels ,airlines, conferences

Content

Majority of the advertisements still focus on the group businesses like IIPM, The Chief Executive forum etc. which gives it the feel of a newsletter. B&E has to come out of the shadows of its business house.

References

1. Mr. Abhimanyu Gosh, CEO, Planman Media
2. Mr. Gautam Sharma, President-Sales & Marketing, Planman Media.
3. Mr. Kedar Sharma, Vice-President, National Readership Survey.
4. www.newswatch.in October 31,2006 5. Indian Council for Market Research (ICMR) Circulation Survey for Planman Media (2005)
6. Website for the registrar of newspapers in India, for the circulation figures (www.rni.nic.in) November 5,2006
7. www.hinduonnet.com/businessline November 10,2006
8. www.planman.org October 22,2006

12

Mergers & Acquisition as Strategic Tool for Corporate Growth - A Case Study on the Merger of Reliance Industries Limited & Reliance Petroleum Limited

Ms. Ritu Srivastava
Assistant Professor
NIILM Centre for Management Studies, New Delhi
rsrivastava@niilm.com
Dr. Ajay Prakash
Assistant Professor
Department of Business Administration, Faculty of Commerce, University of Lucknow
ritukaustubh@rediffmail.com

Introduction to Mergers & Acquisitions as a Strategic Tool

The phrase mergers and acquisitions (abbreviated M&A) refers to the aspect of corporate strategy, corporate finance and management dealing with the buying, selling and combining of different companies that can aid, finance, or help a growing company in a given industry grow rapidly without having to create another business entity. Economic and political stability across the globe have facilitated the same, encouraging corporate growth which in turn is generating more and more M&A activities. Although they are often uttered in the same breath and used as though they were synonymous, the terms merger and acquisition are different strategies by definition. When one company takes over another and clearly established itself as the new owner, the purchase is called an acquisition. When merger happens when two firms, often of about the same size, agree to go forward as a single new company rather than remain separately owned and operated. This kind of action is more precisely referred to as a "merger of equals". Both companies' stocks are surrendered and new company stock is issued in its place. A purchase deal will also be called a merger when both CEOs agree that joining together is in the best interest of both of their companies. But when the deal is unfriendly - that is, when the target company does not want to be purchased - it is always regarded as an acquisition. This is challengeable. An acquisition can be either friendly or hostile. An example of a friendly takeover was when Microsoft bought Fast Search and Transfer (OSE Stock Exchange, Ticker FAST).CEO of the acquired company (FAST) revealed that they had been working with Microsoft for more than 6 months to get the deal which was announced in January, 2008.

Classification of Merger & Acquisition :

I On the basis of formation of new legal entities-

Consolidation: Merger of equals, with new legal entity being formed. A + B = C

Acquisition of Stock (Tender Offer): Tender Offers: It involves an invitation to current shareholders of target firm to offer-up their stock for sale. Therefore there is purchase of stock & assets and liabilities of firm. Here shareholder or even management approval is not required

Acquisition of Assets: It involves only purchases of assets. Here approval of only 50% of the shareholders is required. However it would involve high expenditure on account of legal fees for individual transfer of assets. But integration is difficult without 100% shares and any resistance from management or shareholders may raise prices.

Holding Company: Purchases stock in another firm, but does not plan to merge (at least for the present)

II On the basis of expansion of the value chain of business

Horizontal Merger: It refers to merger of firms engaged in the same line of business in the same industry.

Examples: The formation of Brook Bond Lipton India Ltd. through the merger Lipton India and Brook Bond ,The merger of Bank of Mathura with ICICI (Industrial Credit and Investment Corporation of India) Bank

Vertical Merger: It refers to merger of firms engaged at different stages of production of the same good in an industry. For example: Merger of a Leather tannery with a shoe company where the shoe company would be the surviving company. The benefit is improved coordination of activities, lower inventory levels, and higher market power of the combined entity.

Circular Merger: It refers merger of firms for facilitating activities like distribution and R&D since a small company may not be able to get good prices to make the project more viable. For example: Ranbaxy

Conglomerate Merger: It refers to merger of firms engaged in unrelated or assorted fields. This was earlier very popular among cash rich companies as a means to obtain tax advantage of set off of losses by merging with loss making group companies. Other benefits can be reduction or elimination of certain overhead expenses.

Key features in M&A strategies are as follows:

1. A merger must be approved by a vote of the stockholders of each firm. Typically, votes of the owners of 2/3 of the shares are required for approval. Also the shareholders of the acquired firm have appraisal rights. This means that they can demand that their shares be purchased at a fair value by the acquiring firm. Often the acquiring firm and thedissenting shareholders of the acquired firm cannot agree on a fair value, which results inexpensive legal proceedings.

2. A merger is legally straightforward. It avoids the necessity of transferring title of each individual asset of the acquired firm to the acquiring firm. It does not cost as much as other forms of acquisition.The principal economic rationale of a merger is that the value of the combined entity isexpected to be greater than the sum of the independent values of the merging entities. The most plausible reasons for mergers are strategic benefits, economies of scale, economies of scope, utilization of surplus funds, complementary resources, tax shields, economies of vertical integration and managerial effectiveness.

3. An acquisition is a corporate action in which a company buys most, if not all, of the target company's ownership stakes in order to assume control of the target firm. Acquisitions are often made as part of a company's growth strategy whereby it is more beneficial to take over an existing firm's operations and niche compared to expanding on its own. Acquisitions are often paid in cash, the acquiring company's stock or a combination of both. A bidding firm can also buy another simply by purchasing all its assets. This involves a costly legal transfer of title and must be approved by the shareholders of the selling firm. A takeover is the transfer of control from one group to another. Normally, the acquiring firm (the bidder) makes an offer for the target firm. In a proxy contest, a group of dissident shareholders will seek to obtain enough votes to gain control of the board of directors.

4. Acquisitions can be either friendly or hostile. Friendly acquisitions occur when the target firm expresses its agreement to be acquired, whereas hostile acquisitions don't have the same agreement from the target firm and the acquiring firm needs to actively purchase large stakes of the target company in order to have a majority stake. In either case, the acquiring company often offers a premium on the market price of the target company's shares in order to entice shareholders to sell. For example, News Corp.'s bid to acquire Dow Jones was equal to a 65% premium over the stock's market price.

Synergy through M&A:

The synergy from a merger or acquisition is defined as the value of the combined firm V(AB) less the value of the two firms as separate entities V(A) and V(B) or

Synergy = V (AB)-[V (A)-V (B)].

The shareholders of the acquiring firm will gain if the synergy from the merger is greater than the premium.The term synergy comes from the ancient Greek word syn-ergos, meaning 'working together'. Synergical effect occurs when two substances or factors combine to produce a greater effect together than the sum of those together operating independently. The principle of 2+2 =5, this theory expects that there is really "something out there which creates the merged entity to maximize the shareholders value". To put in other words, synergy is the ability of a merged company to create more shareholders value than standalone entity.

Synergy takes the form of revenue enhancement and cost reduction. Speaking of cutting down costs, this goal is typically achieved through economies of scale, particularly when it comes to sales and marketing, administrative, operating, and/or research and development costs. As for revenue synergies, these are achieved through product cross-selling, higher prices due to less competition, or staking a larger market share. When two companies in the same industry merge, the combined revenue tends to decline to the extend, they overlap with one another and some of the customers may also become alienated. For the merger to benefit the shareholders there must be ample opportunities for the cost reduction, so that the initial lost value is recovered in due course through synergy.

Operating Synergies

Operating synergies are those synergies that enable a firm to increase its operating income or increase growth or both. Economies of scale enable the combined firm to become more cost-efficient and profitable. Economies of scale result when a certain percentage increase in output results in a smaller increase in total costs, resulting in reduced average cost. It Profitable Growth by Acquisition doesn't matter whether this increased output is generated internally or acquired externally. When the firm grows to its "optimal" size, average costs are minimized and no further benefits are possible. There are many potential sources of economies of scale in acquisitions, the most common being the ability to spread fixed overhead, such as corporate headquarters expenses, executive salaries, and the operating costs of central computing systems,over additional output.Operating synergies can affect margins and growth, and through these the value of the firms involved in the M&A.

Financial Synergies

With financial synergies, the payoff can take the form of either higher cash flows or a lower cost of capital. Included are the following:

- A combination of a firm with available cash & few project opportunities and a firm with high return project & limited amount of cash can yield a payoff in terms of higher value for the combined firm. The increase in value comes from the projects that otherwise would not have been taken except with the excess cash available with the combined firm. This synergy becomes available when large firms acquire smaller firms.

- Debt capacity also increases when two firms combine thereby making their earnings and cash flows more stable and predictable. This enables them to borrow more than they could have as individual entities. It creates a tax benefit for the combined firm. This tax benefit can either be shown as higher cash flows or take the form of a lower cost of capital for the combined firm.
- Tax benefits can arise either from the acquisition taking advantage of tax laws or from the use of net operating losses to shelter income. Thus, a profitable firm by acquiring a loss making firm may be able to use the net operating losses to reduce its tax burden. Also, a firm that is able to increase its depreciation charges after an acquisition will save in taxes and increase its value.

Motives behind the M&A strategy:

Procurement of supplies:

To safeguard the source of supplies of raw materials or intermediary product; to obtain economies of purchase in the form of discount, savings in transportation costs, overhead costs in buying department, etc.; to share the benefits of suppliers economies by standardizing the materials.

Revamping production facilities:

To achieve economies of scale by amalgamating production facilities through more intensive utilization of plant and resources; to standardize product specifications, improvement of quality of product, expanding market and aiming at consumers satisfaction through strengthening after sale services; to obtain improved production technology and know-how from the offered company to reduce cost, improve quality and produce competitive products to retain and Improve market share.

Market expansion and strategy:

To eliminate competition and protect existing market; to obtain a new market outlets in possession of the offeree; to obtain new product for diversification or substitution of existing products and to enhance the product range

Financial strength:

To improve liquidity and have direct access to cash resource; to dispose of surplus and outdated assets for cash out of combined enterprise; to enhance gearing capacity, borrow on better strength and the greater assets backing; to avail tax benefits; to improve EPS (Earning per Share).

Strategic purpose:

The Acquirer Company view the merger to achieve strategic objectives through alternative type of combinations which may be horizontal, vertical, product expansion, market extensional or other specified unrelated objectives depending upon the corporate strategies. Thus, various types of combinations distinct with each other in nature are adopted to pursue this objective like vertical or horizontal combination.

Corporate friendliness:

Although it is rare but it is true that business houses exhibit degrees of cooperative spirit despite competitiveness in providing rescues to each other from hostile takeovers and cultivate situations of collaborations sharing goodwill of each other to achieve performance heights through business combinations. The combining corporate aim at circular combinations by pursuing this objective.

The purpose for an offeror company for acquiring another company shall be reflected in the corporate objectives. It has to decide the specific objectives to be achieved through acquisition. The basic purpose of merger or business combination is to achieve faster growth of the corporate business. Faster growth may be had through product improvement and competitive position.

Gains from M&A strategy

I.Gains for the Shareholders

Investment made by shareholders in the companies subject to merger should enhance in value. The sale of shares from one companys shareholders to another and holding investment in shares should give rise to greater values i.e. the opportunity gains in alternative investments. Shareholders may gain from merger in different ways viz. from the gains and achievements of the company i.e. through

(a) realization of monopoly profits;

(b) economies of scales;

(c) diversification of product line;

(d) acquisition of human assets and other resources not available otherwise;

(e) better investment opportunity in combinations.

One or more features would generally be available in each merger where shareholders may have attraction and favour merger.

II.Gains for the management

Managers are concerned with improving operations of the company, managing the affairs of the company effectively for all round gains and growth of the company which will provide them better deals in raising their status, perks and fringe benefits.

Mergers where all these things are the guaranteed outcome get support from the managers. At the same time, where managers have fear of displacement at the hands of new management in amalgamated company and also resultant depreciation from the merger then support from them becomes difficult.

III. Gains for the promoters

Mergers do offer to company promoters the advantage of increasing the size of their company and the financial structure and strength. They can convert a closely held and private limited company into a public company without contributing much wealth and without losing control.

IV. Gains to general public

Impact of mergers on general public could be viewed as aspect of benefits and costs to:

Consumer of the product or services;

Workers of the companies under combination;

General public affected in general having not been user or consumer or the worker in the companies under merger plan.

Valuation of Target Firms:

Valuing an acquisition candidate is similar to valuing any investment. The analyst estimates the incremental cash flows, determines an appropriate risk-adjusted discount rate, and then computes the net present value (NPV). If firm A is acquiring firm B, for example, then the acquisition makes economic sense if the value of the combined firm is greater than the value of firm A plus the value of firm B. Synergy is said to exist when the cash flow of the combined firm is greater than the sum of the cash flows for the two firms as separate companies. The gain from the merger is the present value of this difference in cash flows.

Valuation Procedures

The procedure for valuing an acquisition candidate depends on the source of the estimated gains. Different sources of synergy have different risks. Tax gains can be estimated fairly accurately and should be discounted at the cost of debt. Cost reductions through operating efficiencies can also be determined with some confidence. Such savings should be discounted at a normal weighted average cost of capital. Gains from strategic benefits are difficult to estimate and are often highly uncertain. A discount rate greater than the overall cost of capital would thus be appropriate.

The net present value (NPV) of the acquisition is equal to the gains less the cost of the acquisition. The cost depends on whether cash or stock is used as payment. The cost of an acquisition when cash is used is just the amount paid. The cost of the merger when common stock is used as the consideration (the payment) is equal to the percentage of the new firm that is owned by the previous shareholders in the acquired firm multiplied by the value of the new firm. In a cash merger the benefits go entirely to the acquiring firm, whereas in a stock-for-stock exchange the benefits are shared by the acquiring and acquired firms.

Whether to use cash or stock depends on three considerations. First, if the acquiring firm's management believes that its stock is overvalued, then a stock acquisition may be cheaper. Second, a cash acquisition is usually taxable, which may result in a higher price. Third, the use of stock means that the acquired firm will share in any gains from merger; if the merger has a negative NPV, however, then the acquired firm will share in the loss.

In valuing acquisitions, the following factors should be kept in mind. First, market values must not be ignored. Thus, there is no need to estimate the value of a publicly traded firm as a separate entity. Second, only those cash flows that are incremental are relevant to the analysis. Third, the discount rate used should reflect the risk associated with the incremental cash flows. Therefore, the acquiring firm should not use its own cost of capital to value the cash flows of another firm. Finally, acquisition may involve significant investment banking fees and costs.

EPS Method:-

Another method for valuation is Earning Per Share method in this the EPS of both the companies are determined in order to determine the share swap ratio. Example: A company wanted to be Merged with Company B then in this case swap ratio will be : Share Swap Ratio : EPS of Company B (Target Firm)

EPS of Company A (Merging or Acquirer Firm)

The case of the merger of Reliance Industries Limited & Reliance Petroleum Limited

Reliance Industries Limited (RIL)

RIL is India's largest private sector company on all major financialparameters with a turnover of Rs.139269 crore (US$ 34.7 billion), cash profit ofRs.25205 crore (US$ 3.8 billion) and net worth of Rs.81449 crore (US$ 20.3billion) as of March 31, 2008. RIL is the first private sector company from India to feature in theFortune Global 500 list of 'World's Largest Corporations' and ranks 103rd amongst the world's Top 200 companies in terms of profits. RIL is amongst the30 fastest climbers ranked by Fortune. RIL features in the Forbes Global list ofthe world's 400 big companies and in the FT Global 500 list of the world'slargest companies. RIL ranks amongst the 'Worlds 25 Most InnovativeCompanies' as per a list compiled by the US financial publication – BusinessWeek in collaboration with the Boston Consulting Group.

The movement of stocks of RIL over a period of one year starting from January 2, 2006 to December 2, 2006 had been constant except for a sudden increase followed by a fall around the month of May-June. Apart from this secondary fluctuation, the primary trend has been almost constant. The movement in the stock prices of RIL had been almost similar with the overall movement in the market.

Reliance Petroleum Limited (RPL)

RPL is a subsidairy of RIL. RPL was involved in setting up a greenfield petroleumrefinery and polypropylene plant in a Special Economin Zone at Jamnagar inGujarat. With an annual crude processing capacity of 580000 barrels perstream day (BPSD), RPL will be the sixth largest refinery in the world.

The movement of stocks of RPL over a period of one year starting from January 2, 2006 to December 2, 2006 had been constant.

Details of the merger transactions

- Appointed date of 1st April 2008
- Merger ratio of 1 share of RIL for every 16 shares of RPL
- RPL shares held by RIL to be cancelled. No fresh treasury stock created
- RIL to issue 6.92 crore shares to RPL shareholders 4.4% increase in equity base from Rs 1,574 crore shares to Rs 1,643 crore
- Promoter holding in RIL will reduce from 49% to 47%

The Motivations behind the merger strategy of RIL:

The major sources of motivation for the merger of two entities of RIL-RPL were as follows:

Synergy: It refers to the fact that the combined entity can often reduce the fixed costs and other operating costs by removing duplicate departments or operations, thereby, lowering the costs of the company relative to the same revenue stream, thus increasing profit margins. The merger of RIL-RPL is also said to provide the merged entity with the financial and operational synergies. This is because the nature of the existing refinery and the new refinery is same and also the improved capacity and the complexity would give RIL the necessary reduction in the costs of operations.

Increased revenue or market share: RIL will be amalgamating its subsidiary company (RPL) and by doing this, it would be increasing its market power by capturing increased market share to set prices.

Economy of scale: The merged entity would result in the creation of the refinery which would be the worlds largest refining capacity at a single location. The increased complexity and capacity of the new refinery would help the company to maximize the GRM.

Taxation: Availing the tax benefits is another major incentive for the two companies to opt for merger. But in the case of the merger of RIL-RPL, the merger will be tax neutral as after the merger both the entities will continue to enjoy the same tax benefits which they are currently enjoying. Therefore, on a consolidated basis, RIL will get the benefits of being an Export Oriented Unit and RPL will enjoy the SEZ benefits.

The Merger Process

In 2002, RPL, which was the first refinery project, merged itself with its parent company RIL. Now after 7 years, RPL decided to once again merge with RIL. Present RPL was incorporated in October 24, 2005 to set up the second mega refinery complex.

Though the market was surprised by the announcement of the merger between RIL and its subsidiary RPL, it was expected to happen owing to the strategic fit and the changes in the global scenario. The merger of RPL with RIL seems to be a strategic move as it would enable RIL to enjoy Economies to Scale in production and refinery of petrochemicals. It would also help in minimizing the cost of capital and capitalize on the cash flow of RPL

The merger of Reliance Industries Limited (RIL) and Reliance Petroleum Limited (RPL) resulted in the creation of a petrochemical behemoth which would encompass the entire value chain in the business of petroleum giving the merged entity the necessary clout to take on the competition on the national and international level. According to media reports, the merger was supposed to create a new entity which will have a combined market value of about Rs.233,384 crores.

Reliance Industries Limited, after the merger, would become the world's largest refining capacity at a single location. Also, it would become the fifth largest polypropylene manufacturer. The two firms after the amalgamation will continue to function as separate entities from the accounting point of view and therefore, the tax benefits available to RIL as an Export Oriented Unit and to RPL as a Special Economic Zone will be independent from each other. In fact, this merger would give RIL greater flexibility in operational planning.

RPL had its IPO in April 2006. At that time RIL had 75% stake in the company. RIL and Chevron were the joint promoters of the company with a stake of 15% and 5% respectively. But in November 2007 RIL sold its 4.01% equity stake in Indian Stock Exchange. With this RIL was left with 71% of equity shares in the company.

According to the contract between Chevron and RIL, Chevron had an option to hike its stake up to 29%. For this it would have to buy 24% equity shares from RIL. This would have left RIL with only 47% (71-24) stake in RPL, hence reducing it below 51%.

Now, let us look at the probability of Chevron hiking its stake. Following are the reasons, which made it highly unlikely:

Very High Cost to Chevron: If Chevron would have raised its stake to 29% then it would have to buy the shares from RIL at 5% discount to market price. The amount involved would be very costly for the company, which would be almost the cost of RPL refinery at the current market prices. Hence to raise its stake by 29% it would have to bear almost complete refineries cost.

RIL's stake sales: When in November 2007 RIL sold off its 4.01% stake in RPL, it became further more unlikely for Chevron to raise its stake in RPL. As it will leave RIL with less than 51% shares in Reliance Petroleum Limited. Now, it cannot be the case that RIL does not mind letting its stake go below 51% as the debt agreement clearly states that an Event of Default will occur if RIL's share goes below 51% in RPL.

RPL can source crude on its own: As the existing refineries of RIL, RPL also seemed confident of sourcing crude on its own. Hence the hike of stakes of Chevron seems rather unlikely.

From the above stated points we can see that in November 2007 only it became almost clear that RIL might take a step of merging RPL. RIL has had a history of merging its subsidiaries involved in refining petrochemicals. The old RPL which started its operation in FY01 was finally merged with RIL in FY02. IPCL (acquired by RIL in FY03 as a part of privatization in India) was merged in RIL in FY07. Thus, when on March 2, 2009 RIL finally announced the merger of RPL into RIL, it should not have come as a shock to the market.

Synergy of The Merger

RIL to maintain its refining margin well ahead of its competitors, it has contracted with crude oil suppliers for the cheaper heavy sour crude. Moreover, the product blends from the two refineries will also help RIL to produce fuel which matches the Euro 4 and Euro 5 grades, which is a requirement of the western markets.

The RPL refinery will be one of the most complex refineries in the world with a Nelson Complexity Index of 14.0 which will enable the refinery to process various varieties of crude to produce superior quality products which are able to meet the stringent specifications and command price premiums. This is a significant competitive advantage in the current industry scenario of increasingly heavy and sour new crude finds. As the location of the two refineries is adjacent to each other, it provides a strong base for the company to explore the locked synergies between the two refineries. The ability of the merged entity to buy and process different forms of crude (including the heaviest crude) owing to the improved complexity will help the company in lowering its buying cost thereby increasing the overall GRM.

Apart from this, the merged entity will also capitalize on shipping freight flexibilities to overcome the hurdles posed by the Indian customs authorities that do not allow two companies to load products in a single vessel. Therefore, the merger will help the merged entity in unlocking the financial and the operational synergies that exist between RIL and RPL.

The merger would enable RIL to have improved Cash Flows and Balance Sheet along with a lower cost of capital which would in long run benefit the shareholders of the merged entity. The RIL-RPL merger will also result in the optimization of the supply chain as the combined refining capacity of the company will be 1.24 million barrels every day and the ability to deal with the supply chain, the ability to steadfast in transportation is more for the merged entity. Also, the merged entity will save on the dividend distribution tax paid by RPL on distributing dividends at 17.99% to its shareholders.

The merger would unlock significant operational and financial synergies that exist between RIL and RPL. It created a platform for value enhancing growth and reinforces RIL's position as an integrated global energy company. The merger would enhance value for shareholders of both companies. The merger is EPS accretive for RIL. Through this merger, RIL consolidated a world class, complex refinery with minimal residual project risk, while complementing RIL's product range. There would be further gains from reduced opearting costs arising from synergies of a combined operations The merger is expected to reduce the earnings volatility for RPL shareholders and allows them to participate in the full energy value chain of RPL.

Swap Ratio

The Board of Directors approved the merger of Reliance Petroleum Limited with Reliance Industries Limited for a swap ratio of 1:16. This means that for every 16 shares of RPL, 1 RIL share would be issued.

The RIL board had approved a scheme of amalgamation of Reliance Petroleum with the company under the provisions of Sections 391 to 394 of the Companies Act of 1956. Under this scheme, the RPL's shareholders would get 1 fully paid equity share of Rs 10 each of RIL for every 16 fully paid equity shares of RPL held by them. The merger followed the philosophy of RIL of creating enduring value for its stakeholders. CRISIL has affirmed an AAA rating for RIL post merger. Merger, however, reduced the shareholding of institutional investors, while banks and mutual funds would get a higher share in the merged entity.

According to some analysts, the merger would result in the fall in the promoter holding by 2% from 49% to 47% which would be due to the cancellation of the treasury stock. The merger would also lead to an increase in the retail shareholding from 16.1% to 19%.

The swap ratio of 1:16, which is marginally in favor of the shareholders of RPL, would mean a dilution of 4.4% of RILs equity. The treasury stock which had been created as a result of merger would be extinguished which would prove to be positive for the shareholders of RIL. Therefore, the merger can be said to have a neutral effect on the shareholders of both the company.

After the swapping of shares, RIL would have 3.7 million shareholders and the promoter's holding would fall to 47%. RIL is currently holding 70.38% in RPL which would be cancelled on absorption. If the swap ratio would have been 1:15, RIL would have to issue 8.89 crore equity shares as against the outstanding 133.3 crore of RPL shares. As a result, RIL's equity would have risen to Rs 1,662.65 crore, which amounts to a dilution of just 5.6%. Similarly if the swap ratio would have been 1:17, the dilution of the promoter's share in RPL would have been 1.95% [Table 1]

Table 1: Dilution of Promoters

Particulars	(%)	in crores
Total number of RPL Shares		450.00
RIL's Stake (including Chevron's)	75.38	339.21
Non-Promoters Stake	24.62	110.79
Number of RPL Shares for 1 RIL Share		16
Number of Shares to Promoter		21.200625
Number of Shares to Non-Promoters		6.924375
Total number of RIL Shares before merger		157.30
Number of new RIL Shares to be issued in lieu of RPL		28.125
Treasury Shares to be cancelled		21.200625
Total number of RIL Shares post merger		164.224375
Current Treasury Shares in RIL	12.64	19.88272
Net Equity excluding Treasury (Pre-Merger)		137.41728
Net Equity excluding Treasury (Post-Merger)		144.341655
Existing Promoter's Stake	49.03%	77.12419
Promoter's Stake Post Merger	46.96%	77.12419

The total number of shares of RPL was 450 crores which are represented by the promoter's stake which was equivalent to 339.21 crores which accounted for 75.38% of the total number of shares. The remaining 24.62% of the shares are held by the non promoters which is equal to 110.79 crore shares. The swap ratio as decided by the Board of Directors of RIL is 1:16 which implies that for every 16 shares of RPL, 1 share of RIL will be issued. Thus, the number of shares to be issued to the promoters is 21.2 crores and to the non promoters is 6.92 crore shares.

The total number of shares of RIL before the merger are 157.30 crores and after the merger the total number of shares will be 164.22 crore shares. This figure includes 28.125 crores shares representing the new shares that will be issued in lieu of the shares of RPL and 21.2 crore shares representing the treasury stock which will be cancelled by RIL. Currently, the total number of treasury shares in RIL is 19.88 crores.

Hence, after the merger, the promoter's stake will be 46.96% instead of 49.03%. it means that the equity will be diluted due to the merger to the extent of 2.07%.

Investor's Position

It is believed that the RPL shareholders would benefit in the long term from the merger with RIL. This gain would be due to the following reasons:

1. **Gains from upside in the petroleum sector, retail and SEZ:** RPL shareholders, after the merger will be gaining from the upsides from RIL s petroleum business after merger as the company will be gaining from the strong value accretion due to exploration of the large unexplored acreage in the highly prospective areas. The shareholders of the merged entity will even gain from the upsides in RILs diversification in the organized retail sector and SEZs.

2. **Rise more likely in RIL's earnings:** A steady rise in RILs earnings is more likely than in RPLs earnings. There has been a secular rise in RILs earnings since its inception in 1964. Because there are a number of subsidiary companies under the group, any decline in earnings of one subsidiary is set off against the increase in the earnings of the other subsidiaries. That is, RILs earnings decline in any one business is neutralized by strong growth in other businesses. This would not have been possible in the case of RPL as its earnings are mainly from refining only.

3. **Diversification of risk of minority shareholders:** The merger will diversify the risk of minority shareholders of RPL as it would be shifting from standalone refinery to an integrated unit like RIL. Due to the downturn of the refining sector post global slowdown had increased risks for RPL as a standalone unit. Therefore, the merger with RIL would expose RPL shareholders towards a relatively stable exploration business, integrated refining and petro-chemical business and emerging retail business.

4. **Industry scenario:** The demand is expected to rise through the year 2010 at a rate of about 2% per year for oil and 3% per year for gas. Moreover, in the recent past there has been an increase in the demand for oil and gas. It is expected that the demand for oil and gas will continue to increase as they are expected to remain the leading energy sources for some time to come. Also increase in the exploration and production is expected due to advancement in the technology.

Therefore, it would be safe to assume that the shareholders of RIL will be able to earn regular and consistent dividends along with the capital appreciation in the stock prices

5. **Issue price:** The RPL issue price was Rs 60 per share and the proposed swap ratio and the current market price is higher than the issue price. In a market which has seen so much of turmoil in the last 12 months, the swap ratio can be considered as appropriate for the shareholders of both the companies.

Table 2: Ratio of the market price of RIL & RPL on date of announcement

Date	*Closing Price of RIL*	*Closing Price of RPL*	*Ratio*
27-Feb-09	1,265.05	76.20	16.60
2-Mar-09	1,225.15	75.15	16.30
3-Mar-09	1,199.05	73.35	16.35
4-Mar-09	1,209.60	74.00	16.35
1-Apr-09	1,579.45	98.30	16.07
2-Apr-09	1,662.50	103.60	16.05
6-Apr-09	1,672.25	104.20	16.05
8-Apr-09	1,724.05	107.80	15.99

From the above table, we can see that the ratio of the market price of RIL and RPL on the date of the announcement of the merger i.e., February 27, 2009 was 16.6. On the date of the announcement of the swap ratio for the merger i.e., March 2, 2009, the ratio of the market prices of the two companies was 16.3. For the next week, the ratio remained approximately equal to 16. On April 1, 2009, the date from which the merger was to be effective, the ratio still remained 16 (approx). Only after April 8, 2009, the ratio fell slightly below 16.

Therefore, it can be said that the shareholders who purchased the shares of RPL during this time made a breakeven decision as the ratio of the market price of the shares of the company is almost equal to the swap ratio that has been decided for the merger. Hence, the swap ratio will put the RPL shareholders in the same position after the merger as the shareholders of RIL as they are in now.

Stock Position

The closing stock prices for RIL and RPL for the period of two months starting from February 27, 2009, the date on which the announcement for the merger of the two companies was made till April 29, 2009, has been recorded to understand the movement of the share prices due to the announcement of the merger.

On Friday, February 27, 2009, the announcement of the merger of RPL with RIL was announced. Following the announcement the shares of Reliance Industries dropped to an intraday low of Rs 1,213.20, down four per cent on the following Monday i.e. March 2, 2009, while RPL scrip also showed a fall of over eight per cent to an intra-day low of Rs 70 on the Bombay Stock Exchange. When the market closed on Monday, RIL was down by 3.15% to Rs 1,225.15 and RPL was lower by 1.38% at Rs 75.15. In 2002, when the first merger of RPL with RIL was announced, the share prices of RIL shares had dropped by 2.85% to Rs 312.95.

Financial Ratio Analysis

Reliance Industries Limited, India's largest private sector conglomerate, reported an annual turnover of Rs 1, 33,443 Crores and net profit of 19,458.29 Crores in year 2007-2008. With 1453648601 outstanding shares, RIL has an EPS Rs 133.86. Earnings per Share serve as an indicator of a company's profitability. Higher the EPS, higher is the profitability of the company. Reliance Industries have maintained increasing earnings per share from last 5 years. In 2007-2008 it showed a 63% of increment from last years 82.16. Thus, with the data of EPS, the growth of RIL looks promising.

1. DPS: Dividend per Share is the amount that shareholder will receive for the each share they own. Dividend is distribution of a portion of a company's earnings, decided by the board of directors, to a class of its shareholders. RIL has been continuously paying dividend to its share holders from last five years. The value of DPS has increased from 5.25 in 2003-04 to Rs 13 in 2007-08.

As per my observations and understanding, there has been a change in calculating the DPS for the company since 2006-07as the DPS is calculated on total outstanding shares minus shares held by subsidiary companies on which no voting rights are exercisable and petroleum trust.

2. Operating Profit per Share: It is a measure of company's earning power from ongoing operations. This is equal to earnings before deduction of interest payments and income taxes. Operating profit is also called EBIT (earnings before interest and taxes) or operating income. Reliance Industries Limited has been showing a considerable growth in the operating profits. In 2007-08 it has shown a total growth of 13%, it has increased from 163.90 in 2006-7 to 185.74 in 2007-08.

3. Book Value per share: It is the total value of the company's assets that shareholders would theoretically receive if a company were liquidated. It is also called the net asset value of a company, calculated by total assets minus intangible assets (patents, goodwill) and liabilities. RIL has shown an increasing book value of the company for last 5 years. Thus is reduces the risk factor for the investors. Since the inception of the company, it has been trying to increase the net worth of the investors and in the process it has today become the second largest private sector conglomerate in the world.

The Book Value per share has increased from 246.73 in 2003-04 to 649.12 in 2007-08, hence showing a growth of 163%.

4. Leverage Ratio of **Total debt to equity Ratio:** The debt to equity ratio is used for measuring solvency of a company. It indicates how much the company is leveraged, in other words it measures the companys ability to borrow and repay the money.

Debt to equity ratio is closely watched by creditors and investors because it reveals the extent to which company management is willing to fund its operations with debt. Lenders are particularly sensitive to this ratio as an excessive high ratio value will put their loans at risk of not being repaid.

By using debt in the company finances, it is able to have interest and depreciation tax shield due to the tax paid on the debt interest. However no such tax benefit is achieved when fund raising is done through equity.

Ratios	2008	2007	2006	2005	2004
D/E Ratio	0.45	0.44	0.44	0.46	0.61

Thus from the above table it is clear that RIL has maintained its debt to equity ratio around 0.45 over last 5 years. This means that neither the ratio is too high (risky for the lenders) nor it is too low (entitling the business to leverage and earn higher returns on equity).

5. Liquidity Ratio - Current Ratio: The ratio is mainly used to give an idea of the company's ability to pay back its short-term liabilities (debt and payables) with its short-term assets (cash, inventory, receivables). The higher the current ratio, the more capable the company is of paying its obligations.

A ratio under 1 suggests that the company would be unable to pay off its obligations if they came due at that point. While this shows the company is not in good financial health, it does not necessarily mean that it will go bankrupt - as there are many ways to access financing - but it is definitely not a good sign.

The current ratio can give a sense of the efficiency of a company's operating cycle or its ability to turn its product into cash. Companies that have trouble getting paid on their receivables or have long inventory turnover can run into liquidity problems because they are unable to alleviate their obligations.

Ratios	2008	2007	2006	2005	2004
Current	1.78	1.61	1.49	1.66	1.75

Reliance Industries Limited has a current ratio of 1.78, thus it can easily pay off its short term liabilities with its short term assets. This states that the company is in good financial health and it shows no signs of bankruptcy.

Valuation of RPL

Reliance Petroleum Limited was set up to harness an emerging value creation opportunity in the global refining sector by Reliance Industries Limited (RIL), one of India's largest private sector company with a significant presence across the entire energy chain and a global leadership across key product segments.

With an annual crude processing capacity of 580,000 barrels per stream day (BPSD), RPL is the sixth largest refinery in the world. It has a complexity of 14.0, using the Nelson Complexity Index, ranking it amongst the highest in the sector. The polypropylene plant has a capacity to produce 0.9 million metric tonnes per annum. The refinery project is being implemented at a capital cost of Rs 27,000 crore being funded through a mix of equity and debt.

Reliance Petroleum Limited (RPL) has recently commissioned SEZ refinery at Jamnagar and processed 3.6 million tonnes of crude during the quarter ended 31st March 2009. The unaudited financial results for the quarter / year ended 31st march 2009 revealed the 15 day production results. Based on that data, the valuation of RPL has been done.

Financial Ratios	Mar ' 09
Per share ratios	
EPS (Diluted) (Rs)	0.19
Adjusted cash EPS (Rs)	0.44
Dividend per share	-
Operating profit per share (Rs)	0.50
Book value (incl rev res) per share (Rs.)	30.07
Net operating income per share (Rs)	8.17
Profitability ratios	
Operating margin (%)	6.17%
Gross profit margin (%)	3.10%
Net profit margin (%)	2.28%
Adjusted return on net worth (%)	0.62%
Reported return on net worth (%)	0.62%
Return on long term funds (%)	0.32%

The earnings per share, operating profit per share and net operating income per share are so low for RPL because for year 2008-09 the reported net profit is 84 crores and is based on only 15 days production period.

Dividend per Share is NIL for the company as there has no dividend paid till date by RPL.

Similarly for profitability ratios, the figures do not show the accurate financial health of the company, because the production has not been carried out for complete year leading to a nominal profit.

Overall Impact of Merger

- RIL among top 10 private sector refining companies globally
- RIL now owns 2 of the world's 3 largest, most complex modern refineries
- The merger has made RIL the world's largest producer of ultra-clean fuels at a single location
- Among 50 most profitable companies globally
- Among five largest producers of Polypropylene
- Providing the growth platform for creating value-accretive downstream opportunities
- Higher Financial Strength & Flexibility

- The deal enhanced the position of RIL as an integrated global energy major. Markets ascribe higher valuation for integrated energy companies vis-a-vis standalone refiners due to better competitive position and reduced earnings volatility.
- This merger of RPL transformed RIL to be among world's50 most profitable companies; top ten non-state owned refining company globally; top 15 independent upstream companies; and five largest producers of poly propylene in the world.
- RIL has enhanced weight ages in domestic indices, it will also gain significantly from higher financial strength and flexibility.
- It will have operational synergies from combined business in areas such as crude sourcing, product placement, process optimization and logistics, besides consolidation of a world-class operating refinery asset.
- The combined capacity of the two companies expected to be 1.24million barrels of oil a day. At present RIL produces 6.60 lakh barrels and RPL produces 5.80 lakh barrels a day.
- The merger would help the combined entity save on income tax and dividend distribution tax

Future of RPL shareholders

Book value of RIL shareholder as of March 31, 2009, which is likely to be the effective date of the merger, would be 700, while that of RPL would be Rs 30.

How he arrived at book value: Reliance Industries has been in existence for the last 30 years. So there has been an accretion in the value of the fixed assets of the company, while RPL being a new company, there has not been much accretion. The project cost of RPL of Rs 27,000 crore can be taken at about Rs 30,000-33,000 crore as of today.

Therefore, a shareholder of Reliance Industries will be shouting if the ratio is anywhere more than 24 to 1 because that is the ratio working out, based on the book value. If market value is the criteria for swap ratio, it works out to about 16-17.

Ratio would definitely be negative for RPL shareholders.

Future of RIL shareholders

RPL itself is entitled under Section 10AA; therefore RPL's profits would be exempted for the first five years being an EOU (Export Oriented Unit). "This merger is not being mooted or moved with a view to have any tax advantage because RPL as such is entitled, all its profits will be exempted for the first five years to the extent of 100% of Section 10AA being a 100% EOU."

Conclusion

The prime motivating factors for this merger appear to be to gain "dinosaur"-like size which will strengthen RIL's balance sheet. In the short term, it may also help the company play down the expected under-performance in the merging fiscal year. Mukesh Ambani said the merged entity would be an EPS accretive merge as the equity dilution was only 4.4 per cent of RILs expanded equity and they expect RPL to contribute more than that and that would mean that it would be accretive to the RIL share holders and RIL equity from that perspective. On Tax issues, the management made it very clear that the merger was going to be tax neutral and both the entities would enjoy continue with the same tax benefit they are currently enjoying. RPL will continue to get SEZ benefits, while RIL will continue to get EOU [Export Oriented Unit] benefits and on a consolidated basis there would not be much of an impact. The merged entity would be an operational synergy at a scale at which they would be able to use.

Bibliography

1. Manoj Anand and Jagandeep Singh (2008), "Impact of Merger Announcements on ShareholdersWealth: Evidence from Indian Private Sector Banks", Vikalpa, Volume 33, No.1, January – March
2. M. Selvam, S. Vanitha, J. Gayathri, E. Bennet, P. Nageswari (2010), "The determinants of shareholders' wealth of acquiring firms in India", Journal of Modern Accounting and Auditing, Vol.6, No.1 (Serial No.56)
3. Friedrich Trautwein (1990), "Merger Motives & Merger Prescriptions", Strategic Management Journal, Vol. 11, 283-295
4. Vassilis Papadakis, "Growth through mergers and acquisitions:how it won't be a loser's game", Business Strategy Series, Vol. 8 No. 1 2007, pp. 43-50
5. http://economictimes.indiatimes.com/
6. http://www.business-standard.com/

13

Corporate Social Responsibility at FAB India

Ms. Ruchika Jeswal
Institute of Management Studies
ruchikajeswal@yahoo.com

Abstract

Corporate Social Responsibility (CSR) can be defined as the "economic, legal, ethical, and discretionary expectations that society has of organizations at a given point in time". The concept of corporate social responsibility means that organizations have moral, ethical, and philanthropic responsibilities in addition to their responsibilities to earn a fair return for investors and comply with the law. This case study aims to explore the concept of CSR at Fab India Pvt. Ltd. FabIndia works closely with artisans by providing various inputs including design, quality control, access to raw materials and production coordination. Fab India is Trying to work with its artisans closely and is trying to maintain a supplier base . Today Fab India has a number of retail outlets selling several products and trying to pass the benefits to its artisans.

Introduction

Social responsibility is an organization 's obligation to engage in activities that protect and contribute to the welfare of society . Social responsibility is a matter of intense debate. At one extreme, there are those who strongly believe that organizations are in business solely to produce goods and services that societies want –be they atomic weapons , legal advice ,or life saving drugs – and that they are entitled to make profits in return. For these people , social responsibility is, simply not an issue .At the other extreme ,there are those who believe that organizations should be allowed to do business only if they do not harm ,help solve social problems, and put some of the profits they earn back to work for society.

Concept Of Corporate Social Responsibility

Corporate Social Responsibility (CSR) can be defined as the "economic, legal, ethical, and discretionary expectations that society has of organizations at a given point in time". The concept of corporate social responsibility means that organizations have moral, ethical, and philanthropic responsibilities in addition to their responsibilities to earn a fair return for investors and comply with the law. A traditional view of the corporation suggests that its primary, if not sole, responsibility is to its owners, or stockholders. However, CSR requires organizations to adopt a broader view of its responsibilities that includes not only stockholders, but many other constituencies as well, including employees, suppliers, customers, the local community, state, and federal governments, environmental groups, and other special interest groups'

Company Profile

Fab India was established by John Bissel in 1960 in order to fuse the best aspects of East/ West collaboration. He was determined to showcase Indian handloom textiles while providing equitable employment to traditional artisans and also to develop India's export potential in it's emerging textile industry. Over the years the focus of Fabindia's marketing shifted from exports to the local Indian retail market. What started as an export house has today become a successful retail business presenting Indian textiles in a variety of natural fibers, and home products.

Case Body

FabIndia was founded with the strong belief that there was a need for a vehicle for marketing the vast and diverse craft traditions of India and thereby help fulfill the need to provide and sustain rural employment. They blended indigenous craft techniques with contemporary designs to bring aesthetic and affordable products to today's consumers. Their endeavor is to provide customers with hand crafted products which help support and encourage good craftsmanship.

Their products are sourced from villages all over India. FabIndia works closely with artisans by providing various inputs including design, quality control, access to raw materials and production coordination. The vision continues to be to maximize the hand made element in their products, whether it is handwoven textiles, hand block printing, hand embroidery or handcrafting home products.

FabIndia's managing director William Bissel, who conceived and steered the model, says that unlike many Indian companies he doesn't believe in setting up a department to promote corporate social responsibility(CSR). He created an air of hope ,anticipation and excitement in the sleepy village of Chanderi in the Ashok Nagar district of Madhya Pradesh .The local people include about 1000 –odd weavers who were disappointed not just by no rain or no water but by disappearance of the demand of their cherished fabric–Chanderi.

They were then introduced to the concept of becoming owners of shares in a community owned company .They were unsure but bought shares because they thought that it could change their lives in some ways.

That way has been paved by Fab India, A retail outfit that has grown from one store in mid 1990's to 85 .Dabbling in fabric , apparel, handicrafts and other products, it began an experiment with community –owned companies nine years ago in an attempt to include artisan in the wealth creation process. Fab India has created a fully owned subsidiary Artisans Micro Finance, a venture fund .It is owned 49 percent by the fund, 26 percent by the artisans ,15 percent by private investors and 10 percent by the employees of the community –owned company .The investment by these four categories of investors provides the paid up capital .The company promotes the sales of its artisan community to FabIndia ,Which is the principal buyer.

Walk into any of Fab India's high end retail outlets in major cities across India, and around the world - you would be tempted by their unique clothing and furnishing collection, surprised by the store's relentless focus on the customer and would probably walk out with a big bag in your hands. However, you would never guess that the profits made from that store and many others across the country are partly distributed among the weavers, about 20,000 of who are 'shareholders' of subsidiary companies floated by Fab India.

The artisans gain in many ways .The value of their shares goes up .They earn dividends when the company is in a position to declare them Eventually the company will try and offer loans to the artisans ,arranged through banks. The loans can be used to buy new looms or expand production of other products. Although the villagers see it as a gamble they are convinced that it would work.

William Bissel is convinced that involving artisans and sharing benefits of growth with them is the most sustainable of all models. The shares offer the artisans a divisible asset class and community owned companies help convert FabIndia's artisan base into an asset .

But the model is not desirable from a social point of view alone. Fab India has moved from being a primarily export house in the 1960's to a turnover of Rs 300 crore ,of which 90 percent is domestic sales.Its aim is to be a " lifestyle lternative to mass produced "

Artisans Microfinance Director Smita Mankad Quit ABNAmro to do something she believed was worthwile.

'If you want grow at the pace we have grown , you have to carry your supplier base with you," she says, emphasizing that FabIndia's growth will be hampered unless the artisans grew with it.

If FabIndia is changing the way the artisans work, the new model is changing the way FabIndia works .The typical central warehouses owned by community –owned companies from which goods travel directly to stores across India , This reduces logistics costs and minimizes the role of Middlemen.

While the system seems to be working for all concerned , challenges remain .One of them is developing secondary markets so that the companies can stand on their own feet .Critical to that will be introducing a consciousness of the design element in the artisans so that their products have a wider appeal. Bissel says the model will depend on the artisans beginning to understand the benefits of joining together in something that's not cooperative". A cooperative imposes many restrictions upon them and doesn't give them much in return ,If you get together ,you must create something that's bigger than the sum of it's parts. FabIndia's entry made the biggest difference as it began to source fabric worth Rs 1 crore a year from Chanderi .

Fabindia sources its products from over 15000 craft persons and artisans across India. They support the craft traditions of India by providing a market and thereby encourage and sustain rural employment. Today they have retail outlets in all major cities of India - 85 at last count - in addition to international stores in Rome, Italy; Dubai, UAE and Guangzhou, China.

Today FabIndia has expanded beyond textiles into furniture, stationery, pottery, organic foods and bodycare products. All merchandise is sold under the single FabIndia brand and the company owns all its stores as Bissell feels this helps the brand to maintain its identity.

FabIndia works closely with artisans and villagers to develop designs and colour palettes and to optimise production techniques and raw material inputs. For the textiles, mostly natural fabrics and vegetable dyes are used.

"We attract a specific type of customer and decided we want to give that customer the spectrum of products," Bissell says of the product diversification strategy, adding that FabIndia's customers do not fit an age or demographic profile, but are a loyal base of people who want to support craft.

But Bissell is also candid in admitting that some of the diversifications have had unexpected problems. For example, FabIndia's range of organic foods, which it launched in 2004, has a limited audience and as it is perishable has a shorter shelf life than other FabIndia products.

FabIndia recently forayed overseas and has had some early success. For example, its store in the Gulf has been quick to take off. But this has only reinforced Bissell's conviction that it is the Indian diaspora that makes FabIndia a profitable business. Penetrating overseas markets is a "focus but not a large focus", says Bissell, who sees customers in India as the mainstay. The business derives 90% of its revenues domestically. "Our global expansion will be targeted at places where there are a large number of Indians," clarifies Bissell.

Bissell is clear that it is the firm's decision to stay focused over the decades of its existence that is responsible for its success. "We have consistently operated in the niche we identified initially," sums up Bissell, explaining the firm's philosophy. "We are like a restaurant which serves only one kind of cuisine." And with takers abounding for that one type of cuisine, it is clear Bissell is on to a good thing.

Questions

1. What is the relationship between Fab India, the parent company and the subsidiaries - If the subsidiaries have a claim on Fab India's profits or just act as a supplier unit?
2. What do you think of the model that Bissel has proposed?
3. Would FabIndia really be able to transfer the benefits to its artisans as they have proposed?
4. FabIndia's community-owned companies are converting artisans into assets while sharing the benefits of growth with them. Explain?

5. Would Diversification in some other areas help Fab India to provide better to its shareholders- the artisan community?

Teaching Notes

Overview

Corporate Social Responsibility (CSR) can be defined as the "economic, legal, ethical, and discretionary expectations that society has of organizations at a given point in time". The concept of corporate social responsibility means that organizations have moral, ethical, and philanthropic responsibilities in addition to their responsibilities to earn a fair return for investors and comply with the law. A traditional view of the corporation suggests that its primary, if not sole, responsibility is to its owners, or stockholders. However, CSR requires organizations to adopt a broader view of its responsibilities that includes not only stockholders, but many other constituencies as well, including employees, suppliers, customers, the local community, state, and federal governments, environmental groups, and other special interest groups.

John Bissel , who had worked in India as a consultant for the Ford Foundation, founded FabIndia in 1960 to showcase Indian handloom textiles to the world. He opened the flagship Greater Kailash, New Delhi, store in 1975 to retail home furnishings, and subsequently expanded into garments. At the time, the business largely catered to overseas buyers.

William Bissell his son took over as managing director of FabIndia in 1999 and today heads a network of 87 stores in 39 cities in India as well as branches in Rome, Dubai and Guangzhou with a turnover in excess of Rs3 billion ($68 million). Bissell went one step further in trying to ensure he is sharing the wealth FabIndia creates with those who are helping him to create it. FabIndia floated a wholly-owned subsidiary, Artisans Micro Finance, which will create community-owned companies. For each company, a calculation is done of how much working capital it needs, then this is financed two-thirds through debt and one-third through equity.

Applications

This case study would be best for a management student trying to explore about Corporate social Responsibility and its effects on our Indian community.

Objectives of the Case

This a type of decision case. It will introduce to the reader the following concepts:

1. Corporate Social Responsibility
2. Social responsibility and Organizational Stakeholders

References :

1. www.fabindia.com
2. Business World
3. Vipin Gupta ,Kamala Gollakota ,R. Srinivasan,(2008) Business Policy and Strategic

14

Strategic Brand Building of Lux Soap Bar - A Case Study of the Making of a Nations Beauty Bar

Mr Sukhvinder Singh
Mrs Sarmishta Sarma
sunshinewinner@gmail.com
Institute of Innovation in Technology in Management, New Delhi

Abstract

The process of marketing of a product consists of the element of "brand building" along with the 4 P's of marketing mix. Branding consists of strategically placing a product in the mind of consumer .It is done in such a way that the consumer starts identifying the product with the brand name. Indian market has a number of products that occupy a "cult" status .Some of them are "Surf" for detergent ,"Bata" for shoes , "Lux " for bathing soap to name a few. The present study analyses the branding of Lux as a beauty bar in Indian market.

Lux—derived from the word luxury— was launched in 1899 as a laundry soap in the UK. In 1925, the brand was extended to the toilet soap category. It was positioned as a beauty soap in India, and HUL has since used successful film actors of the time—such as Leela Chitnis, Madhubala, Hema Malini and Kareena Kapoor—to endorse the product.

Lux's secret of longevity has been its consistent evolution—be it the soap colour, packaging or new variants, the brand has banked on innovation to keep its youthful image intact. Extending the soap cake to a range of shower gels, liquid soaps and moisturizing bars has helped the brand keep consumers excited and the competition at bay. What has not changed is the consistency in its communication and its positioning.

Its tag lines—If it's good enough for a film star, then it's good for you too to Play with beauty—have conveyed the same message over the years. "Lux is a brand like Mills & Boon". While the packaging and content could change, the romance angle doesn't. It taps into an emotion very close to humanity's basic need—"social interaction".

The brand has always hired celebrities when they have reached a certain height rather than using them at the start of their careers. This avoids the issue of celebrities overshadowing the brand," says Agnello Dias, national creative director, JWT, which handles the account.

Key Words: Branding, Marketing Mix, Celebrity Advertising.

"A sign of a celebrity is that his name is often worth more than his services."- Daniel J Boorstin

Introduction

Promotion is an important marketing force that provides an extra incentive(usually short term in nature) for consumers, the trade, the sales force and other influential groups. Promotion ranks with advertising and selling efforts as one of the major activities that can be utilized in the marketing of packaged goods. Promotion is directed not only to consumers or the trade but also to the occasion to the sales force and other influential groups.

The great Indian brand wagon of Lux started nearly 8 decades ago. Great brands sometimes outlast their ambassadors as proven by Lux which celebrated its 81st anniversary in India.

The first ambassador Leela Chitnis featured in a Lux advertisement which flagged off the Lux wagon. She gave way to a galaxy of stars which include Madhubala, Nargis, Meena Kumari, Mala Sinha, Sharmila Tagore, Waheeda Rehman, Sairah Banu, Hema Malini, Zeenat Aman, Juhi Chawla, Madhuri Dixit, Sridevi, Aishwaria Rai Bachchan, Kareena Kapoor, Priyanka Chopra and most recently Katrina Kaif.

The last frontier for most actors aspiring to stardom is becoming a Lux ambassador. The brand has outlasted many soaps. From the beginning, Lux became a household name in the country.

Marketing Strategy of Lux

The Lux Marketing Strategy is simple - build a brand based on beauty ("Beauty Begins With Lux") and then throw millions of dollars at the media to support it. There is little to no talk of what makes LUX any better or any worse or any different than any other soap. Essentially, they are doing nothing at all to monopolize their marketplace.

The marketing strategy that LUX Soap uses is no different than 90% of the large corporations out there – "Brand It And Slam It". Meaning they spend time coming up with a catchy tag line, pretty packaging and high priced celebrity endorsements and then spend tens of millions (if not hundreds of millions) of dollars getting the brand out there on radio, tv, store ads etc.

Concept of Celebrity endorsement

The motif behind total branding may be decocted as an attempt to amalgamate diverse activities to win customer preference. The crescendo of celebrities endorsing brands has been steadily increasing over the past years. Marketers overtly acknowledge the power of celebrities in influencing consumer-purchasing decisions. It is a ubiquitously accepted fact that celebrity endorsement can bestow special attributes upon a product that it may have lacked otherwise. But everything is not hunky-dory; celebrities are after all mere mortals made of flesh and blood like us. If a celebrity can aggrandize the merits of a brand, he or she can also exacerbate the image of a brand.

Aristotle's quote on anger can apply to branding ***"Any brand can get a celebrity. That is easy. But getting a celebrity consistent with the right brand, to the right degree, at the right time, for the right purpose and in the right way... that is not easy."***

Celebrity endorsements are impelled by virtue of the following motives:

- Instant Brand Awareness and Recall.
- Celebrity values define, and refresh the brand image.
- Celebrities add new dimensions to the brand image.
- Instant credibility or aspiration PR coverage.
- Lack of ideas.
- Convincing clients.

The scope of a celebrity on the incumbent brand:

Simply stating, a brand is a differentiated product and helps in identifying your product and making it stand out due to its name, design, style, symbol, color combination, or usually a mix of all these.

Before we can scrutinize the effects of celebrity endorsement on the overall brand, we have to ferret the implicit nuances that act as sources of strong brand images or values:

Experience of use: This encapsulates familiarity and proven reliability.

User associations: Brands acquire images from the type of people who are seen using them. Images of prestige or success are imbibed when brands are associated with glamorous personalities.

Belief in efficiency: Ranking from consumer associations, newspaper editorials etc.

Brand appearance: Design of brand offers clues to quality and affects preferences.

Manufacturer's name & reputation: A prominent brand name (Sony, Kellogg's, Bajaj, Tata) transfers positive associations .

The celebrity's role is the most explicit and profound ***in incarnating user associations*** among the above-mentioned points. To comprehend this, let us analyze the multiplier effect formula for a successful brand:

S=P*D*AV—the multiplier effect

Where *S is a successful brand,*

P is an effective product,

D is Distinctive Identity ,

and AV is Added values.

The realm of the celebrity's impact is confined to bestow a distinctive identity and provide AV to the brand; the celebrity does not have the power to improve or debilitate the efficiency and features of the core product. Thus, we are gradually approaching an evident proposition claiming,

"The health of a brand can definitely be improved up to some extent by celebrity endorsement. But one has to remember that endorsing a celebrity is a means to an end and not an end in itself."

An appropriately used celebrity can prove to be a massively powerful tool that magnifies the effects of a campaign. But the aura of cautiousness should always be there. The fact to be emphasised is that celebrities alone do not guarantee success, as consumers nowadays understand advertising. They know what advertising is and how it works. People realize that celebrities are being paid a lot of money for endorsements and this knowledge makes them cynical about celebrity endorsements.

Compatibility of the celebrity's persona with the overall brand image

A celebrity is used to impart credibility and aspirational values to a brand, but the celebrity needs to match the product. A good brand campaign idea and an intrinsic link between the celebrity and the message are musts for a successful campaign. Celebrities are no doubt good at generating attention, recall and positive attitudes towards advertising provided that they are supporting a good idea and there is an explicit fit between them and the brand. On the other hand, they are rendered useless when it comes to the actual efficiency of the core product, creating positive attitudes to brands, purchase intentions and actual sales.

Certain parameters that postulate compatibility between the celebrity and brand image are:

- Celebrity's fit with the brand image.
- Celebrity's fit with the brand image.
- Celebrity—Target audience match
- Celebrity associated values.
- Costs of acquiring the celebrity.
- Celebrity—Product match.
- Celebrity controversy risk.
- Celebrity popularity.
- Celebrity availability.
- Celebrity physical attractiveness.
- Celebrity credibility.
- Celebrity prior endorsements.

- Whether celebrity is a brand user.
- Celebrity profession.

Celebrity endorsement and Branding of Lux

Lux—derived from the word luxury— was launched in 1899 as a laundry soap in the UK. In 1925, the brand was extended to the toilet soap category. It was positioned as a beauty soap in India, and HUL has since used successful film actors of the time—such as Leela Chitnis, Madhubala, Hema Malini and Kareena Kapoor—to endorse the product.

Lux's secret of longevity has been its consistent evolution—be it the soap colour, packaging or new variants, the brand has banked on innovation to keep its youthful image intact. Extending the soap cake to a range of shower gels, liquid soaps and moisturizing bars has helped the brand keep consumers excited and the competition at bay.

What has not changed is the consistency in its communication and its positioning. Its tag lines—If it's good enough for a film star, then it's good for you too to Play with beauty—have conveyed the same message over the years. "Lux is a brand like Mills & Boon". While the packaging and content could change, the romance angle doesn't. It taps into an emotion very close to humanity's basic need—social interaction.

The brand has always hired celebrities when they have reached a certain height rather than using them at the start of their careers. This avoids the issue of celebrities overshadowing the brand," says Agnello Dias, national creative director, JWT, which handles the account.

From the beginning, Lux became a household name across the country. Actor Hema Malini says, "One of the turning points in my career was when I was signed up by Lux. It was then that I knew I had made my mark in Indian cinema as a leading lady. To be a Lux star is a much sought after honour amongst leading ladies and it truly means a lot to me."

After 50 Indian female actors lathering up with Lux, it was the turn of a male actor, Shah Rukh Khan, to say, " I want to tell you about my beauty secret — Lux" .In 1926, Ginger Rogers became the first Hollywood great to appear in a Lux commercial. The first Lux bar made in India was sold for the princely sum of two annas in 1934.

The uniqueness of Lux has been its promotion strategy of constant evolution of tag lines.The present tag line of " Kali se bhi komal" is unique in its catching jingle and presence of Aishwarya Rai and Katrina Kaif.

Conclusion

The story of Lux can be a guide to understand the two very strong marketing concepts of PLC(Product Life Cycle) and Promotion Strategy. "Lux" has effectively outlived its life cycle by constant changes in product features and packaging. In terms of promotion strategy its has proved the celebrity endorsement works ,what is important is the existence of a celebrity, who may change with time. The customer identifies with the celebrity himself. That is the reason Lux enjoys its special position of a "nation's beauty bar" inspite of there being so many soaps in the Indian market.

15

Crossing the Chasm : The Case of Godrej's GoJiyo

Mr Sukhvinder Singh
Dr. Sarmishta Sarma
sunshinewinner@gmail.com
Institute of Innovation in Technology in Management, New Delhi

Abstract:

The present report is a case analysis of Godrej's Gojiyo a unique business model based on the virtual world. It is a step beyond the Games seen in the internet which are so popular among the teens. It is a virtual world where the joiners can own land create structures buy and sell things basically have a world of their own. The company has been in existence since 2010 and is gaining popularity among the early adopters but has not been able to have a consistent base of customers. The problem of the case was to design a market development plan for Gojiyo for sustained growth. The solution to the problem has been derived from the two literary pieces of Geoffery A Moore-"Inside the Tornado" and the "Chasm Champion".

GoJiyo is a virtual world created by Godrej.It was started on 8:00 am March 22nd 2010.It consists of six imaginary planets namely Solaria, Mayuraprastha ,Noom, Turqua ,Snow flash and Re- Janm. It is a virtual world created entirely by its users. This world is crea'ed entirely by its users. This world is created entirely by its virtual "Residents" 6,90,000 of them in this one year of its existence. GoJijo is Indian version of the hugely famous Linden Labs Second Life started in 2008.The priority of Godrej's GoJiyo is to reach out to every internet user in India. It is indeed a unique venture of a business house that has a significant place in Indian consumer durable market.

Virtual World

Virtual worlds are computer simulated world inhabited by its residents called avatar. These virtual worlds are " massively multiplayer online games" (MMOGs) such as world of Warcraft which earned $ 1.1 billion in subscription revenue in 2007 from it's 9 million players. However GoJiyo is first of its kind MMOGs for Indians which is indigenously created.

Indian mythology fantasy of all kinds and science fiction were common MMOG themes. MMOGs achieved persistence through a server connection – if a user logged off then returned the world's state would have changed based on their players actions during the user's absence.

MMOGs were created in 3D graphics and use " physics engines" a software that made movement of avatar realistic. GoJiyo has many attributes similar to MMOGs but is different from MMOGs in three dimensions

a. GoJiyo is not a game , it lacks a story with well defined goals.

b. It is a world entirely created by avtars.

c. The overall business model of GoJiyo is unique which will be discussed in detail below

Gojiyo vs Second Life

Some people are calling GoJiyo the Indian Second Life. Which is a pretty huge compliment given that Second Life is *the* standard for virtual worlds and has been around for 7 years.Godrej looked at Second Life closely and learned from it but chose to use Gojiyo more as a brand communication platform. Looking at all existing worlds from the hugely successful World of Warcraft, IMVU, Vivaty , Twinity, China's Hipihi, to Google's experiment with Lively, to Farmville and Habbo Hotel and at branded environments such as Coke World and Lynx World. Gojiyo has brought togather gaming, social networks, branded and 3D environments. In a way what it went closer to Sony Playstation's Home in the concept (though accessible through a browser and much smaller in scale) than to Second Life. But without the customized spaces aspect PS Home has.

Gojiyo differs from Second Life in following aspects:-

a. Access

1. Second Life needs to be downloaded once (approx 50 MB) and then one has to run that 'viewer' software to enter the world each time. It is not accessible through the browser.GoJiyo is accessible directly through a browser, where it loads. Most other virtual worlds involve a software download. GoJiyo is designed for an Indian broadband bandwidth- to work on an actual download rate of 60 kbps. This means each time one goes to Gojiyo.com the world downloads, but it has cached the first time, so subsequent downloads are quicker. Research tells us that Indians wouldn't want to download a large piece of software. This is perhaps why Second Life and other virtual worlds haven't really taken off in India. GoJiyo works on Unity.

2. The graphical user interface of the Second Life Viewer has, up to now, been pretty difficult to use, to quote one of the team, "we are Linden *Lab* after all" and most Second Life

users have had to be quite tech savvy to be able to use it to its full potential . GoJiyo was designed to be very easy to use in its interface and with simple and fun functionality for less tech savvy users. Aimed at those new to virtual worlds (a step up from Farmville in immersive environments).

b. Features

Second Life is much bigger than GoJiyo- it's absolutely huge with loads of regions built by users, there's sophisticated location-based sound and lipsynching of avatars to their voice etc. Avatar customization is much more developed than GoJiyo's too, because it's user generated, so the team of developers is much larger. One can be a non-human character for instance.

Gojiyo has 6 Regions only, which will refresh continually- Solaria- a beach city; Mauryaavaas - a recreation of the ancient Mauryan Empire, Noom- moon colony; Rejanm - where you can be reborn; an underwater world and an arctic land. Some are very Indian concepts. There is voice chat but GoJiyo is 25 days old compared to 7 years old ad so its features are continually developing. Like with any good software product, features will keep being added continually.

2. One of Second Life's core tenets is giving creativity to the user though allowing them to create their own content (UGC). Users can create their own regions by buying land and building on it. The tools to build are out there to create everything from avatar clothes to gestures and more.

GoJiyo on the other hand, has many mini-games, to name a few: one can go bunjee jumping, surfing, skydiving, fight asteroids falling on the Moon and soon speed date in 3rd Century BCE Mauryavaas. Users can also engage in longer quests like finding who's stolen all the artworks from the city and restoring them; planting algae to save the moon from running out of oxygen. GoJiyo has a points and currency system- Mios and Jios which earns the user rewards online and in the real world and there'll be more links with Godrej and other products. For instance you can win a real trip to climb Kilimanjaro with some of your GoJiyo friends.

3. In GoJiyo there's a friendship engine that tracks one's behaviour in GoJiyo, say someone likes doing adrenalin type activities, it will suggest similar new friends for him to meet, from the GoJiyo Tribe. Second Life doesn't have a feature like that. In fact one can't import friends from other networks, it is one's world apart from the rest of someone's online life.Yes in both worlds one can party at clubs. And in both avatar can fly and teleport.

c. Audience

Second Life's audience is more Western-centric- the majority of Residents are Americans and Europeans, with 7% from Japan and Brazil. Indian user figures are negligable. But 12.1m Residents over the 7 years of operations. A virtual world is, after all, simply an architecture until filled with people. GoJiyo is aimed at young Indians, who are populating it (at time of writing 72,000 avatars in India had been created in 25 days).

d. Business Model & Reason For Doing It

Second Life's mission is "To connect everyone to an online world that advances the human condition." It seems Linden Lab are focusing much more towards UGC and customization of the world- you make what kind of fantasy world you want to inhabit. A virtual meeting between people, including companies, through their Enterprise Grid is another growing area. The exchange rates, Linden dollar to USD also mean Linden have a strong business model for this product.

GoJiyo is a branded environment- Godrej and other brands will be present; but it is not a business Godrej is entering, simply a communication platform for the brand. The aim is to build a conversation with a younger target group than it currently has. And give to them some new, hopefully unique, experiences online.

Target Market:

The target customer for GoJiyo is the internet user above 18 years of age. More specifically speaking the target group of customers is the enterprise customers and the educators. The teen market is given tough competition by the MMOGs besides the presence of fee for owning land and creatively contributing to Second Life makes things difficult. The teen market gets divided into two groups. This group has one section that has purchasing power and another that does not have a purchasing power. The one that does not have purchasing power is because they are largely dependant on their pocket money from parents for fulfilling their needs. In that case spending much money on such pleasures when similar can be got for free through MMOGs takes less priority.

The focus therefore is on three types of target markets teens with purchasing power and the desire to enjoy differently, enterprises that want to use the internet for unique promotion strategies and the educators.

The marketing problem that Gojiyo is facing now is to sustain the interests of the Early Adoptors and bridge the gap between the Early Adopters and the Pragmatists.The gap is called the 'chasm'. Crossing the chasm will show the sustained growth for the company.

Chasm Theory :

The solution to the marketing problem for GoJiyo can be found from the two marketing masterpieces from Geoffery A Moore-'Inside the Tornado ' and 'Crossing the Chasm'. Moore suggests a model for technology marketing in its technology adoption Life Cycle. He says that as a company progresses through the technology adoption life cycle there is gap in its credibility. "Chasm" is the slump in market development that takes place after the visionary (early adopter) market is saturated. The pragmatists who are reference dependant will not come in. The Gojiyo's position is this when it is trying to bridge the gap among the early market, early adopter and the early pragmatists.

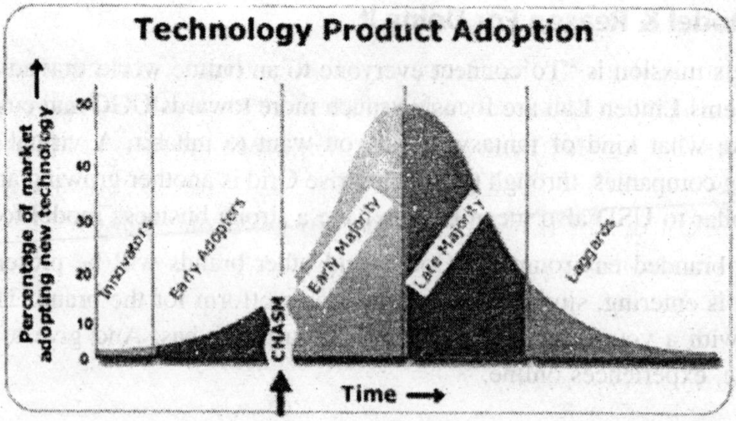

Crossing the Chasm is closely related to the technology adoption lifecycle where five main segments are recognized; innovators, early adopters, early majority, late majority and laggards. According to Moore, the marketer should focus on one group of customers at a time, using each group as a base for marketing to the next group. The most difficult step is making the transition between visionaries (early adopters) and pragmatists (early majority). This is the chasm that he refers to. If a successful firm can create a bandwagon effect in which enough momentum builds, then the product becomes a de facto standard. However, Moore's theories are only applicable for disruptive or discontinuous innovations. Adoption of continuous innovations (that do not force a significant change of behavior by the customer) are still best described by the original technology adoption lifecycle. Confusion between continuous and discontinuous innovation is a leading cause of failure for high tech products.(1)

Crossing the Chasm for sustaining growth:

Moore's solution is to target vertical industrial market segment by penetrating the low risk products. The given metaphor of Moore is borrowed from a game of bowling alley. A similar app is seen when the pragmatists adopt as pins in a bowling ally a tornado of demand is created that the pragmatists adopt en mass. For conversion of the product to mass market a section of Gojiyo should have completely free tools. Strategy to popularize it by giving Gojiyo option in phones and tie-up with hardware solutions providers and telecom service providers can be adopted. The present techniques of giving Gojiyo as the plateform for brand promotion will be fruitful in future. When it becomes mass market it will live in the growth stage of Product Life Cycle for longer time and then with other innovations of the product the growth would be sustained. In short breaking the chasm, moving to newer market and collaborative efforts with similar players in the market can be the winning formula for market development for Godrej's Gojiyo. The chasm theories by Geoffery A Moore find relevance in hyper-growth technology markets and Gojiyo being a unique product of the internet based market the application of the theory seems feasible.

Reference:

1. "Ten Reasons High-Tech Companies Fail". High Tech Strategies Inc.. http://www.hightechstrategies.com/10_reasons.html. Retrieved 2007-03-13.
2. Crossing the Chasm: Marketing and Selling High-tech Products to Mainstream Customers (1991, revised 1999) - ISBN 0-06-051712-3
3. Inside the Tornado: Marketing Strategies from Silicon Valley's Cutting Edge (1995) revised as Inside the Tornado: Strategies for Developing, Leveraging, and Surviving Hypergrowth Markets (2004) - ISBN 0-88730-824-4
4. The Gorilla Game: An Investor's Guide to Picking Winners in High Technology (with Paul Johnson and Tom Kippola, 1998) revised as The Gorilla Game : Picking Winners in High Technology (1999)
5. Living on the Fault Line : Managing for Shareholder Value in the Age of the Internet (2000), revised as Living on the Fault Line, Revised Edition: Managing for Shareholder Value in Any Economy (2002)
6. Dealing with Darwin: How Great Companies Innovate at Every Phase of Their Evolution (2005)
7. Escape Velocity: Free Your Company's Future from the Pull of the Past (2011)

16

Dell Computer: Virtual Company using Real E-commerce

Mr. Sundeep
Bharati Vidyapeeth University
Institute of Management and Research, New Delhi

Introduction

Dell Computer has been pushed by itself and others as a typical Internet company. The Internet has given Dell a means for extending the reach and scope of its direct sales business model at a relatively low marginal cost. It has done so in part by automating functions such as product configuration, order entry, and technical support, enabling the company to grow revenues without a corresponding increase in customer service costs. Also, it has used the Internet to coordinate a network of suppliers and business partners who carry out many of the processes involved in building, distributing and supporting personal computers.

In early 2000, Dell began to redefine itself as the company that "knows how E works."

Capitalizing on its reputation as an e-commerce pioneer, Dell has offered to share that expertise with its customers as they develop their own e-commerce capabilities. However, Dell remains focused on the fact that it is still a hardware company. Its e-commerce efforts are aimed at improving its own efficiency, enhancing customer satisfaction, and reaching new product markets, rather than transforming itself into a services provider as its competitors such as IBM, Compaq, and Hewlett-Packard are becoming.

A close analysis of Dell's use of the Internet and electronic commerce illustrates the strategic and organizational challenges that face any company that is serious about embracing the Internet and trying to tap its potential. It also offers insights into a new form of business organization that may become more prevalent in the networked economy.

Company Background

Dell Computer was founded by Michael Dell in 1984, while he was a student at the University of Texas, Austin. Dell began by selling upgrades of IBM-compatible PCs and in 1985 began to sell its own brand of PCs. From the beginning, Dell operated on the direct sales model, taking orders over the phone and building PCs to the customer's specifications. Dell entered the retail PC channel for several years in the early 1990s, but a downturn in business in 1993 led it to return to its roots as a direct vendor (although the company does work with resellers in some markets).

Dell grew rapidly and in the mid-1990s, its sales reached a point, starting from $3.5 billion in 1994 to $25 billion in 1999. By 1999, Dell had become the number one PC seller in the United States, and was number two worldwide. More importantly, profits were rising, thanks to the cost structure of the direct, build-to-order model. By turning its inventory over 60 times a year, Dell minimized the rapid depreciation costs that mark the PC industry, and by receiving payment from its customers before it paid its suppliers for components, Dell operated on a negative cash conversion cycle. This minimized Dell's working capital requirements and allowed it to achieve high rates of return on its invested capital. The result was an exceptional run for Dell's stock, which outperformed even stars such as Microsoft and Intel in the 1990s.

This success has taken place against the falling PC prices, brutal competition, and enormous losses by other PC makers. Dell has not only survived, but also flourished in this environment thanks to the fundamental advantages of the direct model, and to its continued efforts to improve its execution of that model. It also has taken advantage of its direct model to build strong, stable relationships with the large corporations and other organizations that are its core customers. Unlike indirect vendors, Dell knows who its customers are and has a great deal of information that it uses to provide a high level of service and support, to target customers for retention and expanded sales, and to sell additional third party hardware and software. But even Dell has not been protected to the turmoil in the PC industry. While its most recent 26% growth rate continues to outpace the industry as a whole, it has not been able to match its earlier growth rates of 50% a year, and was hit hard by the slowdown in PC sales in late 2000. The result has been a sharp fall in Dell's stock price and a reminder that Dell is open to the brutal price competition and cyclical demand of the PC industry.

Competitors

Dell's major competitors in its core corporate PC market are Compaq, IBM and Hewlett-Packard. In the consumer and small business market, it faces competition from fellow direct vendor Gateway, and from Compaq, Hewlett-Packard, Apple, and newcomer eMachines. In the portable PC business, the key competitors are Toshiba, IBM, and Compaq. In the critical server and Internet infrastructure markets, Dell competes with Sun, Compaq, HP, and IBM. As Dell moves into new service businesses such as Internet hosting, it faces new competitors such as Exodus and Corio, some of whom may also be Dell customers. Outside the U.S., Dell competes with regional and local vendors in many markets, such as NEC, Fujitsu, and Toshiba in Japan,

Fujitsu-Siemens and Olivetti in Europe, and Legend in China. It also faces strong competition from Compaq and IBM in Europe, Latin America, and the Asia-Pacific region.

Business Strategy

Dell's business has been built on direct sales, build-to-order strategy for producing and selling PCs. While Dell originally sold to regular and experienced individual PC users, by the late 1980s, it was making its way into the corporate market. Dell's direct approach appealed to MIS departments in large organizations who often didn't need or want the various services provided by corporate resellers. Dell concentrated its efforts on working closely with those departments to simplify their lives and lower the total cost of ownership for PCs. Gradually, Dell developed its own sales force to deal directly with CIOs and other top executives, helping penetrate corporate accounts that had long been dominated by established IT vendors such as IBM, HP and DEC. Dell offered competitive prices, high levels of support, and a focus on selling and supporting PCs without the distraction of offering a full line of hardware and services. Dell has capitalized on the inherent advantages of its business model to grow rapidly and profitably. A key advantage of direct sales and build-to-order production is that expensive inventory does not build up in the channel and lose value before it can be sold, and new products can be introduced without having to clear out old inventory in the channel. Dell's inventory turnover rate of 60 times per year compares to 12-15 times for most indirect vendors. Also, customers often pay for the final product before Dell pays suppliers for the parts that go into the PC, so that Dell operates on a negative cash conversion cycle. Perhaps most important are the benefits that Dell gains from the direct customer relationship. Unlike indirect vendors whose channel partners generally refuse to reveal even who the final customer is, Dell knows who the end user is, what equipment it has bought from Dell, where it was shipped, and how much the customer has spent with Dell. Dell uses that information to offer add-on products and services, to coordinate maintenance and technical support, and to help the customer plan its PC replacement and upgrade cycle. With many of its customers, Dell has become what it calls a "PC outsourcer," taking responsibility for managing part or a customer's entire PC inventory, from purchase to disposition. Dell's manufacturing operations are set up to support this business model by building PCs to a customer's specifications, pre-loading software and a hard drive "image" in the factory, and providing an asset tag that can be scanned to keep track of the PC throughout its lifecycle. The build-to-order process has been carefully practiced for years, and involves the entire production cycle and supply chain. Thus, a Dell PC is designed to minimize human touches in production, suppliers are selected to ensure high product quality, suppliers are physically integrated into production, and the entire order fulfillment process is managed by a sophisticated combination of internal and external information systems.

Redefining the Business Model: Dell as an E-commerce Company

Dell was an early and enthusiastic change to the Internet, creating its first web site in 1994 and moving many of its business activities to the Internet ahead of its competitors. The company saw that its direct model gave it an advantage in selling online. Unlike indirect vendors such as

Apple, IBM, HP and Compaq, Dell did not have to worry about channel conflict with resellers and distributors when it began selling online. Also its build-to-order manufacturing processes were already in place, making it easy to offer customers the opportunity to configure products online just as they already did on the telephone. By 2000, Dell was doing $50 million a day in web-enabled sales, but this figure was not the whole story. Dell also used the Internet to link itself more tightly to its large customers by developing extranets called Premier Pages (now renamed Premier Dell.com). Dell had developed over 50,000 Premier Pages for thousands of business customers by mid-2000. These are used for configuration, ordering, services, and support, all customized to the customer's systems and needs. Smaller companies and consumers could buy PCs, peripherals, software and other items online from Dell.com, and receive technical support and other services at the Dell web site.

Equally important was Dell's effort to use the Internet to coordinate its entire value network, including suppliers, logistics providers, and distributors of third-party products, system integrators, and service providers. All of this was driven by the tight information linkages between Dell and its customers.

Dell's successful use of the Internet drew the attention of the media and other companies, including its customers. The company saw an opportunity to capitalize on its growing reputation as an e-commerce innovator and redefine itself as a knowledgeable provider of ecommerce infrastructure to its customers. Dell's public relations machine, with Michael Dell as point man, drove home the message that Dell knows the Internet and could help its customers achieve similar success online. Dell began to market itself as the company that "knows how 'E' works" and can provide the infrastructure that companies need to make it work for them.

Dell has executed its "E-Works" strategy through a new Information Infrastructure sales force and through partnerships with service and software providers, rather than by transforming itself into a services company. Dell brings its corporate customers to the table and offers itself as a model for success on the Internet, but lets its partners do the actual labor-intensive consulting business. Thus Dell manages a high growth market and improves its margins without needing to hire an army of consultants. Dell does make money from services, but most of its revenues still come from selling hardware as part of the e-business solution. This hardware includes high margin items such as large servers and storage devices needed to support e-commerce, as well as commodity desktops and laptops.

Dell has expanded and restores its product line to meet the demands of the e-commerce market. It built Dell.com on Dell servers running Windows NT, and was quick to adopt Windows 2000 internally and in its server line to take advantage of the capabilities of the upgraded operating system. It also has designated Linux as one of its three core operating platforms (along with Windows and Novell), taking advantage of the capabilities and popularity of Linux with ISPs and e-commerce application providers. Dell has increased its R&D investments to enhance the capabilities of its server line, while still sticking to the Intel hardware platform.

Another piece of Dell's e-commerce strategy has been Dell Ventures, which has invested $700 million in about 50 Internet companies (as of July 2000), in areas including broadband and wireless communications, business-to-business and business-to-consumer e-commerce, ASPs, server and storage infrastructure, Internet content, and e-consulting. These investments give Dell access to new technologies without expanding its own R&D activities, and may pay off financially if the companies go public.

Organization of Business Activities

Internal Organization

Dell is organized along geographic lines into the Americas, Asia-Pacific and Japan, and Europe. Corporate headquarters is in Round Rock, Texas, near Austin. The company decided in the mid-1990s that in order to manage a company that was growing at 50% a year, it needed to decentralize decision making rather than try to control everything from the U.S. Each of the regions has its own regional headquarters (Japan has a separate headquarters), its own manufacturing facilities, and its own IT infrastructure. Dell's business activities are organized in each region around different customer segments. These vary somewhat, but generally include (1) relationship (large corporate) customers, (2)home and small business (sometimes called transaction customers), and (3) public sector (government and educational) customers. This segmentation is reflected in Dell's product mix, which has different lines for each segment, in its marketing strategies, which vary by segment, and in its e-commerce and Internet strategies. For instance, services such as DellPremier.com extranets are geared toward large relationship customers, while a more limited set of online services is offered to home and small business customers on Dell.com.

Product development

Dell's product line is similar across different geographies, with adaptations for local requirements such as language, communications protocols and power sources.

Dell customers can order PCs with a variety of configurations for items such as processor speed, memory, storage, sound and video, networking, and monitors. For the most part, however, Dell keeps its configurations fairly limited, with only a few options for each item. But even so, there are thousands of possible permutations for each product, and several products in each line. One estimate is that Dell offers a total of 1.6 million different possible product configurations for all its product lines.

Dell works with partners such as Microsoft and Intel on product development, and with contract manufacturers such as Quanta for product engineering. By controlling the innovations of the PC industry value chain, Dell minimizes its R&D costs. Its own R&D budget is only about 1.6% of revenues, compared to 4-7% for IBM, HP, Compaq and Apple, who are supporting their own technology platforms.

Dell also offers a wide range of third party software and accessories for sale through its DellWare (for relationship and public sector customers) and Gigabuys (HSB) channels. Software also can be installed at the factory—standard applications such as Microsoft Office for all customers, and non-standard or custom applications for relationship customers. In general, then, Dell's product strategy is aimed at enabling it to capture both new customers and a larger share of its current customers' dollars—from PCs to servers and storage; from software to services; and from its own products to third party products. In return, Dell gives customers the convenience of buying a full range of products and services from one source.

Component Sourcing

Dell's main suppliers come from the same group as those of other PC makers, e.g., Intel for microprocessors; Seagate, Quantum, Maxtor and IBM for hard drives; Samsung, Toshiba and Micron for DRAM; Sony, Phillips, Nokia, Samsung and Acer for monitors; contract manufacturers (CMs) such as SCI and Solectron for printed circuit board assemblies; Hon Hai for box builds and connectors; and a variety of Taiwanese original equipment manufacturers (OEMs) for other components and contract manufacturing. Dell's lower-end notebook computers are manufactured entirely by Taiwanese suppliers (mainly Quanta and Arima), whereas only the base units of higher-end notebooks are outsourced as Dell now does final configuration itself. Unlike other PC makers, Dell has relied on Intel as a sole source of microprocessors, a decision that simplifies product development, but which can be costly if Intel is unable to meet the market's demand, as happened in late 1999 and early 2000. About 70% of Dell's procurement is done in the Asia-Pacific region, even though its manufacturing is concentrated in the U.S.

Manufacturing and logistics

Dell organizes manufacturing by region, operating one or more assembly plants to serve its major markets. Plants in the Austin, Texas area and Nashville, Tennessee serve North America; Eldorado do Sul, Brazil serves Brazil and South America; Penang, Malaysia serves the Asia-Pacific region; Xiamen, China serves China; and Limerick, Ireland serves Europe, the Middle East and Africa.

Dell's build-to-order manufacturing process can turn an order around in under a week from the time an order is received until the PC is delivered to the customer. The actual time of assembly is as little as seven hours, including software installation and extensive system testing.

A key to manufacturing is managing inbound logistics with suppliers and contract manufacturers. To have the parts it needs at the right time to assemble a PC, Dell requires suppliers to hold inventory in warehouses within a 15-30 minute drive of its plants. Dell then informs the warehouse when parts must be replenished, and they are trucked to the plant, where they are pulled off of the trucks as needed. When a PC is fully assembled, it is sent to an outbound logistics hub where it is joined with the monitor and peripherals so that the complete system arrives at the customer's site together. All of these logistics are coordinated by Dell through its internal IT systems and via electronic linkages with suppliers, its own logistics hubs, shipping companies, and distributors who handle third party items.

Sales and marketing

Relationship and public sector customers account for about 65% of Dell's revenues overall, and as much as 80% in Europe. All these accounts are initially secured by field-based sales representatives. They are serviced by these field reps and a support team of telephone service reps dedicated to these accounts. Small businesses and consumers are served by several thousand phone reps that can call up historical sales records to assist the customers in choosing systems that match their prior purchase pattern. Approximately one-third of Dell's employee base is in sales and marketing.

The biggest change in Dell's sales and marketing operations has been the introduction of the Internet to handle online sales and to support Dell's sales representatives. At first there was resistance on the part of the country managers and sales reps, who feared losing commissions if customers purchased online or through outbound call centers. To resolve this potential internal channel conflict, Dell changed its incentive system so that country managers and sales reps would receive credit for a sale to their customer accounts, whether it was made on the phone, online, or in person.

External Relationships: From Value Chain to Value Web

Dell's core PC business was organized along the lines of a traditional value chain. Like most other PC companies, it concentrated on building and selling systems, relying on others to provide components, software and services. Unlike most others, however, it sold directly to the end user, thus cutting out the distributor and reseller (Figures 1 and 2).

In terms of designing, building and delivering PCs, this is still roughly the way Dell operates, although a significant share of Dell's products (particularly notebooks) are built by contract manufacturers and shipped directly to the customer. However, as Dell expands its boundaries beyond simply selling PCs, it has replaced the simple value chain with a new model that we call the value web or the virtual corporation.

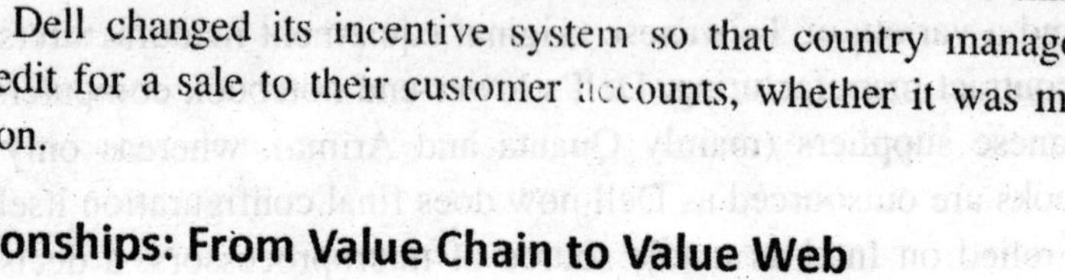

Figure 1. Indirect PC value chain

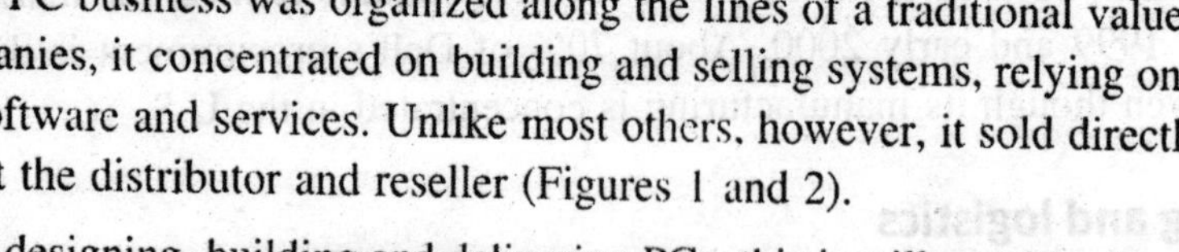

Figure 2. Direct PC value chain: Dell's hardware delivery system

Three key points stand out in the value web model (Figure 3). **First** is Dell's powerful role in coordination and control of the value network, which its direct relationship with the end user allows it to play. Whatever the customer wants or needs, it turns to Dell to provide. Dell then relays the necessary information to its suppliers and business partners who provide the actual service. This is shown by the fact that all of the information flows in Figure 3 are channeled through Dell.

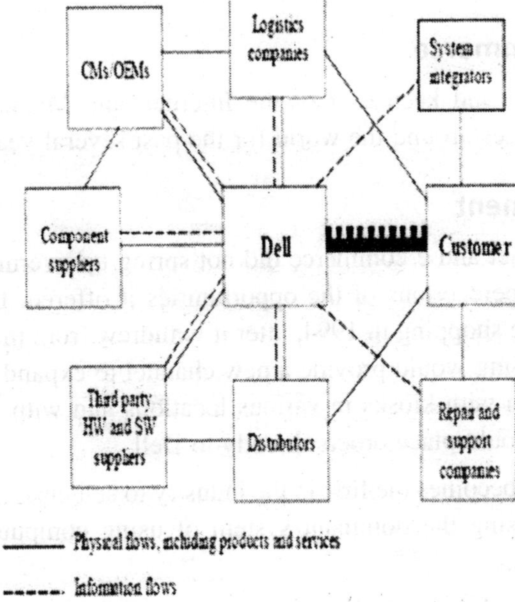

Figure 3. Value Web: Dell's virtual company

Second is the close physical integration of Dell with its suppliers and business partners. Dell's suppliers are not only located close to the plant, but supplier personnel are actually located on the plant floor calling for material from the warehouse using information from Dell's extranet. For example, suppliers not only manage the flow of materials to the plant, but also within the plant, holding inventory until the moment that it actually becomes part of each computer that is built. Similarly, the building of boxes for shipping is done by the box supplier on the factory floor just prior to the moment the computer is loaded into the box. Such physical integration not only reduces Dell's inventory holding costs, but creates personnel efficiencies for its suppliers and builds a closer partnership between Dell and the suppliers.

Third is the importance of information technology, the Internet, and other electronic communications (e.g., e-mail, EDI) in enabling Dell to coordinate this web of close and distant relationships. Information flows back and forth between Dell and the customer via the Internet, triggering orders, service calls and other communications to other parts of the value web. For instance, if a customer's hard drive crashes, the information goes from a Dell technical support person into Dell's internal service and support systems. A new drive is ordered and shipped to a Dell service provider, which dispatches a repair person to install the drive. Information about the drive that crashed goes into Dell's databases and is relayed to the supplier and plant that provided it.

These are just a few examples of hundreds or thousands of different types of actions that must be coordinated internally and with external partners. Without effective information systems, such a structure could not function in a rapidly changing business. Much of that information flow now takes place over inter-organizational systems linked to the Internet.

The Internet and E-commerce

Dell has been an early and keen user of the Internet, and Michael Dell has preached the Internet message to audiences around the world for the past several years.

Evolutionary Development

Dell's use of the Internet and e-commerce did not spring up overnight, but evolved with the technology and with new perceptions of the opportunities it offered. Dell began experimenting with the Internet and online shopping in 1994, after it withdrew from the retail market in the U.S. It hoped that electronic selling would provide a new channel to expand sales and restore growth. Initially, Dell experimented with kiosks in various locations and with online shopping services, through which customers could place orders directly to Dell.

- **1984 The** company becomes the first in the industry to sell custom-built computers directly to end-users, bypassing the dominant system of using computer resellers to sell mass-produced computers.
- **1986 Dell** unveils the industry's fastest-performing computer, pioneers the industry's first thirty-day money back guarantee, and offers the industry's first onsite service program.
- **1996 The** company's quiet bid to sell custom-built computers over the Internet quickly becomes a public revolution when the company announces that sales over http://www.dell.com/ have exceeded $1 million per day. Dell introduces also its first custom custom-made web links for customers. Called "Premier Pages", the links allow customers to tap directly into the company's own service and support databases.
- **1998 Dell** establishes web-based connections with its suppliers to speed the flow of inventory and quality information.

The Internet and e-commerce are fundamental to Dell's business, as befits a company that now defines itself as an Internet infrastructure company. The incorporation of e-commerce into the core of the business is manifested in three ways. These include Dell's use of the technology (1) in its relationships with customers, (2) in coordinating its value web, and (3) in refocusing its market message to emphasize its ability to provide e-commerce solutions to its customers.

Dell's use of the technology in customer relationships

Dell has applied the Internet to all aspects of customer relationships, from sales and marketing to order entry to technical support. It does so partly to support existing channels such as the direct sales force and call centers by providing them with better information and automating their routine tasks. It also has provided self-service tools to customers so that they can order online, track order status, or solve a technical problem via the Internet or an extranet. These applications make Dell's sales and call center staff more effective and productive and reduce staffing required to support a growing customer base. They also give customers access to the same information and tools available to Dell's own personnel, such as product configurators, product specifications, and technical support documents.

For instance, while Dell relies heavily on its direct sales force to win corporate contracts, it supports its sales force with the Internet from the beginning. Dell's sales teams can build a prototype Premier Page extranet for the customer to demonstrate the types of capabilities the customer will enjoy if they select Dell as a supplier. "We often set up Premier Pages for prospective customers before we've won their business. It blows them away," says Chris Halligan, who runs business-to-business e-commerce.16 Also, sales people working on existing accounts can tap into Dell's customer database via the Internet.

Online sales

Dell sells its own products at the dell.com website. Customers in the U.S. are segmented on the home page into home and home office, medium and large organizations, Internet providers, health care businesses, federal government, state and local government, and education. Each customer segment has a different mix of products and services available.

Customers can select and price different configurations with Dell's online configurator. When they are ready to buy, their order is sent to a shopping cart. They can also select various addons such as software, peripherals, digital cameras, PDAs, etc. on the Gigabuys or DellWare sites and add those to the same shopping cart. Once an order is entered, the customer receives an order number that can be used to track order status until it is delivered.

Dell created over 50,000 Premier Page extranets for corporate and small business customers in 13 languages around the world.17 Premier Pages are customized for each customer and include capabilities for procurement, asset management, software upgrading, and technical support. Large relationship customers can have Premier Pages customized further to link to their own internal procurement systems, allowing orders to be sent directly from the customer's information systems to Dell's order management system.

Online service and support

Service and support is an expensive and labor-intensive activity for PC companies, which must provide technical support for complex systems with a wide variety of hardware and software configurations, many of which are added on by the customer. Dell is at an advantage in that much of its business is with large organizations that have their own MIS departments and help desks to support users. Home and small business support is usually provided directly to the end user, and costs more per PC to provide.

Online support was originally developed by the Support Technology Online (STO) team, which grew up in the HSB segment as support.dell.com. In late 1999, Dell created separate STO groups for relationship and transaction customers, each part of those groups' service organizations.

Dell offers several service tools online. These are available to home and small business Customers at support.dell.com, and to relationship customers via the DellPremier.com extranet:

_ *Order status tracking* — Once an order is placed, customers can track it until it is delivered.

_ *Resolution Assistant* — software pre-loaded on a Dell PC that gathers information and sends it to a technician when the customer has a problem. The information is matched against an automated knowledge base. If possible, a MAP—an executable module that automates resolution—is sent to the PC and the fix is done automatically. Resolution Assistant cuts the length of service calls and improves accuracy in diagnosis. It also reduces the number of dispatches for onsite support.

_ *Dell Knowledge Base* — A database containing product information, frequently asked

Questions, third party knowledge and other documents specific to a particular Dell product.

_ *Ask Dudley* — A natural language searchable database of technical information using a

Customized version of the Ask Jeeves search engine.

_ *File Library* – Downloadable drivers, utilities and other updates for Dell systems.

_ *Dell Software Tips* –Library of quick hints and tips for operating systems and office applications.

_ *Pro-active services* – Pro-active notification services on warranty status, system age related information, file drivers, and order status.

_ *Dell Talk*—a monitored bulletin board for Dell customers to share information. Dell has built a community where its customers and loyalists can help each other with technical problems and questions. Dell doesn't censor the discussion, but monitors it to ensure accuracy. Users sometimes give out incorrect information and Dell will intervene with correct information. The volume of activity on Dell Talk is growing fast, increasing more than tenfold in the first few months of 2000. Users are about equally divided between relationship and transaction customers. With the launch of Dell Premier Support.dell.com in September 2000, Dell relabeled its Help Tech service as "Premier Support" for relationship customers.19 Technical Support for corporate and public sector clients is handled by the Relationship Support Technology Online (STO) group. The primary customers for the Relationship STO are the individuals that support the corporate and public sector end users. This includes the help desks, MIS departments, IT professionals and technicians. Dell's relationship customers have access to all of the tools available to HSB customers online, and also have customized applications specific to their account for multiple systems and platforms. Unlike individual users, help desks and MIS organizations must deal with multiple systems, and with problems that arise from networking and client-server environments. For some large accounts, Dell may act as the help desk function for Dell equipment, as Dell's technicians and online offerings are highly experienced in troubleshooting and diagnosing system issues.

The customer profile and history is very important in providing service and support. If the user enters a customer number or system identification number, he or she can get a personal support site that has the machine configuration and the history of what has happened with that machine since it was bought. The support strategy is based on what Dell calls virtual integration—

getting customers closer to the knowledge, and inside out/outside in—giving the internal technicians the same set of tools and knowledge content as the outside customer.

Dell gives customers a choice of venues for support, including phone and online support. They like people to use the web, but don't force them to. The breakdown of help incidents for HSB customers as of mid-2000 was as follows:

- 37% of incidents use the web alone for support
- 13% use both web and phone
- About 50% use the phone alone

Dell finds that people who buy a PC online are more likely to get service and support there, while people who buy by phone will use phone service.

Summary

Dell uses its online sales, premier pages and online support to open up some if its own internal systems to its customers. It also allows corporate customers to link up their own systems such as finance, procurement, MIS, and help desk to Dell's systems via the Internet and extranets. These links enable Dell to keep track of every customer, to inventory equipment upgrades and add-ons, to handle service and support requests directly, to facilitate entry into service and support partners, and to capture feedback on customer satisfaction with its products and service partners. For some large corporate customers, the information network is richer still, including the complete inventory of PCs worldwide for an individual company, the replacement cycle, and the disposition plans.

This extensive information bridge binds Dell more closely with its customers and allows Dell to provide better service to its customers. The Internet and e-commerce enrich the direct customer relationship that is at the core of Dell's business model. Through this relationship, Dell can channel the capabilities of its value web to provide a wider range of services to its customers.

Conclusion: IT, E-commerce, and The Virtual Corporation

Dell started out as a specialist company in the PC industry's horizontally segmented industry structure. It assembled its own computers from standard parts and components manufactured by others and delivered its products directly to customers. Dell focused on the relationship with the customer, but in order to sustain a high growth rate while providing necessary customer service, Dell built a complex web of relationships rather than doing everything itself. With its build-to-order model, Dell viewed final assembly as a core competency, which was kept in house, but it outsourced components, pre-assembly and logistics. Service and support were also viewed as a key part of relationship selling, so Dell kept control of the function but outsourced some service delivery functions to business partners (resellers, system integrators, service companies) who would help customers to install, support, and service Dell PCs. Thus, Dell became a virtual corporation as a matter of business strategy. The key to the strategy was fully exploiting information technology, the Internet, and e-commerce.

In a 1998 interview, Michael Dell explained how he was using information technology to blur traditional boundaries in the value chain among suppliers, the manufacturer, service and support partners and end users to evolve in a direction that he called the virtual corporation. Dell's innovation was not the individual pieces of the strategy—customer focus, supplier partnerships, mass customization, or just in time—although these were certainly important. The real innovation was how to combine them using information and IT to coordinate across company boundaries to achieve new levels of efficiency and effectiveness for the entire value system. The fundamental insight was that IT could allow Dell to achieve coordination of the system and keep its control over the customer relationship.

To do so, Dell focused on using IT and the Internet to improve internal processes such as ordering, assembly, delivery and support, to coordinate its broader value web, and to enhance the customer relationship. A key idea governing process improvements is that information should be diffused as widely as possible throughout the value web to enhance the performance of the entire network and provide rapid feedback to the center. This means that Dell can analyze trends, problems, solutions, performance, and customer satisfaction in real time, creating positive feedback flows that keep the whole system functioning well. Several examples illustrate the powerful role of information and IT in coordination.

- To help its sales organization, Dell has codified information about its product offerings to simplify ordering by phone or the Internet. Dell logs all interactions with its customers so it can determine purchasing behavior, demand patterns and satisfaction levels. This direct contact with the end customers gives Dell insights into how customers buy computers, and what motivates people in different markets. It also enables Dell to use its customer records to anticipate demand. By learning about replacement cycles in different markets, Dell has been able to forecast demand carefully and to target customers with its direct sales force.
- To help its production organization, Dell passes information from sales directly into logistics and assembly, letting its suppliers and the factory floor know the real time demand for PCs and components. By logging all of its customer service interactions, Dell also gets real time information about the performance of its products, enabling it to respond to problems faster and avoid costly refunds and service calls. A good example was provided by Dell's ability to respond rapidly when Intel shipped faulty Pentium chips to computer makers in the mid-nineties. Dell knew exactly where the problem chips were and could easily help customers to replace them. Competitor firms did not know. They had to stop production and go to channel partners to find the problem chips thereby incurring considerable time and cost. The delay, plus the fact that Dell could shift to faultless chips immediately because it had no inventory, caused new customers to look to Dell rather than its competitors.

To help its support organization, Dell mapped out how the support staff could use information within the firm to answer customer questions and provided that knowledge online. It has also provided support staff with online access to each customer's original system configuration and service history. It connected the technical specialists staffing the support lines with Dell marketing, manufacturing and product design groups, exposing many employees in diverse positions to support issues. And, it has provided its service partners with access to the same technical and customer information available to its own support staff. As a result, support staff throughout the value web can perform their function easier, faster and better. Because information is shared no matter where it is collected, the center has the same information available as the periphery.

17

Creation of HLL's Umbrella Brand and Captive Retail Chain Management through Activating Public Distribution System

Ms. Tritali
IMS, Ghaziabad

Study Introduction

Controlled by world giant Unilever (an Anglo-Dutch company), Hindustan Lever Limited (HLL) is the largest consumer products company having 35 strong brands with a powerful presence in key categories – personal care products, foods, soaps/detergents in India. HLL, with a strong and efficient distribution network of millions of retail outlets and thousands of distributors, established itself in the Indian market as a leader. Its products reach every nook and corner of the country. This formidable presence has been built over decades of operations in India, during which it steadily introduced well know brands like Lifebuoy, Lux. Surf, etc. Later, in the early 90s when India-based multinationals were allowed more freedom to operate, HLL went on a takeover spree buying brands and companies like Kwality. Kissan, Tata Oil Mills, etc. there was no looking back for HLL from the heights to had achieved.

For managing sales operations, HLL divides the country into four regions, with regional branches in Delhi, Kolkata, Chennai and Mumbai. Headed by a Regional Manager, they comprise Regional Sales Managers and Area Sales Managers, assisted by dedicated filed forces, consisting of Sales Officers and Territory Sales In-charges.

In Marketing, each category has a Marketing Manager who heads a team of Brand Managers dedicated to each or group of brands.

The Commercial team of a Division is responsible for its supply chain management. There are teams dedicated to sourcing, planning and logistics. Each Division has a nationwide manufacturing base, with each factory peopled by teams of Production, Engineering, Quality Assurance, Commercial and Personal Managers.

In today's consumer market, many big retail chains like 'Big Bazar', 'C3', 'Spencers', 'Shoppers Stop' and many more are taking birth to provide exclusively to their targeted customers. But none of them has the channel exclusively designed to reach 100% mass. All these current retail chains are targeted largely on the upwardly mobile people and thus, HLL was looking at various options for considerations to reach out to the masses creating an 'umbrella' brand of HLL and to acquire readily available captive customers in the following :

1. To create branded retail shops exclusively as 'HLL outfit' in major cities and towns, and gradually spreading over to the other low-income areas
2. To outsource the entire retail chain outfits and its logistics
3. To convert the Public Distribution Outlets (Ration Shops) into a profitable channels as exclusive HLL outlets for families and offering price advantage over the competitors brands.

Based on the options HLL had with them, the project was conferred on me to study the basic opportunities that HLL may exploit by considering the PDS in India, considered as the largest retail chain in the world having four and half lakhs of Fair Price Shops serving 180 million Ration Card holders/families, though very ill organized, inefficient and corrupted to the cause of its objective. The excerpts of the project are reproduced.

Public Distribution System – its evolution, efficacy and opportunity for HLL

Introduction:

Public Distribution System (PDS) is a poverty alleviation program and contributes towards the social welfare of the people. Essential commodities like rice, wheat, sugar, kerosene and the like are supplied to the people under the PDS at reasonable prices. PDS is a boon to the people living below the poverty line. PDS is the primary social welfare and antipoverty program of the Government of India.

The Public Distribution System (PDS) in India is more than half-a- century old as rationing was first introduced in 1939 in Bombay by the British Government as a measure to ensure equitable distribution of food grains to the urban consumers in the face of rising prices. Thus, rationing in times of crisis like famine was the historical precursor to the national policy of stabilization and management of food grains.

Revamping the PDS

In 1984, Government of India created the Ministry of Food and Civil Supplies with two departments namely Department of Food and Department of Civil Supplies: the latter being in charge of PDS. During the Seventh Five Year Plan, an Advisory Committee on PDS headed by the Union Minister for Food & Civil Supplies was constituted by the Government of India to review its working from time to time.

The Government initiated, in consultation with the State Governments and the Union Territory(UT) administrations, steps to revamp to improve its reach based on an area approach (GOI, 1991-92, Part II, p. 53). Preference was planned to be given in this revamped system to the population living in the most difficult areas of the country. This included areas such as drought prone areas, desert areas, tribal areas, certain designated hilly areas and the urban slum areas (GOI, 1991-92, Part II, p. 53). A Revamped Public Distribution System (RPDS) was thus launched in June 1992 in 1700 blocks. For the tribal, hill and arid area populations remotely located and having poor infrastructure, additional items like tea, soap, pulses, and iodized salt were made available under the RPDS. The retail end prices for PDS and RPDS are fixed by the State Governments, taking into account the transportation cost and the dealer's commission (GOI, 1995-96, p.87).

The Program Evaluation Organization of the Planning Commission identifies four major weaknesses of the RPDS. These are

- proliferation of bogus cards
- inadequate storage arrangements
- ineffective functioning of vigilance committee
- failure to issue ration cards to all eligible households (Dev and Renade, 1997, p. 67)

Targeted Public Distribution System (TPDS):

Following the recommendations of the Chief Ministers' Conference held in July 1996, an effort was made to streamline the PDS. Thus, the Targeted Public Distribution System (TPDS) was launched in June 1997. This coincided with the celebration of completion of fifty years of India's independence. The PDS, as it was being implemented earlier, had been criticized for its urban bias and its failure to serve effectively the poorer sections of the population. The latent problem was that a sizeable number of marginalized people, in the absence of cash income that can be transformed into purchasing power are excluded from the planning process because they do not constitute effective demand. This is true after the technological (Green) revolution after the mid-sixties in India. Thus, the TPDS came to replace the erstwhile PDS from June 1997. This system divides the potential beneficiaries into families Below Poverty Line(BPL) and those Above Poverty Line(APL). The State Governments were assigned the task to streamline the PDS by issuing special cards to BPL families and selling essential items under TPDS to them at specially subsidized prices, with better monitoring of the delivery system.

The essential features of the TPDS are as follows

- States to identify families Below Poverty Line(BPL) who would be issued 10 kgs of food grains per month per family at prices less than the Central Issue Price (CIP)
- Population above the poverty line (non poor) now under PDS to continue to receive

normal entitlement at the full CIP

- The Centre should guarantee supply of food grains for the BPL at 10 kgs per month per family to States. Additional quantities required by states would depend on the availability of stocks in the Central Pool
- States will be free to add to the quantum, coverage and the subsidy from their own resources.

HLL's opportunities :

India is on the move and reaching out to the world. After five decades of industrial development based on active Public Sector involvement, regulation of industry and restriction on imports and foreign investment, India embarked upon an ambitious and bold programme of economic reforms since July 1991 to utilize the potential of her vast resource base and to improve her international competitiveness. Notwithstanding the efforts to globalize the Indian economy, the country still presents a very contrasting picture. Familiar picture of poverty and underdevelopment co-exist with wide expanding areas of affluence and modern diversified industrial and service sectors, catering to a vast and thriving market for all types of consumer products. For a country like India having population strength of more than 1 billion, it is not surprising that aggregate private consumption expenditure is one of the higher in the world. Despite low levels of per capita income, there exists in India a large class of consumers for packaged consumer goods and many branded durables and non-durable goods.

Today, PDS is plagued with inefficiencies and corruption. Many intellectuals are suggesting that GoI should completely dismantle PDS. The objective of the project undertaken was not to dismantle PDS, but to utilize possibly this biggest retail chain productively on economies of scale for targeting the top-line of HLL and to reach out to 100% mass by presenting the Fair Price Shops (FPSs), branding them as "Family Value Shop" of HLL.

Methodology :

The methodology was based on data collection. The process of data collection was divided into two parts- primary data and secondary data. Primary data was collected through field research and secondary data was collected through desk research. Primary data collection was based on the structured questionnaire for interviews among three groups – Households, Dealers and Officials.

Goals of PDS :

More specifically, the goals of PDS are:

- Make goods available to consumers, especially the disadvantaged/vulnerable sections of society at fair prices;
- Rectify the existing imbalances between the supply and demand fro the consumer goods;
- Check and prevent black marketing in essential commodities;
- Ensure social justice in distribution of basic necessities of life;
- Even out fluctuations in prices and availability of mass consumption goods.

Erosion of PDS :

There has been gradual erosion of PDS for number of reasons. Some of them are as follows :

- Food grain production has increased vastly. This has partly satisfied the sectional demand;
- Government's procurement expenditure has mounted. Budgetary support increased resulting fiscal problem;
- Storage problem developed and millions of tonnes of food stocks are beyond human consumption;
- The ration units are unwilling to take-off the rotten lot of food stocks;
- Successive dose of price rise of the FCI products has made those items unattractive;
- Rationing units also find it difficult to mobilize fund for off-take under such uncertain response from the people to ration products;
- Open market price and APL price being almost equal, people opt for the former with further advantage of open choice and better welfare gain.

Strength of PDS

The strengths of PDS as perceived for the purpose of this project are as follows :

- It is the largest single retail system in the world;
- Ration cards today are considered as the Identity Card of the family. Therefore, to keep the Ration Cards alive, every family needs to visit the ration shop at least twice a month in order to buy something;
- They got a large godown space;
- Present at the heart of the 'Residential Areas'.

Commercial viability of selected FPSs

An annual return of 12% on PDS transactions can be justified on conditions of commercial viability/bank ability, yet it has been found that of the 67.2% selected FPSs (229) which will earn 12% return with suggested policy package, the 1st, 2nd and 3rd lowest fractiles will only receive a monthly income of Rs.257/-, Rs.488/- and Rs.865/- respectively. This will, trivially not suffice, if PDS is to become a full-time activity of the FPS dealer. Again, 48.7% of them (of the aforesaid 67.2%) still fall below sufficiency criterion. Hence, ensuring the commercial viability of the retailers in PDS and their regular functioning necessitates giving freedom to them to trade in non-PDS items. Recent changes in the regularity of the opening of FPSs and the offer of installments to the consumers reported from Andhra Pradesh after FPSs have been allowed to trade in non-PDS items is strongly indicative.

Weakness of PDS as an opportunity

The present PDS can hardly be described as a 'safety net'. Each and every Indian and also some ghost card holders presently constitute the unorganized crowd that jostles under the ungainly net. While we cannot dispense with the net altogether with millions of poor people living in this vast country, it is crucially important for private sector companies to grab the 'opportunity' of the infrastructure of PDS and mend the net, erect it afresh with the concept of converting the ration shops to "FAMILY VALUE SHOP'.

Weakness or shortcomings in one system of distribution may lead to opening up of new concept of strategic marketing opportunities. The shortcomings of PDS may create new vistas of opportunities to tap the huge "Family Market' which may be defined as the market. signifying purely the daily 'family needs' to the households.

Concept of HLL's Extreme Value Shop

The large private sector companies dealing in FMCG products like HLL may utilize the godown space and selling outlets and make the ration shop owners as their business partners. Such shops may be converted to HLL Extreme Value Shop. Extreme value combines a focused product selection with highly store operations to achieve a singular goal; delivering the most frequently purchased high-quality grocery items to consumers at dramatically lower prices. Extreme value also means delivering savings in an efficient, shopper-friendly store environment. The current ration shops are in dilapidated conditions and these require a face-lift. HLL may standardize the ration shops for better ambience and customer-friendly look in a phased manner. Extreme Value Shop will also create a quicker shopping experience for the customers.

Adaptation to local conditions

However, in the diversified socio-economic conditions of India, it would be a question of 'adaptation to local conditions' which would require be addressing and investigating. While the FPSs in the rural sector are purely designed to cater to the needs of the 'Below-the-poverty-line' (BPL) category, the urban based FPSs on the contrary are more concerned with the 'Above-the-poverty-line' (APL) category. And thus, HLL shall have to consider the FPS channel in such a way that evolves as an expedient adaptation to local opportunities and conditions.

Conclusion

This concept of converting the ration shops to 'Extreme Family Value Shop' might be encouraged by the Government because they are totally incapacitated to provide any more subsidy and to support the PDS. HLL may approach the Government to make one-time capital investment for joint venture initiative by utilizing the amount of subsidy mobilized by the Government in a year. HLL may use the fund for making dispensing outlets attractive.

The starting point for the effective planning of PDS channels shall be to define and determine which markets are to be the target of HLL's mass marketing efforts. It is the part of the determination of over-all HLL's product-market objectives as "the choice of markets and choice of channels are interdependent" [Philip Kotler, marketing management,P-394]. In a broader sense, HLL's objectives shall be decided by unique factors in these current PDS channels which would influence what is desirable and what is possible. Ideally speaking, the PDS retail chain being the single largest mass retail chain in the world could be a model retail network for HLL to reach out to 100% masses. While judging the possibility and viability of converting the FPSs to HLL's 'Family Value Shop', it appears quite a feasible proposition, of course, by step-up method. The step-up method for the purpose is to expand from Metro to Urban to Rural segments through the PDS channels on a graduated scale, based on customer characteristics, product features, characteristics of FPS dealers, competitive characteristics and environmental features prevailing in different geographical segments.

References

1. Sujata Narwal, Management of Public Distribution System
2. Amalesh Banerjee, Food Security and Public Distribution System- Failures and Success.
3. Performance Evaluation of TPDS, Programme Evaluation Organization, Planning Commission.
4. Ahluwalia, D (1993): Public Distribution of Food in India– Coverage, Targeting and Leakages, *Food Policy*, Vol. 18, No.1, (pages 33-54).
5. Government of India (1995) : Evaluation Report on Revamped Public Distribution System, Programme Evaluation Organisation , Planning Commission, New Delhi. *Performance Evaluation of Targeted Public Distribution System (TPDS) -2005.*
6. http://fcamin.nic.in/item22.htm
7. http://indiabudget.nic.in/es2002-03/chapt2003/chap516.pdf
8. National sample Survey, 42nd round,NSSO,1990.

18

Marketing Mix Strategies for Haldiram's Group

Dr. Vinod S. Ingawale
viningawale@yahoo.co.in
Prof. Hrishikesh M. Bhagat
bhagathrishi@gmail.com
Bharati Vidyapeeth University,
Institute of Management and Entrepreneurship Development , Pune

Abstract of the Case:

Over a period spanning six and a half decades, the Haldiram's Group (Haldiram's) had emerged as a household name for ready-to-eat snack foods in India. It had come a long way since its relatively humble beginning in 1937 as a small time sweet shop in Bikaner, in the Rajasthan state of India. In 2001, the turnover of the Haldiram's was Rs. 4 billion. The company employed the best available technology in all its manufacturing facilities in India. Given the increasing popularity of Haldiram's products, the group planned to expand its operations. However, some analysts felt that Haldiram's still had to overcome some hurdles. The company faced tough competition not only from sweets and snack food vendors in the unorganized market but also from domestic and international competitors like SM Foods, Bakeman's Industries Ltd, Frito Lay India Ltd.(Frito Lay) and Britannia Industries Ltd. Moreover, the group had to overcome internal problems as well. In the early 1990s, because of the conflict within the Agarwal's family, Haldiram's witnessed an informal split between its three units as they started operating separately offering similar products and sharing the same brand name. In 1999, after a court verdict these units started operating as three different companies with clearly defined territories. This split had resulted in aggressive competition among themselves for a higher share of domestic and international markets. Now Haldiram's group is seeking the right marketing mix strategies.

Introduction

The Haldiram's Group (Haldiram's) had emerged as a household name for ready-to-eat snack foods in India. The company offered a wide variety of traditional Indian sweets and snacks at competitive prices that appealed to people belonging to different age groups. Haldiram's had many 'firsts' to its credit. It was the first company in India to brand 'namkeens[1]'. The group also pioneered new ways of packaging namkeens.

Its packaging techniques increased the shelf life of namkeens from less than a week to more than six months. It was also one of the first companies in India to open a restaurant in New Delhi offering traditional Indian snack food items such as "panipuri," "chatpapri," and so on, which catered to the needs of hygiene conscious non-resident Indians and other foreign customers. Since the very beginning, the brand 'Haldiram's' had been renowned for its quality products.

The company employed the best available technology in all its manufacturing facilities in India. Given the increasing popularity of Haldiram's products, the group planned to expand its operations. However, some analysts felt that Haldiram's still had to overcome some hurdles.

1. These are spicy snacks made of chickpea floor, processed rice and roasted nuts. 'Namkeens' are very popular in India, especially among people from the northern part of the country. Around fifty varieties of namkeens are available in India.

The company faced tough competition not only from sweets and snack food vendors in the unorganized market but also from domestic and international competitors like SM Foods, Bakeman's Industries Ltd, Frito Lay India Ltd.(Frito Lay) and Britannia Industries Ltd.

Moreover, the group had to overcome internal problems as well. In the early 1990s, because of the conflict within the Agarwals family, Haldiram's witnessed an informal split between its three units as they started operating separately offering similar products and sharing the same brand name. In 1999, after a court verdict these units started operating as three different companies with clearly defined territories. This split had resulted in aggressive competition among themselves for a higher share of domestic and international markets.

History of Haldiram's Group

In 1937, Ganga Bishen Agarwal, (popularly known as Haldiram), opened a small sweet shop in Bikaner, a small district in Rajasthan. Bikaner had a large number of sweet shops selling sweets as well as namkeens. 'Bhujia sev,' a salty snack prepared by Ganga Bishen, was very popular among the residents of Bikaner and was also purchased by tourists coming to Bikaner. In 1941, the name 'Haldiram's Bhujiawala' was used for the first time.

In 1950, Prabhu Shankar Agarwal (Prabhu), along with his father Rameshwar Lal Agarwal (son of Ganga Bishen), expanded the business by establishing a small manufacturing unit for sweets and namkeens in Kolkata. The success of this unit motivated Prabhu to upgrade its machinery to improve the quality of its products. As demand for Haldiram's products increased, it was decided to scale up the company's manufacturing and distribution activities. In 1970, a large manufacturing unit was set up in Nagpur in the state of Maharashtra (India).

In 1983, a retail outlet was set up in New Delhi. The outlet became very popular not only among the Delhiites but also among tourists visiting Delhi. Haldiram's was able to achieve significant growth during the 1980s and 1990s. In 1992, a manufacturing unit with a retail outlet attached to it was set up in the outskirts of Delhi. A year later, Haldiram's syrups and crushes were successfully launched in the Indian market.

In 1995, a restaurant was opened in New Delhi. In 1997, realizing the potential of namkeens, the company set up a manufacturing unit in Delhi exclusively for making namkeens. To add potato products to its existing product portfolio, machinery was imported from the US. Haldiram's maintained high quality standards at every stage of the production process. All its food items were prepared and packaged in a very hygienic environment.

In the mid 1990s, Haldiram's added bakery items, dairy products, sharbats and ice creams to its portfolio. At the beginning of the 21st century, Haldiram's products reached millions of consumers not only in India, but also in several other countries, including the US, Canada, UK, UAE, Australia, New Zealand, Sri Lanka, Nepal, Japan and Thailand.

Analysts felt that the growing popularity of Haldiram's products could be attributed to its constant focus on all the elements of the marketing mix. An article posted on the website apeda.com quoted some of the company's strengths, "To sustain in the competitive market, Haldiram's has endeavored stress on its product quality, packaging, shelf life; competitive price with a special emphasis on consumers satisfaction and its lingering taste is amongst the best available in the world."

Problem Areas

1. According to media reports, Haldiram's lagged behind competitors in the area of customer service. A report in Deccan Herald that Prabhu Shankar Agarwal, the owner of the Kolkata unit, was arrested on charges of manhandling customers only reiterated this opinion.
2. The report also mentioned that few of the company's restaurants did not possess the minimum requirements, such as sufficient seating arrangements and adequate parking lots.
3. Haldiram's also had to deal with problems created by spurious products. Some companies claiming to be close associates of the original Haldiram's of Bikaner used the Haldiram's brand name in their products. For example the 'Haldiram Madanlal' company claimed that its proprietor, Anil Kumar Agarwal, belonged to the Haldiram's family of Bikaner.The consequences of the split were a matter of concern.
4. Though on paper, the three companies had clearly defined boundaries within which they should operate, in practice, they did not stay within their boundaries. They penetrated each other's territories and competed among themselves for a larger share of the snacks market. Analysts felt that competitors would take advantage of this split.
5. Since the scope for increasing market share in India was limited, these companies began to compete aggressively in international markets. They used the internet, not only to

market their products but also compete with each other. Each company claimed that its products were superior to those of the others in terms of quality.

6. Haldiram's Group is currently lagging behind in application of right marketing strategies.

2. Agriculture and Processed Foods Export Development Authority (APEDA) is an autonomous institution, which provides financial, logistics related and promotional assistance to exporters of processed food items from India. Through its website apeda.com, it enables exporters to give a brief account of the company and their products.

Analysis of the Case

The Haldiram's group had presence not only in India but in several countries all over the world. Till the early 1990s, Haldiram's comprised of three units, one each in Kolkata, Nagpur and New Delhi. The Agarwals family that owned Haldiram's were always conscious of the need to satisfy customers in order to grow their business.It had come a long way since its relatively humble beginning in 1937 as a small time sweet shop in Bikaner, in the Rajasthan state of India. In 2001, the turnover of the Haldiram's was Rs 4 billion. Due to several reasons, Haldiram's units were formally split as three separate companies with specific business territories. As a result of this split and weaker marketing strategies, The Haldiram's group is now facing competition among themselves and also from other companies.

The Marketing Mix of Haldiram's Group

Product

Haldiram's offered a wide range of products to its customers. The product range included namkeens, sweets, sharbats[5], bakery items, dairy products, papad[4] and ice-creams (See Exhibit I for details of product range). However, namkeens remained the main focus area for the group contributing close to 60% of its total revenues. By specializing in the manufacturing of namkeens, the company seemed to have created a niche market.

Haldiram's sought to customize its products to suit the tastes and preferences of customers from different parts of India. It launched products, which catered to the tastes of people belonging to specific regions. For example, it launched 'Murukkus,' a South Indian snack, and 'Chennai Mixture' for south Indian customers.

Similarly, Haldiram's launched 'Bhelpuri,' keeping in mind customers residing in western India. The company offered certain products such as 'Nazarana,' 'Panchratan,' and 'Premium' only during the festival season in gift packs. These measures helped Haldiram's compete effectively in a market that was flooded with a variety of snack items in different shapes, sizes and flavors.

Pricing

Haldiram's offered its products at competitive prices in order to penetrate the huge unorganized market of namkeens and sweets. The company's pricing strategy took into consideration the price conscious nature of consumers in India.

Haldiram's launched namkeens in small packets of 30 grams, priced as low as Rs.5. The company also launched namkeens in five different packs with prices varying according to their weights. The prices also varied on the basis of the type of namkeens and the raw materials used to manufacture it. The cost of metallized packing[3] also had an impact on the price,

3. Juice concentrates offered in different flavors.

4. A flat, thin, dried roll of kneaded floor mixed with spicy ingredients. It has a reasonably long shelf life, can be toasted or fried in oil and served as a snack or taken along with food.

5. Packing where in Aluminum was used which helps in preserving the freshness of the products being packed especially in the case of snack foods. The company revised the prices of its products upwards only when there was a steep increase in the raw material costs or additional taxes were imposed.

Place

Haldiram's developed a strong distribution network to ensure the widest possible reach for its products in India as well as overseas. From the manufacturing unit, the company's finished goods were passed on to carrying and forwarding (C&F) agents. C&F agents passed on the products to distributors, who shipped them to retail outlets. While the Delhi unit of Haldiram's had 25 C&F agents and 700 distributors in India, the Nagpur unit had 25 C&F agents and 375 distributors.

Haldiram's also had 35 sole distributors in the international market. The Delhi and Nagpur units together catered to 0.6 million retail outlets in India. C&F agents received a commission of around 5%, while distributors earned margins ranging from 8% to 10%. The retail outlets earned margins ranging from 14% to 30%. At the retail outlet level, margins varied according to the weight of packs sold.

Retailers earned more margins ranging from 25% to 30% by selling 30 gms pouches (priced at Rs.5) compared to the packs of higher weights. Apart from the exclusive showrooms owned by Haldiram's, the company offered its products through retail outlets such as supermarkets, sweet shops, provision stores, bakeries and ice cream parlors. The products were also available in public places such as railway stations and bus stations that accounted for a sizeable amount of its sales.

Haldiram's products enjoyed phenomenal goodwill and stockists competed with each other to stock its products. Moreover, sweet shops and bakeries stocked Haldiram's products despite the fact that the company's products were competing with their own products. Haldiram's also offered its products through the Internet. The company tied up with *indiatimes.com*, a website owned by the Times of India group to sell its products over the Internet. Haldiram's products could be ordered through a host of other websites in India and abroad.

Giftstoindia.com, giftssmashhits.com, tohfatoindia.com and channelindia.com enabled people residing abroad to send Haldiram's gift packs to specified locations in India. Region-specific websites enabled people to send gifts to specified regions. These include indiamart.com (Delhi and surrounding areas), mumbaiflowersgifts.com (Mumbai), and chennaiflowersgifts.com (Chennai and other parts of Tamilnadu). These websites competed on issues such as delivery time, which varied between 48 hrs to one week, delivery charges (some websites offered free delivery of products) and value added services (like sending personal messages along with the gift packs).

6. The Times of India group is owned by Bennett, Coleman & Company Ltd. It is India's leading publishers of newspapers and magazines catering to a wide cross section of customers. The newspapers published by the group include Times of India, Economic Times, Nav Bharat Times and Sandhya Times (Hindi). The magazines published include Femina and Filmfare. Times FM, a music channel owned by the group, broadcasts programs in five cities in India.

Promotion

Haldiram's product promotion had been low key until competition intensified in the snack foods market. The company tied with 'Profile Advertising'[7] for promoting its products. Consequently, attractive posters, brochures and mailers were designed to enhance the visibility of the Haldiram's brand.

Different varieties of posters were designed to appeal to the masses. The punch line for Haldiram's products was, 'Always in good taste.' Advertisements depicting the entire range of Haldiram's sweets and namkeens were published in the print media (magazines and newspapers). These advertisements had captions such as 'millions of tongues can't go wrong,' 'What are you waiting for Diwali?' And 'Keeping your taste buds on their toes.'

To increase the visibility of the Haldiram's brand, the company placed its hoardings in high traffic areas such as train stations and bus stations. Posters were designed for display on public transport vehicles such as buses, and hoardings, focused on individual products were developed. Captions such as 'yeh corn hain' (this is corn), 'chota samosa - big mazaa' (small samosa- big entertainment), 'yeh Kashmiri mix khoob jamega' (this namkeen item will gel well) and 'oozing with taste' (for Rasgoolas) promoted individual products.

For those customers who wanted to know more about Haldiram's products, special brochures were designed which described the products and gave information about the ingredients used to make it. Mailers were also sent to loyal customers and important corporate clients as a token of appreciation for their patronage. Packaging was an important aspect of Haldiram's product promotion.

Since namkeens were impulse purchase items, attractive packaging in different colors influenced purchases. Haldiram's used the latest technology (food items were packed in nitrogen filled pouches) to increase the shelf life of its products. While the normal shelf life of similar products was under a week, the shelf life of Haldiram's products was about six months. The company projected the shelf life of its products as its unique selling proposition.

Posters highlighting the shelf life of its products carried the caption 'six months on the shelf and six seconds in your mouth.' During festival season, Haldiram's products were sold in attractive looking special gift packs. The showrooms and retail outlets of Haldiram's gave importance to point of purchase (POP) displays. Haldiram's snacks were displayed on special racks, usually outside retail outlets. The showrooms had sign boards displaying mouth-watering delicacies with captions such as 'Chinese Delight,' Simply South,' 'The King of all Chats.'

7.An advertising agency based in India.

8. Triangle shaped pastry dough stuffed with spicy potatoes and deep-fried.

9. A traditional Indian snack food item prepared by deep frying potato in oil and mixing it with spices and other vegetables.

Posters highlighting the shelf life of its products carried the caption 'six months on the shelf and six seconds in your mouth.' During festival season, Haldiram's products were sold in attractive looking special gift packs. The showrooms and retail outlets of Haldiram's gave importance to point of purchase (POP) displays. Haldiram's snacks were displayed on special racks, usually outside retail outlets. The showrooms had sign boards displaying mouth-watering delicacies with captions such as 'Chinese Delight,' Simply South,' 'The King of all Chats.'

Posters containing a brief account of the history of Haldiram's, along with pictures of its products, were also on display at these showrooms. Haldiram's also diversified into the restaurant business to cash in on its brand image. The company established restaurants in Nagpur and Delhi.

The restaurant at Nagpur devised an innovative strategy to increase its business: It facilitated people who were traveling by train through Nagpur station to order food from places where stockists of Haldiram's Nagpur unit were located. The customers could order for lunch/dinner by sending a demand draft (DD) or cheque to the Nagpur unit or giving the same to specified local distributors belonging to the Nagpur unit.

Along with the DD/ cheque, customers had to provide information such as the name of the train, its likely time of arrival at Nagpur, their names and coach and seat numbers. Haldiram's restaurants in Delhi also used innovative ways to attract customers. The restaurant located at Mathura road had special play area for children.

To cater to NRI's and foreign tourists, who hesitated to consume snack foods sold by the roadside vendors since it was not prepared in a hygienic manner, the Haldiram's restaurant located in South Delhi used specially purified water to make snack foods including pani puri and chat papri[10]. These promotional strategies helped Haldiram's to compete effectively with local restaurant chains such as Nathus, Bikanerwala and Agarwals and with western fast food chains such as McDonald's and Pizza Hut.

Positioning

The above initiatives helped Haldiram's to uniquely position its brand. Haldiram's also gained an edge over its competitors by minimizing promotion costs. Appreciating the company's efforts at building brand, an analyst said, "Haldiram once was just another sweet maker but it has moved into trained brands first by improving the product quality and packaging. Through its clever products and brilliant distribution it had moved into the star category of brands."

10. Snack items that are prepared with a spicy, water-based sauce. These snacks are commonly sold by roadside vendors.

11. In an article titled 'Brands and Bollywood,' on the website www.indiainfoline.com.

Haldiram's earned recognition both in India and abroad. The Nagpur unit of Haldiram's was conferred the International Food Award by the Trofeo International Alimentacion of Barcelona, Spain for having maintained high standards in quality and hygiene, at its manufacturing unit. The Delhi unit was awarded the Keshalkar Memorial Award by the All India Food Preservers Association in the mid 1980s in recognition of its efforts for popularizing ethnic Indian foods in India and abroad.

In 1994, the unit was awarded the International Award for Food & Beverages by the Trade Leaders Club in Barcelona, Spain. The unit also received the Brand Equity Award in 1998. Manoharlal Agarwal, who played a key role in the success of the Delhi unit, was included in the eighth edition of Distinguished Leadership by the Board of Registrars of The American Biographical Institute. Haldiram's was also admitted as the member of Snack Food Association, US.

The Marketing Mix Strategies for Haldiram's Group

Application of following Marketing Mix Strategies will help Haldiram's Group to overcome the situation.

1. Haldiram's Group should come up with additional new products to sustain the growth and to remain in competitive market situation. For this purpose, they should conduct market research to know the tastes and preferences of the consumers. The group should focus on youngsters, as this is an important segment for their opportunities and growth in the market.
2. The group should take efforts for creation of Brand awareness in market. For this purpose they should focus on the effective advertising. In this case they may take help of advertising agencies, Brand Ambassador, Medias and other promotional activities. Also the sales force should be properly trained to pursued the attention of customers towards Haldiram's Group products.
3. It is observed from the current situation that retailers don't have sufficient stock of Haldiram's Group products to meet customers demand. Proper feedback from the retailers and other channels of distribution should be taken regularly to overcome the situation.
4. As Physical evidence is an important means of marketing communications, the group should apply this marketing mix to improve the situation.
5. All customer facing personnel need to be trained. For this purpose, the Haldiram's Group should concentrate on one of the important services marketing mix i.e. People.
6. For the purposes of the marketing mix, process is an element of service that sees the customer experiencing an organisation's offering. So, the importance must be given to this marketing mix for the growth in the market.

12. It is an international organization in the food processing industry.

13. An award given by "Brand Equity," a publication of the Times of India Group, to companies that are successful in their respective fields.

14. Based in the US, the American Biographical Institute is a publisher of biographical reference works collected from all over the world.

15. 1An international trade association of the snack food industry, representing snack food manufacturers and suppliers.

The Road Ahead

In the financial year 2001-2002, the combined turnover of all three units of Haldiram's was estimated at Rs. 4 billion. The company targeted a growth of 15% for the financial year 2002-2003. Analysts felt that, given the competition in the industry, Haldiram's needed to develop new initiatives achieve this growth.

Frito Lay's product range consisted of a mixture of traditional Indian and western flavors which appealed to younger and older generations. Its products included Leher Namkeens, Leher Kurkure (snack sticks), Lays (flavored Chips), Cheetos (snack balls), Uncle Chips and Nutyumz (nut snacks).

Frito-Lay was the first company to launch small 35 gm packs namkeens priced at Rs. 5 and also the first company in the organized sector to launch Aloo Bhujia. Another competitor, SM Foods, introduced a range of innovative products. The company launched India's first non-wafer chips in 1988. SM offered products under two main brands – Peppy and Piknik.

Under Peppy, it had sub brands such as Cheese Balls, Ringos, Hi Protein Crispies, Potato Rackets, Hearts, Veggie Treat, Mixtures and Minerette. Under Piknik, it had Protein Pin, Junior and Corn Puffs. Haldiram's also faced tough competition from domestic players such as Britannia Industries Ltd., Bikanerwala Foods and ITC.

In addition, FMCG major HLL had also announced plans to enter the snack food market. Analysts felt that Haldiram's lagged behind competitors in offering snack foods targeted at children, who were always eager to try new flavors in every product category. They felt that the company concentrated too much on traditional Indian items such as Bhujia Sev and Moong Dal.

Haldiram's had in fact, taken steps to fill the gaps in its portfolio. Rajendra Agarwal, the owner of the Nagpur unit said, "We want to expand our market by introducing snacks that will appeal to younger people. There will be no growth in the traditional snacks category."[17] The unit planned to launch products such as flavored ready-to-eat popcorn and a product similar to Leher Kurkure.

Though Haldiram's had increased its focus on advertising and promotion in the last couple of years, still more initiatives in this direction were necessary. Frito Lay's expenditure on product promotion was much higher. With successful ad campaigns such as "control nahin hotha" (it is irresistible) for the Leher brand of namkeens, the company made sure that it attracted the attention of viewers.

For instance, an advertisement in 'haldiramusa.com', a web portal that sold the products of the Delhi company in the US, read, "Our items come specially packed from the Original Haldiram's of Delhi offering superior taste and superior quality, the only Haldiram approved by the US FDA

(Food and Drug Administration). Try the Delhi stuff and you will never touch the Nagpur Haldiram packets that most grocery stores store." Analysts were of the opinion that the internal rivalry among its own companies may lead to dilution of Haldiram's brand equity.

16. Paste of mashed potatoes and gram flour, fried and added with salt and spices.

17. In an article 'It All Snacks Up' in Brand Equity, Economic Times dated December 11, 2002.

Teaching Note

Synopsis

The Haldiram's Group had emerged as a household name for ready-to-eat snack foods in India. This group had come a long way since its relatively humble beginning in 1937 as a small time sweet shop in Bikaner, in the Rajasthan state of India. In 2001, the turnover of the Haldiram's was Rs. 4 billion. The company employed the best available technology in all its manufacturing facilities in India. Given the increasing popularity of Haldiram's products, the group planned to expand its operations. In the financial year 2001-2002, the combined turnover of all three units of Haldiram's was estimated at Rs. 4 billion. The company targeted a growth of 15% for the financial year 2002-2003. Analysts felt that, given the competition in the industry, Haldiram's needed to develop new initiatives achieve this growth.

However, some analysts felt that Haldiram's still had to overcome some hurdles. The company faced tough competition not only from sweets and snack food vendors in the unorganized market but also from domestic and international competitors like SM Foods, Bakeman's Industries Ltd, Frito Lay India Ltd.(Frito Lay) and Britannia Industries Ltd. Moreover, the group had to overcome internal problems as well. In the early 1990s, because of the conflict within the Agarwal's family, Haldiram's witnessed an informal split between its three units as they started operating separately offering similar products and sharing the same brand name.

The Marketing Mix of Haldiram's Group includes the following:

1. Product

Haldiram's offered a wide range of products to its customers. The product range included namkeens, sweets, sharbats, bakery items, dairy products, papad and ice-creams (See Exhibit I for details of product range). However, namkeens remained the main focus area for the group contributing close to 60% of its total revenues. By specializing in the manufacturing of namkeens, the company seemed to have created a niche market.

2. Price

Haldiram's offered its products at competitive prices in order to penetrate the huge unorganized market of namkeens and sweets. The company's pricing strategy took into consideration the price conscious nature of consumers in India.

3.Place

Haldiram's developed a strong distribution network to ensure the widest possible reach for its products in India as well as overseas. From the manufacturing unit, the company's finished goods were passed on to carrying and forwarding (C&F) agents. C&F agents passed on the products to distributors, who shipped them to retail outlets. While the Delhi unit of Haldiram's had 25 C&F agents and 700 distributors in India, the Nagpur unit had 25 C&F agents and 375 distributors.

4. Promotion

Haldiram's product promotion had been low key until competition intensified in the snack foods market. The company tied with 'Profile Advertising for promoting its products. Consequently, attractive posters, brochures and mailers were designed to enhance the visibility of the Haldiram's brand.

To increase the visibility of the Haldiram's brand, the company placed its hoardings in high traffic areas such as train stations and bus stations. Posters were designed for display on public transport vehicles such as buses, and hoardings, focused on individual products were developed. Captions such as 'yeh corn hain' (this is corn), 'chota samosa - big mazaa' (small samosa - big entertainment), 'yeh Kashmiri mix khoob jamega' (this namkeen item will gel well) and 'oozing with taste' (for Rasgoolas) promoted individual products.

Following Marketing Mix Strategies are suggested for Haldiram's Group

1. Haldiram's Group should come up with additional new products to sustain the growth and to remain in competitive market situation. For this purpose, they should conduct market research to know the tastes and preferences of the consumers. The group should focus on youngsters, as this is an important segment for their opportunities and growth in the market.
2. The group should take efforts for creation of Brand awareness in market. For this purpose they should focus on the effective advertising. In this case they may take help of advertising agencies, Brand Ambassador, Medias and other promotional activities. Also the sales force should be properly trained to pursued the attention of customers towards Haldiram's Group products.
3. It is observed from the current situation that retailers don't have sufficient stock of Haldiram's Group products to meet customers demand. Proper feedback from the retailers and other channels of distribution should be taken regularly to overcome the situation.
4. As Physical evidence is an important means of marketing communications, the group should apply this marketing mix to improve the situation.
5. All customer facing personnel need to be trained. For this purpose, the Haldiram's Group should concentrate on one of the important services marketing mix i.e. People.
6. For the purposes of the marketing mix, process is an element of service that sees the customer experiencing an organisation's offering. So, the importance must be given to this marketing mix for the growth in the market.

Learning Objectives

A. To acquaint the students with real life market situations.

B. To develop decision making ability among students.

C. To understand how to solve case.

D. To know marketing mix concept.

E. To understand the application of marketing mix strategies for a particular situation.

Assignment Questions

1. Write short notes on –

   A.Haldiram Group Products

   B.Haldiram Group – The Road Ahead
2. In what stage of Product Life Cycle the Haldiram Group products are ? Justify your opinion with examples.
3. Perform SWOT Analysis for Haldiram Group products.
4. Compare Haldiram Group products with their competitors products.
5. Which problems the Haldiram Group is currently facing ? Suggest various alternatives to overcome these problems.
6. Do you think 7 P's of marketing mix will play an important role for the growth of Haldiram Group?
7. Explain the effect of spilt between the three units of Haldiram Group on their business.
8. Suggest different strategies to reduce aggressive competition among three companies of Haldiram Group ?
9. What promotion policy would you recommended for Haldiram Group?
10. Advice distribution strategy to Haldiram Group.
11. If you are appointed as an advisor to the Haldiram Group of companies, what comprehensive strategy would you recommends to its Board of Directors?
12. Develop strategies to maintain long-term strategic advantage for the Haldiram Group product lines.
13. Consider any one product from Haldiram Group products and design marketing mix for that product. Explain your answer with illustrations.
14. Advice branding and product mix strategies to Haldiram Group.
15. What kind of marketing mix strategy the Haldiram Group should adopt to overcome the situation?

Bibliography

Books Recommended:-

1. Marketing Management – Philip Kotler

2. Marketing Management – V.S.Ramaswamy and S.Namakumari
3. Principles of Marketing 12th Edition – Philip Kotler and Gary Armstrong
4. Marketing Models – Lilien & Kotler & Moorthy
5. Marketing Management – Rajan Saxena
6. Marketing – Gandhi

Journals:-

1. Journal of Marketing
2. Indian Journal of Marketing
3. Journal of Marketing Research

Web Sites:-

1. www.icmrindia.com
2. www.haldirams.com
3. www.google.com

19

Coca Cola's Strategies to Tap the Bottom of the Pyramid

Ms. Shradha Vernekar,
Ms. Aakriti Jain
Bharati Vidyapeeth University
Institute of Management and Research ,New Delhi

Coca-cola Company is the world's largest beverage company, largest manufacturer, distributor & marketer of non-alcoholic beverage concentrates & syrups in the world & is one of the largest corporations in the US. The company is best known for its flagships product coca-cola, invented by pharmacist John Stith Pemberton in 1886. It offers nearly 400 brands in over 200 countries or territories and serves 1.5 billion servings each day. Middle East is one of the only regions in the world where Coca-Cola is not the number one soda drink

There were many key Challenges faces by Coca Cola like low penetration in rural market, competition from the organized and unorganized sectors, Shortage of electricity in the rural areas, No proper modes of transportation, Spurious brands or look alike brands available, Poor rural infrastructure and consumption habits, etc.

According to the Rural Market Scenario 70% of our population lives in rural area. No company can survive in future unless they serve rural India in general and b-o-p in particular. NCAER states rural India accounts for the 70% of toilet soap users, and 38% of two-wheelers purchases com from India. Coca-cola is the first global majors to spot the potential spin offs from the rural market. They have a unique supply chain to cater to vast rural markets hinterland, a village retail environment consists of 4-5 kirana shops. They also tapped local forms of entertainment like annual haats and fairs.

Sanjev Gupta, Deputy President-we want to be the hindustan lever limited of the indian beverage business

"Thanda" goes Rural, Thanda Matlab Coca-Cola' was targeted at rural and semi-urban consumers. The idea was to position Coca-Cola as a generic brand for cold drinks. The campaign was launched to support CCI's rural marketing initiatives. CCI began focusing on the rural market in the early 2000s in order to increase volumes

Rural marketing strategy used by coca-cola was based on three A's - Availability, Affordability and Acceptability. They Opted for a hub and spoke distribution system to market in rural areas. It made an investment of Rs 7 million to meet rural demand . Large trucks for transporting stock from bottling plants to hubs and medium commercial vehicles transported the stock from the hubs to spokes. Coca-Cola set out to woo rural consumers by halving the price of a 200-milliliter (seven-ounce) bottle to Rs. 5 (11 cents)

First brand to offer communication that is targeted to the smaller towns would own the rural market , Comprises the other 96% of the nation's population, Primary need is out-of-home thrist-quenching and the soft drink category was undifferentiated in the minds of rural consumers , With an average Coke costing Rs. 10 and an average day's wages around Rs. 100, Coke was perceived as a luxury that few could afford

They started the parivartan program in which they gave training retailers (around 6,000 of them) on displaying and stocking products well and improve inventory management.Presentations in local Hindi language were also given with "Certified Retailer" . Program has covered more than 30,000 retailers

Distribution Strategy used were coke started out by drawing up a hit list of high potential villages from various districts, large distributors were apointed, and they were supplied from the company's depot in large town and cities, full load supplies were offerd twice weekly against payment by demand draft, On their part, the distributors (large) appointed smaller distributors (Spokes) in adjoining areas, the smaller distributors undertook fixed journey plans on a weekly basis and supplied against cash, the distributors also hired rickshaws (cyle operated vans) that travelled to villages daily

Coca-Cola uses Environment-friendly innovation solar cooler to push rural sales. It has capacity to store two crates, which contains 48 glass bottles of 300ml each. Sales of soft drinks have long been blocked by erratic power supply. Sales of soft drinks have long been blocked by erratic power supply so they invented 'eKOCool', a chest cooler, developed internally operates exclusively through solar energy. This innovation gives Coca-Cola a competitive edge to tap new rural markets and ramp up sales of a product

Under promotion Strategy, Communication media used in cities and urban areas would not work in villages because of low penetration of conventional media. Coca Cola India also lauched television commercials (TVCs) targeted at rural consumers, Coca Cola launched Chota Coke in 2002 priced at Rs. 5, In the summer of 2003, Coca Cola India came up with a new commercial featuring Aamir Khan, to further strengthen the Coca Cola brand image among rural consumers, The first ad featured Aamir Khan as a 'tapori' (street smart); in the ad he makes the association between Coca-Cola and the word 'Thanda' , The second commercial in the series featured Aamir Khan as a "Hyderabadi shop-keeper'; here again he equates the word 'Thanda' with Coca-Cola, the third commercial featured Aamir Khan as a 'Punjabi Farmer' who offers Coca Cola to ladies asking for Thanda'Thanda' usually means lassi or nimbu pani, 'garam' is essentially tea. Thanda' generic for Coca-Cola, with the long-playing possibilities of the "Thanda' idea becoming evident, 'thanda' became the central idea

Impact on Rural Economy and Growth of Coca Cola India-Made huge investments in infrastructure for distribution and marketing, Introduced solar cooler for storing their products, CCI draws under 20% of its sales from the rural market, Introduced 2 products vitingo – beverage powder enriched with vitamins, Fanta Fun at Rs 5, Began penetration- Punjab is fully penetrated market, Thus, CCI strategy to tap the B-o-P is getting successful

A suggestion to CCI to Tap the Rural Market by as, 24th September 2011 is celebrated as Girl Child's Day. Sex ratio in India in general and Haryana, Punjab, We suggest CCI and all other big companies to take it as social responsibility to keep aside a share of their profits to protect the girl child by joining hands with government of India

20

IKEA Live Your Life, Love Your Home

Ms. Aditi Sehgal
Ms. Nishtha Sardana
Ms. Simran Dawar
Gargi College, University of Delhi

MISSION STATEMENT

To offer a wide range of well-designed, functional home furnishing products at prices so low that as many people as possible will be able to afford them.

INTRODUCTION

- o IKEA is a privately-held, international, low-cost home furniture retailer that sells modern, utilitarian design furniture, much of which is assembled by the consumer.
- o IKEA = **I**ngvar + **K**amprad + **E**lmtaryd + **A**gunnaryd, South Sweden
- o Cost reduction
- o Customer
- o Presently IKEA has some 230 stores in 42 countries
- o Market share not more than 10-15% but still successful
- o Awareness of the brand is much bigger than the size of the company
- o Success factors :-

  vast experience in the retail market, product differentiation, and cost leadership.

§ It does not bring a new design to market unless it is affordable.

TIME LINE

- o **1943** Ingvar Kamprad registers IKEA as a company.
- o **1947** Furniture is introduced in IKEA's portfolio
- o **1951** The first IKEA catalogue is distributed.
- o **1955** IKEA starts designing its own furniture.
- o **1956** IKEA starts with flat packages.
- o **1958** The first store opens in Älmhult, Sweden.
- o **1973** The first store outside Scandinavia opens in Switzerland.
- o **1963** IKEA began its overseas foray with store in Norway
- o **1985** The first store in the USA.
- o **1991** IKEA buys its own sawmills and factories
- o **1998** The first store in China
- o **20XX** The first store in India?

CASE SUMMARY

- o The case discusses the evolution of Sweden based furniture retailer IKEA's global marketing strategy under various P's of marketing.
- o It illustrates how IKEA built a global brand and its localization strategies in markets including the US and China.
- o The case also details the relationship IKEA had with its customers and details the company's promotional strategies in global markets.
- o It ends with the challenges faced by IKEA in foreign markets

EXPANSION BY FRANCHISING

- o Ikea approaches unknown, relatively small, and high risk markets by franchising.
- o Franchisees have to carry basic items, but have the freedom to design the rest of the product mix to fit local market needs. The basic core items amounts approximately 12,000, simple and functional products.
- o The centralized head office is actively involved in the selection processes and provides advice.
- o In addition, all products have to be purchased from Ikea's product lines. All franchisees pay franchise fees to Ikea holdings. All catalogues and promotional advertising is the responsibility of the headquarters.

PROMOTIONAL STRATEGIES

- o Advertising campaigns were based on unique marketing conditions and cultural sensibilities of each countries
- o Works with different advertising agencies to bring out some of the most creative and un-

conventional ads

- o Also came up with adds which were bold and some times outrageous too
- o These strategies helped create a buzz and kept an unending stream of customers flowing into IKEA

MARKET SEGMENTATION

depending upon innumerable tastes, preference, marketing approach and nature of products

- o IKEA's target market is the global middle class.
- o IKEA concentrated on Local Marketing.
- o Localization of products in whichever country it entered to suit local tastes and preferences.
- o Helped building the brand image
- o Gave respect to the prevalent values and life style of its customers and made necessary product alterations

CONSUMER BUYING BEHAVIOUR

- o Consumer buying behaviour influenced by – cultural social and personal factors.
- o IKEA understood this fact very well and its products went changes accordingly which help in influencing the customer buying behaviour
- o The IKEA BUZZ- the uncanny ability to weave a story around itself

STRENGTHS

- o IKEA have a strong internationally known brand attracting key demographic customer groups.
- o Success has been driven from the price architecture offering value to the customer in innovative but functional products.
- o It has a product portfolio that caters for most consumer lifestyles and budgets from lower to middle income group.
- o Promotional activities followed by the company are one of its major strengths (catalog, radio, word of mouth). It has a good online presence.
- o No direct competition.
- o One stop shop as a typical IKEA has a restaurant, grocery store, supervised play area & baby care room.

WEAKNESS

- o The firm's main weakness is the fact that it is very much reliant on Europe.
- o Large number of out of stock items.
- o Customers not attended properly in case of return of goods.
- o Long queues at the billing section.

- o Traffic jams and accidents due to overcrowding at the opening of new stores
- o Do it yourself.
- o Stores at few locations.

OPPORTUNITIES

- o IKEA should move from international to global status through the expansion into emerging markets in Asia and Eastern Europe.
- o The company should venture into mid and higher price segment
- o Sell some of their furniture in other retail stores across the globe.

THREATS

- o No direct competition but Intertype competition from stores like: Wal-Mart, Kmart, Home Depot and Sears
- o Cultural sensitivity issues.
- o Threat from franchisees as they may demand more control over operations.
- o With economic concerns over rising living costs and depleting disposable income there is an overall threat to the performance of the business in UK and American markets specifically.

QUESTION 1

➢ **IKEA was ranked among the top 50 global brands. Discuss the factors that helped IKEA establish a global brand. What role do you think the founder has played in the success of IKEA?**

o ***Factors that helped IKEA establish a global brand are:***

1. One of the major reasons was that it had vast experience in furniture retail market, and it implemented product differentiation and cost leadership.
2. There were 226 stores across the globe.
3. Effective pricing.
4. The advertising campaign's were based on unique marketing conditions and cultural sensibilities of each country, which varied significantly across markets.
5. The global web of IKEA made it more popular in different countries. It had a global web of 2000 suppliers operating in 55 different countries.

- o Role of the founder:
- o Farsightedness
- o Created an unique IKEA culture that was founded on respect for money and an innovative mindset.
- o As a result of the founder's practices IKEA came up with products that were aesthetically designed and were still affordable.
- o Constantly motivated the employees and praised their hard work and efforts.

- o Self-critism, humility and ability to compensate for one's shortcomings formed the culture of IKEA.
- o Kampard believed that IKEA existed for not just improving peoples lives, but to improve the people themselves.

  IKEA culture emphasizes efficiency and low cost which is not to be achieved on the expense of quality or service.
- o Symbolic policies, such as only flying economy class and stay at economical hotels.
- o Employing young executives and sponsoring university programs would make cost part of corporate culture and would further inspire the influx of entrepreneurship into the organization.
- o All design teams should enjoy complete autonomy in their work, but are expected to design new appealing products regularly.

RECOMMENDATIONS APART FROM THESE ARE:

QUESTION 3

- o ***Reasons for satisfaction of customers:-***
- o It was the one-stop shop for cool, trendy and affordable furniture and home accessories.
- o Significantly varying advertisement campaigns across the world.
- o ***Reasons for dissatisfaction:-***
- o Frenzied crowds and occurrence of stampede during new store openings.
- o Putting in furniture assembling instructions that could not be understood.
- o Out-of-stock items.
- o Long queue at the billing section.
- o ***Solution for customer dissatisfaction :-***
- o Proper inventory levels should be maintained.
- o Increase trained staff base.
- o Improve instruction for assembling.
- o Security staff to avoid incidents.

21

Tasty Foods: Dealing with Difficult Times

Mr. Indranil Mutsuddi
Acharya Institute of Management & Sciences, Bengaluru
indranilmutsuddi@yahoo.com

Mr & Mrs Reddy: The Entrepreneur

Mr. Srinivasan Reddy had left his secure job & started this company in the year 2001 with his wife Mrs. Rekha.

Business Idea came out in the lunch table-back at home.

Mrs. Reddy's Culinary skills particularly in pickles & traditional food items like masala appalams, Puliogere Mix were the key to start the business.

Family tradition & expertise also was a strong motivator.

Food Processing and Pickling in India

Indian food market is currently estimated at Rs. 3230 billion, of which Rs. 1076 billion accounts for processed food.

Fast-paced life, increasing numbers of working women, dual income nuclear families, larger disposable incomes, and the demand for safe, good quality, nutritious food is all factors are influencing the rapid growth of this sector.

Except for a few scattered attempts by some co-operatives and medium scale entrepreneurs, major corporate houses had not done much till date

Exports of Processed Fruits and Vegetables in India (1993 to 2002)

Processed fruit and vegetables

The estimated installed capacity of fruit- and vegetable-processing units in India is 2.11 million tons.

The exports in this category are growing at the rate of 8.68% (1993-94 to 2001-02).

The major export destination for mango pulp is Saudi Arabia, which accounts for one-third of the total exports of mango pulp.

Pickles and chutneys are exported to all EU countries USA, UK and the Middle East. UK and USA account for 30% of Indian pickle exports.

The Indian pickles market

The Indian pickles market is estimated around Rs.800 crores.

Apart from established big players like MTR, Priya, Mother's Recipe, Bedekars, Indiana, Nilons, Pancharanga, Praveen, etc., un-organized sector market is un-quantified and huge.

The Indian pickle industry is growing at around 20-28%

There are abundant investment opportunities in the expanding domestic market and export arena

Tasty Foods: ***Blocks in the beginning***

Operations started with an initial investment of a few thousand rupees and aid from the domestic help.

Initial Investment recovered well enough.

Scale of business was too small

Needed a hefty investment

Need for separate production facility to support large scale production, hire employees (workers) / helps

Need for institutionalizing an effective marketing / sales plan

Initiatives Taken & Consequent set backs

Business Plans submitted to banks were rejected.

Issue of self financing?

Sold property in AP and invested Rs 11Lakhs

Project having shortage of Rs 9 Lakhs

Distant brother in law (Mr. Shankar) agreed to invest Rs 9 Lakhs with 50% partnership

Acceptance of Mr. Shankar's proposal with great hesitation

Tasty Foods: Product Profile

Pickles:

Tasty Mango Pickle

Dried Mango Pickle

Lime Pickle

Tomato pickle

Red Chilli pickle

Mixed Pickle

Plain and masala appalams (pappads), Masala Mix for Rice Bath and Puliogere Mix

Quantity: 100gm & 250 gm

Operations

An old go-down was acquired on lease for 5 years and renovated into factory.

Installation of equipments & machineries

One factory in-charge, 3 semi skilled workers, 10 unskilled workers (House hold Women) and 1 darwan were hired.

One product per batch in the production schedule.

Production closely monitored (trained) by Mr. Rekha

Sales & Marketing

Mr. Shankar: in charge of sales of Tasty Foods

Initial focus on selling the products in and around house holds in locality

With business growth products were distributed to grocery shops.

Working women (employees of Tasty Foods) and even Mr & Mrs Reddy went out to convince shopkeepers for selling their products

Sales & Marketing

Packaging: Simple packaging (plastic); each packet had a small printed leaflet

Our pickles are sold by their taste not by packaging".

Pricing: products quite economical in their pricing as compared to popular brands like MTR.

Promotions and Distribution: products were distributed on the basis of personal contacts

Crisis at Tasty Foods

2003 was a shocker for the Reddys'. Sales figured drastically dropped down.

4 employees had left their job

Employees demanded a hike in their salaries

Need for upgrading the technical facility at their factory to make the production more hygienic

Rumors amongst the employees that Mr. Shankar had changed his attitude towards the employees

Crisis at Tasty Foods

Clash of the Reddy couple with Shankar.

Implications in the poor saleability of Tasty products in local shops.

Customer complaints on the leakage, unattractiveness of the packets

Flaws identified in the records & accounts books.

Crisis at Tasty Foods: Bailing Out?

Getting rid of Shankar by clearing his legitimate claims

Addressing the issues of re-invigorating the company from disaster

Improving the image.

Attracting investment

Motivating and attracting the employees

Finance Cases

1

Model Corporate Governance: Learning Infosys Way....

Dr Anand Sharma
anandsharma.bvimr@gmail.com
Associate Professor Central University of Haryana
Dr Meenakshi Gandhi
drmeenakshigandhi@yahoo.com
Professor, IITM, Janakpuri, New Delhi

Governance: need of the hour

Recent outburst of demand for democratic rights in many countries including India have forced the ruling governance from decades to bring out radical changes in governance approach, core values, structures and systems to transform in a sustainable transparent Governance. Corporate sector is no exception to it. Failures of world's largest banks and financial institutions and global recession has forced corporate sector to rapidly adopt value based sustainable Corporate governance. Corporate governance is vital for the healthy and sustainable growth of business in any country because it influences business from setting objectives to finally transforming them into reality with value system in place.

Corporate governance is the set of processes, policies, practices, laws, and regulations governing the way a corporation (i.e. business organization) should be directed, administered and controlled to optimize productivity and the resulting gains for all stakeholders. Stakeholders include shareholders /promoters, board of directors, managers, financers, employees, customers, vendors, society, community, government, etc. Therefore, a major part of corporate governance also involves exchanging information and managing relationship amongst these stakeholders in order to meet or satisfy their needs and interests. Since large corporations employ a vast quantum of societal resources, the governance process should ensure that these resources are utilized in a manner that meets stakeholders' aspirations and societal expectations.

State of Corporate Governance in India:

Spate of unethical practices of governance in India and abroad are cause of concern for healthy growth of business. Thus now it is much discussed buzzword in business circles. Satyam case has highlighted the worst ethical hazard in India where a complete chain from Chairman , CFO, Bankers to auditors were involved in maligning India's corporate image in the whole world. Even some top business houses Tata group to ADAG have been under scanner in 2 G scam.

KPMG Poll (2008) on Corporate governance in India has revealed;

- Poor Monitoring mechanism: There is weak oversight and monitoring mechanism in corporate governance.
- The independent directors need to be more empowered more rather as a compliance matter.
- Protecting minority shareholders from dominant shareholder is must.
- It is also felt that skill-sets of audit committee to be enhanced

Some reputed Indian information technology (IT) companies are being questioned by the World Bank about their methods of acquiring business orders. A reputed pharmaceutical manufacturer, in particular, is being interrogated about the product quality and safety by the US Food and Drug authority. These reports do not allege corporate fraud (as in the case of companies like Satyam), but bring to light unethical means while acquiring business or producing a critical drug. These are signs of unethical corporate governance, and hold the possibility of adversely influencing the company's long term business goals.

There are some example of good ethical corporate governance in Indian scenario such as ITC, Infosys etc. At this turbulent times Infosys is among those companies which has stood like a strong pillar in unethical wave. Corporate citizens can learn lesson from model governance of Infosys as it has emerged as a benchmark.

Facet of good corporate Governance:

Government has been persuading corporate sector to adopt good governance practices through different means. Corporate sector has also understood that if they do not follow good governance Government may impose strict and compulsory guidelines that is why now corporate sector is increasingly following voluntary guidelines. Following are major aspects of good corporate governance which drives growth of the company with sustainable future.

Monitoring the performance and remuneration of Top management: Usually performance is appraised at lower and middle level there should be effective monitoring of performance of Board of directors and Top management and their remuneration should be linked to performance. It should be continuously monitored by corporate governance audit committee. Kumar Manglam

Birla Committee appointed by SEBI has suggested following items to be disclosed related to remuneration of Directors thus bringing more transparency.

- All elements of remuneration package of all the directors i.e. salary, benefits, bonuses. stock options, pension etc.
- Details of fixed component and performance linked incentives, along with the performance criteria.
- Service contracts, notice period, severance fees.
- Stock option details, if any – and whether issued at a discount as well as the period over which accrued and over which exercisable

Effective implementation of Section 49 concerning Independent Directors: Independent Directors should be effectively utilized and their exclusive meetings should be conducted so that high standards of ethics are maintained. Unfortunately independent directors are a matter of compliance in family run companies. Dearth of competent independent director is also one of the major problems. Ministry of corporate affairs is already looking into this matter.

Rights and equitable treatment of all shareholders: Organizations should respect the rights of shareholders and help them exercise those rights. They can help shareholders exercise their rights by effectively communicating information that is understandable and accessible, and by encouraging shareholders to participate in general meetings.

Protection of interests of other stakeholders: Organizations should recognize that they have legal and ethical obligations to all legitimate stakeholders (employees, customers suppliers, society, etc.). Accordingly, they should devise policies, procedures and rules to govern the business affairs protecting the interests of those stakeholders. This should also include protection of environment and ecology.

Role and responsibilities of the board: the board should be competent enough to deal with various business issues and have the ability and mechanism to review and challenge management performance. It needs to be of an appropriate size and have an appropriate level of commitment to fulfill its responsibilities and duties. The key roles of the chairperson and the chief executive should not be held by the same person. Also, an appropriate mix of executive and non-executive directors (including independent directors) should be maintained so as to balance fairness of decisions and eliminate chances of partiality.

Integrity and ethical behavior: Organizations should develop a code of conduct for their directors and executives to promote ethical and responsible decision-making systems as well as corporate behavior. However, there has to be a controlling mechanism within the organization which ensures that all, irrespective of rank, adhere to that code.

Disclosure and transparency: Organizations should clarify and make the roles and responsibilities of the board and management publicly known in order to provide a level of accountability. They should also implement procedures to independently verify and safeguard the integrity of the company's financial reporting (e.g. external auditing). Disclosures of material matters concerning the organization should be timely and balanced to ensure that investors have access to factual information and are not misdirected. Maximum important information included in annual report will be important for disclosure and transparency. Kumar Mangalam Birla Committee on Corporate Governance appointed by SEBI listed few important items need to be disclosed for better disclosure and transparency.

Why Good Governance? : The moral hazard and some Anna may ....

Recent governance deficit disaster in Public sector has posed new challenges to corporate sector. Today there is a talk from some quarters that now it is turn of corporate sector to shoe good governance else there may unrest in some circles and god knows how far it may go. Corporate sector was targeted in past in some issues like reservations and all corporate bodies came together that we will address our social responsibility in our own voluntary way. This time public sentiments and government influence are different. Thus there is need to urgently address governance issues. Corporate governance at Infosys has been quiet different. Thus in this case study few governance issues have been highlighted and lessons for other Indian companies to follow Infosys way as model in their own settings.

Infosys Philosophy to Corporate Governance:

Infosys philosophy to corporate governance is driven by ethical values, transparency, accountable corporate citizenship and democratic decision making. Infosys corporate governance principles are as follows;

- Trusteeship Principle: Management is trustee of shareholders funds not the owner of funds thus discharge its duties in most trustful manner.
- Transparency: Infosys believes in highest degree of transparency to all internal and external stakeholders.
- Spirit of law not letters of law: Infosys believes in following spirit of law not just wordings of law. Thus it goes much beyond the minimum required standards prescribed by law in respective countries.
- Corporate citizenship: Company believes in responsible and accountable behavior in all the countries by abiding their laws.

Value based leadership:

Mr N R Narayan Murthy, Mr Nandan Nilekani and ...

"Goodbye. Folks, march on with values.... "

These words were not easy to write the history of a value based journey of Commitments, sacrifice, glory, service and innovation of corporate leadership. Infosys leadership is rare example of business acumen with transparency and ethical values. Infosys was created by seven like minded and committed technocrats who started in 1981 with leadership of legendary icon Mr N R Narayan Murthy. He had been heart and soul of Infosys since inception to August 2011.

He was awarded the Padma Vibhushan, India's second highest civilian award, by the Government of India in 2008. Mr. Murthy was ranked as India's most powerful Chief Executive Officer for three consecutive years between 2004 and 2006 by the Economic Times. In 2004,

TIME Magazine identified him as one of ten global leaders who are helping shape the future of technology. In 2005, The Economist magazine ranked him among the ten most admired global business leaders. He has appeared in the rankings of businessmen and innovators in several publications, including those by Business Standard, Business Week, CNN, Financial Times, Forbes, Fortune, India Today and TIME Magazine.

Mr Nandan Nilekani :

Mr Nandan Nilekani along with Mr Narayan Murthy and five other co-founders founded Infosys. While Narayan Murthy stayed in India, Nandan Nilekani shifted to the US to take care of Infosys' operations there. He was the company's marketing face. In 1980s and 90s Nandan Nilekani and his team worked hard to build Infosys. Today Infosys' success story owes to hard work and vibrant thinking of Mr Nilekani. He served company as director since inception and rose to the level of the CEO and managing director of the Infosys.

On the request of Prime minister Dr Manmohan Singh, Mr Nilekani stepped down as the co-chairman and board member of Infosys Technologies in July 2009 to take over as the chairman of Unique Identification Authority of India (UIADI). Now he heads the most ambitious national project for creating a database of citizens. In 2006, Nandan Nilekani was conferred the Padma Bhushan, one of the highest civilian honors of India.

Shareholding pattern of Infosys:

Shareholding pattern of the company reveals that its promoters/Founders have around 16 per cent shares. Equity shareholding of FIIs, Indian financial Institutions and Indian public accounts for 36%, 16% and 13% respectively. ADS counts for 17.6% of total shareholding. It clearly reveals broad based shareholding pattern of Infosys.

Composition of the Board:

The board is balanced with independent, founder executive and non founder executive directors. The board of Director at Infosys consists of 14 directors out of which 8 are independent directors and five are executive and one is non executive. Of the five executive directors three are founder directors. Independent directors includes eminent tycoon like Mr K V Kamanth. Thus this board composition seems to be well balanced. Criteria for board membership is strictly on expertise and experience in Business. It is taken care that Directors' other assignment does not materially affect their performance with the company. For Independent directors strict criteria as per NASDAQ regulation is applied to follow highest standards in this regard. Currently no family member of founder directors (including chairman, CEO and COO) is in the board.

Interestingly roles and responsibilities among Non executive chairman, CEO and COO has been clearly defined and disclosed. They are also supposed to achieve targets and give periodic presentations to show performance in their respective field.

Total remuneration of all Executive directors is performance based. More than 50% part is variable proportion. Interestingly Total compensation is lowest for Chairman among all executive directors. Package of Non founder directors is clearly more than founder directors.

Attendance of all directors' in board meetings is cent percent. It shows commitment of directors in Companies affairs.

Compliance with corporate Governance guidelines:

Infosys has not only complied with all mandatory guidelines but have also followed all Indian and international standards suggested by various bodies such as corporate governance Voluntary Guidelines 2009, Kumar Mangalam Birla Committee 2000, Naresh Chandra Committee, Euro Shareholders corporate Governance guidelines 2000, United nations global compact, OECD principles of corporate governance.

Infosys has got best ratings for corporate governance practices from CRISIL and ICRA over the period of time.

Learning Governance Infosys way:

Lessons for Corporate sector.......

- Good Governance should not be a compliance matter rather is should be voluntary for enhancing wealth in sustainable way. Companies should take advantage of independent directors for fresh thoughts rather taking independent directors as show piece in their compliance report.
- Professionally managed and owned: In a country like India where family owned and controlled business houses are successful Infosys has set a benchmark for professional business without family involvement. Family controlled business houses should encourage innovative thought of professional managers and family successors should come through normal route.
- Sense of ownership among employees: As all employees who joined company before 2010 has been given ownership through shares. This practice has developed sense of belongingness among employees.
- Nurturing talent like none else: Infosys has continuously strived for nurturing talent through education and build dynamic leadership can be well understood by its Infosys Leadership Institute at Mysore. Global Education Centre I and II are the testimony of its strong belief in employee's development and empowerment. Corporations should invest in human capital for long term sustainability.
- Performance based remuneration pattern of executive board members clearly reveals that remuneration at top level is performance based. Accountability of top management and transparent remuneration will lead to morale boosting among employees.

2

Renewal – Cum Enhancement Proposal of Credit Facilities of XYZ Ltd.

Mr. Bijay Krishna Bhattacharya
Associate Professor, Globsyn Business School, Kolkata.
bijaykb_jan2008@yahoo.co.in
bkb@globsyn.com
Mr. Lakshmikanta Sinha Roy,
Chief Manager, West Bengal Financial Corporation,
E-Mail: lksr@rediffmail.com
Mr. Mridul Kumar Ghosh,
Financial Analyst
chithi2007@gmail.com
Ms. Bhawna Duggal
Assistant professor
Bharati Vidyapeeth University, Institute of Management and Research, New Delhi
b16_dhawan@yahoo.co.in

CASE IN DETAIL

The Sutanuti branch, Kolkata of ABC Bank forwarded a copy of their Appraisal Note pertaining to renewal cum enhancement request of XYZ Ltd. XYZ Ltd were sanctioned an expansion project vide regional office (RO) sanction dt having sanctioned a term loan (TL) of Rs 65Lakhs and enhancement of cash credit limit (CC) from Rs 12Lakhs to Rs 40Lakhs with other credit facilities allowed to be continued. The director of the company has been emphasing very now and then having received lesser amount of TL sanction against their application for Rs 87 Lakhs for the purpose which has resulted into tightness in working capital funds as the promoters of the company have exhausted all of their resources and now trapped into accumulation of negative net working capital (NWC) to the tune of Rs 20 Lakhs approximately.

The proposal was initially forwarded to RO for renewal cum enhancement but subsequently the matter was returned to the aforesaid branch stating that it now falls under branch power, considering the same as a corporate borrower where the discretion for Chief Manager (CM) is at Rs 2 Crores. The branch has therefore, processed the same and considered sanction of following need based limits.

As the company has reiterated that short amount of TL has caused a lot of hardship and tightness and the financial data also reveals a negative NWC , therefore, the request of the company for releasing of working capital term loan (WCTL) of Rs 20 lakhs has also to be taken into account and considered.

1. Enhancement of CC limit from Rs 40 Lakhs to Rs 60Lakhs
2. WCTL (fresh) of Rs 20Lakhs repayable in 36 monthly installments of Rs 55556/- to be commenced after 6 months initial repayment holiday.

The branch has although processed and made a comprehensive note for sanction of the credit facilities as above but has to mention that the value of collateral security is falling lesser than 75% for CM's discretion as the value of collateral security considered by Sutanuti branch is 25% of the value given by the approved valuer because the major part of the property is rented out.

The same was already recorded and advised to RO at the time of earlier RO sanction.

THE APPRAISAL NOTE OF THE CASE:

Synopsis

On getting confirmation from its RO Sutanuti Branch of ABC Bank sanctioned a term loan of Rs. 65Lakhs against a proposal of the borrower client for sanction of Rs. 87lakhs together with enhanced CC Limit from existing Rs.12 lakhs to Rs.40 Lakhs. The borrower regretted that the

Term Loan sanctioned amount was low and as a result the business is facing negative NWC of Rs.20 Lakhs (appx). New enhancement proposal was sent by the branch to RO and the same was returned to the branch arguing that it was within the power of Branch Manager. On scrutiny the branch found that the value of collateral security offered by the borrower was outside the branch power. Therefore the proposal was sent again to RO with positive recommendation for their consideration.

TEACHING NOTE

(a) **Case Objective:** Branch of a bank should not sanction any credit facility if it is not within its power.

(b) **Position in Course:** Renewal-cum- Enhancement of Credit Facilities.

(c) **Learning Objectives:** Conception about the followings

(i) Cash Credit against Hypothecation of Stocks (ii) Cash Credit against Hypothecation of Book Debts (iii) Term Loan (iv) Cash Credit against Deposit (v) Letter of Credit **or** Documentary Credit(LC) (vi) Letter of Guarantee (LG) (vii) Working Capital Term Loan(WCTL) (viii) Fund Based(FB) Limit (ix) Non-Fund Based (NFB) Limit (x) Group Exposure (xi) SME (xii) Credit Rating (xiii) Asset Classification (xiv) Income Recognition (xv) Risk Weight (xvi) Loan Policy (xvii) Total Net Worth(TNW) (xviii)Total Outside Liabilities (TOL) (xix) Financial Ratios (xx) Turnover Method (xxi) Maximum Permissible Bank Finance (MPBF) Method (xxii) SWOT Analysis (xxiii) Collateral Securities.

(d) **Teaching Plan:** After introduction of the case in the class the teacher should invite the participants for discussion and should only play the role of facilitator.

(e) **Assignment Questions:** (1) Different types of credit facilities available from the banks (2) How to assess Working Capital Requirements (3) How to prepare Assessment Notes.

(f) **Analysis Suggested:** A detailed Assessment note should be prepared by the branch of a bank if it is not within the Discretionary Power of the branch concerned.

(g) **Suggested Readings:** (a) Banking Law and Practice by P.N.Varshney. Publisher: Sultan Chand & Sons, New Delhi (b) Banking Theory Law & Practice by R.Rajesh and T.Sivagnanasithi. Publisher: Tata McGraw Hill Publishing Co. Ltd., New Delhi.

3

Preet Steel Company – A Case on Letter of Credit

Mr. Bijay Krishna Bhattacharya,
Associate Professor, Globsyn Business School, Kolkata.
bijaykb_jan2008@yahoo.co.in
bkb@globsyn.com
Mr. Lakshmikanta Sinha Roy,
Chief Manager, West Bengal Financial Corporation,
E-Mail: lksr@rediffmail.com
Mr. Mridul Kumar Ghosh,
Financial Analyst,
chithi2007@gmail.com

An irrecoverable documentary credit (at 90 days after shipment date) was opened by London Bank Plc, London, UK (opening bank) in favour of Preet Steel Company Limited, Chowringhee Road, Kolkata (the beneficiary of the documentary credit) for an amount of GBP 325000 on request of Universal Trading Group, London, UK (the applicant of the documentary credit), and the same was advised through Supreme International Bank, Kolkata (advising bank). Goods to be exported were Cold Rolled Galvanised Corrugated Steel Sheets (Non-Alloys).

The beneficiary used to maintain Current Account with Beautiful Bank, Kolkata Branch. They had no credit limit whatsoever INCLUDING in respect of bill purchase as they were very new to export trade.

One fine morning the said beneficiary tendered export compliance documents at the counter of the Beautiful Bank, Kolkata(negotiating bank) with a request to negotiate the documents under the documentary credit and give immediate credit to their current account with the abovementioned bank,as they were in urgent need of funds for the purpose of working capital.

Branches of the said bank was not empowered to negotiate the bills under Documentary Credit without any Regular Limit in favour of any of its client, and, if they have to do so, it is a precondition that they should obtain prior sanction from its controlling office (here it is Kolkata Regional Office) for the purpose.

Under the above backdrop the Branch incumbent had consulted the Departmental in-charge of Foreign Exchange in this regard and advised the later to scrutinize the documents whether they conform to the terms of the Documentary Credit. The Foreign Exchange Department in-charge had scrutinised the documents and also confirmed the conformity of the documents strictly as per Documentary Credit Terms.

On getting the scrutiny report of the documents the Branch Incumbent then instructed the Foreign Exchange In-Charge to negotiate the documents on Ad-Hoc basis and there after write to controlling office for the necessary post-facto sanction i.e. confirmation of action of the branch. He had done/advised the same for the purpose of attainment/fulfillment of branch target for year under consideration.

The department concerned had negotiated the documents and in turn credited the negotiated proceeds to the account of the beneficiary as per their request. After the negotiation the documents were despatched to London Bank Plc, London, UK for the purpose of reimbursement of the proceeds thereof.

On receiving the documents the opening bank further scrutinised the documents and never raised any discrepancy in the documents. The documents were duly released to the applicant on the basis of acceptance of the draft.

The applicant could not release the goods from the concerned shipping company because the Bills of Lading which were issued by the shipping agents did not represent any cargo which was shipped i.e.no shipment of goods was made. It was a fake bill of lading.

The opening bank then returned the documents to the negotiating bank for doing the needful at their end.

The negotiating bank could not realise the proceeds of the bill from the beneficiary' account and the amount advanced in the form of bills purchased facility had turned into a Loss Asset.

The controlling office never confirmed the action of the branch that is Ad Hoc Negotiation of the bill.

The branch incumbent was retrenched together with the Foreign Exchange Department In-Charge and the NPA amount could not be recovered from the beneficiary. The entire matter was handed over to Police Department by the negotiating bank.

Synopsis of the case

An Export Bill was negotiated by a branch of a bank under documentary credit bypassing the branch discretionary power. The proceeds of the bill never realised and turns into NPA.The bill of lading was also fake.

Teaching Note

(a) Case Objective: Not to bypass the branch discretionary power.

(b) Position in Course: Negotiation of bills under documentary credit under the topic Post-Shipment Credit .The goods were sent through seaworthy vessel and the title of goods was obtained by way of Bills of Lading.

(c) Learning Objectives: (i) What is Export Trade (ii) Financing of Export Trade (iii) Documents used in Export Trade (iv) Precautionary Measures to be observed in case of Export Trade (v) Branch Incumbent's as well as Departmental In-Charge's Role of a Bank.

(d) Teaching Plan: After introduction of the case in the class the teacher should invite the participants for discussion and should play the role of facilitator only.

(e)Assignment Questions: (i) What is bill of lading? (ii) Types of bill of lading (iii) What is discretionary power? (iv) What is NPA?

(f) Analysis Suggested: (a) The branch under any circumstances should not bypass the discretionary power (b) Due KYC of the borrower client must be available before granting any credit facility.

(g) Suggested Readings: (a) Practitioners' Book on Trade Finance by Indian Institute of Banking & Finance. Publisher: Taxmann's Academic Publications 2010 (b) Trade Payments under Documentary Credits and Collections (3rd Edition, October, 2007) by G D Awasthi. Publisher: Academy of Business Studies, New Delhi-110 002.

4

Best Way to Invest in the Markets—IPO! Does this Really Hold True? —A Reality Check

Dr.Amit Bagga
Investment Consultant
Mr. Inder Preet Singh
Investment Consultant
inderipsingh@gmail.com

ABSTRACT

Primary Market or Fresh Issue market is supposed to be the safest place for making investments especially for retail investors in Equity Capital Markets. This is achieved by investing in Initial public offerings or popularly known as IPO's of private and public sector companies. Primarily there are two types of objectives for which investors invest in these IPO's. One is to book profits on the listing day (short term) and the other is to hold and carry the investments for a longer period of time which can be a year, 3 year, 5 years or more. This research tries to look at both the prospective and tries to find out the performance of these IPO's both in short term and long term (over a period of 5 years). Also whether in long term (over a period of 5 years) these IPO's outperform or underperform the broad market (Nifty) and "can long term wealth" be created by investing and holding in IPO's is what we have tried to find out the answers for. We have selected 41 IPO's which have been issued in calendar year 2005 on NSE as our sample size for research.

Introduction

The toughest and most complex decision faced by majority of Retail investors when it comes to equities have always been, is to create a separate "investing and trading portfolio".

The horizon for which one remains invested and the risk-reward are the key parameters on which these classifications are done. Usually, trading is considered to be a short term high risk-reward activity spanning from few minutes to few days to few weeks and so on. As for investments, long-term investment horizon, less volatility and better safety is what is looked at. Although the objective from both is profit maximisation but still investing is supposed to be the way for creating "sustainable wealth creation".

Now, once one decides to make investments the next step is to find out which stocks to invest. These stocks can be the one already listed, traded and are available in the secondary market or can be the new ones who are planning to come and raise capital through an IPO in the primary market. Retail investors, who after the Coal India IPO can now invest maximum upto 2 lac Rs. application per applicant, look for more opportunities in the primary market for dark horses or hidden gems. This makes IPO more attractive and lucrative to them.

Unfortunately investing does not provide the exit point which is available in trading and refereed as "stop loss". Therefore once position is made in investing this problem of moving out early is always faced by majority of investors. Therefore stock selection in investing becomes more complex and important because the investment horizon is too long usually more than a year or so and fundamentally to identify the trend reversal is always very difficult. This is the reason why stock selection has left many investors with burned fingers even in long term investing. SKS Micro-finance, Reliance Power, Unitech & Suzlon are few who have eroded the wealth and confidence of investors manifold in IPO's.

Another important factor which results in IPO attractiveness is the overall market sentiment in the period at which IPO is offered. When the markets are in an uptrend or positive growth trajectory it becomes very difficult to separate wheat from chalf i.e. to identify fundamentally strong companies when everything sells like a hot cake. Therefore **timing of an IPO is very important factor.**

For already listed and traded stock its relatively more easy to make a view but to analyse a new company which is coming out with an IPO , a investor has to rely more on the track report of the Merchant Banker to the issue and has to be convinced by the "**investment rational**" being pitched by him. Over subscription and under subscription by different categories of investors especially institutional investor's assists retail investor's confidence building.

Business models such as Infosys, SBI, Punjab National Bank, Coal India, Tata Motors have created wealth creation for investors in IPO to name a few.

Therefore putting money in an IPO for the purpose of selling it on premium on listing is not a part of investment portfolio but becomes a part of trading portfolio. So, it's not only the qualitative & quantitative research which has to be done diligently by the retail investors but also clearly understand the pros and cons of applying in an IPO.

Table- 1. Based on calendar period

Year of Issue	*Number of Issues*	*Capital Mobilised (Rs. Lakh)*	*Nifty's Performance (%)**
2001	2	4,500	-18.44%
2002	2	1,04,399	3.49%
2003	5	1,37,067	41.47%
2004	21	29,33,508	8.09%
2005	50	16,18,142	25.44%
2006	73	23,30,894	28.50%
2007	95	43,16,173	34.72%
2008	36	17,00,380	-107.64%
2009	21	1,93,26,39	41.68%
2010	73	60,19,317	14.71%
2011(Till August)	31	1,34,56,64	-27.23%
Total	**409**	**2,24,42,683**	

Source: www.nseindia.com

Objectives

The objective of our research focuses on:

1. To find out whether investing in IPO's give return in short term (listing price) only, long term (over a period of 5 years) only, in both short term and long term or in none of the situations.
2. To find out whether holding on to investments in IPO's over a period of 5 years do reap fruits of wealth creation and outperform market returns.
3. To find out whether holding on to investments in IPO's over a period of 5 years do reap fruits of wealth creation and outperform risk free returns.
4. To find out the extent to which the sample IPO's return are correlated with Nifty Returns.
5. To find out the extent to which the sample IPO's return are explained by Nifty Returns by determining the Coefficient of Determination (R^2).

Research Methodology

We have taken the list and details of all IPO's & FPO's which have been issued from January 2001 till August 2011 from NSE site. This for our research has given us a population size of **409** (IPO's & FPO's) and out of which we have selected 41 IPO's which have been issued in calendar year 2005 as our sample size for research.

Then for all these 41 IPO's we have compared the difference between the listing price and issue price for each stock individually to find out the short term (listing price) gain or loss % returns.

To find out the long term (over a period of 5 years) total return or total yield for each stock, from each stocks issue price till 25th August 2011, we have found out the Capital Yield (using CAGR wherein ending value is being taken as the stock's closing price on 25thAugust 2011 and beginning value has been taken to be the issue price of the stock) and Dividend Yield (Sum of all years dividend/issue price) for each stock. For NIFTY we have calculated it using closing levels of Nifty as on 25thAugust 2011 and Nifty's level as on 1st January 2005.

· This total yield of each stock is than compared with Nifty's yield to find out whether holding on to investments in IPO's over a period of 5 years do reap fruits of wealth creation and outperform market returns.

This total yield of each stock is than compared with risk free rate over a period of 5 years to find out whether holding on to investments in IPO's over a period of 5 years do reap fruits of wealth creation and outperform risk free returns.

Then from each stocks listing day price till 25th August 2011, based on daily closing price basis we have calculated the ARITHMATIC Return of each stock. Same is being done for NIFTY as well. Based on these, we have calculated each stocks correlation and coefficient of Determination (R^2) with Nifty's Return.

Limitations of the Study

Sample Size is limited to just 41 IPO's issued in 2005 and not to the complete population of 400 IPO's that came out during the period of 10 years. Also the period of comparison for returns with Nifty was taken over a period of 5 years. Hence the findings and analysis can change based on the time frame and sample size selected.

Data Analysis and Interpretation

The data table-2 shows, all individual 41 IPO issues **short term** (listing price) returns that came out in calendar year 2005. The table shows that out of total 41 issues, the best listing gainer performer has been **Emami Limited** giving a return of 298.57% and the worst performer has been **Talbros Automotive Components Limited** giving a return of -36.96% . The NIFTY's return in calendar year 2005 has been 25.44%.

Table- 2

Issuer Company	Issue Size(Rs.Crore)	Issue Price	Listing Date	List Price	Listing Gains/Loss (%)
Emami Limited	3500	70	03-Aug-06	279	298.57%
ABG Shipyard Limited	92500	185	11-Apr-07	370	100.00%
Amar Remedies Limited	4200	28	16-Sep-05	56	100.00%
Sasken Communication Technologies Limited	13000	260	09-Sep-05	460	76.92%
Infrastructure Development Finance Company Limited	137224	34	12-Aug-05	60	76.47%
Provogue (India) Limited	6074	150	07-Jul-05	249	66.00%
Shoppers Stop Limited	13698	238	23-May-05	356	49.66%
Yes Bank Limited	31500	45	12-Jul-05	66	46.44%
Bartronics India Limited	4500	75	12-Jan-06	106	41.33%
Kernex Microsystems (I) Limited	11001	250	20-Dec-05	350	40.00%
Punj Lloyd Limited	64211	700	06-Jan-06	956	36.61%
HT Media Limited	37074	530	01-Sep-05	700	32.08%
Celebrity Fashions Limited	8190	180	12-Jan-06	236	31.28%
Everest Kanto Cylinder Limited	10286	160	15-Dec-05	201	25.63%
Prithvi Information Solutions Limited	13500	270	16-Nov-05	339	25.50%
Suzlon Energy Limited	149634	510	19-Oct-05	639	25.29%
Tulip IT Services Limited	10800	120	05-Jan-06	150	25.00%
Nectar Lifesciences Limited	9288	240	18-Jul-05	300	25.00%
Educomp Solutions Limited	5000	125	13-Jan-06	155	24.00%
Gateway Distriparks Limited	15120	72	31-Mar-05	89	23.47%
AIA Engineering Limited	14805	315	14-Dec-05	387	22.86%
PVR Limited	16650	225	04-Jan-06	270	20.00%
Repro India Limited	4323	165	22-Dec-05	195	18.18%
3i Infotech Limited	20000	100	22-Apr-05	118	18.00%
Gokaldas Exports Limited	13281	425	27-Apr-05	500	17.65%
UTV Software Communications Limited	9100	130	17-Mar-05	150	15.38%
Bombay Rayon Fashions Limited	9433	70	05-Dec-05	80	14.29%
Aurionpro Solutions Limited	2700	90	25-Oct-05	102	13.33%
Allsec Technologies Limited	4241	135	09-May-05	150	11.11%
Shree Renuka Sugars Limited	11400	285	31-Oct-05	315	10.53%
Triveni Engineering & Industries Limited	24000	48	13-Dec-05	53	9.48%
Shringar Cinemas Limited	4320	53	29-Apr-05	57	7.55%
SPL Industries Limited	6300	70	26-Jul-05	75	7.14%
India Infoline Limited	9027	76	17-May-05	81	5.92%
Jet Airways (India) Limited	189937	1100	14-Mar-05	1155	5.00%
Jai Prakash Hydro-Power Limited	57600	32	18-Apr-05	32	0.00%
Bannari Amman Spinning Mills Limited	9450	135	14-Nov-05	101	-25.22%
Talbros Automotive Components Limited	5383	102	29-Sep-06	64	-36.96%

* Piramyd Retail Limited, Shri Ramrupai Balaji Steels Limited, IL&FS Investmart Limited not incl.

The data table-3 shows, all individual 41 IPO issues **long term** (over a period of 5 years) total yield i.e. Capital Yield+ Dividend Yield returns, from the date of listing till 25th August 2011. The table shows that out of total 41 issues, the highest dividend yield has been given by

IL&FS Investmart Limited having 88.40% and the worst has been **Shoppers Stop Limited** giving no dividend.

The highest capital appreciation is being achieved by **Educomp Solutions Limited** of 715.20% while the worst has been **Celebrity Fashions Limited** giving -96.19% over its issue price. For the same period nifty has appreciated by **285.84%.**

Table-3

Issuer Company	Issue Price	Adjusted Price	Capital Yield	Dividend Yield	Total Yield
Educomp Solutions Limited	125	1019.00	715.20%	17.84%	733.04%
UTV Software Communications Limited	130	937.55	621.19%	2.69%	623.88%
Emami Limited	70	467.60	568.00%	40.00%	608.00%
Tulip IT Services Limited	120	734.50	512.08%	14.17%	526.25%
Yes Bank Limited	45	267.35	494.11%	5.56%	499.67%
India Infoline Limited	76	364.00	378.95%	73.68%	452.63%
AIA Engineering Limited	315	1673.00	431.11%	14.92%	446.03%
Bombay Rayon Fashions Limited	70	277.85	296.93%	9.71%	306.64%
Shree Renuka Sugars Limited	285	1093.00	283.51%	9.82%	293.33%
Infrastructure Development Finance Company Limited	34	106.90	214.41%	23.24%	237.65%
Amar Remedies Limited	28	91.70	227.50%	7.14%	234.64%
Gateway Distriparks Limited	72	166.44	131.16%	33.51%	164.67%
Everest Kanto Cylinder Limited	160	349.00	118.13%	21.25%	139.38%
ABG Shipyard Limited	185	343.65	85.76%	5.14%	90.89%
Shoppers Stop Limited	238	390.35	64.01%	0.00%	64.01%
Aurionpro Solutions Limited	90	130.00	44.44%	9.00%	53.44%
HT Media Limited	530	728.25	37.41%	1.85%	39.25%
Triveni Engineering & Industries Limited	48	21.25	-55.73%	71.88%	16.15%
Jai Prakash Hydro-Power Limited	32	32.90	2.81%	12.50%	15.31%
IL&FS Investmart Limited	125	29.00	-76.80%	88.40%	11.60%
Provogue (India) Limited	150	141.00	-6.00%	4.73%	-1.27%
Repro India Limited	165	136.35	-17.36%	10.30%	-7.06%
Shringar Cinemas Limited	53	40.45	-23.68%	0.00%	-23.68%
3i Infotech Limited	100	52.20	-47.80%	17.00%	-30.80%
Bartronics India Limited	75	49.50	-34.00%	2.67%	-31.33%
Talbros Automotive Components Limited	102	42.00	-58.82%	13.92%	-44.90%
PVR Limited	225	115.80	-48.53%	2.67%	-45.87%
Bannari Amman Spinning Mills Limited	135	65.80	-51.26%	4.81%	-46.44%
Sasken Communication Technologies Limited	260	100.55	-61.33%	10.77%	-50.56%
Kernex Microsystems (I) Limited	250	103.07	-58.77%	1.48%	-57.29%
Punj Lloyd Limited	700	272.75	-61.04%	0.97%	-60.06%
Gokaldas Exports Limited	425	154.40	-63.67%	2.59%	-61.08%
Suzlon Energy Limited	510	179.25	-64.85%	2.94%	-61.91%
Jet Airways (India) Limited	1100	272.50	-75.23%	1.36%	-73.86%
Allsec Technologies Limited	135	14.30	-89.41%	7.41%	-82.00%
Nectar Lifesciences Limited	240	18.80	-92.17%	4.38%	-87.79%
Prithvi Information Solutions Limited	270	21.40	-92.07%	3.15%	-88.93%
SPL Industries Limited	70	3.20	-95.43%	1.43%	-94.00%
Celebrity Fashions Limited	180	6.85	-96.19%	0.56%	-95.64%

*Piramyd Retail Limited, Shri Ramrupai Balaji Steels Limited not included.

Based on the total yield comparison of individual stock to NIFTY, the best outperformer has been **Educomp Solutions Limited** giving an excess return of 733.04 % over nifty and the worst underperformer has been **Celebrity Fashions Limited** giving a return of -224.46 % below nifty. As shown in Table-4.

Table-4

Issuer Company	Total Yield	Excess Returns	Nifty
Celebrity Fashions Limited	-95.64%	-224.46%	underperform
SPL Industries Limited	-94.00%	-222.82%	underperform
Prithvi Information Solutions Limited	-88.93%	-217.75%	underperform
Nectar Lifesciences Limited	-87.79%	-216.61%	underperform
Allsec Technologies Limited	-82.00%	-210.82%	underperform
Jet Airways (India) Limited	-73.86%	-202.69%	underperform
Suzlon Energy Limited	-61.91%	-190.73%	underperform
Gokaldas Exports Limited	-61.08%	-189.91%	underperform
Punj Lloyd Limited	-60.06%	-188.89%	underperform
Kernex Microsystems (I) Limited	-57.29%	-186.11%	underperform
Sasken Communication Technologies Limited	-50.56%	-179.38%	underperform
Bannari Amman Spinning Mills Limited	-46.44%	-175.27%	underperform
PVR Limited	-45.87%	-174.69%	underperform
Talbros Automotive Components Limited	-44.90%	-173.72%	underperform
Bartronics India Limited	-31.33%	-160.16%	underperform
3i Infotech Limited	-30.80%	-159.62%	underperform
Shringar Cinemas Limited	-23.68%	-152.50%	underperform
Repro India Limited	-7.06%	-135.88%	underperform
Provogue (India) Limited	-1.27%	-130.09%	underperform
Jai Prakash Hydro-Power Limited	15.31%	-113.51%	underperform
Triveni Engineering & Industries Limited	16.15%	-112.68%	underperform
HT Media Limited	39.25%	-89.57%	underperform
Aurionpro Solutions Limited	53.44%	-75.38%	underperform
Shoppers Stop Limited	64.01%	-64.81%	underperform
ABG Shipyard Limited	90.89%	-37.93%	underperform
Everest Kanto Cylinder Limited	139.38%	10.55%	outperform
Gateway Distriparks Limited	164.67%	35.85%	outperform
Amar Remedies Limited	234.64%	105.82%	outperform
Infrastructure Development Finance Company Limited	237.65%	108.82%	outperform
Shree Renuka Sugars Limited	293.33%	164.51%	outperform
Bombay Rayon Fashions Limited	306.64%	177.82%	outperform
AIA Engineering Limited	446.03%	317.21%	outperform
India Infoline Limited	452.63%	323.81%	outperform
Yes Bank Limited	499.67%	370.84%	outperform
Tulip IT Services Limited	526.25%	397.43%	outperform
Emami Limited	608.00%	479.18%	outperform
UTV Software Communications Limited	623.88%	495.06%	outperform
Educomp Solutions Limited	733.04%	604.22%	outperform

***Piramyd Retail Limited, Shri Ramrupai Balaji Steels Limited**

*Nifty's yield from 1 Jan 2005 till 25th August 2011 is 128.82%

The data table-5 shows, the correlation and coefficient of determination of each stock with Nifty's return. The highest correlation has been 0.7786 for **ICICI Bank Limited** and the minimum correlation has been .0209 for **Tulip IT Services Limited**. Similarly the highest coefficient of determination has been **.6062** for ICICI Bank Limited and the minimum has been **.0004** for Tulip IT Services Limited.

Table-5

Issuer Name	CORRELATION with nifty	correlation^2
ICICI Bank Limited	0.7786	0.6062
Infrastructure Development Finance Company Limited	0.7061	0.4986
Punjab National Bank	0.6747	0.4552
IVRCL Infrastructure & Projects Limited	0.6715	0.4509
Jai Prakash Hydro-Power Limited	0.6288	0.3954
Yes Bank Limited	0.6225	0.3874
Syndicate Bank	0.5987	0.3584
Allahabad Bank	0.5882	0.3459
India Infoline Limited	0.5880	0.3457
Oriental Bank of Commerce	0.5807	0.3373
3i Infotech Limited	0.5737	0.3292
Educomp Solutions Limited	0.5400	0.2916
Triveni Engineering & Industries Limited	0.5072	0.2572
Nectar Lifesciences Limited	0.5068	0.2568
Jet Airways (India) Limited	0.5066	0.2567
Gujarat Industries Power Company Limited	0.4920	0.2421
Sasken Communication Technologies Limited	0.4787	0.2292
Prithvi Information Solutions Limited	0.4741	0.2248
Amar Remedies Limited	0.4725	0.2233
Gateway Distriparks Limited	0.4667	0.2178
Bartronics India Limited	0.4653	0.2165
Everest Kanto Cylinder Limited	0.4643	0.2156
Bombay Rayon Fashions Limited	0.4577	0.2095
Suzlon Energy Limited	0.4485	0.2012
AIA Engineering Limited	0.4292	0.1842
UTV Software Communications Limited	0.4071	0.1657
Kemex Microsystems (I) Limited	0.3944	0.1556
PVR Limited	0.3883	0.1508
Repro India Limited	0.3788	0.1435
Shringar Cinemas Limited	0.3636	0.1322
Provogue (India) Limited	0.3380	0.1142
HT Media Limited	0.3308	0.1095
Shoppers Stop Limited	0.3220	0.1037
Bannari Amman Spinning Mills Limited	0.3195	0.1021
Gokaldas Exports Limited	0.3174	0.1007
Allsec Technologies Limited	0.3167	0.1003
SPL Industries Limited	0.3042	0.0925
Emami Limited	0.2944	0.0866
Jindal Poly Films Limited	0.2890	0.0835
ABG Shipyard Limited	0.2763	0.0763
IL&FS Investmart Limited	0.2758	0.0760
Talbros Automotive Components Limited	0.2734	0.0747
Ginni Filaments Limited	0.2647	0.0701
Celebrity Fashions Limited	0.2577	0.0664
Tulip IT Services Limited	0.0209	0.0004

Conclusion

From the 2005 sample size taken, in the short run performance, 2 stocks have given listing loss, 36 stocks have given listing price gains, and because of unavailability of data 3 have been not included.

In Long Term performance 13 stocks have outperformed nifty, 25 have been underperformer and because of unavailability of data 2 have been not included. The value of correlation ranges from 0.7786 to .0209 and of coefficient of correlation is 0.6062 to .0004.

It is observed that in the short run most of the stocks have generated listing profit whereas in long term most of the companies have underperformed the market return. 19 IPO's over a period of 5 years have given negative returns, 20 positive while data for 2 were not available. Even over a period of 5 years investing in risk-free securities like FD would have at least led to capital protection which was not in the case of these 19 IPO's.

Hence, it is advisable for retail investor to follow upon his own risk-return and holding capacity, any single or combination of all the 3 strategies when investing in an IPO —1st Sell all the allotment on listing day itself, 2nd Partial profit booking on listing and rest holding for long term and 3rd holding for a period of more than 5 years.

Investing in IPO does not necessarily mean "wealth creation". Strategy of pure "invest & hold" does not necessarily generate profits over a long period of time and therefore ,IPO's should be looked at from both the perspectives of short term gains & long term wealth creation that too selectively as an investment avenues.

References

Allen, F and Faulhaber, G R,(1989), 'Signalling by Under-pricing in the IPO Market', Journal of Financial Economics, Vol. 23, 303-23.

Barry, C B and Jennings, R H,(1993), 'The Opening Price Performance of Initial Public Offerings Of Common Stock', Financial Management, Vol. 22, 54-63.

Beatty, R P,(1989), Auditor Reputation and the Pricing of Initial Public Offerings, The Accounting Review ,October, 693-709.

Krishnamurti Chandrasekhar and Pradeep Kumar,(2002), 'The Initial Listing Performance of Indian IPOs',Managerial Finance; Vol. 28, 39-51.

Madhusoonan, T P and Thiripalraju M,(1997),'Underpricing in IPOs: The Indian Evidence', Vikalpa,Vol.22, 17-30.

5

Reengineering of Process for Employee Provident Fund

Ms. Kamaldeep Kaur
Assistant Professor (IT)
kamaldeepkaurkalsi@yahoo.co.in
Ms. Parveen Kaur
Assistant Professor (HR)
NDIM, Okhla

ABSTRACT

The Employees' Provident Fund Organization, India, is one of the principal provident fund institutions in the world in terms of members and volume of financial transactions. The Constitution of India under "Directive Principles of State Policy" provides that the State shall within the limits of its economic capacity make effective provision for securing the right to work, to education and to public assistance in cases of unemployment, old-age, sickness & disablement and undeserved want. The EPF & MP Act, 1952 was enacted by Parliament and came into force with effect from 4th March, 1952. A series of legislative interventions were made in this direction, including the Employees' Provident Funds & Miscellaneous Provisions Act, 1952.

Today is the world of technology; Technology is the application of organized and scientific knowledge to solve practical problems. Automation has had a notable impact in a wide range of industries; Automation has always proved to be an effective plan for most of the industries and companies.

Employee provident fund organization, a statutory body under the ministry of labor and employment, (GOI), has automated the process of EPF.It includes automation of various services like online enquiry and display of current balance of provident fund, EPF status claim, Employee

Provident Fund Appellate Tribunal (EPFAT), EPFiGrievance Management System (EPFiGMS) etc.This case study aims to study the entire reengineering process of employee provident and its potential benefits.

Introduction

Employee Provident Fund [also known as EPF] was one of the main platforms of savings in India for nearly all people working in Government & Public sector Organizations. It was important for every working individual to understand the importance of EPF and how it can benefit him or her.

The Employees Provident Fund Organization (EPFO) was a statutory body of the Indian Government under Labor and Employment Ministry. It administered a compulsory contributory Provident fund, pension and an insurance scheme for Indian Work force. It was one of the largest social security organizations in the world in terms of members and volume of financial transactions undertaken

It was mandatory for every organization that had more than 20 employees on the payroll. If you were working in organizations that have more than 20 employees, and the employer was not giving you EPF benefit, you could lodge a complaint to EPF organization.

Employee Provident Fund Benefits

EPF scheme benefits employees in following essential needs

- Retirement
- Medical Care
- Housing
- Family obligation
- Education of Children
- Financing of Insurance Polices

How EPF works?

Under the EPF Scheme both the employees and employer contribute equally to the Employee Provident fund at the rate of 12% of the basic wages, dearness allowance and retaining allowance, if any, payable to employees per month.

The rate of is fixed at 10% in the case of following establishments:

- Any establishment with less than 20 employees.
- Any sick industrial company and which has been declared as such by the Board for Industrial and Financial Reconstruction
- Any establishment which has at the end of any financial year accumulated losses equal to or exceeding its entire net worth and

- Any establishment engaged in manufacturing of (a) jute (b) Breed (d) coir and (e) Guar gum Industries/ Factories.

How to withdraw EPF accruals?

A member could withdraw up to 90% of the amount of provident fund at credit after attaining the age of 54 years of age or within one year before actual retirement on superannuation whichever is later. EPF form 19 needs to be downloaded, filled and duly submitted to the concerned Provident Fund Office.

You could access entire EPF Acts at official EPF site:

1. Employees' Provident Fund Scheme, 1952
2. Employees' Deposit Linked Insurance Scheme, 1976
3. Employees' Pension Scheme, 1995 (replacing the Employees' Family Pension Scheme, 1971)

Employees' Provident Fund Organization of India

The Employees' Provident Fund Organization (EPFO) was a statutory body of the Government of India under the Ministry of Labor and Employment. It administered a compulsory contributory provident fund scheme, Pension scheme and an Insurance Scheme. It was one of the largest social security organizations in the world in terms of the number of covered beneficiaries and the volume of financial transactions undertaken

Mission

"To extend the reach and the quality of publicly managed old-age income security programs through consistent and ever-improving standards of compliance and benefit delivery in a manner that wins the approval and confidence of Indians in our methods, fairness, honesty and integrity, thereby contributing to the economic and social well-being of Indians."

REENGINEERING OF PROCESS FOR EMPLOYEE PROVIDENT FUND

Traditional Process

In order to simplify and automate the EFP process the government introduced the online access to EPF information for both employers and employees. EPFO initiated online procedure to provide best services to the PF Subscribers. The reengineering efforts of the department were primarily aimed at reducing delays in processing, introducing transparency and providing timely and convenient information to the citizens. The EPF department reengineered and introduced technology to make the process smarter and easier. It roped in several partners who would help the department with little bits of the entire process. The main objective of the reengineering effort was to reduce in ordinate delay in the process of EPF.Its success could be gauged from the fact that the new process was speedier, error free and hassle free.

The initial process of EPF was time-consuming and cumbersome, the entire traditional process has been depicted through the flow chart 2. The manual process of EPF by employees was to submit the form to the accounts department of one's establishment for the initial account opening. Further the accounts department would approach the local EPF office for processing. Once the employee PF account is successfully opened, a monthly deduction from the employee's salary and the contribution made by the employer is deposited in the employees account.

A resigned employee who joins another company would be left with an option of transferring the PF money from his previous PF account to the current PF account, by filling the Form 13. When an employee joins a new company and he wishes to transfer his previous company provident fund amount, he should inform the HR department or accounts department of the new company. The employer will issue Form 13, in which the member had to fill the details of the previous company like - name, address, provident fund account number and address of the provident fund office where the account was held. On form 13, the signature of the previous employer was not required. Once he has filled the required details and submits it to the current employer, the current employer will forward it to the provident fund office for the transferring process. The time taken for transferring the fund from one account to other account normally took about 40 days from date of submission.

Another option available to all individuals was the withdrawal of the PF amount which was again a time consuming and a cumbersome and non transparent task.

Modern Mechanism

The department reexamined the entire process and decided to automate some of the key areas solely for citizen convenience. They decided to automate some process and activities like claim status, balance enquiry, grievance handling which were time taking a causing inefficiency in the departments functioning.

According to Economic Times dated Sep 24, 2006
Nearly four crore subscribers of Employees Provident Fund Organization would be able to access their accounts at a click of a mouse as the EPFO plans to go online soon. "We propose to computerize all our offices and connect to central data base in another one and half years," said Central Provident Fund Commissioner A Vishwanathan. Full-computerization Employees Provident Fund (EPF) offices would be carried out in phased manner. The first pilot project of business process re-engineering would be launched in Kota, Rajasthan on October 2", he said.
www.egovonline.net published news EPF to go online within 4 months on 09 July 2009 which stated
Union Labor Minister Mallikarjun Kharge has said that Employees Provident Fund Portal will be up within four months, enabling people to check their PF account on the click of a button." We are working on the development of the Provident Fund Portal with our people. Director General, Provident Fund is involved in it. It will be up in next three to four months," Kharge said on the sidelines of the launch of the India-US standard's portal. He also said the Labor Ministry will launch the employment portal that was announced in the Union Budget, by the last quarter of this financial year. With a database of 40 million people, the Ministry is

making effort to start the pilot project by January 2010 in five states namely Orissa, Andhra Pradesh, Rajasthan, Haryana and Assam. Union Finance Minister Pranab Mukherjee in his budget speech has proposed to launch a new project for modernization of the Employment Exchanges in public private partnership so that a job seeker can register online from anywhere and approach any employment exchange

[Source: http://www.egovonline.net/news/news-details.asp?newsid=16032]

The new reengineered process was initiated through launching the website http://www.epfindia.com/Index.htm ,which had all the necessary details that could have been accessed by both the employers and employees. The website had features like interfacing with the citizens for access to all EPF related information, claim status , download e-return software, access to regional sites, EPFO directory, balance enquiry,

Figure 1: Benefits of online EPFO

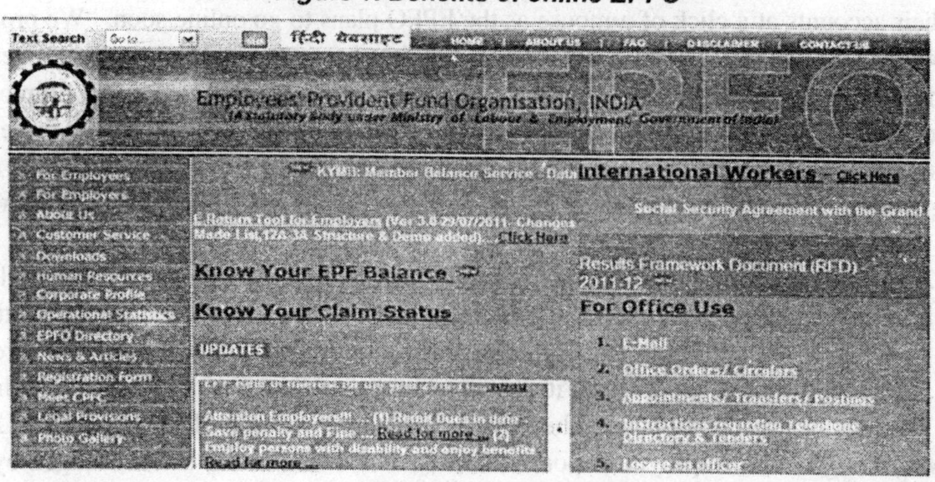

Screen shot 1: Index page of EPFO website (http://www.epfindia.com/Index.htm)

The new reengineered process started with the launch of the website, the department made a lot of changes, both in the activities and the processes of EPF. The first change that was brought about ,was the accessibility of the entire EPF Information and the availability of all the EPF Forms .Instead of queuing up for the forms at the EPF office, the users could download the required form and submit it to the concerned officer. In the previous traditional process, there was no provision to check your current balance in the EPF account, but through this new-fangled technology, the users could easily login to the website and punch in the EPF accounts and enquire about their current balance. This had led to high degree of convenience and transparency in the new website based system.

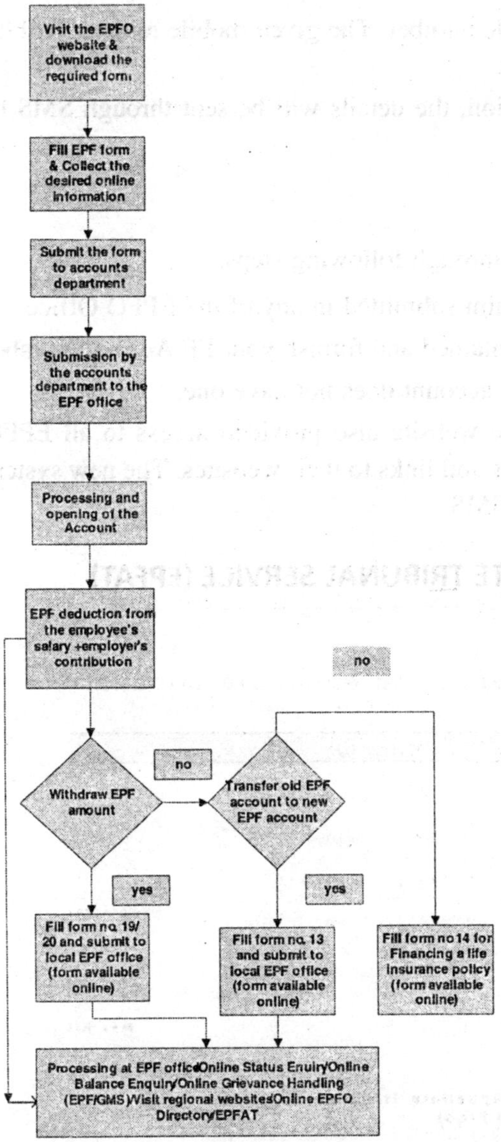

Flowchart 1: the new reengineered EPF process

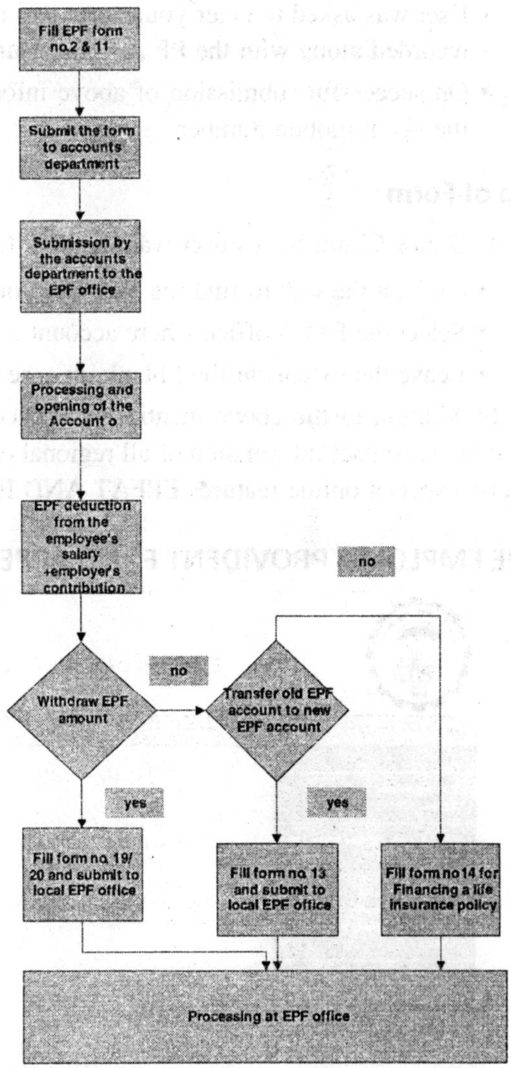

Flowchart 2: the traditional process

Flowchart 1: Employee EPF Process

The other online services that made the system more effective and opportune were the online claim status enquiry in case of the withdrawal of the PF amount. To Know EPF Balance (Service launched on 01/07/2011) the user was required to perform following steps:

- Click on the link to know the balance in your EPF Account up to the date, the accounts are updated, which also includes the latest approved transactions of settlement/advances/ transfer-in/transfer-out, if any.
- Select the EPFO office where account is maintained and furnish your PF Account number.
- Leave the extension field blank, in case account does not have one.
- User was asked to enter your name and mobile number. The given mobile number will be recorded along with the PF Account Number.
- On successful submission of above information, the details will be sent through SMS to the given mobile number.

Top of Form

To Know Claim Status user was required to go through following steps:

- click on the link to find the status of your claim submitted in any of the EPFO Office
- Select the EPFO office where account is maintained and furnish your PF Account number
- Leave the extension field blank, in case your account does not have one.

In addition to the above mentioned services the website also provided access to all EPFO directories, contact information of all regional offices and links to their websites. The new system had two special online features EPFAT AND EPFiGMS.

THE EMPLOYEE PROVIDENT FUND APPELLATE TRIBUNAL SERVICE (EPFAT)

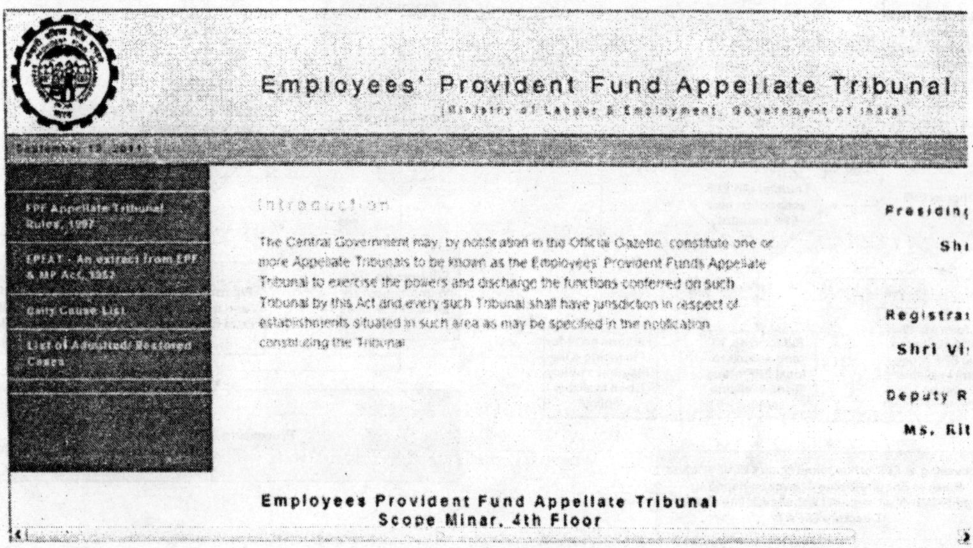

Screen shot 2: index page of EPFAT website (http://www.epfindia.com/EPFAT/epfat.htm)

EPFAT provided information regarding the Employee Provident Fund Appellate Tribunal service ,The employees' provident fund appellate tribunal (procedure) rules, 1997,The employees' provident funds and miscellaneous, Provisions act, 1952 ,Daily cause list and also List of Admitted/ Restored Cases

EPF*i* GRIEVANCE MANAGEMENT SYSTEM (EPF*i*GMS)

The EPF*i*GMS was an online system that allowed the citizens to register their grievances online. The EPFO automated the entire grievance handling process starting with the registration of the complaint to the final status enquiry. In the website, the user initially had to register his complaint. He was asked to enter his personal details and all complaint related details in the online registration form. Next the user could follow up through sending reminders and seek for clarification. Through the registration number provided to him in the initial step user could occasionally go to the website and view the status of the complaint registered.

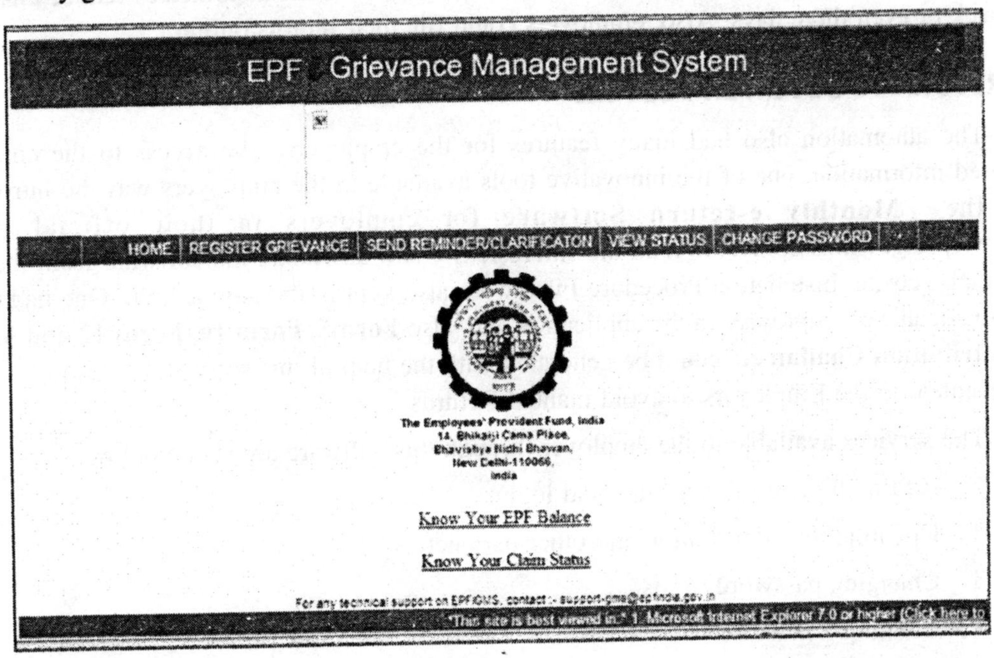

Screen shot 3: Index page of EPFiGMS website (http://epfigms.gov.in/HomePage.aspx)

Another novel feature that had been introduced for pilot testing at some of the regional centers was the provision of SMS service for the information on EPF accounts. This service was started in July 2011.

According to Daily Bhaskar, a national newspaper.

"The EPF system of India (Employees Provident Fund) is all set to go online. Now transferring of money and other transactions are going to be completely online.

On an experimental basis, the information on EPF accounts is being provided on SMS since July. However, the shortcomings would be checked and the procedure will be followed in all the states including Chhattisgarh. This can take a time of around six months to a year.

The headquarters aim to update and correct the EPF accounts by December 31, 2011. The SMS service began from July 1 and six offices were connected with the service in the first phase. These include North Delhi, South Delhi, Lakshmi nagar Delhi, Karnal, Gurgaon and Faridabad. The account holders need to to register their account number and cell phone numbers on the website of EPF to avail the service".

EPF office was also working on software that will verify whether the mobile number registered belonged to the account holder or not. If it was found that the mobile number does not belong to the account holder, the account details would not be sent on the number."

The advantages offered by this process was that a customer wouldn't have to quibble around a lot to get returns, also the customer would know what his month's contribution would be without losing track. Apart from this one can even close his account online. Apart from the digitalization, EPF headquarters was also set to reduce the time involved in various transactions. Currently, settlement of claim takes around a month's time. Officers aimed to reduce this time to a week or even three days. Also, employers could file their returns online.

E-RETURN TOOL FOR EMPLOYERS

The automation also had many features for the employers, like access to the entire EPF related information, one of the innovative tools available to the employers was the introduction of the **Monthly e-return Software** for employers in their official website www.epfo.gov.in.Employers (Who are Interested) could download the software from the EPFO official website. Installation Procedure Files were also kept in the Application. One had to enter all the details of employees in the application and also **Form5, Form 10, Form 12 and Monthly Contribution Challan** etc could be generated with the help of this software .Finally it was most convenient to the Employers to avoid manual Returns.

The services available to the employer through this software are stated below:

1. Add multiple establishments and login
2. Updating the contribution and other parameters
3. Changing password
4. Creating a new user
5. Reset data for a month or period
6. Setting establishment's details
7. Entering/updating establishment master
8. Data entry/upload functions
9. Data entry/upload of member master
10. Data entry/upload of exit details
11. Data entry/upload of monthly wage details
12. Entry of data/generation of challan
13. Data entry/upload of nomination details

14. Generation of returns
15. Generation of form 5
16. Generation of form 2 (r)
17. Generation of form 10
18. Generation of form 12a (r)
19. Generation of broken period 3a
20. Generation of form 3a/6a
21. Generation of integrated monthly return
22. Generation of international workers return

Final Analysis

The new improved system achieved almost all its goals. The following data revealed Outcome/ Impact of activities of Organization/Ministry.

With the automation of the EPF processes in the year 2009 and with the projected details given below, it can be observed that after the automation process the percentage of the grievances registered was projected to increase from NIL in years 2009-10 to 80 in 2011-12 as it was more convenient and an approachable process for the citizens. The grievances once registered would land at the desk of 119 offices of EPFO for further processing.

It was also seen that percentage of claims settled were also projected to increase from 58.72 in 2009-10 to 65 in 2011-12.Also the increase in the numbers of members enrolled as a result of new coverage increased from 2152771 in 2009-10 to 25000000 in 2011-12

Table 1: *EPFO Website,operational statistics. http ://www.epfindia.com/Chapter1_AR200809_El.pdf

	Success Indicator	Unit	2009-2010	2010-2011	2011-2012
1	Settlement of all claims (excluding Form 10A/10D) within 30 days	% of total claims settled	58.73	57.73	65
2	Settlement of monthly Pension claims (Form 10A/10D) within 30 days	% of total claims settled	55.23	49.68	65
3	Disposal of Members Grievances (Including CPGRAMS & epfiGMS).	% of total grievances registered	...	...	80
4	Increase in coverage over previous month as a result of new coverage.	Nos.	40361	46361	43000
5	Increase in enrolment of members as a result of new coverage.	Nos.	2152771	6745990	2500000
6	Recovery of Current Demand (Realisable)by close of following month	% of total Current Demand (Realisable)	79.16	80.92	70
7	Recovery of Arrear Demand (Realisable)	% of total Arrear Demand (Realisable)	53.54	53.19	55
8	Filing of counter reply on receipt of orders of EPFAT/High Courts vacated	Time taken to file counter reply(No. of months)	...	...	2

According to an article by Mr.B.K.Panda, Additioanl CPFC, Information services in the EPF News, (September 2009), a quarterly newsletter of EPFO.

> The 4.4crore members covered under EPF Act & Schemes, 1952 are spread over the length and breadth of the country. In order to take up the challenges of providing efficient, accessible and timely services to the member subscribers and employers, the computerisation project in EPFO is initiated in collaboration with NIC. It will facilitate creation of an environment of transparency and responsiveness which are the essence of e-governance projects.
>
> The revised implementation plan of computerisation, as approved in 182nd C.B.T meeting held on 17.4.2008 will be implemented in two phases. First phase of the plan will focus on automating service areas namely claim settlements to the Provident Fund Members and has provisions for creation of a strong local data base which is largely manual. The second phase will concentrate on consolidating services and database at a central level for 'anytime-anywhere' services with a double entry accounting system. After completion of the first phase, the Provident Fund members will be able to view their Provident Fund balances and status position of their claims on internet. Similarly the employers will get a facility to view the compliance status of their establishments on internet.

***Source** http://www.epfindia.com/EPFO_NewsLetter.pdf.

References

1. http://articles.economictimes.indiatimes.com/2006-09-24/news/27464751_1_computerisation-epfo-plans-national-social-security-number
2. http://epfigms.gov.in/HomePage.aspx
3. http://www.epfindia.com/EPFAT/epfat.htm
4. http://www.epfindia.com/Index.ht
5. http://www.egovonline.net/news/news-details.asp?newsid=16032]
6. http://en.wikipedia.org/wiki/Employees'_Provident_Fund_Organisation_of_India

TEACHING NOTE

SYNOPSIS

The Employees' Provident Fund Organization, India, is one of the principal provident fund institutions in the world in terms of members and volume of financial transactions. The Constitution of India under "Directive Principles of State Policy" provides that the State shall within the limits of its economic capacity make effective provision for securing the right to work, to education and to public assistance in cases of unemployment, old-age, sickness & disablement and undeserved want. The EPF & MP Act, 1952 was enacted by Parliament and came into force with effect from 4th March, 1952. A series of legislative interventions were made in this direction, including the Employees' Provident Funds & Miscellaneous Provisions Act, 1952.

Today is the world of technology; Technology is the application of organized and scientific knowledge to solve practical problems. Automation has had a notable impact in a wide range of industries; Automation has always proved to be an effective plan for most of the industries and companies.

Employee provident fund organization, a statutory body under the ministry of labor and employment, (GOI), has automated the process of EPF. It includes automation of various services like online enquiry and display of current balance of provident fund, EPF status claim, Employee Provident Fund Appellate Tribunal (EPFAT), EPFiGrievance Management System (EPFiGMS) etc. This case study aims to study the entire reengineering process of employee provident and its potential benefits.

LITERATURE REVIEW

Employees' Provident Fund Organization of India

The Employees' Provident Fund Organization (EPFO) is a statutory body of the Government of India under the Ministry of Labor and Employment. It administers a compulsory contributory Provident Fund Scheme, Pension Scheme and an Insurance Scheme. It is one of the largest social security organizations in the world in terms of the number of covered beneficiaries and the volume of financial transactions undertaken

REENGINEERING OF PROCESS FOR EFP

Traditional Process

In order to simplify and automate the EFP process the government introduced the online access to EPF information for both employers and employees. The reengineering efforts of the department were primarily aimed at reducing delays in processing, introducing transparency and providing timely and convenient information to the citizens. The EPF department reengineered and introduced technology to make the process smarter and easier. It roped in several partners who would help the department with little bits of the entire process. The main objective of the reengineering effort was to reduce in ordinate delay in the process of EFP. Its success can be gauged from the fact that the new process was speedier, error free and hassle free.

Modern Mechanism

The department reexamined the entire process and decided to automate some of the key areas solely for citizen convenience. They decided to automate some process and activities like claim status, balance enquiry, grievance handling which were time taking a causing inefficiency in the departments functioning.

Case objectives

- To study the significance of business process reengineering (BPR).
- To study how modern IS are capable of providing numerous organizational benefits including strategic and competitive advantages for the organization.
- To study the use of technology integration for IS activities.

REFERENCES

7. http://articles.economictimes.indiatimes.com/2006-09-24/news/27464751_1_computerisation-epfo-plans-national-social-security-number
8. http://epfigms.gov.in/HomePage.aspx
9. http://www.epfindia.com/EPFAT/epfat.htm
10. http://www.epfindia.com/Index.ht
11. http://www.egovonline.net/news/news-details.asp?newsid=16032]
12. http://en.wikipedia.org/wiki/Employees'_Provident_Fund_Organisation_of_India

Position in the course

The case study can be utilized in following subjects, also mentioned are the topics along with.

S.No	*Subject*	*Chapter*	*Case usage in the course*
1	Management Information System	MIS	This case helps in illustrating the benefits of implementing an Information System for automation.
2	Principles of Management	Business Process Reengineering	This case helps to study how BPR can be used for performance improvement philosophy that aims to achieve quantum improvements by primarily rethinking and redesigning the way that business processes are carried out.
3	Human Resource Management	HRIS (Human Resource Information System)	The case can used to discuss the EPF process and compare the traditional and new process.
4	System Analysis and Design	System Design	The case can be used to illustrate the system design process and also benefits of designing an automated system.

Relevant readings

1. Pressmen, R.S "Software Engineering: A Practitioner's Approach", 6th ed., McGraw-Hill, New York
2. Behforoz, A., and F.J.Hudson. Software Engineering Fundamentals. New York: Oxford university press, 1996
3. O' Brien, James, Maracas, George M. Behl Ramesh "Management Information Systems" 9th ed., McGraw-Hill, New York
4. Ahituv, N., and S .Neumann. "Principles of Information Systems for Management", 3rd ed., Dubuque: Wm.C. Brown Publishers. 1990

5. Page-Jones, M. "The Practical Guide to Structured System Design", 2nd ed. New jersey: Prentice Hall Inc 1988
6. Dessler ,Gary and Biju Varkkey ,"Human Resource Management:,12th ed. Pearson Publication.

Teaching plan

(Assignment questions and suggested possible answers)

Q: Why was it necessary for the government to automate the process of EPF?

A: It was important for government to automate the design process as it served following benefits

Speed: Dramatic compression of the time it takes to complete a task for key business processes. For instance, if process before BPR had an average cycle time 5 hours, after BPR the average cycle time should be cut down to half an hour.

Compression: Cutting major tasks of cost and capital, throughout the value chain. Organizing the processes a company develops transparency throughout the operational level reducing cost. For instance the decision to buy a large amount of raw material at 50% discount is connected to eleven cross checkings in the organizational structure from cash flow, inventory, to production planning and marketing. These checkings become easily implemented within the cross-functional teams, optimizing the decision making and cutting operational cost.

Flexibility: Adaptive processes and structures to changing conditions and competition. Being closer to the customer the company can develop the awareness mechanisms to rapidly spot the weak points and adapt to new requirements of the market.

Quality: Obsession with the superior service and value to the customers. The level of quality is always the same controlled and monitored by the processes, and does not depend mainly on the person, who servicing the customer.

Innovation: Leadership through imaginative change providing to organization competitive advantage.

Productivity: Improve drastically effectiveness and efficiency.

Q: What could be the possible threats or risks that might hamper the successful implementation of an information system?

A:

- Unavailability of dedicated Team
- Non adherence to the Project schedules
- Unavailability of Right technical infra-structure
- Improper Change Management
- Lack of technical support

Q: Explain the process of BPR.

A:

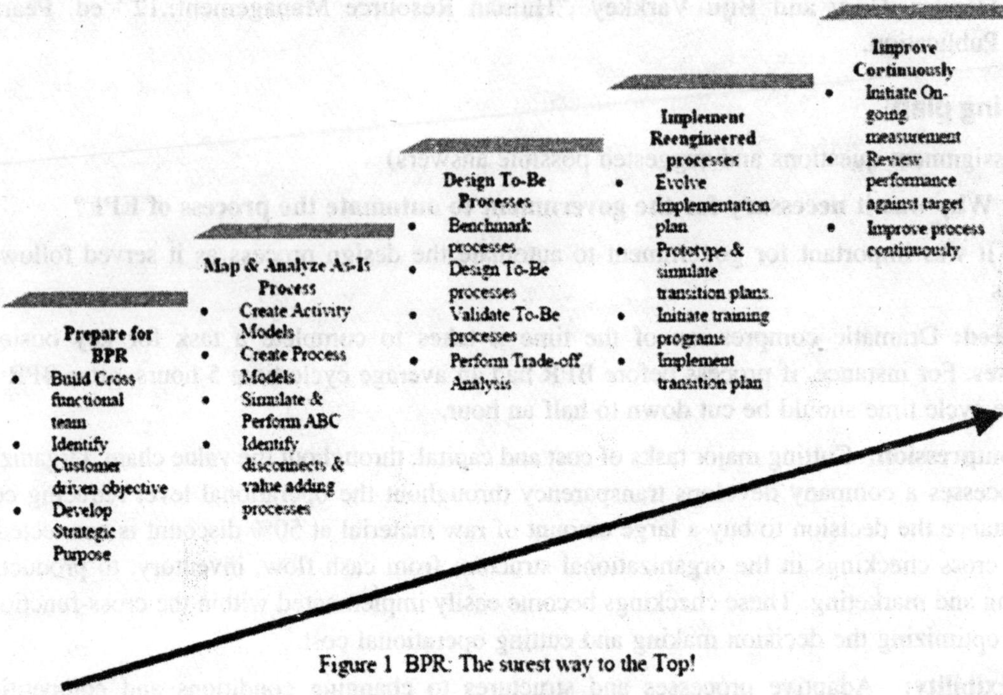

Figure 1 BPR: The surest way to the Top!

Q: Compare and contrast the traditional process and the reengineered process.

A: The new reengineered process had automated various activities like claim status, balance enquiry, grievance handling , which were time taking and causing inefficiency in the departments functioning in the traditional process.

Q: What more features to be added to the existing system to make it more effective?

A:

- Automation of account opening process
- Complete automation of EPFAT

Q: What are the benefits of automating business processes?

A:

— central access

— easy backup

— easy record-keeping

— Report generation or financial statements

— Support decision making

— Online office suite

— Technology used to gain an edge over an organization's competition

— Can be used at all levels of an organization or just a few

— Makes a difference

— Profoundly alters the way an organization does business

— Sustained strategic, competitive advantage

6

Journey of Louis Vuitton from Developed to Developing Economies

Ms. Geetika Chawla
Ms. Kunjana Vasudev
kunjananitk@gmail.com
Amity School of Business, Noida

Abstract:

The case portrays the entry of a premium brand (Louis Vuitton) into low income nations and the problems that the company faces in order to position its brand in the developing nations. The luxury goods manufacturer has faced many practical problems like an increased tariff, maintaing the brand's prestige, identifying the target market and saving itself from the imitation by following a zero counterfeiting policy. The company targeted Indian market through metropolitan like Mumbai, Delhi and China through Shenyang and Nanjing in five star hotels to ensure that its target segment is apt to its brand image on the current world stage. The case would discuss on the movement of Louis Vuitton from developed countries like France and USA to developing countries like India and China.

Keywords: luxury brand, Louis Vuitton, target segment

Learning Objectives:

- To understand the movement of Louis Vuitton to India and China

- Marketing mix of Louis Vuitton
- Challenges faced by Louis Vuitton to position itself in developing countries
- Strategies followed by Louis Vuitton in Developing markets

"LVMH must continue to be synonymous with both elegance and creativity. Our products, and the cultural values they embody, blend tradition and innovation, and kindle dream and fantasy."

Consumers like brand items, while researchers like brand theory. Although scholars also use the word "brand" to refer to the likes of Coca-Cola and McDonald's, there is a vast gulf between these brands and the luxury. I n researchers' brand management theories, one rarely finds mention of representative luxury brands like Louis Vuitton or Dior, or of LVMH.

Creating luxury brands is a difficult marketing exercise. It requires heavy investment in marketing communications, excellent product/service quality, but above all these brands have to try to remain fashionable, which is notoriously difficult. Louis Vuitton is a successful luxury brand that retail to the high-end market. Marketers are moving from the traditional marketing mix approach towards greater use of experiential marketing. This is where customers are treated as both rational and emotional individuals that seek 'experiences' from products. The key is to engage customers in a memorable experience around the product/service, developing a relationship with customers, creating an affinity with them. The central aim of experiential marketing is to create an emotional attachment between the brand and the customer. Louis Vuitton provides this experience through its unique product image and features, its outstanding service, exclusive retail environment, pricing, selective channels of distribution and completes with its distinct packaging. But above all the benefits associated is its unique brand image. To promote a product to the high-market it is important that the customers have the right experience so that the desired feelings, images and perspectives become linked with the product/service and their marketing programme.

Introduction to Louis Vuitton:

The famous brand started out back in the 1850's. The founder was made famous for crafting the luggage for Napoleon. From theses roots the brand has become synonymous with luggage and in particular handbags. Louis Vuitton is very much the envy of the industry, recording an operating margin of 45%, whilst the industry average is only 25% for luxury accessories. The company is famous for its handbags, but also sells a range of wallets, briefcases, eyeglass cases etc. Over recent years, the brand has tried to modernise its image by utilising the talents of young designers and artists in rejuvenating the image of some of their products, whilst maintaining the classic designs. This reinvention has attracted younger buyers into the brand. However no one designer for Louis Vuitton has eclipsed the powerful brand image of Louis Vuitton itself, unlike other design brands.

Louis Vuitton stands out from its peers through its relentless focus on product quality. All products are extensively tested to make sure that they can withstand wear and tear, and that there are no imperfections. The company has blended mechanisation and handmade craftsmanship into their products, boosting their productivity, maintaining that high level of product quality, whilst still holding onto the allure of handmade quality. In an effort, to maintain the prestige image of a Louis Vuitton product, the company operates a pricing integrity strategy amongst its entire distribution network, a Louis Vuitton bag is never reduced in price, there are no sale periods. The company offers customised products such as personal engraving on hand luggage pieces, boosting its appeal further. Furthermore, the company sponsors elite sporting events such as yachting and motorsport events. This is in effort to match the audience of sponsorship property with the target audience of the brand itself.

Some brands like Hermes, a key rival, create even greater exclusivity by having a three-year waiting list before one of their bags can be obtained. These bags are handcrafted, adding to the appeal. China and India are seen as the biggest growth markets for the Louis Vuitton brand. Presently, 55% of its sales are from Japanese sales alone. It has found itself particularly over reliant on the Japanese market, and seeks greater presence in other foreign markets

Target Markets Of Louis Vuitton :

The company uses demographic marketing strategy to target its customers which include both men and women .They make products for all age groups ranging from young adults to seniors. As they focus on the high income group people the income should be above $ 6000 per month.

They sell fashionable as well as durable goods. The goods are for the high society people who practise their ego and power.

Marketing mix of Louis Vuitton:

Product: Their main products have been leather bags and wallets. But they have expanded into other segments like time pieces, shoes, jewellery,sunglasses, belts, scarves and accessories.Their original product line is a Monogram.but they have expanded themselves into Monogram denim, Monogram multicolour , Monogram Vernis and Damier Canvas.

Price: Louis Vuitton works upon certain principles. They have principle of prestige pricing and they prohibit any surprise price changes. Their products are never on sale.The price range for their Handbags: $550- $3,700 and Wallets: $ 200- $ 700.

Place: They are always located on high street, directly operated stores, along with leading department stores, fine jewellers, client suites and online purchasing. Partnerships with jewellers. Louis Vuitton bags are only offered through limited distribution channels. One might go as far as to say Louis Vuitton innovated a method of selling that amounts to "controlling Place" and "not using channels that cannot be controlled". They try to create gallery type feel to store, architectural display cases, limestone floors, warm lighting, clean black and white colours and artwork on display.

Promotion: They emphasise on personal selling. And they don't emphasise on sales promotion. Louis Vuitton, however, does not advertise on television. While Louis Vuitton does advertise in newspapers and magazines like Vogue, Elle , these consist mainly of image ads rather than

"aggressive" sales ads, and more focus is given to publicity (being taken in the media). The age of the House of Louis Vuitton can not be said to have been rabid about promotion, meaning that most of the principles for promotion likely originated with the luxury brand strategy of the holding company LVMH. However, such principles as the Principle of Extravagant Parties can be said to have been given special emphasis in Japan. Endorsements mainly include Jennifer Lopez, Kate Moss, Uma Thurman, and Scarlett Johansson.

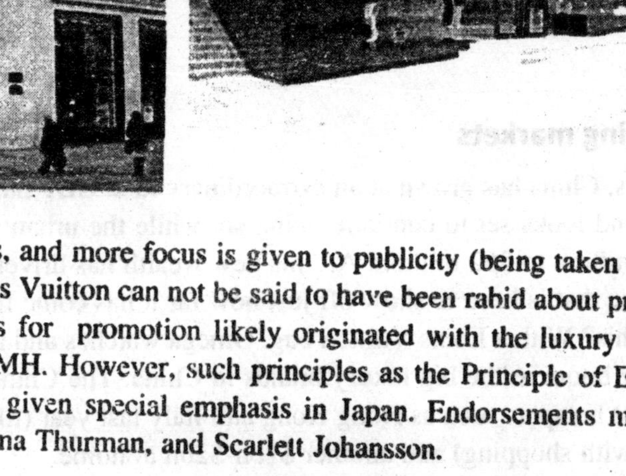

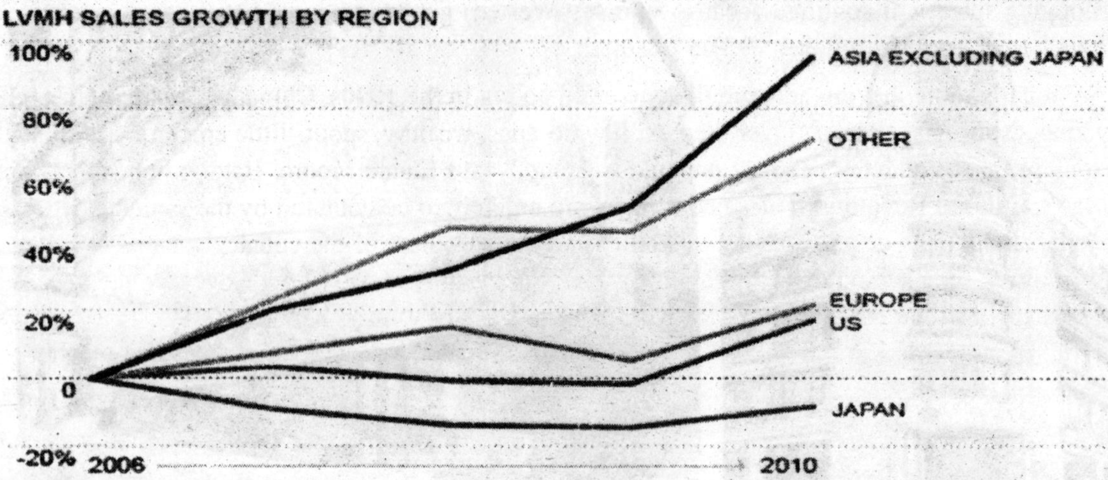

Tapping the Developing markets

Over the last 20 years, China has grown at an extraordinary rate. GDP has expanded at a good 10% a year every year and looks set to continue doing so, while the urban population has more than doubled from 251 million to 562 million. All this new wealth has driven the emergence of a new middle class, and one that is keen to show off just how far it has come from the rice paddies. And the best way to do this? With a Louis Vuitton bag, Omega watches and a bottle of Möet. The result is an extraordinary boom in the big luxury brands in China. The Chinese spent \$4bn-\$5bn on luxury goods in tourist hotspots such as Hong Kong and Italy last year (like the Japanese, they tend to equate holidays with shopping) and another \$1bn-\$2bn at home.

Until now all this money has been pouring out from China's "first tier" cities, such as Shanghai and Beijing, but the real growth area for luxury goods in China is in the smaller second- and third-tier cities. China has about 100 cities with a population of more than a million people and as the spoils of economic growth spread, so will the demand for high-end merchandise. Goldman Sachs estimates that within the next five years the number of Chinese people in a position to spend on such non-essentials will rise from the current 40 million to 160 million. The result? "Citigroup expects that annual sales of luxury goods in China will grow by 21% over the next five years," says Elaine Moore in the FT. Goldman Sachs is just as bullish: it expects the Chinese to be buying nearly 30% of the world's luxury goods within ten years.

This is good news for the big brands. The more sophisticated consumers in the likes of Shanghai have (again in the same way as the Japanese) started to shift towards buying lesser-known brands with an eye to exclusivity. That means that they need second-tier consumers – who are pleasingly interested in getting their hands on the brands that leave casual observers in no doubt about their financial status – to keep sales rising. Luxury goods allows consumers to project an image of success. All this means that the big global luxury brands that have proved popular in China's large cities – Louis Vuitton, Fendi and Möet & Chandon enjoy copy-cat demand from this second round of Chinese consumers. "Even if economic growth slackens, the shopping spree will continue because so many Western goods are 'must-have' status symbols in Asia," says Tom Burroughes in The Business.

What's more, having adopted the one-child policy in the 1970s, China has a bulging class of young, aspiring spenders. "Over the next few decades, wealthy, spoilt 'little emperors' will begin to make up the country's largest population group," says Elaine Moore. Having not experienced Mao's Cultural Revolution, these consumers are unlikely to be bothered by the same anxieties as their grandparents or parents about stability and the weakness of the country's social safety net. As a result, they should drive wave after wave of demand for luxury goods over the next decade. Surveys show that 92% of Japanese women own a Louis Vuitton handbag. There is every sign that the Chinese are in the middle of being gripped by a similar madness.

Of the all the iconic brands that China's second-tier consumers are likely to latch onto, **Louis Vuitton Moet Hennessy** (LVM) – the French luxury powerhouse behind Louis Vuitton, Fendi and Moet & Chandon – owns the ones that look likely to be the most in demand. The company reported a 30% rise in full-year profits in February and is currently establishing stores throughout the country, putting it in a good position to benefit from second-tier consumption. The shares trade on a P/E of 21.7, which is not cheap, but is still something of a discount to Citigroup's estimated sector average of 24.7. This valuation may seem racy, says Elaine Moore in the FT, but given the massive growth potential of the sector, it is probably worth paying. LVMH is on a price to earnings growth ratio of only 1.36 times.

Chinese consumers have buoyed and kept the luxury markets around the world solvent," said Shaun Rein, Shanghai-based managing director of the China Market Research

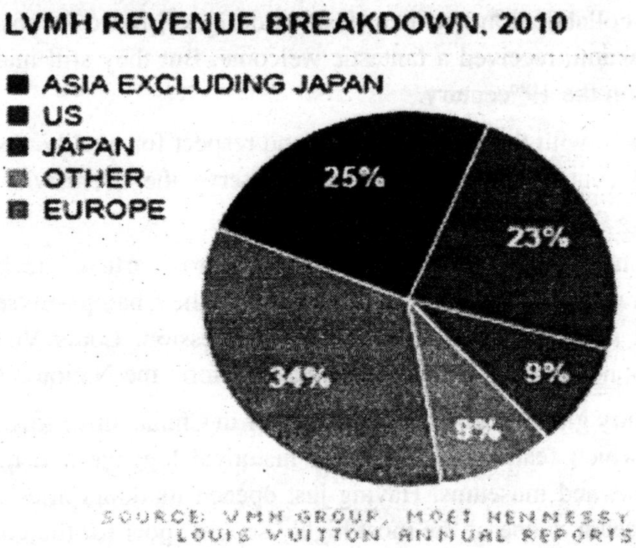

In addition to clamoring for designer goods at stores in Shanghai, Beijing and Hong Kong, Chinese tourists have dominated sales at flagship locations on New York's Fifth Avenue and throughout Europe, where the goods are about 30% cheaper than they are on mainland China.

A Louis Vuitton boutique in London was recently forced to limit shoppers to three purchases to make sure they would have enough left, said Kirk Cheyfitz, CEO of global marketing agency Story Worldwide, at the Bloomberg China Investment Strategies conference. CLSA forecasts that China will become the world's largest market for luxury goods over the course of the next decade, accounting for 44% of global sales by 2020, from 15% today. Chinese buyers are Louis Vuitton's biggest customers already, according to CLSA, and sales will likely keep growing alongside an increase in the number of Chinese millionaires. And demand for luxury goods is likely to pick up even more steam if the Chinese government allows the yuan to appreciate, which would make imports like Louis Vuitton bags less expensive.

"A rising Yuan would give the Chinese much more buying power," said Jonathan Masse, senior portfolio manager of AlphaShares, the fund management company co-founded by Princeton University economist Burton Malkiel, who also authored *From Wall Street to the Great Wall: How Investors Can Profit from China's Booming Economy*. LVMH Moet Hennessy Louis Vuitton (LVMH, Paris), the world's largest luxury goods groups with its 60 brands including its namesakes, Tag Heur and Fendi, is one of the biggest holdings in AlphaShares' global China-linked portfolio.

Louis Vuitton has pursued a consistent approach to developing the market, never compromising in the face of difficult operational obstacles, and, as always, controlling every aspect of the business. This unique approach has powered Louis Vuitton to its current position as the most successful luxury brand in China. In May 2007, the first store in Shenyang was opened. New stores were opened up in Nanjing, Beijing and Tianjin .Today, the mainland Chinese are Louis Vuitton's third-largest customer segment in the world. The fine equilibrium between tradition and innovation reflects the DNA of Louis Vuitton. Products such as the Multicolore Monogram bags, the fruit of a collaboration between [fashion designer] Marc Jacobs and the contemporary artist Takashi Murakami, received a fantastic welcome. But they still make traditional suitcases in the same way as in the 19thcentury.

They have worked with the same creativity and respect for quality. As a leader of the sector, the challenge is to continue growing and still preserve the exclusivity and great quality the company has always offered.

Louis Vuitton has always transcended barriers across artistic, technical, and intellectual disciplines. Inaugurated in 2006 on the seventh floor of the Champs-Elysées Maison, the Espace Louis Vuitton is a space of artistic and cultural expression. Louis Vuitton made a pitch to consumers in a spot no Western brand has ventured before: the National Museum of China.

The French luxury giant, celebrated its 20th year in China, unveiling special summer exhibit titled "Voyages," which featured the brand's historical luggage and handbags, in one of the country's most renowned museums. Having just opened its doors after an epic-long three-year renovation, the museum is one of the most highly-sought spots for the country's tourists.

Louis Vuitton in India

According to ***Forbes***, India has the fastest-growing population of millionaires in the world. But for Western luxury brands operating in the country, grabbing a piece of the market has proven more difficult than anticipated and many are in the process of re-conceiving their India strategies.

Indeed, in order to succeed in India, luxury brands need to localise their marketing strategies. This goes further than just putting an Indian print on a bag or collaborating with a local celebrity. A multitude of cultures, languages, religions, festivals, colours and tastes make up this land of 1.1 billion people. So, it's about understanding the difference between the flamboyant nature of a Punjabi customer and the more reserved nature of a Gujarati, and speaking to each of them in the specific cultural register that they respond to. Louis Vuitton has also localised their approaches, identifying important events and celebrations amongst potential clients and arriving with personalised gifts or a surprise car service for the occasion.

An economy growing at nearly 9 percent has spurred more than 200,000 millionaires, trailing only the United States and China.

The total net worth of "ultra" high net worth individuals defined by net worth of more than $5 million is $1 trillion and is expected to surpass $5 trillion by 2016.

Yet India accounts for only half a percent of the global luxury market at $846 million. Greater China, on the other hand, accounts for 10 percent of the global market at $17 billion.

Trying to sell expensive chic in India faces several challenges: steep import duties of up to 30 percent, inadequate luxury retail infrastructure, real estate regulations and a clientele that prefers to buy its luxury overseas for reasons of cash and cachet.

"India is a tough market, the system is laborious," Gayatri Ruia, Development Director of Palladium in Mumbai, a mall that houses several brands, including luxury and premium.

"And the Indian spending pattern is different. In Japan or China, even an entry level secretary would not be seen without a Louis Vuitton bag." Understanding the consumer behaviour in the Indian market , Louis Vuitton has come up with some localized strategies and initiatives to lure the Indian customers.

Rajeev Sethi, a New Delhi-based artist and scenographer known for bringing contemporary relevance to the work of traditional artists and craftsmen, collaborated with Louis Vuitton to design the Diwali-themed window displays.

From November 5 2010 to mid January 2011, all of Louis Vuitton's 454 stores spanning five continents featured columns of trunks made of banana leaves, which aimed to give passers-by the feeling of gaiety and festivity.

This was the first time in the store's 156-year history that it celebrated a single festival on this scale. Louis Vuitton also confirmed that the store windows would remain unchanged throughout Christmas, a bold move in Western cities where shops compete for the best seasonal display. Luxury brand Louis Vuitton, synonymous with stylish travel paid homage to India's biggest and brightest religious festival through specially-designed store windows, to be unveiled across the world.

World's leading luxury group LVMH is among companies that might be seeking to acquire luxury-hotel chain Amanresorts International Pte. Indian real estate developer DLF Ltd , has received at least five non-binding bids of $400 million to $450 million for Amanresorts. Amanresorts owns and manages 25 small luxury resorts worldwide, according to its website. Private-equity firms are among bidders for Amanresorts. The flagship Amanpuri in Phuket on Thailand's coast was built in 1987 and rooms as the resort start at $525 per night in September. The communications of the Louis Vuitton with the customer in India had started before the opening of the first store in New Delhi. They started with paid personal communications by sending promotional brochures to potential customers, invitations for special viewings of its products and offers of personalized tours to France.

After opening the first store in New Delhi, personal selling also played a crucial role for high sales numbers because salespeople are the primary vehicles in luxury retail market to help customers satisfy their needs through face-to-face communications. They didn't use advertising in media to reach customers and since they were trying to form a new customer segment who wanted acceptable exclusivity, they shouldn't publish "product base" advertisements to everywhere. They need to trigger the excitement of the customers by using emotions. This won't be a hard case for Louis Vuitton because their global campaign is also on the same track. They have managed the financial crises better than their competitors. With similar successful campaigns they will increase the Indian customers' awareness too. Of course the most important thing is to determine the potential customers in India but it wasn't very challenging to find out that segment since the difference between them and the one step lower-income group is very obvious. Unpaid personal communications also had started, where people started to talk about Louis Vuitton and as a consequence of word of mouth method; customers were involved in individual sales requisitions into an order book position. These "special orders" were customized to those individuals in terms of design, color, packaging etc.

About strengths and weaknesses of the methods; in terms of control, Louis Vuitton had the advantage of previously well-organized operations in all around the world. They could decide on the promotions which they offered to potential customers and ideally allocated their budget to those promotions depending on their previous experiences. Time of delivery was specifically important since the special orders were a result of word-of mouth communications and Louis Vuitton had little control over that way of communication. But they had the advantage of flexibility in personal selling and special orders depending on the customers' needs. An addition to what they have done so far, Louis Vuitton also increased their brand awareness through public relations programs. They started to appear in the media with a Bollywood actress, Freida Pinto, at the store opening in Mumbai and Louis Vuitton fashion show in Paris. Also they put a huge suitcase at the Banglore airport to grab the passengers' attention and to put the name of Louis Vuitton into people's minds.

In February, 2006, the Indian government decided to allow 51 percent ownership by a foreign enterprise in a local retail venture of a single brand. This incident became a great incentive for luxury brands to enter India and finally the idea of building a luxury mall had emerged. In cities that did not have luxury retail clusters where the brands spread over several blocks and highlighting their brand personality, Louis Vuitton opened its store in luxury malls. So the first luxury mall opening in New Delhi in 2010 was a very big step for the existence of

Louis Vuitton in Indian market because now, they could reach their first aim of creating a new generation of luxury consumers in India and make them loyal to their brand.

The luxury mall concept would work in India because when we look at the percentage of population below poverty line, it has declined more than 30 percent since 1970s. Also the overall Indian economy is in a path of growing; their gross domestic product (GDP) has increased about 40 percent in 5 years. Finally number of households who have annual income more than 114,940$ is 25 times bigger than it was in 1995. With these economical data, we can assume that India has a huge potential and it started using this potential. For a luxury brand like Louis Vuitton, these developing countries have a clear customer segment that have the financial ability but no place to spend the money. The most challenging part is to make those people loyal to Louis Vuitton because new customers are eager to switch brands at the beginning. But since Louis Vuitton is the largest luxury brand in the worldwide arena and India has a huge potential, with right moves, it would use that potential advantageously and also be very successful in these countries too.

Challenges faced by Louis Vuitton in India and China

The most important challenge for a Global (European Luxury Brand) is the Local Government tariffs and other trade Barriers which are making the retail Cost more than Duty Free Shops or Stores abroad. The most important difficulties that Louis Vuitton faces are:

Import Duties: The figures were rosy, especially since research conducted by a luxury menswear brand said the number of Indian millionaires was growing at a staggering 19.3% annually. But the party poopers came in the guise of infrastructural and regulatory hurdles, if not the challenge to find the right local partner who shared a vision and had a sound track record. Steep duties translate to prices 15% higher than in Europe. Currently, only 51% FDI is permitted, but it applies only to single-brand retail, leaving multi-brand retailers in the lurch. The government has been assuring 100% from a long time.

Local partners, customers lose. Brands win

Louis Vuitton came in when rentals were high, which lowered margins. This led it to pass on high duties to customers, who then preferred to shop abroad rather than pay 25% extra. The luxury segment works on very high margins, but brands refuse to pass these on to local partners.

The Indian high-end retail market is expected to grow to $30 billion by 2015, from the existing $3.5 billion. Louis Vuitton has to re-strategize either alter the arrangement with local partners or invest their own money and run the business before aspiring for a slice of the action, he suggests. Many question whether luxury brands have the credibility to position themselves as art. Louis Vuitton took a little heat, when it opened an art gallery in its Champs Elysees flagship store, showing off an exhibit of nude black and white women spelling out and "L" and a "V" with their bodies.

Louis Vuitton disposed off its manufacturing unit in India

Four years after choosing **Puducherry, erstwhile Pondicherry** for its first manufacturing plant in Asia, French luxury goods giant **Louis Vuitton** decided to sell its Indian unit to a

Chennai-based firm **–Leather Crafts India**. The management made a formal announcement about exiting India on June 13 2011 because of labour problems. **LADP**was set up jointly by **Louis Vuitton** and the Puducherry-based leather fashion brand ***Dilip Kapoor's* HiDesign.HiDesign** did not take a stake in **LADP** but **Louis Vuitton took a 5% stake in HiDesign**. The prospect of a change of management sparked labour unrest with the 200-plus Indian employees on **LADP's** rolls going on strike since**June 13** demanding that the firm regularize their services before winding up its operations and handing over the unit to the new owners.

Long Term returns

Though the luxury sales are high in India and China but the company should not expect a quick return on their investment. The costs of setting up, training staff and building awarness have been high while the demand is still limited. High import duties and consumption taxes also make it difficult to target market segments beyond the economic elite.

Counterfeiting

LV has adopted a zero tolerance policy against counterfeiting .The brand's firm stance led to 13,000 legal actions, 6000 raids and 947 arrests. According to the U.S Embassy in Beijing, the piracy rate in China remains the highest in the world and on an average 20% of consumer products are counterfeit.

Location

There was one big obstacle left in front of the launch of Louis Vuitton in India and that was the location. Typically Louis Vuitton is used to open its stores on fashion streets in the downtown which is very close to rich neighborhoods or in luxury malls. India was lack of both types of location types so it was a big limiting factor to enter the market. Louis Vuitton had also opened stores at luxury hotels in Asia so they decided to try that strategy and opened the first store at the ground floor of The Oberoi Hotel in New Delhi in 2003 and in 1 year ahead, they added another store at Taj Mahal Palace in Mumbai. This was a good strategic decision for a country like India because before scratching a new customer segment from the ground, first they tried to be successful with people who travel around and already know what is going on around the world and their brand image. The French company also hit a rocky patch in China May 2011, when Shanghai's city government required the company to demolish one of its advertisements—a 65-foot-tall suitcase—that violated the city's outdoor ad regulations.

Conclusion

Of course everything was not all dark in India and China. After April 2001, the government removed the ban on imports of leather goods in India so the first obstacle in front of Louis Vuitton was removed. Also according to many surveys, high income level segment of the society is growing very fast and expected to continue its growth. India was recorded as the world's second fastest growing country in the number of high-net-worth customers with 19.5 percent . The size of the luxury market in India was estimated about $4 billion and expected to grow to

$30 billion by 2015 and China has larger figures than India. Since the world luxury market was valued $169 million, the numbers in developing countries may seem small. But Louis Vuitton is the largest luxury brand in the global market so most probably it will also be the largest brand that will get the largest pie in the potential Indian and Chinese luxury market. To get that largest pie, the contrast in the Indian consumer market may help Louis Vuiton. There are too many very poor people in developing countries but on the other hand rich people are very rich that almost all luxury car brands are exceeding their sales targets . According to this information, the customer segment of Louis Vuitton seems like existing in these countries. This customer segment is "the new elite"; which includes people who are the business owners in technology and manufacturing, non-resident Indians returning home, CEOs, Bollywood actors, politicians etc. They don't know Louis Vuitton as a brand and they need to be converted into loyal customers which is a challenging mission for a company even though it successfully proved its brand image and quality to almost the entire world. The crucial thing for that segment is to feel "exclusivity" because the drivers of purchasing for that segment are; pleasure and status symbol. But also they want acceptable exclusivity, when they are spending that much money, they don't want to be alienated by the society. They perceived luxury products as a reward and they are very enthusiastic to show their "success", not to be seen as lavish. They want to prove the idea "I've made it." And the studies shows us that female purchasers are emerging as a distinct voice which is a very good signal for brands like Louis Vuitton whose products are mostly aimed to women consumers.

LVMH had developed its long-term strategy not only to extend in highly developed markets, but also to enter growing ones such as China, India and central Europe. But also there was a historical reason why they chose India, during the Great Depression in 1920s; the orders from Indian royal families helped a lot Louis Vuitton to survive. So it is a fact that the brand image is reputable among Indian ruling class. But besides that gratitude, Wall Street has a pressure on Louis Vuitton to expand in new markets since their numbers are growing very fast in the stock market.

Bibliography/References:

- www.cigaraficionado.com
- www.lvmh.com
- www.chinaapparel.net
- articles.economictimes.indiatimes.com
- www.reuters.com
- www.dlfemporio.com

Questions:

1. What are the key factors to be considered while establishing a brand in a developing market? Is Louis Vuitton able to position itself properly in the developing markets?

2. Discuss how can Louis Vuitton lose its aura of exclusiness and fashion status to other competitive brands.

3. Summarize the major problems and challenges Louis Vuitton has faced in India and China.

4. According to you, what are the main reasons that make Louis Vuitton as a premium and an exclusive brand.

5. Explain in context of Louis Vuitton the importance of concentrating on retail environment which devising strategies for positioning a brand in the market.

7

Film Insurance and Financing in India

Ms. Richa Joshi
Ms. Shipra Taneja
Ms. Shivangi Tewari
Bharati Vidyapeeth University, Institute of Management and Research

New DelhiiCinema entered India in 1896 with the screening of six soundless short films in Bombay. Dada Saheb Phalke, considered to be the father of Indian cinema, made the first fully indigenous feature film 'Raja Harishchandra' in 1913. The first film with sound 'Alam Ara,' was released in 1931, and the first color film, 'Kisan Kanya,' was released in 1937.

In June 2000, when popular Hindi film actress and former Miss World Aishwarya Rai met with an accident, there was another casualty – United India Insurance (UII). Though the accident cost the insurance company a sum of only Rs 1.6 million, it attracted substantial media coverage. The reason was that it was the first instance of the Hindi film industry availing the benefits of film insurance – a practice followed in the US film industry since the era of silent movies.

The credit for pioneering the film insurance business in India however goes to the successful Hindi film producer-director Subhash Ghai (Ghai). Ghai was the first Indian filmmaker to have his film 'Taal' insured for a sum of Rs 110 million with UII in 1998. The move was welcomed by both media and film personalities as opening of a new chapter in the Indian film industry. UII Asst. General Manager, Bhandari said, "'Taal' being the first Hindi film to be insured, the policy had to be formulated from scratch." UII even honored Ghai with naming the policy 'The Cine Mukta Policy' after his company Mukta Arts Pvt. Ltd.

By July 2001, UII had insured around 8-10 films, for sums varying from Rs 25 million to Rs 220 million, with many more in the pipeline. The insured films included YashRaj Films'

'Mohabbatein,' Aamir Khan Productions' 'Lagaan,' Farhan Akhtar's 'Dil Chahta Hai,' Karan Johar's 'Kabhi Khushi. Kabhi Gham' and Dreamz Unlimited's. 'Asoka'. among others.

United India Insurance is a subsidiary of the General Insurance Company carrying on general (non-life) insurance business. It is the second largest insurer in India in terms of premium income and market share of non life insurance. Rai was acting in the movie Mohabbatein, when she met with the accident. The producers, YashRaj Films had insured the movie with UII for Rs 150 million. Yash Raj Films claimed Rs 3.5 million from UII as due to the accident, Rai's shooting schedules were disturbed and a set had to be dismantled. (They were awarded Rs 1.6 million by the UII).

THE PROBLEMS

Analysts remarked that the hesitance of the foreign insurance companies was completely justified. The functioning of the Indian film industry was completely unorganized. To insure (or re-insure) a film project, any insurance company would naturally look for a commercially viable project, backed by detailed reports regarding the risks involved, the financing of the project and completion schedule etc. However, the issue of financing was found to be the biggest stumbling block for the development of the film insurance industry. The three major sources of funds for the film industry were the distributors, music companies and financiers. It was comparatively easier to get finance from the distributors for producers with a good track record. However, in case of a lesser known producer, the distributors frequently asked to see the under-production movie, and forced the producers to make some changes (such as adding or deleting a song/dance/action sequence etc.) to improve the film's success prospects. The music companies, who bought the rights for selling a film's music also provided funds to the producers. However, here also the big banners associated with established music director's had easier access to funds as compared to the others. Thus, the financiers had emerged as the de-facto primary source of funds in India over the years. Financiers – often diamond merchants, brokers, builders and other cash rich businessmen, charged very high interest rates, generally in the range of 36-48% per annum. To get funds at cheaper rates, the film industry gradually moved towards black money, laying the foundations of the underworld mafia and the film industry's association. Industry sources revealed that approximately 30-35% of the films were financed by the underworld.

At various other stages in the course of production of the movie – transactions with the distributors and the music companies for instance – there was always an element of black money involved. Most of the popular stars commanding a high fee, did not take their entire payment in white money in order to escape the taxes. According to estimates, 15-20% of the money paid to stars was always in black money. By the mid 1990s, the industry was facing serious problems with the underworld mafia demanding increasingly higher payments. Often, producers/stars/directors were threatened to pay 'protection money' or the rights for distributing a potentially successful movie. After some celebrities were murdered, reportedly by the underworld, the government had even begun providing police protection to film personalities.

Another problem plaguing the industry was the issue of piracy. The piracy of films, either in the form of illegally showing the movie on cable networks, or the selling/renting of unauthorized video cassettes, VCDs, LDs and DVDs[1], had become a big business in India. In 1995, the industry lost approximately 99% of its total earnings to piracy. Though the figure had come down to 80% in 1998, the threat of piracy was still very significant.

In the late 1990s, the film industry was going through a phase of changes. With increasing concern over removing the underworld influence and the emergence of corporate houses, (such as Mukta Arts, Ajay Devgan Entertainment and Software, Balaji Telefilms, Zee Telefilms, Amitabh Bachchan Corporation Ltd. and Dreamz Unlimited), the demand for the government granting films an industry status intensified. In October 2000, the government finally gave films industry status via notification 2 (C)(XVII) of the IDBI Act 1964. Though the move was welcomed by the industry and banks/FIs in the media, the film financing and insurance business failed to pick up as expected. Analysts remarked that the financing and piracy problems combined with the issues of lack of transparency in operations, disorganized functioning, frequent cost overruns and no physical assets being offered as collateral, resulted in banks and financial institutions shying away from financing film production.

THE SOLUTIONS

In December 2000, a Joint Institutional Committee on Financing Entertainment Industry submitted an interim report that laid down certain norms for offering financial assistance to the film industry. The committee headed by the Department of Banking-Ministry of Finance, had Industrial Finance Corporation of India (IFCI) and Industrial Development Bank of India (IDBI) as its members. The committee's recommendations included:

- Institutions should extend finances only to corporate entities.
- Besides negatives, music rights, satellite TV rights and overseas rights must also be considered as security.
- Insurance companies must extend insurance cover for films and develop more products for the industry.
- When financing a single film, the duration of advance may be restricted to between 6 and 18 months.
- Banks and FIs should work together with producers to evolve standards for financing and insuring films.
- Creating a film industry-rating agency by pooling people from banks/FIs, eminent filmmakers and experts in the media sector to judge a filmmaker's credentials.

The increased transparency as a result of film production companies adopting corporate practices was expected to enable the banks/FIs/insurers to deal with the film industry like any other industry. The changed setup was also expected to result in better films being produced with significant improvement in the overall industry performance levels. Besides helping the film industry in breaking away from the underworld, corporatisation of the film industry was expected to result in multiple benefits for the government as well. Film software was expected to become a \$ 1 billion industry by 2005, employing around 10 million people. Further, ancillary industries like dubbing, editing, sound recording, web designing, web-casting, merchandising and promotion were expected to flourish as well. The government was reported to be working towards developing a comprehensive legal structure for insuring all kinds of movies along with institutes like National Film Development Corporation (NFDC) and Film & Television Institute of India (FTII). This was expected to go a long way in opening up the film finance sector. With transparent accounting practices and assured adherence to targets and time-schedules, a buoyant and flourishing film insurance industry in the country seemed all set to become a reality.

8

The Satyam Saga

Ms. Anjali Singh
Assistant Professor
angel_singh2000@yahoo.com
Prof. S.C. Sharma
H.O.D - Management Department, JIMS , Vasant Kunj.

Background / Early days / Introduction

Satyam Computer Services Limited (Satyam) was a well known name in the IT and consulting services. It was founded by two brothers Mr. B. Ramalinga Raju and B. Rama Raju in 1987 as a private limited company and went public in 1991. The decade of 90 witnessed the rapid growth and diversification of the company. This was the time when various companies like Satyam renaissance, Satyam Infoway, Satyam spark solutions and Satyam enterprise solutions were set up. Satyam Infoway in fact was the first Indian internet company to be listed at NASDAQ.

The company Satyam was increasingly associated with innovation and quality. It counted several Fortune 500 companies like Nestle, Coco Cola and BP as its clients and employed 53,000 people across its offices in places like USA, UK, Canada, Japan, Hungary, Australia and India.

It also won several awards and accolades including Frost & Sullivan's award for competitive strategy in 2001. The World Economic Forum, Davos ranked it as one of the 100 most competitive companies in the year 2000 while in 2006 it was declared as the number two outsourcing vendor globally by the Brown-Wilson Group. Ironically Satyam Computer was also the receiver of the Golden Peacock award for excellence in corporate governance in 2008 (which was later withdrawn).This award is given to Companies which establish new standards and follow best corporate governance practices.

The Financial Performance

The profit after tax in 1999 was Rs. 72.80 crores which increased to Rs. 490 crores in 2002, dipped a little in 2003 and then by March 2008, was Rs.1715.74 crores. Similarly from an earning of Rs. 1.40 per share in 1999 (on a par value of Rs. 2.00 /share) steadily increased to stand at Rs.25.66 by end of March 2008. On the other hand the share capital increased at a negligible rate between 2000 and 2006 while it doubled in 2007 to stand at Rs.133.44 crores and then to Rs. 134.10 crores in 2008. The reserves and surpluses steadily increased to stand at Rs. 7221.71 crores in 2008.

In his foreword to the company's annual report 2007-08, B.Ramalinga Raju the Chairman of Satyam computers noted, "While it took us 18 years to reach U.S. $ 1 billion mark, we crossed U.S. $2 billion threshold in less than 2 years, our net income also grew by 40 percent last fiscal year; to U.S. $417 million. This growth has been the result of several strategic initiatives and continuous investment in our business model." He further added that the Industry analysts had rated the Satyam offerings among the best in the Industry. Detailed analysis of the annual report figures is given in Exhibit "A" and "B"

Of course with the scandal coming to light, it became clear that the figures were incorrect and had been fudged. This obviously meant that the company's performance and financial status had to be reviewed completely in order to arrive at any worthwhile conclusion.

Board of Directors

The board of directors consisted of nine members amongst them the most distinguished and eminent professionals, academicians and bureaucrats in India as independent directors. The composition of the board of directors is given in Exhibit "C".

Satyam Computers appointed Prof Ram Mohan, Mr. T.R. Prasad, Dr. Srinivasan and Prof. V.S. Raju as independent directors to its board. These appointments came in response to the revised clause 49 of the Equity Listing Agreement of SEBI which stipulated that in case the company has an executive Chairman, at least half the board should consist of "Independent directors". In all other cases one third of the board shall consist of Independent directors. The four independent directors were paid a remuneration of Rs. 2.6 crores in 2007-08.

In order to qualify as "independent" the general test is that the person should not have any material pecuniary relationships or transactions with the company, its promoters, its directors, senior management or its holding company, subsidiaries and associates which may affect the independence of the director. Apart from these there are other additional circumstances where a director would be presumed to be not independent if certain conditions are attracted.

The question which is raised is that if an Independent director's appointment, his fee and tenure is dependent on the goodwill of the controlling stakeholder, then how independent is he actually?

Record of Corporate Governance & Social Responsibility

As part of its social responsibility, Satyam established a Trust-Satyam Foundation to transform the lives of less privileged in urban areas by providing help in seven core areas of HIV/AIDS, Health, Livelihoods, Street Children, Education, Environment and Empowering persons with disability.

Satyam also set up an Emergency Management & Research Institute (EMRI), the nonprofit organization to provide free emergency ambulance services across eight states. EMRI works on public-private partnership model where the Government provides funds to the extent of about 95 percent of the expenses, while the promoters funded the rest.

After the scam, the Satyam Foundation was unable to continue its work due to legal issues as well as lack of financial resources while the EMRI charity is being sued in the courts for corruption, land grabbing cases and misuse of funds received from National Health Mission.

A close scrutiny of some of the official papers and practices of Satyam would reveal various cracks in its corporate governance, for example:

- While the board consisted of several eminent personalities none of them had the capability or the experience to understand the financial nuances of the company.
- There were four academicians, one retired IAS officer on board of Satyam Computers not the most well rounded composition of a board. Only one of the members, Mr. Vinod Dham(known as the co-developer of Pentium processor) had served earlier as the Chariman/ CEO of a company and even his expertise was technical rather than financial.
- The board had separated the positions of the Chairman and the CEO but they were occupied by the two brothers who had a big stake in the company, therefore no independent leadership in actual spirit.
- One of the best practices of corporate governance is that the board meets without the executive directors, which was not followed by the board.
- The company did not have a corporate governance committee again a part of the best corporate governance practices.
- Directors like Mr. Vijay Dham and Mr. T.R Prasad served on the boards of 8 other companies.

The World Council for Corporate governance which conferred the golden peacock award for "Best Corporate Governance" to Satyam Computers could have investigated the actual corporate governance practices followed before bestowing this award to Satyam. Global awards like these are used as an indicator by the minority shareholders as a signal that the company is sound and worth investing in.

The unraveling of the fairy tale

On 16th December 2008, the board met and approved of the decision to invest Rs. 8,000 crores in the Maytas properties and Maytas Infra, both promoter related companies. The meeting was presided over by Prof. M. Rammohan Rao, an independent director and chairman of Audit committee. The 28th December 2008 notification to the stock exchanges mentioned that Satyam was to buy the full 100% stake in Maytas properties and 51% stake in Maytas infra for a total of 1.6 billion USD.

The news was met with sharp negative reactions from the shareholders of the company who felt that there was no justification for such a move especially when the deal had not been approved of by the shareholders.

The financial institutions and the papers were unanimous in their condemnation of the deal as a gross violation of all norms of corporate governance. The outrage was primarily due to the board's decision that would, prima facie, benefit only the promoters who owned only 8% of Satyam and 34% of stake in Maytas. The general perception was that the money would move from the company's coffers to that of the promoters.

One of the analysts said "The foreign institutional investors who held nearly 58% of the shares had no inkling of the deal besides which it made no sense that a company would try to invest in a totally unrelated sector where the promoters had no prior experience".

Prof. M. Rammohan put in his papers as independent director in 29th December a day after the notification, and Prof. Srinivasan and other independent directors too resigned subsequently. On 7th January, B. Ramalinga Raju, chairman admitted to fraud and resigned from the board, subsequent to which the various regulatory bodies swung into action.

The Response of the Government and the Regulatory Authorities

When a corporate fraud occurs on a scale like Satyam the regulators need to act swiftly to:

a) Protect the interest of the investors especially small investors

b) Punish the guilty

c) Prevent loss of confidence in the corporate sector

The regulatory & government authorities in India were quick to react and launched a coordinated, multi pronged probe in to the Satyam case, with the case of financial bungling being referred to Senior Fraud Investigation Office.

As one of the steps in a series of moves to restore investor confidence, the Government of India invoked its statutory power and suspended the existing board of directors. A fresh board was constituted, all within a week thereby averting a crisis. The new board had Kiran Karnik as the chairman, and the members were equally eminent and well known personalities like Deepak S. Parekh, C Achuthan, Tarun Das, S. Balakrisha Mainak and T.N Manoharan.

SEBI started its own probe into the scam. It seized the books and records from the registered office of Satyam at Secunderabad. Its report to CBI also suggested that action be taken against the auditors "Price Waterhouse Cooper". The Institute of Chartered Accountants of India (ICAI) also started its own investigations into the dealings and role of Price Waterhouse Cooper.

Role of Independent Directors

According to the market reports, all Independent Directors had unanimously decided to merge the Maytas - the real estate and infrastructure firm with Satyam computers on the ground that the margins in real estate businesses were higher than software business. Mr. Rammohan Rao had, in fact, chaired the meeting which had cleared the merger.

However, T.R. Prasad, one of the independent directors on the Satyam Board and a former Cabinet Secretary of India said, "none of the independent directors were aware of the accounting fraud. We had trusted the audited results prepared by Price Waterhouse Coopers, the independent directors were kept in the dark and we had trusted the company's auditors". However, many independent directors across corporate India said, 'Satyam's board cannot be absolved of their responsibility as they had fiduciary duties towards minority shareholders. A leading corporate lawyer and independent director said, "Such directors have a greater responsibility towards shareholders other than the promoters. If it is proved that the independent directors were aware of the accounting fraud then they can be prosecuted under several provisions of the companies Act."

However, Dr. Alan Greenspan (83) who was Chairman Federal Reserve Board of U.S. for around 20 years and served on the boards of large number of companies during his career spanning nearly 60 years is of the opinion that critical decisions are generally taken outside the boardroom. In his words, "I have served on board with different directors. Only business that was legally required at board meeting got done. Missing from those meeting was the useful exchange of ideas that inform the corporate strategies of the CEO." He further adds, "In practice, directors who are independent of management tend to have very little experience in the business they have been appointed to oversee. They are not likely to know what type of chicanery is possible."

Addressing a large gathering of Chartered Accountants, company secretaries and other professionals at a seminar on corporate governance, a senior officer of Ministry of Corporate Affairs said, "There was a serious erosion of value and credibility. It has impacted all of us. Corporate Governance cannot be legislated, but has to be demonstrated." Another speaker, a former Supreme Court judge said, "Corporate governance should not be restricted to clause 49 of the listing agreement. It should be extended to cover all entities which are engaged in economic activities like education and health care.

Role of Auditors

Satyam's accounts for last several years were audited by Price Waterhouse Coopers (PWC) The role of the Auditor was also under scrutiny given the extent and length of the fraud. Wher asked about the role of the Auditors in the Satyam fiasco, Institute of Chartered Accountants o India, Southern Regional Council, Chairman, C Muralikrishna said, "most SEBI regulations wer intended to be self regulatory" Elaborating on the role of auditors he further opined, "There ar three ways of auditing: verification, confirmation and the certification, depending on the exten of audit and the information to be verified. In the normal circumstances, auditing is differen from investigation. A certain amount of trust is reposed by the auditors in the informatio furnished by a client." However, as per AAS-5 "it is the duty of the auditor to obtain sufficien appropriate audit evidence before forming any conclusions," According to a highly experience chartered accountant, "the company omitted to record a Rs. 1230 crore liability in the books an committed an erroneous recording of assets, which did not exist. The auditing firm could hav raised the question: what the company proposed to do with such a huge cash pile."

The institute of chartered Accountants of India (ICAI), the apex body of chartered accountan initiated enquiry against PWC. In 2007, ICAI had found the partners of PWC guilty of profession negligence in under providing for non performing assets in now defunct Global Trust Bank. In July 2006, PWC's affiliate, Chuo Aoyama, was handed a two month ban on auditing for allegedly certifying false accounts.

The Indian corporate governance norms for audit provide for three basic sets of checks and balances in the audit process – internal audit, statutory audit and the audit committee. Satyam had this system in place and despite it the falsification of accounts at such magnitude could continue for several years. This clearly points to failure of the audit process as the misrepresentation of the financial information was at the core of the fraud.

Satyam Goes on the Block

On 6th March, 2009 SEBI, gave its approval for the sale of 51% of shares of Satyam Computers Services Ltd. through a competitive global bidding process. The new buyer was to be issued 31% of fresh equity and allowed to make an open offer for a further 20% of the equity.

On April 13, 2009 Tech Mahindra Ltd. placed the highest bid to acquire Satyam computer Ltd. at Rs. 58 per share after a global competitive bidding process.

Satyam as India's Enron

The Satyam Fraud is one of the biggest corporate fraud in the Indian corporate history and parallels are frequently drawn with the Enron scandal. Enron, once listed at number seven in the list of Fortune 500 companies filed for Bankruptcy in 2001, and the various investigations that followed revealed one of the largest corporate fraud. One of the after effects of the Enron scandal was the dissolution of the accounting and consulting firm "Arthur Andersen" and more importantly the passing of the "Sarbanes-Oxley Act" in 2002 which sought to prevent the future occurrences of any such corporate governance failures.

There are similarities as well as differences between the Enron Scandal and the Satyam fiasco. Both the companies were high profile companies felicitated and held in high regard by the corporate world and top class performers in the stock exchange arenas. Both companies had acquired the reputation for being a "true blue chip "company and were well known "brand" names in their respective sectors. The differences mainly lay in the way the regulatory bodies and respective governments reacted after the fraud came to light.

Similarities between the two companies:

1. Both Satyam and Enron had grown to dizzy heights in a short period of around fifteen years. Both Companies had major presence in the country of their origin and had expanded to global markets as well.
2. This meteoric rise can be attributed to the political patronage and all round support they managed to buy for pursuing their goals.
3. Both the companies used creative accounting, fudging of financial statements, falsification of records and similar criminal activities for a long period of time before the scams busted.

4. Both the Companies successfully manipulated their share prices by inflating their profits and deceiving the shareholders into believing that the audited financial reports were correct and financially sound.
5. In both the cases the auditing firms, credit rating agencies the money markets and capital market regulators and even the board of directors failed to detect and prevent the rot. Or else they choose to maintain their silence for a price.

The differences between the two companies can be categorized into two broad areas.

1. The Modus operandi – Enron's modus Operandi was to use transfer pricing and the existence of SPEs to siphon out debts and losses from its balance sheet and abuse the special provision of not consolidating the balance sheet of the SPES with Enron. In case of Satyam false invoices were generated to boost up the sales. Further to shore up the revenues and profits the liabilities and assets were interchanged every quarter from 1995 onwards. The Company maintained false receipts and there were several bank accounts which had no money in it, during the course of the investigation it was also revealed that there were around 10,000 employees which were shown on the records but who did not exist. The fall in the prices of real estate in the wake of the global crisis led to the drying up of liquidity to such an extent that a blue chip global company failed to get loans for meeting the monthly wage bill.

2. The US government did not intervene into the Enron crisis except for the regulatory and judicial bodies. Enron filed for bankruptcy making it the biggest corporate bankruptcy in the corporate history of United States of America. By contrast the Indian Government was quick to react and took several steps in order to restore the confidence of the investors. Besides referring the matter for investigation to the necessary agencies, one of the earliest decisions of the government was to appoint a fresh board which was entrusted with the responsibility of selling the company and safeguarding the livelihood of the various employees.

The concept of checks and balances and corporate governance has been in existence for decades. A number of efforts have been made throughout the OECD countries and the emerging economies to lay down a whole host of new institutions and practices, regulatory apparatus and mechanisms, disclosure principles, standardization of accounting standards. However all these have failed to prevent or even detect the designing and bursting of corporate scandals. The causes for this dismal situation lie in the very structure of corporate functioning.

Most of the Corporates are driven by promoters, even though they might be holding a small proportion of the total shares. The appointments to the board of directors and its committees are essentially proposed by the promoters. Such selections and appointments are guided by the utility of such directors and their reputation for lending credibility and enhancing visibility of the company in the eyes of investor- both domestic and global- bankers and lenders, credit rating agencies and regulators. The compensation that board members receive cannot be explained and justified except by a tacit acceptance to the fact that such large payments to them is paid as a price to buy their "silence" This conclusion has universal applicability, cutting across national boundaries, elaborate and highly sophisticated and complex regulatory systems. The actual solution to these frauds lies in carrying out business objectives in accordance with ethical values based on honesty and transparency.

References:

1. Greenspan Alan (2008), Age of Turbulence : Adventures in A New World, 1st Edition, Penguin Books
2. Satyam Computers, 2009. Annual Reports 2008-2009, Hyderabad: Satyam Computers
3. Satyam Computers, 2008. Annual Reports 2007-2008, Hyderabad: Satyam Computers
4. Satyam Computers, 2007. Annual Reports 2006-2007, Hyderabad: Satyam Computers
5. Souvik Sanyal and Anto Anthony (2009) Registrar of Companies to submit a report by Jan 14 on Satyam Computers. Economic Times. 9th Jan 2009
6. Karthik Subharaman (2009) No action against Raju: Police. Economic Times. 7th Jan
7. George J. Benston (2003). "The Quality of Corporate Financial Statements and Their Auditors before and after Enron." Cato Institute, Policy Analysis no. 497, Washington D.C., p 12
8. Healy, Paul M. and Palepu, Krishna G (Spring 2003) "The Fall of Enron", Journal of economics Perspectives, Volume 17, Number 2, pp. 3
9. Clause 49 of Listing Agreement, SEBI available online at http://www.sebi.gov.in/circulars/2006/cir12006.html accessed on 24th June 2009
10. Stuart Gillan and John D. Martin (2002) "Financial Engineering, Corporate Governance, and the Collapse of Enron", Alfred Lerner College of Business and Economic, The University of Delaware, p 21
11. Post James E, Varma Jayanth R, Menon Krishnagopal , Desai Ashank, Raghavan Achal, Srinivasan Vasanthi and Et al (Jan –Mar 2009) Vikalapa, Vol34, No.1, p 69
12. Bajpai G N, (4th Nov 2003) "Corporate Governance & development? Why it matters?" Speech delivered at Global Corporate Governance forum's meeting at Paris.
13. Chairman Y.C Deveshwar's speech "Corporate Governance. Making markets work for CSR." Available online at http://www.itcportal.com accessed on 10th July 2009.
14. Report of the SEBI Committee on Corporate Governance (Feb 2003) available online at http://www.sebi.gov.in/commreport/corpgov.pdf accessed on 13th July 2009.
15. The Enron Scandal available online at http://en.wikipedia.org/wiki/Enron_scandal accessed on 4th July 2009.
16. http://www.businessweek.com/managing/content/jan2009/ca20090116_465633.htm.

Exhibit "A" Statement Showing Financial Performance of Satyam (1999 – 2008)

Rs. In crores

Particulars	**For the year ended March 31,**									
	1999	**2000**	**2001**	**2002**	**2003**	**2004**	**2005**	**2006**	**2007**	**2008**
Total income	378.45	679.01	1.241.67	1.803.10	2.051.51	2,623.28	3.546.78	5,012.22	6.410.08	8,394.48
Operating profit (PBIDT)	146.69	252.56	466.71	652.32	646.39	774.31	971.7	1,571.42	1.710.73	2,085.74
Profit after tax	72.80	134.86	316.16	490.13	459.88	555.79	750.26	1.239.75	1,423.23	1.715.74
EPS on per value of Rs. 2 (Rs.)*	1.40	2.45	5.62	7.89	7.31	8.82	11.81	19.26	21.73	25.66
	As at March 31,									
	1999	2000	2001	2002	2003	2004	2005	2006	2007	2008
Share Capital	26.02	56.24	56.24	62.91	62.91	63.25	63.85	64.89	133.44	134.1
Reserves and surplus	140.9	293.82	756.66	1,867.49	2,071.97	22,517.52	3,153.17	4,268.75	5,648.07	7,221.71
Fixed assets (Gross block) & CWIP	338.19	438.63	630.75	777.31	802.88	869.33	1,002.38	1.230.00	1,570.45	1.945.16
Current assets	183.01	391.25	674.64	1,623.21	2.126.37	2,590.22	3.272.82	4,468.97	5.936.26	7,357.74
Number of associates	3,582	5.067	8,370	8.634	9,759	14,032	19,164	26,511	35,670	45.969

* Adjusted for issue of bonus shares in the ratio of 1:1 allotted in October 2006.

Source: Annual Report 2007-08.

Exhibit "B" Important Financial Ratios of Satyam

Ratio		2007-08	2006-07	2005-06	2004-05	2003-04
Growth ratios						
Software revenue growth	%	30.65	34.40	33.78	36.30	25.59
Total income growth	%	30.96	34.97	33.91	35.20	27.87
Operating profit growth	%	19.58	28.12	34.23	28.38	11.98
Net profit growth	%	20.55	37.70	37.76	34.99	20.86
EPS growth	%	18.09	35.39	35.90	33.90	20.66
Operating ratios						
Export sales to software revenues	%	96.95	95.71	96.27	97.06	97.26
Domestic sales to software revenues	%	3.05	4.29	3.73	2.94	2.74
Personal expenses to software revenues	%	62.01	59.50	58.28	57.66	52.64
Operating & administration expenses to software revenues	%	14.51	14.99	14.69	15.12	18.24
Marketing expenses to software revenues	%	1.01	0.96	1.28	1.55	1.87
Financial expenses to software revenues	%	0.07	0.12	0.06	0.02	0.03
Depreciation to software revenues	%	1.70	2.09	2.65	3.00	4.39
Other income to total income	%	3.06	2.83	2.42	2.33	3.12
Other income/PBT	%	13.25	11.54	9.73	9.52	12.35
Effective tax rate - Tax/PBT	%	11.64	9.53	12.64	13.47	16.04
Dividend payout ratio (including dividend tax)	%	15.90	18.97	25.23	24.06	25.72
Return / Profitability ratios						
EBITDA margins	%	22.47	24.55	25.75	25.67	27.25
EBITDA per associate	Rs. In lakhs	4.48	4.92	5.23	5.36	5.82
Net profit to total income	%	20.44	22.20	21.76	21.15	21.19
Return on capital employed	%	26.09	28.14	29.67	25.81	22.92
Return on net worth	%	26.10	28.11	27.37	25.88	23.57
Return on invested capital	%	64.73	84.03	88.77	83.58	68.67
Market price/Adjusted public offer price	Times	789.10	940.70	848.70	817.00	587.00
Software revenues to gross block	Times	5.47	4.86	4.02	3.69	3.00
Liquidity ratios						
Debtors days outstanding	Days	98	95	87	80	84
Cash and bank balance to total assets	%	60.45	68.24	70.20	73.23	70.14
Current ratio	Times	5.11	5.83	6.32	7.25	7.33
Debt / Equity ratio	%	0.32	0.24	0.29	0.31	0.28
Valuation ratios						
Enterprise value/software revenue	Times	2.71	4.40	5.29	3.09	2.94
Market price to book value	Times	3.59	5.32	6.30	4.04	3.58
Price earning multiple	Times	15.38	21.64	26.43	17.32	16.64
Per-Share ratios						
Dividends	%	175	175	175	125	100
Book value of shares	Rs.	110.03	88.41	67.34	50.63	40.96
Earning per share (without extraordinary items)	Rs.	25.66	21.73	16.05	11.81	8.82
Dividend per share	%	3.51	3.55	3.55	2.51	2.01

Note: Data for previous fiscals has been adjusted wherever applicable, for issue of bonus shares in the ratio of 1:1 allotted in October 2006

Exhibit "C" : Board of Directors – Satyam Computers

B. Ramalinga Raju: Founder and Chairman of Satyam Computers, winner of awards like CNB's Asian Business leaders. corporate citizen of the year (2002) and The Ernst & young entrepreneur of the year (2007). He had also served as the Ex-chairman of NASSOCOM, the industry body of Indian IT Services Company of 1,100 members.

B.Rama Raju: The Co-founder and Managing Director of the company who had been on the company's board since its inception in1977 and was appointed as Managing Director in 1991.

Mr. V.K. Dham: was on board of the company since January, 2003 and had previously held positions of vice president of Intel's Microprocessor Products Group and General Manager of the Pentium Processor Division. Mr. Dham was also on the Boards of Several Companies including New Path ventures L.L.C., NEA-Indo us ventures I.I.C. etc.

Prof. Ram Mohan Rao: The Dean, Indian School of Business, Hyderabad who had been on the board of the company since July 2005. Prof. Rao has been on the Boards of several companies including Bharat electronics Ltd and Mazagon Dock and he was the vice president of the Association of Indian Management Schools. (Compensation: Rs. 13,20,000 + 10000 shares sold at a nominal value of Rs. 2.00 (Market price of share Rs. 500/=)

T.R. Prasad: A retired officer of Indian Administrative Service and Ex. Cabinet Secretary of India. (Compensation: Rs. 12,53,333 +10,000 shares sold at a nominal value of Rs. 2.00 (Market price of share Rs. 500/=)

Dr.(Mrs) Mangalam Srinivasan: a management consultant and a visiting professor at several U.S. universities. She was scientific advisor to government of India and held several key advisory positions during her long career. She was former independent non Executive Director, Member of Audit Committee and Member of Compensation Committee, Satyam Computers Services Ltd. (Compensation: Rs. 12,80,000 +5,000 shares sold at a nominal value of Rs. 2.00 (Market price of share Rs. 500/=)

Prof. V. S. Raju : a former Director of the Indian Institute of Technology, Delhi and professor & Dean at the Indian Institute of was appointed to the board of directors of Satyam in April 2007 as an independent director. He was the Chairman of the Naval Research Board, Defense Research and Development Organization, Government of India. Compensation: Rs. 12,53,333 +10,000 shares sold at a nominal value of Rs. 2.00 (Market price of share Rs. 500/=)

The Satyam Saga – Teaching notes

About the case

This case can be used to explain the concept of the Corporate Governance, the need for corporate governance, the role of independent directors and board in corporate governance, the debate about legislation versus voluntary regulation.

The case study is aimed at MBA level student to whom this could serve as an illustration of how the theory of corporate governance translates into actual practice.

The teaching notes contain the following:

- Case Study synopsis
- Corporate Governance
- Rationale of Independent directors
- Role of Legislation versus Voluntary regulation
- Case Study questions
- Concluding remarks

1. Case Synopsis

Background/ Early days / Introduction

Satyam Computer Services Limited (hereafter referred to as Satyam) was a well known name in the IT and consulting services, ranked 4th amongst the IT companies in India. It started as a private limited company in 1987 and went public in 1991. The decade of 90 saw the company diversifying, growing tremendously and gaining several clients including Fortune 500 clients.

It also won several awards and accolades including the golden peacock award in 2008 for excellence in corporate governance.

The Financial Performance

Please see exhibit "A" and "B" for the financial performance and analysis over the years.

Board of Directors

The board of directors consisted of nine members, independent directors amongst it numbering five. The composition of the board of directors is given in Exhibit "C" The revised clause 49 of the Equity Listing Agreement of SEBI stipulates that in case the company has an executive Chairman, at least half the board should consist of "Independent directors". In all other cases one third of the board shall consist of Independent directors. The four independent directors were paid a remuneration of Rs. 2.6 crores in 2007-08.

In order to qualify as "independent" the general test is that the person should not have any material pecuniary relationships or transactions with the company, its promoters, its directors, senior management or its holding company, subsidiaries and associates which may affect the independence of the director. Apart from these there are other additional circumstances where a director would be presumed to be not independent if certain conditions are attracted.

The question which is raised is that if an Independent director's appointment, his fee and tenure is dependent on the goodwill of the controlling stakeholder, then how independent is he actually?

Record of Corporate Governance

A close scrutiny of some of the papers filed with SEBI and practices of Satyam would reveal cracks in its corporate governance, for example:

- While the board consisted of several eminent personalities none of them had the capability or the experience to understand the financial nuances of the company.
- There were four academicians, one retired IAS officer on board of Satyam Computers not the most well rounded composition of a board. Only one of the members, Mr. Vinod Dham (known as the co-developer of Pentium processor) had served earlier as the Chariman/ CEO of a company and even his expertise was technical rather than financial.
- The board had separated the positions of the Chairman and the CEO but they were occupied by the two brothers who had a big stake in the company, therefore no independent leadership in actual spirit.
- One of the best practices of corporate governance is that the board meets without the executive directors, which was not followed by the board.
- The company did not have a corporate governance committee again a part of the best corporate governance practices.
- Directors like Mr. Vijay Dham and Mr. T.R Prasad served on the boards of 8 other companies.

The World Council for Corporate governance which conferred the golden peacock award for "Best Corporate Governance" to Satyam Computers could have investigated the actual corporate governance practices followed before bestowing this award to Satyam. Global awards like these are used as an indicator by the minority shareholders as a signal that the company is sound and worth investing in.

The unraveling of the fairy tale

On 16th December 2008, the board met and approved of the decision to invest Rs. 8,000 crores in acquiring companies -Maytas properties and Maytas Infra - both promoter related companies. The meeting was presided over by Prof. M. Rammohan Rao, an independent director and chairman of Audit committee.

The news was met with sharp negative reactions from the shareholders of the company and the various financial institutions who felt that there was no justification for such an acquisition. The overwhelming perception was the deal would result in siphoning off the money from Satyam into the promoter's pockets who held 34% share in the Maytas group.

The financial institutions and the papers were unanimous in their condemnation of the deal as a gross violation of all norms of corporate governance. The rationale that the company wanted to diversify and that the real estate had better returns was met with disbelief.

As the protests and negative reactions, escalated the independent board members resigned one after another except for one and the whole crisis culminated with the resignation and confession to fraud by B. Ramalinga Raju on 7th January, subsequent to which the various regulatory bodies swung into action.

The Response of the Government and the Regulatory Authorities

When a corporate fraud occurs on a scale like Satyam the regulators need to act swiftly to:

a) Protect the interest of the investors especially small investors

b) Punish the guilty

c) Prevent loss of confidence in the corporate sector

The regulatory & government authorities in India were quick to react and launched a coordinated, multi pronged probe in to the Satyam case, with the case of financial bungling being referred to Senior Fraud Investigation Office.

As one of the steps in a series of moves to restore investor confidence, the Government of India invoked its statutory power and suspended the existing board of directors. A fresh board was constituted, all within a week thereby averting a crisis. The new board had Kiran Karnik as the chairman, and had members Deepak S. Parekh, C Achuthan, Tarun Das, S. Balakrisha Mainak and T.N Manoharan.

SEBI started its own probe into the scam. It seized the books and records from the registered office of Satyam at Secunderabad. Its report to CBI also suggested that action be taken against the auditors "Price Waterhouse Cooper". The Institute of Chartered Accountants of India (ICAI) also started its own investigations into the dealings and role of Price Waterhouse Cooper.

Role of Independent Directors

According to the market reports, all Independent Directors had unanimously decided to merge the Maytas - the real estate and infrastructure firm with Satyam computers on the ground that the margins in real estate businesses were higher than software business. Mr. Rammohan Rao had, in fact, chaired the meeting which had cleared the merger.

While the independent directors at Satyam defended their action saying that they were unaware of the accounting fraud, others insist that they should have exercised greater responsibility and cannot be absolved of blame.

One interesting viewpoint is that of Dr. Alan Greenspan (83) who was Chairman Federal Reserve Board of U.S. for around 20 years and served on the boards of large number of companies. He says that critical decisions are generally taken outside the boardroom, with only business that is legally required at board meeting gets done. Also is his opinion the independent directors that are appointed tend to have very little experience in the business they have been appointed to oversee and are unlikely to know the wrong doings that are possible.

Role of Auditors

Satyam's accounts for last nine years prior to the scandal coming to light were audited by Price Waterhouse Coopers (PWC). The role of the Auditor was also under scrutiny given the extent and length of the fraud. The auditors were either absolutely inept or negligent or they were actively involved in the fraud, is the commonly held perception.

One of the steps that the experts feel it can take is recommend blacklisting of Price Waterhouse which will bar the global audit firm from practicing in India. As the institute can only recommend, its decision can be challenged in the Courts.

The Indian corporate governance norms for audit provide for three basic sets of checks and balances in the audit process – internal audit, statutory audit and the audit committee. Satyam had this system in place and despite it the falsification of accounts at such magnitude could continue for several years. This clearly points to failure of the audit process as the misrepresentation of the financial information was at the core of the fraud.

Satyam Goes on the Block

On 6th March, 2009 SEBI, gave its approval for the sale of 51% of shares of Satyam Computers Services Ltd. through a competitive global bidding process. The new buyer was to be issued 31% of fresh equity and allowed to make an open offer for a further 20% of the equity.

On April 13, 2009 Tech Mahindra Ltd. placed the highest bid to acquire Satyam computer Ltd. at Rs. 58 per share after a global competitive bidding process.

Satyam as India's Enron

The Satyam Fraud is one of the biggest corporate fraud in the Indian corporate history and parallels are frequently drawn with the Enron scandal. Enron, once listed at number seven in the list of Fortune 500 companies filed for Bankruptcy in 2001, and the various investigations that followed revealed one of the largest corporate fraud. One of the after effects of the Enron scandal was the dissolution of the accounting and consulting firm "Arthur Andersen" and more importantly the passing of the "Sarbanes-Oxley Act" in 2002 which sought to prevent the future occurrences of any such corporate governance failures.

There are similarities as well as differences between the Enron Scandal and the Satyam fiasco. Both the companies were high profile companies felicitated and held in high regard by the corporate world and top class performers in the stock exchange arenas. Both companies had acquired the reputation for being a "true blue chip "company and were well known "brand" names in their respective sectors. The differences mainly lay in the way the regulatory bodies and respective governments reacted after the fraud came to light.

Conclusion

The concept of checks and balances and corporate governance has been in existence for decades. A number of efforts have been made throughout the OECD countries and the emerging economies to lay down a whole host of new institutions and practices, regulatory apparatus and mechanisms, disclosure principles, standardization of accounting standards. However all these have failed to prevent or even detect the designing and bursting of corporate scandals. The causes for this dismal situation lie in the very structure of corporate functioning.

Most of the Corporates are driven by promoters, even though they might be holding a small proportion of the total shares. The appointments to the board of directors and its committees are essentially proposed by the promoters. Such selections and appointments are guided by the utiiity of such directors and their reputation for lending credibility and enhancing visibility of the company in the eyes of investor- both domestic and global- bankers and lenders, credit rating agencies and regulators. The compensation that board members receive cannot be explained and justified except by a tacit acceptance to the fact that such large payments to them is paid as a price to buy their "silence" This conclusion has universal applicability, cutting across national boundaries, elaborate and highly sophisticated and complex regulatory systems. The actual solution to these frauds lies in carrying out business objectives in accordance with ethical values based on honesty and transparency.

2. Corporate Governance

Corporate governance is concerned with the relationships between a company's owners, managers, board of directors and other stakeholders. The central issue of corporate governance is the relationship between these four stakeholders. Corporate governance can also be referred to as the set of checks and balances within the corporate structure that helps create long-term value enhancement for stakeholders in a company.

In India, changes in the overall economic and business landscape post 1991 led to significant changes in the outlook towards corporate governance. In 1992, SEBI – Securities and Exchange board of India, was set up to regulate the securities market in the country. In 1998, the confederation of Indian Industries (CII) set up a national task force to recommend a code for desirable corporate governance. Thereafter the Kumar Managalam Birla Committee was set up and based on its recommendations (which were influenced by the Cadbury committee) the clause 49 of the listing agreement was adapted. Changes in corporate governance in other parts of the world as well as the drafting of Sarbanes Oxley act in USA, led to the formation of the Narayana Murthy committee on corporate governance and the subsequent revision of the clause 49 of the listing agreement.

The primary corporate governance challenge in a developed market such as the U.S. is the principal-agent problem between shareholders and managers, which arises because of the separation of ownership and management. Managers have limited ownership and equity ownership itself is widely dispersed. The principles of corporate governance developed in such countries therefore address this agency problem. For example the mechanism of independent directors serves as a check on the managers and protects the rights of the shareholders. Similarly the act of certifying the financial statement is an attempt to curb the powers of senior managers like CEO and CFO and to ensure that they are acting in the interest of the shareholders.

On the other hand in India, the corporate landscape is dominated by family owned and run business groups (with a few exceptions). The average equity share of "promoters" typically exceeds 50 %. The primary corporate governance challenge in emerging markets like India is the potential expropriation of minority shareholders. The agency problem that is encountered here is that of conflict between the majority shareholder and minority shareholders.

3. Role of Independent Director – Need and Rationale

The opening up of the Indian Economy in 1991 brought about several changes in the corporate landscape. In 1992, SEBI the securities exchange board to oversee the working of the stock exchange market was set up. In the late 1999, Kumar Mangalam Committee was set up, followed by Naresh Chandra Committee in 2002 and the Narayan Murthy committee in 2004. The appointments of these various committees and the various recommendations were a result of the belief that the corporate governance in India should confirm to the international norms.

The concept of "Independent directors" was introduced in India by the Kumar Mangalam Committee and subsequently by the other committees as well. It defined independent directors as those directors who do not have any material relationships or transactions with the company, its management or its subsidiaries which in the judgment of the board may affect their independence of judgement.

However in India, barring a few exceptions, the appointment of the independent directors was simply a matter of legal compliance. If the board meetings are held infrequently, for short period of time and the relevant information is not passed on to the independent directors then it is obvious that the effectiveness of such directors will be limited.

The definition of an Independent director is given by SEBI, (listing agreement given in clause 49) which defines an independent director as a person who:

- Has no material pecuniary transactions with the company or its associates
- Has no relationship with the promoters or senior management
- Has not been an executive with the company in the preceding 3 years
- Neither is, nor has been for the past three years, a partner with an audit firm, legal firm or consulting firm to the company
- Is not a material supplier or lessee to company
- Does not own more than 2% of the company's shares
- Is over 21 years of age

There are several benefits that result from having independent directors on board which can range from long term survival to improved internal controls. They can:

- lend management strength to managerial pool in a company.
- ensure legal and ethical behavior at the company, while strengthening accounting controls
- extend the "reach" of a company through contacts, expertise, and access to debt and equity capital.
- be a source of well-conceived, binding, long-term decisions for a company.
- help a company survive, grow, and prosper over time through improved succession planning through membership in the nomination committee etc.

The Independent directors are therefore also seen as a check on the management of companies, as an oversight mechanism, apart from the value addition that they bring to board deliberations. The shareholders, especially the minority shareholders, look to independent directors providing transparency in respect of the disclosures in the working of the company as well as providing balance towards resolving conflict areas. In evaluating the board's or management decisions in respect of employees, creditors and other suppliers of major service providers, independent directors have a significant role in protecting the stakeholders interests. One of the mandatory requirements of audit committee is to look into the reasons for default in payments to deposit holders, debentures, non-payment of declared dividend and creditors.

Perhaps the single most important role that independent directors play as board members is the objective view that they bring in while evaluation of the board and the management decisions creating a balance in the interest of the shareholders. As members of the board, Independent directors are required not only to comply with the code of conduct but also establish and monitor adherence by other senior management and set an example for others. Clause 49 provides that independent directors be appointed to key committee's like nomination, remuneration, investor relations and audit committee.

The Satyam episode has raised questions about the integrity of the boards, even the blue chip boards. If directors now rethink and accept posts only in companies with clean management it will help investors identify good boards from a bad one. At present the corporate governance structure depends on the independent directors who are appointed to bring objectivity to the oversight function and improve the effectiveness of the board. Perhaps the expectation is misplaced as long as the appointment and remuneration of the independent director continues to be in the hands of the majority shareholders.

Also critical is the fact that the Indian corporate governance norms do not specify the roles of independent directors. It is not entirely clear whether independent directors ought to act as advisors to management from a business strategy perspective or whether they ought to act as a guardian of shareholder especially the minority shareholders. Plus the fact that the role of Independent director is more critical in the separation of management and ownership as seen in countries like US and US rather than in India where the promoters or owners are actively involved in the management of the company.

4. Role of Legislation versus Regulation[1]

Some of the key institutions and players that are a part of the corporate governance are corporate law, securities law, securities regulation, professional associations, business associations, financial accounting standards, public disclosure and auditing standards. The corporate governance institutions comprise of both formal and informal rules which includes a country's generally accepted business practices and ethical standards though these are unwritten.

These institutions and actors impose three kinds of disciplines on the corporates:

- Self discipline
- Market discipline
- Regulatory discipline

[1] Adapted from the speech delivered by Shri G.N. Bajpai, (then Chairman-SEBI) at the global corporate governance meeting held on Nov 4, 2003 at Paris.

The management and controlling shareholders are the ones responsible for the quality of a company. They set the standards of ethics and performance which is used to judge the Company. The system works when the controlling shareholders or management are highly ethical and minority shareholders are treated fairly. When the internal checks and balances such as independent board committees, internal and external audit do not function well, it can result in system failure or lack of self discipline.

When self discipline alone does not work, market enforces discipline on the management. The fear of losing in the market place forces management to behave responsibly. Regulatory discipline is required when self and market disciplines fail to conduct the corporate in the best interest of all the stakeholders. The regulators will set the rules of the game often in consultation with the private sector, and enforce these agreed rules. There must be discipline to take necessary enforcement action in case of cheating or fraud.

5. Case Study Questions

a. Critically evaluate the role of the Independent directors and external auditors in the Satyam fraud?

b. Do you think there is need for more legislation with regard to corporate governance?

c. Critically examine the role of the government and other regulations post the scandal.

d. What do you think are the pillars of corporate governance? Why did they not work in case of Satyam?

6. Conclusion

The long term issue which still remains to be addressed is the feeling that the Satyam issue far from being an arbitrary exception was representative of the problems that exist in other Indian companies. Though the fall out of the Satyam fraud was contained, investor faith in the audited account of the Indian companies has still to be restored.

The Satyam scandal was a good opportunity for the government to put into place effective corporate norms by pushing through reforms which would be resisted by powerful vested interests. But it has not been able to push these reforms through.

The Companies Bill, 2009 was introduced in the Lok Sabha in August 2009. The idea behind the new bill is to foster a regulatory environment which consists of the best international practices and help develop entrepreneurship and growth.

Some of the salient features are:-

- It provides a single comprehensive legal framework that covers all aspects of the operation of a Corporate from incorporation to winding up. It also includes all aspects of internal governance. It also synchronizes the Company Law framework with that of the specialized regulation for sectors.
- It emphasizes the protection of the minority stakeholder's rights, stresses self regulation, and internal corporate accountability as opposed to government control. It seeks to put an

end to shares with differential voting rights as well as provide a mechanism for valuation and allotment of shares for non-cash considerations.

- Help facilitate easy transition of Companies operating under the Companies Act,1956 to the new act.
- Provision for at least 1 director to be resident in India. The provision for independent directors to be at least 1/3rd of the total strength of directors. The attributes which would determine "independence" to be prescribed as well.
- Key Managerial Personnel (KMP) includes the CEO, CFO and the Company Secretary. It also provides for statutory recognition to audit committee as well as remuneration and stakeholders grievances committees of the Board.
- Recognition of both accounting and auditing standards. Redefining the role and duties of the auditors as well as his rights in order to maintain the neutrality and integrity of the audit process. Mandatory provision to club the financial statements of the subsidiaries along with that of the holding companies.
- Enabling the Shareholders / Association/ Group of Shareholders to take legal action in case of any fraudulent action by the company. Provision of investor protection activities and "Class Action Suits"

As per Mr. Salman Khurshid, Minister of Corporate Affairs, the Bill has taken into account the Satyam scandal and that the provisions of the Bill were such that future such episodes could be prevented. He also mentioned that the new Bill had provisions to ensure that the integrity and independence of the audit process is maintained by the audit firms. In order to deal with misconduct by CAs and CSs, the government had also amended the Chartered Accountants Act and the Company Secretaries Act in order to enforce a more effective regulatory framework.

For good corporate governance, while the regulatory framework can provide the basic guidelines and legal structure, the actual spirit of corporate governance will prevail with companies functioning in a highly ethical manner based on honesty and transparency.

9

Life Insurance Corporation of India

Mr. Sanjay Manocha
Assistant Professor
manochas26@gmail.com

Mr. Parul Agrawal
Associate Professor
parul_agrawal@yahoo.com

Bharati Vidyapeeth University, Institute of Management and Research, New Delhi

Insurance offers security and so peace of mind to the individual. The concept of insurance is that the losses of a few are made good by contribution from many. It is based on the law of large numbers. Life Insurance provides protection to your family - your family gets a specified sum in a lump sum when they need it the most i.e. when you are not around. While the emotional loss cannot be mitigated, the lump sum received from an Insurance company can help take care of your family's financial future. Finally, Life Insurance contracts allow an individual to save money in a tax efficient manner and allow savings to grow to help meet our future financial obligations.

The present case explains about Life Insurance Corporation of India which is the largest state-owned life insurance company in India, and also the country's largest investor. It is fully owned by the Government of India. It also funds close to 24.6% of the Indian Government's expenses. It has assets estimated of ₹13.25 trillion (US$295.48 billion), It was founded in 1956 with the merger of 243 insurance companies and provident societies. Details about the IT initiatives taken up by the LIC in its technology drive are also covered in the present case.

Case study

Concept of Insurance[1]

On the one hand, human life is subject to various risks—risk of death or disability due to natural or accidental causes. Humans are also prone to diseases, the treatment of which may involve huge expenditure. On the other hand, property owned by man is exposed to various hazards, natural and man-made.

When human life is lost or a person is disabled permanently or temporarily, there is a loss of income to the household. The family is put to hardship. Sometimes survival itself is at stake for the dependants.

When it comes to property, loss or damage to property it results in either whole or partial loss in income to the person or entity.

Risk has the element of unpredictability. Death/disability or loss/damage could occur at anytime. Losses can be mitigated through insurance. Insurance is a commodity which offers protection against various contingencies.

Insurance products available for life and non-life are many. In non-life, apart from personal covers such as accident covers and health insurance, there are products covering liabilities under a particular law and or common law. The various products are designed to cater to different needs of an individual or industry such as fire insurance policy on multi-storied building, householder's policy.

An insurance contract promises to make good to the insured a certain sum in consideration for a payment in the form of premium from the insured.

Human life cannot be valued. Hence the sum assured (or the amount guaranteed to be paid in the event of a loss) is by way of a 'benefit' in the case of life insurance. Life insurance products provide a definite amount of money to the dependants of the insured in case the life insured dies during his active income earning period or becomes disabled on account of an accident causing reduction/complete loss in his income earnings. An individual can also protect his old age when he ceases to earn and has no other means of income by purchasing an annuity product.

A Personal Accident cover is also for protection. In the event of death or disability, permanent or temporary, of the insured, it provides for compensation which is either the whole or a percentage of the Capital Sum Insured depending on the kind of loss.

In the case of Health Insurance, the policy seeks to cover expenses towards of treatment of diseases and or injury upto the Sum Insured opted for by the insured.

In respect of insurance relating to property, there are many products available. Property may be covered against fire and perils of nature including flood, earthquake etc. Machinery may be insured for breakdown. Goods in transit can be insured under a marine cargo insurance cover. Insurance covers are also available for ships and other vessels. A motor insurance policy covers third party damage as well as damage to the vehicle.

Insurance of property is based on the principle of indemnity. The idea is to bring the insured to the same financial position as he /she was before the loss occurred. It safeguards the investment in the property. Where there is no insurance, losses can mar a project or an industry. General Insurance offers stability to the economy and to the society.

Insurance offers security and so peace of mind to the individual. The concept of insurance is that the losses of a few are made good by contribution from many. It is based on the law of large numbers. It stemmed from the need of man to find a solution for mitigation of losses. It also reflects the nature of man to find a solution collectively.

Need of Life Insurance[2]

Very often it is said that before you let the worry get into your head, buy Life Insurance.

Why? Life Insurance provides protection to your family - your family gets a specified sum in a lump sum when they need it the most i.e. when you are not around.

While the emotional loss cannot be mitigated, the lump sum received from an Insurance company can help take care of your family's financial future. Life Insurance policies also offer tax benefits though tax saving should not be the primary reason an individual should look at a Life Insurance policy. Finally, Life Insurance contracts allow an individual to save money in a tax efficient manner and allow savings to grow to help meet our future financial obligations. The most important question is what is the value of your Life? Heard of this Yaksha question: What is the greatest mystery on earth? Yudhisthir answers, "Everyone has to die. But no one thinks that for himself. This is the greatest mystery. That is the paradox that makes people avoids Life Insurance! That also makes agents take the wrong line of selling Insurance as a tax saving and/or Investment product (ULIP). So what should we do? Start with calculating the Human Life Value (HLV). A very simple way of looking at it is as following: Imagine a monthly income of Rs 10000 and the net income provided to the family are Rs. 8000 after deducting Rs 2000 for personal expenses. Thus the annual income provided to your family is Rs 96000.

The amount of money that will earn Rs 96000 p.a. at 8% interest rate is Rs 12, 00,000. This is only a representation of the value of HLV. It is not the exact way of calculating your HLV. The future income growth, your income generating assets, liabilities, spouse income, children's education, etc are also to be factored in. Various private insurers like Bajaj Allianz, Met Life etc. have placed on their websites the HLV calculators to make you understand the HLV and your Life Insurance needs better.

History of Insurance in India

In India, Insurance has a deep-rooted history. It finds mention in the writings of Manu (***Manusmrithi***), Yagnavalkya (***Dharmasastra)*** and Kautilya (***Arthasastra***). The writings talk in

[1] http://www.irdaindia.org/iac/conceptofinsurance.htm

[2] http://www.niapune.com/images/UserFiles/New%20Article%201%20Pg%2041-55.pdf Bimaquest - Vol. VIII Issue I, January 2008 q 41

terms of pooling of resources that could be re-distributed in times of calamities such as fire, floods, epidemics and famine. This was probably a pre-cursor to modern day Insurance.

Ancient Indian history has preserved the earliest traces of Insurance in the form of marine trade loans and carriers' contracts. Insurance in India has evolved over time heavily drawing from other countries, England in particular.

1818 saw the **advent of Life Insurance Business in India** with the establishment of the Oriental Life Insurance Company in Calcutta. This Company however failed in 1834. In 1829, the Madras Equitable had begun transacting Life Insurance business in the Madras Presidency. 1870 saw the enactment of the British Insurance Act and in the last three decades of the nineteenth century, the Bombay Mutual (1871), Oriental (1874) and Empire of India (1897) were started in the Bombay Residency. This era, however, was dominated by foreign Insurance offices which did good business in India, namely Albert Life Assurance, Royal Insurance, Liverpool and London Globe Insurance and the Indian offices were up for hard competition from the foreign companies.

In 1914, the Government of India started publishing returns of Insurance Companies in India. The Indian Life Assurance Companies Act, 1912 was the first statutory measure to regulate Life business. In 1928, the Indian Insurance Companies Act was enacted to enable the Government to collect statistical information about both Life and non-Life business transacted in India by Indian and foreign insurers including provident Insurance societies. In 1938, with a view to protecting the interest of the Insurance public, the earlier legislation was consolidated and amended by the Insurance Act, 1938 with comprehensive provisions for effective control over the activities of insurers.

The Insurance Amendment Act of 1950 abolished Principal Agencies. However, there were a large number of Insurance companies and the level of competition was high. There were also allegations of unfair trade practices. The Government of India, therefore, decided to nationalize Insurance business.

An Ordinance was issued on 19th January, 1956 nationalising the Life Insurance sector and Life Insurance Corporation came into existence in the same year.

The LIC absorbed 154 Indian, 16 non-Indian insurers as also 75 provident societies—245 Indian and foreign insurers in all. The LIC had monopoly till the late 90s when the Insurance sector was reopened to the private sector.

This millennium has seen Insurance come a full circle in a journey extending to nearly 200 years. The process of **re-opening of the sector** had begun in the early 1990s and the last decade and more has seen it been opened up substantially. In 1993, the Government set up a committee under the chairmanship of RN Malhotra, former Governor of RBI, to propose recommendations for reforms in the Insurance sector. The objective was to complement the reforms initiated in the financial sector. The committee submitted its report in 1994 wherein, among other things, it recommended that the private sector be permitted to enter the Insurance industry.

They stated that foreign companies are allowed to enter by floating Indian companies, preferably a joint venture with Indian partners.

Following the recommendations of the Malhotra Committee Report, in 1999, the Insurance Regulatory and Development Authority (IRDA) was constituted as an autonomous body to regulate and develop the Insurance industry. The IRDA was incorporated as a statutory body in April, 2000. The key objectives of the IRDA include promotion of competition so as to enhance customer satisfaction through increased consumer choice and lower premiums, while ensuring the financial security of the Insurance market.

The IRDA opened up the market in August 2000 with the invitation for application for registrations. Foreign companies were allowed ownership of up to 26%. The Authority has the power to frame regulations under Section 114A of the Insurance Act, 1938 and has from 2000 onwards framed various regulations ranging from registration of companies for carrying on Insurance business to protection of policyholders' interests.

In December, 2000, the subsidiaries of the General Insurance Corporation of India were restructured as independent companies and at the same time GIC was converted into a national re-insurer. Parliament passed a bill de-linking the four subsidiaries from GIC in July, 2002.

As on 13/09/2010 there are 24 general Insurance companies including the ECGC and Agriculture Insurance Corporation of India[3] and as on 06/04/2011 there are 23 Life Insurance companies operating in the country[4].

Life Insurance Corporation of India (LIC)

The **Life Insurance Corporation of India** (**LIC**) (Hindi: भारतीय जीवन बीमा निगम) is the largest state-owned life insurance company in India, and also the country's largest investor. It is fully owned by the Government of India. It also funds close to 24.6% of the Indian Government's expenses. It has assets estimated of 13.25 trillion (US$295.48 billion), It was founded in 1956 with the merger of 243 insurance companies and provident societies.

Headquartered in Mumbai, financial and commercial capital of India, the Life Insurance Corporation of India currently has 8 zonal Offices and 113 divisional offices located in different parts of India, around 3500 servicing offices including 2048 branches, 54 Customer Zones, 25 Metro Area Service Hubs and a number of Satellite Offices located in different cities and towns of India and has a network of 13,37,064 individual agents, 242 Corporate Agents, 79 Referral Agents, 98 Brokers and 42 Banks (as on 31.3.2011) for soliciting life insurance business from the public.

The slogan of LIC is "Zindagi ke saath bhi,Zindagi ke baad bhi" (Hindi: जिन्दगी के साथ भी जिन्दगी के बाद भी) which means "during life and after life".

At present, online premium collection facility is being offered in selected cities as LIC has tied up with some banks and service providers. For providing customer satisfaction the organization has introduced various schemes such as ECS, ATM premium payment facility, IVRS, Info centers which are set up in various cities including Mumbai, Bangalore, Chennai, Kolkata, New Delhi, Pune and many more. It has also come up with SATELLITE SAMPARK offices providing

[3] http://www.irda.gov.in/ADMINCMS/cms/NormalData_Layout.aspx?page=PageNo264&mid=3.2.10

[4] http://www.irda.gov.in/ADMINCMS/cms/NormalData_Layout.aspx?page=PageNo129&mid=3.1.9

easy access to policyholders. LIC has crossed many milestones and set standards for itself fostering unmatched performance. There are various objectives of the organization:

- Holding the money with obligation and using it in the best possible manner in the interests of the policyholder and the community.
- Bringing attractive savings plans and making them easily accessible to the policyholders.
- Giving attractive returns to the people and keeping in mind national priorities.
- Being trustworthy to the customers and develop the spirit of corporate social responsibility.
- Spreading insurance in both rural and urban areas and covering all the insurable persons at a reasonable cost.
- Bringing in plans and policies favorable to the changing environment.
- Providing efficient service and involving people in the organization for their satisfaction.

Information Technology and LIC

LIC has been one of the pioneering organizations in India who introduced the leverage of Information Technology in servicing and in their business. Data pertaining to almost 10 crore policies is being held on computers in LIC.

1964 saw the introduction of computers in LIC. Unit Record Machines introduced in late 1950's were phased out in 1980's and replaced by Microprocessors based computers in Branch and Divisional Offices for Back Office Computerization. Standardization of Hardware and Software commenced in 1990's. Standard Computer Packages were developed and implemented for Ordinary and Salary Savings Scheme (SSS) Policies.

FRONT END OPERATIONS

With a view to enhancing customer responsiveness and services, in July 1995, LIC started a drive of On Line Service to Policyholders and Agents through Computer. This on line service enabled policyholders to receive immediate policy status report, prompt acceptance of their premium and get Revival Quotation, Loan Quotation on demand. Incorporating change of address can be done on line. Quicker completion of proposals and dispatch of policy documents have become a reality. All LIC 2048 branches across the country have been covered under front-end operations. Thus all 100 divisional offices of LIC have achieved the distinction of 100% branch computerization. New payment related Modules pertaining to both ordinary & SSS policies have been added to the Front End Package catering to Loan, Claims and Development Officers' Appraisal. All these modules help to reduce time-lag and ensure accuracy.

METRO AREA NETWORK

A Metropolitan Area Network, connecting 74 branches in Mumbai was commissioned in November, 1997, enabling policyholders in Mumbai to pay their Premium or get their Status Report, Surrender Value Quotation, Loan Quotation etc. from ANY Branch in the city. The System has been working successfully. More than 10,000 transactions are carried out over this Network on any given working day. Such Networks have been implemented in other cities also.

WIDE AREA NETWORK

All 7 Zonal Offices and all the MAN centres are connected through a Wide Area Network (WAN). This will enable a customer to view his policy data and pay premium from any branch of any MAN city. As at November 2005, LIC have 91 centers in India with more than 2035 branches networked under WAN.

INTERACTIVE VOICE RESPONSE SYSTEMS (IVRS)

IVRS has already been made functional in 59 centers all over the country. This would enable customers to ring up LIC and receive information (e.g. next premium due, Status, Loan Amount, Maturity payment due, Accumulated Bonus etc.) about their policies on the telephone. This information could also be faxed on demand to the customer.

LIC ON THE INTERNET

LIC Internet site is an information bank. Information about LIC & its offices is displayed on LIC website.. Efforts are on to upgrade LIC web site to make it dynamic and interactive. The addresses/e-mail Ids of Zonal Offices, Zonal Training Centers, Management Development Center, Overseas Branches, Divisional Offices and also all Branch Offices with a view to speed up the communication process.

PAYMENT OF PREMIUM AND POLICY STATUS ON INTERNET

(Policyholders need to register for these services)

LIC has given its policyholders a unique facility to pay premiums through Internet absolutely free and also view their policy details on Internet premium payments. There are 11 service providers with whom LIC has signed the agreement to provide this service.

INFORMATION KIOSKS

LIC has set up 150 Interactive Touch screen based Multimedia KIOSKS in prime locations in metros and some major cities for dissemination information to general public on our products and services. These KIOSKS are enabling to provide policy details and accept premium payments.

INFO CENTRES

LIC also has set up 8 call centres, manned by skilled employees to provide customers with information about LIC Products, Policy Services, Branch addresses and other organizational information.

Insurance Sector Reforms[5]

Since nationalization, the state-owned Insurance companies have grown into monoliths, lumbering and often inefficient, but with no other alternative. They have been criticized for their

[5] http://www.damodarcollege.org/dhiru_final/meenaxivol6.2.html dated 25/04/11

huge bureaucracies. Despite these criticisms, they still have millions of policyholders. Earlier attempts to even suggest letting private players into this vital sector had met with resistance and agitation from the powerful Insurance employees' unions. However, the Narasimha Rao Government (1991-96) unleashed liberal changes in India's rigid economic structure.

In 1993, the Government set up a Committee under the chairmanship of Shri R. N. Malhotra to propose recommendations for reforms in the Insurance sector. The Committee suggested the following changes:

1. Government stake in Insurance companies be brought down to 50%.
2. The takeover of the holding of the GIC and its subsidiaries in order to facilitate their functioning as independent corporations.
3. Allowing the entry of private sector companies having a paid up capital of a minimum of Rs. 100 crore into the sector.
4. No single entity to function in both Life and general Insurance segments.
5. Foreign companies to be allowed only in combination with an Indian partner.
6. Changes to be made to the Insurance Act.
7. An independent Insurance regulatory authority to set up.
8. Reduction in the mandatory investments of LIC Life Fund in government securities to be brought down from 75% to 50%.
9. GIC and its subsidiaries are not to hold more than 5% equity in any company.
10. Popularization of pension schemes in rural areas
11. Rapid computerization of branches
12. Payment of interest on delayed claims.
13. Use of revised mortality tables by LIC and revision of premiums after every 10 years.
14. Issues of long-term unit linked Insurance plans.

The Insurance sector began its reform process with the passage of the IRDA (Insurance Regulatory and Development Authority) Bill in Parliament in December 1999. The IRDA was constituted as an autonomous body to regulate and develop the Insurance industry. The key objectives of IRDA were to promote competition so as to enhance customer satisfaction through increased consumer choice and lower premium, while ensuring the financial security of the Insurance market. The IRDA opened the market to private enterprise in August 2000 with an invitation for application for registrations. Foreign companies were allowed ownership of up to 26%.

Companies were required to submit business plans detailing the proposed capital structure, the nature of business they planned to carry out and their plans for selling Insurance to the rural and social sectors.

It is important to note that the exclusive privilege granted to the LIC and the GIC to market life insurance and general insurance products respectively has been knocked down. These insurers will now have to compete with more players for the patronage of insurance customers and prospects.

The turn of events, however, should not have come as a surprise for the insurers. It has taken quite some time for the sector to be thrown open for competition, since the Malhotra Committee made its recommendations in early 1994. Both the insurers have had time to gear up for the new challenges. As regards the LIC, the Malhotra Committee had wanted the government ownership reduced to 50 per cent.

In its preparatory exercise, the LIC may suggest changes that may necessitate a Government re-look at the structure and holding pattern of the LIC. The Centre has, however, decided not to tinker with the existing structure or holding pattern in view of t he tremendous resistance faced by it in getting the reforms going. It is to be seen whether the Government decision to maintain the LIC as a fully-held financial-sector entity would help the insurer cope with the situation.

The opening up of the sector will see new players with latest business models and products, backed by state-of-the-art technology, in direct competition with the LIC. The increased awareness and adoption of information technology has brought about a perceptible change in the profile of financial sector customers. They have become more quality- and cost-conscious.

The LIC may not be able to maintain its market share because of its size and financial strength. But it still has the advantage of locking in its agents, as the IRDA norms indicate that an agent can do business with only one insurer. And it continues to have the advantage of government guarantee. Yet, the LIC could face a major challenge, as new insurers would target different business segments — such as corporate houses — and sell aggressively to high-net-worth individuals to gain quick market share and recognition. It would, thus, be worthwhile to examine the need for internal structural changes, making the LIC/GIC more sensitive in their dealings with both internal (agents and employees) and external (the policyholders and prospects) customers.

To deal with the emerging competitive environment, the LIC had appointed international consultants, Booz Allen and Hamilton, to make a diagnostic study and assist in chalking out the transformation process. In this context, it would be a good idea for it to combine the suggestions of the consultant with those of the Malhotra Committee. Urgent attention might have to be paid to make the main operating branches critical to the entire setup, as these are the points of contact for the customer — giving the branches the required powers could help.

Quick decision-making is often not possible in big organisations, as they have several tiers/ hierarchies to contend with. The corporate office continues to be saddled with enormous powers, with zonal and divisional offices being used for collecting information and data. Even within the corporate office, all decision-making — big or small — tend to get gravitated to the top. This trend has to be reversed. The senior executives at the corporate, zonal offices need to be encouraged to take decisions so that the operating units do not suffer. This calls for breaking down status barriers, improving communication and fostering the 'whole-team' idea. The tiers of an organisation need not be top-down. It could be horizontal, as each team-member contributes t o the achievement of its objectives and goals. The top management's commitment to changes and empowerment can make down-the-line staff more receptive and enlightened.

The LIC has, to its credit, adopted various proactive measures — such as greater use of technology — to enhance customer satisfaction through efficient services. But more needs to be done in this area. The expected results of enhanced technology support would be visible more quickly if there is wholehearted participation by the different layers within the organisation. This calls for meaningful, constructive, systematic and structured communication at all levels and in all directions.

Though poor delegation, lack of knowledgeable and effective operational control, lengthening lines of communication, delayed decision-making, and so on, are affecting the operational efficiency of the branches, there is no better opportunity for the LIC to forge ahead and overcome its weaknesses. It must build upon its strengths and turn the emerging challenges and threats into opportunities. It has the competence, the knowhow and the trained manpower to do so. An opportunity missed today may not be available tomorrow.

Questions for Discussions

1. What was the rationale for reforms in insurance sector? Discuss.
2. What are the challenges and opportunities for LIC after privatization of the sector?
3. Describe IT initiatives taken up by the LIC in its technology drive.

10

Mergers and Acquisitions (The Rising Tide of Global Capital Flows)

Ms. Devika Seth
Mr. Sanjeev Kumar
swamiveetshiven@rediffmail.com
Mr. Aman Chugh
swamiveetshiven@rediffmail.com
Bharati Vidyapeeth University Institute of Management and Research, New Delhi

SYNOPSIS

India has emerged as one of the fastest growing Asian economy in the past few decades, creating a niche for itself in the global economic scenario. Indian economy's growth has ushered an era of investment opportunities thus attracting the attention of several multinational enterprises across the globe. The success story of Indian growth began way back in1991, after opening up of Indian economy. Since then a whole lot of challenges both in the domestic and international spheres has prompted the Indian companies to go for corporate restructuring for their survival. This was rather a compulsion than strategic choice. The M&As has become flavor of the century for restructuring the business organizations globally and India has emerged as one of the favorite destination amongst other economies. The trends of mergers and acquisitions have changed globally over the past few decades. The immediate effects of the mergers and acquisitions have also been diverse across the various sectors of the Indian economy.

The last decade has witnessed some of the biggest mergers and acquisitions

In the Indian history notably the Tata's audacious acquisition of Corus in 2007 for $12 billion, Aditya Birla Group's flagship company Hindalco's acquisition of Canada based Novelis for $6 billion (the world's biggest producer of Aluminum rolled products), Tata Motor's acquisition of Ford's Jaguar Land Rover operations in 2008 for $2.3 billion, and very recent acquisition of Zain,s African assets by Bharati's for $10.7 billion.

Everyday one or the other news daily's business section announces at least one headline about some kind of mergers and acquisitions transaction. These transactions worth hundreds of millions, or even billions, of dollars are dictating the fortunes of the companies involved. The successful deal enhances operational efficiency, effectiveness and profitability of the companies whereas unsuccessful or sourced deal could be a death knell. The process of mergers and acquisitions is very complex and cumbersome and requires evaluation and analysis at each stage. That is why a lot of emphasis is given now a day, to all the activities associated with mergers and acquisitions.

Case Objectives

The case is intended to throw light on the various important aspects of mergers and acquisitions including defining the terms, forms and types, Rules pertaining , motives, favorable factors, Valuation models, Impacts and ways to overcome, steps initiated by government, key points to remember while going for a deal and steps to exploit global mergers and acquisitions.

The various aspects related to mergers and acquisitions are important not only for the companies involved in process but are also equally important for all the stakeholders including academicians. A careful study of the case will enable all the beneficiaries in broadening their perspective towards the all important aspect of mergers and acquisitions.

Amalgamation defined:

Amalgamation or Merger is said to occur when two or more companies combines in to one company to increase efficiency. One or more companies may merge with an existing company or they may merge to form a new company. There can be variety of mergers for example unlisted with listed and vice versa, subsidiary with holding company, merger with in the group, strong company with sick company, merger through BIFR (Board of Industrial & Financial reconstructions). Asset & Liabilities of amalgamating company becomes assets & liabilities of amalgamated company.

Acquisition defined:

As an act of acquiring effective control by one company over assets or management of another company without any combination of companies. Thus in an acquisition two or more firms may remain independent, separate legal entity, but there may be change in control of companies.

Major Deals in 2010:

The year 2010 ended with 1047 deals as compared to previous year with 1235 deals but the value of deals was three times that is $55 billion as against $20.3 billion. Major deals were:-

- Bharati acquiring Zain,s African assets for $10.7 billion.
- GTL Infra's $1.8-billion purchase of Aircel's tower.
- Essar energy Plc acquiring Navabharat Power Pvt Ltd, for $2 billion.
- ONGC Ltd. acquiring Exxon Mobil's Angolan oil field for $2 billion.
- RIL acquiring 65% of Value Creation Inc, a Canadian company with oil-sands assets for $1.9billion.
- Hinduja acquiring KBL Private Bankers for $1.69 billion.
- RIL acquiring 95% stake in Infotel Broadband Services.
- ICICI Bank & Bank of Rajasthan Merger for $ 320 million.
- RNRL and Reliance Power merger for $1.5 billion.
- Ranbaxy Laboratories acquired by 'Daiichi'.
- Piramal Health care acquired by Abbott.
- Patni Computer system selling controlling stake to i-gate.
- Paras Pharma scooped by Reckitt Benckiser.
- Controversial $9.6 billion Cairn and Vedanta deal (still held for MOF approval).

Source research firm "VCC Edge"

Major deals called off in 2010:

- RIL's $14.5 billion bid for Lyondell Basell.
- Reliance Communications' $10.8 billion merger deal with GTL Infra.
- Singapore's GIC Special Investments' $84.7 million bid for 6.58 % stake in Fortis Healthcare.
- Drug major Abott Laboratories' interest in Wockhardt.
- EIH's, hospitality major witnessed a deal cancellation of $272 million with Max Hospital's founder and Chairman Analjit Singh for 17% stake.
- Jindal Steel and Power (JSPL) was denied stake in Zimbabwe Iron & Steel, estimated to be in the range of $600 million- $1 billion.
- Multiplex chain PVR Cinemas' bid for DT Cinemas and Ingersoll.
- U.S. based Scripps Networks Interactive's attempt to buy stake in NDTV Lifestyle.
- The backtracked Fortis-Parkway (Singapore) deal too underscores the same trend.

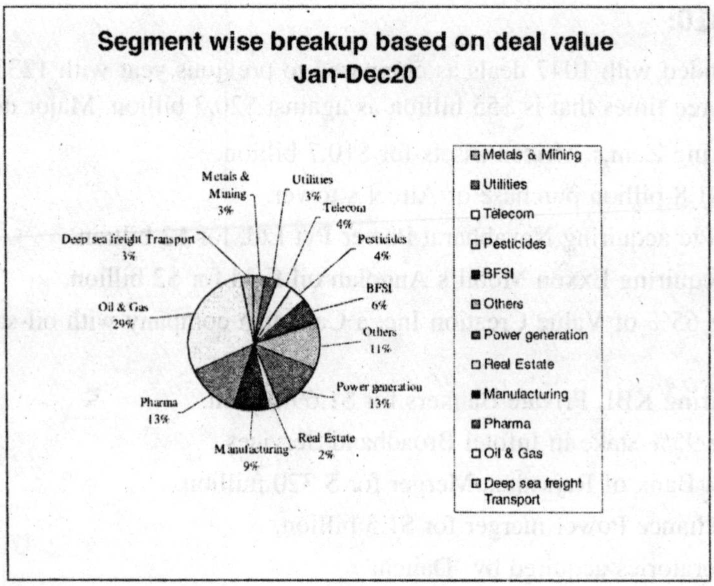

Factors favoring surging trends in mergers & acquisitions:

- Favorable Govt. Policies.
- Buoyancy in Economy.
- Additional Liquidity in corporate sector.
- Dynamics Attitude of the Indian Entrepreneurs.
- A decline in borrowing costs allowing companies to replace debt with cheaper. financing sources such as Euro credits, ADRs and GDRs.

Motives & difficulties:

Motives	*Intricacies*
Accelerated Growth,	Restrict growth of SSI
Restructuring & Consolidation	Increased business complexity
Profit Maximization/Enhanced profitability - Economies of Scale - Financial Synergies - Operating Synergies	Impact on Competition
Diversification of Risk	Resistance to change
Reduction in Tax liability by setting-off accumulated losses & unabsorbed depreciation	Impact on shareholder's wealth-in terms of risk associated with deal
Financial Benefits- surplus cash, Debt capacity, Financing cost, Financing constraints	Restructuring & Consolidation
To acquire Brand name, patents, Licenses, Expert talent	Clash of corporate culture
Influence Investors decision	

Implementing /Augmenting entry barriers in specific markets	Valuation of target
Defensive Reasons- Crown Jewels, white Knight, Green mails, Poison Pills	Problem in achieving synergies
Increased market share	Huge debt financing thereby increasing risk
Increased speed to market	
Lower risk comparing to develop new products	
Avoid excessive competition	

Mergers & Acquisitions types:

Horizontal Merger- Combination of two or more firms in similar type of production, distribution or area of business. It is usually an acquisition of a competitor with an intention to achieve "Economies of scale, reducing investment in working capital, reducing advertising costs, increase market concentration & profitability, and exercising better control over the market.

Vertical Merger- Two or more firms involved in different stages of production or distribution. This type of merger takes place usually with a supplier or a distributor. The merger with its supplier is termed as "Backward integration" and a merger with its distributor/customer is termed as "Forward integration". Vertical mergers impair competition.

Conglomerate Merger- Combination of firms engaged in unrelated lines of business basically for diversification of business. It enhances overall stability and improves the balances in the company's total portfolio of diverse products and production processes. It is also termed as "elimination technique" for eliminating company's potential competitors.

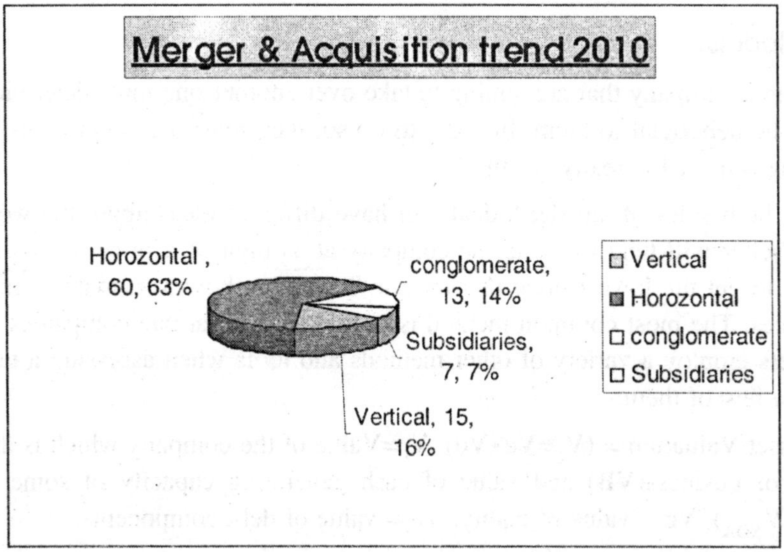

Circular combinations- In circular combinations companies producing distinct products in the same industry seek amalgamation to share common distribution & research facilities in order to obtain economies by eliminating costs of duplication & promoting market enlargement. The acquiring company obtains benefits in the form of economies of resource sharing and diversification.

Forms of mergers & acquisitions:

- Absorption (A+B = A):- In such a case two companies 'A' and 'B' merges such that one company say for example company 'B' looses its identity and company 'A' becomes a larger entity.
- Amalgamation (A+B = C):- In this case two companies say for example company 'A' and company combines to form a third company 'C'. Companies 'A' and 'B' ceases to exist thereafter.
- Spin Offs:- (A-a) + (B-b) = A+B+C where A>a, B>b and C = a+b : A spin-offs occurs when a subsidiary becomes an independent entity. The parent firm distributes shares of the subsidiary to its shareholders through a stock dividend. Since this transaction is a dividend distribution, no cash is generated. Thus, spin-offs are unlikely to be used when a firm needs to finance growth or deals. The subsidiary becomes a separate legal entity with a distinct management and board.
- Equity Alliance (A+B = A_1+ B) :- In this form both entities 'A' and 'B' combine in such a way that no one loose entity, but one of them, say 'A' controls the affair of 'B'. 'A' changes its status to A_1 and becomes the holding company of 'B' by purchasing the controlling stake in 'B'. This is basically a partial takeover.
- Strategic Alliance (A+B = A+B) :- This is a form where both the companies 'A' and 'B' combine to form some strategic alliance on some specific issues to form some cartel or pool. There is no balance sheet impact on two companies.

Valuation Models:

Investors in a company that are aiming to take over another one must determine whether the purchase will be beneficial to them. In order to do so, they must ask themselves how much the company being acquired is really worth.

Naturally, both sides of an M&A deal will have different ideas about the worth of a target company: its seller will tend to value the company at as high of a price as possible, while the buyer will try to get the lowest price that he can. There are, however, many legitimate ways to value companies. The most common method is to look at comparable companies in an industry, but deal makers employ a variety of other methods and tools when assessing a target company. Here are just a few of them:-

- Net Asset Valuation = (V_C=Ve+Vd), V_C=Value of the company which is the sum total of Value of business(VB) and value of cash generating capacity of some non operating assets(V_{NOA}), Ve = value of equity, Vd = value of debt components.

- OPDV (Optimized Deprival Valuation Model): is = ODV, and ODV = minimum of ODRC(replacement cost of the existing fixed assets at modern equivalent asset value which is optimized from technical and engineering standpoint in terms of business life)or Economic value (EV) which refers to the present value of future cash flows if it is more than net realized value.
- Dividend Valuation Model: According to this model, the value of a share is equal to the sum of future streams of dividend discounted at the cost of capital plus the value of share as and when sold in future. Thus the price of a share is expressed as follows:-
  $P_O = D_1/(1+Ke)^1 + D_2/(1+Ke)^2 + \ldots\ldots\ldots + Dn/(1+Ke)^N + Pn/(1+Ke)^N$
- Free Cash Flow Valuation Model: The steps involved in this model are:-
  - o Analyzing the business environment.
  - o Constructing a model of projected financial performance.
  - o Converting projected financial performance in to value.

  Free cash flow = post tax interest payments + dividends + decrease in debt + shares buy back.
- Adjusted Present Value Model (any existing asset that will generate future cash flows): The basic assumption is that business is financed entirely with equity. But because it may not necessarily be financed entirely with equity, adjustments are done with tax shields associated with the financial mix.
- Economic Value Added Model: measures how much better or worse the business did, after meeting the opportunity cost of all resources employed by the business. If:-
  (i) Net income = opportunity cost of equity then nil value added.
  (ii) Net income> opportunity cost of equity then value added.
  (iii) Net income<opportunity cost of equity then value destroyed.
- TDABC (Time Driven Activity Based Costing: This new model of costing assign resource cost directly to the cost objects, requiring only two set of estimates. First, it calculates the cost of supplying resource capacity like personnel, supervision, occupancy, equipment and technology supplied to the department or process. It divides total cost by the capacity of debt to obtain "capacity cost rate". Second, it uses capacity cost rate to derive departmental resource cost to cost object by estimating the demand for resource capacity (basically time) that each cost object requires-**given by S Kaplan & Anderson.**

Ratios to analyses target's value:

- P/E Ratio = Market Price per share / EPS.
- Tobin's 'q' Ratio = Market value of equity & Liabilities / Estimated replacement cost.
- Market value to Book Value= Market price per share / Book value per share.
- Discounted Cash Flow method: A key valuation tool in M&A, discounted cash flow analysis determines a company's current value according to its estimated future cash flows. Forecasted free cash flows (net income + depreciation/amortization - capital expenditures - change in working capital) are discounted to a present value using the

company's weighted average costs of capital (WACC). Admittedly, DCF (Discounted Cash Flow) is tricky to get right, but few tools can rival this valuation method.

- Enterprise-Value-to-Sales Ratio (EV/Sales) - With this ratio, the acquiring company makes an offer as a multiple of the revenues, again, while being aware of the price-to-sales ratio of other companies in the industry.

Rules pertaining mergers & acquisitions in India:

- Section 391-394 of Companies Act, 1956 & companies court Rule, 1959. spells legal procedures to effect M&As.
- Income Tax Act, 1961 specifying various taxable deductions or tax benefits to various parties associated with M&As.
- Competition Act, 2002 requiring regulations of monopolistic powers arising out of M&As.
- SEBI (Substantial Acquisition of Shares & Takeovers) (Amendment) Regulations, 2010 governs takeover of listed companies.
- RBI's 2005 guidelines on merger/amalgamation involving banking companies.
- Stock Exchange(s(s) Norms related to listing.

Impacts of mergers & acquisitions:

There are a number of techniques available to test the impact of M&As on performance of the companies after M&As activity such as **"Event studies"**(comparison of stocks prices of the firm a certain days before and after the merger), **"Regression analysis"** (where we can take after tax rate of returns as dependent variable and size of the firm , rate of increase in capital stock, R&D expenditures etc as independent variables), and 'T'-test paired two samples for mean. Here are few examples of the general impacts of M&As on organizations:-

- Impact on organization.- Revenue loss, customer dissatisfaction, Attrition issues.
- Impact on Employees- Lay-offs, change in corporate culture, Economic Impact, Business procedures, loss of identity, loss of talent, family repercussions, lack of information & anxiety.
- Impact on Management- job loss, cultural clash, high level of stress.
- Impact on shareholders- Economic impact such as dilution of EPS, higher value in case of purchase due hefty payment by acquirer firm.
- Impact on competition- subsided in most cases.

Measures to counter Impact:

- Develop & implement assistance program including advance notification, severance pay extended benefits, retaining program and outplacement activities.
- Communication from the executive team with employees in the pre-acquisition phase.
- Communication between the members of transferor and transferee Company should be open, honest and strategic.

- Involve the employees particularly the key personnel, in the formulation of the action plans, system building and execution of new policies.
- Finance and the Legal departments are essential for the successful implementation of the integration plan.
- Select a right target, but also must have culture in place that accepts the acquisition as quickly as possible.

Why Mergers & Acquisitions Fail:

Despite the highest degree of strategy and planning and investments of hundreds of crores, the majority of the mergers and acquisitions cannot create a value and fail miserably. In 1987, the professor of Harvard, Michael Porter found that around 50% to 60% of the mergers and acquisitions ended in a failure. In 2004, McKinsey also found that only 23% acquisitions ended in a positive note on investment. There are several explanations for failure of mergers and acquisitions. Here are few causes that led to the failure of majority of the mergers and acquisitions deals:-

- No detailed investigations or poor due diligence (that is business review, financial review, acquisition candidate information).
- Cultural difference.
- Flawed intentions.
- No guiding principles.
- No ground rules.
- Poor stakeholder outreach.
- Poor integration techniques (bridging gap between two merging entities).

Important steps to exploit global mergers & acquisitions opportunities:

- Pin Point large economies, growing faster with Industries in which your company competes.
- Identify risk & opportunities in the country's regulations Regarding foreign ownership & other corporate governance practices, capital markets, human capital and its Intellectual Property regime.
- Identify companies/industries in those countries which could be acquisition target.
- Rank those firms based on their fit with your firm's skills & the potential for an attractive investment return. Managers should deicide about the potential target based on the data collected.
- Complete the Acquisition & Integration of the company that best fits these criterions. Execution is fraught with landmines.
- Set Performance Milestones & manage the company to achieve them.

Role of Entrepreneurial Eco-system in mergers & acquisitions deals:

During M&A deals one should take account of targeted markets Entrepreneurial Eco-system elements mentioned below:-

- Transparent & Efficient Financial Markets.

➢ Reliable & Effective corporate governance system.
➢ Human Capital development system.
➢ Clear & supportive IPR protection laws.

-Suggested by Peter S. Cohan & Srinivasa Rangan

Industries to witness positive M&A trends in India:

➢ Infrastructure, services, manufacturing, pharmaceuticals, life sciences, oil and gas, metals and mining companies.
➢ Overseas companies might target Indian pharmaceutical and consumer firms, Retail stores and local enterprises will seek natural resources- said Bank of America.

11

Elephants can Dance ! IBM: The Turn Around Story

Dr. Shashikant P. Valavade
svalavade@gmail.com
Guest Lecturer
Bharati Vidyapeeth University, Institute of Management and Research, New Delhi

The year 1990 was the most profitable year in its history of IBM. .By 1993, the computer industry had changed so rapidly that the company was on its way to losing $16 billions there was a widespread feeling that company was soon on its way to the ICU and sooner or later the IBM would have to file for bankruptcy under chapter 11 unless bailed out by the government as the company was 'too big 'to fail.

Brief History of IBM:

In the early twentieth century Thomas J. Watson, Sr., combined several small companies to form the International Business Machines Corporation. The company had a broad and largely unrelated lineup of commercial products, scales, cheese slicers, clocks ,and typewriters. The company's electromechanical tabulation and punch –card devices introduced computation to business ,government, and academic institutions.

In 1956, Tom Watson, Jr., succeeding his father as CEO started a new product line called the System/360, the original name of the IBM's wildly successful mainframe family. The big shift in technology came with the discovery of the integrated circuit.(the semi-conductor chip) enabling IBM to miniaturize functions and packed onto chips. IBM grew around the mainframe hardware software, sales, services, etc all tied toSystem/360. The runway success and the near monopoly position resulted in IBM becoming insular, creating a self-contained ,self-sustaining world for the company. IBM had ridden one horse, mainframe computers and the franchise built around it. But the horse could carry it only so far before it broke down. This push was first given by UNIX, an 'open' operating environment from companies like Sun, HP.. The push came to a shove when PC makers came along with their desk-tops. Hence the thinking in IBM convert a vertically integrate3d organization into a loose knit confederation of small companies.

Critical Decisions

Prior to the appointment of Gerstner (earlier the CEO of RJR Nabisco, a huge packaged goods company, an earlier the CEO of American Express, a partner of McKinsey &Company) the new CEO of IBM, the company was a one product company producing the mainframe computer the System/390. .Over the years IBM had created a choke point around its main product, the System mainframe, to create a monopoly in the industry and to sell its services and the application software. In an early meeting the mainframe team documented a rapid decline in sales and a precipitous drop in the market share. .The competitors like Hitachi , Fujitsu, and Amdahl were pricing their products 30 to 40 per cent below the IBM price. The main frame team was not lowering the price to match those of the competitors as they felt that IBM would lose substantial revenues and profits when the company needed them most. It was also felt by the earlier management that because the desk-top computers were widely used, the main frame was going to be phased out. Tit was apparent to Gerstner that IBM was milking System /390 main frame while the demand was there.

Gerstner told the team that the milking strategy was over, and an aggressive price reduction would be introduced. The financial people gulped hard . They were further amazed that the company was staying with the mainframe. The alternative strategy , which they expected the new CEO to take was : Keep S/390 prices high for a number of years, since it wasn't easy for customer to shift to competitive products in the near future The revenue-hundreds of millions of dollars –would have been a powerful short-term underpinning of a restructuring of the company. Gesrstner felt that keeping the milking pricing would be painful for the customers and that over the longer term, the present strategy would have destroyed the company's greatest asset around which the entire range of services and the application software was built. Hence the price reduction on the product that vitually created the IBM' profits.

A Lucky Break

In the same meeting the IBM reaffirmed another decision that had been made a number of monthts before Gerstner arrived . The technical team of the mainframe S/390 division had staked a bold move to an entirely different technical architecture for the

System /390: to move from what was known as a bipolar to CMOS (pronounced : C-moss") technology. If this enormously complex project were to be successful, it would permit substantial price reduction in the S/390 without commensurate loss in gross profits, thus improving dramatically the S/390 versus alternative products. If failed, the S/390 was dead. As well as IBM.

This iffy nature of the project had made the previous management and particularly the finance people to postpone the execution of the project as the estimated investment was big, $1 billion. The project execution was given the green signal. Gerstner felt himself lucky that some insightful people had made the decision before he arrived. His job was only to reaffirm it and to protect the billion dollars that the company would spend on it over the next four years. Years later he felt that had the IBM not made the decision to go with CMOSS, the company would have been out of the mainframe business by 1997. For example Hitachi, a major competitor continued development of bigger and bigger bipolar systems, but eventually ran out of gas and Hitachi is no longer in the business.. The CMOSS enabled IBM to build bigger, more powerful systems than anyone had dreamed with bipolar technology. From 1997 with an investment of $1 billion, IBM earned a revenue of $19 billions through the end of 2001.

Keep The Company Together:

During the early years a view had taken hold in IBM that it is a Goliath surrounded by a number of Davids taking sling-shots at the company and that to survive the IBM had to break itself into a number of subunits selling various components, application software and services. A number of investment bankers and consultants had camped themselves in the company to carve out the company in various units so that IPOs could be launched.

When the computer industry appeared on the scene, its model was to deliver to customers a total, integrated package. When a company bought a computer, it came with all the basic technologies, like microprocessors and storage, incorporated in a system, all the software loaded onto the hardware; all the services to install and maintain the system were bundled into the pricing. The customer bought a total system and had it installed for a single price This was a model created by IBM and it had created a monopoly with the choke points. (Decades later this model was adopted by Microsoft to create a monopoly based in application software based on its Windows operating system.)

Only a handful of computer companies , all fully integrated, emerged in the USA(called the BUNCH- Burroughs, Univac, NCR, Control Data and Honeywell). But the leadership position of IBM was intact.

In the mid – 1980s a new model started to appear, which argued that vertical integration was no longer necessary, nor inevitable. The new successful IT companies would offer a narrow , horizontal slice of the total package. The database companies selling only data, companies selling operating systems, storage devices companies and so on. Suddenly there were thousands of companies selling a single, tiny piece of a computer solution.

In this new environment IBM faltered. Thus pundits inside and outside the company argued that the solution lay in splitting IBM into individual segments.

Customers wanted to break IBM's grip on the industry economics i which allowed it to bundle prices and achieve higher margins. The customer was interested in delivering computing power to individual employees (the term was 'distributed computing' in contrast to the mainframe's 'centralised computing.)

As IBM was very slow in delivering distributed computing, many small companies moved to fill in the gap. They were not in a position to deliver an integrated solution, so they offered add-ons to the basic IBM system and built around IBM's central processing hub. (This is what Microsoft and Intel did when IBM reluctantly entered into the PC business.).

To Gerstner, splitting IBM into separate segments was a knee-jerk reaction. When thousands of small specialized companies entered the market, prices dropped and more choices were available..(With the exception of Microsoft, where Microsoft re-created the IBM choke hold in the desktop operating system.)

However the customer had to integrate all the technologies into a usable solution to meet his or her business requirements, the job which earlier done by IBM. This was the undesirable consequence of this development .that there was no integrator.

This was made more difficult by the absence of uniform standards. The , operating system, software, peripherals ,etc. had to be compatible with each company's main hardware. Imagine an electrical appliance industry where the plug or bulbs of say, Phillips could be fitted only in the Phillip's sockets.

Thus the decision was taken to keep the company together because the integrated was needed and at that time only IBM could do this work. Gerstner also could see that gradually computing was moving away from desk-tops to lap-tops, handheld appliances like mobile phones, as well as refrigerators, washing machines, etc, were the 'client/server' model of the desktop was no longer relevant.

At the customers' meeting held soon after the new CEO was appointed, customers vehemently opposed the idea of segmentation, as they were all aware (as opposed to Gurus who did not have to use the systems),. Before the components reached the consumer, somebody had to sit at the end of the line and bring it all together in a way that creates value

Hence the decision was made to keep the IBM together to the relief of employees,(barring a few ambitious managers who were eying at fiefdoms of their own) and a vast number of customers. As a result, IBM threw out the investment bankers who were arranging IPOs of all the pieces of the enterprises along with the accountants and consultants who were creating separate accounting systems and organizational designs for each segment.

This decision to keep IBM a unified enterprise was crucial to the spectacular turnaround of the IBM.

The Vision Thing

In the press conference three months after Gerstner took over on April 1st 1993, he created a flutter of sorts by saying that

"...There has been a lot of speculation as to when I am going to deliver a vision of IBM., and what I would like to say to all of you **that the last IBM needs right now is a vision."**

He added

"What IBM needs right now is a series of very tough-minded, market-driven, highly effective strategies for each of its business processes, - strategies that deliver performance in the marketplace and shareholder value."

:..."The number priority is to restore the company to its profitability. ...The second priority for the company is to win the battle in the customers' premises....Third , in the marketplace , we are moving to be much more aggressive in the client/server area.... Fourth, we are going to continue to be the only full-service provider in the industry.(As well as) a full solutions company (We shall be)more attentive to the customer, faster cycle time, aster delivery time, and a higher quality of service."

In the then corporate religion, the Vision' was a holy cow. Thus the comment evoked a lot of criticism. The more important thing is to enumerate strategies IBM formulated and implemented. This forms the subject matter of Part Two of this case –study.

Following is the brief summary of strategies.

Strategies

Building a new board;

Employee communications;

Creating a global enterprise; Remaking the organization;

Breaking up fiefdoms; Reviving the brand;

Resetting the corporate compensation policy; A services –led model; A networked model;

Building the world's biggest software business

Opening the company store; Un-stacking the stack and focusing the portfolio; emphasis on middleware and services

12

Why Mutual Funds come out as the 'BEST investment option' for Retail Investor?

Ms. Shubhangi Goswami
IMS, Ghaziabad

Retail Investor: Where to Invest?

It is beyond doubt that everyone wants to be secured against unforeseen events of future and financial security is considered to be the most required. The next dilemma for the retail investor is to decide where to invest the little he has. The investment options available to a retail investor range from simple instruments like National Savings Certificates, Provident Fund, Insurance Plans, and Fixed Deposits, Recurring Deposits in Banks to most advanced Unit Linked Insurance Plans, Mutual Funds, Debentures and Shares etc. These instruments have different objectives as tax saving, better returns, providing security, and diversifying the risk etc. Now it depends upon the individual investor's needs, funds available and risk-taking capacity where he would invest. If the amount available is meager, risk-taking capacity is moderate and the objective is good return and growth, the best solution available to him is **Mutual Funds** and that too diversified Equity/ growth fund.

Indian investors who are known to prefer safe and secure investments are gradually developing risk appetite. According to the latest Reserve Bank of India's annual report, the share of mutual funds in household savings has shot up close to 4% from less than 0.5% a year ago (Table-1).

Table-1. Household Savings - Where's the money (2005-2006)

	Household Savings - Where's the money (2005-2006)	
Investment	2005-2006	2004-05
Bank FDs	46.7%	36.4%
Mutual Funds	3.6%	0.4%
Government. Small Savings	12.3%	19.5%
Life Insurance	13.5%	15.1%
Provident and Pension Funds	10.0%	12.9%

Bank deposits also continue to rise on the back of rising interest rates to now command a share of 46% as against 36% the previous year. Share of insurance too has come down from over 15% to a little over 13% now.

In sharp contrast, the share of small saving schemes of the government has fallen to 12% as against 20% the previous year. Contribution to pension and provident funds is also going down, from 13-10%.

According to the RBI annual report, net household investments in mutual funds stood at Rs. 1,500 crore in 2004-05 and jumped to Rs 21,000 crore in 2005-06. Bank deposits meanwhile were up 72% from the previous year. But investments in small saving instruments are down Rs. 13,000 crore to Rs 72,000 crore.

Last year has seen huge inflows into mutual funds and experts say Indians are fast reeling a bit of risk may not be such a bad idea after all.

Mutual Funds: the Fast Growing Industry

The popularity of Mutual Funds has increased manifold in developed financial markets, like the United States. As at the end of March 2006, in the US alone there were 8,002 mutual funds with total assets of over US$ 9.36 trillion (Rs.427 Iakh crores).

In India, the mutual fund industry started with the setting up of the Unit Trust of India in 1964. Public sector banks and financial institutions were allowed to establish mutual funds in 1987. Since 1993, private sector and foreign institutions were permitted to set up mutual funds. As at the end of March 2006, there were 29 mutual funds, which managed assets of Rs. 2, 31,862 crores (US $ 52 Billion) under 592 schemes. This fast growing industry is regulated by the Securities and Exchange Board of India (SEBI) (Table-2 & 3).

Table-2

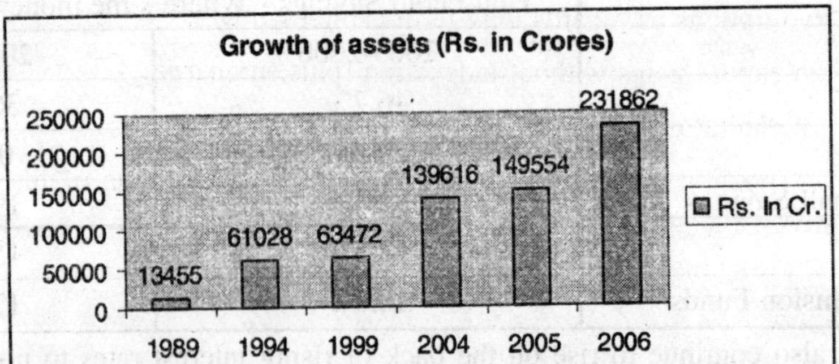

(Source: Association of Mutual Funds in India (AMFI))

Table 3

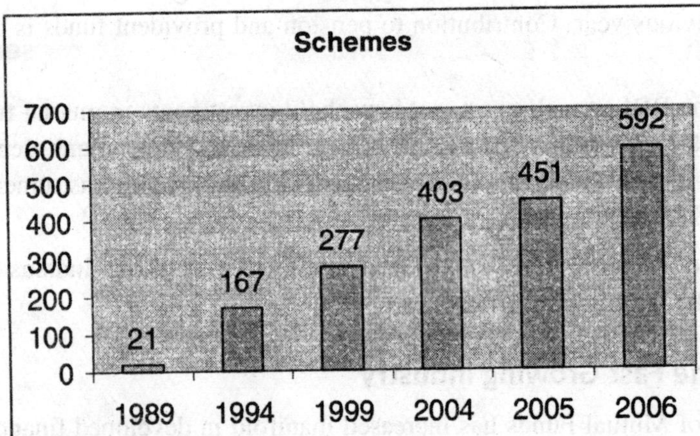

(Source: Association of Mutual Funds in India (AMFI))

Why should one invest in Mutual Funds?

To Reduce risk - Mutual Funds diversify your portfolio by investing in various securities & minimise the risk.

Maximising the opportunities - The fund managers with the strong research take explore new investment options make available opportunities for your investments to flourish.

Liquidity - Mutual Funds can be bought and sold on any dealing day providing **quick access to your money.**

Affordability - Of course you don't need to be millionaire to invest in mutual fund as the minimum investment in mutual fund starts from Rs.500/-. A Mutual Fund because of its large corpus allows even a small investor to take the benefit of its investment strategy.

Low Costs - Mutual Funds are a relatively less expensive way to invest compared to directly investing in the capital markets because the benefits of scale in brokerage, custodial and other fees translate into lower costs for investors.

Tax Benefits - The tax benefits that Mutual Funds investors enjoy at the moment is the treatment of long-term capital gains.

Investors have two options as regards long-term capital gains:

- Tax @ 10% on capital gains without indexation (plus surcharge)
- Tax @ 20% on capital gains after indexation (plus surcharge)

Transparency - The investor gets regular information on the value of his investment in addition to disclosure on the specific investments made by the fund, the proportion invested in each class of assets and the fund manager's investment strategy and outlook.

Regulated for investor protection - All Mutual Funds in India are registered with the regulator of the Indian securities industry - the Securities and Exchange Board of India (SEBI). The funds function within the framework of regulations designed by SEBI and these regulations are intended to protect the interests of investors. The operations of the mutual funds are also regularly monitored by SEBI.

Golden Rules that rule the Mutual Fund world for retail Investor seeking Growth

Invest regularly: The key is to invest regularly i.e. a fixed amount at specific intervals, say every month. By investing a fixed sum each month, you buy fewer units when the price is higher and more units when the price is low, thus bringing down your average cost per unit. This is called rupee cost averaging and is a disciplined investment strategy.

For example if you had invested every month in a mutual fund — referred to as a Systematic Investment Plan — over the past 10 years, you would have been a *crorepati* now.

We studied the SIP returns of the diversified equity funds over the last 10 years. The question was: How much can an investor earn by this straightforward technique of doing something simple and sensible and going at it for a long time? You'll be surprised

If you had invested Rs 20,000 a month for the last 10 years in any one of the better funds, your Rs 24 lakh (Rs 2.4 million) could have grown to almost a crore (Rs 10 million). In fact, the best funds could have left you with a stash substantially more than that.

Mind you, the last 10 years were not exactly a trouble-free period. This decade witnessed a fair amount of crisis in the stock market. But, even in a decade filled with regular crashes and scams, slow and steady really does get you there.

If you had invested Rs 20,000 every month in these funds for the last 10 years, this is how much you would have got (Table-4).

Table-4

Name of the Scheme	Value (Rs/cr)	Annualised returns (%)
Reliance Growth	2.06	40.93
Franklin India Prima	1.87	39.05
HDFC Equity	1.81	38.46
Reliance Vision	1.71	37.38
Franklin India Bluechip	1.57	35.71
Franklin India Prima Plus	1.45	34.25
Magnum Global	1.18	30.39
Prudential ICICI Power	1.18	30.39
Birla Advantage	1.10	28.95
HDFC Capital Builder	1.05	28.07
Taurus Star share	0.96	26.49
Tata Growth	0.93	25.92
Canexpo	0.88	24.89
Magnum Multiplier Plus	0.88	24.79
Canfortune '94	0.80	23.07
Magnum Equity	0.79	22.88
UTI Master Growth	0.75	21.99
J M Equity	0.70	20.64
UTI Master Plus '91	0.69	20.37
Can growth Plus	0.69	20.22
UTI Equity	0.68	19.91
Principal Equity	0.65	19.31
LICMF Growth	0.59	17.32
UTI Master share	0.57	16.69
Taurus Discovery	0.57	16.63

All figures are in Rs / crore.

Value: The amount that you would get after 10 years.

Rs 1 crore = Rs 10million

Annualized returns: The percentage returns every year

Start Early: It is desirable to start investing early and stick to a regular investment plan. If you start now, you will make more than if you wait and invest later. The power of compounding lets you earn income on income and your money multiplies at a compounded rate of return. But make no mistake; the journey will not be as smooth as you would like it to be. There would be sharp declines. The key is that you should not panic and try to figure out where the market will be in the next week or month or year. Focus on being discipline and consistent.

Let's take a fund — **Reliance Growth.**

Investor A began investing Rs 20,000 a month, 10 years ago (August 1996). Investor B began with double the amount every month, five years ago (August 2001).

So, at the end of 10 years, despite investing an equal amount of Rs 24 lakh (Rs 2.4 million), Investor A turns out to be twice as wealthy as Investor B.

By July 2006, Investor A has Rs 2.06 crore (Rs 20 million) while Investor B, Rs 1.06 crore (Rs 10 million).

Find the Best Fund Manager: While equity investments are "risky" an investor is taking a "risk of his lifetime" by not investing in equities if he carries high levels of aspirations.

Let's look at different 10-year periods and see how the Sensex, the barometer of the stock market, has performed.

We looked at the data of different 10-year periods and tried to figure out how much an investor would make if he invested a fixed amount every month.

The best 10-year periods were three: those that ended on December 1992, 1993, and 1995. Each showed an annualized return of over 30%.

The worst was the two 10-year periods ended December 2001 and 2002. They actually showed negative returns.

This will come as a shock to many. Yes, you can lose money by investing in stocks even if you invest consistently over time. But, in all the 18 ten-year periods that we analyzed, just two have shown negative returns. Not selling then but holding on for a few more years would have changed this dramatically.

Good funds managed to outdo the SENSEX! Because the fund manager will keep juggling his stocks and buying and selling to get even better returns than the SENSEX

Collect Right Information: Don't pick a fund simply because it has shown a spurt in value in the current rally. Ferret out information of a fund for at least three years. The one thing to remember while investing in equity funds is that it makes no sense to get in and out of a fund with each turn of the market. Like stocks, the right equity mutual fund will pay off big — if you have the patience. Similarly, it makes little sense to hold on to a fund that lags behind the total market year after year.

Trade off Risk and Return: Certain sector-specific schemes come with a high-risk high-return tag. Such plans are suspect to crashes in case the industry loses the marketmen's fancy. Growth and pure equity plans give greater returns than pure debt plans but their risk is higher.

Check out the Consistency in Performance: While past performance is not an indicator of the future, it does throw some light on the investment philosophies of the fund, how it has performed in the past and the kind of returns it is offering to the investor over a period of time. Also check out the two-year and one-year returns for consistency. How did these funds perform in the bull and bear markets of the immediate past? Tracking the performance in the bear market is particularly because the true test of a portfolio is often revealed in how little it falls in a bad market.

Decide the Investment Horizon: It is the investment horizon of an investor and not the age or so-called risk profile that determines the asset allocation for investors. Longer investment horizon i.e. 3-5 years atleast leaves more headroom for equity to play out, while implying higher risk – price fluctuation – in the short term.

To summarize the whole argument, we would say that, rather than being hostile to you, the market is, at worst, an unpredictable friend with varying mood swings. But it's unlikely to betray you in the end.

References:

1. Abhishek Gupta,Para planner ,Financial Planning Group, Bajaj Capital Limited.
2. Bombay Stock Exchange
3. **"How MFs are scoring over traditional govt schemes"** http://www.moneycontrol.com/india/news/mfnews/indianhouseholdsinvest/howmfsscoringovertraditionalgovtschemes/10/38/article/237741
4. **Moneycontrol**
5. http://www.amfiindia.com/spages/InvestorGuide.pdf
6. www.**mutualfundsindia**.com/**performance**
7. www.**indiainfoline**.com/mufu/whys.html

13

Damsel in Distress

Ms. Supriya Jotshi
Mr. Shrikant Dokhale
IBMR, Pune

Preamble

When India opened its economy in 1991, leftists warned that uncompetitive Indian companies would be killed or swallowed up by multinationals. Fifteen years later, the shoe is on the other foot: Indian companies are taking over giant multinationals.

In 2006, Indian companies raised $19 billion from global markets to finance foreign takeovers and internal expansion. This far exceeded the inflow of foreign direct investment (around $10 billion).

L.N.Mittals's audacious bid and subsequent acquisition of Arcelor seems to have transformed steel industry into an attractive bet for share market investors.L.N.Mittals moves have breathed life into this old economy business.Steel stocks across the world have given strong returns since Tata Steel announced its intention to acquire Corus in early October. All major steel stocks have risen more than 10% since then, some even by over 20%.

The battle for takeover of Corus which would make the new combined entry as the eyeballs of bankers, investors and analysts almost in the same fashion when Mittal Steel acquired Arcelor for $35 billon to become the worlds largest steel producer.

Need For Takeover

Tata :

The acquisition of Corus is likely to confer few principal benefits on tata steel :

- Larger scale, strong downstream business operations, scope for cross fertilization of R& D capabilities (through value-added products in packing, auto and construction)
- Winning Bid for Corus will place Tata among the World's top steel companies with a combined capacity of about 24 million tones.
- Access the European markets, Corus, which controls about 50 per cent of UK steel markets, is likely to offer tata steel a direct gateway into the European market.
- The move also fits well with its de- integration strategy (making primary meal in low-cost countries and having finishing facilities in end- user markets). Its earlier two Acquisitions, of Nat Steel and Millenium Steel, were also carried out with a similar Intent.

Corus :

- Corus is looking for a 'Strategic Fit'. There has be a tremendous rise in the manufacturing sector especially in the automobile sector in the developing countries like china, India, Brazil & some African countries.
- Car manufacturers like BMW, Volkswagen, Mercedes Benz, Porsche and many more from Europe and Toyota, Honda, Nissan from Japan are setting up their plants in these developing countries. Is natural that their would be a high demand for steel and aluminum, to take advantage of this opportunity Corus is trying to merge with either Tata Steel from India or CSN from Brazil.

CSN:

- Offers access to iron ore
- Scope for slab production, if CSN can establish a regular supply flow of slabs to Corus, it will be able to consider expansion projects for slabs that it has put on the Backburner.

Background

1. Tata Steel:

Company Background and Status:

Tata Steel is India's largest integrated private sector steel company. Established in 1907, its steel plant at Jamshedpur produces four million tonnes of hot and cold rolled flat and long products.

The company is backward integrated with owned iron ore mines and collieries. With its competitive advantage in raw materials, efficient operations and the benefits of a recently-completed $2.3 billion programme of modernization, Tata Steel is among the lowest cost steel producers in the world.

Apart from the main steel division, Tata Steel's operations are grouped under strategic profit centres like tubes, growth shop (for its steel plant and material handling equipment), bearings, ferro alloys and minerals, rings, agrico and wires.

Tata Steel's products include hot and cold rolled coils and sheets, tubes, wire rods, construction bars, structurals, forging quality steel, rings and bearings. In an attempt to 'discommodities' steel, the company has recently introduced brands like Tata Steelium (India's first branded cold rolled steel), Tata Shaktee (galvanized corrugated sheets), Tata Tiscon (re-rolled bars), Tata pipes, Tata bearings, Tata Wiron (galvanized wire products) and Tata Agric (hand tools and implements).

Tata Steel is also exploring opportunities in the ferro-chrome and titanium businesses.

Joint Ventures, Associates and Subsidaries

Tata Steel has numerous joint ventures and subsidiaries. Among them are:

- Tinplate Company of India
- Tayo Rolls
- Tata Ryerson
- Tata Refectories
- Tata Sponge Iron

- Tata Metaliks
- Tata Pigments
- Jamshedpur Injection Powder (Jamipol)
- TM International Logistics
- metal junction services
- TRF
- Jamshedpur Utility and Service Company (JUSCO)
- The Indian Steel and Wire Products(ISWP)
- Lanka Special Steel
- Sila Eastern Company.

Strategic Objectives in Acquiring Corus:

If Tata Steels acquires Corus,

- It would get access to global market,
- It would get access to global clients,
- It would get access to the technology of Corus,
- It would enjoy Economics of Scale,
- It would acquire a MNC tag.
- Also get warding "Hostile Takeover".

2] Corus Steel :

Company Background And Status

Corus formed in 1999 through the merger of British steel and Dutch company Koninklijke Hoogovenes, is one of the top-10 steel manufactures globally with manufacturing operations in the UK, The Netherlands, Germany, France, Norway & Belgium. The company also produces Aluminum, besides providing technology and other services to the metal industry.

The company has reported profits of $0.8 Billion on revenue of $18.4 Billion for the last financial year 2005 and employs more than 47000 people Worldwide. The Company was ranked 352 in the Fortune Global 500 list of largest companies for 2006 the company produced 19 million tonnes of stell or 10% of total Europeans output and 0.6 million tones of Alluminium during calendar year 2005.

Corus supplies metal products to a wide range of industries like construction, automotive, packaging, aerospace, energy & Engineering.

Strategic Objectives In Offering Taken Over

Corus has little access to iron ore mines and its steel slab-making facilities turn out products that are more expensive than those in developing countries. Tata's acquisition game plan has been to use its low-cost mines and slab-making facilities to supply to plants near growing markets around the world. If Corus is taken over by either Tata Steel or CSN :

- It would get easy access to cheap labour,
- It would get access to abundant raw material,
- It would also get access to new markets of Asia or South America,
- Its market share also increase considerably,
- They have a chance of monopolizing the resources.
- Also would benefit from "Economics of Scale".

3] CSN :

Company Background and Status

Comphania Siderúrgica Nacional (CSN) is the second major steel-maker company in Brazil. Its main plant is located in the city of Volta Redonda, in the state of Rio de Janeiro. Its current CEO is Benjamin Steinbruch. It was created as a state-owned company in April 9, 1941, during the "Estado Novo", by Brazilian president, Getulio Vargas, after an agreement between the American and Brazilian governments for the construction of a facility that would provide steel for the Allies during the Second World War and later be an aid for Brazil's development. It began its operations in 1946, under Eurico Gaspar Dutra's presidency. It was a state-owned firm until 1993, when it was privatized by

Itamar Franco's government, during the National Program for Privatization led by the federal government, started by Fernando Collor and continued by Franco.

Its main factory are located in Volta Redonda, at the Vale do Paraíba region, southern Rio de Janeiro state, its iron mines at Congonhas and Arcos, both of them cities in the Minas Gerais state, and the coal mines at Siderópolis, Santa Catarina state.

CSN primarily operates as an integrated steel producer in Brazil. It produces a line of steel products, including slabs, which are semi-finished products used for processing hot-rolled, cold-rolled, or coated coils and sheet products; hot-rolled products comprising heavy-gauge hot-rolled coils and sheets, and light-gauge hot-rolled coils and sheets; cold-rolled products, including cold-rolled coils and sheets; and galvanized products consisting of flat-rolled steel coated with zinc or a zinc-based alloy. The company also offers tin mill products, including tin plate; tin free steel, low tin coated steel and black plate products. CSN also mines iron ore, limestone, and dolomite, as well as maintains strategic investments in railroads and power supply companies. The company sells its steel products to customers in Brazil and 71 other countries in North America, Europe, and Asia through its sales force and distributors. It is considered one of the most productive steel-makers in the world, produces more than 6 million tons of raw steel and more than 5 million tons of laminates per year.

Strategic Objectives In Take Over Proposal :

If CSN acquires Corus,

- It can also get access to global markets.
- It can get access to Corus steels high-end technology.
- It can also benefit from "MNC" tag and from Economics of Scale".

The First Mover

Tata Steel: Genesis of Approaches Leading to an Official Bid

On October 20, 2006 Tata steel, the biggest private steel producer, announced that it was in the process of acquiring Corus Group Pluck. Everything about the deal was stunning. The take over, which is expected to be completed by January 2007 for a consideration of about $8.1 billion, will be the biggest buyout by an Indian company. The combine will become one of the biggest steel producers in the world. Almost overnight,Tata Steel will leapfrog in the global ranking from about 50th to the ninth position among the steel majors of the world .Tata Steels acquisition of is thus akin to a minnow swallowing a whale.The corporate India welcomed the deal wholeheartedly.

The Corus Steel's Approach To Tata's Overtures :

Corus has actually accepted Tata Steels bid of 455 pence-per-share offer on 20th October 2006,the approval of which by the shareholders of Corus has being kept pending.

Csn's Entry Into Foray Of Takeover

Companhia Siderurgica Nacional (CSN) had approached the Corus board with an all cash transactions of 475 pence a share or $8.3 billion on November 17, 2006.

CSN has bid for the Anglo-Dutch steel firm Corus, valuing it at 9.6 billion dollars in response to Tata Steel's new offer on December 11. Tata Steel and Corus had already been preparing a merger agreement when CSN barged in on November 17. CSN's bid will be formalized, if Corus' board cooperates, after a due diligence is completed .The Corus board was supposed to vote the Tata offer on December 4, but has postponed its meeting for December 20, thus granting more time for CSN to formalize its bid.The merchant bankers of CSN have purchased about 15% shares of Corus from the open market, clearly indicating the strong intent it has in the deal.

As of 11th December 2006, the board of Corus has formally announced their recommendation of acceptance of the bid by CSN to the amount of 515p per share (approx £4.9 billion total), although it has also confirmed that CSN already owns 3.8% of those shares through previous purchases on the open market. This bid was in response to Tata's increased offer of 500p per share. Agreement has also been reached with both of Corus' main pension bodies on the acquisition.

The Tangle between Tata & CSN

The battle for Corus is all set be a clash of the two steel titans, Ratan Tata of Tata steels and CSN Benjamin Steinbruch.

Firstly, the tangle between Tatas and the CSN to acquire is purely based on financial valuation, After Tata's bid of 500 pence per share; CSN raised its bid to 515 pence. After that the bidding war just continued and the bid value for per share of Corus may reach around 575 pence per share.

Secondly quality raw material to enter into the global market is lacking in case of Tata's on the other hand CSN has got into the problem regarding ownership of Casa De Pedre owned by CVRD.

The battle for Corus is all set to be a clash between the two steel titans, Ratan Tata of Tata Steel and CSN's Benjamin Steinbruch. To survive in a rapidly consolidating industry where scale matters more than anything else, Mr Tata realized that it had to buy something big. Corus fits the bill very well. It produces 18 million tones of steel in various places around the world; it has the latest technology and established relationships with the biggest consumers. But, its price is very high.

For Mr. Steinbruch, the reasons are equally compelling. In his past 10 years he had some successful takeovers first of CSN and then of CVRD, which transformed his profile significantly.

He brought new management, cut production costs and in 6 years, took CSN from a loss of $65mollion to a profit of profit of $1.3 billion.

Benefits to Corus

- Corus through Tata steel has been looking to enter the Asian markets for its construction and auto grade products.
- Corus shareholders will surely get a higher price per share.
- Access to iron ore mines and its steel slabs. Corus has little access to iron ore mines and its steel slab-making facilities turn out products that are more expensive.

The Present Status

In Corus, the situation is now like this. Corus has one highest bid on the table, which is CSN's and which the board has recommended to its shareholders. However, the Tatas have not withdrawn their bid, or made a revised offer, so the Corus is faced with two competing bids under the scheme of arrangement.

And here's what happens next. Under a scheme of arrangement only one bid can go before the court, and an auction is an alternative method for ensuring that both bidders can stay in the race. Once the final date for all revised offers has been agreed to by all parties, in case there continues to be two offers, the final date can be accompanies by a two-way auction.

The takeover panel, in consultation with the parties, will set out a framework for the functioning of the auction. The winner of the auction can then proceed with the takeover either under a scheme of arrangement, or a conventional offer. The auction rules would specify what the terms and conditions of implementing the takeover would be.

The Predictable Outcome

A takeover of Corus by either CSN or Tata Steel would create the world's fifth biggest steelmaker and would be the latest in the industry as companies look for global reach, economies of scale and to secure valuable raw material supplies.

Analysts mostly think CSN holds the upper hand in the battle because it should be able to extract more cost savings from a deal. This is partly because the Brazilian firm will be able to export its iron ore supplies to Corus's business in Europe.

However, analysts also say that Tata Steel, which kick-started the battle with a 455pence per share offers in October, should not be ruled out.

If no company comes out as winner, an auction process would be arranged by the UK take over panel. Here the bidders are usually put through several rounds of bidding where each side is allowed to see the size of the rival bid. The rounds continue for 2-3 days. If there is still no resolution each bidder is asked to submit its full and final offer as a sealed bid and the highest bid is declared the winner.

So the deal is **"Under The Hammer"**.

The Pitfalls In The Take Over Startegies; Tata, Corus & CSN

The bidding war between Tatas and CSN

- **The Broken Hearts**
- **The Vengeance To Win Over The Possible Alliance**

Since the difference the bid of Tatas and CSNs is very marginal, it's likely that the matter will be decided in an open auction. It is also possible that an altogether a new bidder other than Tatas and CSN may take away the 'Damsel Corus'.

Conclusion

This is a real life case study expressing clearly the difficulties; companies from developing countries like India will have to face in their attempts for global inorganic growth through mergers and acquisitions.

There could be unexpressed issues such as ethnicity, corporate- governance, reliability of the alliance over a large period, which might be influencing the minds and actions of Corus board as also the shareholders of Corus.

It is therefore necessary to establish international standard for mergers and acquisitions irrespective of the economic level of countries who desire to expand in the global opportunities.

Global expansion should not be one way track. for the developed countries alone. Their should be equal opportunities for developing countries also to play their might effectively well, in the global economy.

Questions to Ponder :

- Were Tatas over confident in announcing their alliance with Corus before hand?
- Were Tatas really wise to announce the revised bid (500 pence) without CSN opening their cards?
- Is it fair for CSN to act or to intercept in almost concluded deal between Tata's & Corus? Is it really so important for Corus or is it only the super ego as in an internationally known company?
- Are the companies involved (CSN, Corus, Tata) ignoring long term benefit to the shareholders of respective companies & hung on pure financial strengths to win over in the short?

Bibliography

- The Economic Times
- Business Standard
- Frontline Magazines
- Business World

14

Micro Finance in India

Ms. Ritu Sharma
Asst.Professor
Institute of Management Studies, Ghaziabad
Mr. Tushar Jindal
Asst.Professor
Institute of Management Studies, Ghaziabad
tusharjindal1984@yahoo.co.in

Introduction

In the development paradigm, micro-finance has evolved as a need-based policy and programme to cater to the so far neglected target groups (women, poor, rural, deprived, etc.). Its evolution is based on the concern of all developing countries for empowerment of the poor and the alleviation of poverty. Development organizations and policy makers have included access to credit for poor people as a major aspect of many poverty alleviation programmes.

Micro-finance programmes have, in the recent past, become one of the more promising ways to use scarce development funds to achieve the objectives of poverty alleviation. Furthermore, certain micro-finance programmes have gained prominence in the development field and beyond. **The basic idea of micro-finance is simple :** if poor people are provided access to financial services, including credit, they may very well be able to start or expand a micro-enterprise that will allow them to break out of poverty.

Features

There are many features to this seemingly simple proposition which are quite attractive to the potential target group members, government policy makers, and development practitioners. For the target group members, the most obvious benefit is that micro-finance programmes may actually succeed in enabling them to increase their income levels. Furthermore, the poor are able to access financial services which previously were exclusively available to the upper and middle income population. Finally, the access to credit and the opportunity to begin or to expand a micro-enterprise may be empowering to the poor, especially in comparison to other development initiatives which often treat these specific target group members as recipients.

For development practitioners, the success of micro-finance programmes is encouraging. Too often in the past, costly large-scale development initiatives have failed to achieve any sustainable benefits, especially after funds have dried up.

Thus, micro-finance has become one of the most effective interventions for economic empowerment of the poor.

Development Process Through Micro Finance

Micro finance is expected to play a significant role in poverty alleviation and development. The need, therefore, is to share experiences and materials which will help not only in understanding successes and failures but also provide knowledge and guidelines to strengthen and expand micro finance programmes.

In India, a variety of micro-finance schemes exist and various approaches have been practiced by both GOs (Government Organizations) and NGOs. In the development sector, credit has been viewed as one of the missing inputs and therefore, a growing emphasis on re-formulating and re-strengthening micro credit programmes is observed. There are examples of spectacular successes and there are also examples of not-so-successful programmes which experienced high default rates and were unable to provide financial services in the long run. Ultimately the aim is to empower the poor and mainstream them into development. Amongst different approaches of micro-finance schemes, the process and stages remain more or less the same.

The development process through a typical micro-finance intervention can be understood with the help of Chart. The ultimate aim is to attain social and economic empowerment. Successful intervention is therefore, dependent on how each of these stages has been carefully dealt with and also the capabilities of the implementing organizations in achieving the final goal, e.g., if credit delivery takes place without consolidation of SHGs, it may have problems of self-sustainability and recovery. A number of schemes under banks, central and state governments offer direct credit to potential individuals without forcing them to join SHGs. Compilation and classification of the communication materials in the directory is done based on this development process.

Microfinance Development Strategy, aims to ensure permanent access to institutional financial services for the region's poor people and their small businesses.

To achieve this objective, the main focus is on

- creating a microfinance-friendly policy environment
- developing financial infrastructure
- building viable retail institutions
- supporting pro-poor innovations
- supporting social intermediation

Providing the poor with improved facilities to save and to have better access to credit and insurance helps them manage risk, build assets, increase income, and enjoy a better life.

Development Process through Micro-Finance

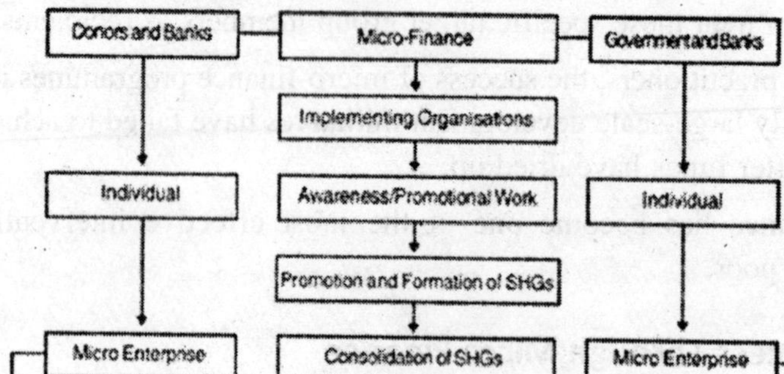

Organisations Providing Micro Finance

There are several Micro-Finance implementing organizations which provide small loans in India. Some of them have successfully expanded their services to thousands of borrowers. Given the fact that most of these borrowers would not have had access to formal financial institutions, that many of the borrowers utilize the loans to enter and/or expand their informal sector micro enterprises, and that the informal sector continues to be an important source of livelihood for many poor people, these Micro Finance Organizations (MFOs) may very well have had a major impact on improving the living standards of millions of poor persons as well as on promoting economic growth. The term MFO has been used for all types of implementing organizations facilitating savings and credit and financial activities at individual and/or group level, not going into details of legal and technical aspects of MFOs.

Some of these organizations have evolved from small NGOs to become important providers of financial services. Realizing the potentially important role that MFOs play in deepening the benefits of economic growth, it is necessary that these MFOs should be strengthened by providing